Research Anthology on Game Design, Development, Usage, and Social Impact

Information Resources Management Association
USA

Volume I

Published in the United States of America by
IGI Global
Information Science Reference (an imprint of IGI Global)
701 E. Chocolate Avenue
Hershey PA, USA 17033
Tel: 717-533-8845
Fax: 717-533-8661
E-mail: cust@igi-global.com
Web site: http://www.igi-global.com

Library of Congress Cataloging-in-Publication Data

Names: Information Resources Management Association, editor.
Title: Research anthology on game design, development, usage, and social
    impact / Information Resources Management Association, editor.
Description: Hershey, PA : Information Science Reference, [2023] | Includes
    bibliographical references and index. | Summary: "Videogames have risen
    in popularity in recent decades and continue to entertain many all over
    the world. As game design and development becomes more accessible to
    those outside of the industry, their uses and impacts are further
    expanded. Games have been developed for medical, educational, business,
    and many more applications. While games have many beneficial
    applications, many challenges exist in current development processes as
    well as some of their impacts on society. It is essential to investigate
    the current trends in the design and development of games as well as the
    opportunities and challenges presented in their usage and social impact.
    The Research Anthology on Game Design, Development, Usage, and Social
    Impact discusses the emerging developments, opportunities, and
    challenges that are found within the design, development, usage, and
    impact of gaming. It presents a comprehensive collection of the recent
    research, theories, case studies, and more within the area. Covering
    topics such as academic game creation, gaming experience, and violence
    in gaming, this major reference work is a dynamic resource for game
    developers, instructional designers, educators and administrators of
    both K-12 and higher education, students of higher education,
    librarians, government officials, business leaders and executives,
    researchers, and academicians"-- Provided by publisher.
Identifiers: LCCN 2022040888 (print) | LCCN 2022040889 (ebook) | ISBN
    9781668475898 (h/c) | ISBN 9781668475904 (eISBN)
Subjects: LCSH: Video games--Design--Research. | Video games--Social
    aspects--Research.
Classification: LCC GV1469.3 .R47 2023 (print) | LCC GV1469.3 (ebook) |
    DDC 794.8/3--dc23/eng/20220930
LC record available at https://lccn.loc.gov/2022040888
LC ebook record available at https://lccn.loc.gov/2022040889

British Cataloguing in Publication Data
A Cataloguing in Publication record for this book is available from the British Library.

The views expressed in this book are those of the authors, but not necessarily of the publisher.

For electronic access to this publication, please contact: eresources@igi-global.com.

List of Contributors

Table of Contents

Section 2
Development and Design Methodologies

Section 4
Utilization and Applications

Section 5
Organizational and Social Implications

Section 6
Critical Issues and Challenges

Preface

Gaming has gained popularity in recent years as more areas of society discover the benefits and opportunities it offers in various sectors. More research is emerging in this area in designing and developing games in order to increase the utility across sectors, and technology is being developed to increase both utility and enjoyment from these games. Recently, the practice of gamification has been applied to education, the medical field, business, and more. However, games, specifically online and video games, often face criticism for a perceived negative impact on society.

It is critical to understand the best practices, challenges, and strategies of gaming design and development to ensure games are utilized appropriately. Research on the social impact of games is also of importance so that a complete view is gained of both the positive and negative attributes of gaming in society.

Staying informed of the most up-to-date research trends and findings is of the utmost importance. That is why IGI Global is pleased to offer this four-volume reference collection of reprinted IGI Global book chapters and journal articles that have been handpicked by senior editorial staff. This collection will shed light on critical issues related to the trends, techniques, and uses of various applications by providing both broad and detailed perspectives on cutting-edge theories and developments. This collection is designed to act as a single reference source on conceptual, methodological, technical, and managerial issues, as well as to provide insight into emerging trends and future opportunities within the field.

The *Research Anthology on Game Design, Development, Usage, and Social Impact* is organized into six distinct sections that provide comprehensive coverage of important topics. The sections are:

1. Fundamental Concepts and Theories;
2. Development and Design Methodologies;
3. Tools and Technologies;
4. Utilization and Applications;
5. Organizational and Social Implications; and
6. Critical Issues and Challenges.

The following paragraphs provide a summary of what to expect from this invaluable reference tool.

Section 1, "Fundamental Concepts and Theories," serves as a foundation for this extensive reference tool by addressing crucial theories essential to understanding the concepts and uses of games and game design in multidisciplinary settings. Opening this reference book is the chapter "A Primer on Gamification Standardization" by Prof. Carlos Filipe Portela from the University of Minho, Portugal; Prof. Alberto Simões of Polytechnic Institute of Cávado and Ave, Portugal; and Profs. Ricardo Alexandre Peixoto de Queiros and Mário Pinto from ESMAD, Polytechnic Institute of Porto, Portugal, which presents a systematic study on gamification standardization aiming to characterize the status of the field, namely describing existing frameworks, languages, services, and platforms. This section ends with "Towards Better Understanding of Children's Relationships With Online Games and Advergames" by Dr. Ali Ben Yahia from LIGUE, Tunis, Tunisia; Prof. Sihem Ben Saad of Carthage Business School, Université Tunis Carthage, Tunisia; and Prof. Fatma Choura Abida from Institute of Computer Science of Tunis, Tunisia, which favors an in-depth understanding of the child's relation with online games and advergames through an exploratory qualitative approach.

Section 2, "Development and Design Methodologies," presents in-depth coverage of the design and development of games for their use in different applications. This section starts with "Augmented Reality Games" by Prof. Baris Atiker from Bahcesehir University, Turkey, which evaluates how augmented reality games interpret gaming concepts and principles through field research methods, new applications, and studies that deal with gamification, presence, immersion, and game transfer phenomena. This section ends with "Eye of the Beholder: Analyzing a Gamification Design Through a Servicescape Lens" by Prof. Adam Palmquist from the School of Informatics, University of Skövde, Sweden and Dr. David Gillberg of Insert Coin, Sweden, which uses the theories from environmental psychology and the servicescape methods to construct a lens to suggest improvements in gamification design for a learning management system used in higher education.

Section 3, "Tools and Technologies," explores the various tools and technologies used within game design. This section begins with "Applied Alternative Tools and Methods in the Replacement of the Game Design Document" by Profs. Pedro Henrique Roscoe Lage de Oliveira and Carlos Alberto Silva de Miranda from Minas Gerais State University, Brazil and Prof. Joao Victor Boechat Gomide from the Universidade FUMEC, Brazil, which proposes alternatives to replace or optimize the use of the game design document (GDD). This section ends with "Towards a Role-Playing Game Procedural Dungeon Generation Strategy to Help Developing Working Skills" by Profs. Esteban A. Durán-Yañez and Mario A. Rodríguez-Díaz from Tecnológico Nacional de México IT Aguascalientes, Mexico and Prof. César A. López-Luévano from the Universidad Politécnica de Aguascalientes, Mexico, which describes the insights towards a proposal to integrate a procedural content generation strategy in a computer role-playing usable and accessible learning video game for gaining replayability to encourage engagement and motivation in learners.

Section 4, "Utilization and Applications," describes how gaming is used and applied in diverse industries for various applications. The opening chapter in this section, "Probability and Game," by Prof. Alessio Drivet from Geogebra Institute of Turin, Italy, emphasizes not only the theoretical aspects but above all the certainty that you always play "against the dealer" with an expected loss assessable for the various games. This section ends with "On Computerizing the Ancient Game of Ṭāb" by Profs. Ahmad B. Hassanat, Ghada Altarawneh, Baker Al-Rawashdeh, and Mohammed Alshamaileh from Mutah University, Jordan; Prof. Ahmad S. Tarawneh from Eotvos Lorand University ELTE, Hungary; Prof. Hossam Faris of The University of Jordan, Jordan; Prof. Mahmoud B. Alhasanat from Al-Hussein Bin Talal University, Jordan; Prof. Alex de Voogt of Drew University, USA; and Dr. Surya V. B. Prasath from Cincinnati Children's Hospital Medical Center, USA, which develops three versions of the game tab—human versus human, human versus computer, and computer versus computer—and employs a genetic algorithm (GA) to help the computer to choose the 'best' move to play.

Section 5, "Organizational and Social Implications," includes chapters discussing the impact of gaming on society. The chapter "Institutions as Designers of Better Social Games" by Prof. Albena Antonova from Sofia University, Bulgaria, discusses how institutions can transform into designers of new types of rules and social arrangements that will be more just and efficient for all within social games. The closing chapter, "The Effects of Fully and Partially In-Game Guidance on Players' Declarative and Procedural Knowledge With a Disaster Preparedness Serious Game," by Prof. Ting Zhou from Fort Hays State University, USA and Prof. Christian S. Loh of Southern Illinois University, USA, investigates the effects of players' gaming frequency, prior knowledge, and in-game guidance received on their declarative and procedural knowledge in a disaster preparedness serious game.

Section 6, "Critical Issues and Challenges," presents coverage of academic and research perspectives on the challenges and issues of games and gaming design. Starting this section is "Gamification Research: Preliminary Insights Into Dominant Issues, Theories, Domains, and Methodologies" by Prof. Kingsley Ofosu-Ampong from the University of Ghana, Ghana and Prof. Thomas Anning-Dorson of the University of the Witwatersrand, South Africa, which explains the idea of game design elements in information systems and provides real-world examples of gamified systems outcomes from developing countries. This section ends with "Digital Games and Violence" by Prof. Arzu Kalafat Çat from Abant Izzet Baysal University, Turkey, which discusses violent elements in digital games within the framework of relevant theoretical approaches through three games that children play most.

Although the primary organization of the content in this multi-volume work is based on its six sections, offering a progression of coverage of the important concepts, methodologies, technologies, applications, social issues, and emerging trends, the reader can also identify specific content by utilizing the extensive indexing system listed at the end of each volume. As a comprehensive collection of research on the latest findings related to games and gaming design, the *Research Anthology on Game Design, Development, Usage, and Social Impact* provides game developers, instructional designers, educators and administrators of both K-12 and higher education, students of higher education, librarians, government officials, business leaders and executives, researchers, and academicians with a complete understanding of the applications and impacts of games and gaming design. Given the vast number of issues concerning usage, failure, success, strategies, and applications of gaming design and development, the *Research Anthology on Game Design, Development, Usage, and Social Impact* encompasses the most pertinent research on the applications, impacts, uses, and development of games.

Section 1
Fundamental Concepts and Theories

Chapter 1
A Primer on Gamification Standardization

Ricardo Alexandre Peixoto de Queiros
(iD) https://orcid.org/0000-0002-1985-6285
ESMAD, Polytechnic Institute of Porto, Portugal

Mário Pinto
ESMAD, Polytechnic Institute of Porto, Portugal

Alberto Simões
Polytechnic Institute of Cávado and Ave, Portugal

Carlos Filipe Portela
(iD) https://orcid.org/0000-0003-2181-6837
University of Minho, Portugal

ABSTRACT

Computer science education has always been a challenging topic for both sides of the trench: educators and learners. Nowadays, with the pandemic state that we are facing, these challenges are even greater, leading educators to look for strategies that promote effective virtual learning. One of such strategies includes the use of game mechanics to improve student engagement and motivation. This design strategy is typically called gamification. Nowadays, gamification is being seen as the solution to solve most of the issues related to demotivation, complexity, or tedious tasks. In the latest years, we saw thousands of educational applications being created with gamification in mind. Nevertheless, this has been an unsustainable growth with ad hoc designs and implementations of educational gamified applications, hampering interoperability and the reuse of good practices. This chapter presents a systematic study on gamification standardization aiming to characterize the status of the field, namely describing existing frameworks, languages, services, and platforms.

DOI: 10.4018/978-1-6684-7589-8.ch001

INTRODUCTION

Nowadays, the games industry is responsible for an important part of the financial market worldwide (Mordor Intelligence, 2020). Several reasons can be identified for this fact from the entertainment of playing a game to its capacity to enhance two typically opposite values such as competition and cooperation. To bring the benefits of the games to non-game contexts, the term gamification appeared and, currently, gamification is applied in several digital applications for several purposes. The most notable examples are to foster the learning of complex domains and to facilitate the integration of workers in companies (on-boarding).

Regardless of the application domain, there is an unsustainable development of gamified applications in terms of specifications, standards and good practices used. Without this type of regulation, the way how gamified apps are created hinders the reuse and interoperability between peers while promoting replication of features which can be error prone and time consuming.

This article focuses on the current state of gamification standardization in the scope of the gamified application development life cycle. As methodology for our systematic study, we will organize all the current contributions for the standardization of gamification in a well-known client-server software architecture pattern called three-tier architecture. In this pattern the three tiers, namely, Data, Business/Logic and User Interface are mapped with gamification contributions such as languages, services, and platforms, respectively.

This work is organized as follows. Section 2 presents the most popular gamification frameworks and their common features. In section 3, we start by presenting the methodology for this study and then, for each tier, we present the most mature contributions for gamification formalization. In the last section, we analyze the study done by making considerations about trends and listing a set of best practices in the design of a gamified system.

GAMIFICATION FRAMEWORKS

A framework can be defined as a conceptual structure which acts as an abstract (or concrete) guide for the building of a software product. In the field of game/gamification design there are no consensus on the use of frameworks. In fact, (Crawford, 1984) states that game design is an activity too complex to be reducible to a formal procedure. Other authors (Julius & Salo, 2013) conclude that it should be treated as an agile process which does not always follow a specific design framework.

Despite the existence of dozens of frameworks worldwide, several researchers (Seaborn & Fels, 2015) and (Hamari, Koivisto & Sarsa, 2014) claim that gamification as an academic topic is still young and only a few well-established frameworks can be useful. To achieve a more empirical study, a literature review was conducted, between 8 and 15 of December of 2020, based on works indexed in three databases, namely, Google Scholar, SCOPUS, and Web of Knowledge. In this review, the search keywords were gamification, game, design, framework, and models.

The study identified 52 articles which either present or refer a gamification framework. From those articles, 12 frameworks were obtained. Despite the high number of frameworks identified, 5 frameworks were referred more than 75\% of the total of articles. These five frameworks will be compared in the next subsections. The Octalysis framework (Figure1) was created by (Choy, 2015) recognized that there are eight different types of **core drive** that motivates people to perform any activity. Visually, the framework has an octagonal shape where the core drives are represented in each corner.

Figure 1. Octalysis Gamification Framework

The right drives (**Right Brain**) represent the creative, artistic, and social aspects, while the left drives (**Left Brain**) represent the logical and intellectual aspects. These drives favors either extrinsic or intrinsic motivation. In fact, most companies aspire to design solely for the extrinsic motivation, which is about reaching a goal or getting a reward. However, Chou states that the intrinsic motivation, the use of creativity and socializing, should be the priority in the gamification strategy design to encourage continuous motivation and make the activity itself rewarding. The framework also distinguishes the bottom and top side of octagon and coined both parts as **Black Hat** and **White Hat**, respectively. The former defines negative motivations where people is being motivated to take a certain action because of the fear of losing, the curiosity of upcoming event or the strive for achieving the things he/she cannot have. The later are considered as positive motivations. These positive drives motivate individuals through creativity, makes them feel powerful due to the sense of control and the impression of a greater meaning. In short, to have a balance strategy, Chou highlights that successful gamification requires the consideration of all the core drives.

Marczewski created a framework, called GAME (Marczewski, 2015) based on two phases. Firstly, planning and designing, which includes the gathering, by means of a survey, of key information such as the user's types in the gamification context. Then, the best solution for goals and engagement is designed, measuring user activities and outcomes. He applies an own motivation framework called RAMP (Relatedness, Autonomy, Mastery, Purpose).

MDA stands for Mechanics, Dynamics, and Aesthetics framework (Hunicke, Leblanc, & Zubek, 2004) and is defined as a formal approach to bridge the gap between game design and development. According to this framework, games can be broken down into three elements: rules, system, and fun. These elements are directly translated into the respective design components, which must be defined when designing a game. The MDA framework has been modified by different authors to be suitable to several contexts. One of the modifications has resulted in the MDE framework (Robson et al., 2015), where the concept aesthetics is replaced with emotions to describe the user experience.

The Sustainable Gamification Design (SGD) is an enterprise gamification framework developed by (Raftopoulos, 2014). This human-centered framework intends to value creation benefits, destruction risks, and be also concerned about being ethically correct. Based on its author, this kind of frameworks could, potentially, produce more responsible and sustainable results. Table 1 summarizes all five frameworks based on their context and scope.

Table 1. Comparison of gamification design frameworks

Model	Creation Date	Context	Scope
Octalsys	Chou, Y. (2015)	Gamification Design	Core Drives Left/Right brain Black/White hat
MDA	Ruhi, U. (2015)	Game Design	Mechanics Dynamics Aesthetics
MDE	Robson, K. (2015)	Gamification Design	Mechanics Dynamics Emotions
SGD	Raftopoulos, M. (2014)	Game Design	Discover Reframe Envision Create Values/Ethics Reflect/Act Understand/Make
GAME	Marczewski (2015)	Gamification Design	Relatedness Autonomy Mastery Purpose

A previous study (Mora et. Al., 2015) gathers more information about these (and more) frameworks.

GAMIFICATION SYSTEMATIC STUDY

The previous chapter focused on identifying and comparing gamification design frameworks that will help in the gamification process of a software system. However, there will come a time when it will be necessary to implement gamification. For this, there are several tools, services, platforms, and languages that can help in the process. However, there is a huge dispersion of technologies and, as expected, poor adherence to standards. This chapter presents a model based on 3 layers to organize the types of technologies that we can find in a gamified system and, for each of these layers, current standards and best practices are presented.

Within a gamification ecosystem there are several agents responsible either to produce, process or consume data that is crucial for the correct functioning of a gamification system.

This section presents the current state of gamification standardization in the scope of a gamified application development life cycle. As methodology for the systematic study all the current contributions for the standardization of gamification are organized in a well-known client-server software architecture pattern called three-tier architecture composed by:

- **Presentation:** exposes interaction for the end users through an UI.
- **Logic:** expresses business rules and expose them as services.
- **Data:** defines domain knowledge and persists it in a storage.

Based on this pattern, a gamification multi-tier architecture was designed for this study representing typical components in a gamification ecosystem (Figure 2).

Figure 2. Gamification Mapping Model

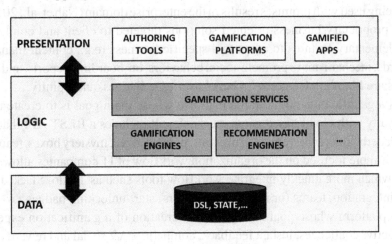

After defining a typical instance of a gamified system, each layer was map to a component. In the next subsection the most popular gamifications platforms in the presentation tier, the most prominent services in the logic tier and the most used domain specific languages for the data tier are presented.

Presentation Tier (Platforms)

Currently, when it comes to develop a gamified application, one of two solutions is chosen: 1) you start creating it from scratch or 2) you use an existing platform to support the gamification features of the application. There are naturally advantages/disadvantages to both approaches.

In the case of the first approach, it requires having a team of multifaceted developers, a deadline not too rigid and servers to store their own game data. On the other hand, flexibility is gained in the development of services and graphical interfaces to be provided to the end user.

In the second approach, it is necessary, firstly, to make a market analysis and identify which platform best supports your needs. Using a platform, weakens flexibility, but development time is saved, as it is not necessary to implement gamification features so developers can focus on business logic.

For the second approach one of the biggest challenges is to choose the most suitable platform considering the current needs.

Gamification platforms can be divided in two main groups:

- Enterprise Gamification Platforms: gathers platforms that implements features typical founded in companies such as worker integration, sales, marketing campaigns, among others.
- Educational Gamification Platforms: dedicated for the teaching-learning process of several domains such as computer programming, math's, medicine, electronics, among others.

The next subsections detail both types of platforms.

Enterprise Gamification Platforms

Gamification is being used with promises results in the enterprise domain (Nah et. al., 2019). In this realm, there are several proprietary business-oriented solutions targeted to client and employee engagement which add complementary features to adapt to a specific business (e.g., content management system, customized rewards, mechanisms to promote social behaviors, on-boarding, reports, and analytics). Some popular examples are Mambo[1], Gametize[2], GameLayer[3], GetBadges, and Spinify[4].

GameLayer is a gamification and rewards platform whose main goal is to create user engagement and consumer loyalty with cloud-based game mechanics. It includes a REST API that exposes several features such as leaderboards, achievements, missions, points, prizes, mystery boxes, teams, and level-ups.

GetBadges.io is more focused on the organization workflow of IT companies allowing the reward of developer teams which more quickly integrate workflow tools such as Trello, Slack, Jira, GitHub, and others. For each integration, teams (or individual workers) start unlocking badges.

Gametize is a platform whose goal is to allow the creation of a gamification experience based on four pillars: interactive challenges, instant feedback, competition \& social and rewards \& redemptions.

Educational Gamification Platforms

Other popular use of gamification is to act as a facilitator for the teaching-learning process of complex domains. Gamification here is typically injected in an ad hoc fashion in so-called open online courses available on the web for several domains.

One of domains that most exploits the use of gamification for enhancing learner's motivation and engagement is the computer programming domain.

In this scope we stress the platforms Coursera[5], Udacity[6], edX[7], Codecademy[8], Khan Academy[9], and Free Code Camp[10] which offer a wide variety of learning material from top universities' courses, with the possibility of get paid certificates.

These platforms typically use gamification to attract learners, adopting elements such as progress indicators, badges, levels, leaderboards, and experience points. For example, Khan Academy uses badges and progress tracking to engage students to enlist and complete courses. Even that it also allows educators to easily create courses for their learners, it is limited to JavaScript-based programming activities

(HTML and CSS are also supported). Codecademy also uses progress indicators and badges. It supports programming languages such as Python, JavaScript, Java, SQL, Bash/Shell, and Ruby. However, creating courses on Codecademy is not yet possible.

In the context of educational institutions, the most widely used approach to create gamified open online courses is to rely on a Learning Management System (LMS) with game mechanics. LMSs were created to deliver course contents and collect assignments of the students. However, many of them evolved to provide more engaging environments resorting to gamification. Some of the most notable examples are Academy LMS, Moodle, and Matrix which include badges, achievements, points, and leaderboards. Moodle also has several plugins which offer a variety of other gamification elements (Paiva, Queirós & Leal, 2015).

One of the most relevant tools is Enki (Paiva, Leal & Queirós, 2016) which is a tool that blends gamification, assessment, and learning, presenting content in various forms as well as delivering programming assignments with automatic feedback, while allowing any stakeholder to create courses freely.

Logic Tier (Services)

Games industry is evolving at an unbridled level. This was one of the reasons for the appearance of Game Backend services.

This trending leveraged the interest of the most important companies (Google, Microsoft, and Amazon) for the creation of gaming integrated development infrastructures. Its architectures are very similar and boils down to a set of tiers responsible for tasks related with the creation, development, storage, and maintenance of a game. In a recent study (Amini et. al., 2018), the tier's architecture was analyzed and organized in five levels depicted in Figure 3:

Figure 3. Levels of Cloud Computing Gaming Services

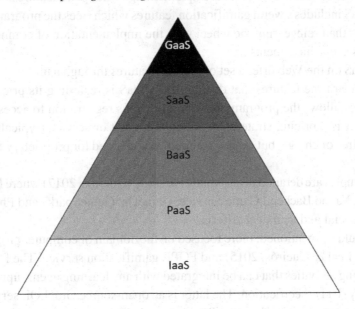

The five tiers are the following:

- **Game as a Service (GaaS)**: revenues model used to deliver game content after its launch (e.g., game subscriptions, gaming on demand and micro-transactions).
- **Software as a Service (SaaS)**: fosters the development, update, and debugging process (e.g., Google Apps, Facebook, YouTube).
- **Backend as a Service (BaaS)**: delivers APIs and SDKs provide many services, such as game elements/mechanics, database management, identity and access management, analysis, and others.
- **Platform as a Service (PaaS)**: offers infrastructure construction and maintenance (e.g., Microsoft Azure, Google AppEngine, Amazon SimpleDB/S3).
- **Infrastructure as a service (IaaS)**: cloud computing that provides virtual computing (e.g., Amazon EC2, GoGrid and Flexiscale).

Based on these tiers we highlighted the BaaS.

The goal of these cloud services is to free the programmer of the implementation of the game infrastructure and give him more time to dedicate in the game logic. The idea is to not replicate the implementation of the game features in each version of the game for several platforms and adhere to a service-oriented architecture providing cross-platform game services that lets you easily integrate popular gaming features such as achievements, leaderboards, remote storage, and real-time multiplayer in games.

A Game-Backend-as-a-Service (GBaaS) is a subset of a Backend as a Service (BaaS) that includes cross-platform solutions for the typical game concepts identified in the previous subsection. During the development process of a game (or a generic application) developers must choose between building their own back-end services

or using an available game back-end platform. This last option is usually preferred since GBaaS include several services specifically tailored for game development. These services allow developers to focus on the game logic by freeing them from implementing boiler plate features.

Typically, a GBaaS includes several gamification features which frees the programmer to the creation of good games rather than reinventing the wheel with the implementation of common gaming features such as leaderboards and achievements.

Most of the GBaaS on the Web offer a set of gaming features through a uniform API and with SDKs in several flavors. One of the features that distinguish GBaaS is regarding its pricing strategy: free or freemium. The former allows the programmer with a previous registration to access all the features of the GBaaS. The latter is a pricing strategy by which a product or service (typically a game or a web service) is provided free of charge, but money (premium) is charged for proprietary features, functionality, or virtual goods.

Most notable examples are detailed in an exhaustive study (Queirós, 2017) where five GBaaS (Google Play Game Services, Yahoo Backend Game Service, GameUp, GameSparks and Photon) are compared based on several on social and technical criteria.

Other services could be mentioned, more focused on the domain of computer programming learning, such as Odin (Paiva, Leal & Queirós, 2015) and FGPE gamification service. The former is a gamification service for learning activities that can be integrated with any learning agent supporting the Learning Tools Interoperability (LTI) specification. The latter is an open-source GraphQL service that transforms a package containing a gamification layer - adhering to a dedicated open-source language (Paiva et.al.,

2021) - into a game. This work was done in the scope of the Framework for Gamified Programming Education Erasmus+ Programme (Swacha et.al., 2020b).

Data Tier (Languages)

The state-of-the-art in the field of gamification currently lacks a main modeling language for gamification concepts. Nevertheless, there are several other established game languages and modeling approaches.

The most notable example of a domain-specific game description language is GaML (Herzig et. al., 2013), a formal and declarative language to define gamification concepts. The language is automatically compliable into gamification platforms without the need to involve IT-experts.

ATTAC-L (Broeckhoven & Troyer, 2013) is a domain specific language which allows the user to specify the game scenario in XML and to build a game using a code generator.

Serious Game Structure and Logic Modeling Language (GLiSMo) is a DSL for serious games. The meta-model includes concepts such as objects, characters, acts, or scenes. Furthermore, the language comprises actions, tasks, and assessments to represent the game's logic.

Other DSL also appeared more tailored to specific aspects of games rather than gamification. This includes the following languages:

- **Card Game Description Language (CGDL)**: focused on the simulation and derivation of novel card games.
- **Strategy Game Description Language (SGDL)**: more specific for the description of emergent strategy games.
- **Video Game Description Language (VGDL)**: used to describe and generate simple video games.

A new language appeared recently to fill the gap of modelling gamification in education called Gamified Education Interoperability Language (GEdIL) (Swacha et. al., 2020). Despite initially designed to fulfil specific requirements of gamification applied in programming courses. These requirements identify a vast collection of rewarding mechanisms such as points, badges, virtual items, and social status (e.g., through leaderboards), to provide extrinsic motivation, but can also affect the educational content directly through unlockable and secret content, different activity modes (e.g., speedup and duels), among others. Nonetheless, GEdIL completely separates the gamification layer from the activities being gamified, which makes it sufficiently generic to be applied to any other educational domains.

Recently several new tools were developed or adapted to help game designers to model, build and analyses games. Unified Modelling Language (UML) is a de-facto standard modelling language used in multiple domains and can be also used to build games. The advantage of UML is that it is well known in the software engineering community. SysML is a general-purpose modeling language for systems engineering applications. That supports specification, analysis, design, and verification of a broad range of systems. SysML has been used for building a training game (Hetherinton, 2014).

Another line of research is the development of modeling languages for formal visual representation of game-based rule systems (Swacha, 2018). In this realm, Machinations and UAREI (Ašeriškis et. al., 2017) are the most popular choices. The models defined in such languages are primarily intended to support the design phase of gamification development. Figure 4 shows a machinations diagram of a Monopoly action scenario.

Figure 4. A Machinations diagram of Monopoly

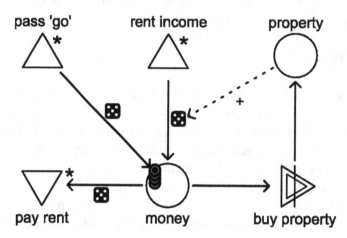

CONCLUSION

In this paper, we present a systematic study on the gamification standardization contributions based on a well-known client-server software architecture pattern called three-tier architecture. For each layer, we shared the most valuable or promising contributions to cover a great part of all gamification design ecosystem.

In the presentation tier, several platforms were depicted that use gamification to empower motivation organized in two flavors: educational and enterprise. In the logic tier, the focus was on services well established in cloud containers known as Game Backend as a Service. Finally, in the data layer, the most popular domain specific languages and modeling approaches were shared.

The paper's contribution is to serve as a synthesis for the contributions that have been shared in the last decade regarding the regulation/formalization of design/implementation strategies in the ecosystem of a gamified application.

Based on this systematic study one can conclude that the gamification ecosystem earns, in this last decade, some contributions trying to fill the huge gap of formalization/regulation in the design of such systems. In this context, several (conceptual) frameworks appeared to give a more formal control to the gamification design strategies. Nevertheless, the efforts are still few requiring more technical contributions and concrete frameworks to shape the future of gamified apps.

REFERENCES

Amini, P., Zahiri Motlagh, S. A., & Nezhadpour, M. (2018). A large-scale infrastructure for serious games services. *2018 2nd National and 1st International Digital Games Research Conference: Trends, Technologies, and Applications (DGRC)*, 27-33. 10.1109/DGRC.2018.8712040

Ašeriškis, D., Blazauskas, T., & Damasevicius, R. (2017). UAREI: A model for formal description and visual representation/software gamification. *DYNA (Colombia)*, *84*(200), 326–334. doi:10.15446/dyna.v84n200.54017

Broeckhoven, F., & Troyer, O. (2013). ATTAC-L: A modeling language for educational virtual scenarios in the context of preventing cyber bullying. *2013 IEEE 2nd International Conference on Serious Games and Applications for Health (SeGAH)*, 1-8. 10.1109/SeGAH.2013.6665300

Chou, Y. (2015). *Actionable gamification - beyond points, badges, and leaderboards. Technical report.* Octalysis Media.

Crawford, C. (1984). *The Art of Computer Game Design.* McGraw-Hill, Inc.

Hamari, J., Koivisto, J., & Sarsa, H. (2014). Does gamification work? A literature review of empirical studies on gamification. *2014 47th Hawaii International Conference on System Sciences*, 3025-3034.

Herzig, P., Jugel, K., Momm, C., Ameling, M., & Schill, A. (2013). Gaml - A modeling language for gamification. *2013 IEEE/ACM 6th International Conference on Utility and Cloud Computing*, 494-499.

Hetherinton, D. (2014). Sysml requirements for training game design. *17th International IEEE Conference on Intelligent Transportation Systems (ITSC)*, 162-167.

Hunicke, R., Leblanc, M., & Zubek, R. (2004). Mda: A formal approach to game design and game research. *AAAI Workshop - Technical Report, 1.*

Intelligence, M. (2020). *Gaming Market - Growth, Trends, Forecasts (2020 - 2025).* https://www.researchandmarkets.com/reports/4845961/gaming-market-growth-trends-forecasts-2020

Janssens, O., Samyny, K., Van de Walle, R., & Van Hoecke, S. (2014). Educational virtual game scenario generation for serious games. *2014 IEEE 3rd International Conference on Serious Games and Applications for Health (SeGAH)*, 1-8. 10.1109/SeGAH.2014.7067106

Julius, K., & Salo, J. (2013). *Designing gamification. Technical report.* Marketing.

Marczewski, A. (2015). User Types. In Even Ninja Monkeys Like to Play: Gamification, Game Thinking and Motivational Design (pp. 65-80). CreateSpace Independent Publishing Platform.

Mora, A., Riera, D., Gonzalez, C., & Arnedo-Moreno, J. (2015). A literature review of gamification design frameworks. *2015 7th International Conference on Games and Virtual Worlds for Serious Applications (VS-Games)*, 1-8. 10.1109/VS-GAMES.2015.7295760

Nah, F., Eschenbrenner, B., Claybaugh, C., & Koob, P. (2019). Gamification of Enterprise Systems. *Systems., 7*(1), 13. doi:10.3390ystems7010013

Paiva, Haraszczuk, Queiros, Leal, Swacha, & Kosta. (2021). *FGPE Gamification Service: A GraphQL Service to Gamify Online Education.* . doi:10.1007/978-3-030-72654-6_46

Paiva, J. C., Leal, J. P., & Queirós, R. (2015). Odin: A service for gamification of learning activities. In *Languages, Applications and Technologies - 4th International Symposium, SLATE 2015.* Springer. 10.1007/978-3-319-27653-3_19

Paiva, J. C., Leal, J. P., & Queirós, R. A. P. (2016). Enki: A pedagogical services aggregator for learning programming languages. In *Proceedings of the 2016 ACM Conference on Innovation and Technology in Computer Science Education, ITiCSE 2016.* ACM. 10.1145/2899415.2899441

Queirós, R. (2017). A Survey on Game Backend Services. In R. Alexandre Peixoto de Queirós & M. Pinto (Eds.), *Gamification-Based E-Learning Strategies for Computer Programming Education* (pp. 1–13). IGI Global. doi:10.4018/978-1-5225-1034-5.ch001

Queirós, R. A. P. (2017). A survey on game backend services. In Gamification- Based E-Learning Strategies for Computer Programming Education. IGI Global.

Raftopoulos, M. (2014). Towards gamification transparency: A conceptual framework for the development of responsible gamified enterprise systems. *Journal of Gaming and Virtual Worlds.*, 6(2), 159–178. doi:10.1386/jgvw.6.2.159_1

Robson, K., Plangger, K., Kietzmann, J., McCarthy, I., & Pitt, L. (2015). Is it all a game? Understanding the principles of gamification. *Business Horizons*, 58(4), 411–420. Advance online publication. doi:10.1016/j.bushor.2015.03.006

Ruhi, U. (2015). Level Up Your Strategy: Towards a Descriptive Framework for Meaningful Enterprise Gamification. *Technology Innovation Management Review*, 5(8), 5–16. doi:10.22215/timreview/918

Seaborn, K., & Fels, D. I. (2015). Gami_cation in theory and action: A survey. *International Journal of Human-Computer Studies*, 74, 14–31. doi:10.1016/j.ijhcs.2014.09.006

Swacha, J. (2018). Representation of events and rules in gamification systems. *Procedia Computer Science*, 126, 2040–2049. doi:10.1016/j.procs.2018.07.248

Swacha, J., Paiva, J. C., Leal, J. P., Queirós, R., Montella, R., & Kosta, S. (2020). GEdIL—Gamified Education Interoperability Language. *Information, 11*(6), 287. doi:10.3390/info11060287

Swacha, J., Queirós, R., Paiva, J. C., Leal, J. P., Kosta, S., & Montella, R. (2020b). A roadmap to gamify programming education. In *First International Computer Programming Education Conference, ICPEC 2020*. Schloss Dagstuhl - Leibniz-Zentrum fur Informatik.

KEY TERMS AND DEFINITIONS

Application Programming Interface: Is an interface that defines interactions between multiple software applications or mixed hardware-software intermediaries.

Backend as a Service: Is a platform that automates backend side development and takes care of the cloud infrastructure.

Domain-Specific Language: Is a computer language specialized to a particular application domain. This contrasts with a general-purpose language (GPL), which is broadly applicable across domains.

Gamification: Application of game-design elements and game principles in non-game contexts.

Interoperability: Is a characteristic of a product or system, whose interfaces are completely understood, to work with other products or systems, in either implementation or access, without any restrictions.

Learning Standards: Are elements of declarative, procedural, schematic, and strategic knowledge that, as a body, define the specific content of an educational program.

Modeling Language: Is any language which can be used to express information or knowledge or systems in a structure that is defined by a consistent set of rules used for interpretation of the meaning of components in the structure.

ENDNOTES

1   Link: https://mambo.io/
2   Link: https://gametize.com/index
3   Link: https://www.gamelayer.co/
4   Link: https://spinify.com/
5   Link: https://pt.coursera.org
6   Link: https://www.udacity.com
7   Link: https://www.edx.org/
8   Link: https://www.codecademy.com/
9   Link: https://pt-pt.khanacademy.org/
10   Link: https://www.freecodecamp.org/

Chapter 2
The Gaming Experience With AI

Preety Khatri

Institute of Management Studies Noida, India

ABSTRACT

There are several uses of artificial intelligence in games that are useful for the better game design. With the help of AI, we can improve the games in different ways by simply playing them. In the game industry, when artificial intelligence of the game enhances to the profitable value of the game, this adds to better game reviews, which results to improve the experience of the player. By using AI, we can control both the player as well as non-player characters of the game. AI emphasizes on optimizing the performance of play, which means to measure the degree to which a player comes across the goals of the game, in case of player character. Whereas the role of AI in case of a non-player character emphasizes automatic game balancing mechanisms as well as allow dynamic difficulty adjustment. The use of AI for the empathetic player experience can improve and drive the design process of games. This chapter explores gaming with AI.

INTRODUCTION

There are several uses of Artificial Intelligence in games which are useful for the better game design. With the help of AI we can improve the games in different ways by simply playing them. In the game industry, when Artificial Intelligence of the game enhances to the profitable value of the game, then this adds to better game reviews. Which results to improve the experience of the player. By using AI, we can control both the characters that is the player as well as non-player character of the game. AI emphases on optimizing the performance of play which means to measure as the degree to which a player come across the goals of the game, in case of player character. Whereas the role of AI in case of a non-player character, it emphasis on automatic game balancing mechanisms as well as to allow dynamic difficulty adjustment. The use of AI for the empathetic of player experience which can improve and drive the design process of games (John & Jeannie, 2008).

In this chapter we will discuss about different Artificial Intelligence (AI) methods for game playing. These methods consists of generating interesting characters in the different types of games. At every stage of game playing, if Artificial Intelligence features are to be added, then it will enhance the game

DOI: 10.4018/978-1-6684-7589-8.ch002

playing features like, in case of winning the game, performing human-like and also provides entertainment .But they experience several of the similar challenges. Actually, there are various reasons why AI methods are used while in game designing as well as while in playing the game (Bob, 2002).

In this chapter we will discuss about different things and challenges while game design. Irrespective of why we want to introduce Artificial Intelligence in a game playing. With the help of different characteristics of the game, we will analyse, which methods be used efficiently to play the game. We will also discuss different Artificial Intelligence algorithms for game playing. Once these algorithms understood then we can make a well-versed choice about AI algorithms that is, which algorithm to play it. Depending upon the characteristics of the game, we could also analyse various methods which can be used in game designing as well as to play the games (John & Jeannie, 2008). We will also discuss about different applications of these methods while game playing. This chapter also emphasis on how Artificial Intelligence methods that can be applied in different types of games. We will demonstrate different types of examples of games using the methods of Artificial Intelligence. In this chapter we will also discuss about different types and most commonly used game-based frameworks. In this chapter we will also compare and analyse for testing AI game-playing algorithms. We will show the comparison between different games with AI features enabled. This chapter mainly discuss the use of AI methods to play to win, but also make several references to the experience-making characteristic of game-playing.

ARTIFICIAL INTELLIGENCE METHODS FOR GAME DESIGN

There are a numerous number of basic AI methods which are commonly used in Games like Finite state machines, behavior trees and utility based AI methods.

Finite State Machines (FSM) Method

A Finite State Machine is the game AI method which conquered the control.

FSMs are signified as graphs and these graphs are abstract representation of an interconnected set of symbols, events, objects, properties or actions of the phenomenon that is required. The graph consists of different states or nodes and these are enclosed with mathematical abstraction and transitions (to represent a conditional relationship between different nodes). A Finite State Machine belongs to the expert-knowledge systems area (Dave & Kevin, 2010).

The main property of FSM s that it can only be in one state at a time. It means if the condition in the equivalent transition is satisfied then the current state can change to another one.

We can define with the help of three main components:

- **States:** It consists of a number of states which are used to store information regarding a particular job.
- **Transitions:** In between states, there are large number of transitions which specify a state change. These transitions are defined by a condition which must be satisfied.
- **Actions:** It consists of a large number of set of actions and these actions must be monitored and followed within each state.

Finite State Machine method is easy to design, visualize, implement and debug. But on a large scale, these may be complex to design and these are limited to certain tasks inside game AI. But the main disadvantage of FSMs is that they are not dynamic as well as not flexible. After the completion of design, these are tested and debugged. Finally the FSMs end up describing with expected behavior in games (Antonios et al., 2013).

Behavior Trees Method

A Behavior Tree is an expert-knowledge system which is correspondingly same as an FSM. It maintains transitions in between a finite set of behaviors. The main advantage of Behavior Trees over Finite state machine is their modularity. It means if designed sound, they can produce complex behaviors which consists of simple tasks (Champandard, 2007).

The Behavior Trees and Finite State Machine both differ in terms of as they are composed of behaviors rather than states. Similar as FSMs, Behavior Trees are easy to design, test and debug. These consists of a tree structure having a root node (parent node) and corresponding child nodes, which represents the behavior of tree structure.

Figure 1.

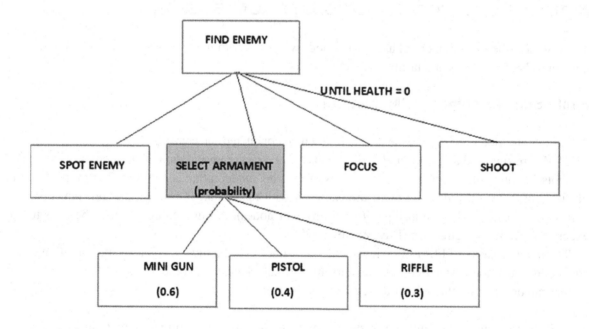

As shown in Figure 1, which represents the Behavior Tree. Here in the Figure, the root is like a sequence behavior, here represented as attack enemy. It implements the child behaviors like find enemy, select Armament, focus and shoot and this procedure should be executed in sequence from left to right. The thickness of the parent-child connecting lines is done with the help of select Armament behavior which is a probability selector giving higher probability. It is indicated by that is the mini gun (0.6) as compared to the pistol (0.4) or the riffle (0.3). Once in the shoot behavior the decorator till health = 0 requests the behavior to run until the enemy dies.

The Behavior Trees traversal start from the root. The operation of execution in between parent-child pairs done as following: if the behavior is still active then the child run, if the behavior is completed then success, if the behavior failed then failure.

There are three different types of nodes in Behvior Tree (Champandard, 2007):

- **Sequence:** If the child behavior get ahead, then the sequence carry on and finally the parent node succeeds if all child behavior succeed else the sequence fails.
- **Selector:** The priority and the probability selectors are the two types of nodes. When the priority selectors are used then the child behavior should be ordered in a list and tried one after the other. Whereas in case of probability selector, when it is used then the child behaviors are selected based on parent-child probabilities (that is set by the Behavior Tree designer). Irrespective of the selector type used, the next child in the order is selected or the selector fails, in case, if the child behavior fails. If the child behavior succeeds the selector succeeds.
- **Decorator:** The decorator node improves the complexity and also develops the capacity of a single child behavior (Damian, 2005).

If we compare Behavior Trees with Finite State Machine, then Behavior Trees are more flexible to design and easier to test. While given that they are static knowledge representations, but their dynamicity is low.

Utility-Based Method

As we know that if there is the lack of behavioral modularity in-game and across games tasks then it is very harmful for the development of high quality Artificial Intelligence. So there is another method for ad-hoc behavior authoring and it removes all the limitations of Finite State Machine and Behavior Tree method. This method is known as Utility-Based AI method and it is used for the design of decision making systems and control in games. By using this method, the instances in the game gets allocated a specific utility function, which provides a value for the importance of the specific instance (Christoffer, Antonios, Julian, & Georgios, 2014).

For example, consider the significance of an enemy which is present at a specific distance or the significance of an agent's health being low (specifically in this particular framework). Given that the set of all utilities available to an agent. The utility-based AI elects which is the most important option should be think at this moment. The utility-based approach is based on utility function design and grounded in the utility theory of economics. This procedure is similar to the design of membership functions (in a fuzzy set) (Michele, 2012).

A utility can extent everything from observable objective data like enemy Health (in this case) to subjective notions like mood, emotions and threat. The numerous utilities regarding possible decisions or actions or these may be accumulated into linear or non-linear formulas. This also helps to guide the agent so that he may take decisions based on the combined utility (Christoffer, Antonios, Julian, & Georgios, 2014). The utility values can also be checked, so the utility-based AI architectures observe all available options and allocates a utility to them. The utility-based AI also select the option which have the highest utility, whereas in case of Finite State Machine and Behavior Trees, these would examine one decision at a time (which is not the appropriate one).

Consider an example of utility-based AI where the utility based on the weapon (armament) selection (Steve & Nathan, 2013).

For selecting an armament, an agent required to consider the following (Christoffer, Antonios, Julian, & Georgios, 2014):

- **The Range Utility Function:** Depending on the distance for instance, it adds value to the utility of a weapon. But if the distance is short, then the weapons (pistols) may be allocated to higher utility.
- **Inertia Utility Function:** To maintain the changes of weapons which are not very frequent, for this, it allocates higher utility value to the current weapon.
- **Random Noise:** To maintain that the agent does not always pick the same weapon (which is given in the same game situation), for this, it adds non-determinism to the selection.
- **Ammo:** It yields a utility regarding the current level of ammunition.
- **Indoors:** It make somebody have to pay the use of specific weapons indoors like a grenade through a Boolean utility function (for example, 1 utility value if the grenade is used outdoors, 0 otherwise). It is the responsibility of an agent to make a regular check of the existing weapons.it also allocates the utility scores (to all of them) and also helps in selection of weapon with the best total utility.

Utility-based AI has like as the decision of the game agent is dependent on a number of different considerations, so it is modular in nature.

AI ALGORITHMS (FOR GAME PLAYING)

Tree Search

Every single AI problem can be cast as a search problem. This may be resolved with the help of finding the best model, plan, function, path etc. there are different search algorithms which may be under the category of tree search algorithms. These types of algorithms being the core of Artificial Intelligence (Bob, 2002). These search algorithms may be understood and analysed as building a search tree, where the root is the node demonstrating the state (from where the search starts). Actions are represented with the help of edges in this tree and the states represented with the help of nodes. In a given state, there are normally various different actions which may be taken into consideration. There are different types of tree search algorithms:

Uninformed Search

Uninformed search algorithms are algorithms which search a state space without any extra information about the goal. The most common uninformed search algorithms like fundamental computer science algorithms (Dave & Kevin, 2010). For example, Depth-first search is an uninformed search algorithm which before backtracking and trying another branch, it discovers each branch as far as possible.

At every iteration of its main loop, the depth-first search first chooses a branch and then in the next iteration, determine the resulting node. After a terminal node is extended, in that case, like depth-first search grows the list of visited nodes till it discovers the one which has unexplored actions. The depth-first search when used for playing a game, it discovers the significance of a single move until the game is in the condition of won or lost and finally taking a different move close to the end states whereas the Breadth-first search is contrary of depth-first search. Breadth-first search Instead of discovering all the significance of a single action, it discover all the actions from a single node before discovering any of the nodes resulting from taking those actions (Vadim et al., 2011).

So, all nodes at depth one are explored before all nodes at depth two, then all nodes at depth three, etc. While the above-mentioned are fundamental uninformed search algorithms. So there are many dissimilarities and combinations of these algorithms, this is the reason is that the new uninformed search algorithms have been developed.

Best-First Search

In best-first search, in the search tree the extension of nodes is informed by having information about the goal state.

By some principle the node that is closest to the goal state is extended first. A* is the familiar best-first search algorithm. The A* algorithm having a list of open nodes and these nodes are next to an explored node.

For each open node, an approximation of the distance of node from the goal is required and prepared. Based on a lowest cost basis, the new nodes are chosen and explore. Here the cost means it is the distance from the origin node and also included the approximation of the distance to the goal. A* can be designed as a two- or three-dimensional space.

In order to manage with large, deceptive spaces there are various alterations of this basic algorithm have been suggested 0which consist of real-time heuristic search, planning algorithms for dynamic game worlds, jump point search for uniform-cost grids, path finding algorithms etc (Kai et al., 2015). As opposed to simply searching physical locations, the A* algorithm may be used to search in the space of game states. The best-first search is used for planning instead of navigation (Michele, 2012).

Minimax

For uninformed or informed search algorithms may be used to discover a path to the optimal game state (Paul & Austin, 2016). But for the two-player games, the other player wants to win and tries for that, then the activities of every player is based on the activities of the other player (Adi et al., 2014). But for these types of games, there is requirement of adversarial search and this search consists of actions of two or more adversarial players.

So, if we talk about the most effective adversarial search algorithm, it is known as Minimax. This Minimax algorithm has been used very effective for playing classic perfect-information two-player board games for example Chess and Checkers. The main concept used in Minimax algorithm which interchanges among player 1 and player 2, for example, in Chess, the black and white player and these named as max and min player (John & Jeannie, 2008).

For every player, the likely moves are explored and for the other player also, all possible moves are also explored., and also explored all possible combinations of moves have been explored till the end of the game. It means it explored whether there is a win or a loss or a draw. The outcome of this whole process is from the root node down to the leaves, the generation of the whole game tree (Antonios et al., 2013). So the result of the game notifies the utility function and that is applied onto the leaf nodes. The utility function identifies about the current game about the status of the current game configuration and how good it is for a player. To find out what action each player would have taken at any given state, the algorithm traverses up the search tree by backing-up values from leaves through the branch nodes.

For this, it consider that each player attempts to play optimally. So from the viewpoint of the max player, it plays and tries to maximize its score and from the viewpoint of min player, it plays and tries to minimize the score of max. This is the reason this algorithm is named as Minimax. A min node calculates the min of its child values whereas a max node of the tree calculates the max of its child values (Paul & Austin, 2016).

But for max, the optimal winning strategy is found. A win is reachable for max for all moves that min can make, on min's turn. For min the optimal strategy is when a win is possible individually of what move max will take (Adi et al., 2014). Start at the root of the tree and choose the moves primary to child nodes of highest value, this is the case, to obtain a winning strategy for max. Whereas in case of min's turn, the child nodes having the lowest value are selected. As shown in Figure 1.2, which shows the basic steps of Minimax.

Figure 2.

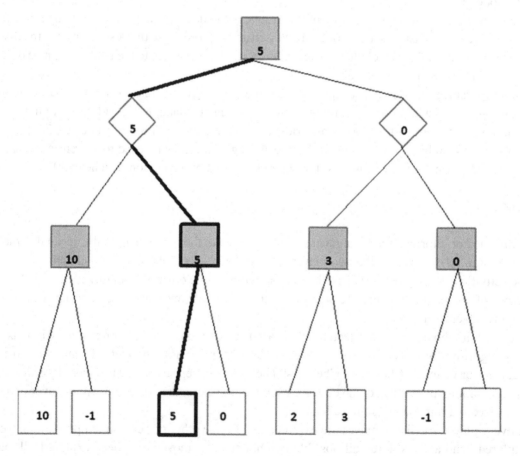

In this Figure 2, which demonstrate an abstract game tree showing the Minimax algorithm. There are two different types of options like for each player max (which is symbolised as red squares) plays first and for min (is symbolised as blue diamonds) plays second and finally the max plays one last time. The terminal nodes symbolised with white squares comprising a positive or winning, a negative or losing or a zero or draw score for the max player.

Succeeding the Minimax strategy, the utility/scores are traversed up to the root of the game tree. Here in this example, the optimal play for min and max are represented in bold and if both players play optimally, then the max successes a score of 5. That is infeasible for any game by exploring all possible moves. All actual applications of the Minimax algorithm, and use a state estimation function to calculate the desirability of each game state at that depth and cut off search at a given depth (Adi et al., 2014). Like, in Chess game, a state evaluation function may be sum of the number of white pieces on the board and minus the number of black pieces (Paul & Austin, 2016). The condition is that, whether this number is higher, similarly the improved the state is for the white player.

Monte Carlo Tree Search

As discussed above, Minimax algorithm can be used for playing various games, but there are many games which Minimax will not play well. In precise way, we can say that the games having a high branching factor, where at a given point of time there are several potential actions to be taken. This results to Minimax which will only forever search a very shallow tree.

Another fact about game playing by using algorithm is that, in case of Minimax, it does not work very well while game playing when it works to construct and evaluate a good state evaluation function (John & Jeannie, 2008). For example, the board game Go is a perfect information and deterministic game which is the best example of both of these phenomena. The branching factor of board game Go isa pprox. 300, however the Chess game play usually has around 30 actions.

The Go game positional nature is all about proximate the adversary, which makes it very tough to correctly evaluate the value of a given board state. For a long time, most of the games like the best Go-playing programs were based on Minimax in the world, these may be hardly exceed the playing strength of a human beginner (Jacob et al., 2011). So in 2007, Monte Carlo Tree Search (MCTS) algorithm was developed. As the evolution of Monte Carlo Tree Search (MCTS) algorithm, there was a change could be seen in board game Go like the playing strength of the best Go programs increased significantly.

Apart from the complex perfect information, the deterministic games which may be for example, Chess, Go, and Checkers. The imperfect information games which were like Poker, Battleship, Bridge. The non-deterministic games for example, like as monopoly and backgammon cannot be solved with the help of Minimax due to the precise nature of the algorithm. In these types of games, Monte Carlo Tree Search (MCTS) not only disables the tree size limitation of Minimax but also, given adequate computation decision. This come close to the Minimax tree of the game (Damian, 2005).

So here the question arises is that how does MCTS handle high branching factors and where there is a lack of good state evaluation functions it also has the lack of determinism and perfect information. To begin with, it does not exploration all the branches of the search tree to an even depth. But instead it focuses on the more favourable branches. This is the reason, it makes it possible to search some confident branches to a significant depth although the branching factor is high.

Additionally, to get around the lack of good evaluation functions, determinism and imperfect information, the standard formulation of Monte Carlo Tree Search (MCTS) uses rollouts to evaluate the quality of the game state, randomly playing from a game state till the end of the game to see the predictable win or loss result. The utility values which is obtained with the help of the random simulations. These can be used efficiently to regulate the policy towards a best-first strategy for example, like a Minimax tree approximation.

At the start of a run of the Monte Carlo Tree Search (MCTS) algorithm, the tree comprises of a single node demonstrating the current state of the game. So we can say that, the algorithm then iteratively forms a search tree with the help of adding and evaluating new nodes which represents the game states. At any time this process may be interrupted and also interpreting MCTS an anytime algorithm. Monte Carlo Tree Search (MCTS) algorithm needs simply two pieces of information to function. The game rules that would, consecutively, produce the existing moves in the game and also the terminal state evaluation, taking into consideration, whether that is loss, a win, a game score or a draw. The vanilla version of Monte Carlo Tree Search (MCTS) algorithm does not involve a heuristic function, which is, in turn, is a key advantage over Minimax (John & Jeannie, 2008).

The basic loop of the Monte Carlo Tree Search (MCTS) algorithm, which may be divided into four steps:

- **Selection,**
- **Expansion (here the first two steps are called the tree policy)**
- **Simulation**
- **Backpropagation**

As shown in Figure 3, which displays the above steps involved.

Figure 3.

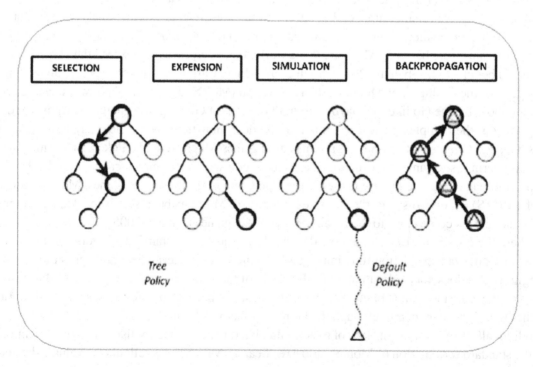

The simulation step might seem counter-intuitive, that is, taking random actions which appears alike no good way to play a game. On the other hand, it delivers a comparatively impartial estimate of the quality of a game state. In actual fact, the better a game state is, the more simulations are probable to end up winning the game. At least, this is correct for games like board game Go, in that case a game will continuously to reach a terminal state inside a definite comparatively small number of moves for example consider it may be 300 for board game Go.

If we talk about some other games, like Chess, it is ideally possible to play an arbitrary number of moves and without winning or losing the game. For many video games, it is feasible that any random sequence of actions will not terminate the game except some timer runs out (John & Jeannie, 2008). It means that most simulations will be extended like it may be tens or hundreds of thousands of steps. But it does not produce useful information. For example, in Super Mario Bros game, the application of random actions would most possible make Mario dance all over the place his starting point this till the time is up.

In most of the cases it is therefore useful to complement the simulation step with the help of state evaluation function and we know that this strategy commonly used in Minimax. So for a set number of steps, a simulation is accomplished. If a terminal state is not reached then a state evaluation is implemented in lieu of a win-lose estimation. But in some cases it may be even be helpful to switch the simulation step exclusively with a state evaluation function. In case of Monte Carlo Tree Search (MCTS) algorithm, It should be take care that there are various variations of the basic MCTS algorithm. So it could be actually be very useful to check the MCTS as an algorithm framework or family instead of a single algorithm.

HOW CAN AI PLAY GAMES

In this topic we will discuss about the core AI methods, and also for each type of algorithms it will go over and examined how they may be used to play games.

Planning-Based Approaches

The different algorithms that select actions with the help of planning a set of future actions in a state Space, these are usually applicable to games, and also these do not require any training time (Bob, 2002). If searching in the game's state space, there is no requirement of a fast forward model. Tree search algorithms are mostly used to play games, either or in supporting roles or on their own in game-playing agent architectures (Kai et al., 2015).

Classic Tree Search

Classic tree search methods, since the very beginning of research on AI and games have been used in game-playing roles. The basic concepts of adversarial tree search have not actually changed since then, there have been several tweaks to some new algorithms and existing algorithms. Overall we can say that the classic tree search methods may be definitely be applied in games that feature a low branching factor, full observability and a fast forward model. Ideally they can solve any deterministic game which is having the features with full observability for the player. They still fail in games consisting of large state spaces. Best-first search, which is a numerous variants of the A* algorithm. So Best-first search is mostly used in modern video games for path-planning (Kai et al., 2015). In the case of A* algorithm, the search is generally done in physical space instead of the state space. So here there is no requirement of forward model.

Because of due to the space is pseudo-continuous, this is the reason the search is generally done on the nodes of a lattice or mesh or overlaid on the area to be traversed. Only for navigation the best-first search is used and it not used for the full decision-making of the agent. Different types of methods like finite-state machines or behavior trees which are used to find out where to go (Champandard, 2007). But in case of A* algorithm, it is used to find out how to get there. There are latest additions to the family of best-first algorithms which consists of the jump point search (JPS) and this may increase the performance by orders of magnitude related to standard A* (under the right circumstances).

Hierarchical path finding which is also the research area and which is based on the idea of dividing up an area into subareas. By using different algorithms is used to decide about how to go between and within the areas (Dave & Kevin, 2010). For a modern video game by choosing a path-planning algorithm is generally a matter of choosing the algorithm and which works best in the given environment. Apart from the path-planning algorithm, the best-first algorithms like A* which may be used for controlling all aspects of game behavior. So the main method is to search in the state space of the game, by using fast forward model.

Stochastic Tree Search

The Monte Carlo Tree Search (MCTS) algorithm came into the picture in 2006. Similarly the board game Go also made its existence in game playing. The classic adversarial search had implemented poorly on Go, because the branching factor is very high. Similarly the classic adversarial search had implemented partly because the nature of Go creates it very hard to take decisions the value of a board state (Christoffer, Antonios, Julian, & Georgios, 2014). The Monte Carlo Tree Search (MCTS) partly overwhelms these experiments with the help of building unnecessary trees, where not all moves required to be discovered to the same depth and by doing random rollout till the end of the game. The AlphaGo software which when came into market in the world in 2016 and 2017, beat two of the best human Go players (Jacob et al., 2011) and is built around the MCTS algorithm.

The success of Monte Carlo Tree Search (MCTS) algorithm on Go has directed practitioners and researchers to discover its use for playing an inclusive range of other games, that consists of real-time strategy games, racing games, trading card games, platform games etc. Obviously, these games be different in various ways from Go. But the Go is a real-time strategy game or a deterministic perfect information game, like StarCraft, a trading card game like Magic.

The other problem which exists in the games having adequate time granularity. To reach a terminal state, which may have an excessively long time for a rollout that is a loss or win. In many video games, without winning or losing the game, it is possible to take an arbitrary number of actions. Without doing something which affects the result of the game.

Given that there are huge number of alterations to all components of the Monte Carlo Tree Search (MCTS) algorithm, which makes more logically to think of MCTS as a general algorithmic framework instead of as a single algorithm. There are a variety of games which may be played either with the help of Monte Carlo Tree Search (MCTS) or uninformed search like breadth-first search or it can be informed search for example A* algorithm. Determining about which method to be used is not at all times straightforward, but these methods are simple to test and implement. The Minimax game playing algorithm which may be used for adversarial games and between two players.

However the other forms of uninformed search are best used for single-player games. Best-first search involves some kind of estimate of a distance to a goal state. But this does not required to be a physical position or the end goal of the game. There are Variations of Monte Carlo Tree Search (MCTS) which may be used for both single-player as well as for two-player games, and usually when branching factors are high then outperform uninformed search.

Evolutionary Planning

The decision making with the help of planning does not required to be built on tree search. Instead, for planning one can use optimization algorithms. Starting from an initial Point, the basic idea is that instead of searching for a sequence of actions, you can enhance the whole action sequence. Otherwise we can say that, you are searching the space of thorough action sequences and this is required only for those which have maximum utility (Christoffer, Antonios, Julian, & Georgios, 2014).

By estimating the utility of a given action sequence, which is ended by simply taking all the actions in the sequence in simulation, also perceiving the value of the state extended after taking all those actions. An optimization algorithm can also explore the plan space in a very diverse manner related to a tree search algorithm (Christoffer, Antonios, Julian, & Georgios, 2014). All tree search algorithms which start from the origin state or the root of the tree and from that point build a tree.

Instead the evolutionary algorithms look the plan as simply a sequence, which may accomplish crossover or mutations at any point in the string. This may help for managing the search at different areas of the plan space so that a tree search algorithm would discover for the same problem. There are variety of optimization algorithms which may be used, as there are lots of research and studies on optimization-based planning in games which may be found in the literature use evolutionary algorithms (Kai et al., 2015). In the specific implementation for the Physical Traveling Salesman Problem, an evolutionary algorithm was used to produce a plan every time step.

The plan was denoted as a sequence of 10-20 actions. To search for plans a standard evolutionary algorithm was used.

The first step of the plan was executed, after a plan was found, as this is the similar case with a tree search algorithm. Evolutionary planning is mostly favourable as a technique for managing very large branching factors. Given the number of actions available per unit or the number of units the player controls, the branching factor is about one million. So only a single turn in advance was planned.

Evolutionary planning in games is a modern discovery, and on this technique there is merely a limited number of studies so far. But it is not well known about under what circumstances this method performs well. The main uncertain problem which is how to achieve evolutionary adversarial Planning, while planning based on tree search works in the presence of an opponent like for example the minimax algorithm.

Planning with Symbolic Representations

While doing planning on the level of in-game actions which involves a fast forward model. But there are other several techniques of using planning in games. In general, one can plan in an abstract demonstration of the game's state space. On the level of symbolic representations, the field of automated planning has studied planning for period of times. Specifically, a language based on first-order logic is required to represent states, events and actions. To find paths from the current state to an end state, the tree search methods are applied. By using the high-level representation, it is required to plan much advance instead of it would be possible when planning on the scale of specific game actions (Kai et al., 2015). This type of representation, instead, involves manually describing actions and states.

Reinforcement Learning

A reinforcement learning algorithm is any algorithm which resolves a reinforcement learning problem. This also consists of different types of algorithms from approximate dynamic programming family or the temporal Difference. The applications of evolutionary algorithms to reinforcement learning which consists of like genetic programming, neuro evolution and other methods also (Champandard, 2004). In this section, so the reinforcement learning consists of the both classic methods (which includes those which involve deep neural networks) and evolutionary methods as they are useful and applied for playing games. For describing the difference between these methods the other ways may be elaborated such as the difference between ontogenetic that is the way through which studies during lifetimes and also the one known as the phylogenetic that is which studies amongst life time's methods (Jacek, 2010).

When there is learning time available then the Reinforcement learning algorithms are appropriate to games. Mostly this means lots of training time that is the furthermost reinforcement learning methods will require to play a game thousands, or possibly even millions, of the times in order to play it well. Consequently, it is very valuable and useful to have a technique of playing the game and is much faster than a very large server farm or the real-time (Antonios et al., 2013). Out of all the reinforcement learning algorithms, there are some of the reinforcement learning algorithms (Jacek, 2010), which also need a forward model. Once this type of model has been accomplished, then a reinforcement-learned policy which may be generally executed but this is a very fast technique.

It is important to note that the planning-based methods which are used for playing games, these methods can't be openly related with the reinforcement learning methods. But they may be solve different problems for example, like the planning involves a forward model and substantial time at each time step. Similarly the reinforcement learning while requires the learning time and which may or may not needs a forward model.

Classic and Deep Reinforcement Learning

The classic reinforcement learning methods (Jacek, 2010) which were used with games primary on. But in some cases with the help of significant success. An algorithm has been devised and this may be explained and stated as the first classic reinforcement learning algorithm and this is came into existence in 1959 to produce a self-learning Checkers player. Instead of the very limited computational resources, to beat its creator, this algorithm manages and learned to play sufficiently well. The other one success for classic reinforcement learning in game-playing which has been came a few decades later, when the modern formulation was used of temporal difference learning (Champandard, 2004) and this was used to teach a simple neural network to play Backgammon (also named as TD-gammon).

After starting with no information and basically playing in contrast to itself, it learned to play unexpectedly well. So during the 1990s and early 2000s, this success motivated considerably interest in reinforcement learning. But, the progress was limited by the non-existence of good function approaches for the value function. Instead there are different algorithms for example, like the Q-learning will possibly come together to the optimal policy under the right conditions. In fact the right conditions are very limiting. In precise, these consists of all the state values or fstate values, which are the types that may be stored separately (Owen et al., 2016). But, for most exciting games there are various possible states for this to be possible that is practically any video game which has however billions of states. It means that the table may be very big to be appropriate in memory, and that utmost states have not to be visited while learning.

It is essential to use a compressed demonstration of the value function and which occupies less memory. This does not needs about the state that is each state to be stop with in order to compute its value., instead, it may be based on adjacent states which have been visited. So we can say that, what is required is a function estimated, for example like a neural network. But with the help of neural networks which composed with time-based difference learning (Jacek, 2010) tries out to be non-trivial. So tt easier to come across catastrophic forgetting and where sophisticated policies are untrained in favour of degenerate policies for example, like same as taking the same action.

But, to automatically understand one of the techniques involved, assume that what would typically takes place for a reinforcement learning agent playing a game. The agent will normally see long stretches of negative reward or no reward. The back propagation algorithm will be trained only with the target value of that reward, only when the same reward is come across for a long time. This is similar to training on a single training example for a long term, this is the case of supervised learning. Irrespective of the input, the expected result is that the network learns to only output that target value. In the use of reinforcement learning, the major success in terms of time-based difference range together with function approximators and that would be come across in 2015.

Every network was proficient to play a single game and this was with the help of inputs being the raw pixels of the game's visuals, composed with the score, and the outcome would be the fire button and controller's directions. Significantly, they achieved to overcome the problems related with using time-based difference methods together with neural networks by using a method called experience replay. So the short sequences of gameplay are replayed and stored to the network in changeable order, so to break up the long chains of related rewards and states. So by using small Batch, this may be realized as similar to batch-based training in supervised learning,

Evolutionary Reinforcement Learning

The other main family is evolutionary methods of reinforcement learning methods. In general, to develop the topology and weights of neural networks or programs this is done with the help of using evolutionary algorithms. The fitness evaluation contains in using the program or the neural network to play the game and using the score or result as a fitness function. Approximately starting around 2005, there are large number of advances had been made by applying neuro evolution to playing various types of video games. This consists of various applications strategy games, car racing, real-time strategy games, classic arcade games such as Pac-Man, first-person shooters etc.

Probably the main takeout from this work is that the neuro evolution is exceptionally useful and which may be functional to a widespread variety of games and this is normally in various different ways for each game. For example, consider in a simple car racing game, it was exposed that developing neural Networks which represented as state evaluators, and in combination with a simple one-step look ahead search significantly, the outperformed developing neural networks working as action evaluators and the input representation matters also (Jacob et al., 2011).

As we know that the egocentric inputs are normally strongly chosen, and also there are supplementary considerations also for specific game types, like how to characterize multiple Adversaries. In cases where the state can be represented using relatively few dimensions, the Neuro evolution has seen abundant success in learning policies, for example, consider fewer than 50 units in the neural network's input layer. This is usually easier to get working and to tune other than the classic reinforcement learning algorithms of the chronological difference range. But, the neuro evolution appears to have problems enlarging up to problems and having very large input spaces which involve deep and large neural networks, for example, like those using high-dimensional pixel inputs.

At present, just about all successful examples of learning which are right from high-dimensional pixel inputs and it use deep Q-learning or related methods. However there are methods that are associated like neuro evolution with unsupervised learning. The main benefit of this association is that the controllers are learned which uses a compressed demonstration of the visual feed as input.

Supervised Learning

By using supervised learning the games can also be played. Or relatively, with the help of supervised learning, the controllers or policies for playing games can be learned. So the main basic idea is that to record and manage the traces of human players which were playing a game. Also to train some function approximator so that it should perform like the human player. These traces are put away as lists of tuples for example, like <features, target>. Wherever the features denote an observation of it that would be available to the agent or the game state. The target is the action which the human took in that state (Jacob et al., 2011). The game can be played only when the function approximator is sufficiently trained and the game may be played the style of the human it was trained on. This is done with the help of just only taking whatsoever action the trained function approximator returns when presented with the current game state. Otherwise, as an alternative of learning to expect what action to take and for this one can also learn to forecast the value of states. In conjunction with a search algorithm, it also uses the trained function approximator which was used to play the game.

Chimeric Game Players

Despite the fact that the reinforcement learning, planning and supervised learning are basically dissimilar methods to playing games and also for solving the game-playing problem in various constraints, but it does not means that they cannot be united. Although, there are various examples of successful chimeras or hybrids of methods from these three broad classes. The dynamic scripting is one of the example and which can be observed as a form of a learning classifier system, where it comprises a script-based or the rule based illustration joined with reinforcement learning. The dynamic scripting regulates the importance of scripts with the help of reinforcement learning at Runtime. This is based on the direct rewards achieved and the current game state also.

Dynamic scripting has seen various applications in games comprising real-time strategy games or the fighting games etc. So this method has been used generally for Artificial Intelligence that familiarises to the skills of the player, in that way pointing at the experience of the player and not essentially at winning the game.

FUTURISTIC APPLICATIONS OF AI IN THE GAMING INDUSTRY

AI's impact to the gaming industry overrides the sector of gaming business, instead of the gaming experience sector. Investors have recognized that the gaming industry is quickly blending with real-world experiences. By considering that the monetization chances of this blended world will only continue to have rising graph, AI powered tools are being won over by them. According to research study it has been found that use of AI on gaming industry has vast impact and we can see and think about the actual nature of games. But, the most stimulating element, possibly, in the visualisation of the future is not just a piece of software that has taken on an creative role in the process of building games, but also that this type of technology could create experiences so tailored to preferences that are continuously dynamic and evergreen. So according to the future impact in gaming industry, should take care some aspects:

- Developer should make smarter games as well as interactive
- Should focus on making games more realistic
- To improve the overall gaming experience
- To transform overall developer skills
- Making PC's as well as smarter mobile games

SUMMARY

In this chapter we have learned about various methods of game playing. We have also discussed here how these methods which are comprises of producing interesting characters in the different types of games. We have also discussed the several reasons about AI methods while game designing and playing (John & Jeannie, 2008) . We have also discussed about challenges and different things while game playing. We have already discussed about which methods may be used proficiently to play the game. In this chapter, we also discussed about various Artificial Intelligence algorithms for game playing and also how Artificial Intelligence methods that can be applied in different types of games with the help of various example.

REFERENCES

Adi, B., M¨uller, M., & Jonathan, S. (2014). Near optimal hierarchical path-finding. *Journal of Game Development, 1*(1), 7–28.

Antonios, L., Georgios, N., & Yannakakis, J. T. (2013). Sentient Sketchbook: Computer-aided game level authoring. *Proceedings of ACM Conference on Foundations of Digital Games*, 213–220.

Bob, A. (2002). *The beauty of response curves*. AI Game Programming Wisdom.

Champandard. (2007). Behavior trees for next-gen game AI. In *Game Developers Conference*. Audio Lecture.

Champandard, A. J. (2004). *AI game development: Synthetic creatures with learning and reactive behaviors*. New Riders.

Christoffer, H., Antonios, L., Julian, T., & Georgios, N. (2014). Generative agents for player decision modeling in games. FDG.

Christoffer, H., Antonios, L., Julian, T., & Georgios, N. (2014). Personas versus clones for player decision modeling. In *International Conference on Entertainment Computing*, (pp. 159–166). Springer.

Damian, I. (2005). Handling complexity in the Halo 2 AI. *Game Developers Conference.*

Dave, M., & Kevin, D. (2010). Improving AI decision modeling through utility theory. *Game Developers Conference.*

Jacek, M. (2010). *Knowledge-free and learning-based methods in intelligent game playing.* Springer.

Jacob, S., Igor, V., & Risto, M. (2011). Human-like behavior via neuroevolution of combat behavior and replay of human traces. *Computational Intelligence and Games (CIG), IEEE Conference on*, 329–336.

John, B., & Jeannie, N. (2008). *Game development essentials: Game artificial intelligence.* Delmar Pub.

Kai, N., Mubbasir, K., Alexander, S., Francisco, G., & Norman, B. (2015). Planning approaches to constraint-aware navigation in dynamic environments. *Computer Animation and Virtual Worlds, Planning, 26*(2), 119–139.

Michele, P. (2012). The use of Fuzzy Logic for Artificial Intelligence in Games. Technical report, University of Milano.

Nathan, R. (2012). Benchmarks for grid-based pathfinding. *IEEE Transactions on Computational Intelligence and AI in Games, 4*(2), 144–148. doi:10.1109/TCIAIG.2012.2197681

Owen, S., Antonios, L., & Georgios, N. (2016). A holistic approach for semantic-based game generation. In *Computational Intelligence and Games*. CIG.

Paul, T., & Austin, S. (2016). Building a near-optimal navigation mesh. *IEEE Conference, AI Game Programming Wisdom, 1*, 298–304.

Steve, R., & Nathan, S. (2013). Path finding Architecture Optimizations. In *Game AI Pro: Collected Wisdom of Game AI Professionals*. CRC Press.

Vadim, B., Yngvi, B., Nathan, R., & Ramon, L. (2011). Real-time heuristic search for pathfinding in video games. In *Artificial Intelligence for Computer Games* (pp. 1–30). Springer.

This research was previously published in Analyzing Future Applications of AI, Sensors, and Robotics in Society; pages 141-157, copyright year 2021 by Engineering Science Reference (an imprint of IGI Global).

Chapter 3
Acceptance of Virtual Reality Games:
A Multi–Theory Approach

Mehmet Kosa

https://orcid.org/0000-0003-1564-2666
Tilburg University, The Netherlands

Ahmet Uysal
Stanford University, Stanford, USA

P. Erhan Eren
Middle East Technical University, Turkey

ABSTRACT

As virtual reality (VR) games are getting more widespread, the need to understand the interaction between players and the VR games is gaining prominence. The present study examines player endorsement of virtual reality games from an amalgamation of technology acceptance, self-determination, and flow theory perspectives. A survey was carried out with participants (N = 396) who had played a VR game at least once and at most five times. Structural equation modeling analyses showed that perceived ease of use was the primary predictor for satisfaction of self-determination constructs (autonomy and competence) and flow constructs (immersion and concentration), which in turn predicted player enjoyment. Accordingly, the results suggest the importance of including self-determination constructs in addition to the flow perspective within the context of technology acceptance model, for explaining the acceptance of VR gaming. Findings also showed that enjoyment resulted in positive attitudes towards VR gaming, and these attitudes predicted intention to play VR games.

DOI: 10.4018/978-1-6684-7589-8.ch003

INTRODUCTION

Virtual Reality (VR) is defined as "A high-end user-computer interface that involves real-time simulation and interactions through multiple sensorial channels." (Grigore and Coiffet, 1994). Providing a higher display and interaction fidelity with respect to regular devices, VR creates a heightened presence and engagement in humans, which make this technology attractive (McMahan et al., 2012; Steed et al., 2016). In general VR is identified with head mounted displays and it was found that head mounted displays are different than desktop monitors in terms of user satisfaction (Santos et al., 2009), arousal, task performance or presence (Kim et al., 2012). These differences signify the prominence of studying the use of VR in addition to the use of traditional devices. In addition to head mounted displays, olfactory stimulation is being integrated to VR systems as well (Feelreal, 2018). VR market is growing (Grand View Market, 2017) and with the investments of key players such as Microsoft, Sony or Nintendo, the cost of the technology will be diminishing in time making the hardware more affordable and VR technology will be reaching a broader audience (Kozlova, 2017). More people are interacting with the VR technology than ever making it important to delineate the factors associated with VR use. VR devices require software to run on them to be functional and the content provided on the software is critical for the overall VR market success (Martin, 2018). Therefore, companies provide software development kits (SDK) for developers to build their own content and contribute to the VR market (i.e. Google VR API).

Gaming is viewed as one of the main driving force for the development and adoption of VR technology in general (Sackville, 2018). Although VR technology can be used for non-leisure purposes such as training or treatment, currently users are more likely to adopt VR devices and consume VR games for leisure use such as gaming. It is reported that VR gaming market is at an increasing trend (Statista, 2016). In present day, VR games come in a variety of genres such as horror games (i.e. Edge of Nowhere), first-person shooter games (i.e. Doom) or role-playing games (i.e. Fallout 4) (Gurwin, 2018) where this variety attracts more players. In addition to personal spaces such as homes, these games are being experienced at VR gaming centers which are places where people can rent VR devices and play (Xiong, 2019; Castillo 2018). This might be another enabler for mass adoption of VR technology for society, resembling internet cafes helping the wide adoption of internet (Lee, 1999).

Hardware for VR is already with us for several decades now (O'Boyle and Willings, 2019). Nevertheless, VR game practitioners and potential investors are facing a major challenge. This challenge is referred as the "content problem" in VR domain and it is described as the scarcity of software and applications that support VR equipment (Matney, 2018). Once end users buy VR equipment, they can quickly exhaust what is available on the market. The shortage of VR applications creates opportunities for businesses. However, it is also a challenge to enter the market since it is a relatively unexplored territory. The lack of knowledge on how VR can be engaging, hinders the proliferation of VR gaming market. For VR gaming to break its current boundaries and become more prevalent, mainstream adoption is required and the users should be encouraged for continued use (ARVRtech, 2019). For that, the "content problem" needs to be solved (Bilyk, 2018). At this point, developers and managers need assistance to make informed decisions on what content should be produced and how this content translates to user motivations, enjoyment and positive player experiences (Bilyk, 2018). With this knowledge, they would feel less hesitant and can enter the market more courageously. Therefore, to create knowledge on VR gaming adoption, this study aimed to bring a perspective on VR gaming player experiences and reveal the factors which might be essential for VR gaming acceptance.

To be able to understand the intentions to use VR in general, researchers adopted the Technology Acceptance Model (TAM, Davis et al., 1989), which provides a helpful foundation and some of these studies have added enjoyment as a predictor in addition to the fundamental constructs of TAM (i.e. perceived ease of use; Huang et al., 2016; Chen et al., 2012; Mütterlein and Hess, 2017). Although enjoyment is relevant to VR gaming as well, VR gaming is fundamentally different than other VR applications in terms of user motivations and experiences. The reason is that, depending on whether a system is designed with hedonic purpose or utilitarian purpose in mind, the reasons for adoption might differ (Van der Heijden, 2004). It was shown that different motivations (hedonic vs utilitarian) can be related to different intentions (hedonic vs utilitarian) and context is important in acceptance (Cai et al., 2018; Childers et al., 2001). Although it is agreeable that some systems might have both hedonic and utilitarian values incorporated in them (e.g. gamified systems), VR applications that are solely designed for entertainment purposes (i.e. gaming) would substantially appeal to hedonic motivations of users. Therefore TAM extensions to non-gaming VR settings might not be directly applicable to the VR gaming domain. The literature on virtual reality gaming is scarce at best, and it is critical to understand what drives players to adopt this emerging technology for gaming purposes. The existing literature on virtual reality gaming is dominantly on learning/training (Vogel et al., 2006; Xu and Ke, 2016), display fidelity (McMahan et al., 2012), pain modulation (Das et al., 2005), traumatic brain injury (Pietrzak et al., 2014), stroke rehabilitation (Saposnik et al., 2010), physical activity (Brütsch et al., 2010; Levac et al., 2010), dynamic body balance (Rendon et al., 2012), prosocial behaviors (Rosenberg et al., 2013), anxiety treatment (Van Rooij et al., 2016), aging with disabilities (Lange et al., 2010) or emotion elicitation (Pallavicini et al., 2018). Although these are important areas, they are not targeted for VR adoption for pure entertainment purposes. It is crucial to understand why VR games are appealing in the first place. It is not clear if VR gaming affords separate player motivations with respect to other forms of gaming and if traditional video gaming motivations are directly applicable in VR gaming as well (Pallavicini et al., 2017). Thus the current study focuses on the leisure use of virtual reality, more specifically on virtual reality games and adopts TAM as its foundation. Main research question of this study is: What are the factors contributing to intention to play virtual reality games? To answer this question, first the literature is reviewed and then a motivational model that is based on technology acceptance model (TAM), self-determination theory (SDT) and flow theory is tested to examine player experience and endorsement of VR games.

BACKGROUND AND HYPOTHESES

Technology Acceptance Model

Technology Acceptance Model (TAM) (Davis et al., 1989), based on the Theory of Reasoned Action (TRA) (Ajzen and Fishbein, 1980) proposes that people's attitude towards acceptance of a technology predicts their intention to use. It also proposes that the people's attitudes are predicted by the perceived ease of use and perceived usefulness of the technology. Several studies provided support for this basic premise of TAM (i.e. Porter and Donthu, 2006; Dishaw and Strong, 1999; Vijayasarathy, 2004). Although, attitudes might not fully mediate the effect of perceived ease of use and perceived usefulness on intention (Davis, 1989; Lederer et al., 2000), research on VR adoption shows that attitude towards the VR technology is important (Liao et al., 1999; Bertrand and Bouchard, 2008). Also positive attitude was found to be higher in more interactive systems (Goh and Ping, 2014).

Majority of research on TAM focuses on utilitarian information systems. Utilitarian information systems can be defined as information systems that are mainly designed to accomplish business-oriented work with effectiveness (Van der Heijden, 2004). For instance, researchers tested TAM in the context of physicians' acceptance of telemedicine technology and found that perceived usefulness and perceived ease of use predicts attitude and attitude predicts intention to use (Hu et al., 1999). Another study found similar associations in the adoption of information technology in business settings (Hernandez et al., 2008). Several other studies supported TAM in adoption of utilitarian information systems (Legris et al., 2003; Marangunić and Granić, 2015).

On the other hand, information systems that are created for entertainment purposes are called hedonic information systems (HIS) (Van der Heijden, 2004). These systems may include games (desktop, console or mobile), mobile applications used for entertainment, music streaming services, gamified apps and so on. In a pioneering study that applied TAM to hedonic information systems, it was suggested that although TAM is a useful theory in explaining acceptance; it is a limited model for explaining the acceptance or adoption of entertainment based information systems, in its basic form (Van der Heijden, 2004). In fact, same study found that enjoyment was the main predictor of intention to use these systems rather than perceived usefulness. Therefore, TAM was updated for hedonic information systems while preserving its other relationships such as attitude-intention to use relationship. For instance, it was found that enjoyment and social image both predicted attitude, which in return, predicted intention to use online video games (Lin and Bhattacherjee, 2010). Another video game study on Massively Multiplayer Online Role-Playing Games found that enjoyment predicted behavioral intentions (Wu and Holsapple, 2014). Similarly, enjoyment and perceived playfulness predicted attitudes toward and intention to use social network games (Shin and Shin, 2011). Direct effect of enjoyment on intention to use was also shown in other but similar contexts such as 3D Worlds (Nah et al., 2011), social networking websites (Rosen and Sherman, 2006), mobile games and music streaming services (Merikivi et al., 2016; Hechler et al., 2016). A recent meta-analysis shows that enjoyment predicts attitude toward HIS, which in turn, predicts the intentions to use (Wu and Lu, 2013), providing support for the predictions on TAM in hedonic information systems. Despite not being in the hedonic context, there are also studies showing that enjoyment of using virtual reality predicts positive attitudes towards using virtual reality technology (Lee et al., 2018; Manis and Choi, 2018).

Consequently, it is also hypothesized that these basic associations of TAM would be also applicable to virtual reality games:

[H1] Positive attitude towards VR gaming positively impacts intention to play VR games.
[H2] Enjoyment positively impacts intention to play VR games.
[H3] Enjoyment positively impacts positive attitude towards VR gaming.

Flow Theory and TAM

Flow is defined as the psychological state when one experiences optimal mental states and experiences (Csikszentmihalyi, 1990). It is the mental state where the individual is fully immersed in an activity and is perfectly concentrated on the task. It is also described as when a person loses the sense of time and space during an activity. This state is associated with greater life quality and absence of boredom and anxiety in the literature (Csikszentmihalyi, 1997).

Although there is robust support for the basic predictions of TAM, researchers also expanded the model with flow (Treiblmaier et al., 2018). In one study (Agarwal and Karahanna, 2000), it was found that cognitive absorption, a construct based on flow (Csikszentmihalyi and LeFevre, 1989) significantly predicted intention to use, along with perceived ease of use in the world wide web context. For hedonic information systems, including games, flow seems to play an important role as well (Cowley et al., 2008; Nah et al., 2014). In a study on online games, flow was found to significantly predict intention to use (Hsu and Lu, 2004). Similarly, it was found that flow plays a pivotal role in mobile game adoption as well (Zhou, 2013). In an extension of TAM, called Hedonic-Motivation System Adoption Model, it was proposed that flow mediates the relationship between perceived ease of use and intention to use (Lowry et al., 2012). Similarly, it was found that flow significantly predicted attitude towards using online games (Wang and Scheepers 2012). Flow is also an essential predictor of enjoyment in games context (Chen, 2007; Sweetser and Wyeth, 2005; Sherry, 2004). Flow-enjoyment relationship was shown to be significant in several gaming settings as well such as MUD games (multi-user dungeon; Voiskounsky et al., 2004), pervasive games (Jegers, 2007), e-learning games (Fu et al., 2009), exercise games (Huang et al., 2018), role-playing games, racing games and jump and run games (Weibel and Wissmath, 2011). Flow was also found to be predicting game enjoyment in games with human-controlled opponents as well as computer-controlled opponents (Weibel et al., 2008). In addition, flow is claimed to be an important factor in online 3D virtual world experiences (Nah et al., 2010; Hoffman and Novak, 2009). For instance, telepresence, one of the key component of flow (Skadberg and Kimmel, 2004), predicts enjoyment in virtual tours in Second Life (Nah et al., 2011). Similarly, research shows that flow is an important factor on fostering enjoyment and positive affect in games with virtual worlds (Faiola, 2013; Chiang et al., 2011). Therefore, it can be hypothesized that flow would predict greater enjoyment in VR games.

GameFlow was selected as the operationalization of flow which is a model developed to explain player enjoyment in games (Sweetser and Wyeth, 2005). It is based on the original theory of flow (Csikszentmihalyi, 1990), where immersion and concentration are two of the major constituents.

Research shows that immersion plays a key role in flow (Draper et al., 1998). Furthermore, a key aspect of virtual reality systems that separates them from other digital systems is their facilitation of high levels of immersion (Slater and Wilbur, 1997). High interactivity and vividness –that are some of the main properties of VR games- results in higher immersion and emotional responses (Sheng and Joginapelly, 2012). Thus, it is important to focus on the role of immersion in endorsement of virtual reality games. Immersion was found to be a construct that is related to loss of self-consciousness, merging of action and awareness and an altered perceiving of time which are also elements of flow (Fang et al., 2013). Although immersion is sometimes referred to as the hardware properties and "presence" to be the measure of subjective experience (Slater, 2018), GameFlow treats immersion as the subjective experience of the player, similar to presence. Overall, it is postulated that immersion would be a unique contributor to enjoyment in VR games:

[H4a] Immersion positively impacts enjoyment in VR games.

At the same time, intense concentration is a key characteristic in achieving flow states (Ghani and Deshpande, 1994; Shin, 2006). Research states that concentration is focused attention and it was found as an antecedent of flow in several game genres such as simulation and avatar-based narrative-driven games (Jinn, 2011). Concentration was also found as a major factor in predicting task engagement in

VR settings (Lackey et al., 2016). Furthermore, focused concentration is referred as a requirement in media enjoyment (Sherry, 2004). Consequently, it is hypothesized:

[H4b] Concentration positively impacts enjoyment in VR games.

Self-Determination Theory and TAM

Self-determination is a grounded theory, comprised of 6 mini-theories, with more than 40 years of research background (Ryan and Deci, 2017). The theory makes the distinction between extrinsic motivation and intrinsic motivation. The former refers to doing an activity for obtaining the gains separate from the activity, and the latter refers to doing something for its own sake since one enjoys the process (Ryan and Deci, 2000a; Ryan and Deci, 2000b). Intrinsic motivation leads people to be more persistent, effective, efficient and satisfied (Deci and Ryan, 2002). The theory also posits that autonomy, competence, and relatedness are the three basic psychological needs, satisfaction of which is essential for intrinsic motivation and well-being. Autonomy is the need to act in accordance with one's true self, as opposed to being controlled and pressured. Competence refers to the need for mastery and feeling optimally challenged. Relatedness is the need to feel connected to others and having a sense of belongingness.

There are studies that incorporated SDT constructs in TAM, for utilitarian information systems. In one recent study, it was found that basic needs (autonomy, competence and relatedness) predicted perceived ease of use and perceived usefulness in mobile-based assessment context (Nikou and Economides, 2017). Similarly, another study found that basic need satisfaction predicted perceived usefulness, which then predicted intention to use (Sørebø et al., 2009). Another study found that basic needs predicted enjoyment which predicted intention to use online knowledge sharing system that is web-based discussion boards (Lee et al., 2015). Also, in the context of e-learning in work settings, autonomy, competence and relatedness significantly predicted perceived usefulness and perceived playfulness (Roca and Gagné, 2008). Therefore in general, satisfaction of autonomy and competence needs positively influences the intentional use of new technologies (Bakke and Henry, 2015).

Although, there is also literature examining TAM and SDT in hedonic or mixed (hedonic and utilitarian) information systems such as virtual worlds (Verhagen et al., 2012), gamified applications (Treiblmaier et al., 2018), computers (Fagan et al., 2008) or internet (Zhao et al., 2011); studies examining TAM and SDT specifically in the gaming context are scarce. Although past studies on the adoption of hedonic information systems, especially games, provides useful foundations, they have not considered need satisfaction in their models where need satisfaction is a vital determinant of gaming motivation (Ryan et al., 2006). According to SDT literature, satisfaction of autonomy and competence needs in games predicts players' enjoyment (Ryan et al., 2006; Przybylski et al., 2010). This is based on the idea that players seek to satisfy their basic psychological needs in games. Thus, it is hypothesized that basic need satisfaction would positively influence enjoyment in VR games:

[H5a] Competence positively impacts enjoyment in VR games.
[H5b] Autonomy positively impacts enjoyment in VR games.

Although the authors posit that relatedness also positively impacts immersion and concentration, because of the design of this study, the authors did not include it in the hypotheses and analyses. Since it was expected that participants to have played VR games at most 5 times (to capture the essence of initial acceptance), it was thought that for the ones who played only single player games, relatedness would be hard to assess if not completely irrelevant.

Intrinsically motivated behavior results in flow experiences and this behavior rises from self-determined actions (Deci, 1992). When basic needs are satisfied during an activity, the individual becomes more and more immersed into and concentrated on that activity and eventually becomes one with that activity entering the flow state. There is ample evidence that self-determined behaviors foster flow states (e.g. Schüler et al., 2013). Research shows that satisfaction of basic psychological needs enhances flow experiences in work settings (Bakker and Woerkom, 2017). Several studies in sports domain also suggest that self-determined behavior and intrinsic motivation predict flow states (Moreno et al., 2010; Kowal and Fortier, 1999; Jackson et al., 1998; Schüler and Brandstätter, 2013). In games context, self-determination and flow are investigated as major constituents of player experiences (Johnson et al., 2013). Similar to other contexts, need satisfaction is stated to be closely related to flow experiences in games as well (Johnson et al., 2018). This is because, by definition, flow requires players to be in control (resembling autonomy need satisfaction) and optimally challenged (resembling competence need satisfaction) during a game. Following this argument and in line with the literature, it is posited that satisfaction of basic psychological needs (i.e. autonomy and competence) enhances the flow states experienced by players.

Research shows that immersion, sub construct of flow, is a construct that is highly correlated with player experience of need satisfaction in video games (Bormann & Greitemeyer, 2015). It was found across different game types and content that as the player experience of need satisfaction increase, immersion levels experienced by the players are enhanced as well (Ryan et al., 2006; Przybylski et al., 2009). In addition, as VR technology is usually characterized with increased immersion levels, it was thought that the immersion-need satisfaction relationship holds for VR games as well. Therefore, the hypotheses become:

[H6a] Competence positively impacts immersion in VR games.
[H6b] Autonomy positively impacts immersion in VR games.

Similar to immersion, satisfaction of basic psychological needs were also found to be associated with higher levels of focused concentration, which is a sub-construct of flow. Studies show that self-determined motivations predict concentration of the individual in the context of sports (Kowal and Fortier, 1999) and school physical education (Ntoumanis, 2005; Standage et al., 2005). This is the case in work (Bakker and van Woerkom, 2017) and schoolwork settings as well (Bassi and Delle Fave, 2012) as well. Similarly, in VR game context, as players feel more competent and autonomous, they would be more concentrated on the game. Therefore, it is hypothesized that:

[H6c] Competence positively impacts concentration in VR games.
[H6d] Autonomy positively impacts concentration in VR games.

With these, it is also inferentially hypothesized that:

[H6e] Immersion mediates the relationship between autonomy, competence and enjoyment.
[H6f] Concentration mediates the relationship between autonomy, competence and enjoyment.

Finally, it can also be suggested that perceived ease of use would facilitate satisfaction of autonomy and competence needs which result in enjoyment. There are studies showing that enjoyment predicts perceived ease of use in utilitarian information systems (Venkatesh, 2000; Sun and Zhang, 2006), however, the authors posit that perceived ease of use would be an antecedent of enjoyment in hedonic information systems, in line with the gaming literature. In video games context, perceived ease of use is determined as the 'backbone' of positive gaming experiences and therefore precedes enjoyment (Shen et al., 2009). Therefore, ease of use is a fundamental requirement for fostering satisfaction in video games. The argument follows that a game that is easy to use may (i.e. easy to use and fun) or may not foster satisfaction (i.e. easy to use but boring) however a game that is not easy to use will likely diminish satisfaction (i.e. not easy to use therefore frustrating). When a game system/interface is hard to use, it is likely to frustrate users, leading to feelings of incompetence. Moreover, not being able to do what they want to do because of a hard to use system would also lower users' feelings of autonomy. In fact, research shows that 'intuitive controls' in games are positively associated with satisfaction of autonomy and competence needs (Ryan et al., 2006) where intuitive controls are considered similar to perceived ease of use in the IS literature (Mantymaki and Merikivi, 2010). Moreover, perceived ease of use was shown to be a major factor in virtual reality adoptions as well (Fagan et al., 2012). Therefore, it is hypothesized that:

[H7a] Perceived ease of use positively impacts competence in VR games.
[H7b] Perceived ease of use positively impacts autonomy in VR games.

Self-Determination Theory and Flow

As explained above, flow is operationalized as in GameFlow which consists of 8 sub constructs: Concentration, Challenge, Player Skills, Control, Clear Goals, Feedback, Immersion and Social Interaction. However, it is also posited that among these 8 sub constructs, 6 of them are already explained by the self-determination constructs. More specifically, challenge ("games should be sufficiently challenging") and player skills ("games should support skill development and mastery") are explained by competence whereas control ("players should feel a sense of control over their actions"), clear goals ("games should provide the player with clear goals") and feedback ("players must receive appropriate feedback at appropriate times") are covered in the concept of autonomy. In addition, social interaction ("games should support social interaction") resembles relatedness. The associative and overlapping nature of these two theories were also mentioned in the literature studying self-determination and flow in an integrative way (Bakker and van Woerkom, 2017; Bassi and Delle Fave, 2012; Fortier and Kowal, 2007). Therefore, flow was operationalized as the remaining two sub-constructs which are immersion and concentration. Previous research also supports the conceptualization of flow as immersion and concentration (Mekler et al., 2014).

CONTROL VARIABLES

It is decided to include age, gender and education as controlling variables, since studies show that these variables can influence technology acceptance attitudes (Kuo et al., 2009; Wang and Wang, 2010; Burton-Jones and Hubona, 2006, respectively). In addition, total years of video game play and hours of video game play weekly are included as well to control for the effects of prior video gaming experiences and video gaming habits of participants. The authors did not want participants' prior (non-VR) gaming experiences or (non-VR) gaming habits to influence the VR gaming acceptance. Finally, hours spent on VR gaming is included to be able to control for the VR gaming experience of players, which could affect their VR gaming acceptance assessment.

The Overall Model

In brief, it is hypothesized that basic need satisfaction would mediate the link between perceived ease of use and enjoyment, as well as the link between perceived ease of use and flow in VR games.

The final research framework is provided in Figure 1.

Figure 1. Proposed model for acceptance of VR games

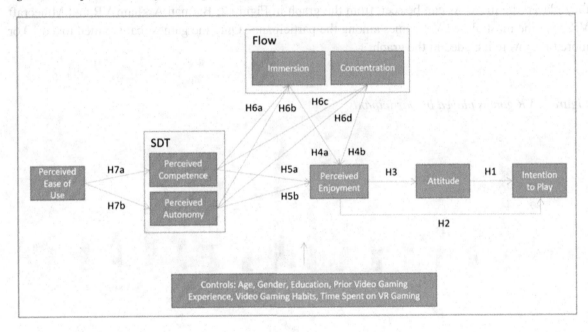

METHOD

Participants

The data is collected from Amazon's Mturk website. The survey was open to the participants residing in USA, and those who had played a VR game at least once were eligible. 400 participants completed the survey. The sample consisted of at least "10 cases per variable" in line with the recommendations of SEM literature (Bentler & Chou, 1987; Kline 2015). Data from four participants were found to be extreme outliers (e.g. 20000 hours of VR play) and were not included in the analyses.

Therefore, there were 396 participants in the dataset (183 male and 213 female). The participants were between 19 and 64 years old (M = 33.78, SD = 9.67). There were 285 white, 46 African American, 6 American Indian or Alaska Native, 36 Asian, 2 Native Hawaiian or Pacific Islander participants, whereas 21 participants preferred not to disclose their ethnicity. The most reported education level was 4-year degree were with 151 participants, and most of the participants (N=263) were full-time employees (Table 1).

Weekly video game play hours varied from 0 to 60 (M = 9.68, SD = 8.45). Years of video game play varied from 1 to 40 (M = 18.50, SD = 8.95). 154 participants claimed that they have played a VR game once. 98 stated that they have played twice, 54 stated that they have played three times, 19 stated that they played four times and 71 stated that they have played five times. To be able to accurately study the "acceptance" of VR games, a threshold of "at most 5 times VR game play" was decided, so that participants would not already be in a continued use state or too experienced to assess their acceptance attitude. However, no participant has played a VR game more than 5 times, therefore no participant was discarded according to the threshold. Most of the participants stated that they have played VR games at home (267). 10 participants claimed that they have played VR games in the office and 36 at the conventions. 83 participants marked "Other" option. Lastly, the participants were asked which three VR games they played the most. As can be seen from the graph in Figure 2, Batman Arkham VR and Minecraft VR were the most played VR games among the participants. Only the games that are mentioned 10 or more times were included in the graph.

Figure 2. VR games played by participants

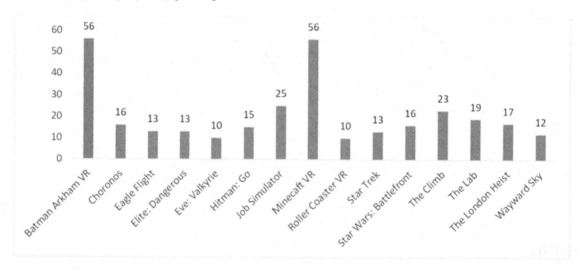

Measures

All of the measures used in the study are adapted from previous studies in video games context and are rephrased to fit in to the VR gaming context. All constructs are measured on a 1-7 Likert scale ranging from "strongly disagree" to "strongly agree".

Table 1. Participant demographic information (N= 396)

Age	18-25	84	21.2%
	26-35	164	41.4%
	36-45	97	24.5%
	>=46	51	12.9%
Gender	Male	183	46.2%
	Female	213	53.8%
Education	High School Graduate	49	12.4%
	Some College	99	25.0%
	2-year degree	57	14.4%
	4-year degree	151	38.1%
	MSc level degree	32	8.1%
	Doctorate	8	2.0%
Ethnicity	White	285	72.0%
	African American	46	11.6%
	American Indian or Alaska Native	6	1.5%
	Asian	36	9.1%
	Native Hawaiian or Pacific Islander	2	0.5%
	Preferred not to say	21	5.3%
Hours Spent on VR gaming	1-25	297	75.0%
	26-50	42	10.6%
	>=51	57	14.4%
Times VR Played	Once	154	38.9%
	Twice	98	24.7%
	Three Times	54	13.7%
	Four Times	19	4.8%
	Five Times	71	17.9%
Total Years of Video Game Play	1-10	93	23.5%
	11-20	161	40.6%
	21-30	116	29.3%
	31-40	26	6.6%
Hours of Video Game Play Weekly	0-20	369	93.2%
	21-40	23	5.8%
	41-60	4	1.0%

Perceived Ease of Use

Perceived ease of use is measured with 8 items from perceived ease of use in gaming scale (Lowry et al., 2012). The internal reliability of the scale was 0.92.

Basic Need Satisfaction

Satisfaction of autonomy and competence needs are measured using the Player Experience of Need Satisfaction Scale, PENS (Ryan et al., 2006). 3 items measure autonomy and 3 items measure competence. Both subscales showed good internal reliability ($\alpha = 0.89$ and $\alpha = 0.88$).

Flow

GameFlow scale is used to measure flow in gaming context (Sweetser and Wyeth, 2005). The immersion (4 items) and concentration (6 items) subscales are used. The internal reliability of the subscales are $\alpha = 0.80$ and $\alpha = 0.81$, respectively.

Enjoyment

For the enjoyment, the scale is used from another study consisting of 3 items (Wang and Scheepers, 2012). The internal reliability is 0.93.

Attitude

Attitude is measured by a previously developed scale (Wang and Scheepers, 2012). It consists of 3 items ($\alpha = 0.90$).

Intention to Play

Lastly, intention to play is measured by a scale consisting of 4 items ($\alpha = 0.94$) (Wang and Scheepers, 2012).

The scales, items of the scales that correspond to the constructs and their citations are summarized in the Appendix.

Procedure

The study was announced on Amazon's Mechanical Turk (MTurk). Mturk is an online platform offering recruitment tools for researchers. It was shown that using Mturk for survey data collection is a valid method provided that rigorous exclusions are employed (Thomas and Clifford, 2017). For that, the participants were required to have an approval rate of at least 95%. After completing the consent form and the demographics measures, participants completed the study measures. The survey took approximately 15 minutes to complete. Those who completed the survey received 30 cents on MTurk.

RESULTS

Preliminary Results

First, the internal reliabilities of the scales are checked. Minimum Cronbach's alpha value was 0.80 and the others were well above the threshold of 0.7 (Nunnelly, 1978). Therefore all of the reliabilities of the scales were within acceptable limits (Table 2).

Table 2. Internal reliabilities of the scales

	Cronbach's Alpha
Perceived Ease of Use	0.92
Autonomy	0.89
Competence	0.88
Immersion	0.80
Concentration	0.81
Enjoyment	0.93
Attitude	0.90
Intention to Play	0.94

Next, the normality of the data is checked. Although there are formal normality tests such as Kolmogorov-Smirnov or Shapiro-Wilk tests, they are unreliable for greater than medium sized samples (n > 300; Kim, 2013). Therefore, the skewness and kurtosis of the data are checked. The maximum value of skewness was -1.5 and the maximum value of kurtosis was 3.1 which were within the acceptable limits for moderate normality (skewness < 2,-2 and kurtosis < 7,-7; Curran et al., 1996; Hair et al., 2010). These limits are also considered critical levels for 'Maximum Likelihood' estimation (Ryu, 2011). 'Maximum Likelihood' estimator was used in the subsequent path analyses, which is also a robust technique against the assumptions of violations of normality (Bollen, 1989; Diamantopoulos et al., 2000).

The factor structure of the model was examined by carrying out confirmatory factor analysis (CFA) using SPSS AMOS software. A model is regarded as acceptable in CFA and structural equation modeling (SEM) analyses, if it satisfies the following fit index conditions: TLI > .90, CFI > .90, RMSEA < .08 and SRMR < .09 (Hu & Bentler, 1999). After dropping the low loading items (CONC4 – 0.38 and CONC6 – 0.45; using the 0.50 cutoff criteria; Hair et al., 2010), the confirmatory factor analysis showed acceptable fit indices (RMSEA = 0.057, %90 CI [0.052, 0.062], CFI = 0, SRMR = 0.049). All of the composite reliabilities were above 0.70 (Hair et al., 2010) and all of the average variance extracted (AVE) values were above 0.50 (Hair et al., 2010) indicating good convergent validity (Table 3). All of the square root of the AVE values of constructs were above their inter-construct correlation values and all the VIFs (variance inflation factors) of autonomy, competence, immersion and concentration were all less than 3, indicating good discriminant validity (Hair et al., 2010). Also, all of the correlations were in the expected direction (Table 3).

Table 3. Correlations, means and standard deviations of constructs

	PEOU	**COMP**	**AUT**	**IMM**	**CONC**	**PENJ**	**ATT**	**ITP**
PEOU	-							
COMP	0.76*	-						
AUT	0.55*	0.69*	-					
IMM	0.32*	0.38*	0.47*	-				
CONC	0.43*	0.50*	0.67*	0.53*	-			
PENJ	0.56*	0.68*	0.76*	0.45*	0.65*	-		
ATT	0.53*	0.62*	0.73*	0.40*	0.62*	0.88*	-	
ITP	0.44*	0.61*	0.69*	0.42*	0.56*	0.85*	0.87*	-
Age	-0.17*	-0.19*	-0.07	-0.04	-0.02	-0.04	-0.05	-0.02
Gender	-0.12*	-0.09	0.01	-0.02	0.08	0.07	0.05	0.01
Education	-0.00	-0.02	-0.00	0.07	0.01	-0.03	-0.05	-0.05
Play Years	-0.11*	-0.10*	0.02	-0.01	-0.04	0.04	0.07	0.11*
Hours/Week	0.17*	0.16*	0.15*	0.13*	0.13*	0.13*	0.13*	0.12*
VR Play	0.03	0.11*	0.05	-0.04	0.02	0.11*	0.10*	0.12*
Mean	4.82	5.14	5.57	4.81	5.07	5.80	5.84	5.77
SD	1.11	1.20	1.03	1.20	0.91	1.08	1.06	1.16
CR	0.92	0.89	0.84	0.80	0.81	0.93	0.90	0.94
AVE	0.60	0.72	0.63	0.51	0.53	0.82	0.76	0.81

*: $p < 0.001$

Zero-order correlations between enjoyment, attitude and intention to play were relatively high (0.88, 0.85 and 0.87). Although these are not more than 0.90 (which indicates common method bias evidence; Bagozzi et al., 1991), a common methods variance test is conducted. Several methods are suggested to conduct common method variance test however Harman's single factor test is the most commonly used by researchers (Edwards and Billsberry, 2010). Although the Harman's single factor accounted for a large variance (46.5%), it was less than 50% which is the heuristic threshold (Podsakoff et al., 2003). Therefore, it is concluded that the dataset did not suffer from common method bias.

Primary Results

SEM analysis is conducted to test the model. After dropping the non-significant paths from the model, the results showed acceptable fit (Figure 3); RMSEA = 0.054, %90 CI [0.050, 0.059], CFI = 0.94, TLI = 0.93, SRMR = 0.056. It is found that the model explains (R^2) 89% of the variance in intention to play VR games. In general, the results showed that perceived ease of use predicted autonomy and competence where autonomy predicted flow as well as enjoyment. Competence predicted enjoyment and enjoyment was an antecedent of attitude and intention to play. These results were mostly in line with the hypotheses. The results are found controlling for age, gender, education, hours spent on VR gaming, total years of video game play and hours of video game play weekly. There were several significant associations between the controlling variables and core variables in the model as well: gender-enjoyment, gender-autonomy, hours spent VR gaming-competence, years playing video games-autonomy, years playing video games-enjoyment associations. Enjoyment and autonomy levels of females were more than the males ($\beta = 0.07$, $p = 0.02$ and $\beta = 0.12$, $p = 0.006$, respectively). People who played more VR games were more competent ($\beta = 0.09$, $p = 0.006$). People who played more video games had more autonomy and enjoyment scores ($\beta = 0.12$, $p = 0.005$ and $\beta = 0.07$, $p = 0.04$, respectively).

As the path estimates between enjoyment and attitude, and attitude and intention to play were extremely high (0.96 and 0.94 respectively). Such high estimates might imply tautology. Nevertheless, enjoyment, attitude and intention to play are separate constructs representing different phenomena. Therefore, a new model was created with the second order latent variable "acceptance", which includes enjoyment, attitude and intention to play as first order variables. The new model showed acceptable fit as well (Figure 4); RMSEA = 0.055, %90 CI [0.051, 0.059], CFI = 0.93, TLI = 0.92, SRMR = 0.062. It was found that this final model explains (R2) 78% of the variance in acceptance of VR games.

Figure 3. Structural and measurement model of VR gaming acceptance

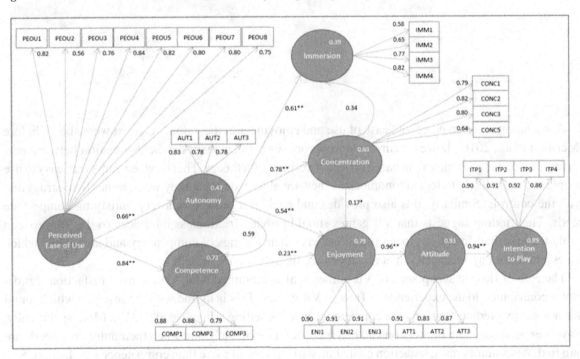

DISCUSSION

In this study, technology acceptance model, self-determination theory and flow theory constructs are used to test a unified motivational model for virtual reality gaming. Results show that perceived ease of use significantly predicted higher autonomy and competence satisfaction, which in turn, predict greater flow and enjoyment. Finally, enjoyment predicts higher intention to play VR games via positive attitudes toward VR games.

Figure 4. Structural and measurement model of VR gaming acceptance (acceptance as 2nd order latent variable)

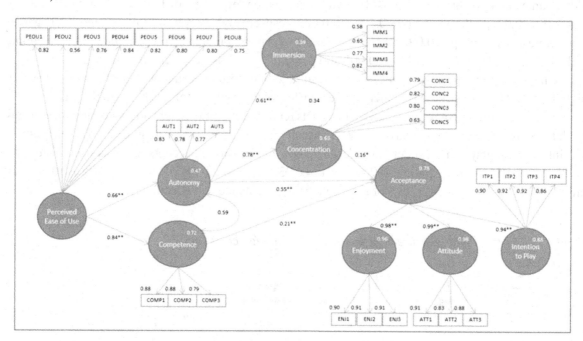

Association between perceived ease of use and enjoyment in the gaming context were shown before (Merikivi et al., 2016), however current study proposes a mechanism for the association between perceived ease of use and enjoyment based on self-determination theory. That is, when games are easy to use people are more likely to feel autonomous as they are able to do what they want, rather than struggling with the controls. Similarly, this also provides and enables a sense of mastery, satisfying competence needs. This finding suggests that VR games should provide frictionless interfaces so that players can easily transfer their intentions to actions, otherwise their feelings of competency and autonomy, which are essential for enjoyment (Ryan et al., 2006) are likely to be frustrated.

The role of flow in acceptance of VR games is also examined. Only autonomy satisfaction significantly contributed to the experience of flow in VR games. This is in line with the research which found that autonomy predicts flow and not competence in a VR setting (Huang et al., 2019). More specifically, players experience more immersion and better concentrate on the game when their autonomy needs are satisfied. Also, autonomy satisfaction contributed to enjoyment more than competence satisfaction. Satisfaction of competence needs could be less important for VR games compared to other digital games, as VR games are more oriented toward providing an immersive experience, rather than challenging the player. Thus, satisfaction of competence needs could be less important for flow in VR games currently.

The rest of the findings are in line with the past research on TAM in gaming contexts (Lowry et al., 2012). Enjoyment predicted intention to play VR games via positive attitudes toward VR games. Nevertheless, they were integrated under the "acceptance" latent variable as the path estimates between these constructs were remarkably high. Although there are several studies which applied TAM in the VR context (Huang et al., 2016; Chen et al., 2012; Bertrand and Bouchard, 2008); to the best of authors' knowledge, this is one of the first study to test TAM in modern "VR Gaming" context with the perspectives of self-determination and flow. Overall, these findings suggest that TAM also provides a valid framework for acceptance of VR games. However, the model is improved by introducing constructs from self-determination theory and flow theory.

Although immersion was found to be associated with positive gameplay experiences (Örtqvist and Liljedahl, 2010) and engagement (Dede, 2009) in the literature; it did not contribute to the prediction of enjoyment in this study. This might be an indication that immersion does not necessarily contribute to enjoyment in VR settings especially when autonomy and competence needs are satisfied. For instance, using immersive VR for treatment of phobias/anxiety or for horror games may not always foster enjoyable experiences. However, explanations on why immersion does not contribute to enjoyment in gaming context should still be researched further. Absence of immersion effect on enjoyment might also be due to choice of the measurement tool. Future studies might consider using an alternative scale to test this. Using standalone immersion scales instead of the flow subscale might reveal alternative findings. In addition, although immersion was assumed as the sub-process of flow in this study, some studies posit that immersion is an objective property of a system and the "presence" construct better captures the subjective perception of being absorbed (Slater, 2018; Slater, 2003). This means that immersion level is independent of the individual and it depends on the modality of the system whereas presence is about the user's subjective feeling of "being there". Therefore, future studies might consider incorporating presence construct rather than immersion in their models when psychological processes in VR use are of interest.

Lastly, some of the control variables were associated with the core variables in the model. For instance, gender was correlated with enjoyment and autonomy where females scored significantly higher than males. Future studies might consider looking into gender differences in terms of VR gaming experiences. Also, prior experience in VR gaming and video gaming in general seem to have an effect on self-determination and enjoyment. Future studies might also consider focusing on the prior experience of players.

Limitations

In the SEM analyses, the path coefficients between attitude, enjoyment and intention to play were very high (i.e. 0.94 and 0.96). These three constructs also showed high zero-order correlations. However, high correlations and high path coefficients around attitude construct were found in other studies on gaming as well (e.g. Hsu and Lu, 2004; Hsiao and Chiou, 2012). Although the developed model passed the tests for discriminant validity and common method bias, these variables could be an indicator of a general acceptance factor (as shown in the final model). Also, some studies do not incorporate attitude in their acceptance models at all (Chesney, 2006; Im et al., 2008). Attitude might be less relevant to adoption (and too similar to intention to play) in the gaming contexts. Future studies might consider dropping some of these constructs (e.g. attitude) or try using different measurements for these constructs.

In addition, two of the concentration items were found to be low loading which were then discarded and not included in the analyses. Still, future studies might consider using alternative scales to avoid measurement problems.

It should be noted that the study is correlational. Although SEM is used to simultaneously test the associations, the findings do not provide evidence for causal associations. The proposed causal associations are theoretical, and it is possible to construct equivalent alternative models. Thus, experimental studies are needed to test causal associations between the constructs. Similarly, longitudinal studies may also provide further insight about the model for long-term endorsement of VR games. Moreover, data collection for the survey was employed through Mturk. Although Mturk is a powerful tool for participant recruiting, it has limitations such as the difficulties of assessing participant qualifications and ensuring data validity (Hunt and Scheetz, 2018). Future studies should corroborate the findings here with other data collection methods. Also, our sample solely consisted of US citizens which might be a threat to external validity of the study. Future studies might consider including participants from different countries as well.

In the current study, there is no relatedness satisfaction in the model. This decision was made due to the fact that it might have been irrelevant for some players who only tried a VR game in a single player mode. Future studies testing this model in other hedonic information systems that involve interacting with other individuals (or more specifically VR games with multiplayer components) might consider examining the role of relatedness satisfaction as it was found that social needs are important in adopting emerging technologies such as social media (Coursaris et al., 2013). Similarly, immersion and flow might be important in VR games context but they might not be essential for other hedonic information systems (Kosa and Uysal, 2018). Thus, whether these constructs in the model are context dependent need to be examined in future studies.

There are several VR hardware brands in the market and different VR systems might have different fidelities which might affect user perception and appreciation. Investigating the differences in terms of VR technology (e.g. Oculus, Vive, Sony) might bring new perspectives to the associations examined here. Future studies might also examine the associations between system characteristics such as objective usability of the system (Venkatesh, 2000), interactivity of the system (Merikivi et al., 2016), appeal and visual aesthetic of the system (Merikivi et al., 2016), novelty of the system (Merikivi et al., 2016), curiosity that the system invokes (Hechler et al., 2016), technical and interaction quality of the system (Lin and Bhattacherjee, 2010) and the model constructs.

Implications

The findings of this study might be important to virtual reality game designers and developers. First, VR game developers need to make sure that the game is user friendly. More specifically, the controls should be consistent and adhering to common conventions. For instance, if a certain button is causing the in-game avatar to jump in similar titles for years, then the designers should seriously reconsider when changing these traditional conventions. These conventions should be consistent throughout the experience as well. It is also often best practice in games to allow users to start interacting within the game effortlessly, without having to refer to the documentations. Ease of use can also be enhanced by providing feedback and informing players on the system statuses. To ensure usability of a game, it is argued that usability heuristics developed for websites and apps can be adapted to games as well (Joyce, 2019). After making sure that the game controls are intuitive and easy to use, VR game designers/developers should focus on supporting the autonomy and competence of players, which consequently will result in higher levels of flow and enjoyment. For autonomy, designers should make sure that the players are in absolute control. Players should be provided with meaningful options and paths to freely choose from, and be able to see the results of their actions. In addition, designers should create obstacles for players to overcome, to boost the feelings of competence. However, designers should set the difficulty of these obstacles mindfully, since extremely hard challenges might frustrate players rather than supporting their competence. Therefore, the challenges in the game need to be beatable with some effort. Moreover, according to the findings, VR game designers should focus more on supporting autonomy and competence satisfaction of players rather than on the immersion considerations. Because this study shows that in the end, immersion itself is not the main contributor to the enjoyment of VR game players but satisfaction of psychological needs is. This study creates knowledge for VR game practitioners and investors, informing them about what they need to focus on during the development of these applications. Although virtual reality hardware related aspects (form factor, price etc.) could be an important aspect of VR technology endorsement, this study shows that the content of VR games and user perception plays a major role in its acceptance as the final model explains 78 percent of the variance in acceptance of VR games.

CONCLUSION

Main contribution of the current study is the creation of a new model, which brings the satisfaction of psychological needs perspective into the VR gaming context. It integrates the self-determination theory constructs with the flow theory and technology acceptance model in the context of virtual reality gaming to explain the player endorsement of VR games. The study also tests the upgraded TAM model in the context of VR games. In brief, it was found that perceived ease of use increases endorsement of virtual reality games via satisfaction of autonomy and competence needs, and concentration experienced through flow. This study shows that, self-determined players, whose psychological needs are satisfied, are likely to play VR games.

REFERENCES

Agarwal, R., & Karahanna, E. (2000). Time flies when you're having fun: Cognitive absorption and beliefs about information technology usage. *Management Information Systems Quarterly*, 24(4), 665–694. doi:10.2307/3250951

Ajzen, I., & Fishbein, M. (1980). *Understanding attitudes and predicting social behaviour*. Academic Press.

ARVRtech. (2019, March 5). *The Greatest Challenges Virtual Reality Companies and Their Clients are Facing and Ways to Overcome Them*. Retrieved from https://arvrtech.eu/blog/greatest-virtual-reality-mistakes/

Bagozzi, R. P., Yi, Y., & Phillips, L. W. (1991). Assessing construct validity in organizational research. *Administrative Science Quarterly*, 36(3), 421–458. doi:10.2307/2393203

Bakke, S., & Henry, R. (2015). Unraveling the mystery of new technology use: An investigation into the interplay of desire for control, computer self-efficacy, and personal innovativeness. *AIS Transactions on Human-Computer Interaction*, 7(4), 270–293. doi:10.17705/1thci.00075

Bakker, A. B., & van Woerkom, M. (2017). Flow at work: A self-determination perspective. *Occupational Health Science*, 1(1-2), 47–65. doi:10.100741542-017-0003-3

Bassi, M., & Delle Fave, A. (2012). Optimal experience and self-determination at school: Joining perspectives. *Motivation and Emotion*, 36(4), 425–438. doi:10.100711031-011-9268-z

Bertrand, M., & Bouchard, S. (2008). Applying the technology acceptance model to VR with people who are favorable to its use. *Journal of Cyber Therapy and Rehabilitation*, 1(2), 200–210.

Bilyk, V. (2018, May 22). *Virtual Reality Apps Development: 8 Problems to Overcome.* Retrieved from https://theappsolutions.com/blog/development/virtual-reality -app-development-problems-to-overcome/

Bollen, K. A. (1989). *Structural equations with latent variables.* Wiley New York. doi:10.1002/9781118619179

Bormann, D., & Greitemeyer, T. (2015). Immersed in virtual worlds and minds: Effects of in-game storytelling on immersion, need satisfaction, and affective theory of mind. *Social Psychological & Personality Science, 6*(6), 646–652. doi:10.1177/1948550615578177

Brooks, F. P. (1999). What's real about virtual reality? *IEEE Computer Graphics and Applications, 19*(6), 16–27. doi:10.1109/38.799723

Brown, E., & Cairns, P. (2004, April). A grounded investigation of game immersion. In *CHI'04 extended abstracts on Human factors in computing systems* (pp. 1297–1300). ACM.

Brütsch, K., Schuler, T., Koenig, A., Zimmerli, L., Mérillat, S., Lünenburger, L., ... Meyer-Heim, A. (2010). Influence of virtual reality soccer game on walking performance in robotic assisted gait training for children. *Journal of Neuroengineering and Rehabilitation, 7*(1), 15. doi:10.1186/1743-0003-7-15 PMID:20412572

Burdea Grigore, C., & Coiffet, P. (1994). *Virtual reality technology.* London: Wiley-Interscience.

Burton-Jones, A., & Hubona, G. S. (2006). The mediation of external variables in the technology acceptance model. *Information & Management, 43*(6), 706–717. doi:10.1016/j.im.2006.03.007

Cai, J., Wohn, D. Y., Mittal, A., & Sureshbabu, D. (2018). Utilitarian and hedonic motivations for live streaming shopping. In *Proceedings of the 2018 ACM international conference on interactive experiences for TV and online video* (pp. 81-88). ACM. 10.1145/3210825.3210837

Castillo, M. (2018, February 9). *Most teens can't afford a virtual reality headset, so they're hanging out in VR arcades instead.* Retrieved from https://www.cnbc.com/2018/02/10/vr-arcades-are-gaming-centers-of-the-future.html

Chen, C. Y., Shih, B. Y., & Yu, S. H. (2012). Disaster prevention and reduction for exploring teachers' technology acceptance using a virtual reality system and partial least squares techniques. *Natural Hazards, 62*(3), 1217–1231. doi:10.100711069-012-0146-0

Chen, J. (2007). Flow in games (and everything else*). Communications of the ACM, 50*(4), 31–34. doi:10.1145/1232743.1232769

Chesney, T. (2006). An acceptance model for useful and fun information systems. *Human Technology: An Interdisciplinary Journal on Humans in ICT Environments, 2*(2), 225–235. doi:10.17011/ht/urn.2006520

Chiang, Y. T., Lin, S. S., Cheng, C. Y., & Liu, E. Z. F. (2011). Exploring Online Game Players' Flow Experiences and Positive Affect. *Turkish Online Journal of Educational Technology-TOJET, 10*(1), 106–114.

Childers, T. L., Carr, C. L., Peck, J., & Carson, S. (2001). Hedonic and utilitarian motivations for online retail shopping behavior. *Journal of Retailing, 77*(4), 511–535. doi:10.1016/S0022-4359(01)00056-2

Coursaris, C. K., Van Osch, W., Sung, J., & Yun, Y. (2013). Disentangling Twitter's adoption and use (dis) continuance: A theoretical and empirical amalgamation of uses and gratifications and diffusion of innovations. *AIS Transactions on Human-Computer Interaction, 5*(1), 57–83. doi:10.17705/1thci.00054

Cowley, B., Charles, D., Black, M., & Hickey, R. (2008). Toward an understanding of flow in video games. [CIE]. *Computers in Entertainment, 6*(2), 20. doi:10.1145/1371216.1371223

Csikszentmihalyi, M. (1990). *Flow: The Psychology of Optimal Experience.* New York: Harper and Row.

Csikszentmihalyi, M. (1997). *Finding flow: The psychology of engagement with everyday life.* Basic Books.

Csikszentmihalyi, M., & LeFevre, J. (1989). Optimal experience in work and leisure. *Journal of Personality and Social Psychology, 56*(5), 815–822. doi:10.1037/0022-3514.56.5.815 PMID:2724069

Curran, P. J., West, S. G., & Finch, J. F. (1996). The robustness of test statistics to nonnormality and specification error in confirmatory factor analysis. *Psychological Methods, 1*(1), 16–29. doi:10.1037/1082-989X.1.1.16

Das, D. A., Grimmer, K. A., Sparnon, A. L., McRae, S. E., & Thomas, B. H. (2005). The efficacy of playing a virtual reality game in modulating pain for children with acute burn injuries: A randomized controlled trial [ISRCTN87413556]. *BMC Pediatrics, 5*(1), 1. doi:10.1186/1471-2431-5-1 PMID:15745448

Davis, F. D. (1989). Perceived usefulness, perceived ease of use, and user acceptance of information technology. *Management Information Systems Quarterly, 13*(3), 319–340. doi:10.2307/249008

Davis, F. D., Bagozzi, R. P., & Warshaw, P. R. (1989). User acceptance of computer technology: A comparison of two theoretical models. *Management Science, 35*(8), 982–1003. doi:10.1287/mnsc.35.8.982

Deci, E. L., & Ryan, R. M. (2002). *Handbook of self-determination research.* University Rochester Press.

Dede, C. (2009). Immersive interfaces for engagement and learning. *Science, 323*(5910), 66–69. doi:10.1126cience.1167311 PMID:19119219

Diamantopoulos, A., Siguaw, J., & Siguaw, J. A. (2000). *Introducing LISREL: A guide for the uninitiated.* Sage Publications. doi:10.4135/9781849209359

Dishaw, M. T., & Strong, D. M. (1999). Extending the technology acceptance model with task–technology fit constructs. *Information & Management, 36*(1), 9–21. doi:10.1016/S0378-7206(98)00101-3

Draper, J. V., Kaber, D. B., & Usher, J. M. (1998). Telepresence. *Human Factors, 40*(3), 354–375. doi:10.1518/001872098779591386 PMID:9849099

Edwards, J. A., & Billsberry, J. (2010). Testing a multidimensional theory of person-environment fit. *Journal of Managerial Issues*, 476–493.

Fagan, M., Kilmon, C., & Pandey, V. (2012). Exploring the adoption of a virtual reality simulation: The role of perceived ease of use, perceived usefulness and personal innovativeness. *Campus-Wide Information Systems, 29*(2), 117–127. doi:10.1108/10650741211212368

Fagan, M. H., Neill, S., & Wooldridge, B. R. (2008). Exploring the intention to use computers: An empirical investigation of the role of intrinsic motivation, extrinsic motivation, and perceived ease of use. *Journal of Computer Information Systems, 48*(3), 31–37.

Faiola, A., Newlon, C., Pfaff, M., & Smyslova, O. (2013). Correlating the effects of flow and telepresence in virtual worlds: Enhancing our understanding of user behavior in game-based learning. *Computers in Human Behavior, 29*(3), 1113–1121. doi:10.1016/j.chb.2012.10.003

Fang, X., Zhang, J., & Chan, S. S. (2013). Development of an instrument for studying flow in computer game play. *International Journal of Human-Computer Interaction, 29*(7), 456–470. doi:10.1080/1044 7318.2012.715991

Feelreal. (2018). *Feelreal.* Retrieved from https://feelreal.com/

Fortier, M., & Kowal, J. (2007). The flow state and physical activity behavior change as motivational outcomes: A self-determination theory perspective. In M. S. Hagger & N. L. D. Chatzisarantis (Eds.), Intrinsic motivation and self-determination in exercise and sport (pp. 113–125, 322–328). Academic Press.

Fu, F. L., Su, R. C., & Yu, S. C. (2009). EGameFlow: A scale to measure learners' enjoyment of e-learning games. *Computers & Education, 52*(1), 101–112. doi:10.1016/j.compedu.2008.07.004

Ghani, J. A., & Deshpande, S. P. (1994). Task characteristics and the experience of optimal flow in human—Computer interaction. *The Journal of Psychology, 128*(4), 381–391. doi:10.1080/00223980 .1994.9712742

Goh, K. Y., & Ping, J. W. (2014). Engaging consumers with advergames: An experimental evaluation of interactivity, fit and expectancy. *Journal of the Association for Information Systems, 15*(7), 388–421. doi:10.17705/1jais.00366

Grand View Market. (2017, May). *Virtual Reality Market Size Growth & Analysis | VR Industry Report 2025.* Retrieved from https://www.grandviewresearch.com/industry-analysis/virtual-reality-vr-market

Gurwin, G. (2018, August 10). *From horror to first-person shooters, these are the best games in VR.* Retrieved from https://www.digitaltrends.com/gaming/best-virtual-reality-games/

Hair, J. F. Jr, Black, W. C., Babin, B. J., & Anderson, R. E. (2010). *Multivariate data analysis* (7th ed.). Upper Saddle River, NJ: Prentice Hall.

Hair, J. F., Tatham, R. L., Anderson, R. E., & Black, W. (1998). *Multivariate data analysis* (5th ed.). London: Prentice-Hall.

Hechler, P., Born, F., & Kroenung, J. (2016, January). Exploring vs. Enjoying: The Choice between Hedonic IS in Post-Adoption Scenarios. In *2016 49th Hawaii International Conference on System Sciences (HICSS)* (pp. 1246-1255). IEEE.

Hernandez, B., Jimenez, J., & Martín, M. J. (2008). Extending the technology acceptance model to include the IT decision-maker: A study of business management software. *Technovation, 28*(3), 112–121. doi:10.1016/j.technovation.2007.11.002

Hoffman, D. L., & Novak, T. P. (2009). Flow online: Lessons learned and future prospects. *Journal of Interactive Marketing, 23*(1), 23–34. doi:10.1016/j.intmar.2008.10.003

Hong, W., Chan, F. K., Thong, J. Y., Chasalow, L. C., & Dhillon, G. (2013). A framework and guidelines for context-specific theorizing in information systems research. *Information Systems Research, 25*(1), 111–136. doi:10.1287/isre.2013.0501

Hsiao, C. C., & Chiou, J. S. (2012). The effects of a player's network centrality on resource accessibility, game enjoyment, and continuance intention: A study on online gaming communities. *Electronic Commerce Research and Applications, 11*(1), 75–84. doi:10.1016/j.elerap.2011.10.001

Hsu, C. L., & Lu, H. P. (2004). Why do people play on-line games? An extended TAM with social influences and flow experience. *Information & Management, 41*(7), 853–868. doi:10.1016/j.im.2003.08.014

Hu, L. T., & Bentler, P. M. (1999). Cutoff criteria for fit indexes in covariance structure analysis: Conventional criteria versus new alternatives. *Structural Equation Modeling, 6*(1), 1–55. doi:10.1080/10705519909540118

Hu, P. J., Chau, P. Y., Sheng, O. R. L., & Tam, K. Y. (1999). Examining the technology acceptance model using physician acceptance of telemedicine technology. *Journal of Management Information Systems, 16*(2), 91–112. doi:10.1080/07421222.1999.11518247

Huang, H. C., Pham, T. T. L., Wong, M. K., Chiu, H. Y., Yang, Y. H., & Teng, C. I. (2018). How to create flow experience in exergames? Perspective of flow theory. *Telematics and Informatics, 35*(5), 1288–1296. doi:10.1016/j.tele.2018.03.001

Huang, H. M., Liaw, S. S., & Lai, C. M. (2016). Exploring learner acceptance of the use of virtual reality in medical education: A case study of desktop and projection-based display systems. *Interactive Learning Environments, 24*(1), 3–19. doi:10.1080/10494820.2013.817436

Huang, Y. C., Backman, S. J., Backman, K. F., McGuire, F. A., & Moore, D. (2019). An investigation of motivation and experience in virtual learning environments: A self-determination theory. *Education and Information Technologies, 24*(1), 591–611. doi:10.100710639-018-9784-5

Hunt, N. C., & Scheetz, A. M. (2018). Using MTurk to distribute a survey or experiment: Methodological considerations. *Journal of Information Systems, 33*(1), 43–65. doi:10.2308/isys-52021

Im, I., Kim, Y., & Han, H. J. (2008). The effects of perceived risk and technology type on users' acceptance of technologies. *Information & Management, 45*(1), 1–9. doi:10.1016/j.im.2007.03.005

Jackson, S. A., Ford, S. K., Kimiecik, J. C., & Marsh, H. W. (1998). Psychological correlates of flow in sport. *Journal of Sport & Exercise Psychology, 20*(4), 358–378. doi:10.1123/jsep.20.4.358

Jegers, K. (2007). Pervasive game flow: Understanding player enjoyment in pervasive gaming. *Computers in Entertainment, 5*(1), 9. doi:10.1145/1236224.1236238

Jin, S. A. A. (2011). "I feel present. Therefore, I experience flow:" A structural equation modeling approach to flow and presence in video games. *Journal of Broadcasting & Electronic Media, 55*(1), 114–136. doi:10.1080/08838151.2011.546248

Johnson, D., Gardner, M. J., & Perry, R. (2018). Validation of two game experience scales: The player experience of need satisfaction (PENS) and game experience questionnaire (GEQ). *International Journal of Human-Computer Studies, 118*, 38–46. doi:10.1016/j.ijhcs.2018.05.003

Johnson, D., Wyeth, P., & Sweetser, P. (2013). The people-game-play model for understanding video-games' impact on wellbeing. In *2013 IEEE International Games Innovation Conference (IGIC)* (pp. 85-88). IEEE. 10.1109/IGIC.2013.6659143

Joyce, A. (2019, May 19). *10 Usability Heuristics Applied to Video Games*. Retrieved from https://www.nngroup.com/articles/usability-heuristics-applied-video-games/

Kim, H. Y. (2013). Statistical notes for clinical researchers: Assessing normal distribution (2) using skewness and kurtosis. *Restorative Dentistry & Endodontics, 38*(1), 52–54. doi:10.5395/rde.2013.38.1.52 PMID:23495371

Kim, K., Rosenthal, M. Z., Zielinski, D., & Brady, R. (2012). Comparison of desktop, head mounted display, and six wall fully immersive systems using a stressful task. *Virtual Reality Conference, IEEE(VR)*, 143-144. 10.1109/VR.2012.6180922

Kline, R. B. (2015). *Principles and practice of structural equation modeling*. Guilford publications.

Kosa, M., & Uysal, A. (2018). Mindfulness, Virtual Reality, and Video Games. In N. Lee (Ed.), *Encyclopedia of Computer Graphics and Games*. Cham: Springer. doi:10.1007/978-3-319-08234-9_164-1

Kowal, J., & Fortier, M. S. (1999). Motivational determinants of flow: Contributions from self-determination theory. *The Journal of Social Psychology, 139*(3), 355–368. doi:10.1080/00224549909598391

Kozlova, A. (2017, October 18). *VR gaming: how industry will propel the technology*. Retrieved from https://teslasuit.io/blog/virtual-reality/vr-gaming-how-industry-push-technology

Kuo, I. H., Rabindran, J. M., Broadbent, E., Lee, Y. I., Kerse, N., Stafford, R. M. Q., & MacDonald, B. A. (2009). Age and gender factors in user acceptance of healthcare robots. In *RO-MAN 2009-The 18th IEEE International Symposium on Robot and Human Interactive Communication* (pp. 214-219). IEEE.

Lackey, S. J., Salcedo, J. N., Szalma, J. L., & Hancock, P. A. (2016). The stress and workload of virtual reality training: The effects of presence, immersion and flow. *Ergonomics, 59*(8), 1060–1072. doi:10.1080/00140139.2015.1122234 PMID:26977540

Lange, B. S., Requejo, P., Flynn, S. M., Rizzo, A. A., Valero-Cuevas, F. J., Baker, L., & Winstein, C. (2010). The potential of virtual reality and gaming to assist successful aging with disability. *Physical Medicine and Rehabilitation Clinics, 21*(2), 339–356. doi:10.1016/j.pmr.2009.12.007 PMID:20494281

Lederer, A. L., Maupin, D. J., Sena, M. P., & Zhuang, Y. (2000). The technology acceptance model and the World Wide Web. *Decision Support Systems, 29*(3), 269–282. doi:10.1016/S0167-9236(00)00076-2

Lee, J. H., Kim, J. H., & Choi, J. Y. (2018). The adoption of virtual reality devices: The technology acceptance model integrating enjoyment, social interaction, and strength of the social ties. *Telematics and Informatics*. doi:10.1016/j.tele.2018.12.006

Lee, S. (1999). Private uses in public spaces: A study of an internet cafe. *New Media & Society, 1*(3), 331–350. doi:10.1177/14614449922225618

Lee, Y., Lee, J., & Hwang, Y. (2015). Relating motivation to information and communication technology acceptance: Self-determination theory perspective. *Computers in Human Behavior, 51*, 418–428. doi:10.1016/j.chb.2015.05.021

Legris, P., Ingham, J., & Collerette, P. (2003). Why do people use information technology? A critical review of the technology acceptance model. *Information & Management, 40*(3), 191–204. doi:10.1016/S0378-7206(01)00143-4

Levac, D., Pierrynowski, M. R., Canestraro, M., Gurr, L., Leonard, L., & Neeley, C. (2010). Exploring children's movement characteristics during virtual reality video game play. *Human Movement Science, 29*(6), 1023–1038. doi:10.1016/j.humov.2010.06.006 PMID:20724014

Liao, S., Shao, Y. P., Wang, H., & Chen, A. (1999). The adoption of virtual banking: An empirical study. *International Journal of Information Management, 19*(1), 63–74. doi:10.1016/S0268-4012(98)00047-4

Lin, C. P., & Bhattacherjee, A. (2010). Extending technology usage models to interactive hedonic technologies: A theoretical model and empirical test. *Information Systems Journal, 20*(2), 163–181. doi:10.1111/j.1365-2575.2007.00265.x

Lowry, P. B., Gaskin, J., Twyman, N., Hammer, B., & Roberts, T. (2012). Taking 'fun and games' seriously: Proposing the hedonic-motivation system adoption model (HMSAM). *Journal of the Association for Information Systems, 14*(11), 617–671. doi:10.17705/1jais.00347

Manis, K. T., & Choi, D. (2018). The virtual reality hardware acceptance model (VR-HAM): Extending and individuating the technology acceptance model (TAM) for virtual reality hardware. *Journal of Business Research*. doi:10.1016/j.jbusres.2018.10.021

Mantymaki, M., & Merikivi, J. (2010). Investigating the drivers of the continuous use of social virtual worlds. In *2010 43rd Hawaii International Conference on System Sciences* (pp. 1-10). IEEE.

Marangunić, N., & Granić, A. (2015). Technology acceptance model: A literature review from 1986 to 2013. *Universal Access in the Information Society, 14*(1), 81–95. doi:10.100710209-014-0348-1

Martin, C. (2018, April 15). *Content Market For Virtual, Augmented Reality Hits $3 Billion*. Retrieved from https://www.mediapost.com/publications/article/317619/content-market-for-virtual-augmented-reality-hits.html

Matney, L. (2018, September 17). *Hear how Oculus is minimizing VR's content problem at TC Sessions: AR/VR – TechCrunch*. Retrieved from https://techcrunch.com/2018/09/17/hear-how-oculus-is-minimizing-vrs-content-problem-at-tc-sessions-ar-vr/

McMahan, R. P., Bowman, D. A., Zielinski, D. J., & Brady, R. B. (2012). Evaluating display fidelity and interaction fidelity in a virtual reality game. *IEEE Transactions on Visualization and Computer Graphics, 18*(4), 626–633. doi:10.1109/TVCG.2012.43 PMID:22402690

Mekler, E. D., Bopp, J. A., Tuch, A. N., & Opwis, K. (2014). A systematic review of quantitative studies on the enjoyment of digital entertainment games. In *Proceedings of the 32nd annual ACM conference on Human factors in computing systems* (pp. 927-936). ACM. 10.1145/2556288.2557078

Merikivi, J., Nguyen, D., & Tuunainen, V. K. (2016, January). Understanding Perceived Enjoyment in Mobile Game Context. In *2016 49th Hawaii International Conference on System Sciences (HICSS)* (pp. 3801-3810). IEEE.

Moreno, J. A., Cervelló, E., & Cutre, D. G. (2010). The achievement goal and self-determination theories as predictors of dispositional flow in young athletes. *Anales de Psicología/Annals of Psychology*, *26*(2), 390-399.

Mütterlein, J., & Hess, T. (2017). Immersion, presence, interactivity: towards a joint understanding of factors influencing virtual reality acceptance and use. *AMCIS 2017 Proceedings*, 7.

Nah, F. F. H., Eschenbrenner, B., & DeWester, D. (2011). Enhancing brand equity through flow and telepresence: A comparison of 2D and 3D virtual worlds. *Management Information Systems Quarterly*, *35*(3), 731–747. doi:10.2307/23042806

Nah, F. F. H., Eschenbrenner, B., DeWester, D., & Park, S. R. (2010). Impact of flow and brand equity in 3D virtual worlds. *Journal of Database Management*, *21*(3), 69–89. doi:10.4018/jdm.2010070103

Nah, F. F. H., Eschenbrenner, B., Zeng, Q., Telaprolu, V. R., & Sepehr, S. (2014). Flow in gaming: Literature synthesis and framework development. *International Journal of Information Systems and Management*, *1*(1-2), 83–124. doi:10.1504/IJISAM.2014.062288

Nikou, S. A., & Economides, A. A. (2017). Mobile-Based Assessment: Integrating acceptance and motivational factors into a combined model of Self-Determination Theory and Technology Acceptance. *Computers in Human Behavior*, *68*, 83–95. doi:10.1016/j.chb.2016.11.020

Ntoumanis, N. (2005). A prospective study of participation in optional school physical education using a self-determination theory framework. *Journal of Educational Psychology*, *97*(3), 444–453. doi:10.1037/0022-0663.97.3.444

Nunnally, J. C. (1978). *Psychometric theory* (2nd ed.). New York: McGraw-Hill.

O'Boyle, B., & Willings, A. (2019, May 16). *What is VR? Virtual reality explained*. Retrieved from https://www.pocket-lint.com/ar-vr/news/136540-what-is-vr-virtual-reality-explained

Örtqvist, D., & Liljedahl, M. (2010). Immersion and gameplay experience: A contingency framework. *International Journal of Computer Games Technology*, *2010*, 6. doi:10.1155/2010/613931

Pallavicini, F., Ferrari, A., Pepe, A., Garcea, G., Zanacchi, A., & Mantovani, F. (2018). Effectiveness of virtual reality survival horror games for the emotional elicitation: Preliminary insights using Resident Evil 7: Biohazard. In *International Conference on Universal Access in Human-Computer Interaction* (pp. 87-101). Springer. 10.1007/978-3-319-92052-8_8

Pallavicini, F., Ferrari, A., Zini, A., Garcea, G., Zanacchi, A., Barone, G., & Mantovani, F. (2017). What distinguishes a traditional gaming experience from one in virtual reality? An exploratory study. In *International Conference on Applied Human Factors and Ergonomics* (pp. 225-231). Springer, Cham.

Pietrzak, E., Pullman, S., & McGuire, A. (2014). Using virtual reality and videogames for traumatic brain injury rehabilitation: A structured literature review. *Games for Health: Research, Development, and Clinical Applications*, 3(4), 202–214. doi:10.1089/g4h.2014.0013 PMID:26192369

Podsakoff, P. M., MacKenzie, S. B., Lee, J. Y., & Podsakoff, N. P. (2003). Common method biases in behavioral research: A critical review of the literature and recommended remedies. *The Journal of Applied Psychology*, 88(5), 879–903. doi:10.1037/0021-9010.88.5.879 PMID:14516251

Porter, C. E., & Donthu, N. (2006). Using the technology acceptance model to explain how attitudes determine Internet usage: The role of perceived access barriers and demographics. *Journal of Business Research*, 59(9), 999–1007. doi:10.1016/j.jbusres.2006.06.003

Przybylski, A. K., Rigby, C. S., & Ryan, R. M. (2010). A motivational model of video game engagement. *Review of General Psychology*, 14(2), 154–166. doi:10.1037/a0019440

Przybylski, A. K., Ryan, R. M., & Rigby, C. S. (2009). The motivating role of violence in video games. *Personality and Social Psychology Bulletin*, 35(2), 243–259. doi:10.1177/0146167208327216 PMID:19141627

Rendon, A. A., Lohman, E. B., Thorpe, D., Johnson, E. G., Medina, E., & Bradley, B. (2012). The effect of virtual reality gaming on dynamic balance in older adults. *Age and Ageing*, 41(4), 549–552. doi:10.1093/ageing/afs053 PMID:22672915

Roca, J. C., & Gagné, M. (2008). Understanding e-learning continuance intention in the workplace: A self-determination theory perspective. *Computers in Human Behavior*, 24(4), 1585–1604. doi:10.1016/j.chb.2007.06.001

Rosen, P., & Sherman, P. (2006). Hedonic information systems: acceptance of social networking websites. *AMCIS 2006 Proceedings*, 162.

Rosenberg, R. S., Baughman, S. L., & Bailenson, J. N. (2013). Virtual superheroes: Using superpowers in virtual reality to encourage prosocial behavior. *PLoS One*, 8(1), e55003. doi:10.1371/journal.pone.0055003 PMID:23383029

Ryan, R. M., & Deci, E. L. (2000a). Intrinsic and extrinsic motivations: Classic definitions and new directions. *Contemporary Educational Psychology*, 25(1), 54–67. doi:10.1006/ceps.1999.1020 PMID:10620381

Ryan, R. M., & Deci, E. L. (2000b). Self-determination theory and the facilitation of intrinsic motivation, social development, and well-being. *The American Psychologist*, 55(1), 68–78. doi:10.1037/0003-066X.55.1.68 PMID:11392867

Ryan, R. M., & Deci, E. L. (2017). *Self-determination theory: Basic psychological needs in motivation, development, and wellness*. Guilford Publications.

Ryan, R. M., Rigby, C. S., & Przybylski, A. (2006). The motivational pull of video games: A self-determination theory approach. *Motivation and Emotion*, 30(4), 344–360. doi:10.100711031-006-9051-8

Ryu, E. (2011). Effects of skewness and kurtosis on normal-theory based maximum likelihood test statistic in multilevel structural equation modeling. *Behavior Research Methods*, *43*(4), 1066–1074. doi:10.375813428-011-0115-7 PMID:21671139

Sackville, S. (2018, April 25). *Gaming Will Take Augmented and Virtual Reality Mainstream | Jabil*. Retrieved from https://www.jabil.com/insights/blog-main/gaming-will-drive-a ugmented-and-virtual-reality-adoption.html

Santos, B. S., Dias, P., Pimentel, A., Baggerman, J. W., Ferreira, C., Silva, S., & Madeira, J. (2009). Head-mounted display versus desktop for 3D navigation in virtual reality: A user study. *Multimedia Tools and Applications*, *41*(1), 161–181. doi:10.100711042-008-0223-2

Saposnik, G., Teasell, R., Mamdani, M., Hall, J., McIlroy, W., Cheung, D., ... Bayley, M. (2010). Effectiveness of virtual reality using Wii gaming technology in stroke rehabilitation: A pilot randomized clinical trial and proof of principle. *Stroke*, *41*(7), 1477–1484. doi:10.1161/STROKEAHA.110.584979 PMID:20508185

Schüler, J., & Brandstätter, V. (2013). How basic need satisfaction and dispositional motives interact in predicting flow experience in sport. *Journal of Applied Social Psychology*, *43*(4), 687–705. doi:10.1111/j.1559-1816.2013.01045.x

Schüler, J., Brandstätter, V., & Sheldon, K. M. (2013). Do implicit motives and basic psychological needs interact to predict well-being and flow? Testing a universal hypothesis and a matching hypothesis. *Motivation and Emotion*, *37*(3), 480–495. doi:10.100711031-012-9317-2

Shen, C., Wang, H., & Ritterfeld, U. (2009). Serious Games and Seriously Fun Games: Can they be one and the same? In *Serious Games* (pp. 70–84). Routledge.

Sheng, H., & Joginapelly, T. (2012). Effects of web atmospheric cues on users' emotional responses in e-commerce. *AIS Transactions on Human-Computer Interaction*, *4*(1), 1–24. doi:10.17705/1thci.00036

Sherry, J. L. (2004). Flow and media enjoyment. *Communication Theory*, *14*(4), 328–347. doi:10.1111/j.1468-2885.2004.tb00318.x

Shin, D. H., & Shin, Y. J. (2011). Why do people play social network games? *Computers in Human Behavior*, *27*(2), 852–861. doi:10.1016/j.chb.2010.11.010

Shin, N. (2006). Online learner's 'flow' experience: An empirical study. *British Journal of Educational Technology*, *37*(5), 705–720. doi:10.1111/j.1467-8535.2006.00641.x

Skadberg, Y. X., & Kimmel, J. R. (2004). Visitors' flow experience while browsing a Web site: Its measurement, contributing factors and consequences. *Computers in Human Behavior*, *20*(3), 403–422. doi:10.1016/S0747-5632(03)00050-5

Slater, M. (2003). A note on presence terminology. *Presence Connect*, *3*(3), 1-5.

Slater, M. (2018). Immersion and the illusion of presence in virtual reality. *British Journal of Psychology*. doi:10.1111/bjop.12305

Slater, M., & Wilbur, S. (1997). A framework for immersive virtual environments (FIVE): Speculations on the role of presence in virtual environments. *Presence (Cambridge, Mass.)*, *6*(6), 603–616. doi:10.1162/pres.1997.6.6.603

Sørebø, Ø., Halvari, H., Gulli, V. F., & Kristiansen, R. (2009). The role of self-determination theory in explaining teachers' motivation to continue to use e-learning technology. *Computers & Education*, *53*(4), 1177–1187. doi:10.1016/j.compedu.2009.06.001

Standage, M., Duda, J. L., & Ntoumanis, N. (2005). A test of self-determination theory in school physical education. *The British Journal of Educational Psychology*, *75*(3), 411–433. doi:10.1348/000709904X22359 PMID:16238874

Statista. (2016, March). *Global VR gaming market size 2020 | Statistic*. Retrieved from https://www.statista.com/statistics/499714/global-virtual-reality-gaming-sales-revenue/

Steed, A., Frlston, S., Lopez, M. M., Drummond, J., Pan, Y., & Swapp, D. (2016). An 'In the Wild' Experiment on Presence and Embodiment using Consumer Virtual Reality Equipment. *IEEE Transactions on Visualization and Computer Graphics*, *22*(4), 1406–1414. doi:10.1109/TVCG.2016.2518135 PMID:26780804

Sun, H., & Zhang, P. (2006). Causal relationships between perceived enjoyment and perceived ease of use: An alternative approach. *Journal of the Association for Information Systems*, *7*(1), 24. doi:10.17705/1jais.00100

Sweetser, P., & Wyeth, P. (2005). GameFlow: A model for evaluating player enjoyment in games. [CIE]. *Computers in Entertainment*, *3*(3), 3–3. doi:10.1145/1077246.1077253

Thomas, K. A., & Clifford, S. (2017). Validity and Mechanical Turk: An assessment of exclusion methods and interactive experiments. *Computers in Human Behavior*, *77*, 184–197. doi:10.1016/j.chb.2017.08.038

Treiblmaier, H., Putz, L. M., & Lowry, P. B. (2018). Setting a Definition, Context, and Theory-Based Research Agenda for the Gamification of Non-Gaming Applications. *Association for Information Systems Transactions on Human-Computer Interaction*, *10*(3), 129–163. doi:10.17705/1thci.00107

Van der Heijden, H. (2004). User acceptance of hedonic information systems. *Management Information Systems Quarterly*, *28*(4), 695–704. doi:10.2307/25148660

Van Rooij, M., Lobel, A., Harris, O., Smit, N., & Granic, I. (2016). DEEP: A biofeedback virtual reality game for children at-risk for anxiety. In *Proceedings of the 2016 CHI Conference Extended Abstracts on Human Factors in Computing Systems* (pp. 1989-1997). ACM. 10.1145/2851581.2892452

Venkatesh, V. (2000). Determinants of perceived ease of use: Integrating control, intrinsic motivation, and emotion into the technology acceptance model. *Information Systems Research*, *11*(4), 342–365. doi:10.1287/isre.11.4.342.11872

Verhagen, T., Feldberg, F., van den Hooff, B., Meents, S., & Merikivi, J. (2012). Understanding users' motivations to engage in virtual worlds: A multipurpose model and empirical testing. *Computers in Human Behavior*, *28*(2), 484–495. doi:10.1016/j.chb.2011.10.020

Vijayasarathy, L. R. (2004). Predicting consumer intentions to use on-line shopping: The case for an augmented technology acceptance model. *Information & Management, 41*(6), 747–762. doi:10.1016/j.im.2003.08.011

Vogel, J. J., Greenwood-Ericksen, A., Cannon-Bowers, J., & Bowers, C. A. (2006). Using virtual reality with and without gaming attributes for academic achievement. *Journal of Research on Technology in Education, 39*(1), 105–118. doi:10.1080/15391523.2006.10782475

Voiskounsky, A. E., Mitina, O. V., & Avetisova, A. A. (2004). Playing online games: Flow experience. *PsychNology Journal, 2*(3), 259–281.

Wang, H. Y., & Wang, S. H. (2010). User acceptance of mobile internet based on the unified theory of acceptance and use of technology: Investigating the determinants and gender differences. *Social Behavior and Personality, 38*(3), 415–426. doi:10.2224bp.2010.38.3.415

Wang, Z., & Scheepers, H. (2012). Understanding the intrinsic motivations of user acceptance of hedonic information systems: Towards a unified research model. *Communications of the Association for Information Systems, 30*(1), 17. doi:10.17705/1CAIS.03017

Weibel, D., & Wissmath, B. (2011). Immersion in computer games: The role of spatial presence and flow. *International Journal of Computer Games Technology, 2011*, 6. doi:10.1155/2011/282345

Weibel, D., Wissmath, B., Habegger, S., Steiner, Y., & Groner, R. (2008). Playing online games against computer-vs. human-controlled opponents: Effects on presence, flow, and enjoyment. *Computers in Human Behavior, 24*(5), 2274–2291. doi:10.1016/j.chb.2007.11.002

Wu, J., & Holsapple, C. (2014). Imaginal and emotional experiences in pleasure-oriented IT usage: A hedonic consumption perspective. *Information & Management, 51*(1), 80–92. doi:10.1016/j.im.2013.09.003

Wu, J., & Lu, X. (2013). Effects of extrinsic and intrinsic motivators on using utilitarian, hedonic, and dual-purposed information systems: A meta-analysis. *Journal of the Association for Information Systems, 14*(3), 153–191. doi:10.17705/1jais.00325

Xiong, D. (2019, January 16). *Richmond opens new virtual reality gaming centre.* Retrieved from https://www.richmond-news.com/business/richmond-opens-new-virtual-reality-gaming-centre-1.23601951

Xu, X., & Ke, F. (2016). Designing a virtual-reality-based, gamelike math learning environment. *American Journal of Distance Education, 30*(1), 27–38. doi:10.1080/08923647.2016.1119621

Zhao, L., Lu, Y., Wang, B., & Huang, W. (2011). What makes them happy and curious online? An empirical study on high school students' Internet use from a self-determination theory perspective. *Computers & Education, 56*(2), 346–356. doi:10.1016/j.compedu.2010.08.006

Zhou, T. (2013). Understanding the effect of flow on user adoption of mobile games. *Personal and Ubiquitous Computing, 17*(4), 741–748. doi:10.100700779-012-0613-3

This research was previously published in the International Journal of Gaming and Computer-Mediated Simulations (IJGCMS), 12(1); pages 43-70, copyright year 2020 by IGI Publishing (an imprint of IGI Global).

APPENDIX

Table 4. Scales used for VR gaming survey

Constructs	Items	Descriptions	Source
Perceived Ease of Use	PEOU1	My interaction with VR games is clear and understandable.	Lowry et al. (2012)
	PEOU2	Interacting with VR games does not require a lot of my mental effort.	
	PEOU3	I find VR games to be trouble free.	
	PEOU4	I find it easy to get VR games to do what I want it to do.	
	PEOU5	Learning to operate VR games is easy for me.	
	PEOU6	It is simple to do what I want with VR games.	
	PEOU7	It is easy for me to become skillful at using VR games.	
	PEOU8	I find VR games easy.	
Enjoyment	ENJ1	I have fun when I am playing VR games.	Wang and Scheepers (2012)
	ENJ2	Playing VR games provides me with a lot of enjoyment.	
	ENJ3	I enjoy playing VR games.	
Attitude	ATT1	I like playing VR games.	Wang and Scheepers (2012)
	ATT2	I like the idea of playing VR games.	
	ATT3	I have a positive attitude toward playing VR games.	
Intention to Play	ITP1	I think I will continue to play VR games.	Wang and Scheepers (2012)
	ITP2	I plan to play VR games in the future.	
	ITP3	I intend to continue playing VR games.	
	ITP4	I predict I will play VR games in the future.	
Autonomy	AUT1	VR games provide me with interesting options and choices.	Ryan et al.(2006)
	AUT2	VR games let you do interesting things.	
	AUT3	I experienced a lot of freedom in VR games.	
Competence	COMP1	I feel competent at VR games.	Ryan et al.(2006)
	COMP2	I feel very capable and effective when playing VR games.	
	COMP3	My ability to play VR games is well matched with the game's challenges.	
Immersion	IMM1	I become unaware of my surroundings while playing VR games.	Sweetser and Wyeth (2005)
	IMM2	I temporarily forget worries about everyday life while playing VR games.	
	IMM3	I feel emotionally involved in VR games.	
	IMM4	I feel viscerally involved in VR games.	
Concentration	CONC1	VR Games provide a lot of stimuli from different sources.	Sweetser and Wyeth (2005)
	CONC2	VR Games provide stimuli that are worth attending to.	
	CONC3	VR Games quickly grab my attention and maintain my focus throughout the game.	
	CONC4	I am not burdened with tasks that don't feel important in VR games.	
	CONC5	VR Games have a high workload, while still being appropriate for my perceptual, cognitive and memory limits.	
	CONC6	I am not distracted from tasks that I want / need to concentrate on in VR games.	

Chapter 4
Videogames and Sensory Theory:
Enchantment in the 21st Century

Kaila Goode
Oklahoma State University, USA

Sheri Vasinda
ⓘD https://orcid.org/0000-0001-6244-3075
Oklahoma State University, USA

ABSTRACT

The act of playing video games is a multimodal experience, immersing the gamer in a sensorial experience in the digital world. Video games incorporate sensory literacies such as haptics, graphics, sound effects, music, auditory dialogue, visual text, and character movement. The sensory literacies allow gamers to connect the digital world to the physical world, becoming engrossed in the world and story of the video game. Thus, due to the multimodal and sensorial nature of video games, they have the potential to be a beneficial tool for increasing student engagement within the classroom and assisting students in further increasing literacy skills and content knowledge. In addition, a review of literature of classroom use of video games as an instructional tool found increased engagement, use of video games as texts, cross-literacies that supported traditional literacy processes and skills.

INTRODUCTION

The first author has been playing videogames since she was four or five. Her parents bought a Sega Genesis for her; this was her very first game system. She remembers playing through the Disney simple story role-playing videogames (RPG) like *Aladdin*, *The Little Mermaid*, and *Pocahontas*. *Aladdin* was her favorite because it was easy; as a four-year-old, she could beat it. Then she got older and started playing more intricate RPG games. For example, one of her favorite games was *The Legend of Zelda: Ocarina of Time*. As she played, she began to get more and more immersed in the story of the game.

DOI: 10.4018/978-1-6684-7589-8.ch004

The game was filled with complex characters like Link, Zelda, Sheik (Zelda's secret identity), and the evil Ganon, and expansive environments like Hyrule, the multiple temples, and Jabu Jabu's (whale-like fish) belly. These characters and environments were brought to life by the visual innovative 3D graphics (for this time period), audio features, and textual story-telling components of the game. The graphics displayed the characters' facial features and reactions, body structures, clothing, weapons, and items with eye-catching colors, artistic lines, and unique character movement. The environmental graphics included details both big and small, from artistically mapping out large structures such as mountains and castles to forming small features such as bushes and trees. The game used music and various sound effects to bring the game to life, drawing her into the game causing various emotional sensations such as excitement, sadness, and terror. After being drawn in visually and audibly, she was further enamored by the game through the textual components: the game's story and the dialogue of the characters in the form of the written word throughout the game. The textual components gave her more insight into the inner-workings of the characters and their world. And, though this game was more difficult and frustrating than the games she had played as a younger child, she persisted, being compelled to discover the ending of the story; she beat the game to know the story.

All of these interactions, visual, auditory, and textual, within the game, created a cohesive and engaging sensory experience, allowing her to know and love the story of the game. Videogames, having complex stories that are compelling and engaging, beckon gamers to revisit and complete the game multiple times. As an adult, she still enjoys playing RPG videogames. She has revisited many games such as *STAR WARS: Knights of the Old Republic*, *The Legend of Zelda: Ocarina of Time*, and *Kingdom Hearts* due to her love for the story or stories that lie within them.

Like traditional literature, videogames have timeless stories that continue to be relevant and exciting. In addition to the sensory experiences that immersed and enchanted her, they also require the use of traditional literacy skills in order to define, interpret, and make-meaning within and of its virtual worlds. However, unlike traditional literature, videogames provide gamers with an engaging sensory experience in which they are digitally immersing themselves into worlds and stories of their favorite characters. Videogames are a multimodal experience, stimulating the gamer through sensory elements and literacies, causing the gamer not only to become part of the story but for the videogame to become part of the gamer's story. Looking back on her experiences, the first author recognizes videogames as a form of literacy, specifically a form of multiliteracies. In her current roles as a teacher of students with identified learning variabilities with personalized Individual Education Plans (IEPs) and as a doctoral student intrigued by the possibilities multiliteracies hold, she is curious about the harnessing potential of videogames as a learning platform for her students, and all students. Her personal experiences and curiosity about the potential of videogames as an instructional tool inspired this review of the literature on utilizing them in classroom contexts and the potential of an emerging literacy theory that may explain the enchantment it has over gamers.

Using a multiliteracies understanding of text expands the notion of text from a static form of paper pages and alphabet to a representation of content and communication of ideas in a variety of evolving forms. This broader representation of texts includes traditional linear texts that are read from top to bottom and left to right (depending on the culture) to non-linear forms that include multimodal texts such as gestures, sounds, and images (Cope & Kalantzis, 2000, 2015; Walsh, 2010). An expanded view of texts includes everything from traditional print-based books to podcasts, movies, images, infographics, webpages, and videogames. Therefore, videogames can no longer be considered 'just a game' (Berger & McDougall, 2013; Gerber et al, 2014; Altura & Curwood, 2015). Rich content such as story, substories, character development, and vocabulary are embedded within videogames such as *Legend of Zelda* and *Star Wars: Knights of the Old Republic* (Haas, 2012). Many videogames require genre-specific (narrative) and discipline-specific (gaming) vocabulary, strategic thinking, collaborative mind-sets, and prior knowledge of themes within the history of humanity. Examples of timeless themes embedded within videogames include good versus evil, foreign entity takeovers, corrupt governments, and the waging of wars.

Furthermore, videogames, specifically RPG videogames, are designed with a story arc. They contain literary elements such as character, plot, setting, and climax. RPGs immerse the gamer in the story to participate in a virtual world full of rich visual images, colors, sounds, movement options, haptic input options, and character choices. There is an element of exploration and the unexpected in which players are not quite sure of what they will encounter. The immersive environment often enchants the players, such as the first author. Enchantment in 21st-century contexts is sparked by surprise, something unexpected (Bennett, 2001). It is "an uneasy combination of charm and disturbance...the charm of wonder co-mingles with the discomforting frustration of dealing with non-linear events..." (p. 104-105). The videogame enraptures the gamer, causing his/her emotions and sensations to become connected with the game. Enchantment is also a sensory experience (Bennett, 2001) well matched to videogames. Because of the interplay of the sensory input, players engage in immersive stories set in complex environments where no real harm comes from taking risks. While playing, gamers can make choices and make meaning of the game's story elements and objectives, causing character paths within the game to be altered and personalized by the gamer. Thus, RPGs require the gamer to use traditional literacy skills and interact with multiple modes of literacy, in order to progress, master the game, and work through the story arc.

The purpose of this chapter is to examine current research on classroom use of videogames as pop culture texts. This builds on a multiliteracies expanded notion of text (Cope & Kalantzis, 2000, 2015) and multimodal literacy (Kress, 2009, Walsh, 2010). The authors also discuss an unexplored connection of sensory theory (Mills, 2016) as a possibility for the appeal of videogames by means of engagement through sensory experiences (Kalantzis & Cope, 2019; Kress, 2009; Mills, 2016) and a sense of modern-day enchantment (Bennett, 2001).

THEORETICAL PERSPECTIVE

Humans have always communicated in a variety of modes depending on the available tools and intentions (Cope & Kalantzis, 2000, 2015; Kalantzis & Cope, 2019; Mills, 2016). In its broadest terms and transcending the schools' hyperfocus on alphabetic modes, literacy is and has been, the ability to communicate with others in a community (Kalantzis & Cope, 2019; Keefe & Copeland, 2011). Before digital literacies and videogame culture were popular and widespread, the New London Group (1996) met to explore the ways in which literacy was evolving because of intersections of diversity and multiculturalism, the disruptions of technology, and economic development (Cope & Kalantzis, 2000, 2015; Kalantzis and Cope, 2019). This group of scholars from the US, the UK, and Australia convened in New London, New Hampshire, USA, thus the name the New London Group (NLG), to grapple with defining the changing nature of literacy. They examined increasing cultural and linguistic diversity in terms of texts and communication modes. In extending beyond the notion of strictly alphabetic texts and communication modes, they considered more multimodal literacy experiences of oral, written, visual, spatial, tactile, gestural, and audio. To capture this multiplicity of modes, NLG invented and introduced the term "multiliteracies", which encompassed all forms of literacy in one word (Gee, 2017). As time and technologies have advanced since the NLG's manifesto, recent scholars have embraced a multiliteracies theoretical perspective that "accounts for multiplicity of communications channels, media and modes, associated with the availability and convergence of new digital" (as cited by Mills, 2016, p. 21).

Literacies and Technology

The New London Group (1996) also focused on the use and disruption of technologies, newer modes of literacy, and the processes people undergo in order to utilize them and interpret them. The New London Group (as cited by Mills, 2016) believed that "multiliteracies accounts for multiplicity of communications channels, media, and modes, associated with the availability and convergence of new digital technologies" (Kindle Location 778). Technology is used by people in a multitude of fashions in order to communicate and interpret messages and meanings. Digital communications provide space for self-expression and interpretation, allowing people to make meaning across multiple technological platforms.

The theory of multimodality examines the modes of literacy in which people communicate (Kress, 2009; Mills, 2016). Kress identified multiple modes of literacy which include the traditional modes of reading, writing, speaking and listening; however, visuals, sounds and varying aspects of technology are also modes of literacy (Kress, 2009; Mills, 2016) With technological advancements, technology has become an important mode of literacy. Technology can be and should be considered a sign system or mode of literacy, as it requires literacy skills to understand and use for communication purposes. The interest in technology as a mode of literacy focuses on the ability to use digital tools to capture, create, modify, combine and share images, text, podcasts, and communication easily and on a wider scale (Mills, 2016).

Multimodalities of Videogames

Videogames are a unique mode of literacy and communication. Unlike traditional books, videogames are a multimodal experience that engages the gamer's senses of sight, hearing, and feeling (Kress, 2009; Compton-Lily, 2007). They incorporate various formats of meaning and messages that go beyond that of linear text. Videogames also use sound, graphics, visuals, style, characters, choices, and format for the gamers to use to make meaning of the game and concepts within the game. As a multimodal text, the game taps into the gamer's auditory and visual cueing systems, allowing the gamer to engage with and within the game (Kress, 2009). Gee (2013) describes videogames as explorative learning environments in which players learn at their own pace through processes of trial and error. He also distinguishes them from simply games played on game platforms and computers, to games, such as the first author describes in her experiences, in which "players take on the role of a virtual character and moving through an elaborate world, solving problems, or in which the player builds and maintains complex entities like armies, cities, or even whole civilizations" (Gee, 2007, p. 1). According to Chess (2018), "the ability to tell stories via experiences and environments is something almost completely unique to videogames" (p. 19). Thus, in the realm of using videogames within classroom settings, they are used as a mode of literacy across content areas and as a mode of learning.

Sensory Engagement in Videogames

The use of multiple senses during the learning and literacy processes allows students to make more meaningful connections to what they are learning and reading. The use of multiple modes of literacy including visual, audible, movement-based, technology, and others, allows students to make-meaning and utilize literacy skills in unique ways that engage them through multiple senses. Sensory literacy theory identifies the relationship between the mind and the body that creates crucial connections during literacy and learning processes (Mills, 2016). The mind and body are not separate from the other, both are essential to literacy and learning. Because literacy is an activity that embodies the principles of interaction and action, both the body and mind play crucial roles within literacy practices and communication exchanges across multiple modalities of learning. Mills (2016) discussed the applications of sensory engagement and literacy:

Sensorial approaches attend to the changing nature and role of the sense and the body in the social process of meaning-making... the body, the senses and their entanglement in the social and material spaces of culture are highly important, as are their relations to the material and forms of literacy practice (Kindle location 3454).

The use of multiple senses during and throughout the learning process assists in increasing student engagement due to the constant interaction of students' senses with the material and concepts in which they are attempting to learn (Mills, 2016). Videogames tap into all human senses, with the exception of smell; they immerse the gamer into a digital environment using elements of multi-faceted graphics, colors, sound effects, music, haptic technology, character movement, physical movement, and traditional text. Thus, in utilizing videogames in the literacy and learning processes, a sensorial engagement is created between gamer and videogame, acting as a text, through the gamer's immersion into the game, reacting to and communicating with sensory literacies.

BACKGROUND

Videogames can be both an activity of enjoyment and a tool for promoting individuality and self-determination. The opportunities of immersion and agency provided within videogames "cannot be duplicated by any other kinds of leisure experiences" (Chess, 2018, p. 19). Because videogames are primarily a leisure activity, most research examining videogames and learning experiences focus on out-of-school settings, such as libraries, after-school clubs, and homes (Abrams & Russo, 2015; Curwood, 2014; Evans, Jones, & Akalin, 2017; Gee, 2007; Squire, 2005). There are fewer studies on the use of videogames in classroom settings and most of them focus on secondary classrooms.

Guthrie and Wigfield (1998) researched motivation and engagement within literacy and learning processes. They discovered that individuals who are intrinsically motivated are more engaged during literacy learning, and are, therefore, more likely to read. They explored various motivational practices in order to assist in the process of engaging readers. Within their research, they discovered that there were "positive effects of motivational practices on students' interest, confidence and dedication in reading" (as cited by Tracey & Morrow, 2017, Kindle location 146). Motivational practices can vary reader to reader or student to student; these practices could include the incorporation of technology-based texts (such as videogames) in order to motivate readers to engage during the reading process.

Videogames are an activity that can be utilized in the classroom to enrich instruction and practice, motivating students to engage and participate in the learning processes. Rich (2020) found that students are motivated by videogame-play due to its risk-free nature, the confidence it instills, and the student's desire to win. Students feel safe within the virtual setting of videogames, unafraid of the ramifications from wrong answers. Videogames allow the student to gradually build up to more difficult levels or tasks; this not only builds upon the student's abilities within the game, but also their confidence within themselves (Granic, Lobel, & Engels, 2014). Through the failure within the trial-and-error process, gamers are motivated to persist, continuing to return to the game regardless of frustration (McGonigal, 2011). Without fear of failure, confidence grows. Videogames motivate students to continue to try until they succeed; they continue to persist until they win (Rich, 2020; Daniels, Tapscott, & Caston, 2003; McGonigal, 2011).

As our digital world and cultural movements continue to blur the lines between in-school and out-of-school literacies, these classroom-based studies have important implications for learning and literacy, such as tapping into the engagement, motivation and agency videogames provide (Hanghoj et.al, 2018; Ye, Hsiao, & Sun, 2018; Israel et al. 2016; Blumberg & Sokol (2004)), as well as improvement of academic skills (Ye, Hsiao, & Sun, 2018; Israel et al., 2016; Berger & McDougall, 2013; Altura & Curwood, 2015; Gerber et al, 2014). These studies also illustrate an expanded notion of texts in terms of choice of text to support teaching and learning goals and objectives.

Increasing the Motivation of Students Who Struggle with Literacy: School at Play

Hanghoj, Lieberoth, and Misfeldt (2018) conducted a study to determine the effects of the utilization of videogames on the motivation and learning of students who are identified at-risk. The determination of at-risk students included those with social difficulties, special needs, and specific disabilities. This three-week study included 190 students within eight classes in Denmark between third and sixth grades. There was a total of 32 students identified as at-risk for academic success in (Danish) literacy and mathematics; four at-risk students in each class. The researchers used commercial videogames within the classroom instructional time frame for three weeks. Researchers were exploring how videogame-play influenced motivated students to learn and how it impacted social engagement with peers. It was also designed to create a safe environment for collaboration and learning. Data was gathered through teacher surveys and rating scales on motivation, achievement engagement, participation, and regulation; the data of the at-risk students was compared to the peer group; the peer group included students considered to be on-target academically per grade-level expectations.

The researchers used the game *Torchlight II,* an RPG game, for its immersive, fantasy story world that provided a rich context for math and literacy concepts. The interventions began with two to three hours of game-playing time. After the game-playing time, the students would participate in classroom discussions over concepts being learned or they would be working on game-related assignments focused on targeted concepts called 'Portal Assignments', Progress Bar", and "Classroom Game". These assignments implicitly and explicitly connected academic concepts and skills to the in-game tasks the students were trying to accomplish.

The data did show a significant increase in intrinsic motivation for literacy and neutral results for math among the at-risk students; the peer group had a decline of intrinsic motivation in both (Danish) literacy and math. They also found a decrease in external regulation, or reminders to stay on-task, of at-risk students in literacy instruction; whereas the peer group did not. Both groups showed a decline in external regulation in math instruction. Data showed that social participation levels increased for both the at-risk student group and the peer group. Hanghoj and colleagues (2018) found students were more willing to participate because the game-based intervention felt more like play than typical classroom participation. The videogame-play seemed to have a positive impact on at-risk students' inclusion within the classroom; they became more involved within the class using of collaborative gaming strategies with peers. The study had varied results among students in relation to levels of engagement and achievement. The data did not show a clear trend of increase or decrease for the group as a whole; however, the data did show that the at-risk student group had unique gains in learning engagement. Academic achievement levels also varied with the at-risk student group not showing clear academic gains that were seen by their peer group. Thus, the study concluded that classroom use of videogames supported increased student motivation for at-risk students, and social participation increased for all. Researchers cautioned that results varied between students since each had unique and varying levels of interest and abilities (Hanghoj et.al, 2018).

Motivation and Concept Knowledge Development:
Angry Birds, Ballance, and Physics

In a two-week study, Ye, Hsiao, and Sun (2018) studied the effects of using videogames as a pre-class learning activity to motivate and engage 77 eighth-grade students; there were three science classes in Taiwan, instructing upon physics. Each class received a different type of instruction. One class received game-discussion (GD), another received game-instruction (GI), and the third received traditional-instruction (TI). The GD group played the commercial 3-D puzzle videogames, *Ballance* and *Angry Birds*, during the pre-class time for 30 minutes and then participated in a cooperative learning activity focused on the science content. The GI group played the commercial videogame during the pre-class time for 30 minutes and then had traditional lecture-based instruction. The TI group did not participate in the gaming activity during the pre-class time and then had traditional lecture-based instruction.

Ballance and *Angry Birds* were chosen because they required the students to practice strategy, trial-and-error based learning skills, and to work through progressively difficult levels within the games. In order to determine how the utilization of these games impacted student learning, the researchers gave the students a multiple-choice exam that evaluated their pre-class self-learning outcomes, or their understanding of the specific concepts being learned. Additionally, the researchers used concept maps in order to measure and track the post-instruction learning outcomes.

According to their statistical data and evidence, the researchers found that the two games were effective pre-class learning tools within the classroom. The games did enhance student motivation, and it helped them to understand specific concepts while also assisting them in identifying their own knowledge deficits within that specific content. The researchers concluded that when using appropriate videogames as a pre-class learning tool, it could help support and motivate student engagement within the classroom learning experiences.

Attitude and Concept Development: You Make Me Sick!, Cell Command, and Crazy Plant Shop

Israel, Wang, and Marino (2016) studied the impact of using video gaming in the science curriculum in relation to the attitudes and capabilities of the students. The study was conducted across three different states using four middle schools, sampling 366 middle school students. The diverse population of students including students of varying abilities and identified learning disabilities.

Throughout the study, the teachers covered three different science units over the topic of physics. Within each unit, they utilized a different science videogame in order to give additional practice with unit-specific content and concepts. The games included *You Make Me Sick!, Cell Command,* and *Crazy Plant Shop.* These RPG games allowed the students to immerse themselves in the science content by playing as a character following simple story arcs, exploring unique environments, and completing missions. Additionally, the games also provided in-game accommodations such as tutorials, dictionaries, and text-to-speech for those that needed extra assistance within the game. The students spent 180 minutes playing the three videogames throughout the course of the six-week study.

At the end of the study, researchers analyzed student and teacher surveys, observations, pre-tests and posttests, and periodic interviews. They noticed that the amount of progress made between the pre and posttests of the units varied between specific units and videogames played during the unit; but progress was made between the pre-test and post-test after students played each game. They attributed these results to the varying student attitudes of interest and motivation to learn specific content from unit to unit, and the level of interest in the specific game being played in each unit. Additionally, the data showed that there was also a significant difference in male attitudes towards using videogames in order to learn science content; they were more motivated to learn through utilizing videogames during instruction than any other subgroup. From the results, Israel et al. (2016) determined that utilizing videogames in the classroom benefits students and teachers; however, when considering using videogames for instructional purposes, teachers need to take special consideration of students' capabilities and interests before selecting videogames to utilize.

Role-playing Games as Texts

Berger and McDougall (2013) studied the use of RPG videogames in relation to reading a traditional novel. The researchers included four groups of teachers and students from different institutions across the United Kingdom within a semester; there were ten students in each group working towards undergraduate studies. The groups played the videogame *L. A. Noire,* in which the gamers play a detective named Cole Phelps. As part of the study, the students and teachers participated in a blog in which they asked and answered questions about the game. This blog, essentially, became a type of study guide for how to play and understand the 'authorless' text of the videogame with the students teaching the teachers how to play the videogame.

Since the story was centered around a white male, some participants of other ethnicities, races, and genders of the group found it difficult to identify with the main character and sought out ways to identify with the story through other characters within the game. This struggle to identify with the main character can impact the engagement and understanding of the 'authorless' text of the videogame. Although relating to the main character was a struggle for some, many students and teachers were able to make text-to-text connections between the game and other classic texts they had read previously. They were also able to determine that there were no distinct boundaries between books and games as far as determining genre; the students were able to identify genre through elements seen both within texts and cinema.

At the end of the study, the researchers determined that *L.A Noire*, an RPG videogame, can be used as a form of literature within the English Curriculum. Within the game, or immersive multimedia text, students were able to make their own choices for their character; this gave students the control to change the story and alter their gaming experience. Berger and McDougall (2013) concluded that RPG videogames such as *L. A. Noire* do "function as a (digitally transformed) novel, in relation to other texts… it contains the utterance of literature, resonating in different media" (p. 148).

CROSS-LITERATE SCHEMA SUPPORTS GAMING AND TRADITIONAL LITERACIES

Commercial-Off-the-Shelf Videogames

In a qualitative case study, Gerber and Onwuegbuzie explored how videogames could promote equitable and cross-literate experiences through a social constructionist lens (Gerber et al, 2014). They also wondered how insights to meaning-making could be revealed through cohesive peer interactions and literate activities in a 10th-grade reading intervention class. Two of the researchers co-taught this game-based course for 18 weeks in a reader/writer workshop framework at an urban high school. They set up the classroom into reading, writing, and videogame workshop stations, or "quest" areas that were used three days per week to support the two-day cycle of whole-class instruction. The five quest areas included a *Videogame Quest Area*, *The Reading Quest Area* (independent reading), *The Writing Quest Area* (independent writing), *The Conference Quest Area* (conferring with the teacher), and the *Metareflection Area* (reflective writing and peer review). Each quest area had activities designed to support the whole class lessons and for students to expand their independent gaming skills. The researchers found that, when given the opportunity to learn through a socially constructed, game-based learning environment, their two case-study students constructed meaning for themselves drawing upon cross-literate experiences, collaborated with peers during learning processes, recognized and used content-specific vocabulary, and made complex inferences both within the games and across texts (Gerber et al., 2014).

Videogames as Cultural Texts

Altura and Curwood (2015) studied the implications of videogames being used as a cultural text within a high school elective class in Australia. The study focused on two specific students as case studies from a class of nine students. The English teacher used videogames as cultural and literary texts with three main projects centered around the games: a research project, a game design project, and a game review. The purpose of these game-based projects was to support research skills and game design while increasing motivation and encouraging participation and engagement during the learning process. Students incorporated literacy skills such as reading and writing while utilizing videogames within the classroom; they treated videogames as if they were a literary text. Students completed analysis critiques of the videogames, developing a deeper understanding of the forms and elements within the literary structure of a narrative. By the end of the semester, they found that students had improved upon multiple literacy skills such as summarizing, synthesizing, and critical and creative thinking, within not only the traditional areas of reading and writing but also within the multimodal literacies of programming, collaborative learning, and creative design.

MAIN FOCUS OF THE CHAPTER

It seems that gamers have come of age and more and more teachers, like the first author, are gamers. In a study of teacher perceptions of videogames, most teachers' perceived videogames as effective for enhancing learning in visually explicit ways and in motivating students (Pastor & Falvo, 2010). These teachers also either had used or intended to use videogames as an instructional tool. Seventy-seven percent of the 53 teachers surveyed also believed videogames were a valuable use of instructional time. Studies of preservice teachers found that those who were gamers had positive perceptions of videogames as learning tools, but also could foresee obstacles in their use in classrooms (Watson, Yang, & Ruggiero, 2012). It stands to reason that these teachers, like the first author, make connections to their experiences as gamers and the possibilities and potential that videogames hold for engaging, immersive, and motivational educational practice with expectations that videogames can also support school-based learning objectives.

A large, national survey entitled Level Up Learning: A National Survey of Teaching with Digital Games conducted by the Sesame Workshop, identified characteristics of teachers who use video games as teaching resources and divided them into four categories: *Naturals, Players, Barrier Busters,* and *Dabblers* (Takeuchi & Vaala, 2014). The first author is a *Natural. Naturals* taught for fewer than 12 years, played digital games often, taught with them weekly, and felt comfortable using them. Naturals made up the largest percentage of this survey (34%) and were the only group that used digital games to teach core content more than as a supplemental resource. *Players* were avid game players, with an average of 14.7 years of teaching experience, and made up 23% of the survey. Even though they played videogames the most in their personal lives, surprisingly this group used games for teaching and learning the least of all four categories of teachers. They cited more barriers than any of the other groups and reported no changes in student behaviors or their teaching when they used digital games. The teacher group that leveraged digital games the most were the *Barrier Busters*. With an average of 13.6 years of experience, they played games as a "common pastime" (Takeuchi & Vaala, 2014, p. 38), but not as much as either the *Naturals* or the *Players*. Although they used digital games and a large variety of digital tools the most, they also reported high levels of barriers to their use. Because they perceived digital game-based learning as an effective tool for developing both content knowledge and 21st-century skills, they worked past the barriers they perceived to incorporate digital games into their instructional repertoire. The most veteran group of game-using teachers were *Dabblers*. They played digital games the least of all four groups and therefore felt the least confident in their use as educational resources. They reported only moderate barriers to their use and used games in their teaching several times per month, more as a supplement rather than to deliver content or as an assessment.

Classroom teachers and researchers have found ways to mediate and enhance traditional literacies, such as reading, writing, speaking, and listening, and disciplinary literacies, such as science, history, and math, through videogame-play (Altura & Curwood, 2015; Berger & McDougall, 2013; Gerber, et al., 2014; Hanghoj et al., 2018; Israel et al., 2016; Takeuchi & Vaala, 2014; Ye, et al., 2018). Videogames are a layered medium incorporating various formats of meaning and messages that go beyond that of text. They are both a sensory and multimodal media in ways that books are not. They involve not only visual input but, also, sound and movement. The videogame text can change and be (re)invented depending on the action of the player(s). Within this sensory experience context, games are immersive texts, in terms of story arc, and games are action, in terms of decision making and agency of the player(s) (Abrams & Russo, 2015; Garcia, 2018).

Videogames can be used to promote student motivation and engagement within the classroom community (Nelson, et al., 2016). Often role-playing and strategy type games challenge students to solve puzzles, assisting them in practicing their problem-solving skills. These are the actions of the game (Abrams & Russo, 2015). They also provide students with unique, independent learning opportunities in immersive environments across diverse content areas. Learning experiences are contextualized in engaging story arcs with characters, personalized actions, and interactions with unique virtual environments, and through concept immersion, connection, and relations. Even games that have more of a mission storyline, such as creating a vaccine, collecting plant specimens, still give the player a sense of agency and competency. Videogames provide learning opportunities across multiple disciplines, offering opportunities for exploration with embedded rewards to encourage and support student effort (Nelson, et al., 2016), which is games as text (Abrams & Russo, 2015).

The review of literature on classroom use of videogames included some inconclusive findings, which will be discussed later. It also uncovered multiple positive outcomes. These positive outcomes included the use of videogames as texts (Altura & Curwood, 2015; Berger & McDougall, 2013), supporting traditional literacies through cross-literate schema (Altura & Curwood, 2015; Gerber, et al., 2014; Isreal, et al., 2018; Hanghoj, et al., 2018), supporting science concept/content development (Isreal, et al., 2018; Hanghoj, et al., 2018), and increased motivation and engagement (Hanghou, et al., 2018; Isreal, et al., 2016; Nelson, et al., 2016; Ye, et al., 2018).

Videogames as Literary Texts

From a multiliteracies perspective, videogames are a text (Cope & Kalantzis, 2000, 2015; Walsh, 2010). Many have classic literary elements such as character, plot, setting, and climax. RPG games, in particular, offer an immersive story experience in which players make choices that help them make meaning of the game and the story within the game. All videogames require the gamer to use literacy and strategy skills, interacting with multiple modes of literacy; thus, allowing them to progress and master the game. When videogames are utilized as text in content area courses positive impacts can be seen, such as with the games *You Make Me Sick!, Cell Command,* and *Crazy Plant Shop*. Even when played for a short duration to provide a contextual introduction to a unit of study, these games yielded an increased conceptual understanding in two cases within the study (Isreal, et al., 2016).

When considering the expanded notion of texts and the story arc of many videogames, like movies, are multimodal texts. The biggest and most striking difference is, as the first author says about her own playing experiences, the player is immersed into the story and compelled to beat the game in order to know the story outcome. Many videogames engage and enact traditional literary elements. Others provide opportunities for collaborative learning requiring communication type literacy skills ranging from using the written word, spoken word, and imagery to convey meaning to other gamers. Furthermore, many have creative components embedded within them, allowing the gamer to have opportunities to reflect their identity and construct creative solutions to problems within the game. Videogames are layered with multiple meanings that can be interpreted, inferred, performed, and conveyed in different ways. Altura and Curwood (2015) suggest that teachers take advantage of the technology we have available, such as videogames, utilizing them as engaging, multimodal texts. They can be a beneficial instructional tool within the literacy classroom, assisting teachers in developing both students' traditional literacy skills and multimodal literacies (Artura & Curwood, 2015).

Cross-literacy Schema or Transliteracy

Learners use all available tools to find meaning and make meaning. The fluid movement across and among a range of texts, technologies, and media is called transliteracy (Sukovic, 2014). Learners may move between paper-based print resources to the internet on a laptop computer, take notes on paper or their mobile phones. Additionally, Gerber et al. (2014) found that students used schema from one text or media type to the other. The eighth-graders in her classes used knowledge of the commercial-off-the-shelf videogames to make connections to print-based literature. Students in secondary science course made improvements to their concept development knowledge using content and experiences from commercial-off-the-shelf games such as *Angry Birds,* a*nd Ballance* (Hanghoj, et al. 2018), as well as specialized videogames such as *You Make Me Sick!, Cell Command, and Crazy Plant Shop* (Israel, et al., 2016). Moving across platforms, content areas, and modes of texts, as being transliterated, and learning from one type of media or text and applying that schema to another type of text, or cross-literacies, supported learners in all modes and media.

Safe Learning Environment: Freedom from Adverse Consequences of Failure

When videogames are utilized for instructional purposes, they support student agency and confidence within their learning through the element of choice. Many videogames offer choices from choosing their avatars to action choices, or strategy choices. Action choices affect the story path, provide opportunities to experience the consequence of choices, as well as opportunities for varieties of outcomes and personalized experiences. Having choice entails having ownership of what one is doing. Specifically, the use of RPG videogames, in which students get to create their own avatar, in the classroom gives the students a sense of identity both within the game and outside of the game. Using role-playing games and avatars allows students to take more ownership of their choices within the game, which then enables them to take more ownership of their learning of the concepts or skills being covered within the game. Personalizing avatars affords the opportunity to express a version of self that is true or a heroic, ideal version of who is possible (McGonigal, 2011).

Many videogames give players the choice to try tasks, skills, and objectives multiple times at different difficulties. When players fail, they can learn from their mistakes, revise their moves, try again, and persist until they complete the task (Gee, 2008). For example, Blumberg and Sokol (2004) studied the use of commercial videogames with fifth-grade and second-grade students. The students played *Sonic the Hedgehog 2,* an RPG game in which they played as characters, either Sonic or Tails, working through levels in order to beat the "bad guy" Doctor Robotnik. The students were observed and surveyed individually one time. Data from the study showed that "children made greater reference to trial and error strategies than to reading the instructions… the use of a trial and error strategy was based on their confidence (Blumberg & Sokol, 2004, p. 157). The students used their prior knowledge of other games to guide their experience of gaming in the classroom; this gave them confidence to play and persist through the game.

Videogames instill confidence in the gamer by giving them multiple attempts or infinite attempts while trying to complete a task (Gee 2007, 2013, 2017) . They provide students with a safe environment within the educational setting to practice, fail, and try again at tasks and academic goals. Though gamers can become frustrated, they are not afraid of the repercussions that come from multiple failures of a task. In turn, they take the knowledge gained from those repeated failures and persevere through difficult tasks within the game until they complete it. Upon completing, they gain a sense of accomplishment, building confidence in their gaming abilities (Rich, 2020; Daniels, Tapscott, & Caston, 2003; McGonigal, 2011; Granic, Lobel, & Engels, 2014).

Videogames, Attitude, and Motivation

Teachers are seeing that videogames can be used to increase students' motivation and engagement within the classroom (Hanghoj et.al, 2018; Ye, Hsiao, and Sun, 2018; Israel et al. 2016). Using videogames as a tool for learning can motivate students since they are familiar with this type of technology and use it daily for entertainment purposes. For example, in a survey conducted by Clarke and Treagust (2010), results indicated that there are "positive attitudes towards games from practitioners working in settings as varied as literacy classes, libraries and prisons with a variety of audiences" (p. 161). Teachers are seeing the potential benefits of using videogames in the classroom to help their students become engaged in the learning process and classroom activities, especially with students who struggle with traditional approaches (Hanghoj, Lieberoth & Misfeldt, 2018). When students begin the learning process in a state of motivation and engagement, they are more likely to be willing to participate in the instructional activities and lessons (Adams, 2009).

ISSUES, CONTROVERSIES, PROBLEMS

Our review of classroom-based studies uncovered the multiple issues, controversies, and problems. There was a lack of data (Clark & Treagust 2010; Lieury et al., 2016), longitudinal studies (Lieberman, Bates & So, 2009), and of controlled experiments (Israel, Wang, & Marino, 2016) within the studies to show the long-term and consistent effects of videogames on learning and literacy processes. Additionally, the literature uncovered possible reasons for these problems and additional challenges involving technology access and infrastructure issues, professional development, and time (Caldwell, Osterweil, Urbano, Tan, & Eberhardt, 2017; Joan Ganz Cooney Center for Research, 2016; Takeuchi & Vaala, 2014; Watson, Yang, & Ruggiero, 2012).

Lack of Data

There was an underwhelming amount of data present within many of the articles, case studies, and experimental design studies showing a significant impact that utilizing videogames has on learning outcomes. In the review of research, Clarke and Treagust (2010) indicated there was a limited amount of research and data, showing videogame's ability to have "significant beneficial impact on learners and on the practitioners, who work with them" and its connection to assisting literacy learning (p. 161). Moreover, much of the literature's data and findings showed little to no statistical difference between the utilization of videogames versus traditional instruction.

Various studies were conducted and analyzed in order to determine the impact of using videogames as an instructional tool. Much of the literature showed inconclusive results regarding the benefits and effectiveness of using videogames for instructional purposes. Many of the studies did not see a significant difference between the different instructional methods or tools. For example, in an experimental study, conducted by Lieury, Lorant, Trosseille, Champault, and Vourc'h (2016), the impact of videogames on cognitive performance was studied. Within the study, the researchers surveyed students within the middle school demographics, and they conducted a battery of assessments to determine the impact that playing videogames had on students' cognitive levels and performance scores. At the end of the study, Lieury et al. (2016) had mixed results:

Results show that there are no positive correlations or small ones between videogames and cognitive/ school tests…(However) there is a positive correlation, although it is a small one, for strategy videogames. As expected, these correlations are with Math and Reasoning tests but also with encyclopedic memory… videogames do not have or have very little relations with cognitive and school tests. These results are consistent with research that shows it requires a high similarity between videogames and learning, so that there is a beneficial effect (p. 1587-1588).

Furthermore, there was a lack of studies and a lack of data specifically on the impact of the utilization of videogames regarding reading instruction in the elementary school setting. Most of the case studies and experimental design studies reviewed and discussed the utilization of videogames within the secondary setting and across various content areas. The authors of this chapter argue that the studies that showed inconclusive findings or negative findings ranged in duration between three to six weeks (Hanghoj, et al., 2018; Israel, et al., 2016). Although the Ye, Hsiao, and Sun (2018) study showed promise after only two weeks and as little as an hour's worth of game-playing with positive trends in terms of science concepts, each of the semester-long studies showed positive learning outcomes. Lieberman, Bates, and So (2009) recommend the explicit need for long-term data in comparison to short-term data:

Longitudinal studies of large numbers of children are needed to identify long-term trends such as the value of using digital media [or videogames] for long periods of time over the course of, say, a school year versus using it in short bursts (p. 278).

Lack of Controlled Experiments

Within the literature, it was also identified that there was a lack of tightly controlled experiments when comparing the use of videogames as instructional tools versus traditional instruction. In reference to their experimental study, Israel, Wang, and Marino (2016) cite their study's limitation in an analysis of students across gaming conditions as not including a control group to analyze how the gaming students' performance on learning tasks compared to a control group that experienced traditional instructional. Controlled experiments are difficult in educational research due to the fact that there are many variables that could impact results, and it is difficult to teach identical content in varying methods of instruction.

Barriers to the Use of Videogames in Classroom Contexts

Even though many teachers and students have positive attitudes toward using videogames as learning tools, or 21st-century texts, as noted in the Level Up Learning survey (Takeuchi & Vaala, 2014) even some teachers who are avid videogame players, perceived many barriers to their use. Watson, Yang, & Ruggiero (2012) found four challenges that affected classroom use of videogames: effective implementation challenges, technological challenges, challenges of working within educational systems, and challenges acquiring the games. Another survey with over 1000 teacher respondents found similar challenges and determined the inclusion of digital games is still a "Do-it-Yourself" endeavor in which teachers are confronted with infrastructure issues of low-internet bandwidth, or speed, and out-dated technology device (Joan Ganz Cooney Center for Research, 2016). This research group also cited lack of professional development as a need. They also referred to the puzzlement of teachers who are gamers (Takeuchi & Vaala, 2014) not using games in their practice even though they are avid players in their personal lives. In addition to lack of high-speed internet and old computers, additional technology challenges reported include one-computer classrooms, lack of access to computer labs, and school firewalls blocking certain downloads (Caldwell, et al., 2017).

Martín del Pozo, Basilotta Gómez-Pablos, & García-Valcárcel Muñoz-Repiso (2017) offer two additional reasons that videogames are not a regular resource in most classrooms. The first reason is one that is also noted by Gee (2007, 2013); immersive games require hours of gameplay that take several days or weeks to complete. It is difficult to create time in classroom schedules that are already overcrowded to include this type of learning. This may be why teachers who do use digital games opt for drill-and-practice and puzzle games as opposed to longer simulations that include role-playing and action/adventure. Second, in terms of K-8 classrooms, there are still few immersive games for younger students. This focus on how to choose games that relate to processes and content is echoed by teachers participating in the Joan Ganz Cooney (2016) survey mentioned at the beginning of this section. They cited lack of a reliable, curated site for game ideas and relied mostly on a game's ability to track performance, research claim on educational impact, and cost as the top three considerations. Their own experience with the game came in fourth, while what other teachers said about the game, what children said about the game, game reviews, and a game's rating (Everyone, Teen, Mature) as lesser considerations, in that order.

SOLUTIONS AND RECOMMENDATIONS

Teacher and Classroom Considerations

More teachers like the *Naturals* and the *Barrier Busters* (Takeuchi & Vaala, 2014), who find incorporating digital games into their teaching a natural process or see so much potential in their use that they are willing to work through perceived barriers to their use, are needed. More curated repositories to help teachers make decisions about games are also needed (Caldwell, et al., 2017). It is important for teachers to take special consideration when choosing the type of videogame and its content applications to use within instruction. The type could improve or negate the goal of engaging students in the learning process. Some types are more beneficial for specific students, content, and learning situations (Israel, et al., 2016).

There is an overabundance of videogames both commercial and educational that can be used in the classroom can be overwhelming, and there are many factors to consider when choosing the appropriate videogame for classroom purposes. Specific types of videogames can promote the practice and growth of specific skill sets within students and people. According to Lieberman, Bates and So (2009) "young children have improved in problem-solving skills, spatial cognition, spatial representation, iconic skills, and visual attention skills when using computers and videogames in school" (p. 276). Additionally, Lieberman et al. (2009) concluded that "well-designed computer-based learning activities and games can improve skills of abstract thinking, reflective thinking and analyzing and evaluating information" (p. 276).

When choosing a videogame for an academic tool, it is important to gauge the difficulty of the game and the content of the game, and how it will correlate to the knowledge and interest of the students (Caldwell, et al., 2017; Israel, et al., 2016). Videogames can assist teachers in differentiating instruction, developing unique goals, tasks, and instructional plans for students based upon their individual needs and interests (Nelson et al., 2016). Different types, styles, and versions of videogames can provide students with different experiences and varying levels of difficulty within a task. Since videogames can differentiate the gaming and learning experience based upon the abilities of the gamer, then they can also, when combined with or related to learning processes and goals, assist in differentiating instruction based upon the needs of the students. Using videogames can assist teachers in differentiating instruction and learning activities, establishing developmentally appropriate goals and tasks, and creating meaningful learning experiences for a diverse population of students (Nelson et.al, 2016). They also provide immediate feedback loops that contribute to engagement, persistence, and authentic assessment and meaningful learning (Abrams & Gerber, 2013; Willis, 2011) while creating learning environments where it is safe to fail (Gee, 2007, 2013).

Thus, when using videogames for instructional purposes it is essential for teachers to take special consideration when choosing the type of game in relation to the content being taught and in relation to the needs and interests of the student. Each student has different interests, levels of ability, and levels of motivation. The teacher must consider the needs and interests of the students when choosing a videogame for instruction; these factors will impact the effectiveness of the videogame in its ability to assist in student progression through the academic material.

Sensory Literacies, Videogames, and Memory: An Unexplored Possibility

Videogames use elements of sensory theory in order to engage gamers in a multimodal experience. Due to their complex sensory nature, they create memorable connections for gamers as the game's story and their story become intertwined. Knowledge, senses, and emotions all coexist both within the physical and virtual world, cohabitating within the mind of the gamer in order to make-meaning and bridge the gap between the two worlds. In creating a link between the virtual and physical world, the gamer can develop a deeper sense of self and build upon individual confidence and agency through acts of perseverance within the game.

Moreover, memory plays a crucial role in the act of videogame-play, requiring the gamer to both retain and access different memories or moments of game-play at all times. The sensory components of videogaming assist the gamer in making meaningful memories that are more readily accessed and retained. There are different types of memory that humans use in order to connect with and remember new concepts, procedures, and ideas. According to the multistore model of memory, developed by Atkinson and Shiffrin (1968), information is input and then enters the sensory memory. From sensory memory, it enters the short-term memory, where it is recalled and rehearsed. Finally, after being rehearsed and recalled multiple times, the information enters the long-term memory, where it can later be retrieved when needed. Regarding sensory memory, there are different types of memory within sensory memory that assist people in remembering information. There is iconic memory and echoic memory. Iconic memory is the type of memory that is triggered by visuals or things that people have seen (Norman, 2008). Echoic memory is the type of memory that is triggered by sounds or spoken words that people have heard (Norman, 2008).

As the first author considered her own playography, while playing videogames, she constantly triggered both her echoic and iconic memory systems (Norman, 2008) through repeated interactions with sensory literacies such as graphics, motion, texts, auditory dialogue, sound effects, and music. These interactions better assisted her in retaining information through the multiple sensory connections made during her meaning-making process (Atkinson & Shiffrin, 1968). Thus, in using videogames, the sensory literacies could be what assisted her in better engagement during the reading process. The visual and auditory features of videogames allowed her to remember the concepts or stories she was reading through repeated interactions with her iconic and echoic memory systems. Furthermore, the visual and auditory features of videogames kept her interest and attention, causing her to be more motivated to read and more engaged during the reading processes within the game.

FUTURE RESEARCH DIRECTIONS

A Need for More Data, Longitudinal Studies, and Controlled Studies

There was a lack of significant data showing an increase in literacy skills, a lack of controlled experimental designs, and a lack of longitudinal data. It is important for researchers within the topic of videogames and instruction to get in-depth research and data to determine if using videogames within instruction is an evidence-based teaching method. More teacher research and experimental design projects need to be done, exploring the topic of videogames and their impact on literacy and learning. When conducting studies on the utilization of videogames for instructional purposes, Israel et.al (2016) recommended that future researchers incorporate both a control group and an independent group within their study to compare the benefits of videogames as an instructional tool against that of traditional instruction.

Technology and videogames are constantly evolving and changing with both educational gaming and commercial gaming. Thus, it is essential that studies are conducted that explore the long-term impact that utilizing videogames for educational purposes has on students' learning. By conducting longitudinal studies, it can give researchers and educators a better idea of the true impact and effects of utilizing videogames in the classroom for instructional purposes. Without longitudinal studies, no conclusions, either positive or negative can be determined. Therefore we need more long-term studies to provide more evidence for whether or not utilizing videogames as an instructional tool will assist students within the learning process.

A Need for More Sensory Literacy Theory Research

Because sensory theory is newly identified as part of the "digital turn" in literacy and learning theories (Mills, 2016) there is little research connecting the visceral, or sensory experiences, of videogames to a framework of sensory theory. Sensory literacy theory and videogames seem logically connected as multiple sensory components that are embedded within the game: audio, visuals, haptic technology, and both physical and graphic movement. The first author was enchanted by games, drawn into them by their sensory experiences and intriguing stories, motivating her to persist and win. Neuroscientist and teacher, Judy Willis (2011), explains this process through the brain's dopamine reward system in which the brain recognizes the process of persisting and meeting the challenges of videogames and opens the channels to the brain's reward system. The expectation of success and rewards are part of the sensory experience. Game designer Jane McGonigal (2011) calls this feeling of elation from an epic win, "fiero", a jubilant feeling of beating adversity. It is a "fist-pumping", gestural embodiment of celebration. Videogames spark these sensory reactions through the immersive experience of being part of the game. By activating and using multiple senses, gamers are engaged with the videogame and are motivated to make progress throughout the game. Similarly, when videogames are used within literacy instruction, students are activating and using multiple senses in tandem with alphabetic literacy skills and visual literacy skills in order to make meaning of the game; this engages students both in the gaming process and in the literacy-learning or content-learning processes. It could be the enchantment that motivates players to persist and make progress within the game and towards their learning goals. Thus, in considering videogames as the virtual embodiment of sensory literacy theory, more research on the sensory connections and videogame-play could shed more light on its enchanting characteristics.

CONCLUSION

Videogames can engage and motivate students to participate in literacy processes and content learning. This engagement, motivation, and persistence are aligned with Bennett's (2001) notion of 21st-century enchantment. The first author, so enchanted by the videogame, did not realize at the time, she was using literacy skills and knowledge to engage with both the textual and sensorial literacies of the game in order to fully know the story of the game; motivation and engagement came naturally and willingly. The games were challenging, but she didn't give up, she persisted. Gee (2007, 2013, 2017) has documented this persistence over and over again. Thus, when students are engaged and enchanted within the multimodal and sensorial experiences of immersive virtual worlds, they willingly immerse themselves not only into the world of gaming but also into a world in which the definition of literature is broader, encompassing both traditional and contemporary literacies interwoven within the stories of videogames. These storyworlds are embedded in disciplinary literacies, such as math and science, too, where learners can become scientists, archaeologists, explorers, detectives, and rulers. This is a world where the identities of avatar, gamer, reader, learner, and student become one. This is a pathway to enchant 21st-century learners.

REFERENCES

Abrams, S., & Gerber, H. (2013). Achieving through the Feedback Loop: Videogames, Authentic Assessment, and Meaningful Learning. *English Journal, 103*(1), 95–103. www.jstor.org/stable/24484067

Abrams, S. S., & Russo, M. P. (2015). Layering Literacies and Contemporary Learning. *Journal of Adolescent & Adult Literacy, 59*(2), 131–135. doi:10.1002/jaal.447

Adams, M. G. (2009). Engaging 21st-Century Adolescents: Video Games in the Reading Classroom. *English Journal, 98*(6), 55–59.

Altura, G. J., & Curwood, J. S. (2015). Hitting Restart: Learning and Gaming in an Australian Classroom. *Journal of Adolescent & Adult Literacy, 59*(1), 25–27. doi:10.1002/jaal.438

Atkinson, R. C., & Shiffrin, R. M. (1968). Human memory: A proposed system and its control processes. In K. W. Spence & J. T. Spence (Eds.), *The psychology of learning and motivation* (pp. 89–195). Academic Press.

Bennett, J. (2001). *The enchantment of modern life: Attachments, crossings, and ethics.* Princeton University Press. doi:10.1515/9781400884537

Berger, R., & McDougall, J. (2013). Reading videogames as (authorless) literature. *Literacy, 47*(3), 142–149. doi:10.1111/lit.12004

Blumberg, F. C., & Sokol, L. M. (2004). Boys' and girls' use of cognitive strategy when learning to play videogames. *Journal of General Psychology, 131*(2), 151–158. Retrieved from http://search.ebscohost.com/login.aspx?direct=true&db=aph&AN=13198165&site=ehost-live

Caldwell, K. E., Osterweil, S., Urbano, C., Tan, P., & Eberhardt, R. (2017). "I Just Don't Know Where to Begin": Designing to Facilitate the Educational Use of Commercial, Off-the-Shelf videogames. In M. Ma & A. Oikonomou (Eds) Serious Games and Edutainment Applications, (pp. 625-648). Academic Press.

Chess, S. (2018). Power on: Why videogames Matter. *Phi Kappa Phi Forum, 98*(1), 17–21. Retrieved from http://search.ebscohost.com.ezproxy.osu

Clarke, G., & Treagust, M. (2010). Gaming for reading. *APLIS, 23*(4), 161–165. Retrieved from http://search.ebscohost.com.argo.library.okstate.edu/login.aspx?direct=true&db=aph&AN=56486052&site=ehost-live

Compton-Lilly, C. (2007). What can video games teach us about teaching reading? *The Reading Teacher, 60*(8), 718–727. doi:10.1598/RT.60.8.2

Cope, B., & Kalantzis, M. (2000). *Multiliteracies: Literacy learning and the design of social futures.* Routledge.

Cope, W., & Kalantzis, M. (2015). What you do to know: An introduction to the pedagogy of multiliteracies. In W. Cope & M. Kalantzis (Eds.), *A pedagogy of multiliteracies: Learning by design* (pp. 1–37). Palgram MacMillan.

Curwood, J. S. (2014). Reader, writer, gamer: Online role-playing game as literary response. In H. Gerber & S. Abrams (Eds.), Bridging literacies with videogames. Sense Publishers.

Daniels, A. C., Tapscott, D., & Caston, A. (2003). *Bringing out the best in people.* McGraw-Hill.

Evans, M. A., Jones, B. D., & Akalin, S. (2017). Using videogame design to motivate students. *Afterschool Matters,* (26), 18–26. Retrieved from http://search.ebscohost.com.argo.library.okstate.edu/login.aspx?direct=true&db =eric&AN=EJ1160875&site=ehost-live

Games and Learning Publishing Council. (2016). *Level Up Learning: A National Survey on Teaching with Digital Games*. Author.

Garcia, A. (2018). Space, time, and production: Games and the new frontier of digital Literacies. In K. Mills, A. Stornaiuolo, A. Smith, & J. Zacher Pandya (Eds.), *Handbook of writing, literacy, and education in digital cultures*. Routledge.

Gee, J. P. (2007). *What videogames have to teach us about learning and literacy*. Palgrave Macmillan.

Gee, J.P.(2013). Games for Learning. *Educational Horizons, 91*(4), 16–20. doi:10.1177/0013175X1309100406

Gee, J. P. (2017). *Teaching, learning, literacy in our high-risk high-tech world: A framework for becoming human*. Teachers College Press.

Gerber, H. R., Abrams, S. S., Onwuegbuzie, A., & Benge, C. (2014). From Mario to FIFA: What case study research suggests about games-based learning. *Educational Media International, 51*(1), 16–34. doi:10.1080/09523987.2014.889402

Granic, I., Lobel, A., & Engels, R. C. M. E. (2014). The Benefits of Playing Video Games. *The American Psychologist, 69*(1), 66–78. doi:10.1037/a0034857 PMID:24295515

Guthrie, J. T., & Wigfield, A. (1998). *Reading engagement: motivating readers through integrated instruction*. International Reading Association.

Haas, L. (2012). *A quantitative content analysis of leveled vocabulary embedded within massively multiplayer online role-playing games (MMORPGs)* (Doctoral dissertation). ProQuest. (UMI No. 3511601)

Hanghøj, T., Lieberoth, A., & Misfeldt, M. (2018). Can cooperative videogames encourage social and motivational inclusion of at-risk students? *British Journal of Educational Technology, 49*(4), 775–799. Retrieved from http://search.ebscohost.com.argo.library.okstate.edu/login.aspx?direct=true&db=eric&AN=EJ1186232&site=ehost-live

Israel, M., Wang, S., & Marino, M. T. (2016). A Multilevel Analysis of diverse learners Playing Life Science videogames: Interactions between game content, learning disability status, reading proficiency, and gender. *Journal of Research in Science Teaching, 53*(2), 324–345. doi:10.1002/tea.21273

Joan Ganz Cooney Center. (2016). *Mind the Gap: Improving Access to High Quality Digital Media*. Retrieved from http://www.gamesandlearning.org/wp-content/uploads/2016/04/Mind-the-Gap.pdf

Katlantiz, M., & Cope, W. (2019). *A Grammar of Multimodal Meanings. Literacy Education at Illinois*. Retrieved from https://www.youtube.com/watch?v=BUQez2U2Jsc&t=256s

Keefe, E. B., & Copeland, S. R. (2011). What is literacy? The power of a definition. *Research and Practice for Persons with Severe Disabilities, 36*(3/4), 92–99. doi:10.2511/027494811800824507

Kress, G. (2009). *Multimodality: a social semiotic approach to contemporary communication*. Routledge. doi:10.4324/9780203970034

Lieberman, D. A., Bates, C. H., & So, J. (2009). Young children's learning with digital media. *Computers in the Schools, 26*(4), 271–283. doi:10.1080/07380560903360194

Lieury, A., Lorant, S., Trosseille, B., Champault, F., & Vourc'h, R. (2016). videogames vs. reading and school/cognitive performances: A study on 27000 middle school teenagers. *Educational Psychology*, *36*(9), 1567–1602. doi:10.1080/01443410.2014.923556

Martín del Pozo, M., Basilotta Gómez-Pablos, V., & García-Valcárcel Muñoz-Repiso, A. (2017). A quantitative approach to pre-service primary school teachers' attitudes towards collaborative learning with videogames: Previous experience with videogames can make the difference. *International Journal of Educational Technology in Higher Education*, *14*(11). Advance online publication. doi:10.118641239-017-0050-5

McGonigal, J. (2011). *Reality is broken: Why games make us better and how they can change the world.* Penguin Press.

Mills, K. A. (2016). *Literacy theories for the Digital Age: Social, critical, multimodal, spatial, material and sensory lenses.* Multilingual Matters.

Nelson, N. J., Fien, H., Doabler, C. T., & Clarke, B. (2016). Considerations for realizing the promise of educational gaming technology. *Teaching Exceptional Children*, *48*(6), 293–300. doi:10.1177/0040059916650639

New London Group. (1996). A pedagogy of multiliteracies: Designing social futures. *Harvard Educational Review*, *66*(1), 60–93. doi:10.17763/haer.66.1.17370n67v22j160u

Norman, K. L. (2008). *Cyberpsychology: An Introduction to human-computer interaction.* Cambridge University Press.

Pastore, R. S., & Falvo, D. A. (2010). Video Games in the Classroom: Pre- and in-service teachers' perceptions of games in the K-12 classroom. *International Journal of Instructional Technology and Distance Learning*, *7*(12), 49–57.

Rich, J. D. (2020, January 28). What videogames Get Right about Motivation. *Psychology Today*.

Squire, K. (2005). Changing the Game: What Happens When Video Games Enter the Classroom? *Innovate: Journal of Online Education, 1*(6). Retrieved from https://nsuworks.nova.edu/cgi/viewcontent.cgi?article=1168&context=innovate

Sukovic, S. (2014). iTell: Transliteracy and digital storytelling. *Australian Academic and Research Libraries*, *45*(3), 205–229. doi:10.1080/00048623.2014.951114

Takeuchi, L. M., & Vaala, S. (2014). *Level up learning: A national survey on teaching with digital games.* The Joan Ganz Cooney Center at Sesame Workshop.

Tracey, D. H., & Morrow, L. M. (2017). *Lenses on Reading: an introduction to theories and models. Place of publication not identified.* GUILFORD.

Walsh, M. (2010). Multimodal literacy: What does it mean for classroom practice? *Australian Journal of Language and Literacy*, *33*(3), 211–239. https://www.alea.edu.au/documents/item/63

Watson, W. R., Yang, S., & Ruggiero, D. (2012). *Games in schools: teachers' perceptions of barriers to game-based learning.* Paper presented at the 2012 AECT International Convention, Louisville, KY. Retrieved from https://www.aect.org/pdf/proceedings13/2013/13_32.pdf

Willis, J. (2011). A neurologist makes the case for the videogame model as a learning tool. *Edutopia.* Retrieved from https://www.edutopia.org/blog/neurologist-makes-case-video-game-model-learning-tool

Ye, S.-H., Hsiao, T.-Y., & Sun, C.-T. (2018). Using commercial videogames in flipped classrooms to support physical concept construction. *Journal of Computer Assisted Learning, 34*(5), 602–614. doi:10.1111/jcal.12267

KEY TERMS AND DEFINITIONS

Avatar: A character that gamers create and play as within a videogame.

Commercial Videogames: Videogames created for the purpose of entertainment and not necessarily education.

Educational Videogames: Videogames that have instructional concepts and components embedded into the objectives or story of the videogame.

Gamer: A person who plays videogames; a person who considers being a 'gamer' as part of their identity.

Haptic Technology: Sensations and interactions had with gaming consoles and technology through touching; this includes the feelings of vibrations, movement, and forces against human extremities such as hands-on controllers, screens, and other interactive videogame devices.

Massive Multiplayer Online Role-Playing Videogames (MMORPG): Videogames that allow gamers to play with other gamers online within the same game in real-time; these games usually require gamers to collaborate to progress through the game and to complete game objectives.

Playography: A gamer's resume, including a history and/or list of videogames played or experienced.

Role-Playing Videogames (RPG): Videogames that incorporate role-playing as a specific character, or creating a character within a game, and playing as the character, making decisions for that character, and progressing through the game as the character.

Videogames: Games played using technology such as gaming consoles and computers; these games are presented virtually, using audio-visual effects and animation graphics interacting with the gamer's senses.

This research was previously published in Disciplinary Literacy Connections to Popular Culture in K-12 Settings; pages 162-183, copyright year 2021 by Information Science Reference (an imprint of IGI Global).

Chapter 5
Fun and Games:
How to Actually Create a Gamified Approach to Health Education and Promotion

Helena Martins

https://orcid.org/0000-0002-0749-917X

Lusófona University, Portugal

Artemisa Dores

Polytechnic of Porto, Portugal

ABSTRACT

Gamification is a relatively new approach that allows the use of videogame design techniques in contexts that are originally not game related, including for the promotion and education of health outcomes. Gamification has been used in many contexts, but healthcare practices, which include often boring, frustrating, or painful tasks, can especially benefit from the fun enjoyable games people play for entertainment purposes. Games can be helpful both promoting an increase in health knowledge and behaviors, as well as the positive emotions elicited by health-related contents and behaviors. This chapter begins by discussing the concept of gamification, the gamification toolbox, and gamer taxonomies and the different uses of gamification and game-based approaches in the healthcare context are explored, to figure out what the key success elements are and why this promising approach has yet to achieve its wide-spread potential use.

INTRODUCTION

Gamification is a relatively new concept that proposes the use of elements from video games in non-game applications (Deterding et al, 2011). Gamification's popularity has been increasing in the past years, drawing attention to different strategies, tools, and fields of implementation (Gentry et al, 2019). This approach aims at changing human behavior by engaging people and can be used in a myriad of possible

DOI: 10.4018/978-1-6684-7589-8.ch005

areas of business and society. Although it has been explored primarily in the marketing area, the potential of gamification's application has been extended to other areas such as Environment, Government, Education, and of course, Health (Simões et al, 2012). This chapter aims at creating a practical framework for planning and designing gamified approaches for health purposes, providing the much-needed conceptual clarity and practical implications for successful gamified approaches in health education and promotion.

Engaging people in health education and promoting health behaviors may be challenging. Often these include repetitive, sometimes unpleasant behaviors, that may be boring at times, and whose consequences are not immediately felt. Fenerty and colleagues (2012), for example, report that 30% to 50% of patients have poor adherence to medication use. Lack of adherence is a major problem because the intended outcomes of the interventions – improved health outcomes - are not likely to be achieved. This means that the costs associated with providing health services - often founded on costly and scarce resources - are wasted (Fenerty et al., 2012). The issue is amplified when access to healthcare is delayed due to waiting lists, given to the possibility of further deterioration of patients' conditions and the additional costs involved in managing those ailments (Richards & Caldwell, 2016). Games, on the other hand have shown to be effective in the increased motivation and involvement of players in game tasks (Simões et al. 2012) and go so far as to determine the release of dopamine in users (Koepp et al, 1998). Games are defined here as voluntary activities structured by rules, with defined outcomes (e.g., winning/ losing) or other quantifiable feedback (e.g., points) that facilitates reliable comparisons of in-player performances (Thai et al, 2009) are becoming more relevant. We seem to be moving from a paradigm of survival and efficiency into a new era where people are mostly focused on what is pleasurable (Deterding et al, 2011).

Gamified education has the potential to provide a quality, cost-effective, novel approach that is flexible, portable, and enjoyable and allows interaction with tutors and peers (Gentry et al., 2019). Such an impactful transversal trend involves many opportunities and risks (Gartner, 2011), as well as ethical concerns (Stetina et al, 2012). Still, the pervasiveness of games and gamification in society cannot be ignored by the healthcare sector, whose systems benefit crucially form individual engagement and positive behaviors.

Health education as a tool for health promotion has a relevant role in the improvement of populations' health, individually and at the community level which can be key in individual well-being as well as society's health, as is the case of outbreaks and pandemics, like COVID-19. Many studies have shown that inadequate health education can have a significant impact on health outcomes, in the use of health care services and health costs. Different factors have limited the attention paid to this area and the success gathered by health education strategies, among them, the limited understanding of health education by those who work in this field; lack of consensus on many different theoretical frameworks and concepts; and the difficulty in demonstrating the efficiency of the actual practices (WHO, 2012). To face these challenges new tools and strategies are urgent to promote the engagement of the public (including healthy people, patients and relatives) and professionals in effective health education practices. Further, game-based and gamified approaches, especially when based on digital technologies and internet have the potential to reach developing countries and vulnerable populations where healthcare resources, especially professionals are missing and the populations' needs are most dire. Gamification can be useful to this endeavor, promoting health education core competencies, supported by leading practices. In general, gamification uses the potential developed by the video game technology to shape user behaviors or embed values in users (Deterding et al, 2011) and some authors go as far as to say that games can make us better (McGonnigal, 2011). All definitions seem to perspective gamification with the goal of user engagement (Xu, Hi & Honolulu, 2011), which is key in the healthcare sector.

Further, play is an important element for healthy personal development (especially in children) (Ginsburg, 2007), including learning development. Hence, more than being a distraction, games can be an integral part of learning and intellectual development, since they stimulate cognitive functions (e.g., imaginative play) and intended behaviors (Ke, 2009), a feature that is crucial in promoting health behaviors. Thus, gamification can be effective in promoting and sustaining healthy behaviors, tapping into playful and goal-driven aspects of human nature with strategies such as goal setting, feedback on performance, reinforcement, comparing progress and social connectivity, techniques that share key elements with established health behavior change techniques (Edwards et al, 2016).

However, the popularization of gamification has been posing some challenges to the construct, with authors like Bunchball (2010) calling out that many approaches are nothing but a "pointification" instead of a true gamified approach, where fun is crucial and other elements should also be considered. Authors often hope to find the outcomes touted for gamification using a simple task-reward system that, despite having its own benefits and applications (even in games), is far from being what gamification is all about (Bunchball, 2010). This chapter is aimed at professionals in the healthcare sector and gaming. The framework of the chapter is presented in figure 1, where we will begin by bringing conceptual clarity to the construct of gamification, differentiating it from other similar constructs, and move on to the essential aspects of gamification, namely tools, components, strategies as well as gamer taxonomy, establishing an appropriate theoretical background, where fun is highlighted as a key (and often forgotten) element of games and gamification design. We will analyze some applications of the gamification approach in the field of health education, and reflect on advantages and disadvantages, as well as ethical concerns. The book chapter will conclude with recommendations for practice and deliver specific guidelines for creating a successful gamified approach in health education, as well as future research directions.

Figure 1. Framework and key takeaways of the book chapter

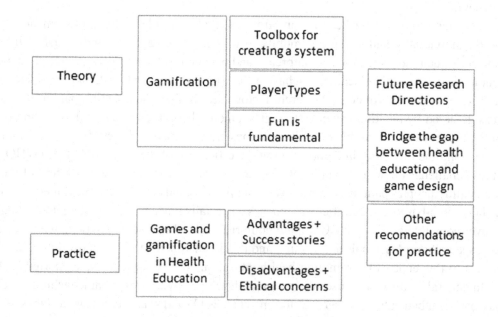

BACKGROUND

Gamification: What it is and What it is not

Although gamification has become a buzz word in the past few years, gamification as a concept is not clearly defined in the research literature (Marston & Hall, 2016).

Generally speaking one can say that gamification is "the use of game design elements in non-game contexts" (Deterding et al., 2011, p.9). In this definition, four terms can be singled out: (1) game, (2) elements, (3) design, and (4) non-game contexts. The term (1) game reflects the set of rules that involve players as opponents or team members and tend to lead to a quantifiable outcome; (2) elements denotes that gamification merely uses some of the game components, as is the case of points, badges and leaderboards; (3) design indicates the intentionality of strategies implemented in a gamification system; finally, (4) non-game context refers to the transcendence from entertainment that the approach has, encompassing a diversity of contexts and areas (Deterding et al., 2011).

Although there are many definitions in the literature (e.g., Deterding et al., 2011; Huotari & Hamari, 2017; Werbach, 2014) originated from distinctive perspectives and contexts, there seems to be consensus in three different aspects (Martins et al, in press):

1. Gamification is based in games and game theory;
2. Gamification is used in non-game contexts;
3. Gamification's goal does not merely entail entertainment, it aims at incentivizing behaviors and supporting added value for the stakeholders.

Gamification can be seen as a form of persuasive or motivational design (Alahäivälä & Oinas-Kukkonen, 2016). Generally, gamified systems are complex interventions, that require thoughtful consideration of the context, content, structure, and delivery of the program and its components which should be articulated with the strategically intended outcomes (Alahäivälä & Oinas-Kukkonen, 2016). Although gamification has been often linked to digital technologies, a gamified approach does not require this aspect and can be analogically driven.

Gamification is not the same as a game. There are several definitions of what a "game" is. In general, a game is a system within which players traditionally engage in an artificial conflict, trying to solve a specific problem. A game is defined by rules and measured by a quantifiable outcome (Deterding et al., 2011). According to McGonigal (2011), a game has four key elements: (a) a specific goal that people are willing to work for, (b) rules that stimulate creativity, (c) a feedback system that lets individuals know how they are doing regarding the goal, and (d) voluntary acceptance of the goal, rules, and feedback systems.

Gamification is more than the simple transformation of everyday activities in a game: it is the redesign of tasks and processes in game mechanisms, in order to stimulate the emergence of motivation in otherwise unappealing processes (Martins et al, in press). Another way to look at the difference between gamification and game-based approaches is that in game-based approaches, a game is used as an artifact to create an extra layer of motivation (typically extrinsic motivation) to the task/mission/goal, whereas a gamification system creates aims at creating a sort of parallel reality where the tasks at hand (usually not very appealing) are transformed into the tools to achieve a certain outcome in a fun way. As such it is important to ensure the necessary conditions for the correct development of a gamified system as to capture user interest when it is applied and must unequivocally consider the diverse and complex user motivation mechanisms (Martins et al, in press).

Gamification is also not the same as serious games. Serious games are the use of interactive computer software for one or more players (e.g., computer simulations), developed to be more than entertainment, explicitly aiming to develop skills and competences in players (Deterding et al., 2011).

Finally, gamification is not the same as pervasive games, which detain one or more characteristics and expand the game dimension in space, time, and social circles, as is the case of the app "Pokemon Go" (Martins et al, in press).

The Gamification Toolbox: Dynamics, Mechanics and Components

The elements in the gamification toolbox are responsible for motivating players and should be selected according to the purpose of the system, the players and software; in order to be effective, gamification strategies should be bespoke to the specific needs of the contexts they are applied to, shunning one size fits all solutions (Martins et al, in press).

Game dynamics are the more conceptual elements of the game, responsible for attributing coherence and standards to the gaming experience: they structure the gamification strategy conceptually. Game dynamics include emotions (e.g., joy or surprise), narrative/story/theme of the game, progression, relationships and game restrictions (Werbach & Hunter, 2012).

Less abstract than dynamics, game mechanics can be compared to verbs in gamification, because they decide what players are doing in each moment (e.g., compete, reward, cooperate); they determine not only the participants to be involved in each step but also how they interact in a gamified system (Robson et al., 2015). Mechanics include challenge, luck, competition, cooperation, feedback, acquisition of resources, rewards, transactions (e.g., buying or exchanging things among players), player turnover, and the feeling of winning (Werbach & Hunter, 2012). Although mechanics build the experience of gamification, since they remain constant and control the course of player action (Robson et al., 2015), by themselves they are not enough to produce the sought after behaviors: they must be aligned with game dynamics and components (Bunchball, 2010).

Components are the more superficial, yet visible elements of a game. They are how higher-level actions are executed and they derive from both game dynamics and game mechanics. They include avatars, virtual goods, artifacts, final fights, collections, conquests, social graphs, quests, levels, gifts, teams, points, badges, and leaderboards (Werbach & Hunter, 2012). Werbach and Hunter (2012) call points, badges and leaderboards the PBL triad and they are an extremely used group of elements in all types of games and gamification strategies.

Points aim at incentivizing users to complete certain actions in a game and especially impact more competitive and focused players (Werbach & Hunter, 2012). Badges represent visually the conquests and achievements and can be attributed spontaneously to upturn player motivation and engagement (Werbach & Hunter, 2012; Zichermann & Cunningham, 2011). Leaderboards allow for the intuitive comparison and interpretation of several players performance simultaneously (Zichermann & Cunningham, 2011). When compared to points and badges they are a more direct element that publicly states each player's progression, but it's application should be cautious to not compromise player experience by generating exacerbated competitiveness (Werbach & Hunter, 2012), and also because not all players enjoy this type of game element (Jia, Liu, Yu, & Voida, 2017).

In sum, components are the pieces of the gamification puzzle, per say: they are the elements that execute the mechanics which in turn embody the dynamics of the game. When designing a gamified or game based approach, the game master would be wise to start with the goals of the game (e.g. lose weight, stop a bad habit, take the medication on time, etc.), then create a game dynamic strategy (e.g. Nike released an app where the user would pretend to be evading zombies to motivate him or her to run: the zombie attack narrative would be the dynamic here). Game mechanics would refer to how the dynamic comes to fruition in terms of interaction with the game and other players (in the previous example, are other players zombies [competing] or allies [collaborating]?) and finally components are what materializes these elements (how are points attributed? How do you know if you "survived"? Are there quests within the game? Are there Easter Eggs?).

Aside from these considerations regarding the goals and available tools, the gamification/ game-baed approach designer would do well to consider the target of the game and bear in mind what type of players they will be catering to.

The Gamification Customer: Gamer Types

Players are at the core of gamification and as such, the effectiveness of any gamified system depends on a profound knowledge of its target audience (Zichermann & Cunningham, 2011). Every player thinks, acts, and interacts in a particular fashion in the game and everyone has their specific distinctive reasons to play, adding to the fact that every game should be disputed with its own purpose (Yee, 2006).

There are many player typologies, but the most popular to date is Bartle's (1996) achievers, explorers, socializers, and killers. A well designed game will contemplate these four types in a sort of balanced ecosystem, which is key for capturing as many players as possible (Yee, 2006; Martins et al, in press).

Achievers are most interested in acting in the game world: they play to win, establishing goals and committing fully until they achieve them. Explorers prefer to *inter*act with the game world; they like to be surprised by the game and have fun exploring it. The joy of finding things out is their main motivation. Socializers represent most players, circa 80% of the overall population (Vianna, Vianna, Medina, & Tanaka, 2013). The main motivation for this type of player is the social interaction that happens in the game. The more collaborating players strongly believe that they can achieve higher and better accomplishments with the synergies they establish. Although socializers can be the least competitive players, they are equally active and ambitious (Vianna et al., 2013). Finally, killers have the most aggressive posture and like to interact with other players as to overpower them and create more difficulties and stress through the game tools and elements (Bartle, 1996).

Other taxonomies have been developed that could be referenced but considering that we are here connecting gamification with learning, we'll simply mention Heeter (2008) and Quick and colleagues' (2012) taxonomies.

Quick, Atkinson and Lin (2012) performed a cluster analysis of personality characteristics with 21 aspects of game play which revealed six types of player: (1) Dutiful Companion, (2) Extroverted Fidelitist Companion, (3) Introverted Fidelitist Explorer, (4) Conscientious Companion, (5) Introverted Challenger, Seeking Fidelitist, and (6) Calm Challenge-Seeking Companion. This analysis overcame the limitations of analyzing isolated individual aspects of game mechanics.

Heeler (2008) on the other hand, established four game playing types: (1) Achiever (high scores, fast times), (2) Lost (low scores, slow times), (3) Explorer (high scores, slow times), and (4) Careless (low scores, fast times). This taxonomy relates to intrinsic motivation for education and requires further testing regarding game play fun or enjoyment (Heeler, 2008).

When creating a game, it is fundamental to consider different gamer typologies as to maximize the involvement of the target audience; this means that the choice for game elements itself should be strategic to enable the achievement of healthcare goals without being detrimental to gamer motivations (Xi & Hamari, 2019).). Individual differences in personality and game play provide a potentially important perspective for understanding who experiences what kinds of fun, and perhaps tailoring game design features to characteristics of the player to maximize their experience of fun (Mellecker et al, 2013).

In sum, considering gamer typologies allows for game design to strategically focus on gamification outcomes without overlooking player involvement, enjoyment, and fun – key aspects to keep subjects playing the game and motivated for the task.

MAIN FOCUS OF THE CHAPTER

The Gamification X Factor: The Elements of fun, Play, Enjoyment, and Gamefulness

Mellecker and colleagues (2013, pp. 142) remind us: "ostensibly games are played for fun or enjoyment". Games have a spontaneous quality, a potential for joy and flow, and are characterized by intrinsic motivation (Stetina et al, 2012). Werbach (2004) proposes that gamification, as a process of making activities more similar to games, should include both game elements referenced in the previous sections of this chapter as well as the holistic experience of playing a game, usually referred to as *gamefulness* (McGonigal, 2011).

Fun has not been a common topic in behavioral theory (Mellecker et al, 2013), but it is important to keep in mind that games hare inexorably connected to the concepts of play and fun. This means that, although gamification is composed of a series of explicit rule bound systems where players interact in an artificial conflict to reach quantifiable results (Huizinga, 2000) to really achieve gamification/game-based approach goals the attitude of play and playfulness must be contemplated (Nicholson, 2015).

The power of playfulness is well known across the healthcare interventions research. For instance Stetina and colleagues (2012) refer that playfulness in psychological intervention can dramatically increase insight processes in patients (e.g., modeling problematic situations with the help of plasticine, building blocks, paper and felt pens) and that this characteristic also keeps players motivated to engage in gamified approaches, for example, to exercise and lose weight. Playfulness which can be construed as an intrinsically motivating game characteristic can be instrumental in creating a lasting therapeutic alliance with the patient, empowering, engaging and encouraging therapeutic adherence, even in pediatric settings (e.g. pediatric incontinence) (Richards & Caldwell, 2016).

Literature has been indicating that games enable the release of dopamine in individuals (Koepp et al., 1998), and make the experience more pleasurable. This leads to the assumption that games are perceived as fun and played continuously only for the pleasure they provide and translate an increased intrinsic motivation. Thus, the fact that games are so pervasive in our society due to the convergence of social, economic, cultural, and technological factors gives gamification an auspicious perspective in the power it may have to motivate individuals. Societies have been shifting focus from survival and effectiveness to a more hedonistic one, in which motivations seem to stem mostly from the pleasure provided by the experiences themselves (Schell, 2008).

Research indicates that fun or enjoyment in games has psychosocial, physiological, and embodiment dimensions (Mellecker, 2013) and different types of people may experience different game design features and mechanics as fun. For example, extroversion (a personality trait) seems to be related to experiences of videogame ecstatic and sociability fun, agreeableness is associated with experiences of sociability and lower experiences of sensual fun, openness was linked to achievement fun (McManus & Furnham, 2010).

Lazzaro (2004) refers that a motivating game offers at least three out of the four following types of fun: 1) hard fun – fun associated with problem-solving and overcoming obstacles; 2) easy fun – fun related to game exploration, more casual and joyful; 3) people fun – associated with socializing and teamwork and 4) serious fun – related to achieving something significant for the community.

The different types of fun are not only responsible for the neurochemical activation of players (Werbach & Hunter, 2012), they are also important in diluting the "imposed fun" factor and increasing engagement (Mollick & Rothbard, 2014). Gamification should be developed in such a way that it attracts the interest of players in the short and long run and ensures that there is a balance between player skills and game challenges in all moments of the process, enabling the emergence of flow experiences (Csikszentmihalyi, 1990).

The experience of flow is another approach to the element of fun and playfulness in games (Koster, 2005). Flow is highly associated with positive mental status, including enjoyment (Csikszentmihalyi, 1990) and it happens when a game incentivizes gameplay and exploration on the behalf of a player through the setting of goals that are perceived as challenging but not unattainable. Flow may even be defined as an equilibrium between the challenge and the competencies/skills of a player to meet said challenge, where the challenge is only slightly over skills, and the gap is perceived as being easily to overcome. Flow is a positive state of mind and is translated as the total immersion in activities and can even be accompanied by the loss of track of time and forgoing basic needs like sleeping or eating (Csikszentmihalyi, 1990).

For players achieve this psychological state, goals must be perceived as non-trivial but achievable, that players must be motivated to pursue these goals under arbitrary and externally imposed restrictions and believe that game actions are voluntary under those restrictions (Landers et al., 2018).

Self Determination Theory (Ryan & Deci, 2000), which emphasizes motivation to perform a behavior, has been used to identify the psychosocial characteristics for enjoying videogame play (Mellecker et al, 2008). Intrinsic motivation is the ultimate motivation in Self Determination Theory, and the enjoyment derived from doing the behavior is a defining characteristic of intrinsic motivation (Ryan & Deci, 2000).

It is thus clear that gamification can access both extrinsic and intrinsic motivation processes. Extrinsically motivating game mechanics are added via the token economy (Richards & Caldwell, 2016). Extrinsic rewards can be a prize or benefit explicitly given as a consequence of players doing what game designers intended; intrinsic rewards come from the players' will to win and succeed in the game (whatever that may be for each player) as well as the fun (whatever type) involved in playing the game.

The experience of enjoyment in playing a game has been detailed as a result from player perceptions, namely autonomy (making in-game choices), competence (being good at playing the game), and relatedness (relating to significant others or to personal values) (Ryan, Rigby & Przybylski, 2006). Further, Klimmt, Hartman and Frey (2006) found that personal characteristics of players (namely effectance, a mix between the concepts of self-efficacy and outcome efficacy) and not situational characteristics (specifically control), were the primary determinant of game enjoyment.

The fun, enjoyment, playfulness and gamefulness of a gamification strategy is extremely relevant because it is the key to keep players interacting with the game despite a lack of immediate health results, or even in the event of boring, frustrating, or painful tasks required. The longer a player is engaged, the more likely a game will be a hit; commercial of the shelf (COTS) videogames, for example, strive for many hours of initial gameplay followed by long-term re-playability (returning to a game after completion for more experiences) (Buday, 2012). During an exercise game (exergame), for example, play should enhance the intensity and duration of physical activity, and thereby the health benefits associated with this intervention (Mellecker et al, 2013).

Boring games happen when you are focused on the outcomes as opposed to the experience of play (Mellecker et al, 2013). From the Design, Play, Experience framework, enjoyment or fun is the experience of game design features (Mellecker et al, 2013) and is therefore impossible to dissociate from gamification. With this in mind it is extremely important that when designing a gamification strategy for health, health outcomes are considered and used as goals, but that the game proposes activities that captivate the user as a priority; it is preferable to have less ambitious health outcomes and motivated, involved players than to have perfect health outcomes for a game that does not captivate users.

The general attributes of playing a game involve spontaneity, intrinsic motivation, defined levels of active engagement and distinction from any other behavior with a make-believe quality (Stetina et al, 2012). Mellecker and colleagues (2013) refer that fun and/or enjoyment in games are inherently laden with psychosocial, physiological, and embodiment aspects and that research is needed to integrate these levels of experience and to identify the game mechanics that enhance, and even maximize, the fun or enjoyment experienced, to consequently increase the potential health benefit.

How Have Games Been Used in the Health Context: A Panoramic View of the Field

Preventing diseases through a healthy lifestyle, supporting autonomy in the management of treatments, and creating public awareness are increasingly being carried out using new technologies (Alahäivälä & Oinas-Kukkonen, 2016).

The urge for "health games" research since 2008 can be attributed to advancements in gaming technology (e.g., Microsoft Kinect® or Nintendo Wii®), the use of smartphones (bringing forth mHealth apps such as Fitbit and Runtastic) as well as the establishment of special conferences (e.g. "Games for Health Conference") (Stetina, 2012).

Smartphone use has increased rapidly in recent years in developed and developing countries: there were over 2 billion smartphone users globally in 2016 (Edwards et al, 2016). Digital games have become very popular not only for adolescents, but for adults and elder people too, composing a 25-billion-dollar industry (Stetina, 2012).

Game-based approaches for health and gamification among them are therefore at the center of this constellation of cultural, behavioral, and technological factors. Health behavior change is one of the most prominent areas of action, and physical activity intervention systems specifically have proven to be a viable application domain (Alahäivälä & Oinas-Kukkonen, 2016)). There are over 100000 health applications (apps) available worldwide for smartphones with exercise, diet and weight management apps being the most popular downloads (Edwards et al, 2016). A systematic review of literature conducted by Kharrazi and colleagues (2012) indicted that notable clinical/health domains attracting most of the health game studies included physical activity (27.1%), nutrition (10.3%), stroke (9.7%), balance (5.8%), cerebral palsy rehabilitation (5.2%), and pain distraction (5.2%).

Many of the gamified applications are designed to support individuals in adopting good health behaviors via positive reinforcing experiences with good results in different areas such as physical activity, diet and weight loss, hygiene, healthy working habits, and medical treatment; the use of an app provides a contingent feedback for situations in which outcomes may not be immediate (Alahäivälä & Oinas-Kukkonen, 2016)).

Although it is acknowledged that eHealth and mHealth interventions have the potential to significantly improve the quality and safety of healthcare processes and outcomes (Richards & Caldwell, 2016), unfortunately, so far only a few games for health have undergone a scientific evaluation to validate their effectiveness (Stetina et al., 2012).

Despite a rapid increase in the use of gamification in the commercial and education sectors, smartphone applications using gamification for promoting health are currently limited (Edwards et al, 2016).

There is a certain trend in the last years on the outcomes of exercise and rehabilitation games and the games concentrate on physical activity and nutrition, focusing on exercise and fitness. (Edwards et al, 2016). Literature suggests however suggests, that with the appropriate design and use, digital games have the potential to be very effective psychotherapeutic tools (Stetina et al, 2012).

The use of videogame consoles as an analgesic treatment alternative has also been studied, as is the case of burn patients who reported with better performance in physical tasks and recovery after a game treatment, as well as higher levels of motivation and faster increase in functional mobility (Yohannan, Kwon & Yurt, 2010).

Older people can benefit from digital games as well. Games have a positive impact on their health condition and improve the capability to carry on everyday life activities. The key factors of interest in games for health are challenge, socialization, escape from a daily routine, and (we cannot stress this enough) fun (Stetina et al., 2012).

Yet, there is little evidence that public health practitioners and users participate in the design of health apps and surprisingly or not, most apps do not contain theoretically consistent behavior change techniques or have had their effectiveness formally assessed, leading to concerns about lack of benefit or even potentially harmful apps (Edwards et al, 2016).

In the following section, we discuss positive effects of games for health as well as negative aspects, including ethical concerns in this area. It is highly important to consider negative side effects, such as excessive gaming behavior as well as social isolation before activating gamified healthcare interventions (Stetina et al., 2012).

Advantages and Success Stories vs Disadvantages and Ethical Concerns

Although research generally indicates positive results with gamified systems, there is plenty of work yet to be done in assessing the effectiveness of strategies for evidence based practice, considering most results refer to the aforementioned PBL triad (Koivisto & Hamari, 2019).

Gamification seems to be an adequate strategy to attract, develop and retain players from Gen Y (millennials) and Gen Z (Narayaan, 2014; Trees, 2015), due to its interest and proximity to games.

Playing a game for health means change in the sense of self-actualization as well as in the sense of treating disorders with many additional possibilities that real life cannot offer (Stetina, 2012).

Edwards and colleagues (2016) found that self-regulatory behavior change techniques were most commonly used (feedback and monitoring including self-monitoring of behavior) in games for health but also in non-gamified apps targeting physical activity, healthy eating and alcohol reduction which is understandable since the effectiveness of these techniques in achieving behavior change is supported by findings from a wide range of studies. Edwards and colleagues (2016) found that frequently used behavior change techniques were comparison of behavior and reward, and threat but also social support, nonspecific incentive and reward and focus on past success. The same authors proposed that although these are effective techniques, the decision to use some of the strategies might be driven mostly by the ease of implementation in smartphone games with an internet connection (e.g. sharing activity on social media) (Edwards et al, 2016).

Further, smartphone-based intervention could provide a potentially cost-effective platform for health promotion and, thus, could have a substantial public health impact (Edwards et al, 2016).

Although fashionable and full of potential, gamification has been strongly criticized on two fronts: 1) it's not engaging enough and 2) it is too engaging and even addictive.

On the first front, Bunchball (2010) calls out most gamification strategies as "pointification" due to the simple attribution of points to tasks and other superficial elements that – as previously discussed is not enough to develop an effective gamification strategy. The pointification of a system is arguably no different than other previous approaches such as behaviorism, remaking that although these game elements are great tools for communicating and regarding player progress, they do nothing for creating value and meaning in the experience, not to mention that the excessive use of rewards may backfire and diminish player motivation (Bunchball, 2010; Koivisto & Hamari, 2019).

The gamification approach may not be suitable for everyone, as each person's characteristics may affect the outcomes of different gamification types, which needs to be taken into consideration (Alahäivälä & Oinas-Kukkonen, 2016).

On the second front, ethical concerns have been raised claiming that there can be a fine line between addicted and engaged players (Stetina et al., 2012), in the sense that creating a gamified experience to deal with an issue might be contributing to create a different one (i.e. gaming addiction); further, regulations and deontological guidelines concerning health data and healthcare professionals conduct in digital settings is still scarce.

Regarding the gaming addiction argument, several definitions, criteria and descriptive symptoms make it very difficult to characterize the maladaptive behavior of problematic computer gaming (Stetina et al., 2012). However, the International Classification of Diseases recognized a gaming disorder, i.e., a behavioral (non-substance-related) addiction (ICD-11; WHO, 2018). For gaming disorder to be diagnosed, the behavior pattern must be seriously compromised and result in significant impairment in several areas of functioning, including personal, family, social, educational, occupational; further, it would normally have been present for at least 12 months (WHO, 2018).

Some authors suggested that the elements such as mood change, tolerance and cognitive (and not behavioral!) preoccupation should be explained better by using the term "highly engaged gamers", because the players show merely symptoms according to a high level of interest in the given activities. Therefore, it makes sense to distinguish between an "addictive" and an "engaged" behavior (Charlton & Danforth, 2004). There are significant differences between highly engaged players and "addicted" players, with highly engaged players often mistaken as addicted. "Addicted" players spend significantly more time playing and there are more negative consequences in their lives (resulting in poorer quality of life), in comparison to highly engaged players.

Different societies (e.g., International Society for the Study of Behavioral Addictions [ISSBA]) and international programs, such as the European Cooperation in Science and Technology (COST) Action Program, have addressed the study of behavioral addictions, which include problematic video game use (e.g., CA16207 - European Network for Problematic Usage of the Internet). Researchers have been studying these disorders, but additional research is needed, including into the phenomenology, etiology, assessment, epidemiology, brain-based biology, socio-health-economic impact, empirically validated intervention, and policy approaches (Fineberg et al., 2018).

Concerning documentation guiding/ regulating professional practices in eHealth, although they are available in some countries, a legal or normative void still exists in others. For example, guidelines have been released for on-line practice and use of digital technologies in Psychology in some countries, as the result of the work of several national and international associations and bodies (e.g., American Psychological Association, European Federation of Psychologists' Associations), but also here the information is still scarce to ensure best practices, including in ethical terms (Mendes-Santos et al, 2020).

In sum, there seems o be plenty of potential concerning gamified and game-based approaches to health education and even healthcare, including the possibility to reach effectively younger generations and to effectively change behavior in a pleasurable manner. However, gamification is not for everybody and all situations without distinction, and ethical concerns regarding game addiction and deontological guidelines regarding professional conduct should be considered when using such an approach.

SOLUTIONS AND RECOMMENDATIONS

Health Theory vs Games Practice: A Major gap That Needs to be Bridged

Interestingly the focus of research on game-based approaches and gamification has more or less neglected the developmental side of intervention strategies (Stetina et al., 2012). A major gap of theory *vs* practice, healthcare professionals *vs* game and app designers seems to exist.

A popular opinion seems to be that educators and health professionals tend to "suck the fun out" of videogames, meaning that when these professionals are put in charge of game design they tend to focus on outcomes and sacrifice the element that attracts and retains players: fun! (Buday et al., 2012).

Healthcare professionals have been mostly focusing on theoretical issues and definitions, while game designers and app developers have mostly been presenting products that can be monetized. This means that not a lot of theory has been built on how to actually transpose healthcare principles and know-how to practice and conversely, practice has been preoccupied with creating products without previous research or consultancy from health care providers and experts.

Good game design is difficult to achieve and not possible for most healthcare providers. Successful COTS game development involves well-oiled teams of creative game designers and artists working hand-in-hand with software programmers (Buday et al, 2012). Multiprofessional teams and respectful interaction in those teams are needed to create an effective intervention with the aforementioned fun aspect (Stetina et al., 2012). There are differences between game developer and researcher-led projects, but this gap must be breached in order for gamification and game-based approaches, in general, to avoid being boring and alienating players (Buday et al, 2012). The skeptics remain, and for many, the problem is not one of intent, but of execution (Buday et al, 2012). The ideal intervention design would be one were experts on gaming behavior would be acknowledged for their knowledge and skills to would enhance the development of interventions (Stetina et al., 2012) and healthcare professionals and experts would be recognized for their knowledge of illnesses and health in general, as well as the more important *de facto* changes that subjects should be making in their lifestyle, etc. This is to say that healthcare professionals should be defining priorities in terms of health behavior outcomes whereas game designers should be given the freedom to decide game strategies and negotiate the goals of the interventions. A creative's job is building entertainment value, measured by the game's ability to emotionally connect and immerse players (Buday et al., 2012).

In a game for health, the designing team, along with game creatives and coders, there should be doctors, psychologists, nurses, nutritionists, exercise specialists, occupational therapists, physical therapists, qualitative methods specialists, public health professionals, among other professionals involved (Buday et al, 2012).

Evidently games created for health purposes do not enjoy the type of budget that COTS videogames possess, and such a reality is unlikely considering the relatively low return on investment prospects of health promoting games. Considering this reality two things should be taken into consideration: 1) the economics of production and scale of delivery could potentially give smartphone apps an advantage over other health promotion interventions; similar methods of assessing cost-effectiveness could be used as for other health technologies (Edwards et al, 2016) and 2) it is unrealistic to expect a gamified approach to health to be on the same level as a COTS; thus, instead of setting the stage for direct comparisons, serious games might consider a different strategy (Buday et al., 2012).

It may also be wise to consider that different health outcomes may require long-term socio-emotional relationships with users, including trust, rapport, and therapeutic alliance, to enhance adherence to treatment as is the case of some mental health interventions; in these cases, the use of computational artifacts or other forms of relational agents may be a relevant strategy (Richards & Caldwell, 2016).

Alahäivälä and Oinas-Kukkonen (2016) identified reinforcing behaviors through positive feedback as a major gamification strategy. A lower-difficulty game that produces less feedback about failure seems to lead to greater game excitement (a proxy for game enjoyment) (Chumbley & Griffths, 2006).

Flow can be a design feature and can be reflected in the way a game is played (Mellecker et al, 2013). It is reflected in experiences of immersion in the activity and control over one's environment; flow increases intrinsic motivation and enjoyment and results from a person's increasing skill dealing with an increasingly difficult environment (Csikszentmihalyi, 1990). When considering flow, the presence of a story or narrative accompanied by the player's immersion in or transportation by the story offers appealing opportunities to promote behavior change (Baranowski et al, 2008).

From this perspective, it also is very important to match the level of difficulty of tasks with player level of skill: low skill in a high-difficulty environment leads to frustration or anxiety, and high skill in a low-difficulty environment leads to boredom (Sherry, 2004). Thus, an engrossing story in which a player is faced with challenges that surpass their skills in such a way that they can increase skills quickly enough to overcome the difficulties but not so hastily to get bored by the challenges appears to provide an important game design structure for enhancing fun or enjoyment (Mellecker et al, 2013).

For a sustainable behavioral change however, an attitude change is ultimately needed, so it is arguable that the designers of gamification interventions should target the attitudes of users more often (Alahäivälä & Oinas-Kukkonen, 2016).

Finally, it is important to consider that also point out that managers and healthcare professionals may not be familiar with the gamification approach and may deem it not credible: careful attention must be paid to concerns such as ethics, confidentiality, and personal privacy when designing gamification for healthcare (Alahäivälä & Oinas-Kukkonen, 2016).

We suggest that strengthening collaboration between app developers, behavioral scientists and public health practitioners is necessary to realize the full health benefits of this game-based approaches like gamification, which could be substantial (Edwards et al, 2016). The gamified approach does not aim at entertaining for the sake of entertainment: it has specific non-game related goals; however, those goals are very unlikely to be met if the gamified strategy is not entertaining or fun.

FUTURE RESEARCH DIRECTIONS´

Health game research has grown constantly over the past years. Despite occasional setbacks due to limited research funding, the general trend shows positive progress toward adapting new gaming technology in specialized health contexts (Kharradzi et al, 2012). On the theoretical front, at this point in gamification and game-based approaches development, there is already a lot written about what gamification is and what the best goals and strategies for attitude and behavior change are. On the practical front, there are many teams (often missing either game designers, coders, or healthcare specialists) developing game-based approaches and gamified systems for healthcare, which brings us to our first future research direction. Carrying out research on the health behavior change field should always be based on the theoretical groundwork, not just the recent trends of the software industry (Alahäivälä & Oinas-Kukkonen, 2016). It is imperative to promote cooperation and synergies between health experts and game designers for research to advance in the near future. (Kharradzi et al, 2012)

Although gamification has become a buzz word in the past few years, interventions that test gamification components for effectiveness in healthcare interventions or clinical applications are still scarce (Marston & Hall, 2016). The immense gap in the testing of such games means that thus far, both research and practice are blind to whether or not the gamification and game-based approaches this far implemented are working and what are the exact elements that make it thrive with different pathologies and populations. Research is in dire need in the area of game efficiency testing, where quantitative results and qualitative insights, for example, with focus groups are equally pertinent (Kharradzi et al, 2012).

The majority of apps seem still be focused on exercise and diet, focusing on the global obesity epidemic (WHO, 2003), but also on beauty standards and in the fact that people are living longer. This is an area that might be a good investment due to the financial return made possible by the millions in revenue generated yearly by this industry. However, there is a great deal of potential in gamification and game-based approaches for other areas such as the strengthening of upper strength for wheelchair users, people recovering from an injury or even mental health benefits which can benefit from research and investment.

In the general discussion, gamification is often dismissed as adding systemic game elements, such as points or badges, to the user interfaces of existing systems. However, gamification strategies may also be carried out using little to no technology as well as through novel or existing full-fledged games or virtual worlds (Alahäivälä & Oinas-Kukkonen, 2016). While using COTS and other such technologically enhanced games can be appealing, it is important to remark that studies indicate that solely framing an activity as a game may be as effective as implementing actual game mechanics (Liberoth, 2014). This means that these types of strategies can be implemented with little to no budget and with a multitude of technologies (digital and analogical) that should be equally studied beyond apps.

Future studies on the topic should inspect further the impacts of game elements and the game frame, as well as the differences between using "full" games and game-inspired interaction design elements (Alahäivälä & Oinas-Kukkonen, 2016).

Further, game-based approaches and gamification in the healthcare context are hardly a "one size fits all" issue, and efficiency of different strategies will most likely depend highly on context, including not only sociodemographic characteristics of the target population, but also of the type and stage of the ailment being addressed. That is, if we are dealing with preventive, clinical or palliative medicine, physical or mental disorders, games for expanding existing care or games for coping with a lack of resources, short-term or long-term interventions, focused on compliance with medication protocols, therapy, lifestyle change or others. Identifying the contextual factors is critical for designing gamification in systems that support actual user needs (Alahäivälä & Oinas-Kukkonen, 2016). Individual differences in personality and game play provide a potentially important perspective for understanding who experiences what kinds of fun, and perhaps tailoring game design features to characteristics of the player to maximize their experience of fun (Mellecker et al, 2013).

The authors propose that game-based and gamification strategies should be the focus of more systematic reviews of literature, following the Cochrane principles, in order to get a truly panoramic view of the field when trying to decide the next steps in both theory and practice.

To add to the above-described entropy there is no agreed-upon baseline, follow up period or assessment protocol for assessing the effectiveness of these strategies which can make things even more confusing (Kharradzi et al, 2012). This means that studies vary immensely on the intervention period being assessed and user-game interaction time (Kharradzi et al, 2012). Therefore, is crucial to develop guidelines and protocols and require their use in order to not only truly advance game-based and gamification strategies knowledge but also to legitimize its use, not a mere fad but as efficient, cost-effective, and adequate approaches to healthcare interventions.

CONCLUSION

Games are important because they tap into key elements of the human experience, namely engagement, enjoyment, fun, play, social interaction, learning. Gamification can be effective because it uses this important part of human nature to achieve its goals of promoting and sustaining healthy behaviors.

Gamification and game-based approaches, the use of game design and principles to non-game areas of life (e.g., work, management, training, health) is an intuitive approach that allows for the benefit of gamefulness and playfulness to pervade other areas of life. In health as in other contexts, gamification aims generically at increasing results while decreasing perceived effort, augmenting persistence, and reducing turnover and helping people cope with less than ideal situations (e.g., burn patients [Yonan, Kwon & Yurt, 2012]). Gamification strategies such as goal setting, providing feedback on performance, reinforcement, comparing progress, and social connectivity share key elements with established health behavior change techniques (Edwards et al, 2016). These have the potential to reach developing countries and vulnerable populations where healthcare resources, especially professionals are sorely missing.

While adherence is a multifaceted problem and the context will differ for each patient, gamification has the potential to improve this aspect of health interventions. Game-based approaches and gamification can help overcome health literacy barriers by improving medical knowledge, and encouraging healthy behavior; more importantly, gamification can be used to provide therapy, treatment advice, and support similar to the ones provided in the traditional clinical practice (Richards & Caldwell, 2016).

In this chapter we discussed key aspects of the game-based and gamification approach to health education and promotion, reflecting on theory and practice and offering some guidelines and considerations when designing one such intervention. This brief overview reveals that gamification and game-based approaches are extremely promising, but the fulfillment of this promise is dependent of a few key aspects, of which we focused two: the importance of not sacrificing fun, enjoyment, gamefulness and playfulness to obtain the desired healthcare outcomes (when it's not fun, it is no longer a game but a chore or assignment) and the importance of multiprofessional teams when designing these approaches, where subject matter experts (healthcare professionals) and game designers respectfully create a synergy that promotes great healthcare strategies and goal setting that has great health outcomes in an engaging entertaining fashion.

REFERENCES

Alahäivälä, T., & Oinas-Kukkonen, H. (2016). Understanding persuasion contexts in health gamification: A systematic analysis of gamified health behavior change support systems literature. *International Journal of Medical Informatics*, *96*, 62–70. doi:10.1016/j.ijmedinf.2016.02.006 PubMed

Baranowski, T., Buday, R., Thompson, D., & Baranowski, D. (2008). Playing for real: Video games and stories for health-related behavior change. *American Journal of Preventive Medicine*, *34*(1), 74–82. doi:10.1016/j.amepre.2007.09.027 PubMed

Bartle, R. (1996). Hearts, clubs, diamonds, spades: Players who suit MUDs. *Journal of MUD Research*, *1*(1). http://www.mud.co.uk/richard/hcds.htm

Buday, R., Baranowski, T., & Thompson, D. (2012). Fun and Games and Boredom. *Games for Health Journal*, *1*(4), 257–261. doi:10.1089/g4h.2012.0026 PubMed

Bunchball. (2010). Gamification 101: An introduction to the use of game dynamics to influence behavior. Retrieved April 7, 2019, from Bunchball website: https://www.bunchball.com/gamification101

Charlton, J., & Danforth, I. (2004). Differentiating computer related addictions and high engagement. In *Human perspectives in the Internet Society: Culture, Psychology, Gender. Southhampton*. WIT Press.

Chumbley, J., & Griffiths, M. (2006). Affect and the computer game player: The effect of gender, personality, and game reinforcement structure on affective responses to computer game-play. *Cyberpsychology & Behavior*, *9*(3), 308–316. doi:10.1089/cpb.2006.9.308 PubMed

Csikszentmihalyi, M. (1990). *Flow: The psychology of optimal experience*. Harper & Row.

Deterding, S., Dixon, D., Khaled, R., & Nacke, L. (2011). From game design elements to gamefulness: Defining "gamification". Proceedings of the 15th International Academic MindTrek Conference: Envisioning Future Media Environments, 9–15. doi:10.1145/2181037.2181040

Edwards, E., Lumsden, J., Rivas, C., Steed, L., Edwards, A., Thiyagarajan, A., Sohanpal, R., Caton, H., Griffiths, C., Munafò, M., Taylor, S., & Walton, R. (2016). Gamification for health promotion: Systematic review of behaviour change techniques in smartphone apps. *BMJ Open, 6*(10), e012447. doi:10.1136/bmjopen-2016-012447 PubMed

Fenerty, S., West, C., Davis, S., Kaplan, S., & Feldman, S. (2012). The effect of reminder systems on patients' adherence to treatment. *Patient Preference and Adherence, 6,* 127–135. PubMed

Fineberg, N., Demetrovics, J., Stein, D., Ioannidis, K., Potenza, M., Grünblatt, E., Brand, M., Billieux, J., Carmi, L., King, D. L., Grant, J. E., Yücel, M., Dell'Osso, B., Rumpf, H. J., Hall, N., Hollander, E., Goudriaan, A., Menchon, J., Zohar, J., ... Chamberlain, S. R. (2018). Manifesto for a European research network into Problematic Usage of the Internet. *European Neuropsychopharmacology, 28*(11), 1232–1246. doi:10.1016/j.euroneuro.2018.08.004 PubMed

Gentry, S., Gauthier, A., Ehrstrom, B., Wortley, D., Lilienthal, A., Tudor Car, L., Dauwels-Okutsu, S., Nikolaou, C., Zary, N., Campbell, J., & Car, J. (2019). Serious Gaming and Gamification Education in Health Professions: Systematic Review. *Journal of Medical Internet Research, 21*(3), e12994. doi:10.2196/12994 PubMed

Ginsburg, K. (2007). The importance of play in promoting healthy child development and maintaining strong parent-child bonds. *Pediatrics, 119*(1), 182–191. doi:10.1542/peds.2006-2697 PubMed

Heeter, C. (2008). Playstyles and learning. In R. Ferdig (Ed.), *Handbook of Research on Effective Electronic Gaming in Education* (pp. 826–846). IGI Global., doi:10.4018/978-1-59904-808-6.ch047.

Huotari, K., & Hamari, J. (2017). A definition for gamification: Anchoring gamification in the service marketing literature. *Electronic Markets, 27*(1), 21–31. doi:10.1007/s12525-015-0212-z

Jia, Y., Liu, Y., Yu, X., & Voida, S. (2017). Designing leaderboards for gamification: Perceived differences based on user ranking, application domain, and personality traits. Proceedings of the Conference on Human Factors in Computing Systems, 1949–1960. doi:10.1145/3025453.3025826

Ke, F. (2009). A qualitative meta-analysis of computer games as learning tools. In R. E. Furdig (Ed.), *Handbook of Research on Effective Electronic Gaming in Education* (pp. 1–32). IGI Global., doi:10.4018/978-1-59904-808-6.ch001.

Kharrazi, H., Lu, A., Gharghabi, F., & Coleman, W. (2012). A Scoping Review of Health Game Research: Past, Present, and Future. *Games for Health Journal, 1*(4), 153–164. doi:10.1089/g4h.2012.0011 PubMed

Klimmt, C., Hartmann, T., & Frey, A. (2007). Effectance and control as determinants of video game enjoyment. *Cyberpsychology & Behavior, 10*(6), 845–847. doi:10.1089/cpb.2007.9942 PubMed

Koepp, M., Gunn, R., Lawrence, A., Cunningham, V., Dagher, A., Jones, T., Brooks, D., Bench, C., & Grasby, P. (1998). Evidence for striatal dopamine release during a video game. *Nature, 393*(6682), 266–268. doi:10.1038/30498 PubMed

Koivisto, J., & Hamari, J. (2019). The rise of motivational information systems: A review of gamification research. *International Journal of Information Management, 45,* 191–210. doi:10.1016/j.ijinfomgt.2018.10.013

Koster, R. (2005). *Theory of Fun for Game Design*. Paragraph Press.

Landers, R. N., Tondello, G. F., Kappen, D. L., Collmus, A. B., Mekler, E. D., & Nacke, L. E. (2018). Defining gameful experience as a psychological state caused by gameplay: Replacing the term 'gamefulness' with three distinct constructs. Journal of Human Computer Studies. Advance online publication. doi:10.1016/j.ijhcs.2018.08.003

Lazzaro, N. (2004, March). Why we play games: Four keys to more emotion without story. Paper presented at the Game Developers Conference, San Jose, CA.

Lieberoth, A. (2014). Shallow Gamification: Testing Psychological Effects of Framing an Activity as a Game Games and Culture. DOI: doi:10.1177/1555412014559978

Marston, H., & Hall, A. (2016). Gamification: Applications for Health Promotion and Health Information Technology Engagement. Handbook of Research on Holistic Perspectives in Gamification for Clinical Practice. DOI: doi:10.4018/978-1-4666-9522-1.ch005

Martins, H., Silva, D., Dores, A. R., & Sousa, R. (2020 in press). Jogar a trabalhar: o impacto da gamificação no trabalho e na gestão de pessoas. [Play while working: the impact of gamification on work and people management] In T. Proença & A. Veloso (Eds.), *Tendências no Trabalho e na Gestão de Pessoas* [Tendencies at work and on people management]. Academic Press.

McGonigal, J. (2011). *Reality is broken: Why games make us better and how they can change the world.* Penguin.

McManus, I., & Furnham, A. (2010). "Fun, fun, fun": Types of fun, attitudes to fun, and their relation to personality and biographical factors. *Psychology (Irvine, Calif.)*, *1*(03), 159–168. doi:10.4236/psych.2010.13021

Mellecker, R., Lyons, E., & Baranowski, T. (2013). Disentangling Fun and Enjoyment in Exergames Using an Expanded Design, Play, Experience Framework: A Narrative Review. *Games for Health Journal*, *2*(3), 142–149. Advance online publication. doi:10.1089/g4h.2013.0022 PubMed

Mendes-Santos, C., Weiderpass, E., Santana, R., & Andersson, G. (2020). Portuguese psychologists' attitudes toward internet interventions: Exploratory cross-sectional study. JMIR Mental Health, 7(4), e16817. doi:10.2196/16817 PubMed

Mollick, E., & Rothbard, N. (2014). Mandatory fun: Gamification and the impact of games at work. The Wharton School Research Paper Series. doi:10.2139/ssrn.2277103

Quick, J., Atkinson, R., & Lin, L. (2012). Empirical taxonomies of gameplay enjoyment: Personality and video game preference. *International Journal of Game-Based Learning*, *2*(3), 11–13. doi:10.4018/ijgbl.2012070102

Richards, D., & Caldwell, P. (2016). Gamification to Improve Adherence to Clinical Treatment Advice: Improving Adherence to Clinical Treatment. Handbook of Research on Holistic Perspectives in Gamification for Clinical Practice. DOI: doi:10.4018/978-1-4666-9522-1.ch004

Robson, K., Plangger, K., Kietzmann, J. H., McCarthy, I., & Pitt, L. (2015). Is it all a game? Understanding the principles of gamification. *Business Horizons*, *58*(4), 411–420. doi:10.1016/j.bushor.2015.03.006

Ryan, R., & Deci, E. (2000). Self-determination theory and the facilitation of intrinsic motivation, social development, and wellbeing. *The American Psychologist*, *55*(1), 68–78. doi:10.1037/0003-066X.55.1.68 PubMed

Ryan, R. M., Rigby, C. S., Przybylski, A., McManus, I., & Furnham, A. (2010). "Fun, fun, fun": Types of fun, attitudes to fun, and their relation to personality and biographical factors. *Psychology (Irvine, Calif.)*, *1*(03), 159–168. doi:10.4236/psych.2010.13021

Sherry, J. L. (2004). Flow and media enjoyment. *Communication Theory*, *14*(4), 328–347. doi:10.1111/j.1468-2885.2004.tb00318.x

Simões, J., Redondo, R., & Vilas, A. (2012). A social gamification framework for a K-6 learning platform. *Computers in Human Behavior*. Advance online publication. doi:10.1016/j.chb.2012.06.007

Stetina, B., Felnhofer, A., Kothgassner, O., & Lehenbauer, M. (2012). Games for Health: Have Fun with Virtual Reality! In C. Eichenberg (Ed.), *Virtual Reality in Psychological, Medical and Pedagogical Applications*. IntechOpen.

Thai, A., Lowenstein, D., Ching, D., & Rejeski, D. (2009). Game changer: Investing in digital play to advance children's learning and health. Joan Ganz Cooney Center at Sesame Workshop.

Vianna, Y., Vianna, M., Medina, B., & Tanaka, S. (2013). *Gamification, inc.: Como reinventar empresas a partir de jogos* [Gamification, inc.: how to reinvent companies through games]. MJV Press.

Werbach, K., & Hunter, D. (2012). *For the win: How game thinking can revolutionize your business*. Wharton Digital Press.

World Health Organization. (2003). Diet, Nutrition and the Prevention of Chronic Diseases. Report of a Joint WHO/FAO Expert Consultation. World Health Organization Technical Report Series 916. World Health Organization.

World Health Organization. (2018). International Classification of Diseases 11th Revision. Geneva: The World Health Organization (WHO).

World Health Organization, Regional Office for the Eastern Mediterranean. (2012). Health education: theoretical concepts, effective strategies and core competencies: a foundation document to guide capacity development of health educators. https://apps.who.int/iris/handle/10665/119953

Xi, N., & Hamari, J. (2019). Does gamification satisfy needs? A study on the relationship between gamification features and intrinsic need satisfaction. *International Journal of Information Management*, *46*, 210–221. doi:10.1016/j.ijinfomgt.2018.12.002

Xu, Y., & Hi, H. (2011). Literature review on web application gamification and analytics. CSDL Technical Report 11-05, available in https://csdl.ics.hawaii.edu/techreports/11-05/11-05.pdf

Yee, N. (2006). Motivations for play in online games. *Cyberpsychology & Behavior*, *9*(6), 772–775. doi:10.1089/cpb.2006.9.772 PubMed

Yohannan, S., Kwon, R., & Yurt, R. (2012). The Potential of Gaming in Rehabilitation of the Burn-Injured Patient. *Games for Health Journal: Research, Development, and Clinical Applications*, *1*(2), 65–70.

Zichermann, G., & Cunningham, C. (2011). *Gamification by design: Implementing game mechanics in web and mobile apps* (M. Treseler, Ed.). O'Reilly Media.

ADDITIONAL READING

Alahäivälä, T., & Oinas-Kukkonen, H. (2016). Understanding persuasion contexts in health gamification: A systematic analysis of gamified health behavior change support systems literature. *International Journal of Medical Informatics, 96*, 62–70. doi:10.1016/j.ijmedinf.2016.02.006 PubMed

Buday, R., Baranowski, T., & Thompson, D. (2012). Fun and Games and Boredom. *Games for Health Journal, 1*(4), 257–261. doi:10.1089/g4h.2012.0026 PubMed

Edwards, E., Lumsden, J., Rivas, C., Steed, L., Edwards, A., Thiyagarajan, A., Sohanpal, R., Caton, H., Griffiths, C., Munafò, M., Taylor, S., & Walton, R. (2016). Gamification for health promotion: Systematic review of behaviour change techniques in smartphone apps. *BMJ Open, 6*(10), e012447. doi:10.1136/bmjopen-2016-012447 PubMed

Gentry, S., Gauthier, A., Ehrstrom, B., Wortley, D., Lilienthal, A., Tudor Car, L., Dauwels-Okutsu, S., Nikolaou, C., Zary, N., Campbell, J., & Car, J. (2019). Serious Gaming and Gamification Education in Health Professions: Systematic Review. *Journal of Medical Internet Research, 21*(3), e12994. doi:10.2196/12994 PubMed

Kharrazi, H., Lu, A., Gharghabi, F., & Coleman, W. (2012). A Scoping Review of Health Game Research: Past, Present, and Future. *Games for Health Journal, 1*(4), 153–164. doi:10.1089/g4h.2012.0011 PubMed

Koster, R. (2005). *Theory of Fun for Game Design.* Paragraph Press.

McManus, I., & Furnham, A. (2010). "Fun, fun, fun": Types of fun, attitudes to fun, and their relation to personality and biographical factors. *Psychology (Irvine, Calif.), 1*(03), 159–168. doi:10.4236/psych.2010.13021

Mellecker, R., Lyons, E., & Baranowski, T. (2013). Disentangling Fun and Enjoyment in Exergames Using an Expanded Design, Play, Experience Framework: A Narrative Review. *Games for Health Journal, 2*(3), 142–149. Advance online publication. doi:10.1089/g4h.2013.0022 PubMed

KEY TERMS AND DEFINITIONS

eHealth: Is the use of internet technologies to deliver health content and interventions.

Enjoyment: Is the emotional benefit from being involved in a pleasurable activity.

Fun: Is the positive emotional state that derives from taking part in activities that are amusing and engaging.

Game-Based Approaches: Broad specter term that encompasses all strategies that use games as a resource for motivating and engaging users in activities that are not games *per se*. These approaches can be digitally or analogically based and include serious games, gamification and learning games, etc.

Gamefulness: Is the characteristic of an activity that imbues it with the spirit of playing a game, promoting a level of abstraction from the context the player is in and giving them focus to interact with and achieve the goals of the game with a positive emotional state. Gameful players are not filled with fear of losing the game, they are excited to achieve the goals and develop the skills they need to win the game.

Gamification: Is the use of videogames strategies, principles and elements to non-game contexts in order to gamefully promote desired and pre-established outcomes.

mHealth: Is the use of mobile devices (e.g. smartphones) to deliver health content and interventions.

Play: Is the element in an activity that allows for experimenting with reality and learning from it, without facing the harshest level of consequence; play usually elicits positive emotions and even flow; a crucial part of human development (children especially learn by playing) and experience it permits testing attitudes, behaviors and strategies because it temporarily suspends the effect of consequences, while informing subjects of what the results of their actions would be.

Playfulness: Is the characteristic of an activity that imbues it with a playful attitude, meaning that the activity can become autotelic (an end in itself) and that it produces a positive and active spectrum of emotions, such as joy and laughter but also mischief and rule-testing/breaking.

This research was previously published in the Handbook of Research on Solving Modern Healthcare Challenges With Gamification; pages 258-278, copyright year 2021 by Medical Information Science Reference (an imprint of IGI Global).

Chapter 6

Towards Better Understanding of Children's Relationships With Online Games and Advergames

Ali Ben Yahia
LIGUE, Tunis, Tunisia

Sihem Ben Saad
🆔 https://orcid.org/0000-0003-3034-9206
Carthage Business School, Université Tunis Carthage, Tunisia

Fatma Choura Abida
Institute of Computer Science of Tunis, Tunisia

ABSTRACT

Since the child is at the heart of current managerial and ethical challenges imposed by digitalization, digital marketing to children is henceforth calling for new territories of studies in connection with the phenomenon of "gaming" in particular. This chapter favors an in-depth understanding of the child's relation with this phenomenon through an exploratory qualitative approach. Focus groups and in-depth interviews were conducted with children and their parents. Findings suggest that psychological states of users during navigation and playing are the feeling of pride, the state of flow, the experience of tele-presence and the feeling of socialization. Given the specificities of this form of communication and the ethical implications, the relationship with the advergame has also been investigated.

INTRODUCTION

Children represent an important target for companies (Fusaro & Hildgen 2013; Capella & Terlutter 2013; Chen et al., 2010; Dessart et al., 2015; Chen & Leung 2016). They are considered as "multi-taskers, risk-takers, explorers, early adopters of new technologies" (Capella & Terlutter, 2013; Chen et al., 2010, Dessart et al., 2015; Chen & Leung, 2016). Companies are aware of the potential of this target (Fusaro

DOI: 10.4018/978-1-6684-7589-8.ch006

& Hildgen, 2013) and are increasingly using experts such as psychologists and anthropologists to study behaviors of those young consumers. With the proliferation of technologies, access to children through direct communication is becoming easier. In fact, screens occupy a significant part of children's leisure time, a phenomenon that is amplified with mobile telephony, social networks and the advergame (Chester & Montgomery, 2008; Chen et al., 2010; Dessart et al., 2015; Chen & Leung, 2016; Vashisht & Sreejesh, 2017). Similarly, the influx of brands in social networks promotes direct communication with the target population on these virtual platforms that allow an important and extremely fast dissemination of information and interaction possibilities, developed through the advergame (Capella & Terlutter, 2013; Vashisht & Sreejesh, 2017).

The purpose of this chapter is to provide a better understanding of children behaviour and perceptions towards games and advergames on the Internet as a digital servicescape. As one of the most significant sectors in the global gaming market, online games continue to experience a substantial increase in popularity. Indeed, the number of online gamers worldwide has surged from 20 million in 2010 to 250 million in 2018, representing an average growth of over 20% per year1. Being one of the children's favourite online activities (Rideout, Foehr, & Roberts, 2010), online games have become an advertising medium with great potentials for companies whose advertisements are targeted at children to influence their choices.

Compared to adults, children are much more vulnerable to marketing techniques, which explains why they are the main target of ads for unhealthy and non-nutritious products. Internet represents a digital servicescape in which children are exposed to a wide variety of stimuli and particularly to advergames that are gamification tools. Moreover, when they are inside this servicescape, children may lose themselves and be affected by an important flow. So, their capacity initially limited to analyze advertising may become more limited in the digital environment when they are exposed to advergames.

The persuasive dimension of advertising associated with online games can be very effective when young children are the target. Indeed, children are very susceptible to advertisements because they do not always understand its persuasive dimension (Kapferer 1985; Chen & Leung, 2016). A child is affected by the pleasure of online gaming (Vashisht & Sreejesh, 2017). In addition, the large share of children in household expenses, the degree of interactivity of the child with the family, the influence of social and individual factors, the degree of parental control, the degree of involvement of the child in this digital world, his state of flow, his feeling of socialization, his telepresence experience are all variables that can influence his relationship with the Internet (Yadav et al. 2013; Pelet, Ettis & Cowart, 2014; Chen & Leung, 2016; Vashisht & Sreejesh, 2017). These findings led to an all-out reflection on children's relationship with online games and advergames (Hamari et al. 2014; Huotari & Hamari, 2017; Vashisht et al., 2019). Using the exploratory approach, this chapter aims to provide an in-depth understanding of the advanced problem. The target chosen is directly concerned by the questions raised, the children and their parents in this case.

The remainder of this chapter is organized as follows: Next section discusses the theoretical framework of gamification on the Internet as a digital servicescape and the psychological states that may be induced in this environment. It also debates the ethical dimension of marketing targeting children on the Internet. Methodological details about the empirical process, sample and tools used to collect requested information are then developed. The main results are developed in the last section. Finally, a discussion of findings, implications and new perspectives of research concludes the chapter.

CHILDREN AND DIGITAL MARKETING: STUDY OF THE PHENOMENON OF THE GAMIFICATION AND ADVERGAME

Gamification

In the last few years, gamification has gained considerable attention from practitioners; however, academic research on gamification has been largely confined to the human–computer interaction and game studies domains (Huotari & Hamari, 2017). The term gamification was first coined by Brett Terrill (2008). The author describes the word as taking game mechanics and applying them to other web properties. Then, the term entered more widespread use in the industry in 2010 (Deterding et al. 2011) and in academia (Hamari et al. 2014; Huotari & Hamari, 2017). These definitions have relied on the notion that gamification proceeds from the use of game design elements.

According to Huotari and Hamari (2017) "gamification refers to a process of enhancing a service with affordances for gameful experiences in order to support users' overall value creation". Huotari and Hamari's definition highlights the goal of gamification, the experiences that it attempts to give rise to – rather than the methods domains (Bitner, 1992; Mari & Poggesi, 2013; Huotari & Hamari, 2017; Vashisht et al., 2019; Helmefalk & Marcusson, 2019). Other definitions go in the same direction as the previous one, stipulate that: "in order to support user's overall value creation, gamification is a process of enhancing a service with affordances for gameful experiences" [Huotari & Hamari, 2017; Helmefalk & Marcusson, 2019). This definition suggests that in order to achieve a marketing outcome, such as purchase behaviour, companies can employ various game mechanics in their offerings.

In a nutshell, the goal of gamification is to influence behavior, motivate individual/group, create dedication, achieve loyalty and achieve benefit. Gamification is also characterized by digitalization and use of game mechanics.

Advergame

The advergame is a new form of interactive marketing characterized by its immersive and interactive nature, designed to be fun and playful (Vashisht & Sreejesh, 2017). The advergame is perceived as a new communication lever. It is a strategic alternative for companies seeking consumer awareness. Advergames are usually free and downloadable on the brand's website.

According to Cavallini (2006), to advertise brands and products, the notion of advergame could be defined as a strategy for marketing that uses games, mainly electronic. The Internet and video game consoles are great environments to use this strategy. Mobile media (smartphones and tablets) are already being tested by companies, which chose this marketing strategy too. Balasubramanian, (1994) adds also, that advergames can be considered as hybrid messages. Indeed, hybrid messages "include all paid attempts to influence audiences for commercial benefit using communications that project a non- commercial character" (Balasubramanian, 1994:30). Also, to place brands and products with commercial purposes, advergames use video games.

Chen & Ringel, (2001) stipulate that based on the way brands or products are placed in them, advergames can be classified in three different levels: The first level refers to associative advergames where the product is linked to a particular activity featured in the advergames (e.g., a sport). The second level refers to the illustrative advergames in which the brand or product plays a significant role in the game.

The demonstrative advergames represent the third level in which the player allows to experience the product in its natural context as reproduced in the gaming environment.

However, according to Panda (2004, p 42), product placement refers to "the practice of including a brand name product, package, signage or other trademark merchandise within a motion picture, television or other media vehicles for increasing the memorability of the brand and for instant recognition at the point of purchase". The term product placement is used to refer to the positioning of images of a brand or product in an entertainment medium such as an online game.

Balasubramanian, Karrh & Patwardham, (2006) distinguish between product placement in video games and advergames. In fact, product placement uses existing video games which are developed by an independent third party. However, advergames are totally funded, developed and controlled by the marketer. Also, the nature of advergames as hybrid messages creates some controversy. In advergames consumers can played online or downloaded the game for free. The authors add the idea that, as with product placement, when using advergames, ethical concerns arise.

Several researchers claim that advergames have become quite ubiquitous and announce food products, most of them unhealthy (Vashisht & Sreejesh, 2017). At the heart of this important diversity of online communication formats, there is a sensitive, impulsive and often vulnerable target whose reactions deserve serious attention. The persuasive dimension of advertising is not easily identifiable for a child. Indeed, several questions are raised about the treatment that children make of these new advertising formats and the reactions that they generate on the cognitive, affective and conative levels.

Flow of Children in Games

As a form of entertainment, video games have deeply infiltrated the child's everyday life. These digital games provide him with optimal experiences, described as happiness (Pelet, Ettis & Cowart, 2014). Because it is an essential arrangement to describe human-machine interactions, Yadav et al. (2013) chose the term "flow" to describe these moments of capacity, also called optimal experiences. The concept of flow has been introduced by Csikszentmihalyi (1975) and has been particularly studied in the context of Internet browsing (Novak, Hoffman & Yung, 2000; Pelet, Ettis & Cowart, 2014). These authors describe the flow as a state lived by Internet users who are highly involved in a given activity. The flow state is considered to be a psychological concept (Gharbi, 1998; Yadav et al., 2013). Ghani and Deshpande (1994) characterize it by the feeling of playfulness and total concentration. Other researchers believe that the activities that lead to the flow state make the user highly focused (Fornerino, Helme-guizon & Gotteland, 2006; Yadav et al., 2013; Pelet, Ettis & Cowart, 2014). On the basis of this observation, the flow state seems to be a fundamental component to describe human-machine interactions.

Several researchers value its relevance by describing the experience of interaction in a mediated environment (Csikszentmihalyi, 1990; Yadav et al., 2013; Pelet, Ettis & Cowart, 2014). According to Gharbi, Ettis and Ben Mimoun (2003) the state of flow is a perfect experience that can be lived by a user in a mediated environment.

Several researchers show that the video game is a real flow distributor. His design sometimes aims unknowingly the flow, which consists here of being totally immersed in the game, totally focused, totally passionate and chaining victories despite increasingly difficult challenges (Pelet, Ettis & Cowart, 2014; Plangger et al., 2016). Players of all ages can stay fully focused on playing (Yadav et al., 2013; Pelet, Ettis & Cowart, 2014, Plangger et al., 2016). This may raise questions about the degree of awareness of particularly young targets during the game in their treatment of advertising information or stimuli; hence the problem of the ethics of marketing actions addressed to children.

The Ethical Dimension in Marketing for Children on the Internet

Ads inserted into games are becoming more and more ubiquitous for all ages. A child is confronted at nearly 200 advertising messages per day (Capella & Terlutter, 2013). Children have become the target of a large number of companies; like the toy makers, video game publishers, etc. Recent research advances the idea that a child is seen as an active member of the decision-making process. Eventually, he will represent a customer with a high degree of loyalty. In this case, the company assigns him a triple role: buyer, prescriber and consumer of the future (Capella & Terlutter, 2013; Charles & Benabadji, 2015; Vashisht & Sreejesh, 2017).

Children are a vulnerable target; they are inexperienced and immature compared to adult (Zichermann & Cunningham 2011, Panic, Cauberghe & De Pelsmacker, 2013). To a child, ads are entertaining (Panic, Cauberghe & De Pelsmacker, 2013, Palmer & Hedberg, 2013, Charles & Benabadji, 2015). Exposed to advergames, children are not able to evaluate the relevance of the information they visualize. They do not understand that games are tools for collecting information about them (Zichermann & Cunningham, 2011; Panic, Cauberghe & De Pelsmacker 2013). This information gathering through online games can be performed without Children's knowledge. The younger the child, the more malleable he is and therefore suggestible (Vashisht & Sreejesh, 2017). Similarly, these researchers argue that the majority of children trust the advertisements that they are exposed to, and that is because they do not have the cognitive defenses needed to decipher the messages they have encountered (Palmer & Hedberg 2013; Charles & Benabadji 2015).

TOWARDS A BETTER UNDERSTANDING OF THE BEHAVIOR OF CHILDREN FACING SCREENS: EMPIRICAL INVESTIGATION

The objective of this chapter is to understand the behavior of children on the Internet, focusing on their psychological state during game online activities and on their relationship with the other advergame. To do so, we conduct a qualitative study containing three steps. Our sample includes children aged from 6 to 12 years and parents of children of the same age group. The consent of the Children's parents has been obtained in order to conduct our investigations.

Step 1: Preliminary Brainstorming: Understanding the Child's Relationship with the Internet

The purpose of this step is to explore the subject and better understand the problem and the information needs. A focus group was organized with 7 children aged from 6 to 12 years. The method of the focus group was privileged to encourage exchanges between participants who, at that age, can express a certain shyness to speak in the context of an experience they all discovered for the first time. At the beginning of the meeting, the moderator presents and explains the sequence of this group interview. The interview guide is organized into three main parts. Firstly, children were asked about their general Internet knowledge and they had to cite everything they associate with it. Secondly, we tried to discover the ideas related to their actions and behavior when they are connected. Thirdly, the issue of digital games online was addressed to try exploring the familiarity of the target with this phenomenon and the possible uses that they make of it. This first step of the study was important to define the best way the lines of investigation in the framework of the subsequent steps. The objective of the second step of the study is to understand in depth the behavior of children on the Internet and their relation with the present contents, the games and the advergame in particular.

Step 2: Focus Group and Observation: Children's Behavior on the Internet and Relationship with Games and the Advergame

In this step, we group together children of the same age, in a cyberspace, in order to be able to see the participants during their browsing on the Internet. Two meetings were organized with 7 participants during each one. The interview guide followed a phased approach and was organized in three parts. The introductory theme was intended to understand participants' cognizance with the Internet and how they use it. The theme focused on two aspects: the relationship of children with digital games and that with advertising on the Internet.

The last part of the interview focused on the psychological states of children when they are connected to the Internet. During the focus group, a break was scheduled for the children. Then they were asked to connect to the Internet again. The moderator explained that they could connect freely as if they were at home or in the usual connection spaces.

This allowed us to observe the behavior of children when they are connected. The first two steps were important to better understand the relationship of this young target with fun content and advertising on the Internet. In order to better understand the phenomenon from different points of view, we opted in the last part for interviews with the parents of targets to investigate the perceptions and attitudes of parents towards the relationship of children with fun content and advertising on the Internet.

Step 3: Individual Interviews with Parents: Comprehension of Attitudes and Perceptions of Parents towards Uses of their Children of Playful and Commercial Contents on the Internet

It is important to understand parents' perceptions and attitudes about children's relationship with new information and communication technologies. In-depth individual interviews were conducted with 13 parents, all recruited from a preliminary questionnaire that verified the target's membership (parent of a child between 6 and 12 years old and connecting and playing online games on the Internet). The individual interview approach was chosen at this stage to allow parents to easily talk about the behavior of their children and to develop ideas they wish hidden from others. Our guide followed funnel logic. First, parents were asked about the behavior of their children on the Internet in general, to explore in a second time the psychological states of the child during the game time. In the last part of the interview, the question of the advergame has been treated in order to understand its influence on the behavior of the child.

RESULTS

In this section, we present all results relating to the different steps of the study. A classical thematic analysis was performed to identify themes and subthemes in accordance with objectives of each step. The method of Evard, Pras et Roux, (2009) was carried out in this study without using any program.

Step 1: Preliminary Brainstorming: Understanding the Child's Relationship with the Internet

For children, the Internet is only search engines or social networks. Interviewees say they use the Internet with their friends or family to play, hence the phenomenon of social games. Most of them prefer to connect alone via multiple media such as tablets and mobile phone. Content analysis has also revealed a lack of parental control when children are browsing, which can increase the risk of exposure to inappropriate content. This may negatively influence children behavior. The analysis of the qualitative study shows a great interest of the children in the online games. In fact, they spend a lot of time in virtual warm environment. In Table 1, we identify the different themes and examples of verbatim extracts from interviews.

Our results converge with those advanced in the literature, claiming that digital has dominated the life of the human being, in particular the child.

The screens are part of the daily lives of children, whether through phones, video game consoles, computers or tablets (Vashisht & Sreejesh, 2017). Thus, the lack of parental control and the daily confrontation of the child with screens increase the risk. Children are more easily exposed to inappropriate content, which can negatively influence their behavior (Marigo, 2014).

Step 2: Focus Group and Observation: Children's Behavior on the Internet and Relationship with Games and the Advergame

In this step, findings are consistent with those of the first step. Indeed, children give a heavy weight to the Internet. They spend most of their time connecting to social networks and playing online. The relationship between the child and the virtual environment is considered personal and warm. In the same way, the online games are massively present in the daily life of our questioned target. This phenomenon was observed in children during the group interview when we asked them to browse a moment on the Internet. Most of the participants systematically connected to their gaming sites and quickly became immersed in the virtual environment. In addition, advertising is hated by most respondents. They say that it disturbs them. Concerning psychological states felt young people on the Internet, the perceived risk is identified. In fact, it's mainly related to the content they are exposed to on the Internet. Children think that they are generally annoyed by violence, scenes and images which are not adapted to their expectations. The paying aspect of games and the problem of downloading games are also found as sources of irritation. However, the feeling of socialization, pride, telepresence and the state of flow are identified as psychological states strongly felt by the child during his navigation. The main identified results are presented in Table 2.

Table 1. Occurrence frequencies and verbatim excerpts from the different themes identified

Themes	Subthemes	Verbatim	Frequency of occurrence
1. Theme: Relationship of the child with the Internet	Definition of the Internet	Children interviewed associate the Internet with a search engine (Google ....)	**5**
	as a search engine *a social network*	(Facebook,....)	**2**
	A game	(*game, FRIV, counterstrike, GTA, Pro- game motos- playstore, ...).*	**10**
	Reason for using the Internet	(*music, youtube ; painting, Facebook, watch the videos, ...*)	**8**
	place of connection	The majority connects at home ("*I also play at home, I go on FB at home, but I prefer to come to the publinet to play with my friends, ...*).	**9**
	The supports used	The supports used by children are tablets (*I have a tablet, ... 2*), the Ipad (*We have an IPad at home, ..*), the computer (*I have a computer at home, ... 6*) and the phone (*my mother's phone too, .. 3*).	**11**
2- Theme: The actions and behavior of the child on the Internet	*Using the Internet with friends and family members*	Interviewees say that they use the Internet with their friends or family to play, hence the phenomenon of social games "(I play with my big sister (13 years), My cousin and my friends put the game on the computer, sometimes my brother (13 years old) plays with me, I play Subway with my little brother ...).	**11**
	Using the Internet alone	However, many argue that they connect and play alone (I stay alone when I play, no one accompanies me, I choose the game alone, .. and I play alone, ...).	**21**
	Absence of parental control	The content analysis also raised a certain lack of parental control at the moment of navigation of their children ("*my brother and my sister control me, whether it is research for school or other things ...*)".	**5**
3. Theme: Familiarity of the child with the phenomenon of online games	*Major interest for online games*	The analysis of qualitative material has brought out a major interest of children for online games. Indeed, they would spend most of their time playing online, hence the feeling of socialization (*I play Subway, We play Counter Strike, everyone on his post, we start together and we play together, I play at Counterstrike, I play Counterstrike, I play, My favorite game is maincraft, ...*).	**14**
	Warm relationship with the virtual environment	the relationship with the virtual environment is considered human and warm ("*I talk to Pok, he's my friend, I find him on Skype, he sometimes gives me his password to play, I discuss with him on Skype, I did not see him, he loves me, he always talks to me, you play with other people, your friends for example, people on dating sites ... "*).	**14**

Step 3: Individual Interviews with Parents

The analysis of the corpus reveals that the Internet is considered a necessity for children. It represents a means of escape, distraction and interaction. Parents add the idea that their children spend on average between 2 hours and 30 minutes per day connected to the Internet. The study also reveals an increase in the rate of equipment in digital technologies such as smartphones and tablets. The analysis of the qualitative results focuses on the online games. The main findings show a relationship lack of affection, impersonal and dehumanized between the child and his relatives. Regarding the psychological states, the state of flow would be the feeling mostly felt by the children at the time of the online game. According to the statements, all children are intensely playful, fully focused and truly confronted with challenges during these moments of play.

Table 2. Occurrence frequencies and verbatim excerpts from the different themes identified

Themes	Subthemes	Verbatim	Frequency of occurrence
1. familiarity and behavior of the child on the Internet	*Knowledge and definition of the Internet*	Interviewees associate Internet with online games and social networks ("FRIV games - you tube - counterstrike - GTA - motorcycle – music, games, download movies, facebook, ...").	15
	Actions on the Internet	Interviewees spend most of their time playing online and consulting social networks (*"I stay alone when I play, I put alone FB, games, subway, games, counterstrike games, games, games, you tube, FB, Google, Skype ... "*).	10
2. Relationship of the child with advertising and digital games	*Kids play online frequently*	The analysis of the results shows that children play online frequently (*"I play Subway, We play Counter Strike, each one on his post, we start together and we play together, some win, others lose, ..."*) .	16
	Children know about advertising	The analysis of qualitative material shows that the majority of the people questioned knows the publicity (*"We know the pub On the Internet, we see pubs of pens, but especially food products, ...*).	4
	Children do not like advertising, they disturb them	They argue that they do not like advertising (*"I do not like advertising because I do not want to be cut when I look at things, I can not stand it, it bothers me, I do not like it, it's bad, ... "*).	21
3. Theme: Understanding the child's psychological states at the time of navigation	Irritability factors on the Internet	According to the interviewees, the main irritants factors on the Internet are violence, scenes and images not adapted to the target "The big words in the rap songs, I do not like to hack the accounts on FB and the big words in the rap songs, the videos I do not like also the big words in the rap songs, the violent videos ...). Some others add the pay aspect of games and download problems (*A game at my brother's, it's with guns, sometimes we do not say it's forbidden at least ...*).	28
	Perceived risk	The analysis of the results shows that the perceived risk is the feeling felt by some interviewees *"With the history of FB, when we enter, we realize that other people have connected to your account FB, Once when I was trying to log into my FB account, I could not, I kept trying and when I entered, I knew who hacked me and I blocked it. ... "*	7
	A sense of pride	Some others show a sense of pride "(*I'm proud because I learned things, for example instead of using the mouse I speak on the computer ...*).	4
	flow State	The feeling of flow has been experienced by some children. Indeed, at the time of their navigation on the sites of games, they were totally absorbed (*I feel that my heart beats and my brain evolves, I learn things, I am happy when I am on the Internet, we are with the friends When I'm on the Internet, concentrated, I do not like people talking to me, I do not want to be disturbed, I can not stand, if someone talks to me and I'm not conscious, I do not listen to it ...*).	7
	The telepresence experience	A feeling of telepresence was mentioned in the corpus ("*I feel that I am in another world Yes, we feel that we have entered the Internet ..*).	3

The phenomenon of the advergame also seems to influence the behavior of children in their particular food preferences and which mainly concern unhealthy products. Table 3 summarizes the main results of the content analysis of the interviews.

Table 3. Occurrence frequencies and verbatim excerpts from the different themes identified

Themes	Subthemes	Verbatim	Frequency of occurrence
1. The behavior of the child on the Internet	*Internet connection time*	Following the interviews, the majority of parents suggest that their children spend an average of 2 hours a day to connect to the Internet (*"2 hours per day, except weekends and holidays ..). Some others think that their children connect on average 20 to 30 minutes online ("it all depends on the days 20 to 30 minutes, ...").*	12
	The equipment used to connect	The study also reveals an increase in the rate of equipment in smartphones, tablets and mobile phones (*"my Smartphone, that of their father, their grandmother as soon as they find a laptop they want to play on, the boy has a tablet.. ").*	15
	Activities on the Internet: play online	The analysis of qualitative material has brought about a major interest for online games. The respondents think that their children spend most of their time playing online (*"Playing in a group online, Yes, they play on the Internet, Iyadh is rather influenced by online games, Yes, she plays on the internet ... .).*	12
	Nature of the relationship with the environment: Cold and dehumanized relationship	The relationship of their children with their surroundings is described as cold, impersonal and dehumanized (*"do not argue with each other, they do not argue with us, sometimes we talk to them but they do not respond, we have to repeat things many times and they are very absorbed by the game, do not want to stop until they have finished the game, disconnected from reality, ...).*	21
	importance of the Internet	Finally, the Internet seems to be a necessity for children. Indeed, for some it is considered as a means of distraction and escape *"A way to escape, to have fun, to decompress after school, it's very important for her, ..."* For some others, it is considered as a means of interaction *"Internet for him represents an opening for the world, it allows the interaction with people who are not in his immediate environment, It becomes a fundamental need! .. ".*	26
2. Psychological states at the time of play	*Flow State*	The content analysis suggests that the feeling felt by the child when he plays online can be considered a state of flow. It can, indeed, express a feeling of playfulness and total immersion. This state is characterized by a feeling of total concentration that also corresponds to an extraordinary experience. It is a state lived by children very involved in a given activity. *"They are concentrated in the game, Very absorbed by what they watch on the screen, they do not listen to what is happening around, Hyper busy in the game and very concentrated above! We must interrupt the game each time, Disconnected from the world ... ").*	27
3. The phenomenon of the advergame and its impact on the behavior of the child	*The significant impact of the advergame on the behavior of the child*	Children's food preferences mainly concern unhealthy products (*"Yes, especially for chocolates, cereals, sweets, etc. Yes, sometimes they want to buy what's in advertising without even understanding what it is, without even tasting the product just because they have seen the ad shot several times on the video, mom I want to buy the games that sells in this or that shop ..).*	29

DISCUSSION OF RESULTS AND GENERAL CONCLUSION

The important use of the Internet and Smartphones by children suggests that children should be considered at the heart of current managerial and ethical challenges imposed by digitalization.

In fact, digital Marketing targeting children is henceforth an important issue as it is strongly appealing for several areas of research: Gamification, Ethical Marketing, Advergame and Psychological reactions on the Internet especially the state of flow. The problems of the behavior of the child on the Internet and its relation with the online games and the advertising contents were at the origin of the investigations carried out within the framework of this study.

The interest is focused in this work on the target of the children, considering that the study of this target can raise questions in particular on the ethical plan, as it was largely underlined in the literature on the marketing intended for children. This issue is also at the center of the concerns of companies and advertisers in this new digital media, with considerable potential.

This study has been explored through focus groups and in-depth interviews the children' psychological states and behavior, during online games. We also investigate children's attitudes towards the advertisements to which they are exposed during these activities. The results of this exploratory study underscored the importance of online games in children' lives and highlighted the possible effects of the ubiquity of this phenomenon on their psychological states. Thus, the feeling of socialization, pride, telepresence and the flow state proved to be psychological states strongly felt by the child at the time of his navigation. The results obtained are consistent with the results of previous studies (Pelet, Ettis & Cowart, 2014) that argue that living a flow state while playing needs to be intensively cheerful, fully focused and truly confrontational with challenges. These dimensions: playfulness, concentration, control and challenges perception are generally identified in studies on flow state (Csikszentmihalyi, 1975, Yadav et al., 2013, Pelet, Ettis & Cowart, 2014). Playfulness relates to the pleasure achieved during the navigation in a mediated environment. Csikszentmihalyi (1997) also states that the playfulness is a feeling of joy that goes beyond pleasure. According to Csikszentmihalyi (1990), concentration expresses the idea that the Internet user becomes totally absorbed by the activity. Several researchers claim that because of the concentration on activity, the Internet user loses consciousness (Ghani, 1991; Yadav et al., 2013). The sense of control refers to "exercising control without actively seeking control over one's actions" (Csikszentmihalyi, 1990, p22). Csikszentmihalyi (1990) describes the perception of challenges as the balance between challenges and skills. Csikszentmihalyi (1990) states that online activities may generate a flow state. In the same vein, many researchers say that for the surfer to live a flow state, he must be playful, focused, perfectly in control of his navigation and in confrontation with challenges (Sandales & Buckner, 1989; Yadav et al., 2013).

To reach the flow state, Csikszentmihalyi (1997) suggests that challenges and skills need to be balanced. Digital games are not only games, they have also become more involved in the psychological states of the child (Pelet, Ettis & Cowart, 2014).

These psychological states can determine the child's positive attitude to the advergame, as pointed out by Chen & Leung (2016) and Pelet, Ettis & Cowart (2014). This rather omnipresent phenomenon, generally announces unhealthy food products (Zichermann & Cunningham, 2011) to a sensitive and impulsive target, the child consumer, in this case. Hence the problem of the ethics of marketing actions addressed to children (Capella & Terlutter, 2013; Charles & Benabadji, 2015; Vashisht & Sreejesh, 2017; Terlutter & Capella, 2017). Because he is affected by pleasure, the feeling of playfulness, the total concentration and the feeling of being physically present in a virtual environment, the child is more vulnerable to the phenomenon of the advergame. He does not understand his persuasive dimension and his behaviors can be significantly affected. It is also relevant to retain the perceived risk that has been revealed in the body of qualitative study as a feeling felt in a virtual environment. Forsythe and Shi (2003) argue that the perceived risk refers to the feeling of anxiety that a user may feel in such environment. It can, in fact, counterbalance the feeling of pride, the state of flow, the feeling of socialization and the feeling of being physically present in a mediated environment (Volle, 1995; Durand, Ezan & Vanheems, 2015). The results of this work make a contribution to the current state of the art on marketing for children by focusing on the phenomenon of the advergame in digital marketing. The issue of the ethics of communication actions aimed at children is also at the center of our work and suggests more in-depth investigations, especially in a virtual context which promotes a total immersion of the target and therefore, the risks of a greater possible manipulation.

Since results of this research don't allow us to give precise answers to this question "who is responsible for this, is the children, parents, or the companies?", they allow us to better understand the general context of this children behavior and may be to analyze the responsibility of children, parents or companies in this case. While we cannot as, Marketing researchers, give instructions to parents on how they should raise their children, this study can provide companies some recommendations on the ethical dimension of communication and advergame on the digital servicescape.

These risks are amplified in the case of a sensitive and vulnerable target and where the means of control are still not accessible or possible. In this regard, parental control has been raised in the case of our study and it has, in fact, been limited. This raises questions about the reasons and potential impacts of this behavior (Marigo, 2014) and also on the means to be put in place as part of awareness-raising actions on the potential dangers of uncontrolled exposure of children to the content of games on the Internet.

The legal track is also to investigate to understand the legal framework which would be or should be put in force to regulate these different phenomena. If this study brings relevant insights into the behavior of children on the Internet and their reactions toward the advergame, the possibilities of generalization remain limited because of the limited sample interviewed. In the same way, this study opens the way towards new perspectives of research in digital marketing. Quantitative studies on representative samples would make it possible to identify the behavioral trends of this target in this study context and to test relationships between the different variables identified.

REFERENCES

Balasubramanian, S. K. (1994). Beyond advertising and publicity: Hybrid messages and public policy issues. *Journal of Advertising*, *23*(4), 29–46. doi:10.1080/00913367.1943.10673457

Balasubramanian, S. K., Karrh, J. A., & Patwardhan, H. (2006). Audience Response to Product Placements: An Integrative Framework and Future Research Agenda. *Journal of Advertising*, *35*(3), 115–141. doi:10.2753/JOA0091-3367350308

Balasubramanian, S. K., Karrh, J. A., & Patwardhan, H. (2006). Audience Response to Product Placements: An Integrative Framework and Future Research Agenda. *Journal of Advertising, 35*(3), 115–41.

Bitner, M. J. (1992). Servicescapes: The Impact of Physical Surroundings on Customers and Employees. *Journal of Marketing, 56*(2), 57–71. doi:10.1177/002224299205600205

Brée, J. (2007). *Kids Marketing*. Edition Management et Société.

Brée, J. (2012). Kids Marketing. Ouvrage collectif, Colombelles: Editions EMS.

Bree, J., & Masserot, B. (2010). Publicité et obésité enfantine: L'impact des annonces publicitaires télévisées sur les choix alimentaires des enfants. In: Actes du 26ème Congrès International de l'AFM – Le Mans-Angers, 6 et 7 mai 2010.

Capella, M., & Terlutter, J. (2013). The Gamification of Advertising: Analysis and Research Directions of In-Game Advertising, Advergames, and Advertising in Social Network Games. *Journal of Advertising*, *42*(2–3), 95–112.

Cauberghe, V., & De Pelsmacker, P. (2010). The Impact of Brand Prominence and Game Repetition on Brand Responses. *Journal of Advertising*, *39*(1), 5–18. doi:10.2753/JOA0091-3367390101

Cavallini, R. (2006). *O marketing depois de amanhã*. São Paulo, Brazil: Digerati Books.

Charles et Benabadji, I. (2015). Le marketing destiné aux enfants: entre profits économiques et atteintes psychologiques, Concours national Promotion de l'Ethique Professionnelle co-organisé par le Rotary et la Conférence des Grandes Ecoles.

Chen, H., & Leung, M. (2016). Exploring web users' optimal flow experience. *Information Technology & People*, *13*(4), 263–281. doi:10.1108/09593840010359473

Chen, J., & Ringel, M. (2001). Can advergaming be the future of interactive advertising? Available at http://www.locz.com.br/loczgames/advergames.pdf

Rozendaal, E., Slot, N., van Reijmersdal, E. A., & Buijzen, M. (2015). Children's Responses to Advertising in Social Games. *Journal of Gaming and Virtual Words*, *6*(2), 159–178.

Csikszentmihalyi, M. (1990). *Flow: The Psychology of Optimal Experience*. New York: Harper and Row.

Csikszentmihalyi, M., & Le Fevre, J. (1989). Optimal Experience in Work and Leisure. *Journal of Personality and Social Psychology*, *56*(5), 815–822. doi:10.1037/0022-3514.56.5.815 PMID:2724069

Dessart, L., Veloutsou, C., & Morgan-Thomas, A. (2015). Consumer Engagement in Online Brand Communities: A Social Media Perspective. *Journal of Product and Brand Management*, *24*(1), 28–42. doi:10.1108/JPBM-06-2014-0635

Deterding, S., Dixon, D., Khaled, R., & Nacke, L. (2011a) 'From game design elements to gamefulness: defining gamification', In *Proceedings of the 15th International Academic MindTrek Conference: Envisioning Future Media Environments*, ACM, pp. 9–15. 10.1145/2181037.2181040

Deterding, S., Sicart, M., Nacke, L., O'Hara, K., & Dixon, D. (2011b). *'Gamification. Using game-design elements in non-gaming contexts'*, *CHI'11 Extended Abstracts on Human Factors in Computing Systems* (pp. 2425–2428). ACM.

Dias, M., & Agante, L. (2011). Can Advergames Boost Children's Healthier Eating Habits? A Comparison between Healthy and Non-Healthy Food. *Journal of Consumer Behaviour*, *10*(1), 152–160. doi:10.1002/cb.359

Fornerino, M., Helme-Guizon, A., & Gotteland, D. (2008). Expériences cinématographiques en état d'immersion: Effets sur la satisfaction. *Recherche et Applications en Marketing*, *23*(3), 93–111. doi:10.1177/205157070802300306

Fusaro, M., & Hildgen, B. (2013). Vaincre l'insécurité numérique et dépasser le sentiment de vulnérabilité: Le cas des adolescents au Québec. *Journal of Advertising*, *19*(5), 539–573.

Deterding, S., Khaled, R., Nacke, L. E., & Dixon, D. (2014). Gamification: Toward a Definition. *Journal of Personality and Social Psychology*, *56*(5), 815–822.

Gensler, S., Volckner, Y. L., & Wiertz, C. (2013). Managing Brands in the Social Media Environment. *Journal of Interactive Marketing*, *12*(4), 242–256. doi:10.1016/j.intmar.2013.09.004

Ghani, J. A. (1991). *Flow in human-computer interactions: Tests of a model. Human factors in management information systems: An organizational perspective.* New Jersey: Ablex.

Ghani, J. A., & Deshpande, P. (1994). Task characteristics and experience of optimal flow in human-computer interaction. *The Journal of Psychology*, *128*(4), 381–391. doi:10.1080/00223980.1994.9712742

Gharbi, J., Ettis, S., & Ben Mimoun, M. S. (2003). Impact de l'atmosphère perçue des sites commerciaux sur leur performance", document non publié.

Hamari, J., Koivisto, J., & Sarsa, H. (2014). 'Does gamification work? – A literature review of empirical studies on gamification', In *Proceedings 2014 47th Hawaii International Conference on System Sciences (HICSS)*, IEEE, pp. 3025–3034. 10.1109/HICSS.2014.377

Harris, C. (2016). *Integrated game mechanics: Get the boring out of customer support.*

Helmefalk, M., & Marcusson, L. (2019). Gamification in a servicescape context: A conceptual framework. *International Journal of Internet Marketing and Advertising*, *13*(1), 22–46. doi:10.1504/IJIMA.2019.097894

Hoffman, J., & Novak, T. P. (2009). Flow online: Lessons learned and future prospects. *Journal of Interactive Marketing*, *12*(1), 23–34. doi:10.1016/j.intmar.2008.10.003

Chen, E., Cohen, S., & Miller, G. E. (2010). How Low Socioeconomic Status Affects 2-Year Hormonal Trajectories in Children. *Business Horizons*, *3*(1), 1–18. PMID:20424019

Huotari, K., & Hamari, J. (2017). A definition for gamification: Anchoring gamification in the service marketing literature. *Electronic Markets*, *27*(1), 21–31. doi:10.100712525-015-0212-z

Kapferer, J. N., & Laurent, G. (1985a). Consumers' involvement profiles: new empirical results. *Association for Consumer Research, 12*(3), 290-295.

Kapferer, J. N., & Laurent, G. (1985b). Consumers' involvement profiles: A new practical approach to consumer involvement. *Journal of Advertising Research*, *25*(6), 48–56.

Mari, M., & Poggesi, S. (2013). Servicescape cues and customer behavior: A systematic literature review and research agenda. *Service Industries Journal*, *33*(2), 171–199. doi:10.1080/02642069.2011.613934

Panda, T. K. (2004). Effectiveness of product placements in Indian films and its effects on brand memory and attitude with special reference to Hindi films. *The ICFAI Journal of Marketing Management,* August, 42-56.

Pelet, J. É, Ettis, S., & Cowart, K. (2014). Understanding Optimal Flow on Time Distortion in Social Media Experience Enhanced by Telepresence. *19ème colloque de l'AIM, AixenProvence,* May 19-21, 2014.

Rideout, V., Foehr, U., & Roberts, D. (2010). Generation M2: Media in the lives of 8 to 18-year-olds, Kaiser Family Foundation Study.

Terlutter, H., & Capella, J. (2016). The Gamiðcation of Advertising: Analysis and Research Directions of In-Game Advertising, Advergames, and Advertising in Social Network Games. *Cognitive Technology, 14*(2), 5–15.

Terlutter, R., Diehl, S., Koinig, I., & Waiguny, M. (2013). *Who Gains, Who Loses? Recall and Recognition of Brand Placements in 2D, 3D, and 4D Movies,* preprint, EMAC, Istanbul.

Trevino, L. K., & Webster, J. (1992). Flow in Computer-Mediated Communication. *Communication Research, 19*(5), 539–573. doi:10.1177/009365092019005001

Vashisht, D., Royne, M. B., & Sreejesh, S. (2019). What we know and need to know about the gamification of advertising. *European Journal of Marketing, 53*(4), 607–634. doi:10.1108/EJM-01-2017-0070

Vashisht, K., & Sreejesh, I. (2017). Impact of Game Speed and Persuasion Knowledge on Brand Recall and Brand Attitude.

Webster, J., Trevino, L. K., & Ryan, L. (1993). The dimensionality and correlates of flow in human-computer interactions. *Computers in Human Behavior, 9*(1), 411–426. doi:10.1016/0747-5632(93)90032-N

Zichermann, G., & Cunningham, C. (2011). *Gamification by design: Implementing game mechanics in Web and mobile apps.* San Francisco, CA: O'Reilly Media.

KEY TERMS AND DEFINITIONS

Flow State: The concept of flow has been introduced by Csikszentmihalyi (1975) and has been particularly studied in the context of Internet browsing. The flow is a state lived by Internet users very involved in a given activity. The flow state is considered to be a psychological concept.

Perceived Risk: It is the feeling of worry that felt a user in an act of buying online.

Socializing Feeling: It's the sense of belonging to the community.

The Advergame: Is a new form of interactive marketing characterized by its immersive and interactive nature, designed to be fun and playful.

The Telepresence Experience: It's the feeling of being physically present in a virtual environment.

This research was previously published in Utilizing Gamification in Servicescapes for Improved Consumer Engagement; pages 175-193, copyright year 2020 by Business Science Reference (an imprint of IGI Global).

Section 2
Development and Design Methodologies

Chapter 7
Augmented Reality Games

Baris Atiker
(iD) https://orcid.org/0000-0002-4622-7409
Bahcesehir University, Turkey

ABSTRACT

Augmented reality strengthens its ties with the gaming world every day. The fact that smartphones can be used as an augmented reality tool, in particular, shows this interest as a remarkable phenomenon for both gamers and game producers. The development of augmented reality applications is of great importance for the future of the gaming world, as it is not only limited to mobile phones but also covers more sophisticated devices. This research intends to evaluate how augmented reality games interpret gaming concepts and principles, through field research methods, new applications, and studies that deal with gamification, presence, immersion, and game transfer phenomena. It is also aimed to make inferences about how our daily life can be gamified in the near future thanks to augmented reality.

INTRODUCTION

One of the fastest-growing areas of digital technologies is undoubtedly the gaming industry. In addition to hardware and software developments, subjects such as digital storytelling, character design, realistic simulations, artificial intelligence, and user experience increase the connection of technology with the concept of gaming day by day.

The relationship between gaming technologies and the concept of reality has been one of the most challenged areas throughout history. Computer visualization is one of the most essential parts of the gaming experience and has become competitive with cinematic visual effects thanks to software and hardware advancements that require high processing power. In addition, the ability of computer games to make this visualization simultaneously within the experience itself has made it more effective and persuasive than the cinema.

Video games often prefer to separate the user from the real world. This isolated world, where imagination and actions are limitless, is one of the main motivations for most players to play the game, even if they are not aware of it. Because this virtual world is more exciting, fun, passionate, and competitive than the ordinary lives of the gamers.

DOI: 10.4018/978-1-6684-7589-8.ch007

Augmented Reality technology offers never-before-seen experiences in terms of matching the immersive gaming world with real life. Removing the boundaries between the virtual and real world means making these unique experiences a reality, not just for gaming, but for gamification as well.

AUGMENTED REALITY GAMES

Augmented Reality, under the umbrella of Extended Reality (XR), is an interdisciplinary subject of artificial intelligence and human-computer interaction. Augmented Reality is a technology that organically integrates physical (visual and auditory) information between the real and virtual world through computer simulation, which is difficult or impossible to experience in a certain time and place in the real world. Augmented Reality devices instantly calculate the user's position and angle framed by the camera and superimpose the digital images by matching them with the real objects in the three-dimensional environment.

Virtual and Augmented Reality games, which have become increasingly popular in recent years, have led to the need to look at the concept of reality from a different perspective. In virtual reality games, the user is fully surrounded by an artificial image, while in Augmented Reality real world is still visible. In Augmented Reality games, players can only partially disconnect from the real world. At this point, the player's presence is challenged not only mentally but also physically.

Augmented Reality uses three-dimensional motion graphics to blend digital images with the user's point of view. Unlike Virtual Reality, which creates a completely artificial environment, Augmented Reality aims to keep the user inside by creating add-ons to the real world. Because of this feature, Augmented Reality is a subset of virtual reality that is rapidly gaining ground among app developers, businesses, and gamers alike.

Augmented Reality applications have been able to overcome many technological obstacles in recent years, thanks to mobile phones that can integrate face and voice recognition technologies. Also factors such as artificial intelligence and machine learning, the Internet of Things, 5G, and cloud computing are driving the growth of Augmented Reality in coming years, making those technologies an indispensable part of the gaming industry of the future.

Augmented Reality and Gamification

Gamification refers to the use of game design elements in non-game contexts (Deterding et al., 2011). Gamification can be easily applied to almost any industry, such as entertainment and media, gaming, aerospace, defense, manufacturing, retail, education, and healthcare.

According to Alsawaier (2018), gamification is the adoption of game mechanics and dynamics to engage people, solve problems and improve the learning process. Gamification involves the use of elements traditionally found in games such as narrative, feedback, reward system, conflict, cooperation, competition, clear goals and rules, levels, trial and error, fun, interaction, interaction.

Education, which is one of the most widely used areas of gamification, contains very concrete methods both in terms of approach and goals. These concrete approaches are one of the main reasons why Augmented Reality applications have become widespread in the field of education. The relative readiness of educational content allows them to be prioritized in Augmented Reality and digital transformation.

Figure 1. JFK Moonshot AR (2019)
Source: www.jfkmoonshot.org

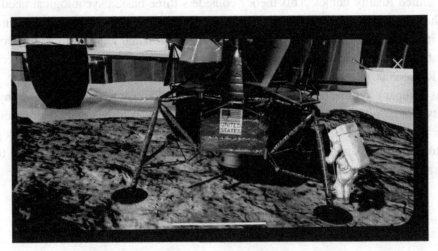

JFK Moonshot (2019), for example, relives the Apollo 11 experience that first set foot on the moon in 1969 as an Augmented Reality game and documentary (Fig. 1).

According to Kapp (2012), gamification can be broadly divided into two types: (a) Structural Gamification; (b) Content Gamification. Structural Gamification is characterized by the use of game mechanics such as badges, scoreboards, and leaderboards. In general, awards are an incentive to engage students and encourage them to continue. The content of the learning material is not like a game, only the structure around the content is gamified. The learning objectives should be clear from the start because that's how rewards can be earned. Structural Gamification "drags" the learner through the content and tries to engage it by handing out rewards.

Content gamification, on the other hand, takes advantage of game mechanics such as challenge, storytelling, feedback loops, freedom to fail, to involve students from the beginning and even without knowing their learning goals in advance. It is also perfectly possible to add these game mechanics to increase interaction and learning without designing an entire game (Kapp, 2012).

According to Barker (2017), four key components are needed to gamify any task: (a) winnable (b) promises new challenges (c) sets clear achievable goals, and (d) provides performance feedback. It is seen that Augmented Reality games easily respond to these four basic components. In particular, the interaction in form of transferring the information to the user is much more convincing and efficient, since it also contains elements from real life.

Conceptually, many games contain real-life simulations. This is the reason why gamification can be adapted to almost any real-life scenarios. These simulations have evolved from just verbal expression simulations to sensory simulations with today's technologies. Especially the proficiency of Augmented Reality games in terms of abstract, stylized, realistic, and unreal simulations brings it to the center of game and gamification studies. Of course, not only the game itself but also the player's relationship with the content and context is a simulation. This relationship determines the continuation of the game. Here, player motivation is one of the most basic tools handled in Augmented Reality games, both psychologically and physiologically.

Self-Determination theory, which is an important study on human motivation, guides us in our view of Augmented Reality games. This theory considers three basic psychological needs: (a) having meaningful choices, referring to the need for freedom and autonomy; (b) the desire to gain mastery and success rate; and (c) connecting with others who need interaction and relationships. It is very important for the player to understand what (content) and why (process) goal pursuit and goal-directed behavior is. (Deci and Ryan, 2000).

Photonlens company synthesizes the concept of physical exercise with gamification by using Augmented Reality glasses and Fighting Fit (2021) application (Fig. 2). It is a known situation that people who have exercise habits have higher motivation for being fit and healthy. Users who are separated from the gym due to Covid 19 are adding some fun and sociability to their lives by redesigning their exercise routines in a safer way in their home environment.

Figure 2. Photonlens Fighting Fit (2021)
Source: www.photonlens.com

What makes augmented reality games more advantageous than other games is that they respond to these psychological and physiological needs while increasing them in a sensory sense. Augmented reality is undoubtedly an excellent tool for gamification, not just for gaming but for all types of industries.

Serious Games and Gamification

The concept of gamification is often confused with serious games. Both terms share many common elements but it is necessary to distinguish them. Gamification uses game codes and other elements commonly found in games, for example, to make an existing training more interesting and fun. Elements such as awards, recognition, and competition are added to the training.

A serious game, on the other hand, is an education offered in the form of a game or simulation created to meet the specific needs of a group and serve a non-entertainment purpose. (Deterding et al., 2011; Laamarti et al., 2014). Serious games can be seen as games that involve targeted missions, with both real-world and non-real scenarios aimed at improving the gamers' performance and cognitive abilities (Shi and Shih, 2015).

A significant proportion of simulation-based Augmented Reality applications are seen in the serious games category. These applications that mainly focus on medicine, military, and industry are preferred because they minimize the cost, risks, margin of error and user concerns of training in a basic sense. Augmented Reality games, which can be evaluated in the field of gamification, mainly aim to entertain, focus, compete and share during training. In a comparative analysis of gamified and non-gamified balance exercises, gamified versions outperformed traditional ones. (Brumels et al., 2008)

In 2021, Microsoft signed an agreement with the US Army for five years and 21 billion dollars over the HoloLens II platform (Palladino, 2021). The use of Augmented Reality technology by military personnel both off the field and during the operation is a remarkable development within the scope of serious games (Fig. 3).

Figure 3. Microsoft HoloLens II for Military Use (2021)
Source: Microsoft

According to Deterding et al. (2011) gamification depends on four semantic components. (a) rule-based or goal-oriented structure, (b) elements as game building blocks in a real-world context, (c) design as elements of technology, and (d) non-game contexts in which gamification can be applied.

Augmented Reality games are preferred because they are one of the most suitable environments for these four components. It is seen that the training given in Augmented Reality Games, especially for educational purposes, fully overlaps with the rules and objectives of the game, real-world objects can be used as game elements, interface and digital graphics are integrated into the real world, and the place where the players are in is a part of the interaction as a non-game context.

The incorporation of gamification methods into educational context known as 'Serious Games' is still the subject of much debate, particularly among educators and society. It is used to reinforce certain learning behaviors with game elements and mechanics such as points, badges, and leaderboards (Werbach & Hunter, 2012). Particularly, the risk of falling behind the weight of educational content in general interaction compared to factors such as entertainment, competition, and immersion is the focus of discussions on this subject. However, while the personalization of the learning experience with Augmented Reality applications provides great advantages in terms of high focus and development while competing, the training content should be at the forefront as much as these factors.

CatchyWords AR (2018) is an incredibly simple yet unique and immersive word game made specifically with the Augmented Reality approach in mind (Fig. 4). To form a word, all the player has to do is move around with the device and tap the virtual objects with their phone to catch the letters.

Figure 4. Catchywords AR (2018)

Augmented Reality in the Gaming Industry

Due to social isolation along with Covid-19, Augmented and Virtual Reality tools are spreading at an accelerating rate from online shopping to entertainment and gaming. Augmented Reality technologies are facing an unprecedented demand for product imaging, interactive clothing, and games. Gamified marketing activities and even the games themselves, which are offered to consumers under the name of a pleasant experience during shopping, have started to take a much more place in our daily lives as Augmented Reality products.

Augmented Reality games are cheaper and more common in terms of accessibility than other reality (VR and MR) approach. Mobile phones, which became widespread after the 2000s, started to be used as powerful Augmented Reality tools with their visual, auditory, and tactile responses, and with this a different experience gate was opened to the game world.

Augmented Reality games promise to make this world more interesting and fun without isolating the user from the real world. Released in 2016, Pokémon Go (2016) is perhaps one of the most popular games in the Augmented Reality world. Pokémon Go became an overnight sensation, with a record 7.2 million downloads in its first week. One of the main reasons for this interest is that it not only brings an already beloved game to the world of Augmented Reality but also makes it possible to experience it simultaneously with millions of players in different parts of the real world.

Robbins (2016) has pointed out that it is so rare for a game that fundamentally changed the way we socialize and use technology to be defined as a real game. Poké Stops and Pokémon Gyms that Pokémon players use while developing their Pokémon characters with various tools, items, and training are actually physical places such as the library and gym on the maps, and the necessity of the player to walk close to these places helps to strengthen his relationship with the game and the real place (Fig. 5). The relationship between the game and the real spaces can be considered as a match rather than an overlap. Pokémon Go is an excellent example of looking at this potential for making learning fun, as it has already shown that emerging technology creates opportunities to connect and educate users in unexpected ways (Spina, 2016).

Figure 5. Pokémon Go (2016)
Source: Niantic

The increasing use of Augmented Reality technology in the gaming industry increases the market size on an accelerating scale. According to research by Facts & Factors (2021), the global Augmented and Virtual Reality Market is expected to reach US$305 Billion by 2026.

The use of Augmented Reality in gaming applications, with the inclusion of visual, auditory, and even tactile content, allows users to interact with the physical environment in different ways and further improve their gamification experience. Technology is the key driver for the Augmented Reality gaming market. Major technology providers collaborate with device and game manufacturers to provide users with immersive gaming features and experiences.

Digital Presence

In Augmented Reality games, the matching between the real and virtual worlds takes place both by tracking the user's physical movements and by the simultaneous response of digital objects to these movements. According to Riva and Mantovani (2012), it is possible to exist in the virtual environment as well as in the physical environment, because "presence" is a neurocognitive phenomenon in which the cognitive system plans actions, performs these actions, and examines the degree to which these actions are completed as intended.

In this case, the person's location is the first key to the numeric entity. These games, categorized as Location-Based Mobile Games (LBMG), mostly use the GPS features of mobile phones to act according to the user's location (de Souza e Silva, 2006).

According to Lombard and Ditton (1997), presence can be considered from six different perspectives. (a) Being as Social Wealth is primarily concerned with notions of intimacy and intimacy applied to unmediated interpersonal communication. (b) Being as realism; It concerns the degree to which an environment can produce seemingly accurate representations of objects, events, and people. (c) Being as transportation; moving the user to another location or moving the location and its contents to the user; It's about taking two or more users to a place they share. (d) Being as immersion; perceptually and psychologically related to the idea of diving (e) Being in the environment as a social actor; (f) The presence of the environment as a social actor; it is about involving users' social reactions to cues (not people or computer characters) provided by a medium itself.

The concept of presence in Augmented Reality games can be easily applied to the approach of Lombard and Ditton. First of all, social interaction in Augmented Reality games has reached great potential, although it is still in its infancy. The fact that users are in communication and interaction at the same time gives great speed to network games in terms of social wealth. In terms of realism, the concept of being is the closest environment to reality because Augmented Reality games consist of virtual interfaces superimposed on the real world. From a transportation perspective, Augmented Reality games have the power to convincingly change the look of the environment, both with virtual portals and overlay graphics. From an immersion perspective, as the user gets used to the virtual images in their world, they tend to accept them as part of reality after a while. In terms of social interaction, players from different locations can affect each other's status simultaneously. Finally, in terms of the social actor, presence can be observed as the feeling of comfort and confidence that comes from being in the actor's environment in Augmented Reality games.

Of course, the most fundamental reason for the success of Augmented Reality applications is the perfect alignment and mapping between the real and virtual worlds. Objects in the real and virtual worlds must be properly aligned with each other, otherwise, the illusion that the two worlds will coexist is jeopardized (Azuma, 1997). Augmented Reality applications rely on several matching technologies to ensure this alignment is perfect.

Similarly, the development of application contents in the field of Augmented Reality brings along the design principles of this world. Vuforia's Augmented Reality System Development Kit (SDK) uses computer vision technology for real-time detection and monitoring of image targets and three-dimensional objects (Fig. 6). The three-dimensional tracking feature uses images such as cubes, blocks, or cylinders as targets. The quick installation method is one of the main advantages of Vuforia AR SDK. This feature makes it possible to create an easy development environment for the designer and get results quickly.

Figure 6. Vuforia AR Interface.
Source: https://www.ptc.com/en/products/vuforia

Mediation Theory

The physical world is a unique source of information that provides humans with a continuous stream of images, sounds, and emotions that cannot be fully simulated by the computers yet. Mainstream games aim to fully exploit the richness of the physical world as a game resource by interlacing digital media with our daily experiences (Broll et al., 2006).

Ihde's (1993) conceptualization of technological mediation has led to a discussion of technology in mediated experiences. So, technology transforms experiences between people and the real world, and creates that subjectivity. In this respect, technology cannot be said to be neutral, but it is thought to have a subjective role in mediated experiences.

Lombard and Ditton (1997) define the concept of presence as 'the illusion of non-mediation'. This illusion effectively redefines what it means to be in one's own body. This redefinition places the virtual world and the real physical world of natural perception on an equal playing field. At this point, the artificiality of Augmented Reality images does not create any negative perception in experiencing it, and on the contrary, it ensures that it is adopted more as a means of adding the difference to the mediocrity of real life.

Many factors promote a sense of presence, such as variables related to the perception of motion, color and size of visual screens, fields of view created by various camera techniques, image quality, size, and viewing distance. Several new technologies, including Virtual and Augmented Reality, simulation rides, video conferencing, home theater, and high-definition television, are designed to provide media users with the illusion that a mediated experience is not mediated.

The "illusion of non-mediation" arises when a person cannot perceive or accept the presence of a tool in the communication environment or react as if the tool has changed there. In a sense, although all our experiences are driven by our internal sensory and perceptual systems, they are defined here as experiences without "agents", that is, without man-made technology. According to this definition, even hearing aids and glasses are "interfering" environments.

The illusion of mediation can occur in two different ways: (a) the media can be invisible or transparent and act as a large window through which the media user and media content are shared in the same physical environment; (b) the environment may seem to have changed from being a social entity to something other than a tool (Lombard & Ditton, 1997).

Augmented Reality games have started to show themselves in two different ways. Especially applications such as Google Glass are built on the principle of hiding themselves as much as possible. Augmented Reality games allow the user to react naturally to the interaction, with maximum harmony with physical environment in terms of social presence.

Although Augmented Reality becomes widespread in our lives with smartphones, it will accelerate its real development with wearable technologies. Google Glass experiences show that we are not ready yet, but soon an inclusive world is waiting to open its doors. The recent evolution of Augmented Reality tools from heavy glasses to contact lens sizes is also part of this trend.

Wearable technologies play an important role in the future of augmented reality, with their shrinking size and increasing processing power as portable computers. Contactless Augmented Reality devices such as glasses, lenses, or motion tracking devices are gradually making Augmented Reality tools invisible and unnoticeable. This will undoubtedly result in much more inclusive, inseparable, and "non-mediated experiences" in Augmented Reality games.

Physical Perception and Shared Experiences

Because interaction is an essential part of the definition of Augmented Reality, an efficient and easy-to-use experience must be provided. Augmented Reality improves a user's perception and interaction with the real world. Virtual objects show information that the user cannot perceive directly with the senses. Information transmitted by virtual objects helps a user perform real-world tasks (Azuma, 1997: 3).

Augmented Reality applications use three different approaches to provide bridging between the virtual and real-world in terms of physical perception. (a) Sign-based Augmented Reality applications use image recognition technology that relies on beacons to overlay and display Augmented Reality content in user's real-life environments. For example, MaxST Augmented Reality platform, uses two- and three-dimensional image tracking technology while superimposing virtual images on the real world through signs placed on real maps (Fig. 7).

Figure 7. MaxST Interface
Source: www.maxst.com

(b) Location-based Augmented Reality applications, operating without signs, use GPS, accelerometer, or digital compass to detect the user's location and then overlay the digital data in physical locations. They include additional features that allow them to send user notifications about new Augmented Reality content available based on their location.

Available only for iOS devices, ARKit is one of the powerful Augmented Reality creation tools. The tool uses Visual Inertial Odometry (VIO) to accurately monitor the environment (Fig. 8). Powerful face and object tracking capabilities allow 3D features and facial effects. The system also includes methods for detecting objects with simultaneous image rendering tools such as Unreal and Unity.

(c) Real-time location system (RTLS) is a location and technology-based application that operates based on technologies such as Wi-Fi, Bluetooth, Ultra-wideband UWB, and other radio frequency identification (RFID). These platforms are used in fleet tracking, navigation, inventory and asset tracking, personnel tracking, network security, and other applications.

Figure 8. ARKit 5 Demo.
Source: Apple

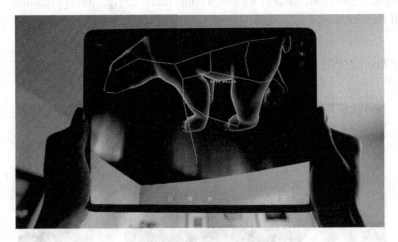

In fact, Augmented Reality games also have to consider the user's interaction with their physical environment. There is already a concern that the use of Augmented Reality games in physical spaces, and especially in public spaces, can cause distraction and unwanted accidents.

Augmented Reality games can be defined as an uninterrupted flow of user experience somewhere between real and virtual environments. This is one of the important factors that allow players to perceptually stay in the flow between physical and virtual reality.

Csikszentmihalyi (1990) defined flow as a state of mind of absolute concentration and absorption in the task at hand. In those moments when time, worries are forgotten and integrated into an activity, the flow appears. Csikszentmihalyi also discussed what facilitates flow formation and what keeps it alive, and proposed nine dimensions that should represent the optimal psychological flow state. (a) the challenge-skill balance as a challenge to the user; (b) the action-awareness dimension that combines activity with a sense of effortlessness as perceiving spontaneously or automatically; (c) clear objectives stating what users should do; (d) precise feedback that allows people to check their progress; (e) Concentration on the task, forgetting all the unpleasant aspects of life; (f) A sense of control as a release from the fear of failure; (g) Loss of self-consciousness due to not worrying about self-evaluation; (h) Time transformation as a perception of time; and (i) the autotelic experience as a fun experience at the end.

Augmented Reality games can be more advantageous than video games or virtual reality games in all nine dimensions of the flow concept. These advantages increase especially in terms of feedback, concentration, and sense of control.

Meaningful interaction in games like Neyon Clash (2020) cannot be achieved through ordinary user interfaces due to the nature of Augmented Reality experiences (Fig. 9). As a team game, Neyon Clash creates the opportunity for gamers to experience virtual interaction in the real world simultaneously. Players struggle to capture target areas in open spaces such as parks, and not being alone during this experience is an important part of the flow.

Azuma (1997) envisioned two similar approaches about Augmented Reality applications and flow connectivity, which inspired many applications in use today. Navigation systems, as one of the first approaches that come to mind for Augmented Reality, make it easier to find a way by automatically performing the virtual and real-world association step. If the user's location and direction are known, and the system has access to a digital map of the space, the Augmented Reality system can draw the map in three dimensions directly from the user's view. Today, many navigation applications are transitioning to the Augmented Reality world.

Figure 9. Neyon Clash (2020)
Source: Reaktor Berlin

The second approach is to visualize locations and events as they were in the past or as they will be after future changes have been made. They are apps available to tourists visiting historical sites such as the site of the Civil War or the Acropolis in Athens (Azuma, 1997).

The MauAR (2019) application has a documentary-like structure that conveys the Berlin Wall, which was destroyed in 1989, along with the important events of the period. Users can experience the Berlin wall, watchtowers, and military vehicles in their real size and location on a location-based basis via their mobile phones and tablets (Fig 10).

Figure 10. MauAR (2019)
Source: ZDF

Flow is also essential in learning activities. Goerner points out that augmented reality "can attract users to experience in a way that makes learning more meaningful" (Goerner, 2016).

The experience of the user in Augmented Reality games gains a significant depth when combined with the purpose of learning. Zhu et al. (2016) defines ten characteristics that an intelligent learning environment should have: (a) location sensitive; (b) context-sensitive; (c) social awareness; (d) interoperability; (e) seamless connectivity; (f) adaptable; (g) is ubiquitous; (h) the entire record; (i) natural interaction; and (j) high interaction properties.

All of these components are available in Ingress Prime AR (2018). It is the current version of the Ingress game released by the Niantic company in 2012. The game, which has the same logic as Pokémon Go, aims to transform players into heroes instead of virtual characters. (Fig. 11) Ingress is a game that pioneered the concept of Augmented Reality and location-based games, and its success has allowed Niantic to work on two of the world's largest popular culture brands.

Figure 11. Ingress Prime AR (2018)
Source: Niantic

Transformation

Augmented Reality applications can capture the perfect transition between the real and virtual worlds, with the perfect transformation of the two worlds into each other. Although this transformation may seem to be one-sided from the virtual world to the real world, the transformation is two-way. Making this calculation in two-sided transformation also includes converting the real world into digital data.

Mobile inertial measurement units (IMUs) consist of 9D sensors (acceleration, gyroscope, magnetic field) that can be worn with their small size or can be directly integrated into the auxiliary device and can detect the horizontal and vertical deviation or possible bending of the user. In this way, the user's position and viewpoint can be calculated very precisely. This transformation enables the creation of numerical graphics that will affect the user's field of view.

One of the transformations from the real world to the virtual world is the transformation of gestures as interfaces and interaction tools. Motion and gesture tracking technologies have an important place in the future of Augmented Reality games. Instead of clicking virtual buttons, users can use body language with more natural responses, simplifying the interaction interface. The ability of devices such as Microsoft Kinect and Nintendo Wii Remote to track the player's movements will be one of the biggest needs for Augmented Reality games in terms of a natural interface that changes according to the instant movements and gestures of the player. Transformation to digital media will increase both the quality of the matched object and the interaction positively.

Tokuyama et al. (2019) developed a simple and experimental Augmented Reality mirror game using a Kinect device for the activation of the brain and the exercise of the lower limbs, especially for the elderly, (Fig. 12). The game acts when the user presses virtual buttons created with Augmented Reality. The player's movements are monitored simultaneously, and the foot and button relationships are evaluated and converted into points.

Figure 12. Tokuyama AR Game (2019)

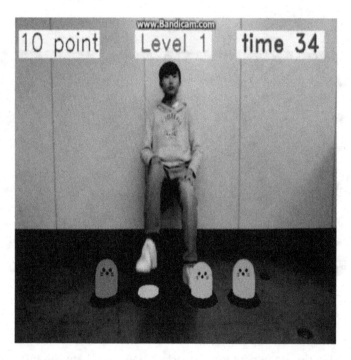

Another transformation in Augmented Reality games is the increase of the photorealistic effect of digital images. Photorealism in digital graphics is successfully achieved in movies and computer games through visual effects, but this is much more difficult to achieve in an interactive and simultaneous application. Lighting conditions, surface reflections, shadow values, and other properties should be measured automatically and in real-time. The physical properties of the real-world environment such as light, shadow, texture, and depth should be calculated digitally and immediately reflected on the user. More sophisticated lighting, texture rendering, and shading capabilities should run at interactive speeds in future scene generators (Azuma, 1997).

The capacity of today's image processors is not yet sufficient to create full realistic images simultaneously. Instead, low-quality images are deliberately and acceptably stylized and used over a small number of polygons and shading features.

Three-dimensional scanning technologies are a great way to combine real-world objects in digitized, even low resolution. LiDAR scanner technology provides ultra-detailed three-dimensional mapping that allows Augmented Reality systems to place their data in a precise and reliable location. Seeing what's going on with a smartphone is not the same as having a full 3D map of the area. The point cloud scanner created by LiDAR greatly improves the accuracy of the Augmented Reality experience. It may even be a step towards a fully developed 3D user interface.

Apple specializes in two key areas such as shrouding and motion capture, with a brand-new set of tools focused on three-dimensional Augmented Reality, called RealityKit. This technology places a virtual three-dimensional object in a real space, allowing the application to understand and evaluate where the actors are on the stage. This feature is of great importance in multiplayer scenarios of Augmented Reality games. The motion capture feature of RealityKit also makes it possible to track the joints and even facial expressions of the players, thus maximizing the interaction between the application and the user.

The speed of transformation between the virtual and real-world is just as important as the interaction itself. The emergence of 5G technology has brought with it the ideal three main features of Augmented Reality devices, namely high speed, large capacity, and low latency. These features enable the system to establish a fast and stable connection to the cloud network and provide a foundation for large-scale commercial use of augmented reality equipment and completing tasks that require high-performance computing.

Immersion

The concept of immersion experienced by many users in virtual environments refers to a user's level of physical or psychological immersion in a virtual space relative to the user's awareness of the real-world environment (Emma-Ogbangwo et al., 2014). While VR applications are undoubtedly much more advantageous in terms of immersion, they also provide important clues for Augmented Reality games.

First of all, although this concept is thought of as the abstraction of the user from his real environment, the level of immersion should be considered together with the concept of flow. While most users use a virtual reality application, they first adapt to the new environment, and the user's awareness of the environment decreases as the experience time increases. The immersion experience here is therefore not only due to the perception of being in a different environment but also to concentrate more on the experience itself after getting used to the new environment.

The continuity of the flow is directly proportional to the isolation of the actor from real space and time. The necessity of virtual and real-world matching in Augmented Reality games comes from this continuity. Any disruption greatly disrupts the immersion effect along with the flow.

Harry Potter: Wizards Unite is an Augmented Reality game that continues the success of its novels and movies, and brings reality to fantastic experiences. In the highly immersive game, players can personalize their selfies with Wizarding World-inspired lenses, frames, deformations, accessories, stickers, and many more customizable features to take their place as an official member of the wizarding world and the Stealth Statute Task Force (Fig. 13).

Figure 13. Harry Potter: Wizards Unite (2019)

When we look at the basic tools of the concept of immersion, it is seen that the psychological elements are much more dominant than the physical elements. Even the experience of reading a book is counted as an active immersion experience, although it does not contain any physical elements in itself. Similarly, the psychological immersion effect of Augmented Reality games is much greater than media such as books or movies. This is because both the psychological and physical elements match together, enriching and deepening the experience.

Another advantage of Augmented Reality games is the emphasis on personalized experience. Especially, users who experience Augmented Reality games in their natural environment are under the influence of the psychological sensations created by a safe and comfortable environment without being aware of it. This naturally strengthens the immersion experience in Augmented Reality games.

One of the important elements that increase the immersion effect is that the actions of the player find their response in the virtual world without any delay. As mentioned before, the users' facial expressions and body language as an interaction tool simplifies and facilitates both the interaction and the environment interface. Tracking hand movements, such as the user touching a virtual object in Augmented Reality games, can be seen as both guidance and a control system. In perfect match scenarios, the user will more easily adopt the illusion that virtual objects belong to the real world. Body/system feedback establishes a perceptual continuity in a relationship where the body feels in an area that "feels" the body (Domingues & Miranda, 2019).

Matching Augmented Reality applications with the real world in terms of immersion concept is possible by calculating depth perception. If the virtual object is positioned behind the real object, the real object must cover the virtual object. Visualization of occluded objects often misleads users' perception if this situation is not properly addressed (Kasapakis and Gavalas, 2017). In other words, the positions of the objects on the depth axis reveal the concept of occlusion in the matching of virtual and real-world objects.

The concept of occlusion is related to the fact that the interaction between two different worlds is in a continuous flow and cannot be separated from each other, just like immersion. With occlusion, digital images are placed not only on top of real-world images but also between them. Google ARCore can calculate the distance between objects using its computer visualization (Raw Depth API) to perfectly place virtual objects between real objects (Fig. 14). This means that a virtual object is created not only from the user's point of view but also associated with real objects.

Figure 14. Google ARCore Occlusion (2020)
Source: Google

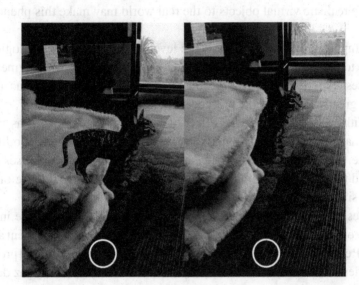

The approach to addressing the problem of covering virtual objects in Augmented Reality consists of three steps. The first step is the selection of an object to cover the virtual object. Here, all pixels in the image are divided into two classes, object, and background. In the second step, the edge boundaries of the object are tracked and averaged based on the displacement of the tracking points. In the third and final step, all pixels within the object boundaries are redrawn according to the position between the real and virtual object (Tian, Guan, & Wang, 2010).

Game Transfer Phenomenon

The effects of the transformation between the virtual and real-world on the user indicate an interesting phenomenon both during and after the experience. In terms of simulations of real-world environments, there is an integration between Augmented Reality games and the use of Virtual Reality headsets. This integration challenges our perceptions of reality for two important reasons: (a) virtuality allows us to live parallel lives in unreal worlds by embracing virtual identities and materializing fantasies (Ryan, 1999) and (b) the results of virtual immersion, seeing or hearing elements in the game after playing may facilitate and/or promote post-game phenomena that occur as hallucinatory-like experiences (Ortiz de Gortari and Griffiths, 2017).

The Game Transfer Phenomenon (GTP) is the habit of bringing gaming experiences to the real-world. It is a psychological phenomenon encountered by the reflection of audio-visual and even scripted elements in the player's real life after an intense and long gaming experience. According to many studies conducted since the 1990s, when the human mind encounters a different situation after intense activity, it cannot quickly adapt to the new situation. In addition, while the natural conditioning reflex of the human brain is shown as one of the reasons for this phenomenon, the similarities between the game and the real-world can trigger some behaviors in users.

In Augmented Reality games, the probability of experiencing GTP is greatly increased due to the interaction with the digital world without leaving the real world completely. The user may not be fully aware of the distinction between the two worlds subconsciously. Even with advancing technologies, the perfect match of more realistic virtual objects to the real world may make this phenomenon even more uncertain.

One of the most important factors for GTP is the level of physical or psychological immersion in a virtual space relative to the user's awareness of the real-world environment. Augmented Reality applications offer the closest experience to reality as they contain digital elements placed in the real world. This experience also greatly facilitates the presence and immersion experience.

Gortari and Griffiths (2014) revealed the effect of GTP on behaviors such as visual and auditory perceptions such as images, visual effects, sounds and music related to the game, bodily perceptions such as acting as in a game, and mental processes such as automated thoughts, impulses or repetitive tasks; LaViola (2000) stated that these perceptual effects are directly related to the use of highly immersive technologies such as simulators and head-mounted displays.

Virtual experiences like Augmented Reality have proven to be commonplace in the lives of many gamers. The interplay of physiological, perceptual, and cognitive processes is evident among the different manifestations of GTP experiences. This is particularly important given the gradual proliferation of highly immersive technologies that are expected to amplify the effects of the GTP (Ortiz de Gortari, 2015).

CONCLUSION

Despite the increasing interest in recent years, there are still significant challenges for Augmented Reality applications to overcome. One of the most important factors hindering the development of Augmented Reality applications is ergonomic problems. Devices that are being developed in the field of wearable technologies such as augmented reality glasses, which have a much greater impact and efficiency compared to the limited interaction of mobile phones, struggle with a number of problems in terms of both hardware and accessibility on the ergonomic axis.

Pribeanu (2012) describes the ergonomics quality of augmented reality applications; it deals with 3 aspects on the axis of usability; ease of understanding, ease of learning how to operate, and ease of operating with a software system. In this case, physical, mental and software issues that affect usability should always be considered.

The most important physical problem is that the weight of augmented reality devices is not yet at an acceptable level. This weight reveals physical discomforts such as pain, dizziness and nausea in long-term use. This problem will begin to disappear as the sizes of components such as processor and ram, which are required for the conversion of HMD and glasses into image processing devices, become smaller.

The bridging feature of AR applications between the real and virtual worlds brings along many ergonomic mental problems. These AR experiences, which are much more "interesting" than real life, can cause addiction due to the level of immersion. The length of time users stay in the AR world will increase as wearable AR devices become more and more common in our lives. In fact, Game Transfer Phenomenon, which is the situation where virtual objects continue to be detected after leaving the augmented reality world, contains important determinations about this problem. (Ortiz de Gortari, 2017)

Finally, the interface design and software features of augmented reality applications can have a negative impact on the instinctive behavior of users. If the system does not warn the user of these dangers, it is very likely that unwanted accidents will occur. Security is a vital issue in placing users of Augmented Reality applications between the real and virtual world. In the perfect immersion experience, which is indistinguishable from the real, especially in theoretical matters, the user may think that real items are virtual. Such applications must be strictly controlled by security and various regulations.

Sharks in the Park (2016) is the first release of Geo AR Games' world's first geospatial Augmented Reality game for kids. By enclosing the real playground with virtual borders, it prevents children from encountering dangerous situations such as getting on the road. (Fig. 15).

Figure 15. Shark in the Park Game Warning Screen

Another problem regarding the accessibility of AR is the high prices of devices such as glasses and lenses, which offer a more immersive and high-quality experience. The main reason for this is hardware features such as high-capacity processors and display, which are mandatory to match the application with the real world.

The fact that Augmented Reality technologies still have a limited number and variety of content is one of the biggest challenges for society to realize its Augmented Reality use potential. Although face-altering applications such as Instagram filters, aging, and Snapchat are attracting a lot of attention, they provide a one-way experience that is far from gamification.

Augmented Reality for the gaming industry, which has accelerated in recent years, will not be limited to a few new technology use cases as in previous years. Augmented Reality will undoubtedly be everywhere and will touch every sector. Beyond its default application in the gaming and entertainment industries, Augmented Reality has groundbreaking potential in healthcare, education, marketing, business, as well as government and non-governmental sectors.

One of Azuma's (1997) predictions is that Augmented Reality applications are perceived as technological innovations that will replace employees in many companies. Augmented Reality can do a good job in this respect when it is designed as a tool to facilitate the user's work rather than a phenomenon that completely replaces the human worker. At this point, social and political concerns should not be ignored before many experimental applications reach the end-user.

In terms of future developments, the use of Augmented Reality environments that can allow collaborative and spatial learning everywhere through computer simulations, games, models, and virtual objects in real environments may become strongly widespread (Broll et al. 2008). 5G technology, especially in mobile-based Augmented Reality games, with shorter latency, less vibration, and less data loss, can bring the world closer together and provide a more realistic perception of real cloud gaming services.

A great development is observed around cloud computing and the Internet of Things. Average consumers own between five and eight mobile-connected devices. In the gaming world, this means that the number of devices that can be directly connected to the network, from smartwatches to Augmented Reality glasses will increase, the wire will be cut forever, and three-dimensional games will bring people much closer together. In addition, cloud network technology will significantly alleviate Augmented Reality devices, as it can solve the need for hardware with high processing power through remotely accessed powerful computers.

The next decade will begin to see some significant developments that will allow cloud computing and cloud-based Augmented Reality games to become more general opportunities for end-users and companies. With the development of Cloud Augmented Reality technology, it is expected that wearable Augmented Reality devices will be rapidly developed and become popular. The mobility demand of AR technology will increase immediately and the demand for 5G technology will grow.

In the future, Augmented Reality will reshape the way people interact with computers, such as holographic graphical user interfaces that will completely change the relationship between the real and digital worlds. Tilt Five AR (2021) is one of the prototypes for the future of Augmented Reality games. It transforms traditional tabletop games through the Augmented Reality and hologram approach, uniting all players at the same table regardless of location (Fig. 16).

Figure 16. Tilt Five AR (2021)
Source: www.tiltfive.com

Sheridan (1992) has asked "What do new technological interfaces add beyond the ways in which our imaginations (our mental models) have been mobilized by writers and artists for centuries, and how do they affect this emotion? His answers given to the questions also give us important clues about the future of Augmented Reality games. The first answer is the degree of sensory information, namely resolution, colors, sound quality, naturalness of movement, etc. elements are reaching new levels of reality that have never been before. Second, the player can control the actions in the game, react to certain changes in the environment and respond to stimuli created by the environment or expressions as simulated figures. Thirdly, the player can control not only his movements but also all the parameters of the virtual environment, so that he can even play against himself.

Artificial intelligence and the Internet of Things will play a major role in overcoming today's obstacles in terms of Augmented Reality games. Torres Vega et al. (2020) state that there are two challenges in combining AR/VR applications with the Internet of Things. Integration and management of direct connections between two AR/VR devices and the semantification of AR/VR data for its interoperability as offered by appropriate IoT platforms. Current peer-to-peer connections are far from allowing the management of both Iot and AR/VR devices. They also state that there is need for a holistic solution that combines data from traditional IoT devices (sensors) with AR/VR data in a single platform, combining semantic interoperability with state-of-the-art techniques for achieving a high quality of service at the connection layer. Applications that can perform more and more successful predictive analysis will be able to offer users much more reliable interactions through Augmented Reality devices. In addition, computer vision will increase human vision more than ever by analyzing real-world objects around the user more thoroughly.

REFERENCES

Alsawaier, R. (2018). The effect of gamification on motivation and engagement. *International Journal of Information and Learning Technology*, *35*(1), 56–79. doi:10.1108/IJILT-02-2017-0009

Azuma, R. T. (1997). A survey of augmented reality. *Presence (Cambridge, Mass.)*, *6*(4), 355–385. doi:10.1162/pres.1997.6.4.355

Barker, E. (2017). *Barking up the wrong tree: The surprising science behind why everything you know about success is (mostly) wrong*. HarperCollins.

Broll, W., Lindt, I., Herbst, I., Ohlenburg, J., Braun, A. K., & Wetzel, R. (2008). Toward next-gen mobile AR games. *IEEE Computer Graphics and Applications*, *28*(4), 40–48. doi:10.1109/MCG.2008.85

Broll, W., Ohlenburg, J., Lindt, I., Herbst, I., & Braun, A. K. (2006). Meeting technology challenges of pervasive augmented reality games. *Proc 5th ACM SIGCOMM Workshop Network System Support Games*, 28–39. 10.1145/1230040.1230097

Brumels, K. A., Blasius, T., Cortright, T., Daniel, O., & Brent, S. (2008). Comparison of efficacy between traditional and video game based balance programs. *Clin Kinesiol*, *62*, 26–31.

Csikszentmihalyi, M. (1990). *The psychology of optimal experience*. HarperCollins.

de Souza e Silva, A., & Delacruz, G. C. (2006). Hybrid reality games reframed: Potential uses in educational contexts. *Games and Culture*, *1*(3), 231–251. doi:10.1177/1555412006290443

Deci, E. L., & Ryan, R. M. (2000). The "what" and "why" of goal pursuits: Human needs and the self-determination of behavior. *Psychological Inquiry*, *11*(4), 227–268. doi:10.1207/S15327965PLI1104_01

Deterding, S., Dixon, D., Khaled, R., & Nacke, L. (2011). From game design elements to gamefulness: defining "Gamification". *15th International Academic MindTrek Conference*. 10.1145/2181037.2181040

Domingues, D. M., & Miranda, M. R. (2019). Affective presence in enactive immersive space: Sensorial and mobile technologies reengineering life. In E. Simão & C. Soares (Eds.), *Trends, Experiences, and Perspectives in Immersive Multimedia and Augmented Reality* (pp. 23–51). IGI Global. doi:10.4018/978-1-5225-5696-1.ch002

Emma-Ogbangwo, C., Cope, N., Behringer, R., & Fabri, M. (2014). Enhancing user immersion and virtual presence in interactive multiuser virtual environments through the development and integration of a gesture- centric natural user interface developed from existing virtual reality technologies. *HCI International*. https://bit.ly/3w5uzIn

Goerner, P. (2016). Augmented reality: What's next? *School Library Journal*, *62*(9), 19–20.

Ihde, D. (1993). *The philosophy of technology*. Paragon House.

Kapp, K. (2012). *The Gamification of Learning and Instruction: Game-based Methods and Strategies for Training and Education*. Pfeiffer.

Kasapakis, V., & Gavalas, D. (2017). Revisiting design guidelines for pervasive games. *International Journal of Pervasive Computing and Communications*, *13*(4), 386–407. doi:10.1108/IJPCC-D-17-00007

Laamarti, F., Eid, M., & Saddik, A. (2014). An overview of serious games. *International Journal of Computer Games Technology*, *2014*, 1–15. doi:10.1155/2014/358152

LaViola, J. A. Jr. (2000). Discussion of cybersickness in virtual environments. *SIGCHI Bulletin*, *32*(1), 47–56. doi:10.1145/333329.333344

Lombard, M., & Ditton, T. (1997). At the Heart of It All: The Concept of Presence. *Journal of Computer-Mediated Communication*, *3*(2), 0. Advance online publication. doi:10.1111/j.1083-6101.1997.tb00072.x

Ortiz de Gortari, A. B. (2015). What can game transfer phenomena tell us about the impact of highly immersive gaming technologies? In *Proceedings from ITAG'15:2015 International conference on interactive technologies and games* (pp. 84–89). 10.1109/iTAG.2015.15

Ortiz de Gortari, A. B. (2017). *Game Transfer Phenomena and the Augmented Reality Game Pokémon Go: The prevalence and the relation with benefits, risks, immersion and motivations. 22nd Annual Cyber Psychology, Cyber Therapy & Social Networking*.

Ortiz De Gortari, A. B., & Griffiths, M. (2017). Beyond the Boundaries of the Game: The Interplay Between In-Game Phenomena, Structural Characteristics of Video Games, and Game Transfer Phenomena. In Boundaries of Self and Reality Online. Academic Press.

Ortiz de Gortari, A. B., & Griffiths, M. D. (2014). Automatic mental processes, automatic actions and behaviours in game transfer phenomena: An empirical self-report study using online forum data. *International Journal of Mental Health and Addiction*, *12*(4), 432–452. doi:10.100711469-014-9476-3

Palladino, T. (2021). *Microsoft emerges from the trenches with more details behind the army edition of Hololens 2*. Retrieved from https://hololens.reality.news/news/microsoft-emerges-from-trenches-with-more-details-behind-army-edition-hololens-2-0384713/

Pribeanu, C. (2012). Specification and Validation of a Formative Index to Evaluate the Ergonomic Quality of an AR-based Educational Platform. *International Journal of Computers, Communications & Control*, *7*(4), 721–732. doi:10.15837/ijccc.2012.4.1370

Riva, G., & Mantovani, F. (2012). Being There: Understanding the Feeling of Presence in a Synthetic Environment and Its Potential for Clinical Change. *Virtual Reality in Psychological, Medical and Pedagocical Applications*. IntechOpen., *28*. Advance online publication. doi:10.5772/46411

Robbins, M. B. (2016). The future of gaming. *Library Journal*, *141*(15), 59.

Ryan, M. L. (1999). Immersion vs. interactivity: Virtual reality and literary theory. *SubStance*, *28*(2), 110–137. doi:10.1353ub.1999.0015

Sheridan, T. B. (1992). Musings on telepresence and virtual presence. *Presence (Cambridge, Mass.)*, *1*(1), 120–126. doi:10.1162/pres.1992.1.1.120

Shi, Y., & Shih, J. (2015). Game factors and game-based learning design model. *International Journal of Computer Games Technology*. *Article ID*, *549684*, 1–11.

Spina, C. (2016). Libraries embrace Pokémon Go. *School Library Journal*, *62*(8), 12–13.

Tian, Y., Guan, T., & Wang, C. (2010). Real-time occlusion handling in augmented reality based on an object tracking approach. *Sensors (Basel)*, *10*(4), 2885–2900. doi:10.3390100402885 PMID:22319278

Tokuyama, Rajapakse, Yamabe, Konno, & Hung. (2019). A kinect-based augmented reality game for lower limb exercise. *Proc. - 2019 Int. Conf. Cyberworlds*, 399–402.

Torres Vega, M., Liaskos, C., Abadal, S., Papapetrou, E., Jain, A., Mouhouche, B., Kalem, G., Ergüt, S., Mach, M., Sabol, T., Cabellos-Aparicio, A., Grimm, C., De Turck, F., & Famaey, J. (2020). Immersive Interconnected Virtual and Augmented Reality: A 5G and IoT Perspective. *Journal of Network and Systems Management*, *28*(4), 796–826. doi:10.100710922-020-09545-w

Werbach, K., & Hunter, D. (2012). *For the win: How game thinking can revolutionize your business*. Wharton Digital Press.

Zhu, Z., Yu, M., & Riezebos, P. (2016). A research framework of smart education. *Smart Learning Environments*, *3*(1), 1–17. doi:10.118640561-016-0026-2

This research was previously published in Next-Generation Applications and Implementations of Gamification Systems; pages 221-243, copyright year 2022 by Engineering Science Reference (an imprint of IGI Global).

Chapter 8
How to Engineer Gamification:
The Consensus, the Best Practice and the Grey Areas

Alimohammad Shahri
Bournemouth University, Poole, UK

Mahmood Hosseini
Bournemouth University, Poole, UK

Keith Phalp
Bournemouth University, Poole, UK

Jacqui Taylor
Bournemouth University, Poole, UK

Raian Ali
Bournemouth University, Poole, UK

ABSTRACT

Gamification refers to the use of game elements in a business context to change users' behaviours, mainly increasing motivation towards a certain task or a strategic objective. Gamification has received a good deal of emphasis in both academia and industry across various disciplines and application areas. Despite the increasing interest, we still need a unified and holistic picture on how to engineer gamification, including the meaning of the term, its development process, the stakeholders and disciplines which need to be involved in it, and the concerns and risks that an ad-hoc design could raise for both businesses and users. To address this need, this article reports on empirical research which involved reviewing the literature and a range of gamification techniques and applications as secondary research, and an expert opinion study of two phases, qualitative and quantitative, as primary research. Based on the results, we provide a body of knowledge about gamification and point-out good practice principles and areas of gamification that are debatable and need further investigation.

DOI: 10.4018/978-1-6684-7589-8.ch008

1. INTRODUCTION

Games have long been a part of culture as a means of entertainment, building relationships, and learning and training (McGonigal, 2011). In recent times, the digitization of games has caused a spike in their use and involvement in everyday lives of many people. According to ESA (ESA, 2014), the average game player is now aged 31 years, 48% of players being female thus shaping the gamers population. The success of games in keeping their users engaged and motivated has led researchers studying the phenomena in more depth to identify constructs in games that enable such engagement and sustainability in users' motivation and utilize them for goals beyond mere entertainment (Seaborn & Fels, 2015). These studies have resulted in various strategies, such as gamification, to pursue these goals.

Gamification is used to increase motivation and engagement in its target users in favor of changing their behaviors towards desired ones. There are several successful applications of gamification available in the literature encouraging various goals, such as adopting a healthier lifestyle (Johnson et al., 2016; Pløhn & Aalberg, 2015), increasing students' engagement with class activities in order to achieve better results (O'Donovan, Gain, & Marais, 2013; Simões, Redondo, & Vilas, 2013), or increasing quality and productivity in a business environment (Robson, Plangger, Kietzmann, McCarthy, & Pitt, 2016; Rodrigues, Oliveira, & Costa, 2016). For example, in a business environment, such as a call center, various game elements such as points and leader-boards could be used to reflect the performance of employees, e.g., the number of calls answered, the number of issues solved, the time taken for finishing tasks, and the customers' satisfaction (InterAksyon, 2012).

In order to understand gamification, the differences between play and game need to be addressed. According to Caillois & Barash (1961), play (paidia) is described as free-form, expressive, improvisational behaviors and meanings. Game (ludus), on the other hand, is rule-based engagement with pre-determined goals. Gamification, as the name suggests, is more focused on ludus, nevertheless, as (Alfrink, 2011) suggests, users are not given much flexibility to improvise their behaviors, and they have to do/achieve pre-determined tasks/goals. Despite the opinions of (Abt, 1987; Bogost, 2011) for excluding playfulness, playful design, and playful interaction from gamification, it is believed that gamification can also facilitate playful behaviors and entertainment to achieve its goals (Groh, 2012). However, including entertainment in a gamification design does not guarantee its success (Berkling & Thomas, 2013).

Since coining the term, several attempts have been made to establish a standard and commonly accepted definition (Deterding, Dixon, Khaled, & Nacke, 2011; Huotari & Hamari, 2012; Werbach & Hunter, 2012). However, there are still many gaps, debates, and ambiguities within the literature that are yet to be investigated. For example, it is not clear which constructs and properties shape gamification, and how it can be differentiated sharply from other similar concepts, such as serious games or games with purpose. Moreover, despite some attempts made towards introducing a methodology for designing gamification from a business-oriented point of view (Herzig, Ameling, Wolf, & Schill, 2015a), it is not yet clear which stakeholders and which fields of study need to be involved in the design process of gamification in a wider perspective, e.g., impacts on social and mental aspects. In addition, there are several debates on when gamification can be introduced to an environment, what concerns it produces and which considerations may lead to a successful design of gamification in that environment. Finally, what issues, from legal or ethical perspective, may arise by the use of gamification and how these issues need to be tackled.

In this paper, we conduct empirical research to gather opinions from experts in the domain of gamification and reflect on that to identify best practice guidelines and point out dissimilarities and areas that need further investigation. Finally, we provide a body of knowledge with regards to gamification design, which informs researchers and practitioners in their future work.

2. LITERATURE AND RESEARCH MOTIVATION

Deterding et al., (2011) define gamification as "the use of game design elements in a non-game context", emphasizing that the final product will not be a game. Despite this emphasis, there are several instances of considering gamification as serious games or even considering both to be the same concept (Kapp, 2012). An alternative definition of gamification is introduced by Huotari & Hamari (2012) as a rules-based service system that provides feedback and interaction mechanism to the user with an aim to facilitate and support the users' overall value creation. In addition to increasing motivation and engagement, their definition of gamification emphasizes that adding gamification to a working environment should lead to the creation of added value to the business, for example., increasing staff engagement with the affordance of graceful experience. However, Deterding et al., (2011) criticize this definition for being not specific enough, indicating that with this definition, even a touch screen on a vending machine would be considered as a gamified application.

Other criticisms to gamification, mainly from experts in gaming, suggest that gamification is focused on the least important aspects of games and is being used as a tool for mere "pontification", whereas games have storylines and valuable contents for their players (Chorney, 2013) that are missing in gamification. The lack of aforementioned features removes the entertainment and makes the task only challenging, whereas games should be "interestingly hard and difficult", giving players joy while performing and achieving a goal (Robertson, 2010). In addition, Antin & Deterding (2012) suggest and stress the importance of intrinsic motivation and "meaningful play" for gamification and state a gamification design that does not understand the needs and requirements of its stakeholders is destined to fail.

The design of gamification can target both intrinsic and extrinsic motivation. A design of gamification that targets the intrinsic motivation can deepen the motivation and engagement. It is argued that introducing extrinsic motivation through gamification in order to motivate users may only have short-term positive results (Antin & Deterding, 2012; Lazzaro, 2011). Despite this argument, it is suggested that extrinsic motivation should not be excluded or should not be considered as a separate a source of motivation, considering extrinsic motivation to be equally important as intrinsic motivation (Reiss, 2012; Ryan & Deci, 2000). This suggestion is made based on the fact that not everyone is intrinsically motivated and the presence of extrinsic motivation can persuade these people to be more engaged.

Gamification is a multidisciplinary field and research on gamification has been conducted within computer science (Pedreira, García, Brisaboa, & Piattini, 2015), psychology (Linehan, Kirman, & Roche, 2015; Scekic, Truong, & Dustdar, 2013), sociology (Huotari & Hamari, 2012), health (McCallum, 2012; Pløhn & Aalberg, 2015), and marketing (Hamari & Lehdonvirta, 2010; Hofacker, de Ruyter, Lurie, Manchanda, & Donaldson, 2016). Regarding the discipline, gamification is focused on changing the behavior of its users and is mainly based on software technology. Therefore, it is crucial for the design to consider the needs and requirements of end-users in the design process. This aspect of gamification urges a user-cantered design process. An ad-hoc design of gamification, without considering its compliance with its users' needs and perceptions, not only may hinder the ultimate goal of motivating users, but also may cause adverse side effects such as discouragement or demotivation, or even threaten the well-being of its end-users in a business context (Shahri, Hosseini, Phalp, Taylor, & Ali, 2014). Therefore, it is necessary for a successful gamification design to follow a systematic approach towards implementing gamification to avoid such pitfalls.

(Herzig, Jugel, Momm, Ameling, & Schill, 2013) provided *GaML,* which is a modelling language intended for designing gamification. GaML is built on atomic motivational elements that is based on (Deterding et al., 2011) taxonomy, and adds visual motivational elements, such as avatars. Moreover, Herzig et al., (2015) have proposed a methodology specifically designed for gamification, suggesting four high-level phases of business modelling and requirements, design, implementation, and monitoring and adaptation. They consider gamification as a software development and define five main stakeholders to be involved in the gamification process; end-users, gamification experts, domain experts, business experts, and IT experts. These methods and languages are acceptable from a business point of view, aiming at increasing user engagement and productivity. However, it is argued that measuring the success of a gamification design should not be narrowed down to the business goals of the environment, and should consider the social and mental well-being of its users in addition (Shahri et al., 2014). Gartner Group in their report (Gartner.com, 2011) predicted that "more than 50 percent of organizations that manage innovation processes will gamify those processes", and later suggested that poor design will lead to 80 percent of gamified applications failing to meet their organizational and business goals (Gartner.com, 2012). Therefore, we argue that a systematic approach and involving more stakeholders should lead to a better design of gamification.

3. METHODOLOGY

We adopted a sequential mixed methods approach (Creswell, Plano Clark, Gutmann, & Hanson, 2003). Initially, interviews with six experts were used to collect rich qualitative data and form the basis for the survey questions. The survey, completed by 40 experts, was used to collect quantitative data and analyzed using descriptive statistics. The survey was followed by interviews with 12 gamification users, namely five managers and seven employees, to enable a variety of perspectives to be included.

3.1. Exploratory Phase

Semi-structured interviews were used, which allowed some flexibility in both the order that questions were asked and the prompts required to request elaboration, stimulate discussion, or creation of new questions. The new questions were used in the next interviews and were also added to the survey.

3.1.1. Identification of Experts for Interviews

The aim of this phase was to gather important aspects of gamification from a design perspective. To identify experts, we looked for high impact peer-reviewed publications available in the literature, and to gather a diversity of viewpoints, we invited experts from different affiliation types (academia and industry), fields of expertise (business, management, gaming, education), and countries. To prevent biased or skewed results, the selected interviewees had no work in common. Since we were looking for opinions from different perspectives, we invited people who have implemented gamification in practice, along with those who only worked with theoretical foundations of gamification.

Six experts agreed to participate in the interview phase of our research; four from academia (with one of them collaborating closely with industry), and two from industry. Three were involved in developing theoretical frameworks for gamification, and three others had developed and applied gamification in practice. Experts with more focus on academic and theoretical aspects had also implemented gamification in practice as part of their studies for evaluation purposes. Hence, they also encountered practical complications. The experts came from different countries and had different level of expertise with gamification; UK 4 years, South Africa 3 years, USA 4 years, Portugal 3 years, Germany 4 years, and Canada 10 years of expertise.

3.1.2. Interview Process

The average time per interview was 39 minutes (minimum 27, maximum 50). Questions were sent to the interviewees in advance which made the actual interview more efficient and focused. After describing the aims of the study, interviewees were asked for their consent for recording the conversation. Once ethical procedures were confirmed, interviewees were asked to talk about their expertise with gamification, to ensure we had gathered the correct information through their public profiles (e.g., for how long they worked on gamification, where and in which domain). Before the interviews started, we tested and refined the interview questions via one pilot interview.

3.1.3. Data Analysis

The recorded interviews were transcribed and the text was content-analyzed to extract important issues. These issues were then grouped together to form a number of sub-themes. Two researchers worked on the analysis and when a disagreement emerged, a third researcher was consulted to take a final decision. The questionnaire items, discussed in the next section, were formed based on the agreed themes.

3.2. Confirmatory Phase

This quantitative phase used a survey study designed to confirm and enhance the findings of the first qualitative phase, i.e. the interviews. The questionnaire included multiple-choice questions and an open text box at the end of each general question for participants to add any additional comments. The questionnaire was piloted on two participants and refined to ensure any ambiguity was removed.

3.2.1. Identification of Participants

We invited authors of peer-reviewed and published papers via email to take part in the survey. The survey was designed to do find consensus, grey areas, and debatable aspects of gamification amongst the experts. A link to the questionnaire was then sent to each expert who accepted the invitation. The characteristics of the participants are summarized in Table 1. Given the novelty of the concept, the participants who specified their level of practical experience with gamification as medium are still experts in areas which are core for gamification, e.g., incentive-centered design, cyber-psychology and HCI. One expert stated low practical expertise, since their expertise was on the psychological aspect of gamification. However, their participation was valuable as it helped in balancing the view and opinions elicited from industrial and academic perspectives.

Table 1. Characteristics of the participants

Years of Experience			Level of Practical Experience		
Min	1		Expert	7	18%
Max	10		High	18	45%
Mean	3.12		Medium	14	35%
Median	3		Low	1	3%
Mode	3		None	0	0%

As in the qualitative phase, experts from different affiliations were invited to ensure diversity of perspectives and opinions. The distribution of participants based on their field of study and country can be found in Table 2.

Table 2. Distribution of participants

Participants per Country				Participants per Area of Expertise			
UK	11	Switzerland	2	Education	11	Exertion Interfaces	1
USA	6	China	1	Psychology	7	General	1
Netherlands	6	Italy	1	Enterprise	4	HCI	1
France	3	Japan	1	Tourism	4	Marketing	1
Germany	3	Taiwan	1	Linguistics	3	Modelling and Theory	1
Portugal	2	Norway	1	Game Design	2	Sociology	1
Spain	2			Software Ergonomics	2	Software Engineering	1

3.2.2. Survey Procedure

Forty-eight experts started the survey and 40 of them successfully completed it. In addition to the descriptive statistics, we have analyzed the comments given by the experts at the end of each question to identify further insights and explanation for the statistics.

4. RESULTS

The data from the two phases have been integrated and therefore the results are presented here under the following eight areas:

- Defining gamification
- Relevant fields and disciplines
- Stakeholders
- When to use gamification
- Concerns and considerations in development

- Systematic approaches
- Ethics
- Best practice recommendations

In the following, we present the results of our study in percentages. Hereafter, we use SD for strongly disagree, D for Disagree, N for neutral, A for agree, and SA for strongly agree throughout the paper.

4.1. Definition and Differences in the Perception of Gamification

The interviewees were asked to give their definition of gamification, its core elements and peculiarities in comparison to other closely-related concepts such as serious games and games with purpose. We asked these questions as we observed different definitions and understandings in the literature about gamification. There is no agreed definition currently available, or a taxonomy which accommodates the commonality and variability of those definitions, although attempts to put a standardized definition have been made (Deterding et al., 2011; Groh, 2012; Huotari & Hamari, 2012). We extracted 10 themes from the interviews which were developed into 10 statements, see Table 3.

The results show there is a considerable amount of diverse opinion on the nuances of some statements. Experts do not share a common view on gamification relation with serious games and games with purpose. One debatable statement was S1.1 where there was a belief that gamification will convert a task into a game. Despite several statements in the literature that gamification only uses game design elements, and is not a game per se, a considerable proportion of opinions (29%) did not agree with this statement. Moreover, S1.9 shows that despite gamification being reasonably defined in the literature, still it cannot be differentiated from serious games and games with purpose. Only eight per cent disagreement was observed on S1.10, while the same question was debatable when applied on serious games and games with purpose in S1.8. One view believed that there is a "grey area between gamification and serious games" and deciding whether it is gamification or serious games depends on the "perspective of people who are making the decision". On the other hand, some others believed that "gamification is about adding game elements to a non-gaming context" where serious games are "applied games used to deliver more than just entertainment".

Another debatable statement was S1.4 where an uncertainty amongst the opinions can be observed about should gamification be added to an already designed business process or it can be designed and added to an environment before or while designing the business processes.

4.2. Relevant Fields of Study

The next question in the interview was designed to collect opinions about the fields of study that should be involved in the development process of gamification. From the interviews, we retrieved seven different fields of study, and then confirmed and enriched the list through the survey. The statements and the results are provided in Table 4.

User experience, HCI, psychology, and game design seem to be highly recommended fields to be involved in the development process of gamification. The percentages suggest that management and human resources, behavioral economics, and software engineering could be involved in the process as well, perhaps with less importance in comparison to the others. It was signified that gamification might not be always software-based, e.g., bulletin boards with ticks for points in small teams, or it might use technology very limitedly, such as screens in public places with some indicators of collective performance. These settings make software engineering and HCI less relevant. Finally, by analyzing the added comments, social science was recommended by a number of respondents as a relevant field, e.g., to study group dynamics.

Table 3. Statements for Definitions and Perspectives

	Statements	Results in Percentages					Stn. Dev.	Mean
		SD	D	N	A	SA		
S1.1	Gamification will convert a task to a game	28	31	13	21	8	0.12	2.42
S1.2	Gamification is meant to achieve a certain users' behavior when doing certain tasks, e.g., more engagement and motivation	0	5	5	56	33	0.25	4.15
S1.3	Gamification is not standalone and it should be always designed to work in conjunction with certain task(s)	0	0	8	39	53	0.26	4.51
S1.4	Gamification should be applied on tasks which are being used already (not before or in parallel)	10	21	21	33	15	0.09	3.12
S1.5	Gamification has its own added value, i.e., it is a part of user value creation at work, not only those related to behavior change when performing specific tasks	0	15	26	49	10	0.17	3.55
S1.6	The main goal of gamification is to increase motivation	3	18	15	49	15	0.17	3.56
S1.7	Gamification must lead to enjoyment	5	18	13	49	15	0.18	3.53
S1.8	Serious games and games with purpose are games by nature	5	21	21	38	15	0.13	3.50
S1.9	Serious games and games with purpose can be considered a kind of gamification (when you make the task as a game, then you gamify the task)	10	36	13	26	15	0.09	2.82
S1.10	Gamification is not a game.	0	8	10	49	33	0.19	4.08

Table 4. Statements for relevant fields of study

	Statements	Results in Percentages					Stn. Dev.	Mean
		SD	D	N	A	SA		
S2.1	User Experience: e.g., to understand users' behavior towards the business and tasks and also game mechanics	0	0	0	36	64	0.28	4.58
S2.2	HCI: e.g., gamification requires careful, sometimes novel, design of Human Computer Interaction	3	3	10	36	49	0.22	4.26
S2.3	Psychology: e.g., for motivation and engagement, and also deciding when a task or a gamification technique becomes boring	0	3	5	36	56	0.24	4.43
S2.4	Game Design: game mechanics come originally from Gaming. Expertise in Game Design is thus needed, e.g., game rules and reward mechanisms	0	0	10	36	54	0.25	4.49
S2.5	Management and Human Resources: e.g., gamification could have an impact on the performance and the social relationship between employees (users)	3	8	36	38	15	0.16	3.58
S2.6	Behavioral Economics: e.g., whether competition and leader-board would increase the performance and quality of doing a certain task for certain groups of users	3	10	21	46	21	0.18	3.71
S2.7	Software Engineering: e.g., to systematically construct gamification from requirements, to design, to implementation and testing	0	25	26	38	21	0.16	3.61

4.3. Stakeholders

After enquiring the fields of study that should be involved in the design process of gamification, we investigated the stakeholders that should be involved in the design process. This information would aid gamification developers to know whom to consult. We deduced a set of eight main stakeholders which are presented in Table 5 with their respective results.

It was highly agreed by participants that end-users, IT developers, researchers, and domain experts should be considered as stakeholders or consultants. However, the degree of consensus seems that there is less need for strategy makers and management, legal departments, security and privacy engineers, and behavioral economics experts. In this research, we tend to consider these areas as part of the eco-system to which gamification belongs. They would inform its decisions and maximize the chance of its correct implementation and integration. An interesting insight came from one expert who further added that it is mandatory that the legal department should be involved, since "gamification may be used as exploitation-ware" and gamification is not just about "[the technical side] of designing BPL [(badges, points, and leader-boards)]". It was also suggested that a professional game designer could also be considered as a stakeholder or consultant, given that gamification borrows most of its techniques from game industry.

Table 5. Statements as to who are development stakeholders

	Statements	Results in Percentages					Stn. Dev.	Mean
		SD	D	N	A	SA		
S3.1	Strategy makers and management: e.g., gamification may lead to changes of behavior and thus affect the organization social structure (when using leader-boards, reputation, etc.)	0	10	18	46	26	0.16	3.84
S3.2	Legal department: e.g., collected points indicate whether the employee is doing the work. Can that be used by managers when deciding to promote an employee?	5	28	28	23	15	0.13	3.07
S3.3	Security and privacy engineers: e.g., listing the top 10 in leader- boards, means others are not in the top 10. Points reflect a person's performance.	3	32	18	26	21	0.14	3.10
S3.4	End-users: e.g., for testing and validation and feasibility study	0	0	5	44	51	0.24	4.36
S3.5	Behavioral economic experts: e.g., for gamification design which is informed by the effect of social and psychological aspects on business objectives.	5	5	16	45	29	0.16	3.91
S3.6	IT developers: for managing the development and maintenance of information technology e.g., real-time communication, video server, communication channels	0	5	23	38	33	0.19	4.04
S3.7	Researchers: e.g., research is needed in most gamification projects as we still do not have ready-to-use solutions or templates for such an emerging field	0	5	18	36	41	0.17	4.06
S3.8	Domain experts: e.g., experts in the business being gamified will inform the design of correct gamification	0	3	8	44	46	0.23	4.27

4.4. When to Use Gamification

When to apply gamification in an environment was another aspect we investigated. The knowledge about this will help organizations to decide whether they need to apply gamification and whether it is feasible and cost-effective to apply it. We retrieved five insights which are presented with their respective results in Table 6.

A high rate of agreement on all the statements in this section was observed and no additional recommendation was made by any of the respondents.

Table 6. Statements about when to use gamification

	Statements	Results in Percentages					Stn. Dev.	Mean
		SD	D	N	A	SA		
S4.1	Theoretically, gamification can address any task, any user and enterprise. This does not mean it is easy to implement correctly, but the idea itself has no restrictions	8	15	3	46	28	0.20	3.86
S4.2	Gamification should be used to achieve another goal, e.g., behavior change. Gamification by itself is not an objective	0	15	8	46	31	0.18	3.82
S4.3	Gamification requires that the users' characteristics, enterprise, and context of the use are known very well, Gamification is not "one size fits all"	0	0	5	29	66	0.29	4.62
S4.4	Gamification is not a cheap solution from both technical and organizational perspectives. It should be used to support long-term goals and also when users/employee's loyalty is a key	0	10	13	46	31	0.19	3.97
S4.5	Gamification requires that we have clear business objectives and metrics to measure success and failure. This is preliminary to decide the suitability and feasibility of gamification.	0	8	18	38	36	0.17	3.99

4.5. Concerns and Considerations in the Gamification Development Process

The next statements presented in Table 7 cover the concerns developers and business owners should take into account while developing gamification so that they can avoid the negative impact it may have in both the short and long term. Knowing these concerns and issues beforehand can prevent organizations from applying gamification in a way which is not cost-efficient, and sometimes is detrimental for them. The cost here does not only refer to monetary development expenses, but to those related to the side-effects of applying it.

While some of the statements (S5.3 to S5.9) had a high rate of agreement, the others had a considerable amount of neutral responses or disagreeing responses. This could mean that we still lack enough knowledge to confirm or reject such statements and further research is still needed. For example, one of the experts strongly disagreed with the statement that removing the rewards will eliminate the intrinsic motivation with it. This was advocated based on an empirical study that the expert conducted. Some others stated that "knowing your players is a key" and believed that each type of user or environment needs their own design of gamification. This should not discourage developing engineering approaches which take that variety of users into account and perhaps provide patterns and adaptation mechanisms for gamification.

4.6. Systematic Approaches for Developing Gamification

The next question in the interviewing phase was related to whether there exist practical systematic approaches for the development of gamification. Our reason to ask this question was that the clear majority of papers apply gamification techniques as ready off-the-shelf solutions in a business context without explaining how decisions are made. We still lack a clear picture whether we should build gamification in conjunction with the business task and software supporting it or apply it in a plug-in style with some configuration steps. By analyzing the interviews, we identified 12 insights, which were subsequently confirmed by the questionnaire. The statements are presented in Table 8 with the respective results.

Table 7. Statements for concerns and considerations in the gamification development process

	Statements	Results in Percentages					Stn. Dev.	Mean
		SD	D	N	A	SA		
S5.1	Gamification should not be used when there is doubt about users' perception of gamification, e.g., certain users see gamification as trivialization of their job	0	23	44	28	5	0.19	3.02
S5.2	It should not be used when it could change management style against the company norms. e.g., transparency about who has the highest performance would affect the way promotions are given by managers	15	31	23	26	5	0.12	2.69
S5.3	Users should not feel they are forced to use gamification as this will lead to negative impact on the enterprise and the well-being at work	0	0	21	38	41	0.19	4.14
S5.4	Gamification should not lead to undermining the task. Users should not forget that gamification is for making the task more interesting, but it is still their job to do the task	3	15	8	51	23	0.18	3.64
S5.5	It is hard to guarantee that every user will see gamification positively regardless of how testing and validation were conducted. It is highly personal	0	10	13	49	28	0.20	3.81
S5.6	Not all game mechanics are applicable for any kind of task, e.g., leader-boards might not be suitable for the task of a collaborative editing of a shared document	3	0	3	34	61	0.25	4.42
S5.7	The desire to win the reward may affect the quality of the work negatively, e.g., users may do tasks in a cursory manner to collect points and win	0	5	13	24	58	0.18	4.14
S5.8	A game mechanic has a lifetime. That is users might get disinterested with it and reject it after a while	0	5	18	58	18	0.23	3.79
S5.9	Gamification may lead to clustering users and changing the original structure of the organization, e.g., good students could group together to win all the t-shirts given as a reward in gamified learning	3	16	18	50	13	0.17	3.51
S5.10	Not all game elements can be applied together, e.g., using competitive and collaborative elements together might not be a good idea	11	18	18	32	21	0.07	3.16
S5.11	Rewards are not good for intrinsically and already motivated users. If you remove the reward after a while, the intrinsic motivation goes with it	8	32	21	16	24	0.12	3.03
S5.12	Rewards are good for tasks which are not creative or intellectual. Rewards could distract users from applying their mind on the task.	8	24	26	29	13	0.12	3.2

Table 8. Statements relating to systematic approaches for developing gamification

Statements		Results in Percentages					Stn. Dev.	Mean
		SD	D	N	A	SA		
S6.1	There is not any established systematic/rigorous approach available in the literature	5	5	23	41	26	0.16	3.84
S6.2	There are guidelines on certain facets of gamification. Guidelines are a looser form of systematic approaches	0	13	15	62	10	0.25	3.82
S6.3	There is not necessarily a systematic approach to build gamification, it is a highly creative activity and systematic approaches could hinder success	3	23	21	44	10	0.14	3.34
S6.4	The engineering of gamification could be seen as a variation of user cantered design	0	13	28	44	15	0.15	3.61
S6.5	User cantered design is supportive but not enough for the engineering of gamification	0	18	15	59	8	0.25	3.71
S6.6	The engineering of gamification is not simply an assembly of other approaches, e.g., motivation theory, gaming, business analysis, etc. It has its own challenges and requires novel engineering approaches	0	8	15	51	26	0.21	3.9
S6.7	Business objectives should be considered from the start, i.e., gamification alignment with business objectives is core	0	5	8	51	36	0.23	4.02
S6.8	There is a lack of standard metrics and criteria for analyzing the feasibility of gamification	3	4	23	47	23	0.18	3.83
S6.10	There is no guarantee of the success of gamification	0	3	11	47	39	0.22	4.2
S6.11	There are tools to aid the design of gamification, e.g., tools offering templates and patterns and check-lists, but not rigorous approaches	5	5	28	51	10	0.23	3.58
S6.12	It is a mistake to think of gamification as a piece of software to engineer. It is a technique to customize and apply in the first place	0	0	13	42	45	0.21	4.52

The results show that there exists a high percentage of agreement on the lack of practical systematic approaches, e.g., "there is a lack of standard metrics and criteria for assessing the efficacy/feasibility of gamification". However, some thought that "there are some good guidelines" and "approaches but they have many key failings". This would mean that even guidelines are still not validated. Interestingly, there is a debate whether we ever need such systematic approaches. Some thought that "gamification development is not software engineering, [but] it is a game design". Others still think that there should be engineering approaches that "combine conceptual theories and technical practicalities". Engineering gamification could borrow certain techniques from user-cantered design, although it has its own unique challenges and we would still need "to standardize the instantiation of gamification" to fit its own peculiarities.

4.7. Gamification and Ethics

The use of gamification is a new trend in business, motivated mainly by increased productivity, though we argue that it may not always be cost-free. Gamification could raise ethical issues and affect the mental and social well-being of employees, and might be detrimental to the team. For example, leader-boards could demotivate those who never appear in them, and giving points upon completing a task could be overly stressful for some and lead employees to complete tasks hastily and without care. In the interview phase, we discussed the ethical issues and professional practice that may need to be considered when applying gamification in a business environment. These statements and their respective results are presented in Table 9.

A high rate of agreement on the statements in this section was observed. Participants unanimously agreed that introducing gamification to a business environment can have potential ethical issues. If contextual elements such as culture, norms, and personality of users are not considered in the design process, gamification may lead to problems such as adding stress and pressure on people, drive them to sacrifice privacy, or create clusters of users and isolate some others.

4.8. Notable Recommendations

In the last question, we asked the interviewees about best-practice recommendations for developing and applying gamification. By doing this, we aimed to produce a body of knowledge coming from previous experiences. We gathered 11 recommendations which are presented with their respective results in Table 10.

A high rate of agreement on the statements in this section was observed. There was a consensus on considering the business environment and the end-users in the design process of gamification. Users can differ from various aspects, namely their personality, age, gender, and cultural and social background, which seem to have high impact on how gamification should be designed. In addition, the environment that gamification is being applied to has various aspects, such as management style, culture, work style, and nature of the job that have to be considered in the design process of gamification. Neglecting these aspects may lead to a gamification design that does not satisfy some users' requirements, or is against norms, nature, or goals of the business which in both cases, can be detrimental to the ultimate goal of adding gamification to a business environment.

5. DISCUSSION

In this section, we discuss our findings in two sub-sections. First, we discuss aspects of gamification that gained a collective agreement and provide a body of knowledge that can aid gamification designers in increasing the quality of a gamification design. Then, we discuss the implications of our findings, in particular noting those areas where there was disagreement, or ongoing debate, which need further investigations.

5.1. A Body of Knowledge on Gamification

In this section, we discuss the agreed aspects of gamification from the perspective of practitioners and researchers, see Figure 1.

5.1.1. Definition

In this sub-section, we elaborate on the findings in section 4.1 and discuss what defines gamification and how it is differentiated from serious games and games with purpose.

Table 9. Questions for gamification and ethics

	Statements	Results in Percentages					Stn. Dev.	Mean
		SD	D	N	A	SA		
S7.1	Gamification can lead to tension in the individuals/groups relations, e.g., when applying a leader-board	3	5	13	51	28	0.17	3.9
S7.2	Gamification can lead to exposure of information users are not necessarily willing to expose, e.g., saying who are the top per- formers	0	10	15	44	31	0.18	3.83
S7.3	Gamification can create tension in the person, i.e., it can be looked as a monitoring system on how well a person is performing	0	13	5	51	31	0.20	3.9
S7.4	It could lead to rating people and creating classes, i.e., additional pressure on some people and change in the equity principles	0	13	15	49	23	0.17	3.67
S7.5	Gamification ethics are highly dependent on the norms and culture of the organization	0	5	10	51	33	0.22	4.21
S7.6	Gamification captures a lot of personal data, e.g., about performance. Privacy policies and data protection need to be augmented by ethical awareness	3	5	26	38	28	0.16	3.7
S7.7	The desire for winning could drive some users to overlook how data is gathered and to whom it is exposed. This makes some users, at times, vulnerable	0	18	15	44	23	0.17	3.67
S7.8	Ethics in gamification could be seen analogous to those in marketing, i.e., gamification could make some tasks attractive to users who would not ethically like to perform without gamification	0	8	33	46	13	0.20	3.56
S7.9	Gamification, in certain cases, could mean trying to get from people more than what their job requires, i.e., using gamification as an "exploitation-ware"	0	23	13	38	26	0.15	3.6
S7.10	Ethics should be seen case by case and even at the individual user level, e.g., the same game mechanic for the same task may be seen differently from ethical perspective according to the user	0	5	26	50	18	0.24	3.84
S7.11	Freedom of Information. Users' ability to see what is stored about them is an ethical issue	0	8	10	44	38	0.19	4.16

Figure 1. A reference model for engineering gamification

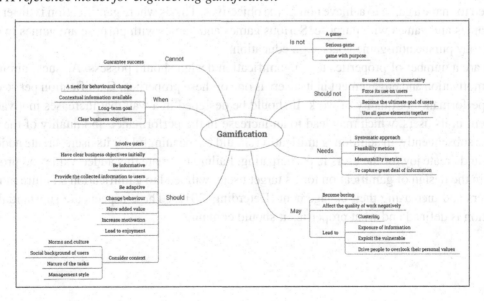

Table 10. Statements of best-practice recommendations for gamification

	Statements	Results in Percentages					Stn. Dev.	Mean
		SD	D	N	A	SA		
S8.1	Gamification should focus on end-users. Adopting gamification without a rich knowledge of users could turn to be harmful on users' experience and consequently the business	0	8	3	41	49	0.23	4.3
S8.2	Age is a distinguished user attribute, e.g., elders might not like virtual rewards	5	28	18	36	13	0.13	3.12
S8.3	Gender is a distinguished user attribute, e.g., males may like competition, females may like cooperation	10	26	13	46	5	0.16	2.97
S8.4	Social background is a distinguished characteristic of users to consider, e.g., some cultures are reputation-oriented while some others are not	3	10	23	54	10	0.19	3.54
S8.5	Gamification should be informative, people like feedback on how they are doing	0	5	3	49	44	0.26	4.41
S8.6	Users should not feel they have to rely on gamification, i.e., they should be still able to do the task perfectly without gamification	0	3	21	44	33	0.19	4.04
S8.7	We cannot decide the applicability and efficiency of a game mechanic per se; amongst other aspects, an analysis of the task and users should be made	0	5	13	54	28	0.21	4.04
S8.8	Gamification should be configurable by managers, e.g., the tasks, the user groups, and the periods to activate and deactivate	5	3	46	31	15	0.19	3.55
S8.9	Management and work style, hierarchical vs. non-hierarchical, need to be considered, e.g., leader-boards may seem odd in highly collaborative teams	3	5	21	38	33	0.15	3.84
S8.10	The word gamification might lead to a negative reaction by some managers, e.g., trivializing the work. Words like behavior change, employee engagement could be used interchangeably	5	28	28	33	5	0.15	2.96
S8.11	It is desirable that gamification is designed as an adaptive mechanism, e.g., depending on the type of users, the culture of the group, the business status, etc.	0	0	8	58	34	0.25	4.21

There seems to be a tendency towards accepting the definition provided in (Deterding et al., 2011). Despite what the name suggests, gamification is not a game. It merely uses a number of elements that are used to shape a game to achieve non-game objectives. This is where gamification is different from serious games and games with purpose. Serious games and games with purpose are games in essence, however, they pursue non-game goals, e.g., education.

There are a number of properties that a gamification design should possess. As such, aiming at increasing motivation and engagement in its users is one of these properties. Gamification per se does not increase performance or quality of work. It should be designed in a way that increases motivation and engagement in its users, which may lead to an increase in the performance and quality of the work of employees subsequently. In addition, gamification should be meaningful for its users, create added value for them, and create joy for the users in participating. Failure to create this added value and provide the meaning in the design of gamification for its target users, will lead to gamification's failure in motivating its users and increasing their engagement (Deterding, 2012). These aspects are substantial in how gamification is defined and what properties it should contain.

5.1.2. Relevant Fields of Study

In this sub-section, we elaborate on the findings in section 4.2 and discuss the list of relevant fields of study that their involvement in the design of gamification can be beneficial to the final artefact. Based on our findings, in addition to the fields mentioned in (Herzig, Ameling, Wolf, & Schill, 2015b), the relevant fields of study that should be involved in the development of gamification are as follows:

- User Experience (UX)
- Human Computer Interaction (HCI)
- Psychology
- Game Design
- Management
- Behavioral Economics
- Software Engineering

Gamification targets the end-users and has direct interactions with them. Therefore, involving the knowledge from user experience (UX), human computer interaction (HCI), psychology, and behavioral economics seems reasonable. These fields of study can provide the information about which strategies gamification should follow in order to be successful in changing the behavior of its users and observe considerable increase in their motivation and engagement.

Gamification borrows its main elements from the games. Therefore, game design is relevant to gamification as it provides information about how game elements can be embedded in the business environment in an interesting and enjoyable manner. Management is relevant as well since they should advise on what goals gamification should achieve and how to resolve possible conflicts that adding gamification to the business environment may introduce.

Finally, software engineering is needed to model and engineer the design of gamification. This involves features such as feasibility analysis, cost efficiency analysis, and measurability of the success for a design of gamification before it is implemented in the business environment.

5.1.3. Stakeholders

In this sub-section, we elaborate on the findings in section 4.3 and add to the list of stakeholders proposed by (Herzig et al., 2015b). We list the stakeholders that their involvement will benefit the design of gamification as follows:

- Management
- End-users
- Behavioral Economics
- IT Developers
- Researchers
- Domain Experts

These stakeholders should provide rich information that can guide the design of gamification in the correct path.

Management can inform the design with what the business objectives are and how they should be followed and achieved. End users will enrich the design of gamification with valuable information of what aspects of gamification will motivate or demotivate them. Behavioral economics and domain experts will enrich the design with what behaviors are beneficial and how they can be achieved. IT developers will inform the design with the possibility and feasibility of requirements from a technical point of view. Finally, researchers will try to enhance gamification and resolve problems that gamification may introduce and have.

5.1.4. When to Use Gamification

As our findings in section 4.4 suggest, when there is a need for behavioral change, gamification can be used as one solution to achieve this goal. Gamification per se will not add to the performance of the employees or increase the quality of their work. It is useful when there is a lack of motivation and engagement in the environment, or bad habits that the organization wants to eliminate by rewarding the desired behaviors.

Another important aspect to consider is the availability of contextual information, that is, clear information about the environment, business objectives, and the users' characteristics that will be involved in gamification. Designing gamification without considering aforementioned contextual information can fail in meeting its ultimate goal and have detrimental effects.

5.1.5. Concerns and Considerations

According to our findings in section 4.5, the engineering process of gamification would need to cater and provide countermeasures for a variety of concerns which may hinder its success and introduce risks

One of the recommendations is that in case of uncertainty of the outcome of gamification; it should not be introduced to the business environment. These uncertainties can be related to the impact gamification may have on the business environment or the perception of it amongst the users. In any of these uncertainties, introducing gamification may not only fail in achieving its goal of motivating its users, but also may be detrimental, such as demotivating users which are already intrinsically motivated. Although there is no guarantee to the success of introducing gamification to a business environment, reducing the uncertainties can decrease the risk of failure.

In addition, it is noteworthy that gamification should not be forced upon the users who must be able to opt-out from using gamification. Although, it is arguable that the peer pressure of using gamification by others may prevent employees from opting out. Moreover, gamification should not become the goal of the employees and they should remember that their actual goal is to achieve their business objectives successfully and gamification is introduced to the business environment in order to help them to do so.

Game elements used in gamification have their own nature and characteristics. For instance, some game elements promote competition and some others, in contrast to competition, focus on increasing collaboration amongst their users. Therefore, a successful design of gamification should take all the characteristics of these elements and choose those that comply with each other and do not cause conflict. In addition, the alignment of game element characteristics with contextual situations is important. Contextual situations refer to the tasks, users, and business environment that gamification is being introduced to.

For various reasons, users may lose their interest in a gamification design. Therefore, a dynamic and adaptive design of gamification is advised where users are constantly monitored in order to detect the need for a change in the design and trigger the need for a new solution, such as introducing a new game element.

It should be taken into account since gamification can assess users according to their strengths and skills, shaping clusters of users is not an unexpected occurring. Although, it was mentioned that this is not necessarily defective for the business objectives, there is potential danger in having clusters of users, especially when it leads to isolation of some others who cannot maintain their performance with the top performers.

Finally, a gamification design may drive employees to decrease the quality of their work, especially when gamification is rewarding the speed of production and does not consider the quality of work while rewarding. It is a very important concern for businesses planning to facilitate gamification, where increasing the quality of work is a major goal.

5.1.6. Systematic Approach

Gamification is different from commercial video games as it aims at fulfilment of business goals through game elements and *play* is a secondary goal for businesses. Therefore, we advocate a systematic approach towards the design and implementation of gamification which can reduce risks and side-effects related to relying on the creativity of its designers and prevent possible losses in the business.

Despite the presence of templates and guidelines for how gamification should be designed and implemented e.g., (Herzig et al., 2015b, 2013), our findings in section 4.6 suggest that there still seems to be a lack of systematic approach, and feasibility and measurability metrics for designing gamification. This is crucial to any system design as lack of them will cause uncertainty in its success or its introduction to the business may cost more than expected since the feasibility of adding it to the business was not analyzed properly beforehand. In addition, the lack of a systematic approach in designing gamification will make it hard to evaluate and analyze its success before implementation.

Moreover, a gamification design should involve its users and employ user centered design techniques in order to identify user requirements in the design process and also have clear business objectives beforehand. This should help achieving a design which is closer to what is expected from a successful gamification.

5.1.7. Ethics

The findings in section 4.7 suggest that, as with any persuasive technology, gamification deals with psychological aspects of its users. Therefore, the engineering process of it should be performed with due consideration of any ethical aspects and impacts it may have.

Gamification relies on collecting personal and work related information from the users and the business environment. However, how this collected information is used can impact whether gamification will lead to ethical issues. Since gamification often collects very detailed work information, it can be used as a very accurate and detailed monitoring mechanism by managers. This can create a great deal of tension among employees as managers can retrieve work habits of employees and put pressure on them to work constantly.

Also, competitive elements of gamification can shape clusters of users with the same skill-sets or similar performance level. As mentioned earlier, this is not necessarily problematic on its own. However, there are potential risks such as users with the same abilities and performance level cooperate with each other to stay in the top performers by helping each other and isolating others.

Moreover, the design of gamification may exploit the vulnerable users, driving them to work more than their contract, without extra payment from the organization, or be less concerned about their privacy just to achieve virtual goods. This, in the long run, can be defective for the social and mental well-being of the users involved.

Furthermore, a gamification design should consider the norms and culture of the society or organization it is being applied to. Promoting competition in a society that competition is defamed in, is going to be ignored by the users or force them to perform in a way that they are reluctant to do.

Finally, gamification should allow the users to have access to what has been collected about them by the use of gamification. This should be available to the users in addition to the feedback that gamification provides. Feedback is one of the main drivers for employees as they will know how they are performing and allows them to decide in which part of their job they need to put more effort.

5.1.8. Recommendations

In this section, we elaborate on the findings in section 4.8 and discuss the best practice recommendations of experts regarding the design of gamification. There are several recommendations about how gamification should be designed and implemented. However, here we discuss the ones that have collective agreement.

One important aspect that is recommended to be considered while designing gamification is the context gamification is being applied to and choose game elements that are compatible with those contextual elements. These contextual elements could be the end-users, the business objectives, or culture of the organization gamification is being introduced to.

Another important aspect is the managerial style in the business environment. There are various reasons that this becomes of concern as how managers will use gamification and the data captured by means of it can change its impact and perception amongst users. If the managerial style tries to value collaboration and hard work through positive reinforcement, this is usually acceptable from the users' point of view, however, having a negative reinforcement and punishing users for being in the bottom of the list in performance monitoring, could be very detrimental.

In addition, it is recommended that gamification should be configurable by either managers or end-users. This is a very important feature that gamification could have which can allow resolving many conflicts that gamification may introduce or even change the design when necessary to avoid boredom and sustain motivation in its users. It is important for the design of gamification to be adaptive. This can be achieved by the use of social adaptation (Ali, Solis, Omoronyia, Salehie, & Nuseibeh, 2012) and social sensing (Ali, Solis, Salehie, & Omoronyia, 2011) to detect when the setting and design of gamification is not working or users have lost interest in it. Then, it can trigger the need for a change in the design to avoid its harmful side effects.

Finally, it is important for the design of gamification to be supplementary to the environment, and it should not become the goal. Users should be reminded all the time that gamification is there to help them, and not to be the goal of the business.

5.2. Debates on Gamification

In this subsection, we provide the debatable statements on gamification reported in Section 4. We considered statements debatable where the rate of agreement and disagreement were close and a definite decision could not be made from the results.

5.2.1. Debates on the Definition

The first debate is whether gamification should be applied to a task after the users have already become familiar with it. The first view advocates that this should be the case as gamification should not be seen as an intrinsic part of the task and could be removed eventually, but the task would remain and the user should still be able to perform it. The second view expresses that this is not necessarily the case. This view argues whether we can consider gamification as a general paradigm that includes serious games and games with purposes.

The first view believed that there is a possibility of designing gamification as a game, similar to serious games and games with purposes. The second view on the other hand, preferred a neat definition of gamification and excluded the possibility of gamification to be designed as a game.

5.2.2. Stakeholders

There was a debate whether legal departments and security and privacy engineers should be considered as stakeholders. The first view advocated this opinion as gamification means changing the work contract in certain cases, e.g., monitoring of performance. The other view preferred to detach that aspect from gamification and advocated that it has to do with the strategy of the company and the way gamification is used is not a concern for gamification engineers.

5.2.3. Concerns

There are three debates here. The first debate relates to users' reaction and opinion about gamification. That is whether we need to avoid violating users' experience, or gamification is meant to lead to behavior change and uncertainty about its usage should be expected. The second debate is whether we should apply gamification if it is going to change the management style. Disagreeing views were analogous to the first debate. The third debate is whether the use of rewards, mainly tangible rewards, is not good for tasks which require intellectual contribution as they would be distracting. One view advocated it, with preference to use intangible rewards, e.g., social recognition, while the other view still sees rewards of all kinds the core of gamification regardless of the task types.

5.2.4. Recommendations

The first debate related to whether age and gender are main factors in the success of certain game mechanics. Different experts had different experiences regarding this aspect, which would call for further studies to investigate this. The other debate related to whether managers should be able to configure gamification or a pre-planned gamification should be applied. The debate mainly emerged because of the fear that this configuration could lead to subjective decisions, e.g., trying to exploit users. However, this seems to be an issue of management style rather than gamification. The third debate relates the perception of gamification itself. Some experts had experiences where managers viewed it as trivializing the work and therefore preferred to avoid using the term, while some other experts believed that this is not applicable and the term is now widely known and accepted.

5.3. Threats to Validity

Our expert study involved 46 experts (six in the interview phase and 40 in the survey phase) and was proceeded by a secondary research on the literature and distinguished projects on gamification and followed by another study to gather users and managers' perspective so that we enrich our analysis and reflections. The survey questions were appended by text boxes so that experts could add further insights, which explained their choices in many cases. The questions were developed based on an initial qualitative phase and literature review, so we ensured their relevance to our study. The experts were selected based on their contribution to the field of gamification, demonstrated via published works so that the credibility of their opinions is maximized. We also ensured that the experts were from different institutes and countries to avoid bias towards specific views of gamification. In spite of these careful arrangements, our study still has some threats to validity, as outlined below:

1. Most experts had only academic expertise, which means that the opinions presented in this paper have an academic flavor. However, the majority of experts still applied gamification in practice, e.g., via case studies to test their contribution and research questions. This would mean that their opinions are not purely theoretical, but also substantiated by some practical experience.
2. We recognize that some of our statements were about problems which still need to be investigated. Experts' opinions about these statements were to some extent speculative. However, their responses and comments enabled us to identify those issues which are still a focus of debate or need further research, and we presented them in subsection 5.2.
3. The study was, to some extent, biased towards gamification in a business environment. Some experts observed such business emphasis in the questions. That observation itself would mean the domain in which gamification is used could affect their answers. We suggest that our results are feasible for a business context and the generalizability of these results to other domains is still to be explored.

6. CONCLUSION

In this paper, we conducted an empirical research to provide a holistic picture of gamification and foundations for its engineering process. This included the meaning of the term, recommendations on the use, concerns to take into account, stakeholders and fields of study to involve, ethical issues that it may create, and best-practice recommendations. Our goal was to provide a body of knowledge, which informs researchers and practitioners in their future work. This research also identified issues which were debatable and required further investigation.

Findings of this research suggest that there is a need for the alignment of gamification and its characteristics with the environmental contexts it is being applied to. Nevertheless, the constituents that give characteristic to gamification and the environmental context are not yet clear. Hence, as future work, we will try to identify these constructs and properties of gamification and the business environment it is being introduced to. This should help in creating a domain specific modelling language for gamification, with the ability to analyze the compliance of the business environment and the gamification being introduced to it and point out any risk that the design of gamification may introduce to the business environment. This can pave the way for software support and automated analysis of the gamification design. Moreover, this modelling language should be able to provide the evolution of gamification according to the changes in the requirements of the stakeholders. These changes can occur for various reasons; users may lose interest in motives over time or even as a result of contextual changes in the business environment. The detection of the changes in the requirements of the stakeholders for the purpose of gamification evolution remains a challenge which needs to be tackled.

ACKNOWLEDGMENT

The research was supported by an FP7 Marie Curie CIG grant (the SOCIAD Project) and by Bournemouth University through the Graduate School PGR Development Fund. We would like to thank the experts who participated in our study for their valuable input and Dr. Sherry Jeary for her feedback on the paper.

REFERENCES

Abt, C. C. (1987). *Serious games*. University Press of America.

Alfrink, K. (2011). *New games for new cities* (Presentation). FutureEverything Std.

Ali, R., Solis, C., Omoronyia, I., Salehie, M., & Nuseibeh, B. (2012). Social adaptation: When software gives users a voice. Retrieved from http://dec.bournemouth.ac.uk/staff/rali/index_files/Papers_PDF/Raian_Ali_et_al_ENASE12_Social_Adaptation_When_Software_Gives_Users_a_Voice.pdf

Ali, R., Solis, C., Salehie, M., & Omoronyia, I. (2011). Social sensing: when users become monitors. *Proceedings of the 19th ACM SIGSOFT symposium and the 13th European conference on Foundations of software engineering* (pp. 476-479). ACM. Retrieved from http://dl.acm.org/citation.cfm?id=2025196

Antin, J., & Deterding, S. (2012). Gamification: Designing for Motivation. *Interactions, 19*(4), 14-17. Retrieved from http://dl.acm.org/ft_gateway.cfm?id=2212877#page=16

Berkling, K., & Thomas, C. (2013). Gamification of a Software Engineering course and a detailed analysis of the factors that lead to it's failure. In *2013 International Conference on Interactive Collaborative Learning (ICL)*, (pp. 525–530). 10.1109/ICL.2013.6644642

Bogost, I. (2011). Gamasutra - Persuasive Games: Exploitationware. Retrieved from http://www.gamasutra.com/view/feature/6366/persuasive_games_exploitationware.php

Caillois, R., & Barash, M. (1961). *Man, play, and games*. University of Illinois Press.

Chorney, A. (2013). Taking the game out of gamification. *Dalhousie Journal of Interdisciplinary Management, 8*(May). Retrieved from http://dalspace.library.dal.ca/handle/10222/16030

Creswell, J. W., Plano Clark, V. L., Gutmann, M. L., & Hanson, W. E. (2003). Advanced mixed methods research designs. In Handbook of Mixed Methods in Social and Behavioral Research (pp. 209-240).

Deterding, S. (2012). Gamification: Designing for Motivation. *Interaction, 19*(4), 14–17. doi:10.1145/2212877.2212883

Deterding, S., Dixon, D., Khaled, R., & Nacke, L. (2011). From game design elements to gamefulness: defining gamification. In *International Academic MindTrek Conference Envisioning Future Media Environments* (pp. 9–15). Retrieved from http://dl.acm.org/citation.cfm?id=2181040 doi:10.1145/2181037.2181040

Entertainment Software Association (ESA). (2014). *Essential Facts About The Computer and Video Game Industry*. Retrieved from http://www.theesa.com/wp-content/uploads/2014/10/ESA_EF_2014 .pdf

Gartner.com. (2011). Gartner says by 2015, more than 50 percent of organizations that manage innovation processes will gamify those processes. Retrieved from http://www.gartner.com/newsroom/id/1629214

Gartner.com. (2012). Gartner says by 2014, 80 percent of current gamified applications will fail to meet business objectives primarily due to poor design. Retrieved from http://www.gartner.com/newsroom/id/2251015

Groh, F. (2012). Gamification: State of the art definition and utilization. In *Proceedings of the 4th seminar on Research Trends in Media Informatics*. Retrieved from http://vts.uni-ulm.de/docs/2012/7866/vts_7866_11380.pdf#page =39

Hamari, J., & Lehdonvirta, V. (2010). Game design as marketing: How game mechanics create demand for virtual goods. *International Journal of Business Science and Applied Management, 5*(1). Retrieved from http://www.hiit.fi/u/hamari/2010-game_design_as_marketing.pd f

Herzig, P., Ameling, M., Wolf, B., & Schill, A. (2015a). Implementing Gamification: Requirements and Gamification Platforms. In Gamification in Education and Business (pp. 431–450). Springer.

Herzig, P., Ameling, M., Wolf, B., & Schill, A. (2015b). Implementing Gamification: Requirements and Gamification Platforms. In Gamification in Education and Business (pp. 431–450). Springer. doi:10.1007/978-3-319-10208-5_22

Herzig, P., Jugel, K., Momm, C., Ameling, M., & Schill, A. (2013). GaML - A modeling language for gamification. In *Proceedings - 2013 IEEE/ACM 6th International Conference on Utility and Cloud Computing, UCC 2013* (pp. 494-499). doi:10.1109/UCC.2013.96

Hofacker, C. F., de Ruyter, K., Lurie, N. H., Manchanda, P., & Donaldson, J. (2016). Gamification and Mobile Marketing Effectiveness. *Journal of Interactive Marketing, 34*(July), 25–36. doi:10.1016/j. intmar.2016.03.001

Huotari, K., & Hamari, J. (2012). Defining gamification: a service marketing perspective. In *Proceeding of the 16th International Academic MindTrek Conference* (pp. 17–22). Retrieved from http://dl.acm.org/citation.cfm?id=2393137

InterAksyon. (2012). In stress-filled BPO world, "gamification" could offer relief. Infotek News: Inter-Aksyon.com. Retrieved May 29, 2015 from http://www.interaksyon.com/infotech/in-stress-filled-bpo-world-gamification-could-offer-relief

Johnson, D., Deterding, S., Kuhn, K.-A., Staneva, A., Stoyanov, S., & Hides, L. (2016). Gamification for health and wellbeing: A systematic review of the literature. *Internet Interventions*, *6*, 89–106. doi:10.1016/j.invent.2016.10.002

Kapp, K. M. (2012). *The gamification of learning and instruction: game-based methods and strategies for training and education*. John Wiley & Sons.

Lazzaro, N. (2011). Chasing wonder and the future of engagement. *Talk*. Retrieved from http://www.slideshare.net/NicoleLazzaro/chasing-Wonder-and-the-Future-of-Engagement

Linehan, C., Kirman, B., & Roche, B. (2015). Gamification as behavioral psychology. In The Gameful World: Approaches, Issues, Applications (pp. 81-105). MIT Press.

McCallum, S. (2012). Gamification and serious games for personalized health. *Studies in Health Technology and Informatics*, *177*, 85–96. Retrieved from http://www.ncbi.nlm.nih.gov/pubmed/22942036 PMID:22942036

McGonigal, J. (2011). *Reality is broken: Why games make us better and how they can change the world*. Penguin.

O'Donovan, S., Gain, J., & Marais, P. (2013). A case study in the gamification of a university-level games development course. In *Proceedings of the South African Institute for Computer Scientists and Information Technologists Conference on - SAICSIT '13* (p. 242). New York, New York: ACM Press. 10.1145/2513456.2513469

Pedreira, O., García, F., Brisaboa, N., & Piattini, M. (2015). Gamification in software engineering – A systematic mapping. *Information and Software Technology*, *57*, 157–168. doi:10.1016/j.infsof.2014.08.007

Pløhn, T., & Aalberg, T. (2015). Using Gamification to Motivate Smoking Cessation. In *European Conference on Games Based Learning* (p. 431). Retrieved from https://www.scopus.com/inward/record.uri?eid=2-s2.0-84955100411&partnerID=40&md5=576d6e9b7d4e44ddeb625dc9b082bb9f

Reiss, S. (2012). Intrinsic and Extrinsic Motivation. *Teaching of Psychology*, *39*(2), 152–156. doi:10.1177/0098628312437704

Robertson, M. (2010). Cant play, wont play. *Hide and Seek*. Retrieved from http://www.hideandseek.net/2010/10/06/cant-play-wont-play

Robson, K., Plangger, K., Kietzmann, J. H., McCarthy, I., & Pitt, L. (2016). Game on: Engaging customers and employees through gamification. *Business Horizons*, *59*(1), 29–36. doi:10.1016/j.bushor.2015.08.002

Rodrigues, L. F., Oliveira, A., & Costa, C. J. (2016). Playing seriously - How gamification and social cues influence bank customers to use gamified e-business applications. *Computers in Human Behavior*, *63*(May), 392–407. doi:10.1016/j.chb.2016.05.063

Ryan, R. M., & Deci, E. L. (2000). Intrinsic and extrinsic motivations: Classic definitions and new directions. *Contemporary Educational Psychology*, *25*(1), 54–67. doi:10.1006/ceps.1999.1020 PMID:10620381

Scekic, O., Truong, H.-L., & Dustdar, S. (2013, June 1). Incentives and rewarding in social computing. *Communications of the ACM*, *56*(6), 72–82. doi:10.1145/2461256.2461275

Seaborn, K., & Fels, D. I. (2015). Gamification in theory and action: A survey. *International Journal of Human-Computer Studies*, *74*, 14–31. doi:10.1016/j.ijhcs.2014.09.006

Shahri, A., Hosseini, M., Phalp, K., Taylor, J., & Ali, R. (2014). Towards a Code of Ethics for Gamification at Enterprise. In *The Practice of Enterprise Modeling* (pp. 235–245). Springer Berlin Heidelberg. doi:10.1007/978-3-662-45501-2_17

Simões, J., Redondo, R. D., & Vilas, A. F. (2013). A social gamification framework for a K-6 learning platform. *Computers in Human Behavior*, *29*(2), 345–353. doi:10.1016/j.chb.2012.06.007

Werbach, K., & Hunter, D. (2012). *For the win: How game thinking can revolutionize your business.* Wharton Digital Press.

This research was previously published in the Journal of Organizational and End User Computing (JOEUC), 31(1); pages 39-60, copyright year 2019 by IGI Publishing (an imprint of IGI Global).

Chapter 9
Techniques on Multiplatform Movement and Interaction Systems in a Virtual Reality Context for Games

Konstantinos Ntokos

Solent University of Southampton, UK

EXECUTIVE SUMMARY

When a student works on a VR game design project, the input scheme is often bypassed because it is considered to be one of the easiest things to implement. But should design affect the inputs, or the other way around? The author attempts to solve this with the creation of a unified communication tool among students, academics, and developers. This proposed tool will define which movement and/or interaction technique is best suited, depending on the following factors: platform, constraints, context, physique, space, immersion, and user experience. The game design framework will be described, discussed, and presented in a table format to address all of the above when working on VR games. This chapter will also include a section that will define what the player can do and how.

ORGANIZATION BACKGROUND

Solent has become a university since July 2005, but it has a long and complex educational history. Incorporated as an independent higher education institution in 1989, the University's origins can be traced back to a private School of Art founded in 1856. Mergers between Southampton College of Art, the College of Technology and the College of Nautical Studies at Warsash has laid the foundations for what is now Southampton Solent University. Since becoming a university, Southampton Solent has helped nearly fifty thousand students from all walks of life to make the most of their potential. Guided by three Vice-Chancellors in turn, the University has changed dramatically over the past ten years – from campus improvements to the state-of-the-art facilities (Solent University, 2018).

DOI: 10.4018/978-1-6684-7589-8.ch009

INTRODUCTION

There is an urgent need to differentiate all the possible movement and interaction systems game development students would have at their disposal to develop a VR game project. That is especially important when students specialized in game development are in the process of completing their Final Major Project (FMP) that intends to define what a game would be, after considering all types of inputs in the design process. Both movement and interaction systems available to game developers would define whether a game could be built as a mobile or a desktop/console game. Those considerations would greatly affect the game design foundation, and, in turn, affect the nature and quantity of features or mechanics in a game design product. The author has been assigned the task by *PacktPub* to develop two online courses to teach VR Development using Unreal Engine (Ntokos & Eleutheriou, 2017). *PacktPub* is a publisher of technology- or developer-oriented technical textbooks. *PacktPub* also develops online courses that require a careful study of system movements and interactions.

BACKGROUND

As part of the Solent University's curriculum, students will be required to complete a final year project at their last semester of study. Some of them opt to do a VR project which often involves issues of great technical and academic importance. Technically speaking, a significant question is which platform students could choose from to develop their game design project. Academically, the VR project itself could bring a new layer of learning experiences for students that need special consideration before delving into game design or code in the areas of movement and input constraints. These issues as mentioned above are likely to pose many challenges for students, which warrants the proposition of a pedagogical framework to define how a game should be made or constrained by game developers.

Technological Concerns

The technical concerns to justify this pedagogical chapter to teach game design principles is that the game design process needs a principle-based framework that can be used for a multi-platform context. Depending on the type of game project that students want to complete, there would be several VR techniques needed for each of these game platforms. Students may also need a full access to PC and/ or mobile headsets, and even subsequently adjust their own game design projects because of these technological limitations. For example, it might not be practical for students to design a VR game for mobile platforms, with the expectation that all end users always have a mobile-friendly gamepad for interactions. Furthermore, mobile headsets are different from each other. In the mobile context, game developers have frequently relied on *Google Cardboard* (Google, 2014) and *Fibrum* headset (Fibrum Limited, 2017). *Fibrum* headset does not have the hole on the upper right corner to allow a finger to be inserted to tap on the screen. On the other hand, *Google Cardboard* is the cheapest solution for mobile VR and it also allows tapping on screen through a hole.

Academic Concerns

The educational concerns are of higher importance as to developing a pedagogical framework to teach VR or game design that might directly impacts on the learning outcomes of the final year project. Furthermore, it could affect students' understanding that both movement and interaction techniques are core aspects of any VR experience. This book chapter summarizes a list of design principles from a series of observation of existing game products on the marketplace. This chapter aims to develop a student-friendly framework that is used during the development of a VR design project or, possibly. any game design project. The framework itself, should be used as a common language among those who are interested in developing a VR project. Furthermore, this pedagogical framework should also be used to either define game design or be constrained by game design itself, depending on the chosen design approach by the game developer. This pedagogical framework itself should be able to differentiate between both movement and interaction systems, for both PC and mobile platforms, or even any applicable game genres in any platforms. Additionally, this descriptive framework could also help students to narrow down their own design choices in the process of completing their own final year project.

Current Challenges Facing the Organization

The challenge experienced by the author at Solent University is that there is no single framework to define which types of movement or interaction systems students could use for their VR design projects. As a result, at Solent University, there is a need to develop a pedagogical framework with a list of clearly-defined techniques and principles for both students and instructors to follow when teaching game design. This framework to teach game design would be used to communicate how the final year project should be structured, particularly on the components of both movement and interaction techniques. The main challenge experienced by many educators teaching the final project is that the student would focus on game design and gameplay elements in their final VR project, but fail to consider as much on how the player would move or interact during gameplay. The best way to demonstrate their knowledge and skills in learning movement and interaction logic in their code is to look at how other commercially successful games have been developed in the past and learn by imitating the relevant design techniques in their project.

Research Questions

On the basis of the above background, this book chapter aims to provide answers to the following three research qestions:

Research Question 1: What design techniques are used by existing video games to implement movement?
Research Question 2: What design techniques are used by existing video games to implement interaction?
Research Question 3: What will be the most efficient combinations of movement and interaction techniques when developing the most natural VR experiences?

MAIN FOCUS OF THE CHAPTER

Movement Techniques

The solution to the problems above is the creation of a pedagogical framework that would define the ways various controlled characters would move around in a VR game. This is based on several technical limitations the game developer would have on any chosen platform. The first thing to consider will be a differentiation on a plethora of easily perceptible techniques. Two factors need to be taken into consideration. First, game developers need to consider which technique to use (no matter whether they are movement or interaction). Secondly, what will be the best platform (desktop or mobile) to choose from? The author analyzes these techniques as well as the platforms to discuss their superiority and to explain if there are any other technical limitations that might hinder the usage of these techniques in an actual design project.

The starting point is to define what constitute the types of movement techniques a game developer may use. In the context of VR, the primary goal of a movement technique is to avoid motion sickness that users may experience. The secondary goal is to increase the immersion of the player by using a realistic movement pattern significant in a given context.

The context of a digital game is very important to define which movement and interaction techniques will be applicable. For example, when a player controls a car, a movement technique using a steering wheel will provide more immersion and realism. When a player controls an Iron-Man-like character who is seeing the world through a suit's user interface, then the best technique would be *LookAt*, which is analyzed further below.

The first, also the most common technique, for VR games on the market is the *Classic* technique. This technique involves any type of input device in the hands of the player, such as a touch device, a game controller, a keyboard & mouse setup, or a mobile-friendly gamepad. The *Classic* technique is the easiest implementation, as the developer only needs to bind the button presses and axis to a specific in-game movement by the character. An example of the games using this technique is *Resident Evil 7* (Capcom, 2017).

While movement may seem to be a trivial task, it really isn't, because it is not just the translation of an object in a 3D space, but it is also the rotation of that object. Consequently, since players are looking through the eyes of a character in a VR game, it is important that a developer needs to think of a user-friendly way of turning around. Problems can arise if a player wants to make a 180-degree turn. It is certain that players will get motion sickness, if turning and rotating are not implemented properly (Harmony Studios Limited, 2018). Turning players' head around and changing the orientation of the camera with this movement is something that is natural when playing a VR game.

The best solution is assigning a button or axis (like the analog/thumb stick – depending on the controller) to a slight but quick turn in degrees (Mason, 2015). As soon as the player tilts the analog stick to any direction, a very slight rotation would occur, within such a very short timeframe, to allow the player even to notice it. The ideal timeframe needs to be adjusted by the developer is likely to be between 0.1 to 0.3 seconds, which might make the change in rotation almost unnoticeable to players. Another factor that needs to be considered is the angle of rotation to be made. Rotating in increments of 5 degrees around the range of 15-30 degrees seems to be ideal, but it is subject to further experimentation to confirm its applicability when designing a game.

The second technique is the *LookAt* technique. With this technique, the developers could design their characters as stationary objects. These characters would make a move only when the player is looking at a specific object within the game world. That can be executed by having the player look at an object while instantly making a move. Additionally, by adding the parameter of duration, the player can keep staring at the object for a specified amount of time, considered to be meaningful for the game context. An example of using the *LookAt* movement technique would be on flight games where the players always move forward, based on where they are looking at. An example of this type of games is *Froggy VR* (FIBRUM, 2017).

As a movement technique, *LookAt* is very easy to implement, and the way the character moves is going to be scripted in a way that prevents motion sickness. *LookAt* may also be one of the few available options, especially when the developers are constrained by inputs available to them. This specific movement technique only uses the selected headset's stereoscopic movements. It is further implemented with a single raycast from the middle of the screen towards the forward-facing axis of the player's head orientation within a specified or infinite range. Another possible drawback is that the movement does not seem to be realistic or immersive as the player cannot directly control the character's actual movement.

The third movement technique that developers can use in VR games is called *Toggled*. By using this technique, the character is always moving forward at a pre-defined speed, based on the forward-facing vector of the player's head orientation. However, this technique would mean that, unless the players want the character to always move forward, there needs to be a mechanism that toggles the character movement. Constantly moving forward is both unrealistic, not immersive, to say the least, and may be a sign of faulty game design. That is the reason the author comes up with the term *Toggled* as this movement needs to be toggled on and off to optimize players' experiences. A plethora of games that use *Google Cardboard* on mobile devices tends to heavily rely on this technique. One of them is *House of Terror VR* for the *PlayStore* (Lakento, 2018).

This technique can be implemented as follows. Firstly, it can be implemented via as simple as a key on a gamepad. The execution can also be done with a simple tap on the touch screen of a mobile device (provided there is a way for a finger to access the touch screen through the headset). Another implementation method would be to design a specific sprite that, when looked at, the player will stop moving. An example would be a sprite that states "STOP". The same sprite would then be used to make the character moving again. That specific sprite needs to follow the player character around and be placed either high up or on the ground, so it does not interfere with the game environment. However, that sprite is lowering the immersion and can get tiring for the user and not as good for motion-sensitive people. A third implementing approach of the toggling would be to ignore the sprite and have a specific angle-threshold that the player will need to raise his or her head above (or below). This could cause the angle between his or her forward-facing vector to be greater (or lower) than the threshold and toggle the movement. That may also be tiring for the player but at least there is not an immersion-breaking graphic. This type of movement technique is more suitable for mobile game platforms since there are input constraints for VR games in that platform.

The above specific movement technique at first glance seems to be more immersive than *LookAt* technique discussed above since the player has a more active role regarding when he or she wants to move. However, with a bit of consideration, that immersion may be easily broken, especially when toggling happens with head tilting or looking at a sprite. Toggling the movement using a gamepad or a simple tap on a mobile device seems to be the most simple and straightforward method. However, three questions may be brought up: "Is that realistic?"; "Can the mobile headset accommodate the tap?"; and "Is this movement type viable for games that can support gamepads, keyboard, mouse and other types of input?"

The answers to these important questions would come after testing those inputs in an actual game, and the short answers to these questions are often "No", "It depends", and "No", in that order. "No" for the first question because it just does not make sense in a game context to tilt one's head to toggle movement. "It depends" for the second question bcause the type of headset one may have (mobile ones specifically, because some headsets do not allow tapping with any available holes in the headset. Finally, "No" for the third question, as if the developers are having other types of input, they should probably use those instead.

The next movement technique is called "Locomotion". With this technique, the character in a VR game moves if quick changes in the acceleration of the VR headset are identified. This involves the real player making fast movements with his or her VR headset, which is achieved by running (so his/her head is moving up and down). Technically, this measures the acceleration of the headset during specific time intervals, and if those changes in acceleration are present, then the character is moving. This is achieved through either the headset's built-in accelerometer, or the phone's accelerometer in a mobile game.

The main drawback of this movement technique, even if it seems natural and realistic, is that it is not as immersive, as the player is not actually running, but is running in-place, which may seem confusing. Consequently, even though it may be realistic, it is not as immersive. However, that is not the case when the technique is used in conjunction with GPS Sensors of the phone, so movement only happens when acceleration and actual GPS updates occur. Another problem with this technique is that there are also no ways of clearly differentiating the acceleration from different speeds. Finally, the most important factor that will make this technique less favorable is that the player needs to be constantly moving when he or she wants the character to move as well. In addition to that, the technique requires a lot of physical stamina for the player who may not be as fit as the game would require. After all, what needs to be considered is that when a video game is created, the focus is to entertain the player and not exhaust him or her during gameplay. However, that is not the case when the game is focused on fitness, which is a great idea of implementing VR in fitness games or apps together.

The *Locomotion* technique may be more realistic than both *LookAt* and *Toggled* techniques that have been discussed above. After repetitive and excessive testing, it seems that this technique does not cause motion sickness as much as the other two techniques. The player's physical movements and excitement do not allow the player to feel that the movement is any different interacting with the game. It seems conclusive that the *Locomotion* technique could allow the player to have the most active control over the character's actual movement. However, this is the most arduous technique for the player in terms of the requirement for physical stamina and fitness. Finally, this technique is recommended to be used with mobile VR games since the actual headset does not require any cabling around it, so the player can run and jump around freely and without any physical restraint. Being a physically-demanding movement, this technique is greatly paired with fitness VR apps and *exergaming* in general. A game example of integrating this movement technique would be the *BitGym* game for a mobile platform (Active Theory Inc, 2018).

The fifth technique the author has explored in this book chapter is the *Rail* technique. It is assumed that the player has no control over his or her movement and only follows a designated path. This movement technique works on the assumption that the player is either mounting a self-driven vehicle that follows a specific pre-scripted trail (such as a mine cart, a jeep, a boat or an airplane). The game design needs to clearly point out that the player will not have any control over that vehicle. For example, where the vehicle is controlled by some other player such as an NPC (i.e., Non-Player Character) driver or gravity and other means. The *Rail* technique has been mostly used in the *Rail Shooter* game genre that are known for their automatic movement during gameplay, and the only concern of the player should be on pointing his/her gun at something before shooting it. An example of a game using *Rail* technique would be *Zombie Shooter VR* (FIBRUM, 2017) for mobile or *Until Dawn: Rush of Blood* (Supermassive Games, 2016). The *Rail* technique is an excellent design choice when the developer does not want the player to have any control over his or her movement to just "enjoy the ride". The occasion could be a rail shooter where the player character walks on his or her own or when he or she is mounting another vehicle. If the designer uses this technique, the players instantly lose any control over their own movement during gameplay. When this occurs, the only focus of the game design is about the actual interaction with in-game design element in the game world. It is apparent that this technique is only immersive when the character is mounted, and it is a good fit for the mobile devices and platofrms. As an added value, it relieves the game developers of the stress due to input constraints, so they only focus on interaction during gameplay. Technically, the only thing that the developers would implement will be the scripted path that the characters would take.

The sixth movement technique, *Teleport*, is the first technique that requires special touch input devices (i.e., haptic sensors), such as *Oculus Touch, Vive Touchpad, PlayStation Move*, etc. The game developers can assume they cannot use this technique on mobile devices. When this technique is implemented, the players are able to move around when they point with their touch controllers to a specific point in space. When this becomes a *Candidate Teleportation Position*, the players need to have a visual indicator that can show them exactly where the position is located at. Following this graphical indication, the players need to use one of the buttons on the touch control to confirm the teleportation.

A very important note to cover is that, whenever a player uses the teleportation mechanic, the developer must fade the screen in and out instantaneously, so the quick movement is obscured from the player. As a result, the player will not have a strong sense of disorientation or motion sickness. Another drawback of this technique is its lack of immersive or realistic feeling in any way, since these characters are constantly blinking from space to space or doing a scripted movement (such as a well-calculated jump using a trajectory). The only challenging part of this technique is to make the actual movement meaningful to players in the game. The *Teleport* technique is also slightly more complex to implement than the other techniques mentioned above, though it is also constrained to be used to either PC or console platforms due to input limitations. The input scheme also has many known variations like *Teleport by Projection, Teleport by Point, Teleport by Throwing Object* (Carbotte, 2018). An example of Teleportation movement in VR game would be *Doom VFR* (id Software, 2017).

The *Rope* technique is characterized by the way the movement is executed within the game context. Like *Teleport, Rope* also requires touch input devices. This technique also uses the depth from a VR camera sensor to see when users' hands are completely stretched forward and backward. Technically, players need to stretch out their arms and close the grip of their hands by pressing a relevant button on the touchpad. Afterwards, the players keep the button pressed and as they move the arm back in its original position, the character keeps moving forward based on the delta position of their hands. The above description explains the design philosophy behind this technique and to demonstrate why *Rope* refers to the movement made by the hands to resemble the physical movement of pulling a rope. Summing up, the players need to stretch out their arms, close their grip firmly (simulated with a button press) and then move the hand backwards toward the direction of the players. *Vindicta* game uses the *Rope* technique (Game Cooks, 2017).

While that movement technique is constrained on PC and console VR platforms, it still may not be as realistic or immersive, unless the actual game involves hand stretching or, rope pulling. *Rope*, as a design technique, also does not lead to motion sickness because the player may sometimes "pull the rope" harder or softer than usual. On the other hand, the player may feel the need to have more control over the movement of the character.

The eighth technique refers to a very specialized design principle and can only be used in games where the player controls something through a steering wheel from a car, a robot, a go-kart, even a pirate ship as the name *Wheel* has implied. This technique requires a steering wheel controller or a gamepad which includes an accelerometer. Examples of digital game using this design technique are *the DualShock 4* or *the Xbox 360/One/One X controller*. Unless the player has access to a special mobile device, which supports such a controller, this technique is exclusive to PC and console game. However, this limitation has a very positive effect on the player's immersive experiences and thus, ideal for a racing genre or a game genre that simulates a driving experience when the player is sitting down. The way this technique works is that based on the rotation of the steering wheel, the player will be able to turn around, and accelerate or brake as needed. Furthermore, there is a good chance that extra buttons will be on the steering wheel to allow players to gain extra control. This control scheme also appears in non-VR games which have to do with racing that support a racing wheel.

Racing games are a natural extension of this design technique. Even though the immersion level might be maxed out, this design technique may cause disorientation and motion sickness. This is true, as some people are not able to handle great speeds in a virtual environment. It is also natural that players will experience gameplay at a high velocity and, in that case, may cause some players to be susceptible to motion sickness or not.

Another game design technique in the proposed framework is called *Scripted* because the game developer are not able to really use any of the above techniques. It is very constrained based on the input devices available, or the game does not really evolve around move at all. The technique closest to *Scripted* is the *Rail* technique, since the player does not really have direct access over his or her character's movements and rather focuses on interaction during gameplay. *Scripted* and *Rail* are different as explained below. Using the *Rail* technique, the character in the game is constantly following a pre-scripted path, while the *Scripted* technique will only allow the player to move once during a specific number of events when conditions are met or triggered. This movement is accomplished through a path, blinking teleportation, or any other way.

In a zombie shooting game that is implemented by the *Rail* movement technique, the character would keep on walking no matter what, and the player would need to shoot as many zombies as possible. In the *Scripted* technique, the character would be standing still, and all zombie enemies may need to be defeated or a specific timeframe must pass to trigger subsequent movement.

Several *scripted* techniques are also used in puzzle or escape room games, where the character is constrained on a chair and cannot really do much besides looking around at objects in the virtual environment. This technique also gives the game developers the freedom to design for either a mobile, a desktop, or a console platform that does not require any input from the user directly. As such, the main conditions required to trigger the transition are facilitated through player's own interaction with the virtual environment.

The game design framework is further enhanced with two other techniques to supplement both the movement and interaction techniques discussed in this book chapter. The context and implementation change, in the end, will be at the discretion of the game developers as to how to use two supplementary techniques properly: *Voice* and *Kinetic*. The *Voice* technique requires that the player has full access to a microphone of a mobile device, a USB or condenser microphone for a PC/Console, or the *PlayStation* VR headset with a built-in microphone. The player can control the way his or her character moves using either specific voice commands (voice recognition) or just the pitch or volume of his or her own voice. An example of how these techniques have been used can be found in *Star Trek: Bridge Crew* (Red Storm Entertainment, 2017). The way movement is executed is like the *Scripted* technique, but the actual condition that needs to be met is the voice command or pitch/volume itself.

Technically, the *Voice* technique is also one of the hardest things to implement, especially if one is considering using solely voice commands. The *Voice* technique needs an underlying voice recognition software or algorithm to understand simple words at first, and complex sentences at a later stage. However, this is a very immersive movement technique which may also be the only movement technique to move AI-controlled NPCs within a game context. For example, a character may be tied to a chair, may be handicapped, or may even be completely paralyzed. The only method of moving other NPCs is through the character's own voice as a control mechanism. That would be ideal if the character is sitting in a monitor room, observing other NPCs through the CCTV cameras, as they advance in a game environment infested with zombies where voice is the only way to command them.

The final movement technique is the *Kinetic* technique that could enable player's movement to be completed whenever the player is moving specific body parts using the depth sensor of a VR camera. This movement technique is appropriate for the design of *exergaming* and fitness games. Like the *Locomotion* and *Rope* techniques, the *Kinetic* technique will require a great amount of player stamina as the movement process may get strenuous after a while. The actual movement, like *Voice*, resembles the *Scripted* technique, as the player does not control his or her movement directly, but the body movements actually trigger this transition. This technique can be also expressed as *Superman Locomotion* where a player must hold his or her hands towards a direction he or she wants to move. The *Superman Locomotion* is often experienced by a player in *Weightless* (Schubert, 2016), which uses Leap Motion Technology that involves a hand-tracking technology to develop VR games and applications.

The above discussions review different types of movement techniques that are commonly used in game design circle and students majoring in game design. These techniques with a short explanation are summarized in Table 1.

To conclude this section, it is also worth noting here that a movement technique should not be associated with the way a camera is set. There are 3rd Person Platformers for VR that use a *floating head* camera following the character, but the actual movement is done through the *Classic* technique. This movement happens since the game character moves around using axis and button presses from a gamepad.

Interaction Techniques

Moving around can influence the game design and the mechanics to be built or the platform that will be chosen in the design process. Interaction on its own has the same amount of influence in defining game design and platform choice, which becomes important when a movement technique combines with other interaction techniques.

Table 1. Types of movement techniques

Movement Techniques						
Technique	**Recommended Platform**	**Player Immersion**	**Motion Sickness**	**Ease of Control**	**Extra Hardware**	**Recommended Context**
Classic	PC/Console	Medium	Varied	High	Mobile gamepad if possible.	Most VR contexts with complex inputs.
LookAt	Mobile	Low	Medium	Medium	-	Mobile games with input constraints and simple mechanics.
Toggled	Mobile	Low	Medium	Low	-	Mobile games with simple interaction and three toggle modes: toggle via tap, via angle and via look at. Not all headsets support holes for tapping on screen.
Locomotion	Mobile	Medium	Low	Varied by Physique	-	Fitness Game, powered by GPS
Rail	All	High	Low	High	-	Simulate a character that is mounted on something or sits on the passenger's seat.
Teleport	PC/Console	Medium	Low	Medium	Touch Controls, Depth Sensor	Any context that blinking/ teleporting/ jumping on specific spots make sense.
Rope	PC/Console	Medium	Medium	Medium	Touch Controls	Simulate mountain climbing or when hand-stretching is required like controlling a robot monitor
Wheel	All	High	Varied	High	Steering Wheel	Racing or Driving game or simulator. Ideal for simulating cockpits of all types.
Scripted	Mobile	High	Low	High	-	Puzzle or Escape room game, with a focus on interaction input.
Voice	All	Medium	Low	High	Microphone	Games where the player acts as an overlord, tasking the AI with actions or where the character has no legs or hands.
Kinetic	PC/Console	High	Low	Varied by Physique	Depth Sensor	Exergaming or other fitness-related apps/games.

The first interaction technique is *Haptic* that enables the player to use the touch sensors to interact with the environment mainly through gripping. The player in the game can interact with the environment by grabbing objects, throwing them around, and using his or her hands to press buttons or to fire weapons during gameplay. A multitude of game genres has used this interaction technique when the character can use two objects at the same time with the environment. A demonstration of this technique in a game would be *Skyrim VR edition* that allows a player to control a melee weapon on one hand and a spell on the other. Additionally, the player can hold a bow with one hand and load & shoot an arrow with the other (Bethesda Softworks, 2017). *Haptic* is also based on grabbing and gripping mechanics, and as such, the game features should involve those game mechanics. This technique is very similar to *Rope* and *Teleport* movement techniques, which can be used along with the *Kinetic* interaction technique. This technique is by far the most immersive control scheme of all possible interaction techniques, because it is the only technique that uses the touch sense to its full potential. The most challenging part when selecting a *Haptic* interaction technique is to choose a right movement technique to allow game developers to provide the best possible experience for its end user. The *Haptic* interaction technique, however, is not suitable for mobile devices.

The second interaction technique is straightforward and is a counterpart of the *Classic* movement technique. Thus, the *Classic* interaction technique involves controls through a mainstream input controller, such as a gamepad, or mouse & keyboard. Interaction through these devices is achieved through a simple button and a key press, axis manipulation, and a mouse button click. This technique is applicable for PC and Console games, but this technique for mobile devices can be implemented through tapping the touch screen.

In terms of realism, the *Classic* interaction technique seems to be a straightforward choice, and while it may not be as immersive as *Haptic*, it is the most comfortable choice for the end users. Whenever developers want to favor ease of use and user experience over realism and immersion, the *Classic* interaction technique is the definite choice, while *Haptic* will sacrifice some comfort for immersion. The game developers also need to make sure that whenever the *Classic* interaction technique is used for mobile devices, they need to ensure that the mobile headset allows for users to tap on the touch screen.

The third interaction technique is yet another counterpart of the *LookAt* technique. In the context of interaction, it is not only irrelevant of how the character moves, but also the character interacts with his or her environment by looking at the character. More specifically, just as looking at objects for a short period of time, a specific movement would occur for the the *LookAt* movement technique. So, if the player's forward-facing axis is directed towards a usable object, then the character would examine or interact with the virtual object in a way that makes sense for the game the players are currently playing.

The *LookAt* interaction technique is better used in mobile VR games, and is best suited when the players do not have a gamepad or equivalent for input. It is one of the few resources developers can leverage if players do not have any other means of input that could have an impact on the realism and immersion. An example of using the *LookAt* interaction technique would be when a gun always shooting forward after a specific time interval, because there is not a way of manually firing automatically.

The fourth interaction technique is called *VR Gun* that requires a very special sensor to be used an actual gamepad-like gun to be connected to a PC or a console via a USB cable, using a simple Wi-Fi connection. This technique is exclusive for a PC or console platform since it requires that special type of input. The *VR Gun* technique works like the *Classic* interaction technique, though the *VR Gun* can be used to point at objects within the game context based on its own orientation. As the gun comes with an assortment of buttons, the player can easily reload, shoot and perform other types of interaction as well. A game example that has used this technique in its design is *Farpoint* (Impulse Gear, 2017).

The main drawback of this interaction technique is the difficulty in reaching a larger pool of audience, since it requires a very specific input device in the interaction process. Another limitation of this technique is the constraint related to only a few game genres besides FPS and action-oriented games can actually accommodate such a device. On the other hand, the level of immersion is very high. The feeling of control and absolute autonomy will affect the user to enjoy this VR game.

The fifth interaction technique is *Voice* which functions the same way as it does in other movement techniques. The player can interact with the virtual environment using the voice pitch and/or volume as well as voice commands, which relies on a voice recognition algorithm. A microphone will be needed to use *Voice* to interact with the game. If the character is not disabled in any way, then using *Voice* as a secondary interacting tool will increase a sense of immersion. On the other hand, if this is the only way of interacting when the game character is not disabled or constrained to voice only, this will reduce the level of immersion, no matter how simple this technique will be used in designing a VR game.

One final note for the *Voice* technique, whether it is being used as a movement or interaction technique, is that it is the only technique that requires an audio input, which means that the player needs to reply on voice cues in the virtual space. This technical requirement could make the game unappealing or even, unplayable for the player that cannot make any sound in the environment.

The sixth interaction technique is *Kinetic* which shares similarities with the movement technique using the same label. This technique allows the player to interact with the environment via the depth sensor of the VR camera, and thus is only viable for PC/Console VR games. The player can move his or her whole body or individual body parts (depending on the type of VR games) to interact with the environment, such as waving hello or goodbye to someone, or any other real-time gestures. This interaction technique is ideal for action-demanding *exergaming*, fitness games, or VR games which require very specific movements incorporated into the game design mechanic. However, *Kinetic* is the only technique that could be more demanding than all others, in terms of adding realism and immersion.

The seventh and final interaction technique is called *Automatic* which is the only interaction technique used as a fallback when any other technique is not available. This technique is characterized by its automatic interaction because it needs the player to move into a trigger area to execute a specific interaction. Because interaction is done automatically, this technique cannot be used with *Scripted* or *Rail* movement technique, because either technique needs to be directly controlled and influenced by the player and contradicts what *Automatic* means. The *Automatic* technique can be easily implemented through trigger points and trigger areas in the virtual environment and is very simple to use. Also, both mobile and PC/Console VR games can leverage the *Automatic* technique, but is more recommended for mobile devices when inputs are a big constraint. On the other hand, a big disadvantage of this technique is that it is not so realistic or immersive to directly influence the environment. It should be mentioned that it is a necessary sacrifice to simplify interaction with the virtual environment. Furthermore, there are tricks that a developer can use to reduce a sense of removed realism and immersion. Intentionally, placing the character to only investigating and examining objects as part of core gameplay will be likely to address this problem because it is then only action the character can take. Table 2 summarizes the above discussions.

Matching Movement With Interaction Techniques in Game Design

After discussing all the movement and interaction techniques, the author has identified all possible and feasible combinations among these techniques in the design process. Furthermore, these movement and interaction techniques have been mapped out on two tables (PC/Console, mobile context), which are also used as reference points to assist future game developers, students and academics on VR projects. Table 3 and Table 4 present the movement and interaction techniques mapped out on a matrix to guide both professional and beginning game designers to determine how efficiently each of those techniques can be combined for either a PC or console context. All interaction techniques have been placed in the columns horizontally, and all movement techniques have been placed in the rows vertically as shown in Table 3 and Table 4.

Table 2. Types of interaction techniques

Interaction Techniques					
Technique	**Recommended Platform**	**Player Immersion**	**Ease of Control**	**Extra Hardware**	**Recommended Context**
Haptic	PC/Console	High	High	Touch Controls, Depth Sensor	VR Games with dual-object wielding or grip mechanics, like a carnival-simulation game.
Classic	PC/Console	Medium	High	Mobile Gamepad if supported	Most VR contexts with complex inputs.
LookAt	Mobile	Low	Medium	-	Mobile games with input constraints and simple mechanics.
VR Gun	PC/Console	High	High	Special VR Gun	First Person Shooter and heavy action-packed games.
Voice	All	High	High		Games where the player acts as an overlord, tasking the AI with actions or where the character has no legs or hands.
Kinetic	PC/Console	Medium	Varied by Physique	Touch Controls, Depth Sensor	Exergaming or other fitness-related apps/games.
Automatic	Mobile	Low	High	-	Mobile games with a lot of input constraints where the character ideally is performing simple tasks that are environmental context-aware.

Table 3. Combination of techniques to maximize efficiency for pc/console platforms

Technique Combination Efficiency Matrix (PC/ Console)							
Techniques	**Haptic**	**Classic**	**LookAt**	**VR Gun**	**Voice**	**Kinetic**	**Automatic**
Classic	High	High	Medium	N/A	Medium	Low	Low
LookAt	Medium	Low	Low	Low	Medium	Low	Medium
Toggled	Low	Low	Low	Low	Low	Low	Medium
Locomotion	High	Low	Medium	High	Low	High	Medium
Rail	High	High	Medium	High	Medium	Low	N/A
Teleport	High	Low	High	N/A	Medium	Low	Medium
Rope	High	Low	Medium	N/A	Medium	Low	Medium
Wheel	N/A	High	N/A	N/A	N/A	N/A	N/A
Scripted	High	Low	Low	High	Low	Low	N/A
Voice	Medium	Medium	Low	Medium	Medium	Medium	Low
Kinetic	High	N/A	Low	N/A	Medium	High	Medium

These two tables offer game designers a useful tool to determine which techniques should be chosen. For example, when it comes to PC or console games that the player has more input choices, the best choices for interaction techniques would be *Haptic* or *Classic*. *Classic* is working best when combined with either *Classic* movement (since both techniques use the same gamepad or keyboard). The *Wheel* technique will be great because, playing VR racing games, the wheel itself has buttons, making it a great combination of different design principles. The *Haptic* technique can also be best combined with the *Classic* movement technique since there are bound to be buttons on the touch sensors and both can help the developer to use an alternative technique. Another stunning combination is *VR Gun* that is designed with *Rail*, *Scripted* or *Locomotion* movement techniques to address the interactions that involve the player running around and shooting virtual objects common in most games. Finally, the *Kinetic* interaction technique seems to be best used with its counterpart, *Kinetic* movement technique, or with the *Locomotion* technique. Both technique are able to keep input consistent by using physical movements of the body. *Voice* is not a definite way of working on platforms with many other inputs, but it could be a great secondary or supplementary technique for movement or interaction.

Table 4. Combination of techniques to maximize for mobile platforms

Technique Combination Efficiency Matrix (Mobile)							
Techniques	**Haptic**	**Classic**	**LookAt**	**VR Gun**	**Voice**	**Kinetic**	**Automatic**
Classic	N/A	High (if mobile gamepad is supported or headset can support tapping)	Medium	N/A	Medium	N/A	Medium
LookAt	N/A	Medium	High	N/A	Medium	N/A	High
Toggled	N/A	Low	High	N/A	Medium	N/A	High
Locomotion	N/A	Low	Medium	N/A	Low	N/A	Medium
Rail	N/A	Medium	High	N/A	Low	N/A	N/A
Teleport	N/A	N/A	N/A	N/A	N/A	N/A	N/A
Rope	N/A	N/A	N/A	N/A	N/A	N/A	N/A
Wheel	N/A	N/A	N/A	N/A	N/A	N/A	N/A
Scripted	N/A	High (if mobile gamepad is supported or headset can support tapping)	High	N/A	High	N/A	N/A
Voice	N/A	Low	Medium	N/A	High	N/A	Low
Kinetic	N/A	N/A	N/A	N/A	N/A	N/A	N/A

The combinations of different techniques presented in Table 3 and Table 4 are the most useful design considerations, and thus the more powerful when used together. The process of game design depends on what the developers want, what is designed to be done beforehand, and what type of experience the developers attempt to create for users. When game developers are designing for idle/sitting players in front of a computer desk or a TV, an obvious choice for input would be a gamepad or a wheel. When the players are expected to stand and/or have space between them and a depth sensor, then haptics, dual-wielded grips are the obvious choices. Designing a VR game needs to balance both immersion and comfort at the same time.

RESEARCH METHOD

These tables to provide a list of movement and interaction techniques and are based on observations after collecting and analyzing at a sample of 100 VR games using either mobile, PC, or console platforms. The benefits of researching existing digital games are because their input schemes have already based on the developers' perspective. The summary list of techniques is based on actual game examples.

CONCLUSION

Future Research Directions

One of the main constraints when working on input schemes for movement and interaction with VR is the fact that the player needs to use a heavy headset connected to a PC, usually through a cable. Facebook has announced that the company will be publishing the world's first wireless VR headset for PC, with its latest *Oculus Quest* technology. *Oculus Quest* can be a game-changer for VR development as it will be consumer friendly as the headset will be working standalone. (Facebook Technologies, LLC, 2018). The new headset can influence and improve players' overall VR experiences previously constrained by a small environment and will drastically reduce the environmental hazards. Furthermore, this innovation has the potential to release the developers' creative freedom to experiment with more design techniques. This is especially true regarding movement that can be added on the identified movement technique table in the future.

Practical Implications for PC and Console Game

While mobile devices have more input-limitations compared with a PC / console platform, it requires expensive hardware to develop and is not easy for developers and/or students alike. This situation should not be taken for granted that everyone, especially for students, to purchase entire VR headsets with motion sensors and camera setups on expensive PCs to run VR software. The situation is even worse for *PSVR* (Sony Interactive Entertainment, 2016) that demand users to acquire a *PSVR Kit*, a compatible powerful PC and hard-to-get *PlayStation 4 Dev Kit*. This constraint will probably be solved in the future with more accessible VR headsets, such as *Oculus Quest*.

Practical Implications Mobile Platforms

The biggest drawback for mobile devices, besides the reduction in frame rate, the lower-quality graphics, and the constraint in input, is that some devices do not have a depth sensor. However, mobile devices vary with this capability (Wagner, 2018) when this feature is still not "mainstream" and easily accessible. Furthermore, when *VR Gun*, *haptics* or *kinetic* movement techniques are not supported, everything needs to be designed around the player looking at things. However, because mobile devices are not cabled, the player can play any VR game with the constraints of equipment. For mobile VR game, developers cannot provide complex inputs because not everyone will have a mobile VR headset for tapping. Furthermore, not everyone has a mobile-compliant gamepad. A combination of the two *LookAt* techniques seems to be appropriate to ask players to interact by staring at virtual objects. That can be further supported by having either *LookAt* for movement and *Automatic* for interaction, or combining *LookAt* for interaction and *Scripted* for movement in that scenario. For most cases, besides *LookAt*, *Scripted*, or *Automatic* techniques, game developers can have one less layer of difficulty in integrating input in game design.

The design decision to choose the best input mechanism really depends on the development needs of the game designer. The developers need to consider the inputs before designing a game. Furthermore, the platform where the VR game will be played can define the path they can follow and what technique to use. This will immediately result in some gains or losses in terms of possible input hardware available to the end users. A mobile game will require the mobile VR headset and whether it supports tapping on screen. Another possible consideration would be the genre of the game or the experience intended with the game. Finally, some games require a specific physique or physical setup to be experienced adequately by the player, and thus those requirements must be specified for players to be seated or how to deal with disabled player to interact with the virtual environment. The proposed unified game-design framework hopes to provide answers to these requirements, after it tackles all possible cases, multi-platform issues as well as suggests solutions for movement and interaction systems. The framework is also a good starting point that can possibly bridge the knowledge gap for students, academics and developers alike.

REFERENCES

Active Theory Inc. (2018, September 5). BitGym: Virtual Cardio Tours. Google PlayStore.

Bethesda Softworks (2017, November 17). The Elder Scrolls V: Skyrim VR. Bethesda Softworks.

Capcom. (2017, January 24). Resident Evil 7: Biohazard. Worldwide: Capcom.

Carbotte, K. (2018, March 10). *Do the Locomotion: The 19 Ways you walk and run in VR Games*. Retrieved from https://www.tomshardware.co.uk/picturestory/230-virtual-reality-games-locomotion-methods.html

Facebook TechnologiesL. L. C. (2018). Retrieved https://www.oculus.com/quest/

FIBRUM. (2017a, April 11). Froggy VR. Google PlayStore.

FIBRUM. (2017b, May 17). Zombie Shooter VR. Google PlayStore.

Fibrum Limited. (2017). *Fibrum VR*. Retrieved from https://fibrum.com/

Game Cooks (2017, June 20). Vindicta. Game Cooks.

Google. (2014). Retrieved from Google Cardboard: https://vr.google.com/cardboard/

Harmony Studios Limited. (2018). *VR Sickness: What it is and how to stop it*. Retrieved from https://www.harmony.co.uk/vr-motion-sickness/

id Software. (2017, December 1). Doom VFR. Bethesda Softworks.

Impulse Gear. (2017, May 16). Farpoint. Sony Interactive Entertainment.

Lakento. (2018, October 18). House of Terror VR 360 Cardboard Horror Game. Google PlayStore.

Mason, W. (2015, November 16). *Five Ways to Reduce Motion Sickness in VR*. Retrieved from https://uploadvr.com/five-ways-to-reduce-motion-sickness-in-vr/

Ntokos, K., & Eletheriou, O. (2017b). *Exploring Unreal Engine 4 VR Editor and Essentials of VR*. BirPacktPub.

Ntokos, K., & Eleutheriou, O. (2017a). *Creating a VR Shooter Game Using Optimized Techniques*. Birmingham, AL: PacktPub.

Red Storm Entertainment. (2017, May 30). Star Trek: Bridge Crew. Ubisoft.

Schubert, M. (2016, March 10). Weightless. Itch.Io.

Solent University. (2018). Retrieved from https://www.solent.ac.uk/about/our-history

Sony Interactive Entertainment. (2016, October 13). *PlayStation VR*. Retrieved from https://www.play-station.com/en-gb/explore/playstation-vr/

Supermassive Games. (2016, October 13). Until Dawn: Rush of Blood. Sony Interactive Entertainment.

Wagner, D. (2018). Retrieved from https://medium.com/@DAQRI/depth-cameras-for-mobile-ar-from-iphones-to-wearables-and-beyond-ea29758ec280

ADDITIONAL READING

Harmony Studios Limited. (2018). *VR Sickness: What it is and how to stop it*. Retrieved from Harmony Studios: https://www.harmony.co.uk/vr-motion-sickness/

Lee, J., Kim, M., & Kim, J. (2017). A study on immersion and VR sickness in walking interaction for immersive virtual reality applications. *Symmetry*, *9*(5), 78. doi:10.3390ym9050078

Mason, W. (2015). *Five ways to reduce motion sickness in VR*. Retrieved from Upload VR Website: https://uploadvr.com/five-ways-to-reduce-motion-sickness-in-vr/

Ntokos, K., & Eleutheriou, O. (2017). *Creating a VR Shooter Game Using Optimized Techniques*. Birmingham: PacktPub.

Ntokos, K., & Orfeas, E. (2017). Exploring Unreal Engine 4 VR Editor and Essentials of VR. Birmingham: PacktPub.

University of Waterloo. (2018). *Virtual reality motion sickness may be predicted and counteracted*. *ScienceDaily*. Retrieved from www.sciencedaily.com/releases/2018/09/180927083336.htm

Upload (2018). *The Best way to interact within VR*. Retrieved from Upload: https://uploadvr.com/the-best-way-to-interact-within-vr/

Wagner, D. (2018). Depth Cameras for Mobile AR: From Iphones to Wearables and Beyond. Retrieved from https://medium.com/@DAQRI/depth-cameras-for-mobile- ar-from-iphones-to-wearables-and-beyond-ea29758ec280

Wareable (2018). *A new wave of VR motion sickness solutions is here.* Retrieved from https://www.wareable.com/vr/new-wave-vr-motion-sickness-solutions

KEY TERMS AND DEFINITIONS

FMP: Abbreviation of final major project, also known as dissertation or thesis. This is the final project students work on when reaching the final year and complete before graduating.

HMD: Head-mounted display. Refers to the headsets players wear on their heads to experience VR games, apps, and VR-experiences in general, for example, the Oculus Rift, the HTC Vive, and the Steam VR.

Leap Motion: Technology focused in hand-tracking for VR applications.

LookAt: Interaction or movement technique that has the VR player look towards a specific point in 3D space for several seconds to "confirm" movement or interaction. This is used instead of the conventional controllers or motion sensors.

NPC: Non-player character. Usually refers to other characters within a game world that are controlled by the AI.

Unreal Engine: Industry-standard game engine, primarily used in AAA 3D games. Some games created with Unreal Engine include *Bioshock, Mass Effect, Deus Ex, Batman: Arkham City, XCOM: Enemy Unknown*, and the well-known *Fortnite*.

VR: Abbreviation for virtual reality. Refers to the computer-generated simulation of a 3D world, usually in a gaming or non-gaming context, where the user immerses himself/herself.

This research was previously published in Cases on Immersive Virtual Reality Techniques; pages 199-216, copyright year 2019 by Engineering Science Reference (an imprint of IGI Global).

Chapter 10
Software Requirements Definition Processes in Gamification Development for Immersive Environments

Paulo Veloso Gomes
 https://orcid.org/0000-0002-3975-2395
LabRP, School of Allied Health Technologies, Polytechnic of Porto, Portugal

João Donga
 https://orcid.org/0000-0002-8701-2113
LabRP, School of Allied Health Technologies, Polytechnic of Porto, Portugal

Vítor J. Sá
 https://orcid.org/0000-0002-4982-4444
LabRP, Polytechnic of Porto, Portugal & Centro ALGORITMI, Universidade Católica Portuguesa, Portugal

ABSTRACT

The implementation of gamification in immersive environments is a complex and multidimensional process. A socio-technical approach is necessary to cover all the specifications that the system needs to satisfy the needs and the purpose of its genesis. The use of virtual reality (VR) technologies in mental healthcare associated with gamification mechanisms has been gaining popularity. Two projects were developed using VR, one that allows people to experience and better understand mental health conditions through empathy construct and the other can be used to help patients with social phobia or Arachnophobia to reduce their phobias using VR solutions and real-time biofeedback. The authors analyze the aspects that influence the development of immersive environments and gamification mechanisms and propose a socio-technical methodology based on actor-network theory for the survey and definition of requirements.

DOI: 10.4018/978-1-6684-7589-8.ch010

INTRODUCTION

Exposure to immersive environments can have different objectives, from the playful component, to impactful experiences, application to serious games and development of therapeutic programs. Whatever the purpose of the System to develop, there is one aspect in common, its complexity. Thus, designing and developing such a system is a great challenge, not only technological, but above all, in terms of being able to properly exploit its full potential.

Gamification in healthcare implies the involvement between people and technology, creating a socio-technical system in which the different elements interact and influence each other. This chapter analyzes the aspects that influence the development of immersive environments and proposes the use the Actor-Network Theory (ANT) as methodology for the survey and definition of requirements.

Implementing gamification in an immersive environment is a big challenge, involves making important decisions that have a decisive influence on the results to be achieved. The analysis and specification of requirements for such a system is a complex process, and should consider some aspects such as, to whom it is intended, interactivity, hardware, the type of suitable immersive environment (VR, MR, CAVE, Video 360°), real-time biofeedback measurement devices, the interactive narrative, the objectives, the results, report, surrounding space, among others.

IMMERSIVE ENVIRONMENTS FOR EMPATHY CONSTRUCT AND SELF-CONTROL MECHANISMS

Immersive environments create impactful experiences and have great potential to generate emotions that increase the degree of empathy. Real-time biofeedback allows to assess users' reactions to the environment to which they are exposed. Emotions are part of the empathy process, of the complex ability to share the affective state of another individual (de Tommaso et al., 2019; Santamaría-García et al., 2017).

When a system is developed to generate an immersive environment to create emotions, it makes sense to incorporate art elements to enhance its effect. The art in immersive environments influence the individual process that increases the person's receptivity to the construction of emotions.

Stimuli induce emotions, and emotions trigger personalized reactions, each reaction is personal and occurs in a specific spatial, temporal, and circumstantial context. The same stimulus can give rise to different emotions, in different people, or even in the same person at different times (Paulo Veloso Gomes et al., 2019).

Immersive environments explore multimedia potential, the use of multiple devices and different types of multimedia produce different stimuli and induce different emotions, contributing to the audience's involvement (Soleymani, Larson, Pun, & Hanjalic, 2014). Some art projects use EEG (Electroencephalography) as an input to produce or modulate artistic content, such as animations, music and choreography (Grandchamp & Delorme, 2016). Neurofeedback allows the voluntary regulation of brain activity. Its application intends to enhance and recover emotion and cognitive processes, and their underlying neurobiology (Lorenzetti et al., 2018).

The exposure of an individual to an immersive environment generates emotions, emotions trigger feelings, which in turn, promote actions (Paulo Veloso Gomes et al., 2019).

IMMERSIVE ENVIRONMENTS ARE JUST TECHNOLOGICAL ARTIFACTS?

Immersive environments are complex artifacts involving a strong technological component. However, the concept of immersiveness confronts the duality between giving and receiving. It suggests "to enter", "to dive into", "to be part of", but also to "imbue", to impregnate "and "receive it" (Paulo Veloso Gomes et al., 2019) .

An immersive environment contributes to an individual process that increases the person's receptivity to the construction of their own emotions. Emotions make each person react individually to a stimulus. This reaction is personal, because the same stimulus can trigger different emotions in different people, or even different emotions in the same person at different times (Paulo Veloso Gomes et al., 2019).

Gamification can be used as a motivation strategy in training programs and knowledge transmission. The construction of immersive gamification environments faces some multidimensional challenges, especially when it is intended to use the player's biofeedback as an interaction mechanism in order to influence the game's narrative.

It is intended with the use of biofeedback mechanisms measure the player's reaction to stimuli. In a simpler way, the result can be used to measure the impact of the stimulus, but the result of this measurement can also be used as an element of voluntary, or non-voluntary interaction and allows the game to adapt to bioreactions. Thus, biofeedback as an element of interaction is essential for the use of interactive narratives when it is intended that the user is involved in the environment in a natural and continuous way.

Emotional Behavior

Immersive environments are designed to involve and awaken sensations for the user. Exposure to the immersive environment causes involuntary reactions and changes in emotional state, which consequently affect heart and respiratory rate, skin conductivity, brain activity and eye movements.

These reactions are very important because they represent the real impact that the exposure has on the person. Its real-time capture is possible using biofeedback devices capable of identifying, registering, and measuring its intensity. Technological developments have allowed biofeedback devices to be incorporated into VR devices, making their use almost, or even in some cases, imperceptible to the user. Looxid Link™ is an accessory device with EEG sensing capabilities that could be integrated with VR glasses like VIVE Pro Eye™ already equipped with a precision eye tracking system. The use of this type of equipment allows much more than just registering and viewing data, these data can be used as an element of interaction between the user and the immersive system. It allows the use of interactive narratives in the conceptualization and design of the immersive system, opening space for application in areas such as neurogaming and biofeedback therapy.

The construction of an interactive narrative to be applied in an immersive environment can incorporate a strategy to take advantage of the user's emotional behavior, the user takes an active role in the creation, emission, intensity and frequency of the stimuli emitted by the system. The effect of stimuli on the user can be determined from the real-time data obtained on the user's physiological signals.

An emotionally adaptive system, through measurement of user emotional data, can adapt continuously its stimulus to the user emotional state, optimizing his experience (Tijs, Brokken, & Ijsselsteijn, 2008). The use of biofeedback systems in the design of an immersive environment transform it into an Emotionally Adaptive Immersive Environment.

The user's reaction to stimuli can be involuntary or voluntary, an adaptive behavior can be developed during exposure or over several exposures to the environment (Figure 1). The concept of interactivity is very evident in the cycle of influence between the system and the user, where the system's stimuli affect the user, and the user's reactions contribute to alter the stimuli produced by the system.

Figure 1. Characterization of the user's profile according to behavior during continuous exposure to immersive environments.

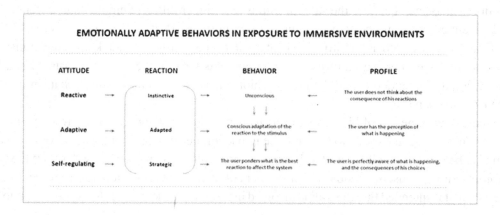

During continuous exposures to immersive environments the human emotional adaptative process affect user's behavior to stimuli (Figure 1). Over time the unpredictable becomes predictable, the time needed to interpret the occurrences decreases, and the environment becomes familiar to the user. The user becomes more confident, can understand better and faster what surrounds him increasing his perception of the system. This emotional adaptative behavior allows to transform a reactive attitude into an adaptive attitude, allowing the user to have a conscious behavior, reacting in a more assertive way to adapt his reactions to the system's stimuli. Continuous exposures can enable the user to interact with the system in a more thoughtful way, being able to determine which reaction is most appropriate to influence the system. When reaching the level of expert, the user designs the best strategy for his own benefit.

This evolutionary behavioral process means that adaptive immersive environments, through real-time biofeedback mechanisms, can also be interesting from a therapeutic point of view, having an important role in the development of self-regulation strategies by the user, in the face of challenges, adversities or threats, which in daily life interfere with his normal activities.

In non-adaptive systems, different tools can be used to assess the user's emotional state, traditionally the feedback obtained allows to analyze and define changes in future exposures. However, in addition to the inconvenience that the analysis result is not in real time and can only be applied afterwards, the tools used do not always produce reliable results, for example, in a questionnaire, the user for the most diverse reasons, may have felt a certain emotion and respond that he felt another type of emotion, or not being able to explain its intensity.

Immersive emotional adaptative behavior systems in addition to providing real-time responses, they can convert unimodal data into multimodal data. The reliability of the system is increased with the use of multimodal data from different sources of biological signals (Paulo Veloso Gomes et al., 2019).

Biofeedback Interactivity

Immersive environments allow multimodal human-computer interaction between the physical and virtual environment, through natural forms of communication. As can be seen, the importance that individual interpretation exerts on an immersive stimulus influences not only the way the individual perceives and interprets the immersive environment, but also the results that the exposure to that environment should produce. This way it is possible to infer that Immersive environments are complex artifacts involving a strong human component.

The use of interactive narratives in immersive environments allows the environment to adapt and react to the actions of each user. The interaction can be made through conscious mechanisms, when the player is faced with a situation of choice and chooses a path, this strategy allows the player to understand the relationship between an action and its consequences. When it is intended that the player has an immediate perception of his reaction to a certain stimulus, the biofeedback mechanisms, by allowing the system to collect the information given unconsciously by the player, can be used in immersive environments, as elements of choice in interactive narratives, to generate and improve self-regulation of behaviors. According to (Marcos, Bernardes, & Sá, 2002), multimedia technology is ideal to register multi-sensorial information.

Interactivity in adaptative immersive environments is based on Biofeedback-Stimuli dynamic cycle (Figure 2). Core Engine is the central unit, it controls the system software and the connected devices. The user experience can be optimized with the continuously adaptation of stimuli to the user reactions.

Stimuli are generated and trigger physiological reactions in the user. Biofeedback devices capture the data corresponding to each bio signal. These unimodal data are recorded and graded separately.

System incorporate the effects of stimuli processing the unimodal data separately, then merges unimodal data in multimodal data (Poria, Cambria, Bajpai, & Hussain, 2017) to interpret the user's response and use that response to generate new stimuli.

The affective algorithm maps the unimodal data and converts it into multimodal data to identify the type and intensity of emotions created by the stimulus. Then, the algorithm adapts the system's response capacity, considering the type and intensity of the stimuli, with the appropriate response to each situation, selecting new stimuli to send and grading their intensity and frequency (Figure 2).

Interactivity is an important factor for the conceptualization of the immersive environments, the design of a dynamic and adaptive model, as Biofeedback – Stimuli described in Figure 2, is fundamental to analyze and define the data flow generated by bio stimuli.

The development of immersive environments consider the four levels of observation, the theoretical information level, physical level, the cognitive level and the intentional mode (Hildebrand & Sá, 2000).

A stimulus can elicit different types of responses. Responses can be involuntary, when the user has no control over it, responds instinctively, without thinking, or responses can be voluntary, when the user is aware of the response he wants to give and chooses to respond to the stimulus in a certain way.

If in a first stage the user has no control over his heart and respiratory rate, brain activity and eye movements, with experience, the self-control of a person's biological status can be developed (Bersak et al., 2001). When the user receives information in real time about a certain aspect of his physiology, he can be able to determine how his mental changes can influence his state. Biofeedback process can control those physiological factors (Bersak et al., 2001).

Emotion sensing and recognition is one of the core areas of affective computing and that provide relevant methods and techniques to affective design (Hudlicka, 2008).

Figure 2. Biofeedback - Stimuli, interactive cycle in adaptive immersive environments.

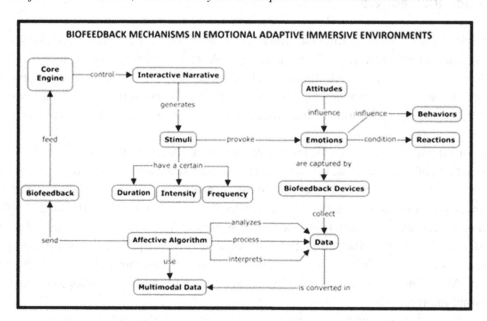

The term affective feedback appears when the concepts of affective computing and biofeedback are related, its application in immersive environments makes biofeedback mechanisms influence the user experience (Bersak et al., 2001).

A SOCIO-TECHNICAL APPROACH IN THE REQUIREMENTS DEFINITION FOR IMMERSIVE ENVIRONMENTS DEVELOPMENT

If an immersive environment as a strong technological and human component, it can be considered a socio-technical system. In that perspective, is a strong socio-technical environment where human and non-human elements come together in a heterogeneous network. The Actor-Network Theory (ANT) offers a different type of analysis, focused on the relational effect of the interaction between human and non-human elements in its heterogeneous network (Iyamu & Mgudlwa, 2018).

ANT focuses on the formulation of heterogeneous networks formed by human and non-human actors and on the relationships established between themselves (Iyamu, 2018). The use of ANT in the design of socio-technical systems, particularly in the definition of requirements (*Figure 3*), has been studied and tested over the last few years in collaborative systems (P. Veloso Gomes, 2004). Recently (Paulo Veloso Gomes et al., 2019) used Actor-Network Theory as an approach to design an immersive artifact of digital media art, the e-EMotion-Capsule, to develop an interactive immersive environment as a socio-technical system, where human and non-human elements have established strong relationships.

The ANT approach allows to decompose and analyze human and non-human elements, such as processes, policies, environment and networks, which involve the development and implementation of Information Systems (Nehemia-Maletzky, Iyamu, & Shaanika, 2018). These elements, human, technological and hybrid, are the genesis of an immersive environment.

One of the benefits of ANT is the recognition that technological and human elements are not distinguished and are related to each other, being equally influential in the environment in which they find themselves (Iyamu & Mgudlwa, 2018). This is a critical and important advance in the health sector, as it is impossible to separate professionals, patients and therapy programs (Iyamu & Mgudlwa, 2018).

Figure 3. Actor-Network Theory in the Requirement Definition Process, adapted from (P. Veloso Gomes, 2004).

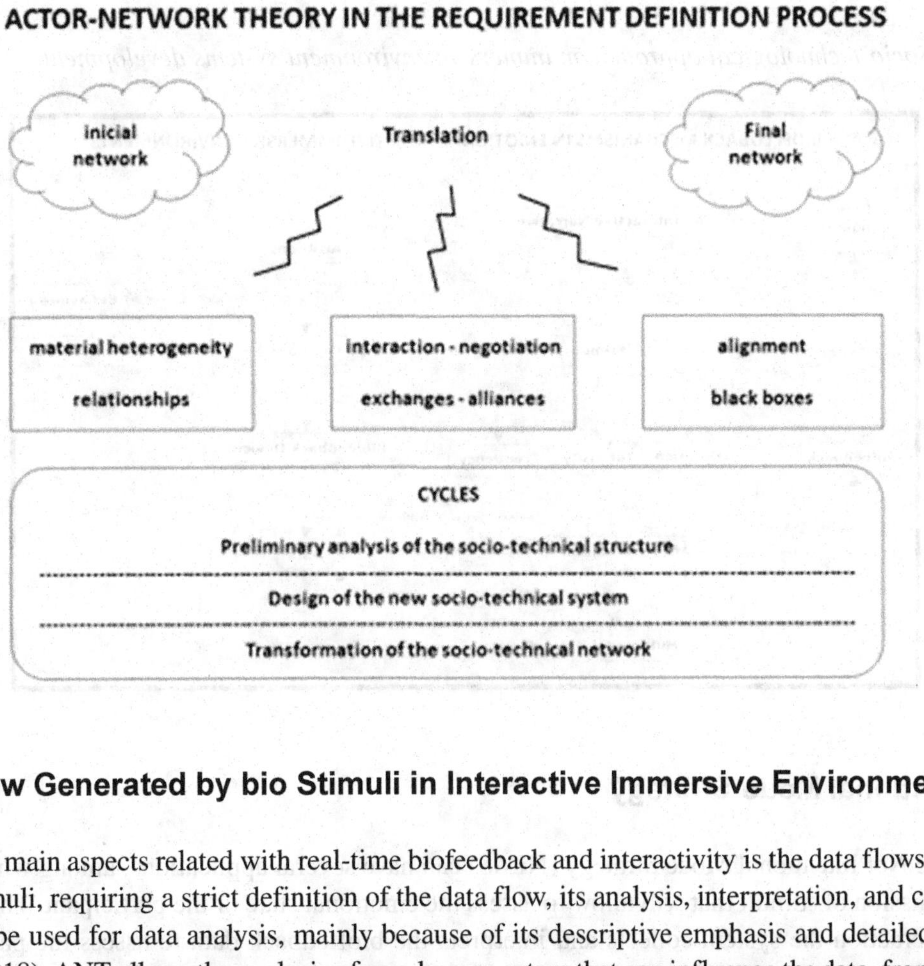

ACTOR-NETWORK THEORY IN THE REQUIREMENT DEFINITION PROCESS

Data Flow Generated by bio Stimuli in Interactive Immersive Environments

One of the main aspects related with real-time biofeedback and interactivity is the data flows generated by bio stimuli, requiring a strict definition of the data flow, its analysis, interpretation, and conversion. ANT can be used for data analysis, mainly because of its descriptive emphasis and detailed narrative (Iyamu, 2018). ANT allows the analysis of non-human actors that can influence the data, from the point of view of size, speed and variety (Iyamu, 2018). This aspect is particularly important since the process of collecting, analyzing and processing real-time data collected by biofeedback, can be influenced by several factors, such as electrical or magnetic interference, collection errors or algorithmic interpretation, sudden movements, errors caused by noise, among others.

Emotionally Adaptive Immersive Environment through affective algorithm can use three types of strategies, the Not Intentional Mode Strategy (NIMS), based on randomness in the stimulus management process, the Intentional Mode Strategy (IMS) that automatically generates stimuli according to pre-defined objectives, and the Controlled Mode Strategy (CMS) through the intervention of a supervisor who controls the system during user exposure to the immersive system (*Figure 4*).

In an initial phase, the system can choose to use the Not Intentional Mode Strategy (NIMS), where stimuli are generated randomly, and the system can assess the participant's emotional state. Subsequently, the system can adopt the Intentional Mode Strategy (IMS), where through the analysis of the obtained biofeedback, the system leads the participant to appropriate behaviors to achieve the intended objectives. The Controlled Mode Strategy (CMS) implies the intervention of a supervisor who controls the system personalizing the type of stimulus while observing the participant's responses.

Figure 4. Socio-technological approach on immersive environment systems development.

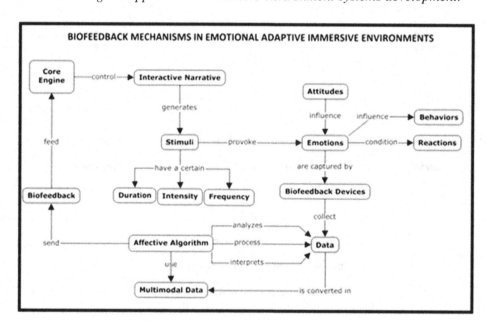

Not Intentional Mode Strategy

The use the Not Intentional Mode Strategy (NIMS) can have several applications, among which stands out, the emission of stimuli that will allow to assess the emotional state of the participant. Through this type of interaction the system collects and interprets the bioffedback data to assess the participant's behavioral pattern, defining his profile.

The use of this game mode allows to determine the condition of the participant through the baseline measurement of his biological signals. Baseline values vary from person to person, it is important that the system determines the values of each participant to be able to personalize their behavior, analyzing and adapting the stimuli to each experience.

When necessary, this IMS mode can also be used to adapt to the immersive environment, or for training, allowing the participant to interact with the system freely, adapting their behavior and reactions to randomly generated stimuli.

Intentional Mode Strategy

The use the Intentional Mode Strategy (IMS) can have several applications, among which stands out, the emission of stimuli that will allow to assess the emotional state of the participant. Through this type of interaction the system collects and interprets the bioffedback data to assess the participant's behavioral pattern, defining his profile.

The registration of the participant's baseline values is essential for a personalized interaction. The affective algorithmic calculates the range of values to issue stimuli appropriate to the participant's profile.

Controlled Mode Strategy

In an initial phase, the system can choose to use the Not Intentional Mode Strategy (NIMS), where stimuli are generated randomly, and the system can assess the participant's emotional state. The Controlled Mode Strategy (CMS) is used when third-party interaction is desired, this mode applies to exposures with specific therapeutic objectives.

The supervisor controls the system personalizing the type, frequency and intensity of stimulus while observing the participant's responses. The supervisor assumes the role of participatory observer, influencing the exposure according to the reactions and responses of the participant.

FUTURE RESEARCH DIRECTIONS

Some challenges are identified in this area, namely the portability of systems, so that they can be taken to people with reduced mobility, develop some even lighter and more sophisticated equipment, making them less invasive, so that the participant does not feel that he is using them, providing a more natural experience, the integration of new elements of interaction like multisensory VR devices such as motorized VR chairs or VR sensitive gloves and smell stimulators, this type of equipment is useful to increase the feeling of immersiveness.

CONCLUSION

Observing that the involvement between the user and the immersive system, considering that the user is also part of the system, and the dynamic interaction generated, it becomes difficult to unequivocally separate human elements from technological elements.

This work used the Actor-Network Theory as methodology to create an Emotionally Adaptive Immersive Environment, through the development of an affective algorithm capable of using three different interaction strategies. The Actor-Network Theory as a socio-technical approach allowed to analyze and design a dynamic, interactive, and self-regulating system.

Adaptive immersive environments can be used to induce emotional changes capable of generating states of empathy and self-control behaviors. The use of biofeedback mechanisms during the participant's exposure to adaptive immersive environments generates unimodal data, which when converted to multimodal data, can be used as an element of interaction between the participant and the system.

Biofeedback allows to identify and quantify emotional states and increase the interaction possibilities between the participant and the adaptative immersive environment. Its use as an interactive element influence the course of the interactive narrative.

The heterogeneous network created by the adaptive immersive environment use the biofeedback-Stimuli interactive cycle as an interaction engine, where the human and non-human elements influence each other and merge into a socio-technical system.

Using real-time biofeedback mechanisms during exposure to adaptive immersive environments allows new types of interaction between the participant and the system, the participant is influenced and influence the system simultaneously.

REFERENCES

Bersak, D., McDarby, G., Augenblick, N., McDarby, P., McDonnell, D., McDonald, B., & Karkun, R. (2001). Intelligent biofeedback using an immersive competitive environment. *Most*. Retrieved from http://medialabeurope.org/mindgames/publications/publicationsAtlanta2001rev3.pdf

de Tommaso, M., Ricci, K., Conca, G., Vecchio, E., Delussi, M., & Invitto, S. (2019). Empathy for pain in fibromyalgia patients: An EEG study. *International Journal of Psychophysiology*, *146*(September), 43–53. doi:10.1016/j.ijpsycho.2019.09.007 PMID:31648023

Grandchamp, R., & Delorme, A. (2016). The Brainarium: An Interactive Immersive Tool for Brain Education, Art, and Neurotherapy. *Computational Intelligence and Neuroscience*, *2016*, 1–12. Advance online publication. doi:10.1155/2016/4204385 PMID:27698660

Hildebrand, A., & Sá, V. (2000). EMBASSI: Electronic Multimedia and Service Assistance. In *Intelligent Interactive Assistance & Mobile Multimedia Computing (IMC 2000)* (pp. 50–59). Retrieved from http://publica.fraunhofer.de/eprints/urn_nbn_de_0011-n-39911.pdf

Hudlicka, E. (2008). Affective computing for game design. *4th International North-American Conference on Intelligent Games and Simulation, Game-On 'NA 2008*, 5–12.

Iyamu, T. (2018). A multilevel approach to big data analysis using analytic tools and actor network theory. *South African Journal of Information Management*, *20*(1). Advance online publication. doi:10.4102ajim.v20i1.914

Iyamu, T., & Mgudlwa, S. (2018). Transformation of healthcare big data through the lens of actor network theory. *International Journal of Healthcare Management*, *11*(3), 182–192. doi:10.1080/20479700.2017.1397340

Lorenzetti, V., Melo, B., Basílio, R., Suo, C., Yücel, M., Tierra-Criollo, C. J., & Moll, J. (2018). Emotion regulation using virtual environments and real-time fMRI neurofeedback. *Frontiers in Neurology*, *9*(JUL), 1–15. doi:10.3389/fneur.2018.00390 PMID:30087646

Marcos, A., Bernardes, P., & Sá, V. (2002). Multimedia technology and 3D environments used in the preservation and dissemination of the portuguese cultural heritage. In Méndez Vilas A., J. A. Mesa Gonzáles, & I. Zaldívar Maldonado (Eds.), *Educational Technology : International Conference on Information and Comunication Technologies in Education (ICTE2002)* (pp. 1335–1339). Badajoz: Consejería de Educación, Ciencia y Tecnología.

Nehemia-Maletzky, M., Iyamu, T., & Shaanika, I. (2018). The use of activity theory and actor network theory as lenses to underpin information systems studies. *Journal of Systems and Information Technology, 20*(2), 191–206. doi:10.1108/JSIT-10-2017-0098

Poria, S., Cambria, E., Bajpai, R., & Hussain, A. (2017). A review of affective computing: From unimodal analysis to multimodal fusion. *Information Fusion, 37,* 98–125. doi:10.1016/j.inffus.2017.02.003

Santamaría-García, H., Baez, S., García, A. M., Flichtentrei, D., Prats, M., Mastandueno, R., Sigman, M., Matallana, D., Cetkovich, M., & Ibáñez, A. (2017). Empathy for others' suffering and its mediators in mental health professionals. *Scientific Reports, 7*(1), 1–13. doi:10.103841598-017-06775-y PMID:28743987

Soleymani, M., Larson, M., Pun, T., & Hanjalic, A. (2014). Corpus Development for Affective Video Indexing. *IEEE Transactions on Multimedia, 16*(4), 1075–1089. doi:10.1109/TMM.2014.2305573

Tijs, T., Brokken, D., & Ijsselsteijn, W. (2008). Creating an emotionally adaptive game. Lecture Notes in Computer Science (Including Subseries Lecture Notes in Artificial Intelligence and Lecture Notes in Bioinformatics), 5309 LNCS(September), 122–133. doi:10.1007/978-3-540-89222-9-14

Veloso Gomes, P. (2004). *Participação e colaboração mediada por computador em instituições universitárias: uma abordagem atraves da teoria Actor-Network.* Universidade do Porto, Porto. Retrieved from https://repositorio-aberto.up.pt/handle/10216/12055

Veloso Gomes, P., Marques, A., Pereira, J., Correia, A., Donga, J., & Sá, V. J. (2019). E-emotion capsule: As artes digitais na criação de emoções. In *ACM International Conference Proceeding Series.* Braga: Association for Computing Machinery. 10.1145/3359852.3359962

This research was previously published in the Handbook of Research on Solving Modern Healthcare Challenges With Gamification; pages 68-78, copyright year 2021 by Medical Information Science Reference (an imprint of IGI Global).

Chapter 11
Crowdfunding Serious Games:
Towards a Framework

Christopher Buckingham
ⓘ https://orcid.org/0000-0001-8417-1007
University of Southampton, UK

Vanissa Wanick
ⓘ https://orcid.org/0000-0002-6367-1202
University of Southampton, UK

ABSTRACT

In serious game design, addressing issues related to the value and opportunity of the development of a game is vital in the early stages, creating a more structured and robust approach by exploring the business case. Present frameworks provide an in-depth analysis of game design models but often fail to state the case of predetermined target markets and new funding options for serious game design. Crowdfunding is an emerging funding path for these games and one that leads the vanguard in breaking with traditional forms of raising funding. This chapter aims to help in addressing an existing limitation in the literature by reviewing an existing framework on game design and blending this with the concept of crowdfunding. This chapter proposes the extension of a framework that reflects the possibility for early crowdfunding of a serious game.

INTRODUCTION

With changes in the workplace promoted by the 2020's coronavirus (COVID-19) global pandemic (e.g., large adoption of remote and online working practices and the implementation of digital transformation within companies' cultural practices), there is an increased demand in the larger market for corporate training, that could be done online and remotely (Baker, 2020). This has not only affected the business sector, but also education. For instance, due to the pandemic, the online education market is expected to reach $350 billion by 2025. Additionally, according to Sonawane (2017) by 2023 the serious games market is expected to be worth more than $9.2 billion. As Kriz (2020) noted, with pupils having to

DOI: 10.4018/978-1-6684-7589-8.ch011

study online, simulations and serious games can be a suitable and effective means to convey educational content that overcome the limitations of Virtual Learning Environments (VLEs). For example, serious games can help students face challenges in a simulated environment through multiplayer collaboration/competition strategies supported by game mechanics (de Gloria et al. 2014).

The global pandemic also caused economic hardship for consumers, businesses and governments, in which financial resources have become scarce (Barker & Russell, 2020). The very nature of crowdfunding results in value being created beyond funding a vision. Demonstrating expertise of the crowdfunding applicant, educating the crowd and engaging that crowd with the possibility to be included in the journey of the vision are some of the major justifications of using crowdfunding.

In fact, the use of crowdfunding by larger corporations is becoming recurrent (Grell et al., 2015) and with new ways of gaining entry to markets more generally are explored. This can be seen in the acceleration of firms like Microsoft moving from a device-centric (focused on hardware development) to a player-centric (focused on user nurture and engagement) firm (McGee, 2020).

The console video game industry is a complex behemoth that captures the creative and independent sole of the electronic game building community and networks them through their monopolised channels of distribution. This is in direct opposition to Benkler (2006) who summarised the two-way evolution and revolution of cultural artefacts through the use of The Web. This was to be a new era of fulfilment on behalf of the creator where they could choose to commercialise their cultural product or simply donate it to the world archive that is The Web (Lessig, 2004). For the video game sector more broadly, this process has been slow to materialise because of the monopolistic characteristic of the distribution process for games for entertainment purposes (Planells, 2015). Of the many elements and components that make up the ludic centred world, change is ever present as ludic constructs are presented and tested in real world conditions (Walz & Deterding, 2014). Game design and building is at the vanguard of this evolutionary process as it sits at the confluence of the academic and the industrial. Evidence of this morphogenesis in the design-to-build process can be witnessed through the various frameworks and models that have been proposed in the literature in the past few years (Robson et al., 2015). The Mechanic, Dynamic and Aesthetic (MDA) framework (Hunicke, LeBlanc & Zubeck, 2004) has a wide application in this space and is implicit in many of the additional frameworks which emerged (Dillon 2011; Kim 2015). The MDA framework has proven to be a stable building block for the implementation of game design (Hunicke, LeBlanc & Zubeck, 2004).

The components of the MDA framework will be explored in this chapter as evidence of the lasting cultural legacy of the original authors. So far, much emphasis has been given in the literature towards the design elements of a digital game. But chronologically these are lacking the design intent to build a game as an opportunity to fulfil a specific set of purposes for a specific audience; thus, here is a lack clarity when addressing the wider possible market opportunity that may exist in the very production of the game.

Using the MDA Framework (Hunicke, LeBlanc & Zubeck, 2004) and its extension, the DPE Framework (Design, Play, Experience) (Winn, 2009), this chapter demonstrates a new conceptual extension that affords the possibility for both a robust cultural product that fulfils needs on an open market and understanding as to how this product could be funded via a crowd of enthusiasts.

This chapter adopts Michael and Chen (2005)'s definition of a serious games as "...games that do not have entertainment, enjoyment, or fun as their primary purpose (p.17)." The specific term 'serious', in this context, is taken to mean non-entertainment as opposed to stern or not fun (Seaborn & Fels, 2015). De Lope and Medina-Medina (2017) offer one of the most comprehensive taxonomies of serious games, for this chapter the serious game has a single purpose in its utility. However, clarity for the business case of the game creation is still required. If we ask for the specific purpose of the games creation to be stated at the outset, we can go some way to enlightening stakeholders that are not involved in the games development but are interested in funding the vision being created (e.g. potential crowdfunder's and investors). This adds immediacy to the understanding of the rationale for the game development and intentions (Asuncion et al., 2011). Additionally, it will also add confidence for investors as they step into the opaque world of entrepreneurship for (possibly) the first time.

By extending the existing Design Play Experience framework (Winn, 2009), this chapter's intention is to show that, theoretically, serious game developers with a Minimum Viable Product (MVP) can gain an understanding of the wider business context for the application of a serious game to an unknown market via crowdfunding. This is especially relevant with the introduction of new trends in work, business, and financial models (i.e. crowdsourcing/crowdfunding) as patterns of production and funding morph in the contemporary context. Although not all serious games are developed for educational purposes, in this chapter the theoretical application of the extended DPE Framework (Winn, 2009) will assume there is a pedagogical requirement in the serious game being developed.

This chapter contends that a more focused approach can be taken via the conceptual introduction of the OPDEPLEX framework. The OPDEPLEX framework aims to provide a bridge by creating the opportunity for the serious game developer to address these issues. It does so by adding the opportunity column to an existing framework, adding value from the perspective of an investor who may influence the game's development, while simultaneously becoming a potential consumer. This is new ground in the brave new world post pandemic for both the games design eco-system and investors, producers, and consumers alike (Planells, 2015).

BACKGROUND

According to Rae (2007), opportunities are either created, discovered or a hybrid of these whereby an individual may have insight to a tangible or intangible situation or object, and act entrepreneurially to profit from that insight. There are four stages that the opportunity must traverse before becoming an enacted entrepreneurial reality, these are: 1) relating the opportunity to personal goals; 2) creating and exploring the opportunity; 3) planning to realise the opportunity; and 4) acting to make the opportunity happen (Rae, 2007, p.10).

This is a linear process which relies on the cognitive abilities of management. If this transition from an entity 'out there' to an entity that has concrete entrepreneurial potential, there must be agential interventions. This takes both an agent's cognition and conceptualisation of the entity and the opportunity that could be a future reality (Eckhardt & Shane, 2010). To date, there is no framework or model that provides a bridge by creating the opportunity for the serious game developer to address these issues and, if it is required, approach this via crowdfunding. Developers might want to commit to the broader picture and create a product that may be scalable into other areas. In this scenario crowdfunding can be used of as a mass focus group. The opportunity in the literature for a robust framework dealing with this paradigm has not been realised.

Economic sustainability of a project relies on sourcing revenue streams that equip management with the ability to create their vision (Rae, 2007). Thus, it is possible that if this is done early in the planning process, the team developing the product will have greater commercial cognition. Conceptualisation of the wider opportunity for the game application and the possibility of crowdfunding is baked-in from the beginning. However, it is also realised that not all serious games are intended for a commercial market or indeed have learning objectives at the core of their design. It may be that the game being built is limited to the game development in hand (Salen & Zimmerman, 2003). This process is partly reliant on an understanding of the various elements that combine to make a game appealing to a predefined target demographic. However, this situation may be less of an issue for the development of games that only tackle a single issue on which the aims and objectives are based. In this instance, it may be required to serve specific objectives for a narrow user group. . For the entertainment game genre, the MDA Framework is sufficient as a reductionist analytical aid in the analysis (or building) process. For serious game with pedagogy at its core, this is found lacking as the depth needed to clarify the pedagogical engagement of the objectives embedded in the game require much broader scaffolding (Winn, 2009).

Building a game as an aesthetic form is a very different proposition from building a game as a strictly commercial proposition. The tension between these two is over the form the worthiness these take to different segments of a market. Worthiness in this model is not pecuniary gain, it is a value ensemble beyond economic reward and, logically, it would follow that motivations must therefore also differ between genres (Cockton, 2006). These are old debates (cf. (Carey, 2006)) and it is sufficient here to conclude that there are valid reasons for the existence of both, serving as they do particular markets that can at times be fused.

EVOLUTION FROM MDA TO DPE FRAMEWORKS

Delivering the possibility of learning objectives results in attention being drawn to the need for a serious game framework that can support the design and building of such an outcome which also positions the need to understand the business rationale and the possibility of crowdfunding for the final outcome. Although there are frameworks and models specific for serious games development such as the GAME framework (Brito et al., 2015), the PLEX framework (Arrasvuori et al., 2011) and the RETAIN model (Gunter et al., 2008), these have not attempted to consider the business case; these frameworks were considered and critically evaluated for their relevance to the process of developing a serious game in the context of aiding fluency for the player.

Mechanics, Dynamics and Aesthetics were the three headline features of the MDA framework from Hunicke, LeBlanc and Zubeck (2004). Further to these three components present in the MDA framework, Winn (2009) saw a need to extend the supporting role this framework played between designer and player. Whereas Hunicke, LeBlanc and Zubeck (2004) introduced a framework for the design principles most salient to the core features of games, Winn (2009) took issue with the framework's holistic approach and proposed a more detailed and focused approach exploring the designer-to-player nexus (see Figure 1).

In addition, criticism has been levied at the MDA framework mainly from the lexical perspective which is often focused on lexicon that may be deemed duplicitous. For game designers, this context can lead to friction through misinterpretation of the term (or terms). An example of this is found in the Robson et al.'s (2015) paper, their emphasis is on the use of the term 'emotion' as opposed to the term 'aesthetic'. They problematize the term aesthetic as it tends to be linked to coding practices. Aesthetic is a term that lends itself well to the game player's state when they engage with the game but not one that readily translates to the wider business context. Their use of the term *emotion* over *aesthetic* provides a business context that places the emotions of the employees or customer's sense of engagement above mere digital game engagement (Robson et al., 2015).

The view Winn (2009) took was that there was too much emphasis on the game play elements in the MDA framework. MDA failed to; "address aspects of game design beyond the game play, including the storytelling, user experience, and influence of technology on design" (Winn, 2009, p.1014). Additionally, the MDA framework had not considered the learning component core to serious game design. To readjust the MDA framework further, components were added extending it so as to encompass the unique "design challenges" (Winn, 2009, p.1014) that are necessary for the building of a quality game fit for the purpose it was intended to fulfil. One of the major issues Winn (2009) raises is the degree of control a designer has with the end result when using the MDA framework.

In effect, designers are constrained by the mechanics and only allowed input at this layer of the game development. There is no further control over the interaction between player and game. Play-testing is encouraged in the MDA framework, but the iterative process this affords is considered much less robust than that emphasised in the Expanded version of the DPE framework (see Figure 1). DPE affords the opportunity for a deeper analysis of the iterative data and an ongoing option to adjust learning, storytelling and gameplay.

Figure 1. The Expanded DPE framework (Winn, 2009)

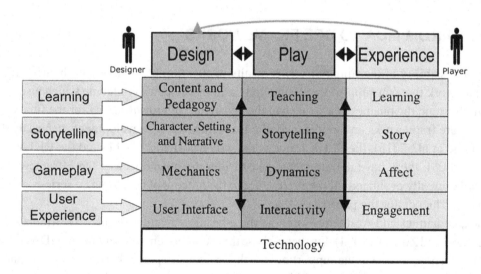

There are several key features of the DPE framework that need to be emphasised. First is the iterative process not just in the central vertical columns but also between the design and the experience. This is vital for an iterative process to be realised and ongoing while engaging the community for whom the game is being developed. This extends the base requirements of a game for entertainment and emphasises the markets need for the development of a serious game. According to Winn (2009) the complexity of a serious game, with learning objectives at its core, requires a deeper cognition in the iterative stages.

Since each player has a different cultural expectation and experience in the game itself, the DPE framework allows more understanding of space and time for the player aesthetic to be realised. This is also where the most salient change in terminology, from 'aesthetic' to 'affect' is introduced. This change is presented as a challenge to the term aesthetic, which is suggested as implying a deeper artistically centred concept "representing the beauty of something" (Winn, 2009, p.1016). The term *affect* has more psychological undertones representing an emotional or desired state or entity, which is not that dissimilar to the change Robson et al. (2015) thought necessary when they changed *aesthetic* for *emotion*. This is perhaps the weakest argument in the extension of the MDA framework. But it does serve to emphasise the conflicting values that terminology can bring to a concept. The intention of Robson et al. (2015) was to diversify the debate and get serious games designed and built to adequately meet their purpose. In the brave new world, this is highly important as markets enter the unknown with exaggerated fear of further economic and social shocks.

Serious games serve learners by allowing them the opportunity to achieve objectives in either a psychological or behavioural manner (Leaning, 2015). In its most basic form, aesthetics deal with the pleasurable affordances for the subjective individual (Mautner, 2005). Not allowing adequate focus on these issues could lead to criticism of failure to recognise the attributions offered through the aesthetic position. Likewise, Winn's (2009) replacement term, 'affect', offers a transparent veneer through which the deeper insights may be seen to be working but are impenetrable and unobtainable to the designer. Aesthetics, alternatively, are cavernous and concern the taste and disposition of the player's cognition. This may become an opaque view when seen through the lens alone

THE OPDEPLEX FRAMEWORK

Extending the original DPE framework has allowed the columns *opportunity* and *crowdfunding* to be added to the OPDEPLEX framework (see Figure 3). The original headline rows of learning, story, gameplay and user experience support the new additional columns. Additionally, to the far left is added ex-ante and to the far-right post-ante. These serve to highlight a product's journey transitioning from untested idea, ex-ante, to tested product, post-ante, with feedback from the target demographic, the linear progression is maintained in the product's development.

Iteration between all layers and their respective columns was strongly encouraged in the original paper by Winn (2009). However, as the columns transition so iterations are possible between the opportunity and the crowdfunding columns. This reflects the nature of crowdfunding where it is necessary to present to the crowd a stable idea that has been well thought through in terms of the business model and strategy (Smith, 2015; Mollick, 2013).

This may, however, lead to potential conflict in that any entrepreneurial venture will inevitably discover new problems and solutions as they develop their ideas further. Both Planells (2015) and Smith (2015) identified this problem for the digital games sector using crowdfunding. Indeed, as Smith demonstrated, it may be possible for the strategy, or for the mechanics, of a digital game to be updated following input from the crowd during the live phase of a crowdfunding campaign.

As the OPDEPLEX framework is enlisting crowdfunding as a potential revenue source to enable the project to at least reach a runway (Ries, 2011), Planells (2015) argues that there must be consideration of the investor, producer and consumer as separate individuals, which are embodied as individuals that comprise the crowd (see Figure 2). For example, an individual member of the crowd can combine all three attributes in one. They may be an investor who is equally a producer, while also consuming (an "Inprosumer" in Figure 2). This identifies this section of stakeholders as both separate and combined members of the crowd. According to Planells (2015) this is a unique characteristic of the crowdfunding genre in that an individual member of the crowd can combine all three attributes in one. They may be an investor who is a producer who is also a consumer.

Figure 2. IPC stakeholder map

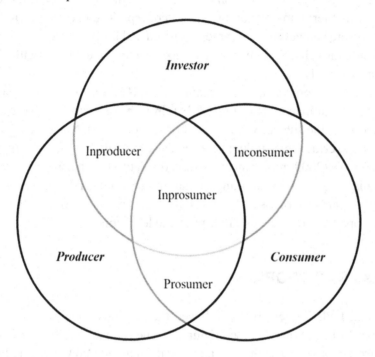

Business models are also problematic in that they are often presented as fixed entities that act as a veneer for the workings behind the scenes. This is disputed by Antonopoulou et al. (2017) who view this as an over-simplification of what can be an emerging process within fields seeking digital innovations. This is supported in the framework with the introduction of extraction in the opportunity column and under the story layer. It is also expected that through the theoretical utility offered by the OPDEPLEX framework (see Figure 3) the potential and levels of each possible revenue stream can be identified and incorporated into the project. The opportunity now becomes part of the design mix and early in this process the wider business case for a serious game can be stated clearly and concisely. In the next subsections, the columns are explained in detail.

Opportunity Column

Targets: The opportunity column starts with targets, which includes stakeholders. As this framework is intended for serious games it is essential that the needs of the stakeholder community are identified and met. Identifying the demographics of these users early in the process will mean a much more targeted approach to understanding their desires and needs later in the framework. Stakeholders are not necessarily the end user or player of the game, but they may have the power to endorse or shelve the project. Funding should not be a set strategy at this early stage since funding from other avenues may be found more appropriate than crowdfunding. As Nagle and Roche (2013) discussed, crowdfunding for the creative

Figure 3. The OPDEPLEX framework

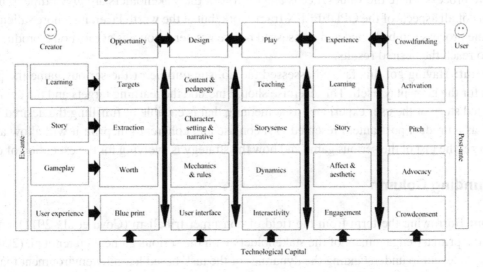

industries is particularly hazardous. Seeking financial aid may mean more traditional financing routes are favourable at the time funding is sought. Alternatively, match-funding could equally be possible. Discounting any means of funding on the grounds of subjective dislike or hearsay with no evidence is a risk resulting in the potential delay or missed opportunity for the creation of the vision.

Extraction: The drawing out of the story to be told to enable targets to be met. Extraction in this context is both the active listening by management to the crowd's input, coupled with the internal organisational dialogues that allow for the emergence of a business model as development proceeds (Antonopoulou et al., 2017). This layer is dependent on understanding of the outcomes and the players that will be expected to use and benefit from the serious game deployment. For this to happen there must be interaction between game builder, teacher and player/learner for the utility of story components and language to emerge. Gunter et al. (2008) identified the benefits of this process as manifest of an emergent story that the player or learner will find most satisfying and conducive for learning. The process of extraction may be in the form of interviews and questionnaires posed to the target stakeholders. There is also an aesthetic value embedded in this extraction process in that the story manifests itself in what the player/ learner will want in terms of engagement. For this to be the case there has to be a certain aesthetic value created for the target user and demonstrable in the final game offer. The process of extraction may be simple enough in the form of interviews and questionnaires posed to the target stakeholders. Dangers lie in vanity metrics (Ries, 2011) becoming the standards that the researcher relies on most. Where extracted content is analysed and the subjectivity of the researcher clouds the meaning of the subject's response. Avoiding this is critical to the realisation of a product worthy of further development.

Worth: Having now developed the targets, uncovered detail concerning the extraction of the story, game worthiness can be assessed in terms of both the sustainability of the game and the gameplay of the proposal. A pivot may be necessary given the insights from the above (Ries, 2011). If the concept is considered worthy of further resources then a more detailed approach can be undertaken in the next layer of the column (blueprint). Therefore, it is possible to ask; What will a successful serious game look like to all stakeholders (especially the player or learner)? How does one measure the efficacy of gameplay? This means metrics are needed for deeper consideration at this step. To get to this point there must be a reflective process where the values, needs and desires of the stakeholders are given time to manifest. This is true of all aspects of the OPDEPLEX framework, but at the worth layer, it is more salient. In this instance the process can be halted and reassessed before greater resources are lost on a production that will fail to reach the desired results.

Blueprint: Having got this far and assessed the holistic outline of the serious game the planning can begin for the gameplay itself. This exercise should include the learning targets and the evidence for the extracted story of the user experience as something that is capable of fulfilling the desired learning outcomes as a product post-ante. Presented as a concise and coherent blueprint it will allow all stakeholders to get the gist of the serious game and how the strategy is evolving for the execution of the plan.

Crowdfunding Column

Activation: Borrowing the term from the field of consumer tribalism (Cova et al., 2011), activation concerns the primary engagement of the stakeholders with the serious game. Gunter et al. (2008) view this as very relevant to understanding the dynamics of the task-based learning environment that is supported through the design and creation of a serious game.

In crowdfunding, the possibility of the triple status from Planells (2015) of members of the crowd can be applicable to the wider crowdfunding and sourcing paradigm. Each status requires different activation of motivational affordance to become a reality. As an investor, the motivational affordance may be the return on capital employed; as a producer, the motivational affordance can be the prospect of positive peer reviews; for the consumer, the motivational affordance could be the possession of knowledge gained through their engagement with the serious game. Crowdfunding is reliant on the crowd's activation to engage with a campaign and the vision being created.

Pitch: Is an essential part of the process where one seeks approval from the crowd in the form of *crowdconsent*. Persuasive discourse is used to position the vision as a worthy cause and one that needs support to enable the future possible reality to exist. Conveyance may be problematic for management particularly if they fail to provide verifiable evidence of their track record to date (Zhang & Liu, 2012). Furthermore, Lins et al. (2016) identified resistance from the crowd if socially accepted norms were being supplanted with new profound ideas. In these more radical situations, the pitch allows a narrative to be formed and conveyed that can help ease this tension (Lins et al., 2016; Rosenfeld et al., 2002; Leary, 1996; Leary & Kowalski, 1990; Goffman, 1959).

Zhang and Liu (2012) found positive language a key component to a construction of a suitable pitch in crowdfunding. Supplication, showing a weakness and need for help in certain areas, is also beneficial when delivered in doses that corresponded with the vision being created. Balancing these issues well in the pitch may result in herding, whereby investors desire inclusion based only on peer effects (Zhang & Liu, 2012; Shen et al., 2010). If the pitch is rejected it is likely that there was no dominant class leading the herd to a positive investment decision. If it succeeds, on the other hand, there were likely a dominant class leading the action. Rejection is thus based on rational observations leading to a negative action decision and no corresponding irrational herding effects.

Advocacy: At this level, the pitch has been accepted, which leads to several outcomes including dissemination of the pitch to the networks of the advocate and discretionary levels of funding being provided. Further active engagement is now made possible with the extension of the networked supporters and the dissemination of the campaigns message. Falk and Ichino (2006) identified this as a result of gaining traction via peer effects. The persuasive discourse employed is also vital for another deeper aspect of impression management that the advocate may be attempting to demonstrate. That is that through the funding and realisation of this vision there is an opportunity to break away from the homogenisation of previous entities and a demonstration of favourable conditions for the new paradigm. For example, this could include, for a serious game designer, integrated learning in the gameplay as an implanted aesthetic. If this has never been done before the designer (and stakeholders more broadly) are faced with higher risks of rejection by the targeted community as the vision they propose may be perceived as something too risky or unnecessary. If the target community reject the new entity then the likelihood of positive advocacy is reduced. Likewise, if they accept the new entity, positive advocacy is likely increased.

Crowdconsent: Crowd acceptance of the visions stated outcome will allow the vision to be realised as *crowdconsent* is granted (Buckingham, 2015). This is the permission granted by the crowd to enable the vision to be created. For the serious game stakeholders this is the approval from the crowd for the idea of the vision, not, however, for the vision itself. This can only be granted once the game is in play by the targeted segment. Their acceptance at this stage of the serious game as a utility that affords the desired outcomes via a set of experiences they deem appropriate, is still hypothetical (ex-ante) and yet to be confirmed as a product that can deliver on the projected promises being made in the crowdfunding campaign.

DISCUSSION

For the designer involved with the creation of a serious game with educational requirements as either objective or outcome, the benefits of the OPDEPLEX framework are that a sound perspective of the application of crowdfunding can be derived from the holistic approach it offers. Thus, the OPDEPLEX framework extends the existing DPE framework (Winn, 2009) but adding two columns: opportunity and crowdfunding. As identified in the literature, existing models and frameworks like GAME framework (Brito et al., 2015), the PLEX framework (Arrasvuori et al., 2011) and the RETAIN model (Gunter et al., 2008) target the development of the serious game from the point of view of game design and its influence in the player experience. The OPDEPLEX framework provides a step before and after the design process, offering game designers and developers an understanding of what can be done to publish a serious game successfully.

Since crowdfunding provides a platform for the crowd, investors and designers to create a shared vision, another option of use for the OPDEPLEX framework is to utilise crowdfunding as a way of testing an MVP and ideas through a business lens. This would mean utilising crowdfunding not necessarily for the funding of the project but as a methodology for understanding how receptive a market may be to the product or concept. For example, crowdfunding could be employed as a mass focus group or where weaknesses are identified in a team or business model then supplication could be employed.

The main contribution of the OPDEPLEX framework is application of crowdfunding for serious games development, derived from a holistic approach and critical review of current game design frameworks. This takes the form of first providing the designer with the recognition of the opportunity within the context of an existing and established framework. The expected utility of this additional column is in the recognition for the designer that they are producing an outcome that has value on an open market. The main principle of the OPDEPLEX framework is that if this is done early in the planning process, the team developing the product will have a greater commercial understanding. Furthermore, there may be broader opportunities to extend this outcome to new applications. Finally, the crowdfunding column provides an initial insight into the possibility of utilising this form of funding for the project.

This is a conceptual framework which builds on the existing DPE framework from Winn (2009). As such, limitations exist in Winn's framework as it has not been tested empirically. It is intended as a discussion on the research topic and to introduce the work as the research moves forward and testing begins in the real world. However, with the main objective of introducing the new columns as a fresh interdisciplinary approach and positioning the OPDEPLEX framework as a potential for a fresh perspective for serious game designers. Reviews of the literature on serious games have thus far been sparse on the area of serious games and crowdfunding. This in part may reflect the novelty of the crowdfunding concept or that the serious games field are yet to embrace this form of funding. This theoretical contribution is intended to address these areas.

CONCLUSION

The opportunity to develop and create a serious game that may be applicable to a varied number of scenarios has not been found in the literature to date. Couple this with new trends in funding vehicles and the need for a framework that can lend itself well to these areas becomes apparent. The OPDEPLEX crowd framework goes someway to empowering serious game stakeholders with the ability to see beyond their initial target and recognise value creation that extends to other market opportunities.

The OPDEPLEX framework is a theoretical framework that extends existent theory to include contemporary forms of funding and the opportunity to create additional value for serious game development. This framework aims at empowering serious game stakeholders with the ability to see beyond their initial target and recognise value creation that extends to other market opportunities. With new trends in funding venues and paradigm changes, it is expected that the OPDEPLEX framework could provide guidance for serious game designers and stakeholders entering and exploring new markets. Further studies could consider the exploration of the application of the OPDEPLEX framework through different stages of serious game design, including its contribution for the MVP stage, value creation and the role that IPC (investors, producers and consumers) stakeholders take in each stage. In the future, it is expected to validate the framework with experts and game developers working in the field. In this changing world, the hope is that some guidance may emerge through the contribution of OPDEPLEX.

ACKNOWLEDGMENT

We would like to thank the editors of this book for putting this publication together.

This research received no specific grant from any funding agency in the public, commercial, or not-for-profit sectors.

REFERENCES

Antonopoulou, K., Nandhakumar, J., & Begkos, C. (2017). *The Emergence of Business Model for Digital Innovation Projects without Predetermined Usage and Market Potential. In Proceedings of the 50th Hawaii International Conference on System Sciences.* HICSS. http://hdl.handle.net/10125/41787

Arrasvuori, J., Boberg, M., Holopainen, J., Korhonen, H., Lucero, A., & Montola, M. (2011). Applying the PLEX Framework in Designing for Playfulness. In *2011 Conference on Designing Pleasurable Products and Interfaces*. ACM. http://www.ekarapanos.com/DPPI13_PLEX.pdf

Asuncion, H., Socha, D., Sung, K., Berfield, S., & Gregory, W. (2011). Serious Game Development as an Iterative User-centered Agile Software Project. *Proceedings of the 33rd International Conference on Software Engineering* 10.1145/1984674.1984690

Baker, M. (2020). 9 Future of Work Trends Post Covid-19. *Gartner.* https://www.gartner.com/smarterwithgartner/9-future-of-work-trends-post-covid-19/

Barker, M., & Russell, J. (2020). Feeding the food insecure in Britain: Learning from the 2020 COVID-19 crisis. *Food Security*, *12*(4), 865–870. doi:10.100712571-020-01080-5 PMID:32837648

Benkler, Y. (2006). The Wealth of Networks: how social production transforms markets and freedom. New Haven, CT: Yale University Press.

Brito, J., Vieira, V., & Duran, A. (2015). Towards a Framework for Gamification Design on Crowdsourcing Systems: the G.A.M.E. approach. In *12th International Conference on Information Technology* (pp. 445-450). IEEE Computer Society. 10.1109/ITNG.2015.78

Buckingham, C. (2015). *Crowdfunding Intelligence: the no-Nonsense guide to raising investment funds on the internet*. LID Publishing.

Carey, J. (2006). *What Good are the Arts?* Faber and Faber.

Cockton, G. (2006). Designing Worth is Worth Designing. In *Proceedings of the 4th Nordic Conference on Human-computer Interaction: Changing Roles* (pp. 165–174). ACM. 10.1145/1182475.1182493

Cova, B., Kozinets, R., & Shankar, A. (2011). *Consumer Tribes*. Routledge.

De Lope, R. P., & Medina-Medina, N. (2017). A Comprehensive Taxonomy for Serious Games. *Journal of Educational Computing Research*, *55*(5), 629–672. doi:10.1177/0735633116681301

Dillon, R. (2011). The 6-11 Framework: a new approach to video game analysis and design. In T. C. Tien (Ed.), *GAMEON-ASIA 2011 Proceedings* (pp. 25–29). Eurosis. Retrieved from http://www.eurosis.org/cms/?q=taxonomy/term/263

Eckhardt, T. J., & Shane, S. (2010). An Update to the Individual-opportunity Nexus. In Handbook of Entrepreneurship Research (2nd ed.). New York: Springer. doi:10.1007/978-1-4419-1191-9_3

Falk, A., & Ichino, A. (2006). Clean Evidence on Peer Effects. *Journal of Labor Economics*, *24*(1), 39–57. doi:10.1086/497818

Goffman, E. (1959). *The Presentation of Self in Everyday Life* (1990 ed.). Penguin.

Grell, K. B., Marom, D., & Swart, R. (2015). *Crowdfunding The Corporate Era*. Elliot & Thompson Ltd.

Gunter, G. A., Kenny, R. F., & Vick, E. H. (2008). Taking Educational Games Seriously: Using the RETAIN model to design endogenous fantasy into standalone educational games. *Educational Technology Research and Development*, *56*(5–6), 511–537. doi:10.100711423-007-9073-2

Hunicke, R., LeBlanc, M., & Zubeck, R. (2004). MDA: A formal approach to game design and game research. *AAAI Workshop on Challenges in Game AI*, 4.

Kim, B. (2015)... *Understanding Gamification. American Library Association*, *51*(2), 1–35.

Kriz, W. C. (2020). Gaming in the Time of Covid-19. *Gaming and Simulation*, *51*(4), 403–410. doi:10.1177/1046878120931602

Leaning, M. (2015). A Study of the Use of Games and Gamification to Enhance Student Engagement, Experience and Achievement on a Theory-based Course of an Undergraduate Media Degree. *Journal of Media Practice*, *16*(2), 155–170. doi:10.1080/14682753.2015.1041807

Leary, M., & Kowalski, R. (1990). Impression Management: A literature review and two-component model. *Psychological Bulletin*, *107*(1), 34–47. doi:10.1037/0033-2909.107.1.34

Leary, M. R. (1996). *Self-presentation: impression management and interpersonal behavior. Social psychology series*. Westview Press.

Lessig, L. (2004). *Free Culture: the nature and future of creativity. London*. Penguin Press.

Lins, E., Fietkiewicz, K. J., & Lutz, E. (2016). How to Convince the Crowd: an impression management approach. *Hawaii International Conference on System Science* (pp. 3505–3514). IEEE. 10.1109/HICSS.2016.439

Mautner, T. (2005). The Penguin Dictionary of Philosophy (2nd ed). London: Penguin.

McGee, P. (2020, Sept. 25). Is It Game Over For The Console? *Financial Times*.

Michael, D. R., & Chen, S. L. (2005). *Serious Games: Games that educate, train, and inform*. Course Technology.

Mollick, E. R. (2013). *The Dynamics of Crowdfunding: an exploratory study*. Rochester, NY: Social Science Research Network. https://papers.ssrn.com/abstract=2088298

Nagle, P., & Roche, C. (2013). *Equity Crowdfunding for the Arts & Creative Industries*. http://www.culturecrowd.co.uk/

Planells, A. J. (2015). Video Games and the Crowdfunding Ideology: From the gamer-buyer to the prosumer-investor. *Journal of Consumer Culture*. Advance online publication. doi:10.1177/1469540515611200

Rae, D. (2007). *Entrepreneurship: from opportunity to action*. Palgrave Macmillan. doi:10.1007/978-0-230-20925-1

Ries, E. (2011). *The Lean Startup: how today's entrepreneurs use continuous innovation to create radically successful businesses*. Crown Business.

Robson, K., Plangger, K., Jan, H. K., McCarthy, I., & Leyland, P. (2015). Is It All a Game? Understanding the Principles of Gamification. *Business Horizons*, *58*(4), 411–420. doi:10.1016/j.bushor.2015.03.006

Rosenfeld, P., Giacalone, R. A., & Riordan, C. A. (2002). Impression Management: building and enhancing reputations at work. In Psychology at work (New ed.). London: Thomson Learning.

Salen, K., & Zimmerman, E. (2003). *Rules of Play: game design fundamentals*. MIT Press.

Seaborn, K., & Fels, D. (2015). Gamification in Theory and Action: A survey. *International Journal of Human-Computer Studies*, *74*, 14–31. doi:10.1016/j.ijhcs.2014.09.006

Shen, D., Krumme, C., & Lippman, A. (2010). Follow the Profit or the Herd? Exploring Social Effects in Peer-to-Peer Lending. *IEEE Second International Conference on Social Computing*. 10.1109/SocialCom.2010.28

Smith, N. A. (2015). The Backer-developer Connection: Exploring crowdfunding's influence on video game production. *New Media & Society*, *17*(2), 198–214. doi:10.1177/1461444814558910

Sonawane, K. (2017). *Serious Games Market*. Allied Market Research. https://www.alliedmarketresearch.com/serious-games-market

Walz, S., & Deterding, S. (2014). An Introduction to the Gameful World. In S. Walz & S. Deterding (Eds.), *The Gameful World: approaches, issues, applications* (pp. 1–13). The MIT Press.

Winn, B. (2009). The Design, Play, and Experience Framework. In R. E. Ferdig (Ed.), *Handbook of Research on Effective Electronic Gaming in Education* (1st ed., Vol. 3, pp. 1010–1024). doi:10.4018/978-1-59904-808-6.ch058

Zhang, J., & Liu, P. (2012). Rational Herding in Microloan Markets. *Management Science*, *58*(5), 892–912. doi:10.1287/mnsc.1110.1459

This research was previously published in Practical Perspectives on Educational Theory and Game Development; pages 112-129, copyright year 2021 by Information Science Reference (an imprint of IGI Global).

Chapter 12
Combining UML Profiles to Design Serious Games Dedicated to Trace Information in Decision Processes

Laure Vidaud Barral
Université Grenoble Alpes, France & IRSTEA, France & ETNA, France

Francois Pinet
Université Clermont Auvergne, France & IRSTEA, France & UR TSCF, Clermont-Ferrand, France

Jean-Marc Tacnet
https://orcid.org/0000-0003-4731-5440
Université Grenoble Alpes, France & IRSTEA, France & ETNA, France

Anne-Laure Jousselme
NATO STO Centre for Maritime Research and Experimentation, Italy

ABSTRACT

An expert assessment consists of an ordered series of decisions that have to respond to time-evolving information contexts. Improving decisions made in a risk context requires better knowledge of reasoning mechanisms. The authors think that serious games can constitute a rich observatory for reasoning and decisions. However, the design of these games is not trivial and is rarely scalable or reusable. This paper proposes a UML profile library for generically modeling expert reasoning in situations using serious games that involve risks. Two main UML profiles are dedicated to both serious games and gamer decisions traceability modeling. Complementary profiles address risk expert reasoning modeling and data quality modeling. The authors illustrate the approach using the design of a serious game about avalanche risk analysis.

DOI: 10.4018/978-1-6684-7589-8.ch012

1. INTRODUCTION

Generally, making a decision requires the consideration of a large amount of heterogeneous information in an uncertain context. The quality and availability of data involved in a decision-making process can vary (Bouyssou, Dubois, Prade, & Pirlot, 2013) and significantly influence decisions. In the field of natural risk management, such as snow avalanche engineering, experts examine multiple factors that describe the phenomena and its stakes to identify the most avalanche-prone areas, design defense structures, and draw risk maps. Experts may need to make real-time decisions, such as decisions regarding road closures if environmental conditions become too dangerous. These decisions are not exclusive to the avalanche risk. Several types of decisions exist; they differ according to the objectives, stakes, environment, participants and quality and availability of data. These decisions need to be explained from a legal point of view (Lacroix, 2005). We need to improve knowledge transfer to users and learn from decisions from the past. In practice, a decision is the risk situation assessment final objective. However, we also admit that the risk situation assessment is composed of many smaller decisions. Therefore, we consider an expert evaluation as a series of decisions (Tacnet, Dezert, Curt, Batton-Hubert, & Chojnacki, 2014).

To observe the decision process and analyze decision makers' behaviors, real conditions need to be simulated, especially in natural risk management. Researchers have to identify the different successive steps of decision-making and link their assessment of phenomena with the availability and quality of information. Decision process traceability is required. This traceability can be implemented in an information system to enable further decision analyses. Therefore, the main goal of our approach is to propose design tools to improve traceability linked to any decision and its implementation in an information system.

The requirement to observe decision makers' behaviors in almost-real conditions led to serious games. According to (Michael & Chen, 2005), serious games intend to deliver a message, teach a lesson or provide an experience without entertainment as the primary purpose but with an explicit thought-out educational goal. Because of the game mechanics, the authors of (Constant, Buendia, Rolland and Natkin, 2015) define serious games as reflexive tools to observe the decision-making of players. These games are relevant supports to analyze the decision-making process, regardless of the game theme. (Abt, 1987) is the first author to consider a player as a decision-maker. To play is to decide. The serious games enable decision makers to play a concrete decision scenario while scientists can study the reasoning scheme that produces a decision. A serious game can be considered an efficient decision observatory. Thus, this aspect raises the question of designing software tools and information systems for the decision process traceability.

As stated by (Combemale et al., 2016), information system designers and software developers use models to address complexity. For various purposes, models are deeply linked with many concerns: system design, alternative solution exploration, mutual understanding among different stakeholders involved in design, and simulation of a not-yet-existing system. Basing a system design on Model-Driven Engineering ensures that paths to address the previously mentioned issues can be identified. The Unified Modeling Language (UML) of the Object Management Group (OMG) is a visual language for specifying systems using many models that may describe static or dynamic aspects (OMG-UML_2.5, 2015). Even if the UML is probably the most widely accepted and utilized modeling language, it remains too general in some situations, especially for modeling applications of specific complex domains. The OMG defines an approach, where the UML can be specialized to be more focused on a concern while respecting the UML metamodel. These specializations are possible by extension mechanisms of the language referred to as UML profiles.

In our approach, we propose and use UML profiles to enable designers to separate systems concerns (decision, information traceability, and data quality) and model decision process traceability in serious games. We show a flexible way to combine UML profiles to design dedicated serious games that involve decision processes. The high level of abstraction of these profiles enables capitalization of knowledge about decision processes but also design, which enables new serious games to be modeled with related concerns. Knowledge and understanding of our design problem and its solution should be acquired in the same "building", as highlighted by (Hevner, March, Park, & Ram, 2004) for design science. The UML profiles provide a visual communication tool that has interesting contexts that involve different types of stakeholders.

These profiles also facilitate the modeling of information systems for the storage of data related to the decision traceability process collected in serious games. We propose some insights into the implementation of our approach, which provides a first step to validate our approach. We design a serious game in which stakeholders have to make decisions in an avalanche risk context. In this application, information imperfections are formalized and stored with the traceability of the stages of the game, the type of information, the moment they are used during the game session and the choices made by the players. The output offers scientists a collected data structure that is adapted to their working practices and a way to retrospectively analyze players' behaviors.

In this paper, we propose the use of new extensions of UML via the combination of UML profiles to observe and analyze decision processes in a serious game. The paper is organized as follows: Section 2 presents fundamental principles on natural risk expertise, serious games and their design, which are required to understand the paper. Section 3 presents the way we combine UML profiles for serious games design. Section 4 focuses on the new UML profiles that we propose: 1) a UML profile dedicated to serious game design based on expert reasoning, and 2) a UML profile dedicated to decisions traceability in a serious game. Section 5 presents an implementation using our UML profiles for a serious game on avalanche risk assessment. Section 6 provides conclusions and perspectives.

2. BACKGROUND AND RELATED WORKS

2.1 Expert Assessment Needs and Significance of Imperfect Data in Decision

Risk management is a complex decision process that is based on several expert assessments. This complexity is broadly linked to a lack of information and knowledge about natural phenomena and the heterogeneity and reliability of available information sources (historical data, and field measurements) (Tacnet et al., 2014).

The need for traceability in an expert evaluation was the subject of a French standard in 2003 (NF X 50-110 standard) (AFNOR, 2003). In a more oriented quality management way, guidelines were proposed to structure expert evaluation activity in an international context with (ISO, 2009). Traceability, which describes the data flow across different reasoning processes and expert assessments, appears as a main requirement in decision-making processes. These standards emphasize the need for an extensive range of information: contextual elements at the origin of the expert evaluation, sources of data that may be reliable, components of expert evaluation, progress of the approach that led to the development of the expert evaluation. Meta-information related to the positioning of expert evaluation in the risk management cycle (M. M. Merad, 2003) (i.e., prevention, crisis, and repair), the context of the realization of the expert evaluation and the nature of applied information (e.g., temporal imperfection, and type of information).

The expert assessment of natural hazards is considered a decision-making process (M. Merad, Dechy, Llory, Marcel, & Tsoukias, 2014) based on imperfect information (Tacnet et al., 2014). These imperfections have distinct impacts on any decision. The imperfection of information can assume several forms: inconsistency (contradiction or conflict), incompleteness (a total or partial absence of information), inaccuracy (lack of quality level) and uncertainty. A lack of formalization of the entire expert evaluation chain in a natural hazard context exists by precisely mapping the imperfections to reliable sources (Tacnet, 2009).

To understand decisions, users and decision makers or magistrates expect traceability and information imperfection elicitation (Tacnet, Lacroix, & Batton-Hubert, 2007).

2.2 Serious Game as a Research Tool?

Thus, we emphasize the importance of a better understanding of decisions to improve the decision process and must find a way to observe them. In many cases, in natural risk management, analyzing the decision process in real conditions and real time is difficult. Many decision processes occur in situations in which we have to consider two sides: a technical approach of the hazard and its vulnerability, and the influence of a social context. Classical approaches for elicitation techniques exist for a long time; (Hoffman, Shadbolt, Burton, & Klein, 1995) evokes analysis of tasks that are usually performed by experts and various types of interviews or contrived tasks, which reveal an expert's reasoning processes. More recent studies highlight the capabilities of serious games/simulations in disaster risk management: capacity of reaching diverse audiences (experts, and communities), realistic simulation of disasters, undertaking preventive actions, empathy triggering and perspective-taking. The effectiveness of a contrived technique as serious games to enhance the risk management process is demonstrated (Schönbohm & Jülich, 2016).

Serious games integrate the mechanisms of classic games but their primary purpose is not entertainment (Michael & Chen, 2005). Serious games are now extensively employed for various purposes: training (i.e., fire-fighters, doctors and bus drivers), awareness (i.e., ecology, and terrorism), learning (i.e., simulation) and analysis (i.e., human behavior). Many serious games address the theme of natural hazards: a serious game to save lives in the case of a tsunami, storm, fire, flood or earthquake; a serious game to learn how to reduce the risk or games that are especially dedicated to flood management (Disaster Risk Reduction, 2018), (Mossoux et al., 2016), (Taillandier & Adam, 2018), (Meera, McLain, Bijlani, Jayakrishnan, & Rao, 2016). In the case of simulation-oriented games, regardless of the skill level of a player's assessment, the game allows her/him to confront her/his decisions to the outputs of a reasoning reference scheme, which is prepared by experts of the field, before the game. Thus, we can analyze the difference between her/his skills and this reference and possibly identify room for improvement in terms of learning.

According to (Brougère, 1997), one of the descriptive characteristics of a game is that the game is a sequence of decisions. The expert evaluation and the game are based on the same mechanics, especially in terms of interactions with other "experts" or "players". Unlike real decision-making, a real-life consequence of decisions made during a game does not exist.

The approach we propose is to use a game as a "reasoning observatory", which led to a final decision. As we consider the game as a sequence of decisions, tracing each step of the game allows the reasoning construction of a player or a team to be followed. The game proposes not only several scenario games for players but also a tool that collects data for researchers. After several iterations with data collection, the game compares game sessions and proposes improvements related to the decision process of the players. Based on reference reasoning, the players manipulate categories of data previously established by the experts. During the games, players' reasoning may differ (while somewhat distant) from the reference reasoning. Since players can be experts, they can offer alternatives to traditional reasoning schemes that can be used to enrich or tune some classical reference reasoning schemes. This aspect raises the question of designing these complex software tools.

2.3 Serious Game Design

As serious games have attracted considerable interest in recent years, methods for designing them have been the subject of research for approximately fifteen years (Thompson, Berbank-Green, & Cusworth, 2007). The main lines of methodologies for the design of serious games, on model-based approaches, were briefly presented in (Hunicke, LeBlanc, & Zubek, 2004), (Altunbay, Metin, & Çetinkaya, 2009) or (Tang & Hanneghan, 2010). Design frameworks have also been proposed by (Yusoff, 2010), (Marne, Wisdom, Huynh-Kim-Bang, & Labat, 2012) or (Ibáñez, Marne, & Labat, 2011). Some initial ideas represented by object-oriented models have been proposed in (Aouadi, Pernelle, Amar, & Carron, 2016) or (Thillainathan & Leimeister, 2014). In the context of ontologies, a formal representation has been introduced in (Tang & Hanneghan, 2011). Design patterns dedicated to serious games have also been proposed by par (Nystrom, 2014), (Bjork & Holopainen, 2004), (Marne & Labat, 2012). An integrated method dedicated to the development of information systems for the serious game traceability has been proposed. We need a system that stores the decision process to enable analysis of the details of its mechanism. In our opinion, this type of system can be useful for the postanalysis of player behaviors in serious games. An information structure with this purpose has not been proposed.

2.4 Traceability and Uncertain Data Modeling

The category of the games that we consider in this paper corresponds to serious games for decision-making, as shown in (Linehan, Lawson, Doughty, & Kirman, 2009), (J. A.-L.and Pallotta Jousselme & Locke, 2015). In this type of game, pieces of information are separately provided to players who must make a final decision. Each new piece of information modifies the game context of the previous round and the player is asked to evaluate how this new piece of information influences her/his position regarding her/his final decision. We model these serious games as successive player's assessments that are related to her/his (un)certainty about decisions and information. For example, imagine that a player has to assess the avalanche risk on a road. She/he may evaluate that the closure of a road in the case of an avalanche event should not be a priority but either may be a good solution or should be absolutely implemented. In this application, a subsequent explanation of the reasons that led to the final decision is often needed. Reproducing a good practice or improving the current practice is interesting. Therefore, traceability related to the decision-making process is a main concern of the game design method proposed in this paper.

Thus, modeling and storing the traceability of the entire process, which leading to a decision, contributes to the characterization of this decision. The challenge is to trace not only information during serious games but also the associated imperfection (incomplete information, imprecision, and inconsistency) and the level of reliability of the corresponding sources. This challenge is essential to understanding the impact of data imperfections and the level of trust of a source in final decision-making. Taking into account uncertainty in reasoning becomes a requirement in numerous cases, including legal cases (Lacroix, 2005). The evaluation made by the players after each new piece of information is processed is mandatory and enables analysis of the impact of the imperfection of information about their decisions.

In other contexts, many computer-based systems enable traceability in a rigorous manner; for example, in food chains, defective product tracking in production chains, and hospital care. Concerning the design of computer-based systems, note the traces of the requirements in computer development and constraint traceability in the transformations from models to code. The modeling of traceability can be facilitated due to different techniques: specific metamodels (Amar, Falleri, Huchard, Nebut, & Leblanc, 2008), (Vanhooff, Van Baelen, Joosen, & Berbers, 2007), UML profiles (Arpinen, Hämäläinen, & Hännikäinen, 2011) or a dedicated Domain Specific Expert System (Guo, 2013). These methods have one point in common: they propose a traceability management with a high level of abstraction. The specific issue of the formalization of the various uncertainty types has been achieved from a computer standpoint in multiple ways; for example, (J. Xiao, 2009) (in the form of UML profile), (Williams, Cornford, Bastin, & Pebesma, 2009) (in the form of XML schema), (Williams et al., 2009) and (in the form of uncertain data patterns).

2.5 Summary of Related Work

To improve the understanding and knowledge of decisions based on expert reasoning, we rely on a model engineering approach. To propose a methodological approach that can be replicated in the future, we explore UML capabilities. UML provides standard notations with a very wide scope; however, UML profiles are extension mechanisms to produce formalizations that are adapted to a targeted application field. As indicated in (Fuentes-Fernández & Vallecillo-Moreno, 2004), the use of UML profiles during a system formalization has several advantages. UML profiles enable the development of concepts that are adapted to a specific application field and the definition of specific constraints on objects. Profiles facilitate model reuse and provide a common representation for a set of models. Another advantage of these mechanisms is that they can be implemented in existing UML-based tools (Selic, 2007) because they are a product of the (OMG-MOF_2.5, 2015). The Object Management Group (OMG) proposes the Meta-Object Facility (MOF), which is a recognized standard for . Another argument in favor of UML profiles is the level of abstraction and modeling. We need to capitalize on the observation of the investigated decisions. Thus, a metamodeling level provides an interesting solution due to its reuse capability.

As previously noted, the serious game can be considered a research tool to work on the decision process. When the game is played several times (with different players), this storage in an information system constitutes a decision observatory that can be queried for decision analyses and learning using player behavior. Thus, we intend to link the model engineering approach (use of UML profiles) to the design of serious games.

From a practical point of view, once implemented, the targeted modeled serious game will enable a rigorous recording of the game stages, information applied during games, choices made by the players and a quality level assessment for the information and its source. Another issue consists of checking how information imperfection influences the decision process (J. A.-L.and Pallotta Jousselme & Locke, 2015): when are decisions made considering the quality of available information? How does the level of quality trigger or delay a decision?

Figure 1. Main steps of guidelines to combine UML profiles to design serious games dedicated to trace information in decision processes

Process step		Purpose of the step	Outcome
Step	Optional step		
1 — Define serious game requirements		- Purpose is to establish requirements for a serious game (type of game, type of game mechanics, type of decisions handled by the game, taking into account the imperfection of the data involved (or not) and how it is planned, etc.)	- List serious game requirements
2 — Select UML profile		- Purpose is to match profiles and requirements in order to select useful profiles and identify missing elements	- List of useful UML profiles - List of missing elements and UML profiles update needs
	2' — Extend existing UML profile	- If necessary, existing UML metaclasses are extended with new stereotypes, attributes and constraints. - Purpose is to enrich UML profiles with every new serious game design.	- Result could be new part of UML profiles to extend possibility of them (more type of decisions, new data quality approach, etc.)
3 — Create model based on selected UML profiles		- Purpose is to select which stereotypes will actually be used and elaborate class diagrams strongly linked with them. Notations and semantics proposed by profiles are guiding the design.	- Result is model and class diagrams of the serious game
4 — Process the model		- Purpose is to automatically generate a data structure which give a storage answer for serious game requirements data	- First result is a data model which express what will be stored in the database and how it will be stored. - Second result is a SQL script with DDL statements able to generate automatically the expected database structure

Thus, the following developments propose on the use of Model Driven Engineering and UML profiles to design serious games that are dedicated to the study of decision processes. We provide designers with a way to build observatory decisions that are dedicated to her/his own concerns.

3. GUIDELINES FOR COMBINING UML PROFILES TO DESIGN SERIOUS GAMES DEDICATED TO TRACE INFORMATION IN DECISION PROCESSES

Handling and analyzing information requires the development of a specific data structure. In this section, we present the main steps of our information system design method for serious game traceability. Designers will be able to integrate other stages in their project management (feasibility analysis, requirement specification, and agile approach). Our approach is based on the joint use of two main UML profiles described in this paper: the first profile is dedicated to the design of serious games and the second profile is dedicated to traceability. In our design method, these two pivot profiles can be combined with several other complementary profiles. In this paper, we propose the use of complementary profiles dedicated to risk expert evaluation and data quality. These profiles are detailed in the following sections. However, other profiles can be employed depending on the game requirements. Our general design approach proposes the five steps listed in Figure 1.

As illustrated in Figure 1, we define a specific data structure that is dedicated to trace information in decision processes for the development of the main steps. We also define an optional step to emphasize the importance of the extension of the profiles when we need to express a new concern. Each time a profile is enriched, knowledge is capitalized as a reusable way.

3.1. Step 1: Define Serious Game Requirements

The purpose of this step is to establish a list of requirements to describe the expected serious game. Four main topics can be established in relation to our proposals:

- About the serious game mechanics: Single-player or multiplayer mode? Internal rules? Ending rules? Required materials – dice and cards.
- About the need to trace decisions: What decisions should be traced in the game? How should decisions be described?
- About the serious game theme: What is the general theme? What kind of information is needed? Do we need to categorize the information? Should we evaluate the information? What criteria should be applied?
- About taking into account the imperfection of the data.

3.2. Step 2: Select UML Profile

The purpose of this step is to establish not only a list of useful UML profiles and associated stereotypes but also a list of missing elements related to specific concerns.

During this step, the designer selects the stereotypes she/he wants to use in the two main proposed UML profiles. She/he must make choices in terms of serious game design (with the profile described in Section 4.2) and the level of traceability (with the profile described in Section 4.3). The profile, which is especially dedicated to serious game design, provides a uniform and generic framework for game representation. As indicated here, additional UML profiles can be implemented and combined. To illustrate this approach, we use a profile that is dedicated to risk-based reasoning (via the profile described in Section 4.4.1) and a profile dedicated to information quality (via the profile described in Section 4.4.2). These profiles put into perspective the conception of a serious game with the reasoning expert evaluation on which it is based by integrating major concerns in our work, including data imperfect information, their sources and reliability. The profile dedicated to risk expert evaluation proposes a way to understand the analysis criteria on which it is based. Existing UML profiles can be combined to address other related issues: geo-referenced information (Pinet, 2012), refined typologies of uncertainty (Jing Xiao, Pinel, Pi, Aranega, & Baron, 2008) or details on game mechanisms (e.g., a deck of cards, and a board game (Altunbay et al., 2009)). This latter aspect can be achieved by specializing our serious game profile.

3.3. Step 3: Extend Existing UML Profile

If designer's concerns are not addressed by UML profiles and if she/he considers that his needs can be generic and reusable for the next time, she/he can enrich proposed profiles with new stereotypes. This premise is the spirit of our proposal: learn by addressing different types of decisions and capitalize on them, guided by specific serious games that are designed in a generic way, and collecting data.

3.4. Step 4: Create Models Based on Selected UML Profiles

The purpose of this step is to elaborate domain models independent from a platform. Once the requirements are refined and the profiles and stereotypes are chosen, the game designer creates the class diagrams that describe the serious game. For example, the simultaneous use of the profiles facilitate the modeling of objects that belong to the chosen game mechanics, traceability mode, and theme of considered risks. Using UML profiles, classes in a model diagram can be built with at least one stereotype.

3.5. Step 5: Process the Model

The purpose of this step is to implement a data structure. In this phase, the information system for game traceability is implemented from the class diagram specifications (and complementary specifications, such as use case definitions). The different technical choices for this implementation are established. The game traceability can be stored in a traditional relational database, Extensible Markup Language (XML) files, Hierarchical Data Format 5 (HDFC5) files. The researchers often work with raw data. The class diagram can be used for more advanced code generations (for instance Java or Python).

To facilitate the insertion and visualization of objects of a game, a Domain Specific Modeling Language can be proposed that would enable modelers to represent, select or display the main instances of the database in a more graphical and understandable way. Various tools can be used to design a Domain-specific modeling Language (DSML); for example, Eclipse Sirius. The goal is not to enter only information related to decision traceability instead of entering data and visualizing the entire database. Other instances can be inserted and viewed in the database via more conventional user interfaces.

The final objective to these design guidelines is to build a data structure that enables researchers to manipulate data for different purposes: compare decision-making during different runs of a game; reconstruct the arguments of the players in terms of stages, choices, and data (with their imperfections and sources); and compare the players' reasoning schemes with a reference reasoning scheme.

4. UML PROFILES FOR DESIGN RISK ASSESSMENT-ORIENTED SERIOUS GAME

Our approach is based on the previously mentioned profile mechanism. In this section, the main aspects of our UML profiles are presented. One UML profile is defined for each aspect that we want to model:

- A UML profile to design a serious turn-based game for decision making
- A UML profile to take into account the needs for traceability
- A UML profile to take into account the risk assessment
- A UML profile to integrate an analysis context with imperfect data and unevenly reliable sources.

Regarding these profiles, our main contribution is the proposal of a detailed profile for serious games for decision, which are associated with a detailed profile for the traceability of decision reasoning. The other profiles mentioned in this paper can be utilized (if needed by the applications). We present them to illustrate the flexibility of using multiple UML profiles; they are not mandatory in all applications.

4.1 UML Profile Usage

In Figure 2, we propose a metamodeling (layer M2) of our domain via the UML profiles described in the following paragraphs. Each profile is an extension of the basic standard UML model (OMG-MOF_2.5, 2015) that is dedicated to one of our four objectives. MOF is often considered layer M3 because it provides a set of schemas by which the structure, meaning and behaviors of objects can be defined. The use of at least one UML profiles enables specific models (layer M1) to be proposed for the development of computer-based tools that are dedicated to particular fields (layer M0).

Figure 2. Overview of the design method according to the layers of modeling pyramid proposed by Object Management Group (OMG)

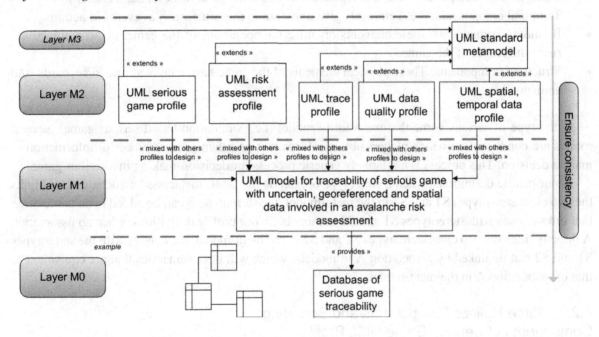

Figure 3. Flexibility of UML profiles reuse

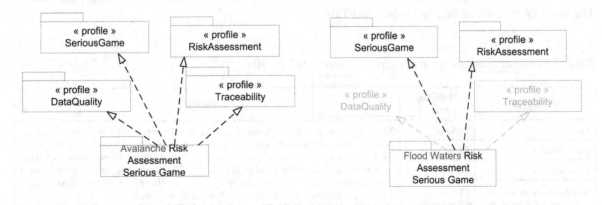

The application used to illustrate our approach corresponds to avalanche risk management (as detailed in our case study in Section 5); however, other uses are possible. The proposed method is sufficiently generic to be applied to any other decision-based system or (natural or not) risk analysis context, such as a torrential risk or a technology risk (as illustrated in Figure 3). Some combinations of profiles may not have any interest depending on the targeted application.

4.2 UML Profile for Serious Game

This section describes the main aspects of the UML profile dedicated to serious games. The four descriptive categories proposed in (Holopainen, 2011) are used to present this profile.

- Game holistic components: these components describe the game with its main features.
- Temporal components: these elements give a rhythm to the game, such as events or actions.
- Bounding components: these elements organize the operations of the game, i.e., the objectives, rules and stages of the game.
- Structural components: These physical elements of the game have a defined role (dice, cards, and animators).

In the type of serious game that we want to model (i.e., simulation-based serious game), several rounds are conducted, in which players obtain information and then process pieces of information to make a decision. This process is a relatively generic process for decision-making in a serious game.

In our profile definitions, when a stereotype S extends the UML metaclass "association" and links the two class stereotypes S1 and S2 in the meta-model, the stereotype S can be added to an association that links classes with stereotypes S1 and S2 in models. In our profile definitions, when an association A directly links the two class stereotypes S1 and S2 in the meta-model, the classes with the stereotypes S1 and S2 can be linked by association A in models, which will have semantics that are equivalent to that of association A in the meta-model.

4.2.1. Game Holistic Components and Bounding Components of Serious Game UML Profile

Figure 4 illustrates the part of the serious game profile that concerns holistic and bounding components. The stereotypes are detailed in Table 1 and Table 2.

Table 1. Holistic components from serious game UML profile

Stereotype	Metaclass UML 2.0	Semantic
Game	Package	The Game package is the container of all features and components of the serious game.
GameSession	Class	A serious game offers several game scenarios (GameScenario) but occurs according to a single game scenario during a session (GameSession). A session is instantiated each time a game is played and contains the team of players. The theme of the serious game is based on a reasoning of reference proposed by a group of experts (RiskAssessmentGrid *). In the example presented in this paper, the theme is the risk assessment.
GameScenario	Class	
RiskAssessmentGrid *	Class	

*Metaclass that is described in "UML profile for risk assessment," Section 4.4.1

Figure 4. Game holistic components and bounding components of serious game UML profile

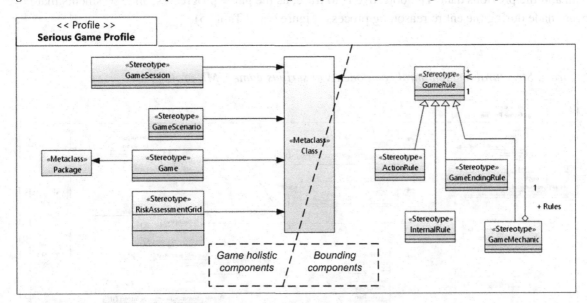

Table 2. Bounding components from serious game UML profile

Stereotype	Metaclass UML 2.0	Semantic
GameMechanic	Class	The two concepts GameMechanic and GameRule allow the functioning of a game to be described by its rules, as detailed in (Thompson et al., 2007). The GameMechanic describes the game as a set of nested rule types (GameRule). The concept of GameRule is adapted based on the game rule metamodel proposed by (Montero Reyno & Cubel Carsí, 2009).
ActionRule	Class	The rules can be classified into different types:
InternalRule	Class	- "ActionRule": rules and constraints on players' actions, which direct the game mechanics (example: the players cannot ask for new information if they did not complete the evaluation of the previous information)
GameEndingRule	Class	- "InternalRule": internal rule that guides the underlying system (example: time constraint for playing the game) - "GameEndingRule": rule that establishes the conditions of game ending (example: when the player draws a card that indicates that the avalanche has fallen)

4.2.2. Structural and Temporal Components of Serious Game UML Profile

Figure 5 illustrates the part of the serious game profile that concerns structural and temporal components. The stereotypes are detailed in Table 3 and Table 4.

4.3 UML Profile for Decision Traceability

This section describes the main aspects of the UML profile that are dedicated to the traceability of a reasoning process. This profile models the reasoning process using a sequence of evaluations, where each sequence is established with regard to a specific context. A context is defined by a set of pieces of information and iteratively grows: the integration of new data creates a new context to gather these new data and the previous data. The objective is to trace, as the game progresses, all assessments that have been made during the entire reasoning process (Figure 6 and Table 5).

Figure 5. Structural and temporal components of serious game UML profile

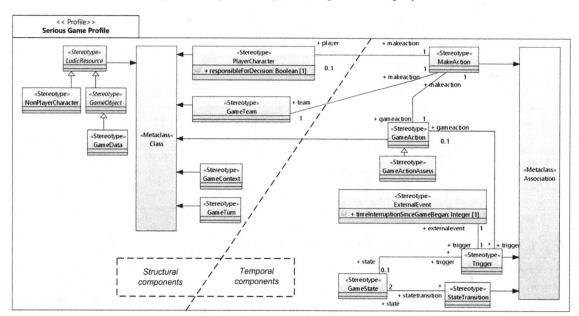

Table 3. Structural components from serious game UML profile

Stereotype	Metaclass UML 2.0	Semantic
GameTeam	Class	PlayerCharacter describes the categories of players involved in the game. In the context
PlayerCharacter	Class	of a crisis simulation game, the players can be experts, elected officials, and people from operational services. This metaclass is similar to the PlayerCharacter metaclass proposed in the metamodel of (Montero Reyno & Cubel Carsí, 2009), which describes the different roles of players. These players are grouped into a GameTeam that can perform actions as a team. Several teams can also play a game.
NonPlayerCharacter	Class	This class contains the different types of players in the game other than the players, such as the game master. This metaclass was proposed by (Montero Reyno & Cubel Carsí, 2009) and describe the main categories of nonplayer characters.
LudicResource	Class	This concept was defined in the model proposed by (Aouadi et al., 2016) to describe the "physical" entities of the game, external to the players. As in (Aouadi et al., 2016), an object of this class can be specialized in a GameObject or NonPlayerCharacter, as subsequently described.
GameObject	Class	These different types of objects will be specialized according to the needs (cards, and dice) used during the game, as described in (Aouadi et al., 2016). These objects actually correspond to data, e.g., conceptually, a die roll or a card draw corresponds to new pieces of data provided to players. Thus, the GameData stereotype inherits from GameObject.

Table 4. Temporal components from serious game UML profile

Stereotype	Metaclass UML 2.0	Semantic
GameState	Class	A session (GameSession) is instantiated at the beginning of each game run. A session is a series of game turns (GameTurn) during which the game can present several states (GameEtat). The characteristics of these states of play are traced (what action, which player, and what assessment). For example, a state can be "Waiting for evaluation by players" or "Selection of information by the player". Transitions from one state of the game to another one are caused by (1) external events (ExternalEvent); for example, the intervention of a nonplayer character (triggered by a game card draw) or by (2) the actions of the players (GameAction); for example, the player performs an evaluation. Each game turn (GameTurn) is associated with a game context (GameContext) that contains all information acquired by the players at a given moment. The start of a game turn is initiated by the modification of the game context when the players acquire a new piece of information, and the game turn ends with the evaluation made by the players. A context (GameContext) is a collection of elements of the game (GameObject).
GameTurn	Class	
GameContext *	Class	
ExternalEvent	Class	
StateTransition	Association	This relationship traces a move from one state to another state (GameState) within a game turn (GameTurn) and defines the traceability between the states of the game.
GameAction	Class	The players (PlayerCharacter) or nonplayers (NonPlayerCharacter) of the game perform different actions (GameAction); for example, use a game object (GameObject), such as "a game card". An example of the class specialization of GameAction is the class GameActionAssess, which is dedicated to "evaluate" actions. A new specialization of this metaclass can be proposed to precisely model new types of actions.
GameActionAssess	Class	
MakeAction	Association	
Trigger	Association	During the game, triggers can cause events or new actions. Trigger associations enable triggering GameStates in response to actions (GameAction) or external events (ExternalEvent). Each Trigger association is ordered (i.e., oriented) to connect a trigger (actions, event, and game state) to the entity that is triggered (action and event).

* Metaclass that will be described in «UML profile for traceability», Section 4.3

Figure 6. Decisions traceability UML profile

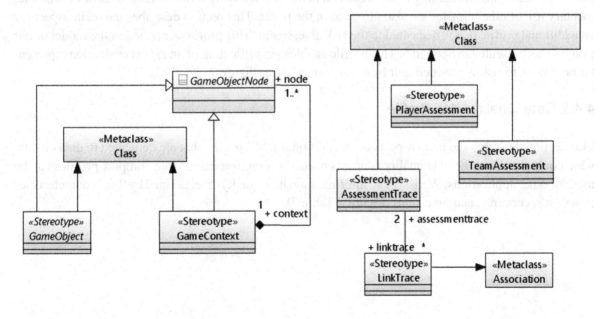

Table 5. Components from traceability UML profile

Stereotype	Metaclass UML 2.0	Semantic
AssessmentTrace	Class	The metaclass AssessmentTrace orderly groups all evaluations made in the game. Each trace is associated with a game context (GameContext), which is a grouping of game data (GameObject) at a given time. GameObject corresponds to all data associated with the objects of the game (cards, etc.), and in particular, those that will be analyzed by the players (for example: a game card indicates a piece of information).
GameContext	Class	
GameObject	Class	
GameObjectNode	Class	This class is a GameContext, which is an object that consists of information but can be constituted by another context with new information (GameObject). We posit that the context observed at a given time is composed of the context at the previous given time embellished with new information.
PlayerAssessment	Class	Each GameContext is evaluated by a player (PlayerAssessment) or a team (TeamAssessment). All evaluations are stored. For example, during an avalanche risk role play, two players can evaluate the closure of a road, as highly recommended, without considering that a certain decision needs to be made, and a third player can decide that the road closure is absolutely needed. The joint evaluation and decision made by the team can be to close the road.
TeamAssessment	Class	
LinkTrace	Association	This relationship traces the move from one assessment to another assessment (AssessmentTrace) and defines the traceability between the assessment and decisions of the game.

4.4 Complementary UML Profiles

4.4.1 UML Profile for Risk Assessment

As previously indicated, the contribution of this paper is a profile for serious games associated with a profile for reasoning traceability (both presented in the previous subsections). Examples of the complementary use of other profiles are also provided in the paper. This section describes the main aspects of an additional profile that is dedicated to the risk assessment. This profile is applied in the model of our example, as presented in Section 5. This profile enables simplification of an expert evaluation representation related to risks by modeling it by evaluation criteria (Figure 7 and Table 6).

4.4.2 Data Quality UML Profile

This section describes the main aspects of an additional UML profile that are dedicated to data quality, which only describes the data quality concepts needed for our use case. More complex profiles can be used for other applications. We associate information with a quality level defined by three characteristics (relevance, certainty, and precision) (Figure 8 Table 7).

Figure 7. Risk assessment UML profile

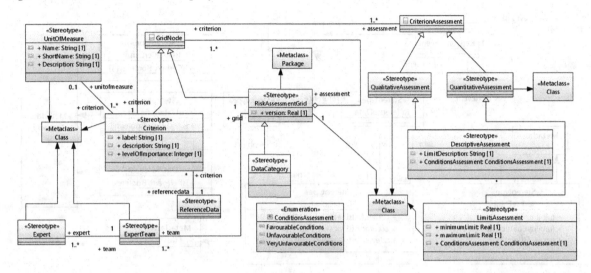

Table 6. Components from risk assessment UML profile

Stereotype	Metaclass UML 2.0	Semantic
RiskAssessmentGrid	Package	The RiskAssessmentGrid package is a grouping into a structure of all elements (criteria, categories) that contribute to a risk assessment. A finer representation is proposed with DataCategory, which enables the evaluation criteria to be organized into categories. For example, for an avalanche risk assessment, a DataCategory can be "snow-weather conditions". This grid of risk assessment criteria (RiskAssessmentGrid) is proposed by a team (ExpertTeam) composed of experts of the application field (Expert).
DataCategory	Package	
ExpertTeam		
Expert		
Criterion	Class	The Criterion metaclass is the smallest element that can store the evaluation of information. Real-life information (ReferenceData*) can be the subject to several criteria. For example, a report on the morphology of an avalanche site can provide assessment criteria for the surface of the departure zone of the avalanche corridor and its average slope.
UnitOfMeasure	Class	The metaclass is used to store different units of measurement.
CriterionAssessment	Class	The CriterionAssessment can be approached quantitatively (QuantitativeAssessment) or qualitatively (QualitativeAssessment). We can establish vague markers to establish categories of appreciation (favorable, unfavorable, and very unfavorable). For example, the amount of snow fallen during the last 72 hours is quantitatively evaluate: a maximum of 50 cm is considered to be favorable; in the range 50 cm <h <100 cm is unfavorable and above 100 cm is very unfavorable. The state of the fragile layer inside the snowpack is evaluated in a descriptive way and can be possible and localized, proven and constant.
ConditionsAssessment	Enumeration	Enumeration to evaluate the criterion as "Favorable", "Unfavorable" and "Very unfavorable"

* Metaclass that will be described in «Data quality UML profile», Section 4.4.2

Figure 8. Data quality UML profile

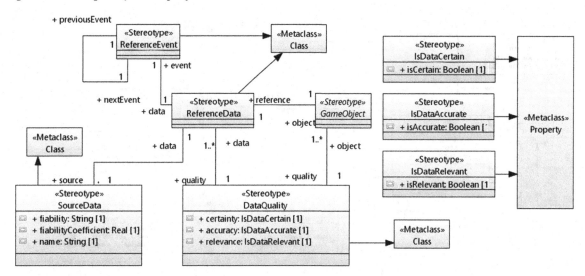

Table 7. Components for data quality UML profile

Stereotype	Metaclass UML 2.0	Semantic
ReferenceEvent	Class	The metaclass (ReferenceEvent) allows representation of a sequence of events and real data (ReferenceData), which will be used as a reference in games.
ReferenceData	Class	
SourceData	Class	The SourceData metaclass is used to assign the source of information (ReferenceData) and provide its coefficient of reliability, which is indicated as a tagged value (reliabilityCoefficient). For example, a source may be a public data agency, which is a meteorological sensor.
DataQuality	Class	The metaclass DataQuality is related to the quality of information; it uses 3 tagged values to indicate if the information is certain (IsDataCertain), relevant (IsDataRelevant), and accurate (IsDataAccurate).
IsDataCertain, IsDataAccurate, IsDataRelevante	Property	
GameObject	Class	The metaclass GameObject is used to store an element that is associated with real-life information (refer to previous subsections). In the game, this GameObject is associated with the quality (DataQuality) of its information.

5. AN ILLUSTRATION OF THE USE OF THE PROPOSED GUIDELINES: AN AVALANCHE RISK ASSESSMENT-ORIENTED SERIOUS GAME

We illustrate the use of our profiles on a serious game that we developed based on a capture expert's avalanche risk assessment. This serious game has been tested with different participants (stakeholders, roads managers, avalanche experts, and mountain practitioners). The game has the form of a physical board game (not a computer-based application).

5.1 Requirements of the Game

5.1.1 Game Purpose

The serious game intends to train players to pay attention to the information that they have to search and the quality of information they have to process to learn about their reasoning (after the session) and compare their reasoning with a reference reasoning. In practice, the topic is a risk avalanche assessment. In winter, snow avalanches can reach roads and hit people, cars, and infrastructures. Risk management consists of making decisions about protecting works above roads (snow fences and tunnels), preventively triggering avalanches or temporarily forbidding access. An example of a decision is to close a road or maintain access to the road (Figure 9).

*Figure 9. Serious game concept (***Vidaud et al., 2018***)*

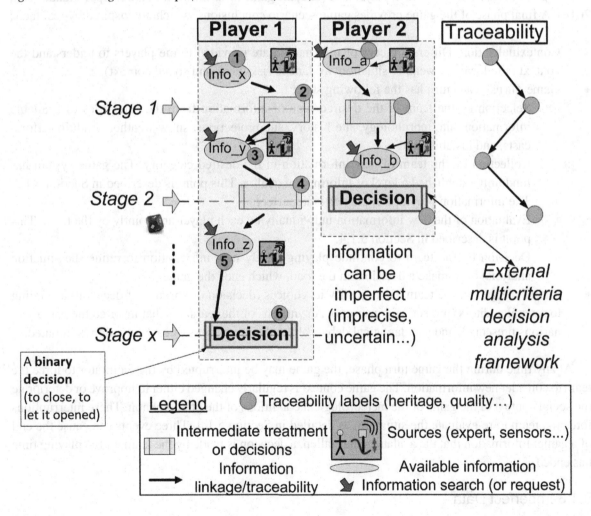

In a serious game, a team of several players has to make a decision in a context of avalanche risks preceding (or not) a period of crisis management, i.e., close (or not) a road exposed to at least one avalanche corridor. This game allows different roles for the players: either a local elected representative, a road manager or an avalanche expert. The research challenge is to observe and analyze decision-making in the context of imperfect data. Each new piece of information provided in the game is first individually evaluated by each player and then jointly by the team. As illustrated in Figure 9, each game stage is rigorously traced. The main objective is to trace the reasoning of each player (but also of the team) for every important moment in the game, particularly the impact of new information. The quality and provenance of the information is also important.

5.1.2 Game Play Mechanics

The game mechanics are easy to understand. In the first step, the facilitator animator explains the context and the game scenario to the team of players. Second, the game turns follow the same steps (Vidaud et al., 2018). A final phase of the game provides game scenario conclusions, which are inspired by real facts:

- Contextualization: Different pieces of information are provided to the players to understand the context (site location, weather situation, avalanche risk level, and social context).
- Game Turns - each turn has the following steps:
  - Selection by the team of the desired type of information from the categories of available information (site morphology, site history, site protections, snow-weather conditions, forecasts, and instabilities)
  - Collection by the team of new information in the desired category. The game system has randomly established a level of information quality. This point is described in Section 5.1.3. The information provided to players is imperfect.
  - Evaluation of the new information individually by each player and jointly by the team. This point is described in Section 5.1.4.
  - Decision by the team to continue playing (apply new information to refine the situation analysis) or to make a decision on the road, which ends the game.
- End of the game: The team has to justify its choices (decision or absence of decision) according to several auditors (prefect, and insurers). A synthesis of the real facts that inspired the game scenario is presented, and a pedagogical debate about the uniqueness of each situation is initiated.

At any time during the game turn phase, the game may be interrupted by the facilitator to force the team to consider new information. The game context is regularly changed either to improve or deteriorate the social context of the game or the meteorological conditions of the phenomenon. These interruptions force the team to re-evaluate the situation, as detailed in Section 5.1.4. Three events can cause the end of a game: Information that the avalanche has fallen, a decision is made by the team, or the playing time has ended.

5.1.3 Imperfect Data

An educational objective of the game is to make players consider the quality of the data they handle, and therefore, the reliability of the data sources. The concept of the information quality has been employed in the game based on the concept proposed by (A.-L. Jousselme, Pallotta, & Locke, 2018). Each piece of information proposed to the player is associated with a quality level. This quality level has been established according to three criteria: whether the information is relevant, whether the information is certain and whether the information is accurate.

5.1.4 Evaluation Traceability Matrix

A dedicated tool has been developed for the game: the evaluation traceability matrix. This tool enables the reasoning of the team and of each player to be traced throughout the game and enables the collection of the most important data provided by the game from the researcher's point of view, i.e., decision traceability data. In each turn, evaluating any new information provided is proposed to the team and each player. A scale of 0 to 1 enables them to evaluate the confidence in decision-making, as shown in Figure 10. In practice, they report the data id (#345Q011, #087Q110; #222Q11) used in the game (in the left column) and provide their corresponding assessment using a scale. If players think that the new information does not considerably influence their decision, they give a low value (e.g., 0.2, and 0.3). If the information enables them to make the final decision, the value will be high (e.g., 0.8 and 0.9).

Each piece of information is uniquely identified in the game and associated with a level of quality (refer to Section 5.1.3). The reasoning progress made by the team can be traced by sequential evaluations. At the beginning of each turn, the choice of the information type highlights the information needed to the team to complete the analysis. In each turn, the different evaluations involve observing if a decision trend is emerging. The impact of the information quality level on the decision-making process can also be captured.

Figure 10. Traceability matrix

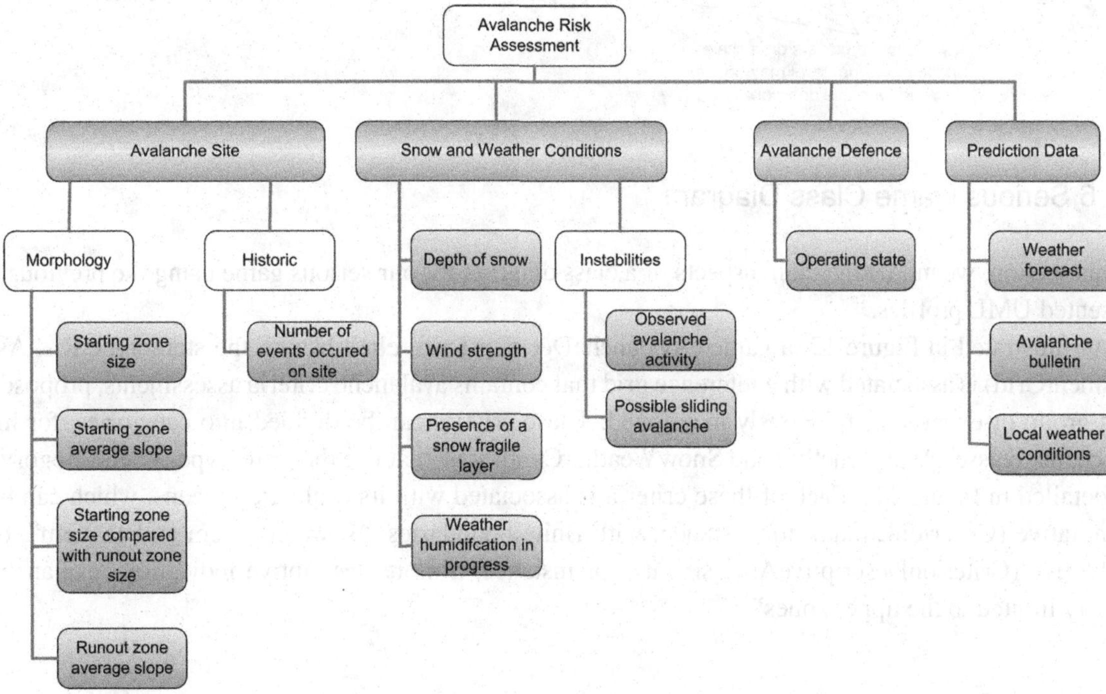

5.1.5 One Reference Avalanche Risk Assessment

The game is based on a reference reasoning scheme proposed by avalanche experts from ANENA and Irstea established upstream of the game design. The categories of information and the analysis criteria illustrated in Figure 11 are proposed to the players. Four criterion categories have been identified: avalanche site description, snow and weather conditions, avalanche defense onsite and weather prediction data. In theory, the players, according to the analysis of the pieces of information they obtain, can evaluate these different criteria. In practice, their personal opinion and experience impact the perceived relevance of some criteria. The evaluation grid of each of the criteria proposed by the experts is also provided to the players and can help nonexpert avalanche players. For instance, experts consider that the risk of avalanche increases according to the increase in the depth of snow observed. Below 50 cm of snow, conditions are considered favorable. They are unfavorable between 50 cm and 100 cm and are highly unfavorable above 100 cm.

Figure 11. Main criteria of one reference avalanche risk assessment

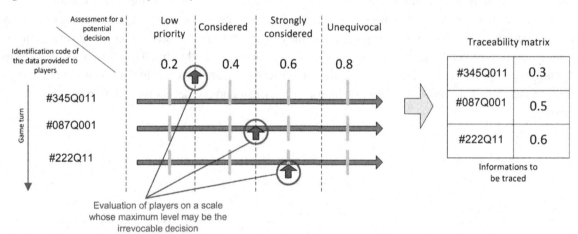

5.1.6 Serious Game Class Diagram

In this section, we model the main aspects of a class diagram for our serious game using the previously presented UML profiles.

As illustrated in Figure 12, a game (AvalancheDecisionTrace class having the stereotype RiskAssessmentGrid) is associated with a reference grid that contains avalanche criteria assessments, proposed by a group of experts, as previously mentioned. These criteria can be divided into categories, for instance, the classes AvalancheSite and SnowWeatherConditions that use the stereotype "DataCategory" (as detailed in Figure 11). Each of these criteria is associated with its evaluation means, which can be quantitative (CriterionLimits), for instance, with finite boundaries "between 50 cm and 100 cm", or qualitative (CriterionDescriptiveAssessment), for instance, a more descriptive indication "avalanche activity limited to the upper zones".

Figure 12. One structure key aspect of risk assessment serious game class diagram: game reference to expert assessment grid

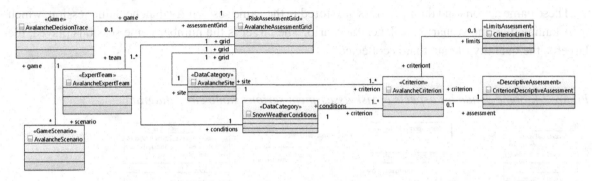

Figure 13. Main purpose of risk assessment serious game class diagram: to trace players assessments

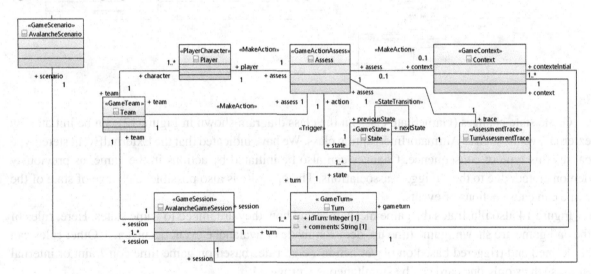

A predefined list of actions is available during the game, as defined by the stereotype "GameAction". For example, possible actions are "Choose a category of information" or "Draw a map that relates to the social context". Figure 13 focuses on a specialization of this stereotype named "GameActionAssess", which is the basis of the actions traced during the game, e.g., evaluations made by the players. Thus, players (Player) or a team (Team) perform the evaluation action (Assess) in a game context (Context). The two stereotypes on associations "MakeAction" and "Trigger" allow (1) for the first stereotype, connecting the action to realize its authors and a given context; and (2) for the second stereotype, triggering the game state change (State). To store all player's evaluations generated by this type of action (during a turn), we use the "AssessmentTrace" stereotype on the TurnAssessmentTrace class.

This method for tracing the evaluations throughout the turns enables the evolution of the reasoning to be subsequently traced and analyzed. These evaluations are linked to the evolution of game context. The game starts with a given context, which contains a determined quantity of information. Any new information is an evolution of the previous context. The new context, is therefore, composed of the previous context and the new information. We create a sequence of contexts that have their individual and team evaluations.

These game actions and their progress are stored in the game session AvalancheGameSession, which is instantiated on the scenario AvalancheScenario. The larger is the number game sessions played, the larger is the quantity of data that is collected.

Figure 14. Some dynamics aspects of risk assessment serious game class diagram

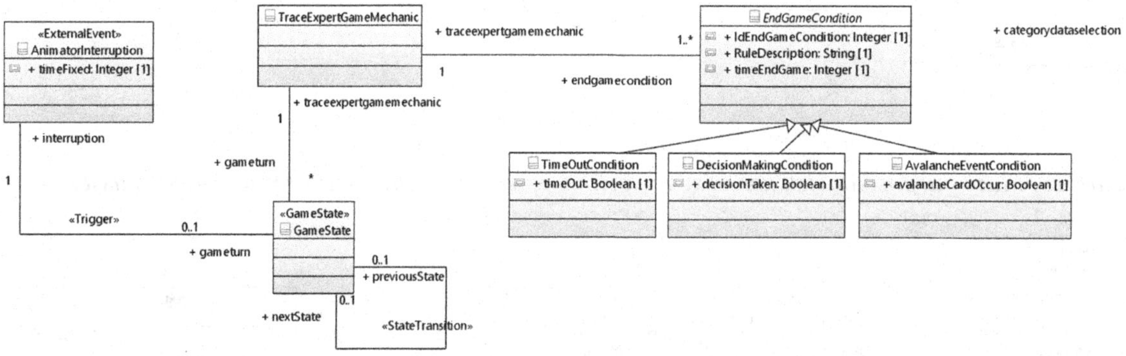

Game state changes (GameState class on the class diagram shown in Figure 12) can be initiated by external events, such as AnimatorInterruption class. We have indicated that the ExternalEvent stereotype causes this type of consequence. Changes can also be initiated by actions in the game, as previously demonstrated, due to the "Trigger" associations. The opposite is also possible: a change of state of the game can cause actions or events.

Figure 14 also illustrates the game mechanics and how they are linked to game states. Here, rules of the end game are shown: game time up, decision made or avalanche event occurrence. Other rules can be defined and triggered based on player actions, e.g., rules based on game time constraint or internal rules, such as only one card can be simultaneously provided.

Thus, a database for the traceability of the game can be directly produced from the class diagram. The database will store the game scenario, the data used in the game, their quality and order of use, and the players' reasoning.

5.1.7 Implementing the Serious Game Data Model: Collected Data and Possible Queries and Analyses

If the previous UML diagrams are implemented in a database, different queries can be used to analyze the data collected in the serious game.

For example, the reference reasoning of the game with their criteria and (quantitative or qualitative) evaluation means can be traced. This information can be determined with the objects of the classes (refer to Figure 12): AvalancheAssessmentGrid, AvalancheSite, SnowWeatherConditions, AvalancheCriterion, CriterionLimits, and CriterionDescriptiveAssessment.

Using the objects of the classes AvalancheScenario, AvalancheDecisionTrace, Assess, State, TurnAssessmentTrace, and Context (Figures 12 and 13), the reasoning of a player or team (or both) for a session can be traced and the following questions can be answered:

- What is her/his knowledge on data or her/his fields of interest (some information may never be obtained from the game); what is the quality level of this information; and in which order did she/he have access to this information?
- What was her/his evaluations at each game context update?
- What scenario did she/he play?

The real scenario that inspired the fictional game scenario from the collected data can be recovered.

These queries can be used to answer the following questions: What information was decisive in the player or team's decision-making? Have they been decisive? What was their level of quality? Are they correlated? We should also be able to compare the reasoning of the players and the reasoning of the team for the same session. Has the decision-maker always respected a consensus or has she/he sometimes imposed her/his opinion? A comparison of the player/team reasoning in relation to the reference reasoning can also be determined.

6. CONCLUSION

This paper proposes some design guidelines based on the combination of UML profiles to design a serious game that is built on experts' reasoning processes related to risk management. The goal of the targeted serious games is to observe decision-making processes. The process traceability and the consideration of imperfect data are the main points investigated in this category of serious games. We have proposed two generic main profiles: a profile dedicated to serious game modeling for decision-making and a profile for decision traceability. Profiles for expert reasoning on risk and data quality are presented in the paper to illustrate the use of additional profiles. The use of these profiles helps to produce class diagrams in a standardized manner and guarantees their consistency. In the next step, designers will generate an SQL structure to analyze the data collected during game sessions.

A future perspective is to develop an advanced description of a method for using our proposal. This method must provide a detailed definition of the design steps. We can apply the work of (Hevner et al., 2004), which shows researchers and practitioners how to conduct, evaluate, and present design-science research. This type of approach provides guidelines to help the creation and evaluation of artifacts, such as a model, a method or an instantiation (such as a prototype application).

In future work, we will also model a new serious game based on an existing board game. This new application will help validate our approach in another case. Many game sessions are also needed to collect sufficient data and conduct research via their analyses. We can also propose a Domain Specific Modeling Language (DSML) that would offer more intuitive visualizations and insertions of instances.

Another perspective is the use of the DMN standard (OMG-DMN_1.1, 2016) to expand the possibilities of making decisions (even if this standard is more dedicated to organizational decision-making).

The serious game traceability can enable scientists to analyze expert behaviors and determine the expert reasoning process. Consequently, in different application fields, such as avalanche risks, this analysis should be used to build decision support systems based on an explainable artificial intelligence paradigm (Došilovi, Brci, & Hlupi, 2018). As indicated in this paper, the decisions in avalanche risks have to be justified by explanations and processes that are understandable by humans, e.g., legal reasons. Even if decision support systems are employed, the decision process must be explainable and transparent for different stakeholders.

ACKNOWLEDGMENT

The authors thank the colleagues involved in this project on the topic of avalanche risk assessment: Sébastien Escande and Xavier Pasquier (ANENA), François Rapin and Michaël Deschâtres (IRSTEA). The serious game development shown in this paper has been founded by Direction Générale de la Prévention des Risque (DGPR), the French Ministry of the Ecological and Solidarity Transition, in the TraceExpert project, elaborated in an agreement with the Service des Risques Naturels et Hydrauliques (SRNH).

REFERENCES

Abt, C. C. (1987). *Serious games*. University Press of America.

AFNOR. (2003). *Norme française NF X 50-110 - Qualité en expertise: Prescriptions générales de compétence pour une expertise*. Saint-Denis La Plaine: AFNOR.

Altunbay, D., Metin, M. G., & Çetinkaya, M. (2009). Model-driven Approach for Board Game Development. *First Turkish Symposium of Model-Driven Software Development (TMODELS)*, Ankara, Turkey.

Amar, B., Falleri, J.-R., Huchard, M., Nebut, C., & Leblanc, H. (2008). *Un framework de traçabilité pour des transformations à caractère impératif*. LMO.

Aouadi, N., Pernelle, P., Amar, C. B., & Carron, T. (2016). MDA Approach for Reusability in Serious Game and E-learning Design. In *International Conference on Web-Based Learning* (pp. 206–212). Springer. 10.1007/978-3-319-47440-3_23

Arpinen, T., Hämäläinen, T., & Hännikäinen, M. (2011). Meta-Model and UML Profile for Requirements Management of Software and Embedded Systems. *EURASIP Journal on Embedded Systems*, *2011*(1), 592168. doi:10.1155/2011/592168

Bjork, S., & Holopainen, J. (2004). *Patterns in game design (game development series)*. Academic Press.

Bouyssou, D., Dubois, D., Prade, H., & Pirlot, M. (2013). *Decision making process: Concepts and methods*. John Wiley & Sons.

Brougère, G. (1997). Jeu et objectifs pédagogiques : Une approche comparative de l'éducation préscolaire. *Revue Française de Pédagogie*, *119*(1), 47–56. Retrieved from http://www.jstor.org/stable/41200719. doi:10.3406/rfp.1997.1166

Combemale, B., France, R., Jézéquel, J.-M., Rumpe, B., Steel, J., & Vojtisek, D. (2016). *Engineering modeling languages: Turning domain knowledge into tools*. Chapman and Hall/CRC. doi:10.1201/b21841

Disaster Risk Reduction. (2018). *Stop disasters* (Playerthree, Ed.). Retrieved from https://www.stopdi-sastersgame.org/

Došilovi, F. K., Brci, M., & Hlupi, N. (2018). Explainable artificial intelligence: A survey. In *2018 41st International convention on information and communication technology, electronics and microelectronics (MIPRO)* (pp. 210–215). IEEE.

Fuentes-Fernández, L., & Vallecillo-Moreno, A. (2004). An introduction to UML profiles. *UML and Model Engineering, 2*.

Guo, Cleland-Huang, & Berenbach. (2013). Foundations for an expert system in domain-specific trace-ability. In *21st IEEE International Requirements Engineering Conference, RE 2013, Rio de Janeiro-RJ, Brazil, July 15-19, 2013* (pp. 42–51). 10.1109/RE.2013.6636704

Hevner, A. R., March, S. T., Park, J., & Ram, S. (2004). Design science in information systems research. *Management Information Systems Quarterly, 28*(1), 75–105. doi:10.2307/25148625

Hoffman, R. R., Shadbolt, N. R., Burton, A. M., & Klein, G. (1995). Eliciting knowledge from experts: A methodological analysis. *Organizational Behavior and Human Decision Processes, 62*(2), 129–158. doi:10.1006/obhd.1995.1039

Holopainen, J. (2011). *Foundations of gameplay*. Blekinge Institute of Technology.

Hunicke, R., LeBlanc, M., & Zubek, R. (2004). MDA: A formal approach to game design and game research. In *Proceedings of the AAAI Workshop on Challenges in Game AI* (Vol. 4, pp. 1–5). AAAI Press.

Ibáñez, B. C., Marne, B., & Labat, J.-M. (2011). Conceptual and technical frameworks for serious games. *Proceedings of the 5th European conference on games based learning*, 81–87.

ISO. (2009). *ISO 9000 : Quality management*. ISO.

Jousselme, Pallotta, & Locke. (2015). *A Risk Game to study the influence of information quality on threat assessment and decision-making*. Technical report CMRE-FR-2015-009, NATO STO Centre for Maritime Research and experimentation, La Spezia, Italy. NATO STO Centre for Maritime Research and experimentation.

Jousselme, A.-L., Pallotta, G., & Locke, J. (2018). Risk Game: Capturing impact of information quality on human belief assessment and decision making. *International Journal of Serious Games, 5*(4), 23–44. doi:10.17083/ijsg.v5i4.258

Lacroix, E. (2005). Risques naturels en montagne: aspects juridiques de l'affichage de l'incertitude dans les expertises. *Master 2 Professionnel Droit et développement de la montagne*.

Linehan, C., Lawson, S., Doughty, M., & Kirman, B. (2009). Developing a serious game to evaluate and train group decision making skills. In *Proceedings of the 13th international MindTrek conference: Everyday Life in the Ubiquitous Era* (pp. 106–113). ACM. 10.1145/1621841.1621861

Marne, B., & Labat, J.-M. (2012). Implémentation de patrons de conception pour l'adaptation des parcours pédago-ludiques dans les jeux sérieux. In *8ème Colloque Technologies de l'Information et de la Communication pour l'Enseignement (TICE 2012)* (pp. 69–79). Academic Press.

Marne, B., Wisdom, J., Huynh-Kim-Bang, B., & Labat, J.-M. (2012). The six facets of serious game design: a methodology enhanced by our design pattern library. In *European Conference on Technology Enhanced Learning* (pp. 208–221). Springer. 10.1007/978-3-642-33263-0_17

Meera, P., McLain, M., Bijlani, K., Jayakrishnan, R., & Rao, B. R. (2016). *Serious game on flood risk management. In Emerging research in computing, information, communication and applications* (pp. 197–206). Springer. doi:10.1007/978-81-322-2553-9_19

Merad, M., Dechy, N., Llory, M., Marcel, F., & Tsoukias, A. (2014). Towards an analytics and an ethics of expertise: Learning from decision-aiding experiences in public risk assessment and risk management. *EURO Journal on Decision Processes*, *2*(1-2), 63–90. doi:10.100740070-013-0022-5

Merad, M. M. (2003). *Apport des méthodes d'aide multicritère à la décision pour l'analyse et la gestion des risques liés aux mouvements de terrains induits par les ouvrages souterrains.* Université Paris-Dauphine.

Michael, D. R., & Chen, S. L. (2005). *Serious games: Games that educate, train, and inform.* Muska & Lipman/Premier-Trade.

Montero Reyno, E., & Cubel Carsí, J. (2009). *A Platform-Independent Model for Videogame Gameplay Specification.* Academic Press.

Mossoux, S., Delcamp, A., Poppe, S., Michellier, C., Canters, F., & Kervyn, M. (2016). Hazagora: Will you survive the next disaster? A serious game to raise awareness about geohazards and disaster risk reduction. *Natural Hazards and Earth System Sciences*, *16*(1), 135–147. doi:10.5194/nhess-16-135-2016

Nystrom, R. (2014). *Game programming patterns.* Genever Benning. Retrieved from http://gameprogrammingpatterns.com/contents.html

OMG-DMN_1.1. (2016). *Object Managment Group : Decision Model And Notation, version 1.1 beta.* Object Managment Group. Retrieved from https://www.omg.org/spec/DMN/1.1/Beta/

OMG-MOF_2.5. (2015). *Object Managment Group : Meta Object Facility core specification v2.5.* Object Managment Group.

OMG-UML_2.5. (2015). *Object Managment Group : Unified Modeling Language, version 2.5.* Object Managment Group. Retrieved from https://www.omg.org/spec/UML/2.5/

Pinet, F. (2012). Entity-relationship and object-oriented formalisms for modeling spatial environmental data. *Environmental Modelling & Software*, *30*, 80–91. doi:10.1016/j.envsoft.2012.01.008

Schönbohm, A., & Jülich, A. (2016). On the Effectiveness of Gamified Risk Management Workshops: Evidence from German SMEs. *International Journal of Serious Games*, *3*(2). doi:10.17083/ijsg.v3i2.117

Selic, B. (2007). A systematic approach to domain-specific language design using UML. In *10th IEEE International Symposium on Object and Component-Oriented Real-Time Distributed Computing (ISORC'07)* (pp. 2–9). IEEE. 10.1109/ISORC.2007.10

Tacnet, J.-M. (2009). *Prise en compte de l'incertitude dans l'expertise des risques naturels en montagne par analyse multicritères et fusion d'information.* Ecole Nationale Supérieure des Mines Saint-Etienne.

Tacnet, J.-M., Dezert, J., Curt, C., Batton-Hubert, M., & Chojnacki, E. (2014). How to manage natural risks in mountain areas in a context of imperfect information? New frameworks and paradigms for expert assessments and decision-making. *Environment Systems & Decisions*, *34*(2), 288–311. doi:10.100710669-014-9501-x

Tacnet, J.-M., Lacroix, E., & Batton-Hubert, M. (2007). *Risques naturels en montagne: aspects juridiques de l'affichage de l'incertitude dans les expertises*. Ecologie Humaine, Edisud.

Taillandier, F., & Adam, C. (2018). Games Ready to Use: A Serious Game for Teaching Natural Risk Management. *Simulation & Gaming*, *49*(4), 1046878118770217. doi:10.1177/1046878118770217

Tang, S., & Hanneghan, M. (2010). A model-driven framework to support development of serious games for game-based learning. *Developments in E-systems Engineering*, *2010*, 95–100. doi:10.1109/DeSE.2010.23

Tang, S., & Hanneghan, M. (2011). Game content model: An ontology for documenting serious game design. *Developments in E-systems Engineering*, *2011*, 431–436. doi:10.1109/DeSE.2011.68

Thillainathan, N., & Leimeister, J. M. (2014). *Serious game development for educators-A serious game logic and structure modeling language*. Academic Press.

Thompson, J., Berbank-Green, B., & Cusworth, N. (2007). *The computer game design course: principles, practices and techniques for the aspiring game designer*. Thames & Hudson.

Vanhooff, B., Van Baelen, S., Joosen, W., & Berbers, Y. (2007). Traceability as input for model transformations. In *ECMDA Traceability Workshop (ECMDA-TW)* (pp. 37–46). Academic Press.

Vidaud, L. B., Tacnet, J., Pinet, F., Pasquier, X., Escande, S., Duclos, A., & Jousselme, A. (2018). How can (serious) gaming help to trace and improve snow avalanche expertise process? An innovative methodology and application to roads risk management. *ISSW 2018 International Snow Science Workshop*.

Williams, M., Cornford, D., Bastin, L., & Pebesma, E. (2009). *Uncertainty markup language (UncertML)*. Academic Press.

Xiao, J. (2009). *Gestion des incertitudes dans le processus de développement de systèmes complexes*. Institut National Polytechnique de Toulouse. Retrieved from http://ethesis.inp-toulouse.fr/archive/00001059/

Xiao, J., Pinel, P., Pi, L., Aranega, V., & Baron, C. (2008). Modeling uncertain and imprecise information in process modeling with uml. *Fourteenth International Conference on Management of Data (COMAD)*, Mumbai, India.

Yusoff, A. (2010). *A conceptual framework for serious games and its validation*. University of Southampton.

This research was previously published in the International Journal of Information System Modeling and Design (IJISMD), 11(2); pages 1-27, copyright year 2020 by IGI Publishing (an imprint of IGI Global).

Chapter 13
Codebook Co–Development to Understand Fidelity and Initiate Artificial Intelligence in Serious Games

Werner Siegfried Ravyse
TELIT, North-West University, South Africa

A. Seugnet Blignaut
TELIT, North-West University, South Africa

Chrisna R. Botha-Ravyse
TELIT, North-West University, South Africa

ABSTRACT

This study aimed to identify and rank the serious game fidelity themes that should be considered for retaining both the learning potential and predicted market growth of serious games. The authors also investigated existing links between fidelity and AI. The methodology unraveled serious game fidelity through the co-development of a theory- and data-driven codebook, applying the constant comparison method for data analysis. The theory-driven codes stemmed from literature while the data-driven codes emerged from a heuristic user interface evaluation of a comic book style game, named ExMan. This article identifies five fidelity themes, with functional fidelity as most important, and postulates that functional fidelity is most suited to AI integration. This study delivers a fidelity-for-serious-games codebook and concludes that observing the suggested fidelity hierarchy could safeguard that neither digital game-based learning is watered down, nor the lustre of digital gameplay dulled. Furthermore, the authors hold that AI for serious games should be given a high design priority.

DOI: 10.4018/978-1-6684-7589-8.ch013

INTRODUCTION

Digital entertainment games can be divided into a genre spectrum comprising of action, adventure, fighting, puzzle, roleplaying, simulation, sport or strategy (Herz, 1997). This division awards game studios the opportunity to appeal to the diverse ludic demands of playing audiences. Although game studios use this genre-based market entry to drive their sales figures, there are some general facets (e.g., graphics, animation, sound, interaction, etc.) common to all game genres that elevate the overall popularity of digital gameplay. Many of these facets are influenced by the entertainment game sector's push for high fidelity gaming and search for cutting-edge artificial intelligence (AI) (REF). Directly pushing high-fidelity onto serious games; however, may result in distractions that are detrimental to digital game-based learning (DGBL) (Ke & Abras, 2013). While adaptivity and user-modelling are popular AI serious game additives, there exists little conclusive evidence on the effects of more entertainment-centric AI in DGBL. In this study, the authors present an empirical investigation with a codebook as the tool toward in-depth understanding of game fidelity, and the role AI plays in this and how these may provide the required insight to preserve the learning potential of DGBL while propagating fidelity's entertainment game appeal to serious games. The authors aim to: (a) determine what the fidelity entry points for initiating AI in serious games are; and (b) establish each identified entry point's relative importance. This study addresses these questions by developing a serious games fidelity codebook underpinned by theory- and data-driven codes, where the latter stem from a heuristic evaluation of a business simulation game the authors designed and developed for a higher education course on food services management. The authors envision that the codebook would serve as a basis for continued qualitative studies in this area and invite other researchers to adapt the codebook's entries as they uncover further truths about serious game fidelity and AI. This study investigates, among inexperienced gamers, what the barebones fidelity characteristics of a serious game should be and identifies the fidelity characteristics that can be used to initiate AI integration to possibly boost learning with serious games. It should be noted that the authors view serious games as an artefact for digital game-based learning (DGBL) and in this study use the term serious game as the noun for the action (or verb) of DGBL.

FIDELITY

Fidelity, in a gaming context, is often affirmed as the accuracy with which a virtual world approximates reality (Alexander, Brunyé, Sidman, & Weil, 2005). This definition is broad with reason. Petridis et al. (2012) unravels fidelity for their engine selection framework into two categories, namely audiovisual and functional fidelity. Petridis et al. (2012) respectively explain these categories under the activities of: (a) rendering, animation, and sound; and (b) scripting, supported AI techniques and physics. Alexander et al. (2005) confirm this categorisation, summarising the three functional fidelity activities as simulation accuracy; and add a psychological fidelity category, with emotional content, noise, and time pressure as its properties. Alexander et al. (2005) further elaborate on psychological fidelity as the extent to which the game is able to elicit similar psychological responses a player would experience when confronted with a similar real-world environment. In a systematic literature review on the success factors of serious games (Ravyse, Blignaut, Leendertz, & Woolner, 2017), the authors note that non-player character (NPC) response can be placed alongside simulation accuracy as an added property of functional fidelity. McMahan, Bowman, Zielinski, and Brady (2012) propose that, with the widespread accessibility of gesture-controlled consoles and games, interaction fidelity with the property, which this article terms as locomotive precision, is also part of the overall depiction of fidelity. Interaction fidelity also includes navigational freedom, or the process of wayfinding and navigation during gameplay (Harrington, 2011). Navigational freedom is noteworthy because it has a significant combinatorial effect, with visual fidelity, on learning with serious games (Harrington, 2011). Figure 1 gives a visual summary of the literature pertaining to fidelity in the context of digital games.

Figure 1. Fidelity in the context of digital games

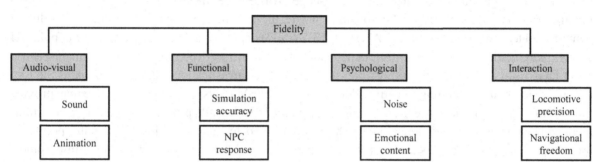

Serious games have a deliberate educational intent without the goal of engaging with them for entertainment only (Abt, 1970). This definition still rings true within today's digital context and many authors in the field of DGBL have accepted and adopted it. In establishing that pedagogy sets serious games apart from entertainment games (Zyda, 2005), the debate of which of these (pedagogy versus entertainment) is more important, has hounded the DGBL field for some time. Notwithstanding, even siding with the pedagogy over entertainment corner, one would be hard-pressed to deny the weight that the entertainment (or fun) element carries for serious games. More so, Giessen (2015) indicates that in order to attain effective DGBL, serious games producers must understand the significance of avoiding a game that is either game (entertainment) or learning (pedagogy) dominant.

Serious games received mainstream recognition with the release of *America's Army* in 2002 and the founding of the *Serious Games Initiative* shortly thereafter (Susi, Johannesson, & Backlund, 2007). Since then, using games to foster learning has gained favour among education practitioners, policy makers, health professionals, advertisers, and training practitioners (Connolly, Boyle, MacArthur, Hainey, & Boyle, 2012); or from the authors' viewpoint, gained favour among the supply side. This is reflected by a predicted compound annual growth rate of 16.38 percent between 2015 and 2020 for the serious games market (MarketsandMarkets, 2015). Yet, no matter how well intended serious games are, satisfying the playing audience (demand side) will most likely determine the realisation of this growth. Given that adventure, puzzle, roleplaying, and simulation games (genres originating within the entertainment games sphere) are well suited to DGBL (Mortara et al., 2014), one would do well to try and understand the game elements that make up the allure of the entertainment games sector. The most prolific game element that has changed the face of entertainment games, is AI. Previously, AI was widely *incorporated* into games Bourg and Seemann (2004), whereas more recently, "nearly all games *need* some amount of AI" (Moss, 2016). This is evidenced by the video games on the Forbes 2017 bestseller (Kain, 2018) list—*Call of Duty: WWII, NBA 2K18, Destiny 2, Madden NFL 18, The Legend of Zelda: Breath of the Wild*. None of these top sellers are without AI.

Fidelity and Digital Game-Based Learning

In this pursuit of balancing learning and fun in DGBL, fidelity has often come under the spotlight. In the earlier period of widespread serious games recognition, fidelity was seen as an antagonist to learning (Kiili, 2005; Papastergiou, 2009; Virvou & Katsionis, 2008) with the majority of arguments concluding that overly realistic scenes are distracting. Five or so years later however, assertions about fidelity and learning started to sway in favour of audio-visually rich games with accurate modelling, texturing and sound depictions of the real world to help players better comprehend their virtual learning spaces (Baranowski et al., 2011; Dickey, 2011). The authors contend that technological advancement leaps in graphics processing during the 2010-2012 period may have largely led to higher player expectations of entertainment video game fidelity, in turn affecting similar demands on DGBL, as noted by Couceiro, Papastergiou, Kordaki, and Veloso (2013). This shift in fidelity opinion may also be attributed to work by Bellotti, Berta, De Gloria, and Primavera (2009) and Annetta, Minogue, Holmes, and Cheng (2009), who both prescribe high-fidelity learning content in low-fidelity surroundings. Whatever the reason, still newer work on DGBL illustrate that high-detail graphics (Chittaro & Buttussi, 2015), voiceovers (Byun & Loh, 2015) and natural NPC responses (Barab, Pettyjohn, Gresalfi, Volk, & Solomou, 2012) promote learning effects and harbour a greater sense of enjoyment from those engaged with serious games. From this exposé on fidelity and learning, it becomes clear that many researchers concentrate on the audio-visual fidelity effect on learning, affording little recognition to the other fidelity themes (functional, psychological and interaction) this article proposes in Figure 1.

Fidelity and Artificial Intelligence

Game AI can be more than just cheating. Taking advantage, as a computer adversary, of access to information that human opponents would typically have to play for (van Lent & Laird, 1998), is one of several deterministic forms of behaviour that game AI could display. Deterministic behaviour refers to predictable NPC actions, predominantly exhibited in chasing algorithms (Bourg & Seemann, 2004). Significantly more complex AI techniques (e.g., decision trees, neural networks, genetic algorithms and probabilistic methods) that form the scope of non-deterministic performance (or NPC behaviour that brandishes uncertainty) are behind the success of bestseller games (Bourg & Seemann, 2004). For example, a neural network (an electronic simulation of how a simplified human brain gathers knowledge from the environment (Sweetser & Wiles, 2002)) is the AI algorithm behind the racing opponents of the game *Forza Motorsport*. In this game, the NPCs continuously learn how good your driving avatar is in order to match your playing ability and as such, keeping the game competitive. From this brief dig into game AI, it is evident that two primary constituents exist—NPCs (or agents) and the algorithms (level of intelligence) that control them through their virtual environment. Agents use sensors to gather information about their in-game environment in order to exact some action on it (Russell & Norvig, 2010). In line with the idea of deterministic and non-deterministic AI for games, agents can be broadly classified according their abilities as: (a) reflex agents, showing limited intelligence in reacting to the observation of their current environment; (b) goal- and utility-based agents, showing simple intelligence in advancing toward some predetermined goal state; and (c) learning agents, showing broad intelligence in combining performance standards and current observations for decision making (Russell & Norvig, 2010). Although it is undeniable that agent-driven AI is well engrained in games, Yannakakis (2012) declares that game AI is being reshaped by research in: (a) player experience modelling; (b) procedural content generation; (c) massive-scale game data mining; and (d) different perspectives on NPC AI. Regardless of how AI for games is approached, Dignum, Westra, van Doesburg, and Harbers (2009) postulate that the AI guiding principles of intelligence and autonomy may be essential for serious games.

Artificial intelligence in serious games uses techniques that are well demonstrated in the entertainment game sector—most notably in the form of reflex agents. The difference, understandably so, is that serious game producers coerce the AI into directing recognized learning aids as opposed to striving for superior entertainment. Bellotti, Berta, De Gloria, and Primavera (2009) propose a game architecture that includes AI for event generation, NPC activation (spawning) and as Connolly, Stansfield, and Hainey (2011) purport, appropriate hinting. The notion of personalized agent (NPC) responses (Thompson et al., 2010), sometimes directed by an NPC's own agenda (Barab et al., 2012), is also an AI practice applied in serious games. Generating user models from player actions, captured and stored in a database, is another conventional AI technique for serious games. These user models manifest themselves in the game's ability to harmonize with player learning styles by adapting the game's content presentation (Hwang, Sung, Hung, Huang, & Tsai, 2012; Soflano, Connolly, & Hainey, 2015). Bellotti, Berta, De Gloria, D'Ursi, and Fiore (2012) use serious game adaptivity for adjusting a game's difficulty level according to the player's recorded ability. There are other authors who, without implementing AI in their games, recognize and proclaim the potential of AI (specifically user modelling) to assist with adaptive feedback (Cheng, Lin, & She, 2015) that will in turn benefit scaffolding and debriefing (Ke, 2008). All in all, the authors are confident in their stance that AI should have more than just a toehold in the serious games arena. A recent literature review (Frutos-Pascual & Zapirain, 2017) on the use of AI in serious games shows that recent work in this area, aims to test whether various AI techniques can be imposed on serious games. In the process however, many of the reported research cases focus on developing AI rich games, often at the cost of equally important fidelity.

Given the fidelity overview and the current sphere of AI practices, it would appear that the entry point for AI integration into games lies with: (a) functional fidelity, where NPC responses can be directly guided by AI techniques; and to some extent (b) psychological fidelity, where user modelling could lead to game behaviour that provokes a deeper emotional connection with the game. What lies ahead, is to: (a) determine whether there may be other fidelity entry points for initiating AI in serious games; and (b) establish each identified entry point's relative importance. This study addresses these questions by developing a serious games fidelity codebook underpinned by theory- and data-driven codes, where the latter stem from a heuristic evaluation of a business simulation game.

The Business Simulation Game

ExMan is a business simulation game that exposes players to management soft skills within the food service industry by letting them roleplay as the manager of a fictitious catering company. The game was originally designed and developed by the authors for a playing audience that have little or no digital gameplay experience in order to research player perceptions about using *ExMan* as part of a Dietetics university course (Botha-Ravyse & Hanekom, 2016). One of the authors was, at the time of this experiment, the active lecturer for the course in question. Given the novice gameplay status of the target audience, the *ExMan* designers stringently followed the recommendations of Alessi and Trollip (2001), whose model prescribes that DGBL is most effective among novice game players when a diminished emphasis on game fidelity is maintained. The planned implementation site and pedagogical approach of the game further outlined the game's design. *ExMan* was designed and developed with no sound as it was intended to serve as a collaborative in-class activity. Moreover, each level of *ExMan* was envisioned as an experiential summary of the lectured theoretical aspects of a particular learning module and would replace the traditional paper-based case studies. The ephemeral nature of sound and that sound for *Ex-Man* would be primarily reading and hearing the same text, which may decrease learning (Alessi & Trollip, 2001), dissuaded the developers from incorporating sound. The lecturer designer also viewed sound emanating from multiple simultaneous gameplay sessions in a classroom environment as possibly distracting. Using earphones was not a solution, as it would have jeopardised the peer-assisted learning that underpins *ExMan*'s pedagogical approach and hampered student to lecturer communication.

Figure 2. Screenshots of ExMan gameplay

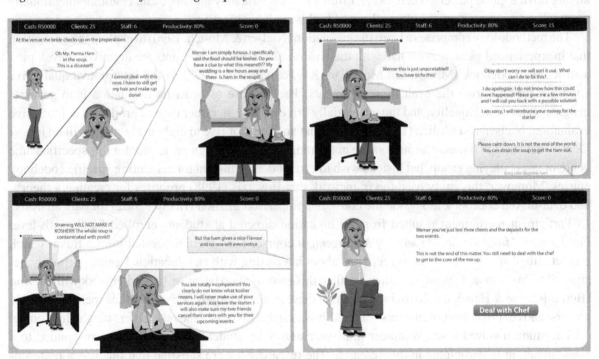

Gameplay is two-dimensional and progresses linearly in the form of an interactive slide show where the interaction is predominantly with NPCs and occasionally with other game assets. Player-character (PC) to NPC communication is by means of textual multiple choices and NPC to PC response is also textual in the form of speech bubbles. Drag and drop is the game's primary mechanic. The reward mechanic comprises an overall money balance to indicate the financial wellbeing of the company and a star rating (0 to 5) for the catering unit's reputation. The game is entirely offline with local scoring only (i.e., no online leader board) and does not have a multiplayer option. The graphics are stylized and presented in a comic book fashion with no animation. Player-character and NPC facial expressions; however, change from one image to another to reflect the emotions that are coupled to gameplay decisions. *ExMan* is silent (i.e., no background music, sounds or voice-overs) and while the game's overall learning outcome is *improved business management*, there is no underlying tale or plot (other than the objective to earn revenue and maintain a healthy reputation for the catering company) for the game. Figure 2 shows a four-slide progression of one of the *ExMan* scenes.

RESEARCH DESIGN AND METHODOLOGY

This study set out to establish the fidelity preferences of students with little gameplay experience, sans the distractions that come with ostentatious graphics (Virvou & Katsionis, 2008), intricate controls (Kiili, 2005), complicated reward mechanics (Chittaro & Sioni, 2015), an overly elaborate storyline (Cheng & Annetta, 2012) and the nuisance of sound in a classroom setting. González-González and Blanco-Izquierdo (2012) underlines the assertions by Kiili (2005), that these distractions are most prevalent among novice game players. Therefore, *ExMan*'s novice gameplay audience and resultant intentionally minimalist design are particularly well suited to this study's objectives.

The methodology comprises a heuristic evaluation (Nielsen & Molich, 1990) to explore the interaction that inexperienced game players had with the *ExMan* user interface and opts for iteratively developing a structured codebook (MacQueen, McLellan, Kay, & Milstein, 1998) as the interpretive qualitative approach for analyzing the evaluation comments. The purpose of heuristic evaluation is to generate insights about design quality, and thus potentially drive re-design, rather than to produce a comparative evaluation. Nielsen and Molich (1990) stipulate that an excess of five to eight evaluations will no longer identify new design issues. The authors are not aiming at general design principles for this specific game genre or target playing group, but instead wish to extract deeper insight for cementing specific codebook entries. Moreover, this study used the framework that Boyatzis (1998) proposes for creating a theory- and data-driven codebook alongside the constant comparison method (Boeije, 2002) for data analysis.

Participant recruitment resulted from an invitation directed at students enrolled for the exit-level *Foodservice Management: Aspects of Management* course. They were requested to join this research project aimed at collecting their perceptions about interacting with an educational game purposely designed for this course. This target audience suited this investigation because: (a) earlier work with *ExMan* (Botha-Ravyse & Hanekom, 2016) indicated that these students largely consisted of inexperienced game players; and (b) this cohort of students was readily accessible, as one of the researchers taught this course.

The study involved seven volunteer third-year university students (one male) who responded to a class invitation to participate in this research. The researchers were satisfied that this was a representative sample of this course's population, which was overwhelmingly female (20 out of 22) with very little gameplay experience (Botha-Ravyse & Hanekom, 2016). The participant ages ranged from 19 to 25 years old. All seven participants had completed the module's coursework. This study was not deterred by the seemingly low turnout of volunteers since user interface drawback identification reaches a juncture of diminishing returns at about 5 to 10 evaluators (Nielsen & Molich, 1990). At the time of data collection, one participant was an active computer game (mainly roleplaying games) player, two participants only played Facebook® games, while the remaining four had little or no prior experience with playing digital games.

To replicate the implementation intention of *ExMan*, the students assembled in a computer laboratory during a scheduled lecture session. *ExMan* was preloaded on the PCs and the study participants played the game while the researchers video recorded their gameplay experiences. Although the lecturer researcher was present to assist with queries and unforeseen technical difficulties, no instruction on how to play the game was given. The group was recorded to capture verbal exclamations during their engagement with the game. These vocalisations were extracted and incorporated into the integrated dataset for analysis. Gameplay lasted 45 to 75 minutes and was stopped for a structured interview with the students that asked about their: (a) current digital gameplay habits (how often and what type of games they played); (b) encounter with *ExMan* and their perception of the game's usefulness; and (c) likes, dislikes and suggested changes for *ExMan*. In order to eliminate influence across participants, each student was interviewed individually away from others.

The questions pertaining to student gameplay habits were used to ensure that the focus on inexperienced gamers was met. These questions had no further bearing on the analysis process. Other irrelevant data, particularly stemming from the video recordings, were also removed. This is in line with the refining of raw information that Boyatzis (1998) prescribes as a first step for data-driven code development. In order to meet the outcomes of steps two (sub-sample theme identification), three (cross-sample theme comparison) and four (code creation) of Boyatzis' framework, the researchers transcribed the video recordings of the gameplay session and the interviews into separate word processor documents on a per player basis. The analysis extracted the likes, dislikes and suggested changes from the individual interviews and merged these into a single document that was used to confirm the coding and as such, establish code reliability—step five of the data-driven code creation procedure. All documents were imported into ATLAS.ti™ (a computer assisted qualitative data analysis system).

Researcher one compiled a structured codebook of theory-driven codes reflecting the fidelity organogram presented in Figure 1. These theory codes were used as a predefined set of codes with the understanding that emergent data-driven codes would be appended to the codebook as comprehension of the data progressed. The codebook evolved over four co-coding sessions with time lapses of one to two weeks between the sessions. The seven documents comprising the video and interview transcriptions were used for the first three coding sessions. The first session included researchers one and two, while researchers one and three co-coded in the second session. Both sessions were coded to consensus and emergent data-driven codes were appended to the codebook throughout. All three researchers co-coded during the third session to consolidate the codes into a unanimous codebook. Although some codes were renamed and some minor definition changes transpired during this coding session, no new codes surfaced. The fourth co-coding session, again with all three researchers, was directed exclusively at the likes, dislikes and suggested changes interview questions. No further changes were made to the codebook during this last co-coding session and the researchers viewed this as confirmation of the codebook content. Figure 3 provides an overview of the research design for this study.

The initial codebook comprised 11 codes (emotional content, noise, time pressure, navigational freedom, locomotive precision, animation, haptic, use of sound, visuals, NPC response and simulation accuracy) derived from a formal systematic literature review investigating the success factors of serious games (Ravyse et al., 2017) and a more specific scrutiny of literature pertaining to fidelity. Although four codes (noise, time pressure, locomotive precision and haptic) were expectedly absent and one code (navigational freedom) surprisingly absent from the *ExMan* evaluation, they were retained in the codebook to provide a more complete theoretical contribution to future studies on serious game fidelity.

The 11 theory codes were classified into four overarching fidelity themes (psychological, interaction, physical and functional).

Figure 3. Overview of the study design

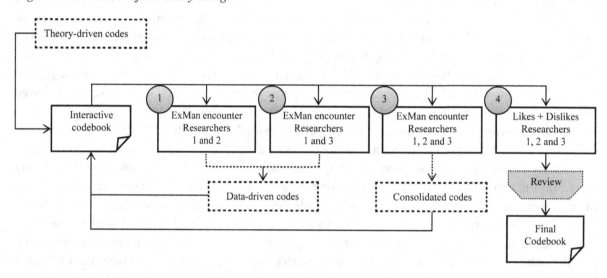

Coding sessions one and two resulted in eight data-driven codes (flow, recovery from error, status, expectation of gameplay components, game progression, type of sound, replayability and reward mechanic) that were classified under the four existing theoretical themes and six data-driven codes (technical flaws, degree of realism, ease of use, interaction efficiency, prior content exposure and prior gameplay experience) that were classified under two additional themes (fidelity evaluation and level of fidelity).

Coding session three (code consolidation) brought about the removal, renaming and reclassifying of several data-driven codes and themes. Most significantly, the authors: (a) deliberated that the degree of realism code was synonymous (and hence merged it) with the simulation accuracy code; (b) renamed the prior content exposure code to supplementing of course content and reclassified it under the functional fidelity theme; (c) removed the level of fidelity theme as there were no remaining codes under this theme; and (d) reflected that fidelity evaluation was not a descriptive enough theme name for the codes it contains and renamed it to technical fidelity. The codebook remained unchanged throughout the fourth coding session.

The researchers reviewed the codebook again after the fourth coding session and opted to exclude prior gameplay experience, gameplay expectation and replayability from the codebook. Prior gameplay experience captured the extent that players engage with other (most likely entertainment) games along with the accompanying fidelity suggestions for serious games. Gameplay expectation encompassed comments pertaining to physical in-game attributes and gameplay possibilities that players expect as part of a game, as well as how players think a typical game should respond to their actions. Although prior gameplay experience and gameplay expectation comments were primarily fidelity directed, the analysis also used the more specific fidelity codes to capture the same comments. In other words, including these codes in the codebook would have constituted double counting and erroneously skewed the data. The replayability code was used when players explicitly commented about their desire to replay *ExMan* or expressed the value of replaying the game. Replayability, although it may have a likely cause-and-effect relationship with fidelity, does not define fidelity and were left out of the codebook. The researchers do however, recognize the significance of these three codes in the greater scheme of fidelity and have not exempted them from further discourse.

DISCUSSION OF FINDINGS

The analysis extracted 219 quotations spread over 24 codes from the interview and video recording analysis. The codes, prior gameplay experience (groundedness = 23), gameplay expectation (groundedness = 32) and replayability (groundedness = 21) were removed from the codebook. Prior gameplay experience co-occurred 17 times with gameplay expectation. This is unsurprising since previous experience forms the basis of expectation when confronted with a new but similar environment, object or activity. Whether this gameplay expectation from game exposure is self-practised or through observing others is unknown, but it led to speculation that novice gamers will draw on their previous contact with games when evaluating the fidelity of a serious game. During the coding phase of this study, the codebook consisted of six headings (code name, short definition, long definition, when to use, when not to use and examples) (MacQueen et al., 1998). In order to report the codebook as a finding however, this study adopts the three-heading structure (code name, full definition and examples) DeCuir-Gunby, Marshall, and McCulloch (2010) propose where the full definition element combines the short definition, long definition, exclusion and inclusion descriptors. Furthermore, because the codes noise, time pressure, locomotive precision, haptic and navigational freedom are absent from the *ExMan* experience, the researchers have provided somewhat contextualized generic examples to augment these codebook entries. Notwithstanding, the researchers consider the resultant codebook (Table 1), containing 21 fidelity related codes that are classified into 5 themes, a trustworthy model of game fidelity that is well suited to further research endeavours.

Noise, time pressure, navigational freedom, locomotive precision and haptic have a groundedness of zero because *ExMan*'s comic-book style does not lend itself to these fidelity elements. Table 2 provides a summary of the consolidated codebook structure, distinguishes between the theory- and data-driven codes and indicates (in parentheses) each code's groundedness—the total groundedness for each theme is also given. This data is presented in Table 2 from highest to lowest total groundedness to express the relative importance of this article's proposed fidelity themes.

Whereas the students were largely regarded as novice game players, the interview analyses suggest that many of their suggestions funnel from expectations created by mainstream games. It is unclear whether their exposure to entertainment games was downplayed during the interviews (perhaps they felt inexperienced in comparison to their immediate peers), or whether the slight acquaintance they have with entertainment games was sufficient to set a bar of expectation for other game applications. In the apparent case that the interview responses flowed from entertainment game influences, the researchers could assume that the students answered the questions from a hedonistic perspective. That is, the answers they gave, pointed out the desired changes that would make them more likely to play the game for fun. This type of internal drive is positively correlated with purposeful cognitive engagement (Walker, Greene, & Mansell, 2006) and since there is no meaningful learning without engagement (Jonassen, 2004), this article asserts that the interview responses confirm the fidelity theme hierarchy it proposes as important for both learning and entertainment.

Table 1. Codebook for serious game fidelity evaluation

Code Name	Long Definition	Examples
Theme: Psychological fidelity		
Emotional content	When the game (through its content) extracts some emotional response from players while they are engaging with the game.	The chef makes me angry; I can't believe I lost my company
Flow	A state of immersion that is induced when the level of difficulty is constantly just beyond the player's capabilities to avoid boredom or entice enjoyment.	The level of difficulty should increase; more scenarios would be more fun
Noise	A gameplay disruption, either from within the game itself or the player's immediate surroundings (including actual noise, interruption or distraction) that causes players to disengage from the game.	Constant talking from other players distracted me; the game's leader board that keeps popping up is irritating
Recovery from error	The opportunity to retry when actions that lead to gameplay setbacks have been selected; also, using the game as a safe haven for experimentation.	Try straining the soup; different choices have different outcomes; firing the chef influences your business
Status	A player's desire to measure their performance against that of other players or the game itself.	I would like the scores posted online; I want to know how my classmates are doing; the game tested my knowledge a little
Time pressure	Any time constraints (or competition against time) imposed on players by the game or their immediate environment causing player anxiety or excitement.	The time limit for the food swapping was too short; we need more class time to play this game
Theme: Interaction fidelity		
Locomotive precision	The accuracy with which the PC replicates movement (particularly with motion sensing input devices)	This is not where I aimed; my character turns exactly like I do
Navigational freedom	The extent or restrictions placed on the directional movement of a game avatar.	I wish I could make my character crawl; this car cannot reverse; it is impossible to jump this high
Game progression	How a player progresses through the game's backstory from start to finish, either linearly (fixed sequence of challenges with every player seeing every challenge every time they play) or nonlinearly (no fixed sequence of challenges, which may mean not all players see all the challenges, in turn implying that there are multiple paths to victory).	I cannot go back to try something else; there is only one way to win the game; if I played it often, I would know what to choose to progress
Theme: Physical fidelity		
Animation	Refers to any movement, which is not related to navigational direction, by game assets (characters and other scenario specific items) or the ambient environment (e.g., heads-up display elements or scenario transitions).	Animation would keep your attention; the facial expressions should change
Haptic	Refers to any physical feedback (proprioceptive, vestibular, olfactory or tactile) players could receive during gameplay	The mouse should get hot when the food is burning; imagine if you could smell the rotten food
Use of sound	Refers to how sound is used or absent within the game either during introductory scenes, cut-scenes or actual gameplay	I wonder if you can add sound; include a voice that reads out the speech bubble; I cannot make out what that sound is
Visual	Refers to the quality, type, style or appropriateness of the visuals within the game—this includes special effects, shadows, lighting and texturing; also refers to icons used on the heads-up display and other inanimate game scene objects	Visuals help me to recall better; I would let the background change; make the pictures more realistic
Theme: Functional fidelity		
NPC response	Indicates the physics (how the NPC response is manifested on the screen), scriptedness (appropriateness of the response content and when the response takes place) or AI (how personal, situationally accurate or agent-like the response is) of the NPC response.	If I hire another chef, the bride will be happier; the character response shows me how to act

continues on following page

Table 1. Continued

Code Name	Long Definition	Examples
Reward	Any reward (gameplay, intrinsic or extrinsic) the player can obtain by playing the game; gameplay reward includes ancillary, environmental progression or practical rewards; intrinsic reward describes the feeling the player is left with after a gameplay session; extrinsic reward occurs because of playing the game.	The star rating does not make sense; the reward should not take the fun out of the course; I will be able to manage staff after playing this game; I want marks for time spent playing the game
Simulation accuracy	How accurately the game's behaviour portrays reality, which includes the physics of gameplay items, logical order of proceedings and naturalness (or appropriate AI) of the response to player actions; this instils an element of trust among the players that the game will convey appropriate knowledge or behaviour.	Appointing more staff means increasing productivity and making more money; The waitress would never be able to know what you are doing; Can replace some of the case studies in class
Supplemen-ting course content	The degree in which the game adds to prior content knowledge and how much prior learning (preparation) is required to play the game	It makes foundational knowledge more concrete; it will not add knowledge; it will be good for somebody who has had the course; I would use it to prepare for class
Theme: Technical fidelity		
Ease of use	The extent to which controls are intuitive and make use of recognisable devices; also refers to how the complexity or player understanding of the UI and Heads-up display elements compares with other learning modes.	It would be an easy way to obtain marks; I had trouble dragging the answer to its correct slot; I would rather use this than my study guide
Interaction efficiency	The interaction effort that is required to perform actions within the game (even to start up the game); also, how quickly the game responds to user inputs.	I would rather click instead of click and drag; reading takes too much time; voice-overs might speed up gameplay
Technical flaws	Any errors during gameplay that cause frustration or irritation among the players	Spelling errors; the game hangs; my scores don't make sense

The students did not comment about the *2Dness* of the game. Taking the findings of Bellotti, Berta, De Gloria, and Primavera (2009) and Papastergiou (2009) into account that a 3D immersive environment is generally preferred over 2D, this was somewhat surprising. This may however, be an indication of their limited game exposure. Still, it does show that the wow factor of physical fidelity (hyper-realistic graphics and animation) is overshadowed by the importance of functional fidelity (simulation accuracy, NPC interaction and random events). Although sound is, by this study's organogram, grouped under physical fidelity, it is just as much functional. The students possibly perceived NPC responses via speech bubbles as less natural than voice-overs and as such demanded (regardless of *ExMan*'s intended classroom-based tuition) higher functional fidelity by way of including voice-overs. Although this study cannot conclude that sound in serious games has to be state of the art, the researchers can categorically state that the addition of sound was requested across the board. Although there were pertinent implementation reasons for excluding sound from *ExMan*'s design, the researchers failed to recognize that including sound might allow *ExMan* to extract play-out-of-free-will value. If sound is one of the factors that encourages students to play the game outside the classroom, it should be included. After all, self-elected gameplay implies that the student is engaging with the learning material when they would otherwise have been doing something else and by extension, engaging with learning material should be viewed as positive for learning. However, to maintain the original intent of classroom collaborative learning, the option to switch off the sound must be built into the game. As much as players requested voice-overs, they did not mention speech recognition. The researchers suspect that this is because it is not mainstream among entertainment games (yet), and therefore, not an expectation.

Table 2. Summary of consolidated codes in order of relative theme importance

Theory-Driven Codes	Data-Driven Codes
Functional Fidelity (113)	
NPC response (15)	Reward (20)
Simulation accuracy (47)	Supplementing course content (31)
Psychological Fidelity (92)	
Emotional content (26)	Flow (36)
Noise (0)	Recovery from error (12)
Time pressure (0)	Status (18)
Interaction Fidelity (47)	
Navigational freedom (0)	Game progression (15)
Locomotive precision (0)	Gameplay expectations (32)
Physical Fidelity (33)	
Animation (7)	
Haptic (0)	
Use of sound (22)	
Visuals (4)	
Technical Fidelity (19)	
	Ease of use (3)
	Interaction efficiency (9)
	Technical flaws (7)

CONCLUSION

Literature, expert comments and the games found on best-seller shelves in stores show that AI has become a necessity for the success of highly popular games. As is the norm with features that find a home in the upper echelons of a given activity, these soon filter down and become an expectation for less intricate examples of that activity. The aim of this study was to provide a clear understanding of game fidelity for serious games and whether there may be fidelity entry points for the initiation of AI into serious games. In trying to gain a handle on game fidelity, this study scrutinizes literature and presents an organogram that became the theory-driven codes for a fidelity codebook. These theory-driven codes were supplemented with data-driven codes from a heuristic user interface evaluation of an unsophisticated serious game. The process resulted in a first-of-its-kind codebook that provides a theoretical contribution for further qualitative evaluation of serious game fidelity. Additionally, this codebook has provided much insight into the continued development of *ExMan*—particularly, with regard to AI infusion.

The student interview responses call attention to the fidelity changes that would lead to an increased appetite amongst the target group for playing the game. The researchers coded the student responses and classified these codes according to their theoretical view of fidelity to produce a ranking of five fidelity themes with functional fidelity as most important, followed (in order of relative importance) by psychological, interaction, physical and technical fidelity. This article argues that changing *ExMan* to suit the hedonistically driven participant responses would lead to higher engagement and as such, advance the learning effect. Thereby advocating that serious game producers, who wish to ensure that the learning potential of DGBL is preserved while sustaining a compelling level of entertainment, should pay heed to this study's proposed fidelity hierarchy.

With functional and psychological fidelity regarded as the most important themes and given that: (a) AI very much underpins these categories through NPC response, simulation accuracy and (to some extent) emotional content; and (b) AI has become an expected feature of entertainment games; there is a strong case for further investigation into suitable AI infusion for serious games. Although current serious game AI practices naturally hover within these categories, they do not often stray far from the relative safety of response-oriented programming (reflex agents) and uncomplicated database store and retrieve techniques. In discovering the relative significance of the fidelity categories that house AI potential, it may be beneficial to introduce stronger AI techniques (e.g., fuzzy state machines, neural networks, decision trees or genetic algorithms) into serious games. Whether these techniques will have a positive impact on the learning construct of serious games is a topic for further research.

From a methodology viewpoint, the researchers conclude that collaborative codebook development is a reliable methodology for unravelling complex topics or elements of serious games. Not just does it provide a sound theoretical contribution, but a codebook also functions practically in providing insight for new game designs as well as the further development of existing games. This article has also shown that, on the back of heuristic user interface evaluation, codebook development can bring about significant findings from unassuming games.

The resulting codebook is limited to the researchers' understanding of literature and the dataset that was accrued through the heuristic user interface evaluation of *ExMan*. With this, the researchers acknowledge that analyses of other games and intentional fundamental research on fidelity may lead to additional codebook entries. Therefore, digital game researchers are invited to use this study's suggested fidelity codebook as a starting point and to amend it according to their continued discoveries on this topic.

The outcomes of this study have set the tone for an in-depth investigation into AI for serious games that will in turn direct the redesign and development of *ExMan*.

ACKNOWLEDGMENT

This work is based on research support, in part, by the National Research Foundation of South Africa. Any opinion, findings and conclusions or recommendations expressed in this material are those of the authors and therefore the NRF does accept any liability in regard thereto.

REFERENCES

Abt, C. C. (1970). *Serious games*. New York: Viking Press.

Alessi, S. M., & Trollip, S. R. (2001). Multimedia for learning: Methods and development (3rd ed.). Needham Heights, MAS: Allyn & Bacon.

Alexander, A. L., Brunyé, T., Sidman, J., & Weil, S. A. (2005). From gaming to training: A review of studies on fidelity, immersion, presence, and buy-in and their effects on transfer in pc-based simulations and games. *DARWARS Training Impact Group*, 5, 1–14.

Annetta, L. A., Minogue, J., Holmes, S. Y., & Cheng, M. T. (2009). Investigating the impact of video games on high school students' engagement and learning about genetics. *Computers & Education*, *53*(1), 74–85. doi:10.1016/j.compedu.2008.12.020

Barab, S., Pettyjohn, P., Gresalfi, M., Volk, C., & Solomou, M. (2012). Game-based curriculum and transformational play: Designing to meaningfully positioning person, content, and context. *Computers & Education*, *58*(1), 518–533. doi:10.1016/j.compedu.2011.08.001

Baranowski, T., Baranowski, J., Thompson, D., Buday, R., Jago, R., Griffith, M. J., ... Watson, K. B. (2011). Video game play, child diet, and physical activity behavior change: A randomized clinical trial. *American Journal of Preventive Medicine*, *40*(1), 33–38. doi:10.1016/j.amepre.2010.09.029 PMID:21146765

Bellotti, F., Berta, R., De Gloria, A., D'Ursi, A., & Fiore, V. (2012). A serious game model for cultural heritage. *Journal on Computing and Cultural Heritage*, *5*(4), 1–27. doi:10.1145/2399180.2399185

Bellotti, F., Berta, R., De Gloria, A., & Primavera, L. (2009). Enhancing the educational value of video games. *Computers in Entertainment*, *7*(2), 1–18. doi:10.1145/1541895.1541903

Boeije, H. (2002). A purposeful approach to the constant comparative method in the analysis of qualitative interviews. *Quality & Quantity*, *36*(4), 391–409. doi:10.1023/A:1020909529486

Botha-Ravyse, C., & Hanekom, S. (2016). "I fired the chef!" Simulation gameplay for enhancing food management skills. *Paper presented at the EdMedia*. Academic Press.

Bourg, D. M., & Seemann, G. (2004). *AI for game developers*. Sebastopol, CA: O'Reilly Media, Inc.

Boyatzis, R. E. (1998). *Transforming qualitative information: Thematic analysis and code development*. Thousand Oaks, CA: Sage Publications.

Byun, J., & Loh, C. S. (2015). Audial engagement: Effects of game sound on learner engagement in digital game-based learning environments. *Computers in Human Behavior*, *46*, 129–138. doi:10.1016/j.chb.2014.12.052

Cheng, M.-T., & Annetta, L. (2012). Students' learning outcomes and learning experiences through playing a serious educational game. *Journal of Biological Education*, *46*(4), 203–213. doi:10.1080/00219266.2012.688848

Cheng, M.-T., Lin, Y.-W., & She, H.-C. (2015). Learning through playing Virtual Age: Exploring the interactions among student concept learning, gaming performance, in-game behaviors, and the use of in-game characters. *Computers & Education*, *86*, 18–29. doi:10.1016/j.compedu.2015.03.007

Chittaro, L., & Buttussi, F. (2015). Assessing knowledge retention of an immersive serious game vs. a traditional education method in aviation safety. *IEEE Transactions on Visualization and Computer Graphics*, *21*(4), 529–538. doi:10.1109/TVCG.2015.2391853 PMID:26357103

Chittaro, L., & Sioni, R. (2015). Serious games for emergency preparedness: Evaluation of an interactive vs. a non-interactive simulation of a terror attack. *Computers in Human Behavior*, *50*, 508–519. doi:10.1016/j.chb.2015.03.074

Connolly, T. M., Boyle, E. A., MacArthur, E., Hainey, T., & Boyle, J. M. (2012). A systematic literature review of empirical evidence on computer games and serious games. *Computers & Education*, *59*(2), 661–686. doi:10.1016/j.compedu.2012.03.004

Connolly, T. M., Stansfield, M., & Hainey, T. (2011). An alternate reality game for language learning: ARGuing for multilingual motivation. *Computers & Education*, *57*(1), 1389–1415. doi:10.1016/j.compedu.2011.01.009

Couceiro, R. M., Papastergiou, M., Kordaki, M., & Veloso, A. I. (2013). Design and evaluation of a computer game for the learning of Information and Communication Technologies (ICT) concepts by physical education and sport science students. *Education and Information Technologies*, *18*(3), 531–554. doi:10.100710639-011-9179-3

DeCuir-Gunby, J. T., Marshall, P. L., & McCulloch, A. W. (2010). Developing and using a codebook for the analysis of interview data: An example from a professional development research project. *Field Methods*, *23*(2), 136–155. doi:10.1177/1525822X10388468

Dickey, M. D. (2011). Murder on Grimm Isle: The impact of game narrative design in an educational game-based learning environment. *British Journal of Educational Technology*, *42*(3), 456–469. doi:10.1111/j.1467-8535.2009.01032.x

Dignum, F., Westra, J., van Doesburg, W. A., & Harbers, M. (2009). Games and agents: Designing intelligent gameplay. *International Journal of Computer Games Technology*, *2009*, 1–18. doi:10.1155/2009/837095

Frutos-Pascual, M., & Zapirain, B. G. (2017). Review of the use of AI techniques in serious games: Decision making and machine learning. *IEEE Transactions on Computational Intelligence and AI in Games*, *9*(2), 133–152. doi:10.1109/TCIAIG.2015.2512592

Giessen, H. W. (2015). Serious Games Effects: An Overview. *Procedia: Social and Behavioral Sciences*, *174*, 2240–2244. doi:10.1016/j.sbspro.2015.01.881

González-González, C., & Blanco-Izquierdo, F. (2012). Designing social videogames for educational uses. *Computers & Education*, *58*(1), 250–262. doi:10.1016/j.compedu.2011.08.014

Harrington, M. C. R. (2011). The Virtual Trillium Trail and the empirical effects of freedom and fidelity on discovery-based learning. *Virtual Reality (Waltham Cross)*, *16*(2), 105–120. doi:10.100710055-011-0189-7

Herz, J. C. (1997). *Joystick Nation: How Videogames Ate Our Quarters, Won Our Hearts, and Rewired Our Minds*. Boston, MA: Little, Brown and Company.

Hwang, G. J., Sung, H. Y., Hung, C. M., Huang, I., & Tsai, C. C. (2012). Development of a personalized educational computer game based on students' learning styles. *Educational Technology Research and Development*, *60*(4), 623–638. doi:10.100711423-012-9241-x

Jonassen, D. H. (2004). *Learning to solve problems: An instructional design guide* (B. Miller, Ed.). Vol. 6). San Francisco, CA: John Wiley & Sons.

Kain, E. (2018). The Best-Selling Video Games of 2017. *#GamingSales*. Forbes. Retrieved from https://www.forbes.com/sites/erikkain/2018/01/19/the-best-selling-video-games-of-2017/#65cd4c4d6226

Ke, F. (2008). A case study of computer gaming for math: Engaged learning from gameplay? *Computers & Education*, *51*(4), 1609–1620. doi:10.1016/j.compedu.2008.03.003

Ke, F., & Abras, T. (2013). Games for engaged learning of middle school children with special learning needs. *British Journal of Educational Technology*, *44*(2), 225–242. Retrieved from http://nwulib.nwu.ac.za/login?url=http://search.ebscohost.com/login.aspx?direct=true&db=eric&AN=EJ1009157. doi:10.1111/j.1467-8535.2012.01326.x

Kiili, K. (2005). Content creation challenges and flow experience in educational games: The IT-Emperor case. *The Internet and Higher Education*, *8*(3), 183–198. doi:10.1016/j.iheduc.2005.06.001

MacQueen, K. M., McLellan, E., Kay, K., & Milstein, B. (1998). Codebook development for team-based qualitative analysis. *Cultural Anthropology Methods*, *10*(2), 31–36.

MarketsandMarkets. (2015). Serious game market worth $5,448.82 million by 2020. Retrieved from http://www.marketsandmarkets.com/PressReleases/serious-game.asp

McMahan, R. P., Bowman, D. A., Zielinski, D. J., & Brady, R. B. (2012). Evaluating display fidelity and interaction fidelity in a virtual reality game. *Visualization and Computer Graphics. IEEE Transactions on*, *18*(4), 626–633. PMID:22402690

Mortara, M., Catalano, C. E., Bellotti, F., Fiucci, G., Houry-Panchetti, M., & Petridis, P. (2014). Learning cultural heritage by serious games. *Journal of Cultural Heritage*, *15*(3), 318–325. doi:10.1016/j.culher.2013.04.004

Moss, R. (2016). 7 examples of game AI that every developer should study. Gamasutra. Retrieved from http://www.gamasutra.com/view/news/269634/7_examples_of_game_AI_that_every_developer_should_study.php

Nielsen, J., & Molich, R. (1990). Heuristic evaluation of user interfaces. *Paper presented at the SIGCHI Conference on Human Factors in Computing Systems*. Academic Press.

Papastergiou, M. (2009). Digital game-based learning in high school computer science education: Impact on educational effectiveness and student motivation. *Computers & Education*, *52*(1), 1–12. doi:10.1016/j.compedu.2008.06.004

Petridis, P., Dunwell, I., Panzoli, D., Arnab, S., Protopsaltis, A., Hendrix, M., & de Freitas, S. (2012). Game engines selection framework for high-fidelity serious applications. *International Journal of Interactive Worlds*, *2012*, 1–19. doi:10.5171/2012.418638

Ravyse, W. S., Blignaut, A. S., Leendertz, V., & Woolner, A. (2017). Success factors for serious games to enhance learning: A systematic review. *Virtual Reality*, *21*(1), 31–58. doi:10.100710055-016-0298-4

Russell, S. J., & Norvig, P. (2010). *Artificial intelligence: A modern approach*. Essex, UK: Prentice Hall.

Soflano, M., Connolly, T., & Hainey, T. (2015). An application of adaptive games-based learning based on learning style to teach SQL. *Computers & Education, 86*, 192–211. doi:10.1016/j.compedu.2015.03.015

Susi, T., Johannesson, M., & Backlund, P. (2007). *Serious games - An overview* (HS- IKI -TR-07-001). Retrieved from Skövde: Sweetser, P., & Wiles, J. (2002). Current AI in games: A review. *Australian Journal of Intelligent Information Processing Systems, 8*(1), 24–42.

Thompson, D., Baranowski, T., Buday, R., Baranowski, J., Thompson, V., Jago, R., & Griffith, M. (2010). Serious video games for health: How behavioral science guided the development of a serious video game. *Simulation & Gaming, 41*(4), 587–606. doi:10.1177/1046878108328087 PMID:20711522

van Lent, M., & Laird, J. (1998). Developing an artificial intelligence engine. Retrieved from http://ai.eecs.umich.edu/people/laird/papers/GDC99.pdf

Virvou, M., & Katsionis, G. (2008). On the usability and likeability of virtual reality games for education: The case of VR-ENGAGE. *Computers & Education, 50*(1), 154–178. doi:10.1016/j.compedu.2006.04.004

Walker, C. O., Greene, B. A., & Mansell, R. A. (2006). Identification with academics, intrinsic/extrinsic motivation, and self-efficacy as predictors of cognitive engagement. *Learning and Individual Differences, 16*(1), 1–12. doi:10.1016/j.lindif.2005.06.004

Yannakakis, G. N. (2012). Game AI revisited. *Paper presented at the Proceedings of the 9th conference on Computing Frontiers*. Academic Press.

Zyda, M. (2005). From visual simulation to virtual reality to games. *Computer, 38*(9), 25–32. doi:10.1109/MC.2005.297

This research was previously published in the International Journal of Game-Based Learning (IJGBL), 10(1); pages 37-53, copyright year 2020 by IGI Publishing (an imprint of IGI Global).

Chapter 14

Requirements-Based Design of Serious Games and Learning Software:
An Introduction to the Vegas Effect

Brock Randall Dubbels
McMaster University, Canada

ABSTRACT

A serious game can be entertaining and enjoyable, but it is designed to facilitate the acquisition of skills and knowledge performance in the workplace, classroom, or therapeutic context. Claims of improvement can be validated through assessments of successful, measurable practice beyond the game experience, the targeted context of the workplace, classroom, or clinical using the same tools as multiple traits and multiple measure (MTMM) models. This chapter provides a post-mortem describing the development of the initial design and development of a measurable model to inform the design requirements for validation for a serious game. In this chapter, the reader will gain insight into the implementation of lean process, design thinking, and field observations for generative research. This data informs the assessments and measurement of performance, validated through the MTMM model criteria for requirements. The emphasis examines the role of research insights for onboarding and professional development of newly hired certified nursing assistants in a long-term care facility.

INTRODUCTION

This article provides a post mortem for developing serious games to answer the question:

How do you know your serious game had the intended impact?

DOI: 10.4018/978-1-6684-7589-8.ch014

This chapter builds upon this theme to emphasize the importance of a Lean Process approach, when integrated with Design Thinking, User Experience Research, traditional psychology and psychometrics, and Agile Development. These approaches to product design potentially provide a synthesis to reduce uncertainty, facilitate action, increase transparency, flexibility, velocity, and learning.

BACKGROUND

In the case study presented here as a post-mortem, the five different fields are presented and synthesized to present an approach to developing a video game to train inexperienced care-givers to become effective certified nursing assistants.

One of the foundations of serious games is that they deliver on a claim. If a claim is made that performance, training, or a health outcome is improved, it must be observable inside the game—the activity is the assessment in a serious game (Dubbels, 2016; 2017)—and that the improvement from playing in the game transfers to improvement in the wild of the non-digital world, and measurable with the same models from the game. This makes a case for having evidence-supported requirements. Although this is not always possible initially, research techniques can be used to generate and test insights as part of an iterative process, culminating incremental improvement of requirements, models, and testing as part of a build, measure, learn process(Ries, 2011, 2013) If we do not have a clear understanding of the activities and how to model and measure the behavior we want out users to learn, we are essentially throwing the dice, hoping we guessed correctly. This does not have to be the case, as there is a history of user research to reduce risk and uncertainty in developing and designing games.

History of Game User Research

What is odd is that game user research is not new. In his keynote address at the Games User Research Summit, Michael Medlock (Medlock, 2014) provided a history of games research, going back to 1972, when Atari hired Carol Kanter. She shared that:

It all started on a bet. I met Gene Lipkin VP of Atari. I asked him how he could tell if his games were good or not. I bet him that in 6 months I could tell which game will do better in the market than the others, and if I could then he needed to hire me full time. I did, and then he did.

Although Kanter is listed as the first in a tradition of game user research, the early games user researchers focused on marketing—showing which games would be successful and why. This approach focused on generative research techniques such as focus group work and field methods. These techniques culminated in the creation of teams at Nintendo, and the creation of guides for usability (Al-Awar, Chapanis, & Ford, 1981).

Recently, more companies are creating new positions in user experience research, user experience design, and even behavioral economics. The intent is to generate insights that guide game development to improve the game experience, and to examine new ways to generate income. However, few game development companies have begun to integrate the field of psychometrics from psychology, and examine whether games can provide services like training, diagnosis, performance enhancement, and skill and knowledge acquisition. This chapter provides a synthesis of traditional psychology and psychometrics with current practices in project management, development, and design.

However, the recent emergence of brain fitness games had led to research psychologists looking at ways that games can be used as cognitive, affective, behavioral, and physiological interventions. Research using video games identified that playing these games can lead to physiological, behavioral, affective, and cognitive changes (Anguera et al., 2013; Bavelier et al., 2011; Dubbels, 2012; Green & Bavelier, 2008; Green, Benson, Kersten, & Schrater, 2010; Green & Bavelier, 2003; Jaeggi, Buschkuehl, Jonides, & Perrig, 2008; Loftus & Loftus, 1983; Merzenich et al., 1996; Smith et al., 2009). This approach had drawn heavily from the research perspective developed by research psychologists, with great emphasis on the ability to objectively measure and differentiate psychological states as categories and constructs for diagnosis, identification of casual origin, and potential treatment.

The ability to identify, describe, diagnose, and treat with psychological tools is the history of psychology. Psychology was once a subfield of philosophy until the1870s, when people interested in psychological processes began to formalize their methods of study with the adoption of objective scientific method. According to historical studies of psychology ("Timeline of psychology," 2015), studies of reaction time by Franciscus Donders, the creation of psychophysics as a field of study in 1860, and the publication of the first textbook of experimental psychology by William Wundt in 1874, which led to academic studies of psychology. William Wundt created a laboratory dedicated to psychological research on the nature of religious beliefs, identification of mental disorders and abnormal behavior, and to study brain structure and function through identification of damaged parts of the brain. In doing so, he was able to establish psychology as a separate science from other topics, but still faced criticism about the methods that relied upon introspection and questioned whether psychology could be called a legitimate science.

With the evolution and growth of psychology as an objective science, new methods have been created to answer the question: *How do you know?*

Serious Games as Informative Assessment

Serious games are already very much like the tools used in psychological assessments and evaluations. Games, by their very nature assess, measure, and evaluate as informative assessments (Black & Wiliam, 2009; Forster, 2009; Wiliam & Thompson, 2007). This makes sense. Informative assessments provide measurement and feedback in the flow of the activity. This is in contrast to formative and summative assessments, which are measures that occur outside the flow of an activity.

In games, assessment is part of the game play. Informative assessment provides an activity where the player learns the scoring criteria through feedback from interaction in the game environment. If a game is to act as an informative assessment, it will stress meaningful, timely, and continuous feedback about learning concepts, and provide adaptive situations through introduction of ambiguity and least/worst situations in game play to expose weaknesses in knowledge and performance, and scaffold learning.

Evidence supports that informative assessments are powerful learning tools. Research findings from over 4,000 studies indicate that informative assessment has the most significant impact on achievement (Wiliam, 2007). When serious games are built as an informative assessment, the scoring criteria becomes the roadmap for learning (Dubbels, 2016). The criteria can also provide a framework for construct validity for learning in the game, as well as a tool for measuring activities outside the game. This approach can increase the likelihood that learning and performance recorded inside the game, can be measured as a training effect outside of the game—avoiding the Vegas Effect.

Currently, most games are not designed as informative assessments. This means that learning in a serious game might suffer from the Vegas Effect—learning that happens in games, stays in games. For a game to act as informative assessment, the learning must transfer. This is accomplished when the learning concepts are accurately defined, measured, and depicted as game play; and the in------game assessment tools can be used in an actual work or clinical environment.

Why Go to All of This Trouble?

When games are used as tools for assessment, diagnosis and performance evaluation, they can have a serious impact on a person's life—whether the game is used for a clinical diagnosis or for a work performance review. If serious games are to be taken seriously, they need to account for two concerns:

1. People are being judged: if serious games are to be used to measure and evaluate the performance and abilities of an individual, the process should be done with great care.
2. Serious games are significant investments: a serious game should provide clear evidence of learning for return on investment (ROI).

The adoption of methods and techniques from psychometrics can reduce the gamble associated with serious game development. Increasing certainty about learning outcomes should be at the top of the list. This can be addressed through adoption of existing models from the research literature, and implementing methods from the field of psychometrics. The integration of validated research models and psychometric methodology can the reduce risk associated with poor assessment, measurement evaluation. This can easily be accomplished through a review of the research letter in the content area being modeled and using the criteria of the construct being described, and building game mechanics based upon valid, reliable, and replicated metrics and outcomes described in the research.

The review of psychometric models, assessments, and data should be modeled prior to the construction of the prototype. This saves time, money, and the sanity of the programmers, artists, and subject matter experts. There will always be learning in development, but when psychometric methods are used to build models from established criteria, analysis can be conducted prior to, during, and after development, rather than waiting until after the game has been finished. This approach is often called an agile approach (Kane, 2003). In academic research, building these models is required prior to experimentation – why should it be different for serious games?

As an analogy, the author worked in construction one summer, and often heard experienced builders laugh when talking about the impatience of customers, and their fear of planning expenses. The veteran builders would say:

Sure, why bother planning—we can always build it twice.

There are many companies that realize that upfront planning and modeling from user experience research can actually reduce expense. Companies like Boeing Co. Fidelity Investments reported that poor user experience can add as much as 50% to the total cost of software. Additionally, the Gardner Group reported that 25% of software development efforts fail outright due to poor planning, and another 65% of efforts result in sub-standard performance (Kwong, Healton, & Lancaster, 1998). User experience research requires a bit of planning up front, but it saves time and resources. Avoiding the Vegas

Effect may lead to serious economic opportunities as saving money and measurable improvements in performance outside of the game.

It is in our nature to make predictions based upon assumption. Can we assume that a serious game delivers on its' promises? When the outcome is high-stakes, such as learning to deliver medical treatment, or operating heavy equipment? We need to know quickly that the games as intervention is effective before we introduce real-world risk. We often draw on assumptions and educated guessing to create requirements and learning criteria. This approach seems not only risky and potentially wasteful, but also a common theme for constructing requirements. It is not enough to start with a business case. Best practice suggests that we can reduce risk and uncertainty by adopting a Lean Process (Ries, 2011), which offers a method for increasing certainty.

The Lean Process seeks to:

- identify how people currently solve a problem (current behavior),
- propose a better process (proposed behavior)
- conduct a gap analysis
- identify the value provided in the proposed behavior (value hypothesis)
- identify a measurement of efficacy to support the business case (growth metric)

These steps provide a powerful approach for the development of software requirements. Better requirements make for better design, development, and customer experience. When requirements for building any type of software are validated with the user needs as a focus, and this focus is informed from research and evidence, we can feel more confident that our software will deliver the experience we claim it delivers.

Using a Lean process (Eisenmann, Ries, & Dillard, 2012; Frederiksen & Brem, 2017; Ries, 2011, 2012, 2013; Womack & Jones, 1997) one can use empirical scientific methods to have greater confidence and certainty in the design and development requirements, as well as greater certainty that what happened in the game experience, leads to improved performance as potential training and therapy.

To start with a Lean Process, we need to take a close look at the business case development of criteria to design models for game mechanics. We need to ask, "what do we know about how people are currently solving this problem?" If the development team thinks of the software as a jigsaw puzzle, the business case should provide framing as corners and edges. If there are gaps in the business case, these gaps can be identified as assumptions. The riskier the assumption, the greater the business risk. This can be achieved through what Jeff Patton describes as user story mapping (Patton, 2002; Patton & Economy, 2014).

The process starts with proposed ideas and goals from the business case, which leads to steps in the process supporting the customer experience:

I want to build X for these reasons, and for these people to experience.

This can be drawn from designing a GIST model. A Gist model (Gilad, 2018) is for the creation of "lightweight plans that are built for change, lower management overhead, improved team velocity and autonomy, better cross-company alignment and ultimately better products and solutions." The GIST model was created to quickly develop, and right-size project planning into simple steps, as compared to waterfall approaches ("Waterfall model," 2018).

This form of planning is a ton of work—just getting all stakeholders to agree is a massive undertaking, yet ROI is very low. The plans quickly go out of sync with reality—the longer they are the more they are wrong. It took me awhile to realize that my fancy roadmaps and project gantts were already outdated the day I published them. Also, it's a waterfall (different from the famous project waterfall), meaning that there is almost no room for agility—changes at the top cause huge ripple effects of replanning and project cancellations at the bottom. Agile development addressed project waterfall, but didn't change planning waterfall. And then there's the impact on innovation and culture. As roadmaps allow only for a few big projects to be funded you have to prioritize and kill many potentially good ideas upfront. In top-down orgs the winner ideas come from management. In bottom-up orgs getting your idea to win became a very big deal, hence pitching, salesmanship and hype are now mandatory product management skills. To me it all felt very mid-20th century. (Gilad, 2018).

Gilad developed the GIST model in alignment with Lean Process and Agile Development. The benefits include:

- No split of ideation, planning and execution—they all happen concurrently all the time
- Goals rather than solutions or vague strategy statements.
- Idea banks rather than product backlogs.
- Short sub-quarter step-projects rather than long multi-quarter/multi-year projects.
- No betting on just a few big ideas that take forever to implement—we test many ideas quickly and pursue the ones that work.
- Iterations—we revisit every part of the plan regularly and systematically and stay agile at all levels.

The intention is to create light-weight plans that are *"built for change, lower management overhead, improved team velocity and autonomy, better cross-company alignment and ultimately better products and solutions"(Ibid)*. The main building blocks of the GIST model are depicted below in figure 1 as: Goals, Ideas, Step-Projects, and Tasks.

Figure 1. GIST Model
(Gilad, 2018)

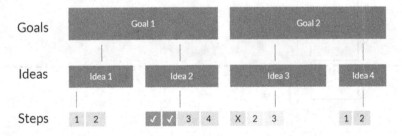

According to Gilad each level of this model embody a principle.

- **Goals:** The principle is to focus on strategy informed by desired outcomes. Whenever there is a question about the rationale behind an activity in design and development, a goal should give an answer. This approach comes from Gilad's experience at Google, where each quarter employees are asked to state and define measurable goals in the form of Objectives and Key Results (OKRs)—(for more on OKRs, read: Doerr, 2018).
- **Ideas:** Ideas and approaches to achieving goals. (author note, I prefer the term *approach* to the term *solution*, as it promotes that this is a testable hypothesis rather than the end of the inquiry and testing).
- **Step-Projects:** These are defined and identified based upon goals and ideas prioritized at the beginning of the quarter.
- **Tasks:** This category i intended to identify tasks as activities necessary to complete step-projects. This category can also be used for identification of tasks within the steps of a customer journey as a finer-grain depiction of the user journey well as identification of customer activities within a journey map for planning.

To formulate steps from an idea, your team can implement a story map methodology as depicted below in figure 2.

Figure 2. User story map

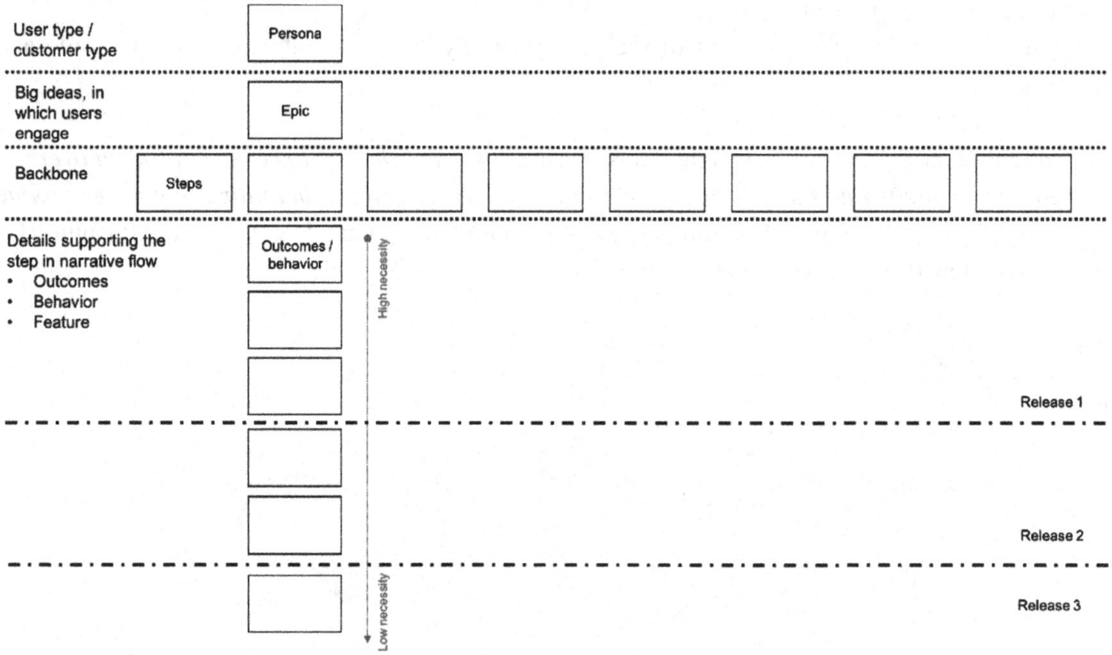

In story mapping, the team can propose Step Plans from Ideas (Patton, 2002; Patton & Economy, 2014). In Figure 2, the team can replace the term "epic" with idea and propose steps as part of the project backbone. The proposed experience is expressed as steps in a user/customer journey. Each step in the journey can be described below the step as a vertical column as details supporting the narrative flow of the story with outcomes, behavior, and features. As the steps on the backbone of the process are identified horizontally, details of each step are built as sublevels below each step. As the story map is refined, the designers and developers can prioritize activity by identifying release for aspects of each step.

As the story map is generated, gaps can be identified for assumptions, opportunity, elimination, and automation. As these decisions are made, prioritization can be made, and research questions can be identified as part of right-sizing. This may include

According to Patton, there are five powerful reasons for using story mapping as a generative methodology:

- User stories let you focus on building small things, it's easy to lose sight of the big picture, resulting in an experience cobbled together from mismatched parts—aka, a "Franken-product".
- User stories provide scope, which provides estimates for timelines, resources, on what is delivered, when, how, and by whom. This improves velocity and morale.
- Story maps serve as documentation techniques. Stories are about conversations, and in the midst of the experience of story, we may forget what they talked about and agreed to in the conversations.
- User stories provide acceptance criteria, common understanding of what needs to be built, and when – helping teams finish the work they plan on in the projected timeframe.
- Even in instances where product features does not seem to have direct users, we may build without any consideration of the potential user. The story map accounts for the parts users may not see or use.

Generative work like GIST models and Story Mapping can help to organize and identify features as a continuous experience, gaps in the experience, and opportunities to provide value, and planning roadmaps for design and development sprints. As the ideas and step-process are defined, riskiest assumptions can be identified and the step processes can be scored for effort and impact. Confidence

As the story map is developed as a step-by-step experience, the team can identify gaps in in steps for activities lacking support, gain new insights, focus on what should be removed from the experience, as well as look for opportunities and actions that can be automated to create value and delight. As the proposed story map is reviewed and discussed, changes can be proposed for prioritization in redesign and development. The gaps identified can be charted as in the Prioritization Matrix depicted below.

Prioritization of gaps as steps typically identifies cost and effort, as shown above. It is important that the category on the x-axis "Effort" is informed by design, development, and research resources. In the category of effort, the assumptions identified in the gap analysis of the story map should identify areas requiring research. The larger and riskier the assumption, the greater the research need.

The identification of gaps should include riskiest assumptions in the redesign and development. When research cannot be conducted due to limited time and resources, the time can create a risk mitigation document, identifying risks and assumptions that were identified, but not addressed. This allows the project to move forward while documenting shortcomings, concerns, and limitations. The goal of Agile, Lean Process, and User Experience Research is to be flexible and willing to pivot as new information becomes available. The risk mitigation plan documents awareness of the riskiest assumptions and provides transparency.

Figure 3. Prioritization matrix as an ICE score
(Ellis, 2010 – modified by Dubbels)

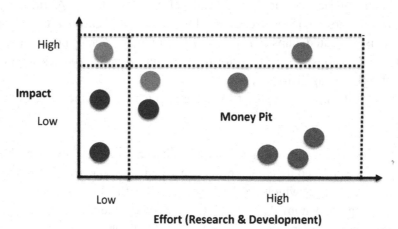

Applied Case With CNA Game

In the context of the certified nursing assistant game, a number of data points were gathered in resource review. The company had great interest in building a serious game and provided a business case that showed the potential value in using a video game as a training system for on-boarding and on-going training. The big idea was that the video game would take the pressure off of experienced care givers by directing new hires to practice in a controlled environment where failure to perform would not result in consequences for the vulnerable populations for whom the provide medical support.

As the team worked to gather requirements, the team did not initially use a story map to elicit and document the experience of the newly-hired certified nursing assistant. This may have led to tension in communications expectations. Upon delivery of the MVP, the stakeholders expressed confusion. The MVP provided a very limited functional training experience, lacking ideas and expectations from the subject matter experts and stakeholders. What resulted from the initial design and development as an MVP (minimum viable product) were very simple case-based experiences, which provided only task-based knowledge as a procedural rhetoric (Bogost, 2007). This provided distress between the design and development team and the customer stakeholders.

In order bridge the gap in the expected product and MVP, the author was brought in to revisit discovery, mend fences, and build trust as product owner and researcher. To do this, stakeholder interviews were conducted, and a story map was created. This story map suggested that the experience of the new certified nursing assistant (CNA) is task-based: following a schedule, doing certain tasks, in specific places, at specific times, for specific people. Although this task-based procedure is important, it was not what the stakeholders or subject matter experts (SMEs) wanted in the game. The stakeholders and SMEs required that game focus on building soft-skills such as relationships, trust, and having the ability to empower the residents of the care facility to become autonomous, thus relying less upon the CNAs for task-based assistance.

Figure 4. Confidence Wheel
(Gilad, 2018 – modified by Dubbels 2018)

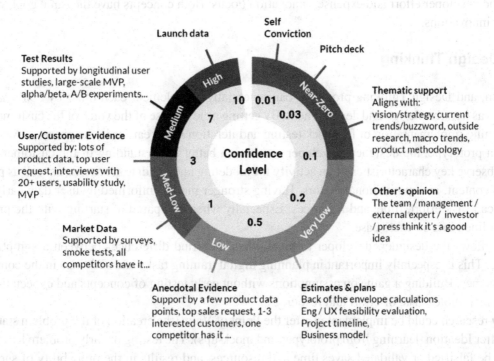

With the new information, the requirements were evaluated and scored for a confidence level Figure 4 (below) (Gilad, 2018). The team used the confidence wheel to identify the types of evidence we needed to move forward. For each category below, the assumptions and gaps from the story map, and our confidence level of what was currently known led to a research plan for incremental development, to gather evidence for requirements and insight as iterative development.

Reducing Assumption and Risk Early

It is a is has always been having substantive data early in the development cycle, especially when a product does not yet exist:

How do I generate data to support dev and design before there is something to test?

There are many techniques for generative research that align with Agile and Lean Process. One popular school of thought is Design Thinking. In Design Thinking, it is important to test early and often as part of a co-design process, connecting with customers, and potential customers early and often. The core expression in Design Thinking is that *"you are not the user."*

Design Thinking is about understanding users and/or customers in the pre-production phase. With Design Thinking methods, generative research can be conducted as means of co-design, between the researcher and the potential user/ customer. More than just generative methods, it is also a mindset (Buchanan, 1992). Design thinking is intended to identify and explore assumptions in early design and development. Design Thinking makes use of extensive user research, feedback loops and iteration cycles to develop models of behavior and assessment, which can be observed and tested as concepts early on, saving the developer effort and expense. Innovation Focus: Both concepts have the same goal, which is to foster innovations.

Lean Design Thinking

The Lean, and Design Thinking processes can potentially complement each other by converging the strategies as iterative design and development. By getting a clear sense of the voice of the customer/ user, and planning implementation of feedback testing and iteration loops earlier in the process, even before there is a prototype, the designer/ developer can have a better understanding of the customers actual needs, observe key characteristics of an activity for modeling and validation criteria, as well as process, required content, and motivational factors. Having stronger models informed by user data early in the process can save effort, time, and resources. Especially when compared to starting with the proposed needs outlined in a business case.

This allows the designer/ developer to pivot when they find differences between assumption and evidence. This is especially important in planning digital training tasks and activities in the contexts of serious games. Building a game on assumptions without early testing of concepts and expectations can result in incredible waste of effort and resources.

Early research could be implemented after the Point of View (the creation of the problem statement) and/or after Ideation (learning from prototypes and mock-ups). The testing of early problem hypotheses, that can be falsified or validated saves time and resources, and results in the probability of successful project results. Although the level of confidence may be low initially, introducing a generative approach from Design Thinking will address assumptions, mitigate risk, and quickly increase confidence, thus increasing viability and confidence in the project.

Although testing in Design Thinking is commonly performed as a qualitative method, the use of quantitative methods and measures are also essential for increasing scope and reducing uncertainty. The transition does not need to be difficult. Observable qualities can be quantified – quantities are qualities, e.g. frequency, quality, etc.

Unlike design thinking, Lean Process does not prescribe how to collect customer input. To increase confidence level, qualitative research methods—e.g. ethnographic methods—can be used to provide context to quantitative data in Lean Process. Additionally, structured frameworks and the generation of a qualitative persona might help designers to better understand and develop their customers and their respective needs and problems. Both Lean Process and Design Thinking should be scheduled at the beginning of the process with emphasis on ideation techniques, as they are applied in design thinking, to develop concept variations.

Although Lean Process usually starts with a concrete business idea, it might be helpful to use structured ideation methods to iterate that idea within the process, specifically before the problem-solution fit is achieved. Consequently, pivoting should be applied earlier (already on the initial concept). And finally, qualitative feedback evaluation, such as qualitative user interviews, could be implemented in the pivoting steps, in addition to the metric-based evaluation techniques.

Serious Games and Generative Research

To make a serious game, scores in the game should be associated should simulate and create improvements in performance that can be measured outside of the game. To do this, progress in the game should represent progress in the real world. A first step must include guided observations of professional CNAs working in situ. A technique for generative research and validation of a story map is field observation.

Field Reporting as Methodological Fit

Field reporting can be used to help validate theoretical models such as empathy maps and personas; provide context and behavior for analytical data; they can also be used as an initial pilot to understand user context, purpose, and need. Designing systems on assumption is risky behavior. It is important to test assumptions with observed behavior in the wild. One should understand that the future behavior can best be predicted from past behavior, and that any type of service design, instructional design, product design, and/or system design should be tested with actual user where they would actually be using it. It is essential to see if the projected behavior of the personas is the way people (which they approximate) actually behave. Conversely, field observation and cognitive ethnography are method-specific for defining personas, and mapping out process for how people solve problems.

Cognitive Ethnography as a Form of Field Reporting

As a methodological approach, cognitive ethnography assumes that cognition is distributed through rules, roles, language, relationships and coordinated activities, and can be embodied in artifacts and objects (Dubbels, 2008). For this reason, cognitive ethnography is an effective way to study activity systems like games, models, and simulations –whether mediated digitally or not.

In its traditional form, ethnography often involves the researcher living in the community of study, learning the language, doing what members of the community do—learning to see the world as it is seen by the natives in their cultural context, Fetterman (1998). Cognitive ethnography follows the same protocol, but its purpose is to understand cognitive process and context—examining them together, thus, eliminating the false dichotomy between psychology and anthropology.

Observational techniques such as ethnography and cognitive ethnography attempt to describe and look at relations and interaction situated in the spaces where they are native, including virtual and natural environments. Cognitive ethnography is methodologically tuned for mapping and describing how cognition and cognitive activities like decision making and problem solving, Specifically, cognitive ethnography assumes that cognition is distributed across systems that may be composed of combinations of tools, roles, and off-loading complexity onto the environment.

Theory of Distributed Cognition

Cognitive ethnography assumes that cognition is distributed. Specifically, cognitive ethnography is used to map the systems created solve complex tasks. When people face a difficult task, they may attempt to recruit others and create a system with tools, cooperation, and language to distribute the complexity. For example, people often coordinate their activities in teams. Members of teams are given roles, they use language to create rules and process, and they use tools. Groups, roles, rules, language, and tools off-load complexity to achieve a purpose. A complex problem is simplified by off-loading the complexity onto a system.

It is important to consider whether cognitive ethnography provides methodological fit with the research problem and questions. The focus of observation in cognitive ethnography is the description of how an activity is distributed across a system. There are three main systems: physical (virtual), social, and conceptual. These observations should inform the design of objects, systems, services, and understanding.

Cognitive ethnography emphasizes inductive field observation, but also uses theory in a deductive process to analyze behavior (. This approach is useful to increase external validity, operationalize terms, and develop content validity through expanding a study across new designs, across different time frames, in different programs, from different observational contexts, and with different groups (Cook and Campbell, 1979; Campbell & Stanley, 1966). Study of these features can help the researcher determine the organization, transfer, and representation of information (Hutchins, 2010; 1995).

Ontology/Purpose of Cognitive Ethnography Methodology

As stated, cognitive ethnography assumes that human cognition adapts to its natural surroundings. Therefore, the role of cognitive ethnographer is to transform observational data and interpretation into meaningful representations so that cognitive properties of the system become visible (Hutchins, 2010; 1995). According to Hutchins (2010), the study of the space where an activity takes place is a primary feature of observation in cognitive ethnography. He lists three kinds of important spaces for consideration:

1. **Physical/Virtual Space:** What is near to what, seen from each position, how bodies fit in space.
2. **Social Space:** Social organization, groups, identities, status roles, rules and how they affect the flow of information.
3. **Conceptual Space:** The conceptual structures of activities determine the content and organization.

Cognitive ethnography offers both an inductive and deductive methodology. It works for contextual inquiry and task analysis, and as a prerequisite for task analysis to model and understand user cognition, engagement, and physical interaction.

Methods

There are many general approaches and techniques that can be used for data collection in cognitive ethnography. What is important is the systematic observation and accurate recording of the varying aspects of a situation. Researchers should always approach their field study with a detailed plan for cognitive ethnography, including what will be observed, where to conduct observations, and the method by which they will collect and record their data. Although there is no rule about data gathering techniques, there are generally accepted and implemented techniques:

- Note Taking
- Video and Audio Recordings
- Illustrations and Drawings
- Artifact collection

Real-Time Observation and Running Records

In data collection, it is essential to continuously analyze observations as a running record. As observations are recorded, look for the meaning underlying the observed actions, coding patterns, themes, and insights in real time. Ask yourself: "What's going on here? What does this observed activity mean? What else does this relate to?" Note that observation and recording is an on-going process of reflection and analysis.

A running record can lead to scope creep in observation. Although one may find the unexpected, it is essential to keep the scope of research questions and purpose in mind during observing. Recording is not a random process, and should not be conducted haphazardly. Field observation requires focus, and emphasis on attending to details. Enter the observation site [i.e., "field"] with a clear plan about what the goals and purpose of the observation, but the researcher should be prepared to adapt to changing circumstances as they may arise.

Conscientious observations, recordings, and analysis will provide focus and what is heard and seen in the context of a theoretical framework. This will simplify the coding, analysis, interpretation, and reporting.

This theoretical focus is also what separates data collection and observation from simple reporting. The theoretical framework should guide observations to help determine what, when, and how observations are reported, and act as the foundation for interpretation for findings. Generally, the following can serve as a framework for things to document:

- **Physical Setting**: The characteristics of an occupied space and the human use of the place where the observation(s) are being conducted.
- **Objects and Material Culture:** The presence, placement, and arrangement of objects that impact the behavior or actions of those being observed. If applicable, describe the cultural artifacts representing the beliefs--values, ideas, attitudes, and assumptions--used by the individuals you are observing.
- **Use of Language:** Don't just observe but listen to what is being said, how is it being said, and, the tone of conversation among participants.
- **Behavior Cycles:** This refers to documenting when and who performs what behavior or task and how often they occur. Record at which stage is this behavior occurring within the setting.
- **The Order in Which Events Unfold:** Note sequential patterns of behavior or the moment when actions or events take place and their significance.
- **Physical Characteristics of Subjects:** If relevant, note age, gender, clothing, etc. of individuals being observed.
- **Expressive Body Movements**: This would include things like body posture or facial expressions. Note that it may be relevant to also assess whether expressive body movements support or contradict the language used in conversation

Along with these suggested items, what should drive your observations and analysis are he research problem, the theoretical perspective that is driving your analysis, and the observations that you make, which determine how to format the field report. Field reports should be written in the past tense. Your reader's only knowledge and understanding of what happened will come from the description section of the report because the reader was unlikely to have been a witness to the situation, people, or events being writing about. Given this, it is crucial that sufficient details are provided as thick description, to place the analysis into proper context; don't make the mistake of providing a description without context. As a general activity flow, figure %% (below) provides a general process once the research problem and purpose have been identified.

Figure 5. Contextual Inquiry as Ethnographic Method

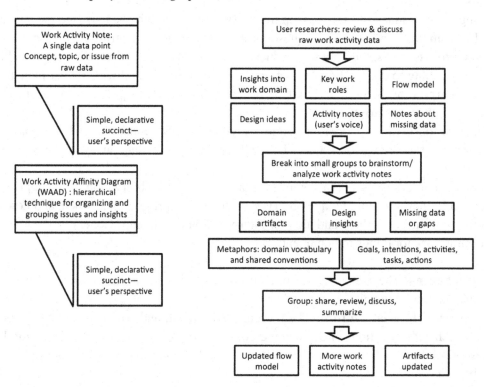

Design and Validity for Methodological Choice

Although cognitive ethnography starts with a clear purpose and research problem, and one or more research questions, the sequence of steps through the process can vary in order (i.e., they are not necessarily linear or unidirectional), and even the question and/or purpose can be revised when needed.

To briefly summarize, cognitive ethnography as a research process model comprises eight distinct steps: (1) determine the research question; (2) determine whether the research design is appropriate; (3) define the methods for sampling and data collection; (4) collect the data; (5) analyze the data; (6) interpret the data; (7) legitimate the data; and (8) draw conclusions (if warranted) and write the final report.

Once these steps are completed, the construction of the final report can be presented in a variety of formats, depending upon the purpose, audience, and methodological/ theoretical orientation. The description section of a cognitive ethnography should align with the format of a field report, which is often similar to a well-written piece of journalism. A helpful approach to systematically describing the varying aspects of an observed situation is to answer the "Five W's of Investigative Reporting."

- **Description:** The "Five W's"
- **What:** Describe what you observed. Note the temporal, physical, and social boundaries you imposed to limit the observations you made. e.g., what is your impression of the application of iPads as a learning device?
- **Where:** Information about the setting, and, if necessary, note important material objects that are present that help contextualize the observation [e.g., arrangement of computers in relation to student engagement with the teacher].
- **When:** Record factual data about the day and the beginning and ending time of each observation. Note that it may also be necessary to include background information or key events, which impact upon the situation you, were observing.
- **Who:** Note background and demographic information about the individuals being observed e.g., age, gender, ethnicity, and/or any other variables relevant to your study]. Record who is doing what and saying what, as well as, who is not doing or saying what. If relevant, be sure to record who was missing from the observation.
- **Why:** Why were you doing this? Describe the reasons for selecting particular situations to observe. Note why something happened. Also note why you may have included or excluded certain information.

What We Learned

In *A Better Life*©, the player faces a dynamic tension. The CNA does not have enough time to meet obligations in the scheduled tasks but must still build relationships. If the CNA does not build relations, the residents become resistant and take more time. Conversely, if the CNA spends too much time in building relations, she may fall behind in completing her scheduled tasks with other residents. An example of this is shown in Figure 1 (below).

Figure 6. Scheduled Tasks for a CNA

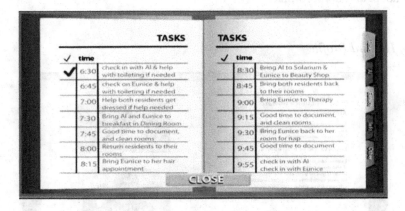

The CNA has a number of things to do in a 15-minute increment. The CNA must prioritize and compromise, as there are no correct answers. A close look at the care recipients shows that both have special needs (figures 2 and 3).

Al Jorgenson has dementia, and if he is not checked on every 15 minutes, he will wonder off. If this happens, he could get hurt, or hurt someone else Figure 2. By knowing Al's needs, what he can and cannot do, the CNA can identify how Al can be independent and what makes him cooperative, such as turning on the radio.

Figure 7. Al Jorgenson Profile

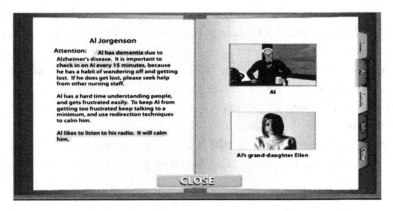

Eunice, figure 3, also needs special care. Although she wants to be independent and autonomous, there are certain things she cannot do such as walking, and she can be argumentative and disagreeable. Because the CNA is new to the care facility, the CNA must navigate the relationship through effective communication and time management. By spending more time with Eunice, she builds rapport and trust, and Eunice becomes more autonomous.

However, if the CNA does not return to check on Al every 15 minutes, he wanders, and this throws the CNA, and other staff off their scheduled tasks, reducing trust, rapport, and autonomy with other residents. All the while the clock is running and tasks must be completed. There is no correct answer. The player must adapt and compromise.

Figure 8. Eunice Howard Profile

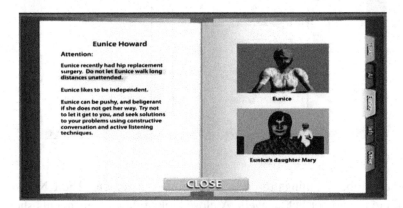

Throughout the day, the CNAs are asked to help their charges participate in the care facility, and this may include dressing, medications, activities, and transportation.

When the CNA spends time building trust, the CNA is rewarded with cooperation and independent behavior, i.e., Eunice will dress herself while the CNA goes to check on Al. The key is managing time and relations. When the residents cooperate, the CNA's job is easier, but the CNA must be careful to know when and where to spend time, otherwise Al may wander, or the CNA will not get time to perform the functional requirements of their job, such as tidying rooms or documenting resident behaviors for the care plan.

Documentation is also an important part of the CNAs job description. It is one of the ways that the business partner is capable of making data driven decisions. The accuracy of observation and interactions is of great importance, and a central part of their workday. According to the SME, the CNAs are trained to enter their observations into data collection programs in the care facility. This game emphasizes that practice (see figure 4 below).

Figure 9. Documentation Screen at Kiosk

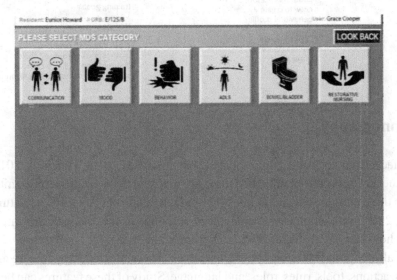

Because observation and documentation are an important part of the CNAs functional role, they were emphasized as a game feature. When the CNA reports their observed ADL, the reports are scored for accuracy based upon their interactions with the residents. The ADL are modeled in game scenarios and scored for accuracy.

What we find through story mapping are opportunities for creating a flow model that can be validated through automation and augmentation through machine learning from learning reinforcement models. In the case of the game, the flow of the game play experience started with a simple set of challenges, where the player cared for two residents of the facility. For each resident there was a flow model for personalization in figure 10 (below).

As the player is onboarded into the game they are presented with choices as the game learns about their functional requirements. As the player moves to their first decision point, the algorithm uses the scoring criteria to assess and evaluate the level of challenge. Challenge is increased through greater ambiguity in resolving a situation (least/worst), and observing to see of the player takes short term actions which undermine their long-term goal. This is how the brief and debrief train the player, and then provide feedback after game play.

Figure 10. Flow model for challenges in game

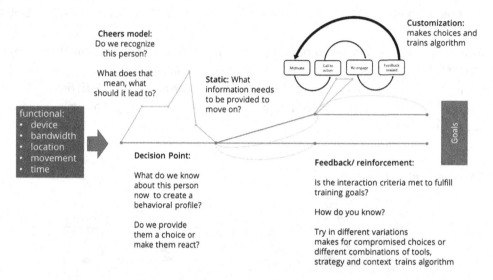

Cognitive Ethnography

The in game artifacts from cognitive ethnography (Dubbels, 2011, 2014; Hutchins, 2011) in care facilities operated by the business partner informed the story map and the flow model. Cognitive ethnography is efficacious for these activities, as it assumes that human cognition adapts to its natural surroundings (Hutchins, 1995, 2010) with emphasis on analysis of activities as they happen in context; how they are represented; and how they are distributed and experienced in space.

More specifically, cognitive ethnography emphasizes observation and key feature analysis of space, objects, concepts, actions, tools, rules, roles, and language. Study of these features can help the researcher determine the organization, transfer, and representation of information (Hutchins, 1995, 2010) and affords an initial qualitative approach which can inform game design, and methodologies leading up to the formation of construct validity (Cook & Campbell, 1979; Campbell & Stanley, 1966) through the creation of a nomological network (Cronbach & Meehl, 1955). Through gathering models of the space, social relations, and the conceptual space (what must be known), the game storyboard is informed, and the game criteria are defined and weighted for coding from the collected theories and tools.

The cognitive ethnography involved taking hundreds of pictures, analysis of artifacts such as schedules, task descriptions, documents, process, and protocol, and chains of interaction. In order to model a long term care facility, it was important to have a strong sense of a facility, and to analyze the gathered data using themes generated from the interviews (discovery process) with SMEs.

The SMEs had proposed a number of factors that could easily inform a construct. The work of the CNA shares some theoretical approaches and tools associated with nursing. These approaches and tools were examined for application, and resulted in a construct proposed here as the *Perceived Quality of Life* (PQoL) construct.

The PQoL construct is conceptualized as having four different skills that are operationalized and modeled in the game play:

- **Complex Relationship Building**: How the CNA interacts with residents.
- **Functional Performance**: Whether the CNA is able to complete scheduled tasks such as transport, assistance in ADL, and housekeeping.
- **Schedule Adherence**: Whether the CNA meets scheduled functional tasks in timely manner.
- **Observation and Documentation:** Of the Activities of Daily Living in the facility documentation software.

The *Perceived Quality of Life* (PQoL) construct is used here to inform the game play as well as performance in the care environment. PQoL is composed of a number of skills, theories, and assessment, just as the construct called Intelligence is mapped to specific skills, theories, and assessments. The value of developing a construct such as PQoL is that the developer can operationalize these skills, assessments to be modeled and tracked in the game as quantified scoring criteria. The relationships informing the PQoL construct are presented below in figure 5.

Figure 11. Weights for Game Play Mechanic and Scoring Criteria

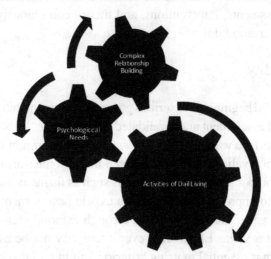

- The central cog in Figure 5, Psychological Needs, draws from Self------ Determination Theory (Deci & Ryan, 2000).
- The base measure, or bottom cog, draws from the Activities of Daily Living (Roper, Logan, & Tierney, 1980; 2000) and is hypothesized to be influenced through interpersonal relations.
- The interpersonal relations were modeled from operationalization of Complex Relationship Building (Bulechek, Butcher, & Dochterman, 2008)

This leads to two testable propositions:

1. When there is a high level of PQoL, the CNAs will enjoy their jobs more, have a longer tenure, and provide a higher quality of care.
2. When there is a high PQoL, the care recipients will improve in their general health and this should reduce training and care costs, with reduced dependence on medication for pain management, catastrophic care, and the need to replace and train CNAs.

Although it is useful to model hypothetical relationships in a game as in figure 5, it should not be enough. A next step to test the model can be taken, before it is modeled as a game mechanic. A conceptual model is a proposition that can be tested. Through testing these propositions, the relationships can be quantified to determine how they work proportionally. This can be done with paper and pencil models for what is called discount usability (Kane, 2003; Nielsen, 1994, 2009; Pagulayan, Steury, Fulton, & Romero, 2005).

Ultimately, the developer must decide if the theories and assessments guiding the interactions being modeled in the game actually inform the training (Medlock, Wixon, Terrano, Romero, & Fulton, 2002). Thus, when the developer conducts analysis and attempts to use the outcomes of that analysis for developing game mechanics, such as weighting relationships between the Activities of Daily Living and Complex Relationship building and examine influence them as mediated by Self-Determination Theory, they are building theory. In the case of this game, the analysis of the initial concepts such as SDT and ADLS, they may find through observation and factorial regression, that they are actually theory building. They are building assessments, interventions, and theory contiguously. In this way, game design becomes a form of research methodology.

Assessment and Validity

Surface level validity is a useful beginning for serious game development, but it should only be considered a step towards having a valid assessment and a validated serious game. It should be considered a gamble to build a serious game on surface validity. A step towards certainty might include attempts at criterion validity. For example, criterion validity can be attempted through measuring learning outcomes with a game and correlating those outcomes with external tools such as formative and summative assessments. Playing the game may lead to improved outcomes with existing assessment tools.

Thus, the success of the game may be evaluated through external measures with criterion validity and reduce the likelihood of a Vegas Effect. However, there may not be assessment tools designed to evaluate, and research design is essential in using criterion validity. In this case, there are four different assessments that could be used to model and measure the PQoL construct. Since these assessment tools were developed to measure specific constructs:

Self-Determination Theory, Complex Relationship Building, and Activities of Daily Living, the use of these assessments may not provide the degree of validity and certainty necessary to avoid the Vegas Effect.

Correlation Does Not Imply Causation

There may be a number of factors that could influence the outcome of an assessment, and it is important to have some certainty that the game actually led to an improvement in outcomes that matter to the business partner. If the game was built to provide an experience, but not based upon the criteria of the external assessment, there is only correlation to support the efficacy of the game. When they play the game, there is an improvement on this assessment.

To really avoid the Vegas Effect, the serious game developer could develop for construct validity. A construct is a concept like intelligence, relationship building, or happiness. In the case of this game, the construct is called Perceived Quality of Life (PQoL). Validating a construct can require significant investment in time and money, however, some methods from psychometrics in the development process can be adopted to reduce time and cost, and reduce the probability of the Vegas Effect.

To do this, it may be in the interest of the developer and business partner to conduct some research and build construct validity. To do this, they can draw from existing assessment tools, and identify important traits for measurement, that lead to an improved Perceived Quality of Life (PQoL).

To ascertain validity in the PQoL constrict, two things need to be examined:

- The validity of the measuring tools (e.g. psychometric test, observational rubric, the scoring criteria in a game)
- The validity of the procedure of the study.

When we claim construct validity, we are essentially claiming that our observed pattern—how things operate in reality—corresponds with our theoretical pattern— how we think the world works. This is an important consideration for modeling activities in a game. To do this, we create a workflow pattern that fit a deductive/ inductive framework:

- **Deductive:** Theory, hypothesis, observation, and confirmation.
- **Inductive:** Observation, pattern, and tentative hypothesis.

Most social research involves both inductive and deductive reasoning processes at some time in the project. It may be reasonable to look at deductive/inductive approaches as part of the development cycle.

To do this, the researcher should provide a theoretical framework for what is being measured, an empirical framework for how it is to be measured, and specification of the linkage between these two frameworks. This is called a nomological network.

The idea of creating nomological network in research came from Cronbach and Meehl (1955) in attempt to provide better assurance of construct validity. Although this was a theoretically sound position, Cronbach and Meehl did not provide a method for operationalizing a nomological network, and it was not until later that Campbell and Fiske (1959) provided the *Multi Trait Multimethod Matrix* (MTMM) for doing so.

Through the use of this methodology, the researcher creates a matrix or table of correlations arranged to facilitate the interpretation of construct validity. The MTMM assumes that you measure each of several concepts by each of several methods (e.g., a paper and pencil test, a direct observation, a performance measure). The MTMM is a very restrictive methodology—ideally you should measure each concept by each method. The reasoning behind this is to know that you are measuring what you say you are measuring.

Figure 12. Multi Trait Multi Method

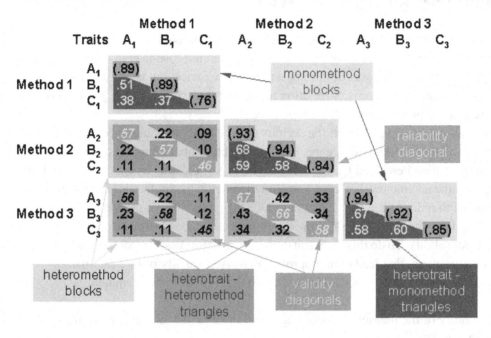

In the case of PQoL, the traits thought to be essential from the Activities of Daily Living (ADL) and Self-Determination Theory (SDT) are aggregated into three assessments. The central traits are then tabulated and compared for reliability and analysis is conducted for convergent and discriminant validity. These traits may be drawn from assessments from the ADL and SDT and the traits used in the matrix.

The new assessments can then be used investigate the influence of Complex Relationship Building on measures of ADLs and SDT. This provides an ability to compare multiple traits through multiple methods. The emphasis in using the MTMM is multiple replication of the same trait across method. In the case of our serious game, we provide in------game measures, observations from the workplace, and surveys of the caregivers and care recipients.

The idea is to provide three measures for construct validity. To construct an MTMM, you need to arrange the correlation matrix by concepts within methods. The figure shows an MTMM for three concepts (traits A, B and C) each of which is measured with three different methods (1, 2 and 3) Note that you lay the matrix out in blocks by method. Essentially, the MTMM is just a correlation matrix between your measures, with one exception—instead of 1's along the diagonal (as in the typical correlation matrix), substitute an estimate of the reliability of each measure as the diagonal.

As these relationships are validated, the game developer and the key stakeholders can depend upon a greater degree of certainty when modeling a game on the quantified relationships attained through this process. For example, the Nursing Interventions Classification suggests that more than one hour of CRB is necessary to promote insight and behavioral change (Bulechek, Butcher, & Dochtman, 2008, p.831). It may be useful to observe this relation to SDT and ADLs to validate the PQoL construct. When this step is taken, in game criteria presented though game mechanics can be modeled on ratios taken from the analysis of the observed behaviors and outcomes from the analysis tools.

Once the initial data collection is conducted in the observational setting, and the outcomes of the analysis used to create the game mechanics, the observational process can be turned inside out.

Figure 13. Design Flow of Serious Game

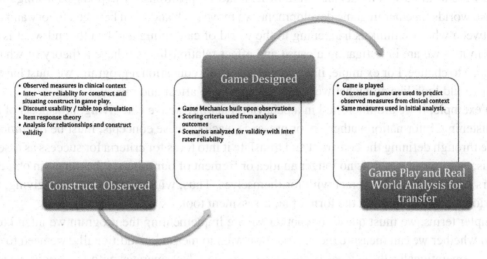

The developer begins with validation of the measures of their construct, in this case PQoL, and then uses the assessment and observation tools to account for quantitative relationships in the form of ratios and probabilities. Thus, if a CNA provides so many minutes in CRB, this may effect improvement in PQoL.

These relationships, qualitative and quantitative are then used to model the behavior in the game. A video game is a serious of calculations that serve as if------then statements, i.e., if this, then that. What is important is whether these relationships modeled in the game, have any external validity to the work environment. Do they extend to other populations and contexts? What we model in the game can be built from what we observe in the world. The effectiveness of what we model in the game depends upon the fidelity and veracity of what we model from.

New Perspectives in Serious Game Development

In this modified model of software development, the developer works with SMEs to define the testable hypothesis and learn how to turn them into tools and an intervention. In the case of the A Better Life© game, a prediction was made that specific communicative and autonomy--supporting behaviors would improve health outcomes and reduce employment attrition. The subject matter experts had asserted that many functionally capable CNAs are hired, but very few have the communication and relational skills. It was the belief of the SMEs that if the caregivers, certified nursing assistants (CNAs) were able to build caring relationships with the residents in the long term care facilities where they worked, several things would happen:

- The CNAs would enjoy their work more and be less likely to quit.
- The residents would build trust with the CNAs and would improve their response to care giving. Trust and improved communication could result in improved health outcomes as measured by the activities of daily living.
- Improved health outcomes could yield greater autonomy, less dependence on pain medication, and reduced catastrophic care.

These were testable statements and were turned into propositions for hypothesis testing. When we bring these worlds together in game development, we move back and forth between theory and observation—between what we think is happening in the world of caregiving and health, and what is actually going on in it— we are investigating a cause and effect relationship, we have a theory of what causes performance to change. For example, if we are testing a new educational program, we must have an idea of what it would look like and what we are ideally trying to affect and measure.

As an example, if we are interested in a behavioral act like active caregiving, or aspects of caregiving like listening, information gathering, or presence, each of these concepts, must be *operationalized*. This done through defining the construct and translate it into tools for criteria for success as assessment, operations, and procedures. It is no longer an idea or figment of our minds, it becomes an object or tool that others can observe and interact with for themselves. Thus, when we describe caregiving, we have an operationalized definition in the form of an assessment tool.

In simpler terms, we must question whether we are implementing the program we intend to implement, and whether we can measure the outcome we want to measure. Additionally, we need to question whether we operationalized the ideas of the cause and the effect operates with fidelity in the activities in the game. We will find ourselves in hot water if we ask those questions after the game is finished, and the answer to those questions is *no*. Quite simply, if we attempt to answer our guiding questions after the game is finished, it will have been too late. We may have to start again, and this can be expensive!

The utilization of the techniques from Lean Process, Design Thinking, and Psychometrics and Cognitive Ethnography provide the generative insights to develop a serious game that is capable of delivering training and providing data for ROI analysis. This is essential when considering the development of training, health, and medical software and evangelizing the value these process, and your team bring to your organization. Although many development teams will jump right into creating a prototype right away, your approach to user experience research can reduce costs and development time, and increase the quality of software.

REFERENCES

Al-Awar, J., Chapanis, A., & Ford, W. R. (1981). Tutorials for the first-time computer user. *IEEE Trans. Profess. Commun, 24*(1), 30–37.

Amazon.com. (n.d.). *The Lean Startup: How Today's Entrepreneurs Use Continuous Innovation to Create Radically Successful Businesses*. Retrieved June 17, 2018, from https://www.amazon.com/Lean-Startup-Entrepreneurs-Continuous-Innovation/dp/0307887898

Anguera, J. A., Boccanfuso, J., Rintoul, J. L., Al-Hashimi, O., Faraji, F., Janowich, J., ... Gazzaley, A. (2013). Video game training enhances cognitive control in older adults. *Nature, 501*(7465), 97–101. doi:10.1038/nature12486 PMID:24005416

Basak, C., Boot, W. R., Voss, M. W., & Kramer, A. F. (2008). Can training in a real--time strategy video game attenuate cognitive decline in older adults? *Psychology and Aging, 23*(4), 765–777. doi:10.1037/a0013494 PMID:19140648

Bavelier, D., Green, C. S., Han, D. H., Renshaw, P. F., Merzenich, M. M., & Gentile, D. A. (2011). Brains on video games. *Nature Reviews. Neuroscience, 12*(12), 763–768. doi:10.1038/nrn3135 PMID:22095065

Black, P., & Wiliam, D. (2009). Developing the theory of formative assessment. *Educational Assessment, Evaluation and Accountability, 21*(1), 5–31. doi:10.100711092-008-9068-5

Bogost, I. (2007). *Persuasive games: The expressive power of videogames*. MIT Press. Retrieved from https://books.google.ca/books?hl=en&lr=&id=vjbOnZw1wfUC&oi=fnd&pg=PP6&dq=ian+bo gost &ots=xkkxhHzOC2&sig=kFr1ICwyE-moUXdfqsN5uywhsM8

Buchanan, R. (1992). Wicked problems in design thinking. *Design Issues, 8*(2), 5–21. doi:10.2307/1511637

Doerr, J. (2018). *Measure what Matters: How Google, Bono, and the Gates Foundation Rock the World with OKRs*. Penguin.

Dubbels, B. (2011). Cognitive Ethnography. *International Journal of Gaming and Computer-Mediated Simulations, 3*(1), 68–78. doi:10.4018/jgcms.2011010105

Dubbels, B. (2014). Cognitive Ethnography as a Mixed-Method for Game User Research. *CHI 2014*.

Dubbels, B. (2016). Pedagogy & Play: Creating Playful Curriculum for Academic Achievement and Engaged Learning. In Learning, Education, and Games. (Vol. 2). Etc. Press.

Dubbels, B. R. (2012). *The Brain Is For Action: Embodiment, Causality, and Conceptual Learning with Video Games to Improve Reading Comprehension and Scientific Problem Solving*. University of Minnesota.

Dubbels, B. R. (2017). Gamification Transformed: Gamification Should Deliver the Best Parts of Game Experiences, Not Just Experiences of Game Parts. *Transforming Gaming and Computer Simulation Technologies across Industries*, 17–47. doi:10.4018/978-1-5225-1817-4.ch002

Eisenmann, T. R., Ries, E., & Dillard, S. (2012). *Hypothesis-driven entrepreneurship: The lean startup*. Academic Press.

Forster, M. (2009). *Informative Assessment—understanding and guiding learning*. Retrieved from http://research.acer.edu.au/research_conference/RC2009/17august/11/

Frederiksen, D. L., & Brem, A. (2017). How do entrepreneurs think they create value? A scientific reflection of Eric Ries' Lean Startup approach. *The International Entrepreneurship and Management Journal, 13*(1), 169–189. doi:10.100711365-016-0411-x

Gilad, I. (2018, February 1). *Why you should stop using product roadmaps and try GIST Planning*. Retrieved July 1, 2018, from https://hackernoon.com/why-i-stopped-using- product-roadmaps-and-switched-to-gist-planning-3b7f54e271d1 ?ref=http%3A%2F%2Fproduct-frameworks.com

Green, C., & Bavelier, D. (2003). Action video game modifies visual selective attention. *Nature, 423*(6939), 534–537. doi:10.1038/nature01647 PMID:12774121

Green, C. S., & Bavelier, D. (2008). Exercising Your Brain: A Review of Human Brain Plasticity and Training-Induced Learning. *Psychology and Aging, 23*(4), 692–701. doi:10.1037/a0014345 PMID:19140641

Green, C. S., Benson, C., Kersten, D., & Schrater, P. (2010). Alterations in choice behavior by manipulations of world model. *Proceedings of the National Academy of Sciences of the United States of America*, *107*(37), 16401–16406. doi:10.1073/pnas.1001709107 PMID:20805507

Hays, R. T. (2006). *The Science of Learning: A Systems Theory Perspective*. Universal-Publishers.

Hutchins, E. L. (2011, December 15). *Cognitive Ethnography*. Retrieved from http://hci.ucsd.edu/102b/

Jaeggi, S. M., Buschkuehl, M., Jonides, J., & Perrig, W. J. (2008). Improving fluid intelligence with training on working memory. *Proceedings of the National Academy of Sciences of the United States of America*, *105*(19), 6829–6833. doi:10.1073/pnas.0801268105 PMID:18443283

Kane, D. (2003). Finding a place for discount usability engineering in agile development: throwing down the gauntlet. In *Agile Development Conference, 2003. ADC 2003. Proceedings of the* (pp. 40–46). IEEE. Retrieved from http://ieeexplore.ieee.org/xpls/abs_all.jsp?arnumber=1231451

Kwong, A. W., Healton, B., & Lancaster, R. (1998). *State of siege: new thinking for the next decade of design. IEEE Aerospace Conference*, 4, pp. 85–93. doi:10.1109/AERO.1998.682158

Loftus, G., & Loftus, E. R. (1983). *Mind at Play: The Psychology of Video Games*. Basic Books.

Medlock, M. (2014, March). *History of Video Games User Research*. Keynote presented at the Games User Research Summit, San Francisco, CA. Retrieved from http://www.gamesuserresearchsig.org/gursig---library.html

Medlock, M. C., Wixon, D., Terrano, M., Romero, R., & Fulton, B. (2002). Using the RITE method to improve products: A definition and a case study. *Usability Professionals Association, 51*. Retrieved from http://www.computingscience.nl/docs/vakken/musy/RITE.pdf

Merzenich, M. M., Jenkins, W. M., Johnston, P., Schreiner, C., Miller, S. L., & Tallal, P. (1996). Temporal processing deficits of language-learning impaired children ameliorated by training. *Science*, *271*(5245), 77–81. doi:10.1126cience.271.5245.77 PMID:8539603

Nielsen, J. (1994). Guerrilla HCI: Using discount usability engineering to penetrate the intimidation barrier. *Cost-Justifying Usability*, 245–272.

Nielsen, J. (2009). Discount usability: 20 years. *Jakob Nielsen's Alertbox*. Available at http://www. useit. com/alertbox/discount-usability. html

Pagulayan, R. J., Steury, K. R., Fulton, B., & Romero, R. L. (2005). Designing for fun: User-testing case studies. In *Funology* (pp. 137–150). Springer. Retrieved from http://link.springer.com/content/pdf/10.1007/1-4020-2967-5_14.pdf

Patton, J. (2002). Designing requirements: incorporating usage-centered design into an agile SW development process. In *Conference on Extreme Programming and Agile Methods* (pp. 1–12). Springer. 10.1007/3-540-45672-4_1

Patton, J., & Economy, P. (2014). *User story mapping: discover the whole story, build the right product*. O'Reilly Media, Inc.

Ries, E. (2011). *The lean startup: How today's entrepreneurs use continuous innovation to create radically successful businesses*. Crown Books.

Ries, E. (2012). *The lean startup methodology*. The Lean Startup.

Ries, E. (2013, May 22). *The Lean Start Up Methodology*. Retrieved May 22, 2013, from http://theleanstartup.com/principles

Smith, G. E., Housen, P., Yaffe, K., Ruff, R., Kennison, R. F., Mahncke, H. W., & Zelinski, E. M. (2009). A Cognitive Training Program Based on Principles of Brain Plasticity: Results from the Improvement in Memory with Plasticity-based Adaptive Cognitive Training (IMPACT) Study. *Journal of the American Geriatrics Society*, *57*(4), 594–603. doi:10.1111/j.1532-5415.2008.02167.x PMID:19220558

Squire, K. (2005). *Game-based learning: Present and future state of the field*. Masie Center e-Learning Consortium. Retrieved from https://pantherfile.uwm.edu/tjoosten/LTC/Gaming/Game-Based_Learning.pdf

Timeline of psychology. (2015, February 17). In *Wikipedia, the free encyclopedia*. Retrieved from http://en.wikipedia.org/w/index.php?title=Timeline_of_psychology&oldid=647514853

Waterfall model. (2018, June 3). In *Wikipedia*. Retrieved from https://en.wikipedia.org/w/index.php?title=Waterfall_model&oldid=844245639

Wiliam, D. (2007). Changing classroom practice. *Educational Leadership*, *65*(4), 36.

Wiliam, D., & Thompson, M. (2007). *Integrating assessment with learning: what will it take to make it work?* Retrieved July 4, 2012, from http://eprints.ioe.ac.uk/1162/

Womack, J. P., & Jones, D. T. (1997). Lean thinking—banish waste and create wealth in your corporation. *The Journal of the Operational Research Society*, *48*(11), 1148–1148. doi:10.1057/palgrave.jors.2600967

This research was previously published in Exploring the Cognitive, Social, Cultural, and Psychological Aspects of Gaming and Simulations; pages 1-34, copyright year 2019 by Information Science Reference (an imprint of IGI Global).

Chapter 15
An ARM Framework for F2P Mobile Games

Marisardo Bezerra de Medeiros Filho
Universidade Federal de Pernambuco, Brazil

Farley Fernandes
UNIDCOM IADE, Portugal & Universidade da Beira Interior, Portugal

Felipe Matheus Calado
Universidade Católica de Pernambuco, Brazil

André Menezes Marques Neves
Universidade Federal de Pernambuco, Brazil

ABSTRACT

This chapter presents an ARM (acquisition, retention, and monetization) framework for F2P (free-to-play) mobile games to be used as to support game design practice and research. ARM strategies are dispersed throughout various sources such as websites, papers, and books, hampering the work of researchers and practitioners in this field. The aim of this framework is to list and organize these strategies into a single source. A literature research about ARM strategies in F2P mobile games was conducted to identify and select elements. Based on surveys with game development professionals, some of these elements were polished, merged, or removed. Finally, these elements were organized into a single framework, consisting of 3 main categories (acquisition, retention, and monetization), 8 subcategories, and 59 specific elements.

INTRODUCTION

To make profitable Free-to-Play (F2P) games, there are some elements used to promote new players acquisition, retain them playing and drive them to monetize the game. Acquisition - Retention - Monetization (ARM) strategies are an important tool to help game developers to understand elements and relations between such stages, increasing the chances to make more profitable F2P games (Fields and Cotton, 2012; Lovell, 2013; Luton, 2013; Thibault, 2013). However, these ARM strategies are dispersed

DOI: 10.4018/978-1-6684-7589-8.ch015

throughout various sources such as websites, academic works and books. During this research the authors did not find any source that listed or tried to organize, formally, a set of ARM F2P game elements. Such listing can be important for knowledge development about free-to-play mobile game design and help game development professionals and researchers to formally identify possibilities and opportunities related to such games.

The general objective of this work is to organize common ARM F2P game strategies in an unique framework, describing and organizing the content of ARM related elements and strategies. It can be used by to design acquisition, retention and monetization features on F2P games and also be used as a foundation to further academic researches on the subject. The specific objectives of this research are:

- Review the academic and professional literature regarding Acquisition, Retention, Monetization, and ARM Funnel, applied to F2P mobile games, this being the aim of this paper;
- Propose the elements and an architecture to organize an ARM framework for F2P mobile games;
- Evaluate the proposed ARM framework with F2P mobile games experienced professionals;
- Based on the evaluation conducted, make the adjustments needed for the final version of the framework.

This paper is organized with the following structure: The next chapter covers the main aspects about ARM in F2P mobile games; the third chapter lists and presents the main elements regarding user acquisition, retention and monetization; the fourth chapter presents the development and version 1.0 of the framework; and the fifth chapter presents the conclusions and discussions of this work.

ARM IN F2P MOBILE GAMES

The term ARM refers to an analytic framework, often used to describe a business model, in mobile game industry. As an acronym, it means Acquisition, Retention, and Monetization. It could be useful as an aid to understand the business models used by F2P mobile games, and also as a guide for developers when applying the concepts at their own games. Acquisition strategies are used to attract new users to the game; Retention strategies aims to keep them playing and lastly, Monetization strategies are used to make users generate revenue for the game (Kuusisto, 2014; Tao, 2014). However, games that are not F2P use a different framework, named B2P (buy-to-play), where its users first buy the game (Monetization), then discover the gameplay (Acquisition), and finally can repeat the experience (Retention) (Davidovici-Nora, 2014). In this context, the retention is at the end of the process and does not have a direct connection with monetization. On the other hand, F2P games business model architecture is way more complex and can generate multiple interactions among stages and not only a one-to-one relationship.

In F2P games, the monetization stage is pushed to the end of the process as payment is optional to a certain extent. Games with F2P business model put emphasis on experience before monetizing it, in order to accumulate a huge user base and make them engaged. Considering that the price to acquire a F2P game is zero, acquisition stage seems to be an easy and automatic stage in such model when compared with B2P ones (Davidovici-Nora, 2014). Figure 1 shows the ARM funnel initially proposed by Kontagent (2011).

Figure 1. Illustration of ARM funnel for video games (THIBAULT, 2013, p.21)

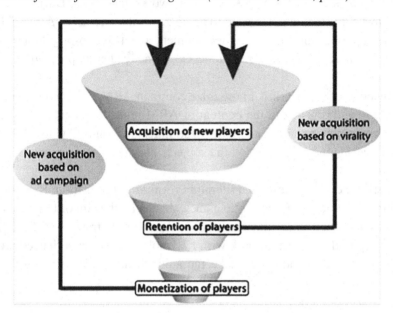

These three stages are strictly linear and act more like a recurring cycle within the overall framework, it can be explained as (Fields & Cotton, 2012): First, the game acquires a large player base (acquisition); Then it should retain some of these players (retention), keeping enough of them coming back so that they will like the game enough to invest their money into it (monetization); Some of the retained players will spread the word about the game and make it viral. They will raise the brand awareness of the game and attract new players (acquisition); Game's profits from monetization can be invested into acquiring more users (advertising campaign). The cycle repeats.

Katkoff (2012a) explained an example that helps understanding how these stages are connected, as can be seen on figure 2. In his example, the player starts building a house, but in order to finish it, he needs some specific items. At this point, the player knows that getting these items require several play sessions and a lot of grinding (retention). The player can skip grinding simply by asking friends to gift these items (something that generates new players acquisition), or, as a third option, just paying to proceed (monetization).

The next chapter of this paper will explain separately every element of the ARM framework applied to F2P mobile games, considering the specific aspects of each one and relations among them.

ARM STRATEGIES

This chapter presents elements used to acquiring, retaining and monetizing through players in F2P games.

Acquisition

In F2P games, player acquisition is the first one to take place, since it is not necessary to buy the game to have it. F2P games have to convince users to spend money after they have already made the acquisition

Figure 2. Most common virality formula (KATKOFF, 2012a)

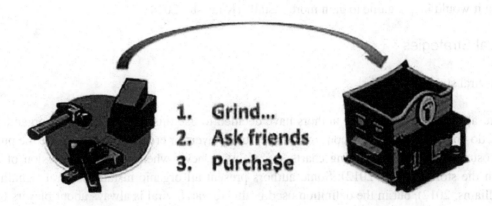

decision. Then, it is usually necessary a large number of players in order to make this model profitable (Alha, Koskinen, Paavilainen, Hamari, & Kinnunen, 2014; Davidovici-Nora, 2014; Nguyen, 2014).

Askelöf (2013) explains that, in the ARM model, user acquisition sources are classified as being either viral or non-viral. Viral user sources refer to new players which have been generated by existing users. Whereas non-viral sources are those that are not generated by existing users, such as: advertising, cross-promotion and offer walls. Based on this research, it was selected a proposal of elements, indicated by professionals and academic researchers as directly related with acquisition in F2P games. Based on Askelöf (2013) explanation, acquisition was divided in two main subcategories: Viral and Non-Viral. The selected categories and subcategories are not excluding among themselves, then an element could also represent, sometimes, more than one of these categories. The selected subcategories are organized below:

Viral Strategies

The Viral strategies are:

- Invitation Mechanics: There are a lot of mechanics to encourage users to invite their friends to try the game, where the player will usually be rewarded with some gifts for every invited person that installs the game (sometimes it is not necessary to install it). This is a way to reward users for sharing the game with some form of free content. This technique is often used by game designers as an incentive for users to invite their friends, increasing the virality. Also, there are some mechanics that encourage players to ask for help to quickly reach some objective, which could attract new players and help their retention as well. Some common examples of invitation rewards are: Boosts, power-ups and gacha tickets (Askelöf, 2013; Katkoff, 2012a; Morel, 2012; Paavilainen, Alha, & Korhonen, 2017);
- Timeline Social Features Sharing: Social features like leaderboards and achievements that players can share on their timeline. It can also increase user base retention and growth (Askelöf, 2013; Maiberg, 2013; Paavilainen, Alha, & Korhonen, 2017);
- Word of Mouth: Natural invitations by players without using actions on the game. If a game is engaging and brings a good experience, it should make more players tell their friends about it (Askelöf, 2013; Kuusisto, 2014; Narinen, 2014; Williams, 2012);

- Chart Position in Market Places: Better chart position in marketplaces will provide more visibility, then it would help a game to gain more installs (Kuusisto, 2014);

Non-Viral Strategies

The Non-viral strategies are:

- Natural Organic Installs: The authors have decided to use this term to represent organic installs that do not take influence by consume of previous players or cross-promotions, like the pure store exposure - without considering charts - or trending news when an updated version of a game is in the store (Kaniel, 2012). Some authors present all organic installs as viral (Khalil, 2016; Williams, 2012), but in the definition used in this research viral is always about players bringing more players;
- Cross-promotions (within other games or Apps): Some companies provide the ability to cross-promote a game with others in their network, allowing reach large audiences at a relatively inexpensive cost basis by mutually advertising. Another example of cross-promotion is to redirect players between other games of the same company. This way, all of the company´s games can get a better chance of exposure (Askelöf, 2013; Luton, 2013; Morel, 2012; Williams, 2012);
- Offer Walls: Through Offer Walls, players can earn in-game currency by performing certain tasks. Examples of such tasks are installing an app or game. However, since the player is often only interested in getting the reward and not in using the offer they signed up for, players obtained through this method tend to quickly abandon. Offer Walls are a common method for monetizing users, but can also be used for player acquisition, by giving offers to players of competitor games (Askelöf, 2013; Morel, 2012);
- Off Game/App Advertising: The authors are considering, in this element, advertising that not occurs through other games or apps. This includes advertisements on websites or on social networks, banners on online stores, or e-mail campaigns (Askelöf, 2013; Kaniel, 2012; Khalil, 2016; Morel, 2012; Nguyen, 2014);

Retention

The second level of the ARM funnel is known as retention. For Thibault (2013), this category is about how to keep players involved into the game and what should be done to retain them on a mid and long-term basis. Retention is a measure of how many players keep playing the game after their initial play session. Since resources have been spent to acquire players, it is important to make them engaged. Then, it is directly linked to player engagement (Narinen, 2014). In a similar way, Luton (2013) explains, as related to retention, that the number of players who are retained over a given time period in a game, indicating how sticky the game is, or how effective it is at keeping players playing.

Askelöf (2013) presents three categories of game mechanics and dynamics used to make a player engage in Social Network Games (SNGs):

- Progress Systems: It is about the common mechanics used in SNGs to manage progress, and how this progress is communicated to the player;
- Social Aspects: These are mechanics that support social interactions;

- Time-Based Limitations: A set of techniques used in SNG to control the length of game sessions.

Then, a set of elements was selected, indicated by professionals and academic researchers, as directly related to retention in F2P games. The elements were divided into three subcategories, as the division proposed by Askelöf (2013) for SNGs. The authors have decided to use the following subcategories since they are self-explanatory and fit better with the selected elements. The name of the subcategory Time-Based Limitations was also changed to Space and Time-Based Limitations, to bear the Location Triggers element. The selected categories and subcategories are not mutually excluding, then an element can represent, sometimes, more than one of these subcategories.

Progress Systems Strategies

The Progress System strategies are:

- Achievements: Often referred to as badges, achievements provide the feeling to reach something, rewarding players who fulfill some required conditions (Askelöf, 2013; Katkoff, 2012b; Lovell, 2013; Maiberg, 2013; Thibault, 2013);
- Points: Players can collect them to reach some task, challenge, better competition position, in-game richness, or more. The following divisions were found in the literature: experience points; redeemable points (or game coins); skill points; karma points; reputation points; progress points (or levelling up) (Askelöf, 2013; Kuusisto, 2014; Lovell, 2013);
- Leaderboards: A leaderboard, sometimes called scoreboard, is a competitive return trigger and its purpose is to make comparisons among players (Askelöf, 2013; Lovell, 2013; Luton, 2013; Nguyen, 2014). In the framework, this element is part of progress system subcategory, as well as social aspects subcategory, because it is about how the player is progressing in relation to others;
- Levels: It is an indication of how far has the player progressed in a game. It is not just about challenge progression, but also about new places and challenges to explore (Askelöf, 2013; Davidovici-Nora, 2014; Luton, 2013; Narinen, 2014);
- Tutorial: Sometimes called onboarding, it is the act of guiding players during specific moments of the game when they need to do something new (Askelöf, 2013; Luton, 2013; Narinen, 2014);
- Objective: An objective is a task, mission, quest or challenge that the player can reach in the game. By giving the player an objective, depth and meaning can be added to the game, creating variety to gameplay and adding constant rewards (Askelöf, 2013; Kuusisto, 2014; Salen and Zimmerman, 2004).

Social Aspects Strategies

The Social Aspects strategies are:

- Leaderboards: Leaderboards are an important social element to keep players competing against each other, while exposing their individual ranking position. Leaderboards can also help monetization when players willing to overcome others pay to do that easier and faster (Askelöf, 2013; Lovell, 2013; Luton, 2013; Nguyen, 2014). As explained before, this element is also part of progress system subcategory and social aspects subcategory as well;

- Achievements sharing: It is a social aspect tool that allows competitive and exposure interactions (Askelöf, 2013; Katkoff, 2012b; Maiberg, 2013; Thibault, 2013);
- Socializing: Also known as goal change, this element refers to a player's willing to play with other friends or teammates, making their goal socialized (Fukada, 2011, apud Askelöf, 2013; Nguyen, 2014);
- Help request: Using invitation mechanics to complete some task or goal in a game, the player can ask for help from their friends. This system encourages players to bring new players in (acquisition) and existing players come back to the game. (Askelöf, 2013; Katkoff, 2012a; Luton, 2013; Morel, 2012; Paavilainen, Alha, & Korhonen, 2017);
- Gifting: That is the possibility to spontaneously give gifts to other players, who are notified and encouraged to join (acquisition) or to come back to the game to return the favor. Reciprocity strengthens the social ties between the players, reminding them to keep playing (Luton, 2013; Paavilainen, Alha, & Korhonen, 2017; Radoff, 2011);
- Challenges: players can invite others to compete with them (Luton, 2013);
- Competition sense: It is about any other kind of situation players competing against the machine, against oneself and against others (Radoff, 2011; Salen and Zimmerman, 2004);
- Cooperation sense: It is about any other kind of situation players interact with each other in a noncompetitive way. Like social commitment, based on the sense that makes players return to complete some waiting action for another player, or helping their guild with some of their specific abilities. The willing to cooperate is the basis of this element (Luton, 2013; Radoff, 2011; Salen And Zimmerman, 2004).

Space and Time-Based Limitations Strategies

The Space and Time-Based Limitations strategies are:

- Energy System: These are common techniques used to limit the length of players' sessions. Each action the players performs consumes energy and, as their energy drains to zero, they need to wait until their energy bar is restored before it is possible to continue (Askelöf, 2013; Katkoff, 2012b; Luton, 2013);
- Time to Complete: Also known as construction time, it is about the time taken to build some object, learn a new ability or complete any other waiting bar that allows new resources in the game, forcing the player to wait or spend money to avoid it (Askelöf, 2013; Narinen, 2014; Luton, 2013);
- Cooldown: It is a time limit on how often certain actions can be used in game. (Askelöf, 2013);
- Reward for Replaying: Also known as incentivize appointment, or reward retention, reward for playing are mechanisms that reward player for returning to the game (Askelöf, 2013; Luton, 2013; Narinen, 2014; Nguyen, 2014);
- Punishment for Absence: It is, in some way, opposite of the reward for replay element. The player receives some penalty for not returning to the game for some specific period of time (Askelöf, 2013);
- Limited-Time Events: Also known as limited time campaigns, these are seasonal events that offer something special for a short period (Askelöf, 2013; Luton, 2013);

- Come Back Message: Also known as nudge triggers, that is appointed as one of the weakest return triggers. These are messages that remember the players about the game when they have not played the game for some time (Luton, 2013; Nguyen, 2014);
- Location Triggers: It is about when the game provides rewards for players playing in some specific places (Luton, 2013).

Monetization

Narinen (2014) explains that, in F2P games, monetization is the act of selling optional services and virtual resources to players within the game. The player can buy these resources with real money, which usually include things like cosmetic changes, virtual items and virtual currencies. Morel (2012) argue it is necessary be prepared to invest money to acquire users, since 2-6% of F2P players pay for something. Regarding free social mobile games, Nguyen (2014) says that two of the most notable ways to monetize them are selling advertisement and virtual items. F2P model lets players play the game without paying up-front, but incentives are constantly given to the user to invest some money in order to further improve their gaming experience. By spending money in the game, a player can boost its abilities, advance quicker and overcome time limitations. About this issue, selling virtual items is consider the main method for monetization in F2P games. Then, instead of requiring players to pay in order to keep playing a game, a F2P one prefers to rely on specific game mechanics to incentivize players to naturally spend money in it (Askelöf, 2013). Appel, Libai, Muller, & Shachar (2017), explain that such products rely on revenues from two sources: paying consumers, and paying advertisers. For Luton (2013) the ways to monetize F2P games are:

- In-app Purchases (IAP): Also known as microtransactions, they are purchases made by a player to acquire virtual goods or virtual currencies, items or usable resources in a game;
- Advertising: Ads provided by third-party suppliers that pay publishers on the number of impressions made in-game (interactions or exhibitions);
- Product placement: It is the practice to insert a real product in a game and reinforce the product estimate among its players by their association. It can be also considered a subtler way of advertising;
- Merchandise: The act of selling of physical goods associated with the game;
- Store Cards: These are physical cards with a code that can be redeemed for credits to be spent in the game. This item can be seen as an alternative to IAPs.

Based on this research, a set of elements was selected, indicated by professionals and academic researchers, as directly related to monetization in F2P games. They were also divided into three subcategories, following the division proposed by Luton (2013), with some adaptations. Store cards were inserted into IPA subcategory since it is another way to monetize by in-app purchases. Furthermore, product placement was inserted into advertising subcategory, because it is just a subtler way of advertising. The selected categories and subcategories are not mutually excluding, then an element can represent, sometimes, more than one of these categories. The subcategories are following bellow.

In-App Purchase Strategies

The In-App Purchase Strategies are:

- Virtual Currencies: These are virtual money that allow players buy things in the game. There are basically two types of them: hard currency and soft currency. Hard currency is rewarded on a finite number of or low frequency of actions and it is commonly purchased, whereas a soft currency is infinitely rewarded through a core loop and commonly earned in large quantities. Hard currencies usually are more used for premium functions (Askelöf, 2013; Kuusisto, 2014; Luton, 2013);
- Content: It consists of more content to explore within the game, such as: maps, levels, new abilities, characters or similar that give players more things to do (Luton, 2013; Radoff, 2011);
- Play Accelerators: Also known as convenience, it consists of the purchase of anything that allows players skips ahead, providing them with something that would usually need time and dedication to reach it (Luton, 2013; Radoff, 2011);
- Competitive Advantage: Stands as anything that provides players with any competitive advantage against the game or other players (Luton, 2013; Radoff, 2011);
- Customization: It is how the game lets players customize their avatar or the game's world, making changes just for vanity or expressive reasons, or changes that could also make difference in gameplay (Askelöf, 2013; Davidovici-Nora, 2014; Kuusisto, 2014; Luton, 2013; Nguyen, 2014; Radoff, 2011);
- Collectibles: These items belong to a set of items that exists only to be collected (Radoff, 2011);
- Gifts: They can help player-to-player interaction, but sometimes also can be acquired by hard currency (Luton, 2013; Paavilainen, Alha, & Korhonen., 2017; Radoff, 2011);
- Store Cards: Physical cards with codes that can be redeemed for credits to be spent in the game.

Advertising Strategies

The Advertising strategies are:

- Banner Ads: It is a thin strip that usually is shown at a top or bottom of the screen (Luton, 2013);
- Interstitial Ads: These are ads that appear between the transitions of two screens and usually are presented full screen. They monetize better than banner ads (Luton, 2013);
- Video Ads: Video ads are one of the most effective ads, but often the most intrusive (Luton, 2013);
- Offer Walls: As a monetize method, offer walls make money through actions that players need to do, as installing another game or signing up for a service. This method is a common way for monetizing users, rewarding players with some limited in-game resources and publishers with monetization (Askelöf, 2013; Luton, 2013; Morel, 2012);
- Affiliate Linking: It is a link to a store, which tracks the player and pays out a percentage of any sales made. For example, the ad takes the players from the game to a store, and if they make some purchase in that store, it monetizes for the publisher (Luton, 2013);
- Product Placement: As explained, it is the use of real products within the game as a way to advertise;
- Merchandise: As explained, it is the act to sell physical goods associated with the game.

THE ARM FRAMEWORK FOR F2P MOBILE GAMES

This chapter presents the development, and the final version, of the ARM Framework for F2P Mobile Games.

The ARM Framework Development

This section explains what approaches were used to define an ARM Framework for F2P Mobile Games, as well any other aspects related to the methodology used to collect the needed data. The development of the *1.0 version* of this framework was made in three main stages. The first was focused on creating a baseline framework.

First Stage: Creating the Baseline Framework

To identify the elements of the baseline framework, an extensive literature review was done, covering authors from the game market and academia, as can be reviewed in chapter 3. A series of elements covered by multiple authors were identified, as well others covered by just one author. The baseline framework elements was selected based on three criteria: What was presented by authors; What is not redundant; What is understood as something that aids the ARM process in F2P Mobile Games.

The subcategories were selected based on what was proposed by the authors and what properly fits all elements founded and selected. Some minor adaptations had to be made to make the framework more intuitive and not redundant, as explained in chapter 3.

Then, forty-five elements and eight subcategories were found and then organized in a cycle graph, to represent the whole first version of the framework, the baseline framework, as presented in figure 3.

Second Stage: Creating a Polished Version

The second step was focused on creating a polished version of the previous one, and on adding new elements, considering feedback from game development professionals. A questionnaire was prepared in order to verify if users could properly identify the meaning of the categories of the ARM framework proposed, just by the label. This was done to minimize the chances of misunderstanding when future interviewees read the next survey, even considering that the label's description will be shown to interviewees on the next survey. In addition, this questionnaire has the goal of evolving the proposed framework, identifying possible problems and opportunities to change.

The survey was conducted through Google Forms, and it was divided into six sections. The first section is called the introduction, where the aim of the study is explained, a necessary basic explanation about ARM and some guidance on the questions; section two is a simple professional profile questionnaire, asking interviewees about subjects such as area of expertise, years of experience, and experience on F2P mobile games; section three presents the baseline ARM framework for F2P mobile games proposed, explaining textually and graphically, how the main categories, subcategories, and elements, are organized; then, sections four, five and six, present the main categories and subcategories with their descriptions, and asks interviewees, based only on their knowledge and perception, to write a short description about how they understand each one of the related elements presented.

Figure 3. Baseline ARM framework for F2P mobile games (the authors)

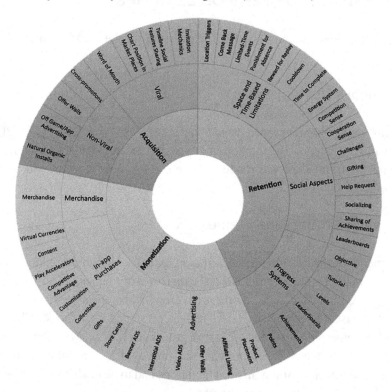

Five game market professionals, with experience in Production, Game Design, Project Management, Game Programming, Game & Data Analysis, Business Development & Marketing, areas, have been part of this survey. All of them have, at least, some experience with game design or production areas, as well as some experience working on mobile F2P games. They work in companies from Germany, Finland, Canada, New Zealand and Sweden.

In this interview the authors presented the framework and explained the meaning of the categories (Acquisition, Retention, and Monetization), and their subcategories as well. The authors did not explain the meaning of the elements inside the subcategories. Then, the interviewees were asked what they understood about each of the elements proposed, considering their categories and subcategories involved. Through this questionnaire, some issues were identified and some adjustments had to be made. The list below presents the analysis and justification for the adjustments:

- Off Game/App Advertising: Although all the interviewees could understand the label, based on an observation made by one interviewee, the authors replaced the term for a more usual one, "Non-Game Media Advertising";
- Objective: The label was changed to "Goals", because it was a more usual term for the interviewees;
- Help Request: This label was changed to "Help Request Mechanics", adding mechanics at the end of the sentence, to make clear that the term refers to some action provided by the game system;
- Gifting: This label was changed to "Gifting Mechanics", adding mechanics at the end of the sentence, to make it clear that the term refers to some action provided by the game system;

- Challenges: Based on three misunderstood labels, the authors perceived that the interviewees understand that as a kind of specific goal or extra challenge, and not a challenge mechanic where the player can invite someone to compete with. To fix this problem, the label was changed to "Challenge Invitation";

- Competition Sense: It was decided to change this label to "Competitive Environment" to make clear that the term does not refer to a specific mechanic, but the whole game environment that involves competitive aspects;

- Cooperative Sense: Like Competitive Sense, the authors decided to change this label to "Cooperative Environment", because it is not about a specific mechanic, but the whole game environment that involves cooperative aspects;

- Time to Complete: Three interviewees understood this as a countdown timer to complete some game challenge. Because of this reductionist interpretation, the authors decided to change this label to "Time to Complete (Waiting Time)" and create a brand new one, called "Countdown Timer";

- Reward for Replay: The authors decided to change this label to "Reward for Return", because two interviewees understood that as the possibility to redo a game challenge;

- Come Back Message: The authors changed this label to "Come Back Message (Push Notification)", just adding "Push Notification" to make clear it's not about a message inside the game;

- Content: The authors perceived it could be confused with any kind of content in the game. Because of that, the label was changed to "Extra Content" to make it more aligned with the original intention;

- Customization: The authors changed this label to "Customization (To Set Up)", because two interviewees understood that the term referred only to cosmetic customizations;

- Collectibles: The authors changed this label to "Collectible Collection", to make clear that the term is not about any kind of item that can be collected;

- Gifts: To make it clearer that ther label refers to a gift the player needs to buy, the authors changed this label to "Purchase Gifts".

The authors also decided to add a new element named "Countdown Timer", which is a time constraint for the player to complete a specific challenge. The element was added because three out of five interviewees identified it, and it is not covered by any other element. This element should be part of the Space and Time-Based Limitations subcategory, inside Retention category. Based on all previous information, the new framework version is represented on figure 4.

Third Stage: Developing the 1.0 Version

After the second step, the authors prepared a questionnaire of evaluation in order to identify how game market professionals rated the proposed framework, and what they thought should be changed. That was done to maximize the chances the framework will be useful to game market professionals, creating a sense of understanding about the elements, its organization, and possibilities related to ARM. In addition, this questionnaire has the goal of helping evolve the proposed framework, identifying possible problems and opportunities to improve it.

Figure 4. Second Version of The ARM Framework for F2P Mobile Games (The Authors)

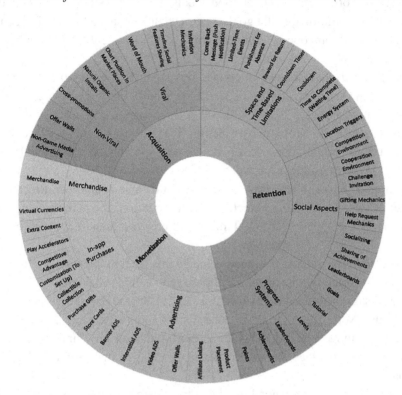

The survey was conducted through Google Forms, and it was divided into three sections. Like the first survey, the first section is called introduction, where the aim of this study is detailed, a necessary basic explanation about ARM, and how to approach and answer the questions is explained; also similar to the first survey, section two is a simple professional profile questionnaire, asking interviewees about subjects related to their professional, mobile, and F2P, experience.

Then, section three presents the Second Version of The ARM Framework for F2P Mobile Games, explaining textually and graphically, how the main categories, subcategories, and elements, are organized, and providing a link with the description of all elements of the framework, as well as their categories and subcategories.

Thirty game market professionals, with experience in Production, Game Design, Project Management, Game Programming, Game Testing, Sound Design, Game & Data Analysis, Academic & Research, Business Development & Marketing areas, have been part of this survey. All of them have, at least, some experience working on mobile F2P games, and 39 of them have experience working as a game designer. They were working in companies from Russia, Finland, Canada, United Kingdom, Brazil, Germany, Australia, Netherlands, India, USA, Romania, Ukraine and Pakistan.

In this interview, the authors presented the second version of the ARM framework for F2P mobile games and explained the meaning of the categories (Acquisition, Retention, and Monetization), and their subcategories as well. Furthermore, as explained before, the authors have provided a link that explains the meaning of the elements in the subcategories.

The authors are also considering the whole group of results related to this section considering the following criteria: At least 2 answers indicating the same issue were found, considering any match of questions; Any kind of feedback that seems to provide good solutions that properly fit into the proposed framework; The authors identified a good opportunity to change the label to something more intuitive, based on suggestions, interpretations or even misunderstandings.

On the second survey, some interviewees identified that there was room for improvement on the framework if the authors keep making changes on it from time to time. Furthermore, it was possible to identify, that new techniques and elements related to ARM practices are continuously being developed, which could make the practice of keeping the framework updated even more relevant.

Therefore, considering the second framework version and the answers of the Likert and open questions of the second survey, these are the changes made to create the third version of the framework:

- Increasing New Elements
  - VIP Subscription / Season Pass: This is an In-App Purchase element, where players pay for exclusive content and advantages. Players that pay for it have temporary access to exclusive content;
  - Up-Sells: This is an In-App Purchase element, that is about the way the game offers better options for buying goods, where the cost savings is proportionally inferior to the quantity purchased. For example, when the game offers a package of 1K gold for 1 dollar and, at the same time, offers 5K gold for 3 dollars;
  - Discounts: It is an In-App Purchase element, where the game offers, for a limited time, an in-game product (or products) cheaper than the normal price;
  - Targeted-Offers: This element is part of the In-App Purchases subcategory. That is an approach where the game offers specific promotions to the players, according to their gameplay style or activity;
  - Gacha: This is another In-App Purchases element. Gacha is a system where players acquire a kind of package, without knowing what comes inside until they open it;
  - Annuities: That is an In-App Purchases, as well as a Space and Time-Based Limitations, element. In this technique, the players pay for rewards but need to keep returning at a specific frequency to get them because they are distributed over some period of time. Generally, the game administrator offers better deals when using this technique. It also increases the retention since the players need to keep returning to get the full value for what they have bought;
  - Clans: That is a Social Aspects element. Also called guilds, this is an in-game structure that allows players to create or be part of a group that allows them to communicate between themselves, share resources, help each other, chase common goals, or to do other special interactions;
  - Visiting Other Players: That is another Social Aspects element. This element is about how the game allows players visit other players' home, and then check how well other players are in the game;
  - Community Management: That is a Social Aspects, as well a Viral, element. It is about how the game company deals with the external and internal community of players, through executing events and contests, expanding and maintaining the online community, supporting the community on social media platforms, and more related issues;

- ◦ Time Gated Rewards: That is a Space and Time-Based Limitations element. Using this technique, the game limits the amount of rewards the player can acquire in some amount of time. Doing this, the player needs to keep returning to try to acquire new rewards, unlocked over time;
- ◦ IP Based: This is a Non-Viral element. It means the game uses established intellectual property (like cartoon or comic book characters), in order to acquire new players. The authors have classified this element as a Non-Viral because it is not something that comes from players, to acquire new players, but something that makes the game more attractive by itself;
- To be Excluded
  - ◦ Socializing, from the Social Aspects subcategory was excluded, because its interpretation could be ambiguous. Also, in some ways, its meaning is covered by the combination of the new Clans element, and other ones, such as Cooperation Environment and Competition Environment;
- Other Changes
  - ◦ The element Collectible Collection, from In-App Purchases subcategory, was added to Progress Systems subcategory, since it was perceived that it could be understood by the player as a long-term goal;
- Keep Developing
  - ◦ Based on some feedback and this work itself, the authors have decided to keep making continuous changes, additions and adaptations to this framework, with the help of the game development community, in the upcoming works;

It is important to note that there were some suggestions proposing elements that are already covered, in some way. Also, there were some suggestions that just do not fit on a framework to design ARM elements on F2P mobile games.

Version 1.0 of The ARM Framework for F2P Mobile Games

Based on all previous feedbacks, the established criteria, and analysis, the new framework version is represented in figure 5, presenting fifty-nine elements. In addition, even though this is the final version of this framework, the authors will keep developing it, based on the feedback of game market professionals, the related literature, and the new trends of the F2P mobile game market.

A brief description, subcategory and category of each element of the third version (version 1.0) framework follows in table 1.

CONCLUSION

The free mobile game design has specific characteristics that demand an investigation. The proper understanding of these characteristics can allow game professionals to create more profitable and successful mobile games. For example, a set of acquisition, retention, and monetization mobile free-to-play game elements, schematically organized, could be helpful to turns these elements formally accessible to be consciously designed on real games.

Figure 5. Version 1.0 of the ARM framework for F2P mobile games (the authors)

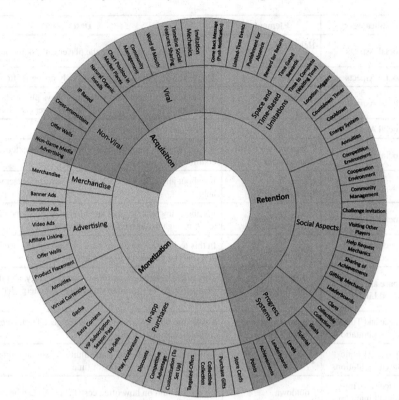

Table 1. Categories, subcategories, elements and descriptions

Category	Subcategory	Element	Description
Retention	Progress Systems	Points	They can be: experience points; redeemable points (or game coins); skill points; karma points; reputation points; progress points (or leveling up)
Retention	Progress Systems	Achievements	Provide the feeling of reaching something, rewarding to players who fulfill the required conditions
Retention	Progress Systems	Collectible Collection	These items belong to a set of items and exist only to be collected.
Retention	Progress Systems	Leaderboards	It is a competitive return trigger, focused on making comparisons between players
Retention	Progress Systems	Levels	It's an indication of how far the player has progressed in the game
Retention	Progress Systems	Tutorial	It is the practice of guiding and teaching players in some moments of the game when they need to do something new
Retention	Progress Systems	Goals	A goal is a task, mission, quest or challenge for the player to clear in the game
Retention	Social Aspects	Leaderboards	Leaderboards are an important social element to keep players competing against each other, while exposing their ranking position
Retention	Social Aspects	Sharing of Achievements	It is a game mechanic that allows players to share what they have achieved
Retention	Social Aspects	Clans	Also called guilds, this is an in-game structure that allows players to create or be part of a group that grants them the ability to perform special interactions between each other

continues on following page

Table 1. Continued

Category	Subcategory	Element	Description
Retention	Social Aspects	Help Request Mechanics	It is a game mechanic where the player can ask for help from their friends
Retention	Social Aspects	Gifting Mechanics	That is the possibility to spontaneously give gifts to other players
Retention	Social Aspects	Visiting Other Players	This element is about how the game allows players to visit other players' homes, and then check how well other players are doing in the game
Retention	Social Aspects	Challenge Invitation	Players can invite others to a challenge
Retention	Social Aspects	Community Management	It is the way the game company deals with the external and internal community of players
Retention	Social Aspects	Cooperation Environment	It's about any other kind of situation players interact with each other to help
Retention	Social Aspects	Competition Environment	It's about any other kind of situation players competing against the machine, against oneself and against others
Retention	Space and Time-Based Limitations	Annuities	In this technique, the player pays for rewards but needs to keep returning at a specific frequency to get them
Retention	Space and Time-Based Limitations	Energy System	This is a system where actions consume energy, and if the players' energy drains to zero, they need to wait until their energy bar is restored to continue
Retention	Space and Time-Based Limitations	Time to Complete (Waiting Time)	That is the time taken to build some object, learn a new ability, or complete any other waiting bar
Retention	Space and Time-Based Limitations	Time Gated Rewards	Using this technique, the game limits the amount of rewards the player can acquire in some amount of time
Retention	Space and Time-Based Limitations	Cooldown	It's a time limit on how often certain actions can be used in game
Retention	Space and Time-Based Limitations	Countdown Timer	That is a time constraint for the player to complete a specific challenge.
Retention	Space and Time-Based Limitations	Reward for Return	These are mechanisms that reward the player for returning to the game
Retention	Space and Time-Based Limitations	Punishment for Absence	The player receives some penalty for not returning for some specific period of time
Retention	Space and Time-Based Limitations	Limited-Time Events	Seasonal events that offer something special for a short period only, like an exclusive quest
Retention	Space and Time-Based Limitations	Come Back Message (Push Notification)	Messages that remind the players about the game when they haven't played the game for some time
Retention	Space and Time-Based Limitations	Location Triggers	Advantages for players playing in some specific places
Acquisition	Viral	Invitation Mechanics	Mechanics to incentivize users to invite their friends to try the game
Acquisition	Viral	Timeline Social Features Sharing	Social features like leaderboards and achievements players can share on their timeline
Acquisition	Viral	Word of Mouth	Things like natural invitations by the players without using actions on the game
Acquisition	Viral	Community Management	It is the way the game company deals with the external and internal community of players
Acquisition	Viral	Chart Position in Market Places	Better chart position in market places will provide more visibility
Acquisition	Non-Viral	Natural Organic Installs	Organic installs that are not influenced by the consumption by previous players or cross-promotions, like the pure store exposure

continues on following page

Table 1. Continued

Category	Subcategory	Element	Description
Acquisition	Non-Viral	IP Based	The game uses established intellectual property, in order to acquire new players.
Acquisition	Non-Viral	Cross-promotions	The ability to cross-promote a game with others
Acquisition	Non-Viral	Offer Walls	Through Offer Walls, the players can earn in-game currency by performing certain tasks
Acquisition	Non-Viral	Non-Game Media Advertising	Advertising that does not occur through other games or apps
Monetization	In-app Purchases	Annuities	In this technique, the player pays for rewards but needs to keep returning at a specific frequency to get them
Monetization	In-app Purchases	Virtual Currencies	Virtual money that allow players buy things in the game
Monetization	In-app Purchases	Extra Content	More content to explore the game, as maps, levels, new abilities, characters, or similar
Monetization	In-app Purchases	VIP Subscription / Season Pass	Players that pay for it, have a kind of temporary access to exclusive content
Monetization	In-app Purchases	Up-Sells	It is when the game offers better options for buying goods, where the cost savings is proportionally inferior to the quantity purchased.
Monetization	In-app Purchases	Play Accelerators	It consists of the purchase of anything that allows players skips ahead, providing them with something that normally would need time and dedication to reach it
Monetization	In-app Purchases	Gacha	It is a system where players acquire a kind of package without knowing what comes inside until they open it
Monetization	In-app Purchases	Discounts	The game offers, for a limited time, an in-game product (or products) cheaper than the normal price
Monetization	In-app Purchases	Competitive Advantage	Anything that provides players with any competitive advantage against the game or other players
Monetization	In-app Purchases	Customization (To Set Up)	How the game lets the players customize the avatar or the game's world
Monetization	In-app Purchases	Targeted-Offers	That is an approach where the game offers specific promotions to the players, according to their gameplay style or activity
Monetization	In-app Purchases	Collectible Collection	These items belong to a set of items and exist only to be collected
Monetization	In-app Purchases	Purchase Gifts	Gifts also can be acquired with hard currency
Monetization	In-app Purchases	Store Cards	Physical cards with codes that can be redeemed for credits to be spent in the game
Monetization	Advertising	Banner Ads	It's a thin strip that is usually shown at the top or bottom of the screen
Monetization	Advertising	Interstitial Ads	Ads that appear between the transition of two screens and are usually full screen
Monetization	Advertising	Video Ads	Video ads are one of the most effective ads
Monetization	Advertising	Offer Walls	Offer walls can monetize through actions that players need to do, such as installing another game or signing up for a service
Monetization	Advertising	Affiliate Linking	It is a link to a store, which tracks the player and pays out a percentage of sales made
Monetization	Advertising	Product Placement	It is the use of real products inside the game to promote advertisement;
Monetization	Merchandise	Merchandise	That is the act of selling physical goods associated with the game.

In this research the authors have organized a 1.0 version of the framework for F2P mobile games, assembling a set of fifty-nine elements, eight subcategories, and three main categories. These elements were put together through a research focused on professional and academic literature. The authors believe this framework can be very useful for free-to-play game design and game production professionals, as well as researches related to this subject. A formally organized list of applicable elements could turn the selection of F2P solutions more effective, as a checklist of possible options on the game design process. Game designers and producers, while using this framework, can verify if they are forgetting any element or consider alternatives that could help the game to be successful. The authors should also consider the use of the proposed framework as the basis for more research about ARM strategies in games.

Figure 6 illustrates the build process of the ARM framework for F2P mobile games, developed in Study 1. After the literature research, the authors identified a baseline ARM framework with forty-five elements. Then, after a comprehension test, the authors created the second version of the ARM framework, with fourteen adjusted elements and one new element. As the final step, after the framework evaluation, the authors finished the version 1.0 of the ARM framework, with thirteen new elements added and one removed.

Figure 6. The build process of the ARM framework for F2P mobile games (The Author)

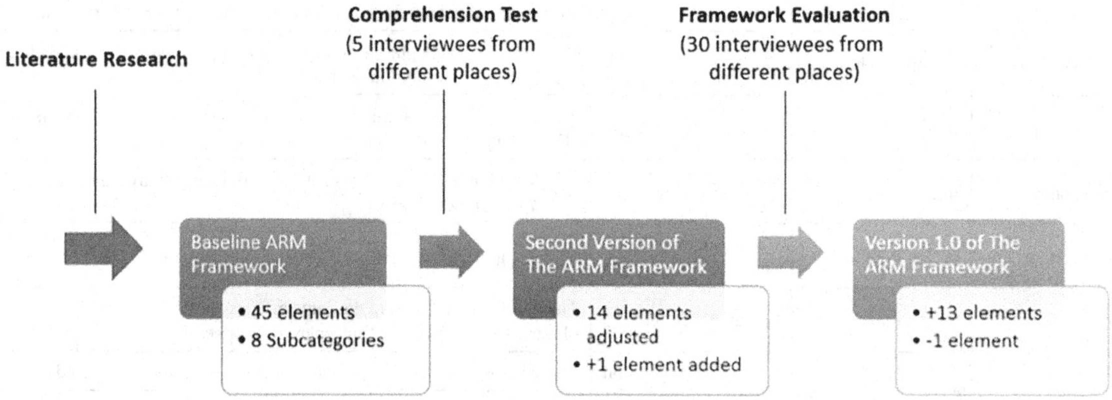

Furthermore, the developed set of heuristics can provide a structured and well-accepted group of guidelines and best practices to help new and experienced game designers when planning F2P mobile games. In addition, this set can be used as an academic reference, providing a structured way to organize heuristics specifically designed for ARM elements in F2P mobile games, since the authors didn't find anything similar during the research.

It is also necessary to consider that the academic room for contributions, about this specific field, is very large since there is scarce academic literature about it. This work itself is directly contributing to creating the academic basis for ARM in F2P mobile games.

As a future work, the authors are going to keep evolving this framework, validating and modifying its structure and elements, as well its labels. It will be done through continuous surveys with F2P mobile game professionals.

REFERENCES

Alha, K., Koskinen, E., Paavilainen, J., Hamari, J., & Kinnunen, J. (2014). Free-To-Play Games: Professionals' Perspectives. In Proceedings of Nordic Digra (vol. 2014). Visby.

Appel, G., Libai, B., Muller, E., & Shachar, R. (2017). *Retention and The Monetization Of Apps*. Retrieved from: http://www.hitechmarkets.net /files/appellibaimullershachar2 017.pdf

Askelöf, P. (2013). *Monetization Of Social Network Games In Japan And The West* (Master's thesis). Lund University, Sweden.

Davidovici-nora, M. (2014). Paid And Free Digital Business Models Innovations In The Video Game Industry. Digiworld Economic Journal, 94, 83.

Fields, T., & Cotton, B. (2012). *Social Gamer Design: Monetization Methods And Mechanics*. Elsevier.

Kaniel, O. (2012). *Events Tracking Technology*. U.S. Patent application n. 13/649,402, 11 out. 2012.

KatkoffM. (2012a). *From Players To Payers*. Retrieved from: https://www.deconstructoroffun.com/ blog//2012/05/from-players-to-payers-4-steps-to.html

Katkoff, M. (2012b). *Mid-Core Success Part 2: Retention*. Retrieved from: https://www.deconstructoroffun.com/blog//2013 /10/mid-core-success-part-2-retention.html

Khalil, H. (2016). *Engineering Viral Growth* (Master's thesis). Aalto University, Finland.

Kontagent. (2011). *The Top 7 Metrics Of High Successful Social Companies*. Retrieved from: http:// static.kontagent.com /whitepaper/knt_wp_top7metrics_p3_finalx.pdf

Kuusisto, M. (2014). *Evaluating Free-To-Play Monetization Mechanics In Mobile Games: Case: Improvement Proposal To Supersonic-Game* (Bachelor's thesis). Tampere University of Applied Sciences, Finland.

Lovell, N. (2013). *The Pyramid Of Free-To-Play Game Design*. Retrieved from: https://www.gamasutra. com/blogs/ nicholaslovell/20130919/200606/the_pyramid_of_freeto

Luton, W. (2013). Free-To-Play: Making Money From Games You Give Away. New Riders.

Maiberg, E. (2013). *Pearl's Peril Is Wooga's Fastest-Growing Game To Date*. Retrieved from: http:// www.adweek.com/ digital/pearls-peril-is-woogas-fastest-growing-game-to-date/

McClure, D. (2007). *Startup Metrics For Pirates: Aarrr! 500 Hats*. Retrieved From: http://500hats. typepad.com/500blogs /2007/09/startup-metrics.html

Morel, R. (2012). *Choosing The Right Business Model For Your Game Or App*. Retrieved from: https:// www.adobe.com /devnet/flashplayer/articles/right-business-model.html

Narinen, A. (2014). *How Player Retention Works In Free-To-Play Mobile Games: A Study Of Player Retention Methods* (Bachelor's thesis). Tampere University of Applied Sciences, Finland.

Nguyen, H. (2014). *Monetization For A Free-To-Play Mobile Game* (Bachelor's thesis). Kajaani University of Applied Sciences, Finland.

Paavilainen, J., Alha, K., & Korhonen, H. (2017). A Review Of Social Features In Social Network Games. *Transactions of the Digital Games Research Association*, *3*(2).

Radoff, J. (2011). *Game On: Energize Your Business With Social Media Games*. Indianapolis, IN: Wiley Publishing, Inc.

Salen, K., & Zimmerman, E. (2004). *Rules Of Play: Game Design Fundamentals*. The MIT Press.

Tao, Z., Cheung, M., She, J., & Lam, R. (2014). Item Recommendation Using Collaborative Filtering In Mobile Social Games: A Case Study. *Big Data And Cloud Computing (bdcloud). IEEE Fourth International Conference*, 293-297.

Thibault, C. (2013). *Game Data Analysis–Tools And Methods*. Birmingham, UK: Packt Publishing ltd.

Think Gaming. (2018). *Top grossing all devices-games*. Retrieved from: https://thinkgaming.com

Williams, J. (2012). *Applying Lessons Learned On Facebook To Mobile App Development*. Retrieved from: https://www.gamasutra.com/blogs/joshwilliams/20120117/90918/applying_lessons_learned_on_facebook_to_mobile_app_development.php

KEY TERMS AND DEFINITIONS

Acquisition Strategies: Strategies to attract users to a game.

Free-to-Play Games: Games that the user does not have to pay to download and play.

Game Design: Field of design focused on the creation of games.

Game Development: The act of creating a game, from the conceptual basis to the final, published version.

Mobile Games: Games made to be played on mobile devices (smartphones and tablets).

Monetization Strategies: Strategies to make the user pay and/or generate profits to the game developers.

Retention Strategies: Strategies to keep the users playing a game, once they already played one time.

This research was previously published in the Handbook of Research on Human-Computer Interfaces and New Modes of Interactivity; pages 177-198, copyright year 2019 by Engineering Science Reference (an imprint of IGI Global).

Chapter 16
Fiero and Flow in Online Competitive Gaming:
The Gaming Engagement Framework

Sharon Andrews
University of Houston-Clear Lake, USA

Robert E. Bradbury
University of Houston-Clear Lake, USA

Caroline M. Crawford
University of Houston-Clear Lake, USA

ABSTRACT

This paper explores the concept of fiero as it relates to online competitive gaming, resulting in a framework focused upon levels of fiero and flow, labeled as the gaming engagement framework. More specifically, the paper describes this framework and its supporting methods as can be applied to measure perceived intensity and engagement levels leading to fiero, and concentration and collaboration levels leading to flow, giving an overall prediction of the level of fiero and flow that a game is capable of eliciting. The use of both quantitative and qualitative data in support of the framework offers a mixed-methods approach towards discovery of both weak areas and strong areas of fiero and flow, along with a collection of literal user perceptions. This framework can be applied at the prototyping phase during game development as well as at incrementally advancing levels of product development through pre- and post-production.

INTRODUCTION

An online competitive video game player can be fully engrossed, fully focused, and all synapses firing while in the flow of online competitive gaming engagement. There can be an intensity often not seen in the day-to-day activities of real life, motivating the player in ways that may have been previously unrealized. Observations of online competitive video game competitons reveal players in intense competitive

DOI: 10.4018/978-1-6684-7589-8.ch016

states while participating in games. Many require high levels of engagement with the game including concentration and collaboration as well as enjoyment. The authors hypothesize that highly successful and highly engaging games are those that require of players high levels of intensity, collaboration, concentration, enjoyment. These traits directly result from game play and are significant factors in determining what makes online competitive video gaming so attractive and popular. There can be other motivations for gameplay deriving from reported benefits from game playing which this article briefly discusses in order to present a larger picture of gaming motivations. These observed traits of intensity of a game, its collaboration required as well as its concentration and enjoyment are contained in the notions of fiero and flow. The authors assert it is a game's fiero and flow that contribute greatly to a game's attraction and engagement ability and present herein a framework which allows for the levels of fiero exhibited by a game to be measured, and to a lesser extent flow. The focus of this paper is the presentation of a theoretical framework for the measurement of this engagement termed fiero, along with an example to illustrate how the framework can be applied in practice.

The concepts of fiero and flow are central to an understanding of what makes games so popular and therefore central to our framework is the concept of fiero; as such, these concepts are specifically focused upon as foundational points of discussion.

The paper briefly describes the benefits of computer games with a focus upon online competitive gaming. Understanding these benefits provided a partial basis for determining measures and traits for this engagement framework, as well as provides indications for future expansions of the framework to assess the levels of some of the benefits noted.

BACKGROUND

Benefits Online Competitive Gaming

The social benefits of online competitive gaming are real and important as they provide gamers who may be socially awkward and isolated at school or work and outlet for human engagement by utilizing online computer games to interact in real-time with hundreds or even thousands of like-minded human players on a regular basis This sense of community, camaraderie and even the competition and team building are all important self-reported social benefits to avid gamers.

Video games have also been reported to help with learning, as well as provide high levels of motivation for learning (Sharritt & Suthers, 2011). Online competitive gaming has been reported to be used to promote second language skills, particularly in MMORPG (massive multiplayer online role-playing games) environments (Dixon & Christison, 2018). Such learning was reported to be a result of inherent collaboration and co-construction activity requirements and partly driven by a participant's high motivation to engage with the game in the required languages (Peterson, 2010, 2016) Such reports provide indications of both a social and cognitive benefit of online competitive gaming.

For online competitive gaming, physically disabled players can compete equally well if they are able to user upper body functions to operative the computer controls and their eyes and mind to think quickly. As quoted within Baig's (2019) article, "Barlet of AbleGamers describes video games as 'the great equalizer. You don't know if I'm disabled. You just know that I'm an ogre or whatever character or manifestation I am in the game. To me, games are about community, about connecting with a shared experience.'" (para. 39). This last statement further illustrating the social benefit of games, but the most far-reaching real-life benefit of online gaming is its ability to bring the physical natures of competition, its intensity, concentration, enjoyment and collaboration, to a world of physically disabled people who without this virtual physical world would have no way to experience what it feels like to compete in such competitive sports. They are able to compete equally along-side with and against physically able competitors and make social connections by virtue of the social interactions afforded by online competitive gaming.

Fiero and Flow

Computer game companies have become masters at creating games that maximize motivational articulations referred to as fiero and flow. The motivational factor of these highly successful and engaging games are realized far beyond the skill-demand balance (Baumann, Lurig, & Engeser, 2016), suggesting that a highly dynamic style of game pacing offers a balanced approach towards high engagement aligned with short breaks in cognitive demand. Baumann, Lurig, and Engeser (2016) suggest that flow is a loop towards achieving fiero, suggesting that "Upon accomplishing a hard part, they arrive at a state of pride ("fiero") that comes with completing a difficult task and requires some frustration upfront." (p. 508-509). Through this initial understanding, flow and fiero are worthy of a closer analysis with respect to online competitive gaming.

Csíkszentmihályi describes flow as, "a state in which people are so involved in an activity that nothing else seems to matter; the experience is so enjoyable that people will continue to do it even at great cost, for the sheer sake of doing it" (1990, p.4.). Csíkszentmihályi (1990, 1996, 1998, 2008) and Chen (2007) engaged in research works towards better understanding this flow phenomenon. The realization was that there are nine common elements associated with a state of flow, with an important recognition that the initial three elements may be external characteristics, while the final six designated elements reflect an internalized sense of characteristics and experiential engagement:

1. There are clear goals every step of the way;
2. There is immediate feedback to one's actions;
3. There is a balance between challenges and skills;
4. Action and awareness are merged;
5. Distractions are excluded from consciousness;
6. There is no worry of failure;
7. Self-consciousness disappears;
8. The sense of time becomes distorted;
9. The activity becomes an end in itself. (Csíkszentmihályi, 1990, as cited by Liljedahl, 2016, p. 1).

Similarly to Csíkszentmihályi's elements of flow, Chen (Chen 2007) described flow as being composed of eight components: a challenging activity requiring skill, a merging of action and awareness, clear goals, direct immediate feedback, concentration on the task, a sense of control, a lack of self-consciousness, and an altered sense of time. Psychological, behavioral, and physiological aspects of flow have had attempts to be defined and measured by numerous researchers (Borderie & Michinov, 2016; Chen, 2007; Csikszentmihalyi, 1975/2000; Keller, Bless, Bloman, & Kleinb'ohl, 2011; Takatalo, Häkkinen, Kaistinen, & Nyman, 2010). However, fiero has not received the same attention nor have researchers attempted to define and measure fiero to this extent.

Flow is present in many endeavors, not just gaming (Chen, 2007; Schachter & Singer, 1962; Tozman, Zhang, & Vollmeyer, 2017). Flow can be present in mundane or tedious tasks which are not tasks of play or enjoyment, or even pleasurable tasks (Liljedahl, 2016). One example of this is computer programming. Programming is not a game or a hobby activity, but instead is a mindful activity that is intense in its requirement of concentration, and mathematical in rigor of detail and syntax. However, flow is present in programming activity, as many experienced or advanced programmers will attest. Flow is directly exhibited when programmers engage in significant time periods of non-stop programming, which they describe as being *in the zone*.

In support of this personal observation, DeMarco and Lister (1987, 1999) characterized the programming profession as one in which flow is often present; programmers experience total immersion within the development process, reflecting an intense sense of flow while coding computer programs. As described by Salt (1993), DeMarco and Lister (1987, 1999) "point out that creative brain-work is done in a state that psychologists call 'flow'. This a meditative, mildly euphoric state, with decreased awareness of the passage of time, when ideas flow without effort" (DeMarco & Lister, 1987, 1999, as cited by Salt, 1993, p. 4). The level of concentration required for the activity and the collaboration required between the "player" (in this example the programmer) and the game unit (in this example, the computer and the software interface) is paramount in contributing to the state of flow.

Flow is exhibited during competitive gaming resulting in long uninterrupted sessions of play (Takatalo, Häkkinen, Kaistinen, & Nyman, 2010). The strength of the flow state emphasizes the ability of one's cognitive engagement to ignore all other aspects of life, concentrating solely on gameplay strategy. Flow is an outcome of activities that require high levels of concentration and collaboration and, as such, tasks and instruments that measure concentration and collaboration may indicate levels of flow.

A game can provide high levels of stimulation and enjoyment to the point of outwardly vocal, physical and physiological expressions of jubilation, or even anxiety and stress (Schmidt, Gnam, Kopt, Rathgeber & Woll, 2020), as occurs in competition such as football or tennis. Such intensity and engagement with the game is reflected by expressions of both triumph and regret such as shouting, throwing of hands, jumping, or even an elevated heart rate, and certainly flow is present (Keller, Bless, Bloman, & Kleinb'ohl, 2011), as well as fiero.

The term *fiero* has been used in conjunction with gaming. McGonigal (2011) asserted that gamers experience and express emotion when they win a round or score points referred to as *fiero*, an Italian word for *pride*, used to describe a level of emotionally laden pride and celebratory fun as well as to express feelings of triumph and great excitement. Fiero is directly derived from emotions elicited by activities that provide success and enjoyment and therefore, fiero is very much a motivating factor driving the return to play of any competitive game. It can be strong enough to contribute to addiction by some to game play, as it links one's emotional senses to more primal senses of chemical reward. Given these definitions of fiero and flow one can surmise, by observation and participation, that the more successful, exciting games most likely put players in states of high fiero and high flow.

The emotional benefits of neurologic fiero, and the mental concentration benefit of flow, work together to improve semantic processing and to enhance the gamer experience, game ability and agility, contributing to the gamer's ability to overcome one complexity after another. Based upon the work of Craik and Lockhart (1972), Calongne, Stricker, Truman and Arenas (2019) describe deep or semantic processing as, "the construct of semantic processing through deep immersion provides connections that support applied learning: The relationship between objects or experiences; The deeper meaning of the experience; The importance of the experience" (p. 181). Deep processing, also referred to as semantic processing, reflects the immersive experience of online competitive games with the relationships between emotional experiences and rewards Csikszentmihalyi (1975/2000).

On the negative side of the discussion, too much flow can contribute to physical burnout as with the programmer or gamer who codes or plays continuously, deprived of sleep and nutrition. Further, too much fiero can be stressful and emotionally draining to the point of cognitive burnout. Taken to the extreme, fiero and flow can begin to look and feel like addiction (Stromberg, 2009; Nardi & Harris, 2006). This was also suggested by Hoeft et al., (2007) from observance in one study that the brain experienced exceptionally intense activation when gamers experienced moments of triumph, or fiero, and suggested this might explain the addiction some gamers feel to a favorite game. As suggested by Snodgrass, et al, (2016), gamers may realize a level of potential compulsion related to online competitive games, with fiero and flow directly supporting the motivation of such intense gamer engagement.

Fiero and flow are arguably strong motivating factors to return excessively to a game to attain neurologic reward. The gaming engagement framework provides a method for evaluating the differentiated levels of fiero and flow, in order to correlate the levels of fiero and flow within a game to support and validate the hypothesis that exciting games most likely put players in states of high fiero and high flow. As fiero is expressed in physical and physiological ways, it can be measured and estimated by observations and recording; as such, the authors include a method for measurement of fiero in the framework.

THE GAMING ENGAGEMENT FRAMEWORK

The qualities of fiero and flow offer the opportunity to measure and evaluate several aspects of a game or gaming environment, namely the attributes of *engagement, intensity, collaboration* and *concentration*. One can begin to measure and estimate these attributes by recording observed and collected measures indicative of fiero and flow. Fiero is a direct indication, and by product of, a game's level of intensity and enjoyment. If users of a game experience high levels of fiero than one can reasonably assert that both intensity and engagement are also high, and vice versa, if fiero is very low. If users of a game experience high levels of flow during a game then one can reasonably assert that the game requires high levels of concentration and collaboration. And low levels of such would predict low levels using the same logic. The levels of fiero and flow together suggest the type of engagement capability of the game.

It is noted that usability testing is related to the engagement framework measurements, as usability can contribute to all aspects of game play. Certainly usability is vital to discerning the success or failure of a competitive game as well as testing using the correct audience (Logan, n.d., para. 11) and the authors concerns of fiero and flow certainly contribute to usability, but the authors refine this notion to an analysis of the engagement level of a game considering the game's enjoyment, intensity, collaboration, and concentration required. As such, a framework through which to analyze and measure fiero and flow, along with a process and measurement methods for its application, have been defined. The frameworks methods are based upon four measureable traits the framework uses to measure fiero and flow: intensity, engagement, concentration and collaboration.

Figure 1 illustrates the Gaming Engagement Framework. This framework defines a method of assessment of these traits using the framework's defined process, which together serve as an evaluative model through which to evaluate gaming environments with respect to fiero and flow. Levels of a player's outwardly exhibited and self-reported intensity, enjoyment, concentration and collaboration are the focus of the framework. The X axis is designated as fiero, which the framework measures by way of the outwardly exhibited attributes of intensity and enjoyment. The Y axis is designated as flow, which the framework measures by way of the outwardly exhibited attributes of concentration and collaboration. The framework uses measureable traits of *physical movements*, *heart rate*, and *user perceptions* to assess the levels of fiero and flow. Fiero is currently more concentrated upon in the framework with respect to the number of measures applied, with future work planned for additional predictors based on future case study analysis.

The actual method of measurement of the attributes of intensity, enjoyment, concentration and collaboration, form the basis of the application of the framework using a process defined by this framework. After application of this framework's process and the measures applied, the resulting levels of fiero and flow are predicted and can be plotted in the graph. Measures resulting in both high fiero and high flow will fall in the upper right quadrant (as illustrated in Figure 1), whereas measures resulting in low flow and low fiero would fall in the lower left quadrant, with remaining quadrants following similar understandings. The framework makes use of live observation via video game-session recording of the measurable traits of physical movements heart rate monitoring and gamer self-reporting of user perceptions to evaluate the four traits of intensity, enjoyment, concentration, and collaboration. Each of these methods of measurement is discussed in the sections following, as to how they can be measured, the specific process one would follow to apply the Gaming Engagement Framework, as well as a theoretical example of the application of the model.

Figure 1. Gaming engagement framework

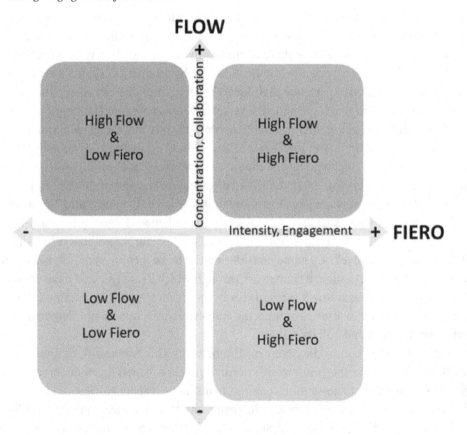

Tables 1-8 collectively illustrate framework's methods and implemention. These tables form the actual data recording and scoring mechanism instrument used during evaluation of fiero and flow. Table 1 illustrates the initialization data required, whereas Table 2 lists the physical movements measured and how to score these, Table 3 is used for scoring the heart rates recorded, Table 4 records the result of users perceptions collected and Table 5 represents the sum total of the fiero and flow scores. Results from each category are plotted over the engagement framework graph. To help with application of the framework, a process has been defined as part of the framework definition. The steps of this process are given below in the section named the Engagement Framework Process. This process provides a set of repeatable steps that guide the evaluator in using the tables to collect and record the measures as defined by the framework. An example of how the framework can be applied follows the process definition. But first, presented below, are the types of data collected and the method of collection.

Types of Data Collected

Use of selected physical traits in exercise video games have been used to assess affects on fitness (Bock et. al, 2019), and heart rate has been used to assess emotional responses associated with video games (Appelhans & Luecken, 2006). The gaming engagement framework makes use of three main instruments of data collection to predict levels of fiero and flow traits of a game: video recording of measurable traits of physical movements, heart rate monitoring, and user perceptions. Each of these three categories of instruments is dedicated to the assessment of traits attributed to either fiero or flow, with particular attention paid to fiero. Video recordings of gameplay are used to record physical reactions that suggest traits of fiero. The physical traits that this framework relies upon to measure fiero are listed in Table 1. Each of the physical reaction types listed in Table 1, along with their frequency, are determined from an analysis of a video recording of a player in a game session. Table 2 illustrates the collection of the players' heart rate during gameplay. Table 3 illustrates the collection of the players perceived perceptions of the game's intensity, enjoyment and collaboration, and concentration required. Each of the instruments of video recording, heart rate monitoring, and user perception survey is explained below.

Video Recording: Capturing Physical Movements

A video is made of the player playing the game for the purposes of capturing measurable traits of physical movements during gameplay. The game screen and the player, the entire body of player, can be viewed in the video, including articulated focus upon the player's face, including shoulders, hands and legs. Two cameras are used, one showing a side view so that the players entire body is seen from the side and one from the players rear viewing both the players monitor showing the gameplay as well as the back of users' head, hands, and body. The video records the gameplay. From these videos, the scenes are studied and data points assessed according to the measures outlined quantitatively and compiled into a data collection spreadsheet as articulated in Table 1. Points for specified observed actions are defined below. This method allows for easy reweighting of the points to refine as needed based on future case studies utilizing the framework.

The video clips are marked digitally for the physical measures of legs jerking, pumping, kicking, staining showing excitement and intense enjoyment and points are awarded for such actions. Scores are applied by points for hands slapping surfaces, legs, the players face or forehead, or other hand movements indicative of intense engagement. The number of points per type of actions is listed in Table 1. The framework allows for easy adjustment of points or addition of new indicators to be measured.

Table 1. Physical indications of Fiero

Points Possible for Physical Indications of Engagement and Intensity During Each Period	
Variable	**Point Allocation**
Legs Jerking or Pumping Excitedly	1
Hands Slapping Desk or Legs or Face	1
Jumping Up Out of Seat or Jumping Where Feet Leave Ground	2
Hands Raised Over Head in Triumph or in Frustration	2
Shouting at the Game	2
Normal Calm Play, No Excited Hand or Leg Movements	0
Bored Expressions or Stopping Play	-1

Survey of Players Perceptions

The player is given a simple questionnaire to answer after completing the game that asks the player to rank the attributes of intensity, collaboration, engagement, and concentration of the game as they perceived it to be. The framework defines collaboration as both the level of collaboration the players has with the game such as collaboration with onscreen instructions and interface interactions, as well as collaboration resulting driven by interactions with other online players or virtual players. Players are given this definition of collaboration. Players are asked to rank the level of intensity of the game in regards to how excited the game made them feel, and are asked to rank the level of mental concentration the game required. Players are also asked to rank engagement and told that while concentration levels are an aspect of a game that demands no interruptions or moments of distraction in order to keep up with the game or to even proceed in the game, to view engagement as the ability of the game to keep one interested in playing but not necessarily require intense concentration. Thus it is possible that one could have a highly engaging game but with a medium to lower demand of concentration, collaboration or intensity. These definitions are given to the player both orally and in writing as part of the survey and the player is asked to provide rankings for each. This form is illustrated in Table 2.

Table 2. Player perception survey form (player rates indications of fiero and flow)

Variable	Intensity of the Game				
	1	**2**	**3**	**4**	**5**
	Boring				Great Intensity/ Excitement
Intensity of the Game (fiero)	1	2	3	4	5
Level of Collaboration the Game Required (flow)	1	2	3	4	5
Level of Engagement the Game Required (fiero)	1	2	3	4	5
Level of Concentration the Game Required (flow)	1	2	3	4	5

Heart Rate Monitoring

A heart rate monitor is attached to the player and in preparation for the heart rate to be recorded over the specified gameplay period. For example, the average heart rate over a 15 second period, for each of 8 periods, would be recorded into the heart rate data collection table as illustrated in the sample in Table 6. Before the player begins playing the game the resting heartbeat is noted and recorded into Table 6 and used to calculate assigned points based on the heart rate recorded at the specified intervals of time during gameplay. The data to be collected and recorded during this step is as follows:

- Record resting heart rate into Table 6 before game play begins;
- At the end of game play, extract the players' heart rate data and average the heart rate over each period defined record it in Table 6.

The underlying implementation of scoring the heart rate collected is illustrated in Table 3 and described as follows:

- The heart rate is considered high range if the recorded value is 25% elevated over resting rate and 2 pts are recorded for every period it is high;
- The heart rate is considered remaining in resting range if the recorded value is less than 15% elevated over resting rate and is assigned 0 points for each such period;
- The heart rate is considered slightly elevated if the value recorded is 15% elevated over the resting recorded heart rate and 1 point is recorded for each such period.

The resting heart rate versus elevation of the gamer's heart rate at predetermined intervals throughout gameplay designates allocation of point structure that is articulated as aligned with appropriate check intervals. This is illustrated in Table 3.

Table 3. Heart rate as physiological indication of fiero

Points for Physiological Indications of Engagement and Intensity	
Point Allocation Rules	
Resting (Heart Rate)	0
Heart Rate > Resting < = 115% Resting	0
Heart Rate > 115% Resting < =125% Resting	1
Heart Rate >125% Resting	2
Max Score = (Number-of-Periods -1)* 2	

Application of the Framework

Measureable traits of physical movement, heartbeat, and user perceptions are collected into Tables 5, 6 and 7 at periodic frequency through-out a designated game play-time. Both the game play-time and period/frequency must be provided to the method before measurement collection can begin. The longer the game playtime and the more frequent/short the plot intervals, the better the prediction accuracy of fiero and flow. The pace of the game itself should determine the frequency of plotting and length of measure time.

The following engagement framework application process dictates the specific framework defined steps to follow for assessment and requires the use of Tables 4-8 for the recording of measures taken. Tables are shown filled with sample data from an example application of the framework. Excel templates implement each of these tables and they can be used to apply the process repeatedly.

The Engagement Framework Application Process

This Enagement Framework Application Process provides a set of repeatable steps that guide the evaluator in using the tables to collect and record the measures as defined by the framework. The process gives explicit instructions as to application of the framework and refers to the tables that must be filled with collected data. An example of how the framework can be applied as a result of this process follows the process steps.

Step 1: Select a game to be measured and record into the initialization table (Table 4).
Step 2: Select total game time length in minutes and record into Table 4.
Step 3: Select the period length in seconds and record into Table 3.
Step 4: Collect together Tables 5-7 to record scoring results.
Step 5: Select and set up two video recording devices to record game play from two angles.
Step 6: Attach heart rate monitor to player.
Step 7: Record the players resting heart rate into Table 6.
Step 8: Start game play and record game play for the time specified in Table 4.
Step 9: At the end of gameplay apply and record the measures as defined into Tables 5-6.
Step 10: Have user take perception survey and record results into Table 7.
Step 11: Table 8 will show the overall scores.

The process allows for multiple people scoring heartrate and video recording sessions and the results can be averaged thereby reducing bias, impartiality or other human errors that could be made in the observation and assignment of scores.

Application Through Tabular Frameworks

Table 4 illustrates the total time of game play that will be evaluated, and the number of periods in the length of play, and total play time. The total play time is divided into a number of periods for the purpose of recording the physical traits and heartbeat within each period. However, the player plays the game continuously for the total length of play specified. The sample herein shows a game play time of two minutes made up of 8 fifteen second periods. Gameplay proceeds uninterrupted for the two minutes, but data is recorded within each of the 8 periods.

Table 5 illustrates an example of data that may be recorded once extracted from the video recording of 2 minutes of game play. Data recorded is a result of the video analysis of the physical indications marked during each of the 8 periods of play. Recording of these movements are indicated in the respective row and column of Table 5. The score is calculated by the excel table according to point allocation for each movement type as defined by the framework shown in Table 1. For example, "shouting at the game "is a 2 point score for each occurrence in period. In this example this occurs in the 6th and 8th period, thus 2 appears the row under those periods. In the below example 14 is the total physical indication score, which is the sum of all movement subtotal scores shown in the column marked Total. The interpretation of the total score for physical indications of fiero are: total >43: very high level of fiero, 28 to 43: high level, 13 to 27: medium level, 2 to 12: low level, 0 to 2: no fiero.

Table 4. Framework initialization data

Variable	Data Recorded
Total Time (in minutes)	2
Time in each period (in seconds)	15
Number of Periods (auto calculated)	8

Table 5. Physical indications of engagement and intensity (application of Table 1)

Variable	Record in Corresponding Period								
	1	2	3	4	5	6	7	8	Total
Legs Jerking or Pumping Excitedly						1	1	1	3
Hands Slapping Desk or Legs or Face					1	1	1		3
Legs Jerking or Jumping Up Out of Sheet							2		2
JumpingWhere Feet Leave the Ground							2		2
Hands Raised Over Head in Triumph or Frustration									
Shouting at the game						2	2		4
Normal Calm Play, No Excited Hand or Leg Movements									
Bored Expressions or Stopping Play									
Total Score for physical indication									14

Table 6 illustrates an example of heart rate data taken before and during each of 8 periods of game play. The resting heart rate is taken before gameplay begins and recorded in the table in the first row. The example below shows 90 bpm recorded as the resting heart rate. The average heart rate is calculated within each period and recorded for that period in the table. The example shows the values recorded in each period as 90, 110, 118, 110, 120, 118,119, and 120. The excel table will automatically fill in the scores and the totals based on the scoring formulas in Table 3. The excel table calculates the score based on the scoring interpretation in Table 3. For example, in period 3 an average heart rate of 118 bpm was calculated over the 15 sec period. According to Table 3, 118bpm is greater than 125% of the resting rate of 90bpm which results in a weighted score of 2 placed in the column marked 3 (3rd period) and in the row for heart rate > 112.5. The totals are interpreted as: Total heartbeat score > than 14 indicates very high fiero, 1-14 indicate high fiero, 7-9 medium fiero, and below 6 indicates low fiero. The weighting of the scores can be easily adjusted to accommodate needed modifications based on future case studies.

Table 6. Sample heart rate data (application of Table 3)

Resting Heart Rate	Point Allocation								
90	Periods of the Game (8)								**Total**
	1	**2**	**3**	**4**	**5**	**6**	**7**	**8**	
	Heart Rate Values Recorded Per Period								
	90	110	118	110	120	119	119	120	
Scoring									
Heart Rate >90 < = 103.5	0								
Heart Rate > 103.5 < =112.5		1		1					
Heart Rate >112.5			2		2	2	2	2	
Max Score possible = 14									
Total Heartbeat Score									12

Table 7 illustrates a players ranking of their perceived levels of intensity, engagement, collaboration, and concentration of the game segment that they played. The player ranks these on a scale of 1 to 5. The totals are auto-calculated by the excel table. The method allows for easy modification of ranking choices and additional weights to accommodate future tweaking based on future case study feedback. A total score of 8 or above for Intensity + Engagement indicates high fiero, and totals of 8 to 10 of collaboration + concentration indicate a high level of flow. A total value of 2 and below would indicate low fiero or flow, and totals in the midrange indicate medium levels. The more players assessed within the same game the more reliable the results.

Table 7. Survey of players perception of the game's attributes (Application of Table 2)

Variable	Scale					Total
	1	**2**	**3**	**4**	**5**	
	Low				Very High	
Level of Intensity of the Game				4		
Level of Engagement the Game Required					4	
Total Perceived Fiero: Intensity + Engagement						8
Level of Collaboration the Game Required					5	
Level of Concentration the Game Required					5	
Total Perceived Flow: Collaboration + Concentration						10
Total Combined						18

Table 8 shows the overall total score of fiero and flow utilizling the heart rate, user perception and physical movement instruments. Overall totals greater than 50 indicate very high fiero and flow, 39 to 49 indicate high levels, 20 to 27 indicate only medium levels and score under 20 indicate low levels. Table 8 shows an overall total score of 44, which indicates a high level of fiero and flow.

Table 8. Scoring final levels for fiero and flow

Level of Fiero and Flow
Physical Movement Total Score 14
Heart Rate Total Score 12
User Survey Total Score 18
Overall Total Score* (44) → (10 25 * 45 55 70)
Fiero and Flow Scale low very high

Collectively, Tables 4-8 show a theoretical example of the application of framework following the Engagement Framework Application Process, with data recorded over a game time of 2 minutes using eight 15-second periods. During each of the periods the data is recorded with respect to video recording of physical movements, recording of heart rate, and survey of user perceptions, and using these results, a final overall score is produced that indicates levels of fiero and flow.

Areas for Further Research

The Gaming Engagement Framework is one method of evaluating levels of intensity, engagement, collaboration and concentration leading to fiero and flow within online competitive gaming environments. The Gaming Engagement Framework offers an opportunity to evaluate gaming environments through innumerable gamer experiences with a specific focus upon fiero and how one can begin to measure this trait. Each of the areas of assessment could be expanded upon with further traits identified for analysis and included into an expanded set of measures. An additional consideration is the differentiation of each gamer's reach towards levels of flow and fiero within differentiated gaming environments. Regarding the issues of gaming benefits, research is needed to determine if people experience lasting significant improvements to their social or cognitive health by gaming. Such would require original research in a multi-discipline approach, including disciplines such as software, gaming, biology, bio-physiology, neurology, psychology, kinesiology, and others. As to the benefits of using gaming to enhance learning, exploration is needed in the application of gaming to the improvement of methods that would benefit changing and adapting pedagogy for adult learners (Crawford, White, & Wallace, 2019).

CONCLUSION

Using the presented framework and its supporting methods as described it is possible to measure perceived intensity and engagement levels leading to fiero, and concentration and collaboration levels leading to flow, giving an overall prediction of the level of fiero and flow that the game is capable of delivering. The use of both quantitative and qualitative data in this framework offers a mixed methods approach towards discovery of both weak and strong areas of fiero and flow as along with a collection of literal user perceptions. Evaluating the online competitive gaming products by this standard offers the game/product developer, tester and end user an evaluative tool through which to potentially evaluate the outcomes desired by the gaming experience. This framework can be applied at the prototyping phase during game development as well as at incrementally advancing levels of product development through pre and post production. Given the benefits of online competitive gaming, it is clear that the game itself must impart significant levels of both fiero and flow to achieve these benefits at their fullest. Fiero, is particularly important, as it appears to contribute more to enjoyment than flow with its high levels of intensity and engagement which are the prerequisites for high levels of fiero.

REFERENCES

Appelhans, B., & Luecken, L. (2006). Heart rate variability as an index of regulated emotional responding. *Review of General Psychology*, *10*(3), 229–240. doi:10.1037/1089-2680.10.3.229

Baig, E. C. (2019, May 9). Video games are a 'great equalizer' for people with disabilities. *USA Today*. Retrieved from https://www.usatoday.com/story/tech/2019/05/09/passionate-vi deo-gamers-dont-let-their-disabilities-stop-them/3661312002/

Baumann, N., Lürig, C., & Engeser, S. (2016). Flow and enjoyment beyond skill-demand balance: The role of game pacing curves and personality. *Motivation and Emotion*, *40*(4), 507–519. doi:10.100711031-016-9549-7

Bock, B. C., Dunsiger, S. I., Ciccolo, J. T., Serber, E. R., Wu, W. C., Tilkemeier, P., ... Marcus, B. H. (2019, April). Exercise videogames, physical activity, and health: Wii heart fitness: A randomized clinical trial. *American Journal of Preventive Medicine*, *56*(4), 501–511. doi:10.1016/j.amepre.2018.11.026 PMID:30777705

Borderie, J., & Michinov, N. (2016). Identifying Flow in Video Games: Towards a New Observation-Based Method. *International Journal of Gaming and Computer-Mediated Simulations*, *8*(8), 19–38. doi:10.4018/IJGCMS.2016070102

Calongne, C., Stricker, A. G., Truman, B., & Arenas, F. J. (2019). Cognitive Apprenticeship for Teaching Computer Science and Leadership in Virtual Worlds. In A. G. Stricker, C. Calongne, B. Truman, & F. J. Arenas' (Eds.), *Recent Advances in Applying Identity and Society Awareness to Virtual Learning* (pp. 180–200). IGI Global. doi:10.4018/978-1-5225-9679-0.ch010

Chen, J. (2007). Flow in games (and everything else). *Communications of the ACM*, *50*(4), 31–34. doi:10.1145/1232743.1232769

Craik, F. I., & Lockhart, R. S. (1972). Levels of processing: A framework for memory research. *Journal of Verbal Learning and Verbal Behavior*, *11*(6), 671–684. doi:10.1016/S0022-5371(72)80001-X

Crawford, C., White, S., & Wallace, J. (2019). Rethinking Pedagogy, Andragogy, and Heutagogy. *Academic Exchange Quarterly*, *22*(4), 4–10.

Csikszentmihalyi, M. (1975/2000). *Beyond boredom and anxiety: Experiencing flow in work and play*. San Francisco: Jossey-Bass.

Csíkszentmihályi, M. (1990). *Flow: The Psychology of Optimal Experience*. New York: Harper and Row.

Csíkszentmihályi, M. (1996). *Creativity: Flow and the Psychology of Discovery and Invention*. New York: Harper Perennial.

Csíkszentmihályi, M. (1998). *Finding Flow: The Psychology of Engagement With Everyday Life*. New York: Basic Books.

Csikszentmihalyi, M. (2008). *Flow: The Psychology of Optimal Experience*. New York, US: Harper Perennial Modern Classics.

DeMarco, T., & Lister, T. (1987). *Peopleware: Productive Projects and Teams*. New York: Dorset House Publication.

DeMarco, T., & Lister, T. (1999). *Peopleware: Productive Projects and Teams* (2nd ed.). New York: Dorset House Publication.

Dixon, D. H., & Christison, M. (2018). The Usefulness of Massive Multiplayer Online Role Playing Games (MMORPGs) as Tools for Promoting Second Language Acquisition. In J. Perren, K. Kelch, J. Byun, J. Cervantes, & S. Safavi (Eds.), *Applications of CALL Theory in ESL and EFL Environments* (pp. 244–268). Hershey, PA: IGI Global. doi:10.4018/978-1-5225-2933-0.ch014

Hasbro. (2020). *Scrabble*. Retrieved from https://scrabble.hasbro.com/en-us

Hoeft, F., Watson, C. L., Kesler, S. R., Bettinger, K. E., & Reiss, A. L. (2007). Gender differences in the mesocorticolimbic system during computer gameplay. *Journal of Psychiatric Research*, 42(4), 253–258. . doi:10.1016/j.jpsychires.2007.11.010 PMID:18194807

Keller, J., Bless, H., Bloman, F., & Kleinb'ohl, D. (2011). Physiological aspects of flow experiences: Skills-demand-compatibility effects on heart rate variability and salivary cortisol. *Journal of Experimental Social Psychology*, 47(4), 849–852. doi:10.1016/j.jesp.2011.02.004

Liljedahl, P. (2016). *Flow: A framework for discussing teaching*. Retrieved from http://www.peterliljedahl.com/wp-content/uploads/PME-2016-Flow-and-Teaching-1.pdf

Logan, B. (n.d.). Video game usability testing-factors to consider. *Spotless Interactive*. Retrieved from https://www.spotless.co.uk/insights/video-game-usability-testing/

McGonigal, J. (2011). *Reality Is Broken, Why Games Make Us Better and How They Can Change the World*. New York: Penguin Press. Retrieved from http://dutchlarpplatform.subcultures.nl/wp-content/uploads/2014/10/Reality-Is-Broken-Why-Games-Make-Us-Better-and-How-They-Can-Change-the-World-2011.pdf

Nardi, B., & Harris, J. (2006, November). 2006 Strangers and Friends: Collaborative Play in World of Warcraft. In *Proceedings of the 2006 20th Anniversary Conference on Computer Supported Cooperative Work* (pp. 149–158). ACM.

Peterson, M. (2010). Massively Multiplayer online role-playing games (MMORPGs) as arenas for language learning. *Computer Assisted Language Learning*, 23(5), 429–439. doi:10.1080/09588221.2010.520673

Peterson, M. (2016). The use of massively multiplayer online role-playing games in CALL: An analysis of research. *Computer Assisted Language Learning*, 29(7), 1–14. doi:10.1080/09588221.2016.1197949

Salt, J. D. (1993). Keynote address: Simulation should be easy and fun! In G. W. Evans, M. Mollaghasemi, E. C. Russell, & W. E. Biles (Eds.), *Proceedings of the 1993 Winter Simulation Conference*. Retrieved from https://www.researchgate.net/profile/John_Salt/publication/221525149_Simulation_should_be_easy_and_fun/links/56636d2008ae418a786bb19c.pdf

Schachter, S., & Singer, J. (1962). Cognitive, social, and physiological determinants of emotional state. *Psychological Review*, *69*(5), 379–399. doi:10.1037/h0046234 PMID:14497895

Schmidt, S., Gnam, J.-P., Kopf, M., Rathgeber, T., & Woll, A. (2020). The Influence of Cortisol, Flow, and Anxiety on Performance in E-Sports: A Field Study. *BioMed Research International*, *2020*, 1–6. doi:10.1155/2020/9651245 PMID:32076623

Sharritt, M., & Suthers, D. D. (2011). Levels of Failure and Learning in Games. *International Journal of Gaming and Computer-Mediated Simulations*, *3*(4), 54–69. doi:10.4018/jgcms.2011100104

Snodgrass, J. G., Lacy, M. G., Dengah, H. F. II, Batchelder, G., Eisenhower, S., & Thompson, R. S. (2016). Culture and the jitters: Guild affiliation and online gaming eustress/distress. *Ethos (Berkeley, Calif.)*, *44*(1), 50–78. doi:10.1111/etho.12108

Stromberg, P. (2009). *Caught in Play: How Entertainment Works on You*. Palo Alto, CA: Stanford University Press.

Takatalo, J., Häkkinen, J., Kaistinen, J., & Nyman, G. (2010). Presence, Involvement, and Flow in Digital Games. In R. Bernhaupt (Ed.), *Evaluating User Experience in Games*. London: Springer; doi:10.1007/978-1-84882-963-3_3

Tozman, T., Zhang, Y. Y., & Vollmeyer, R. (2017). Inverted U-shaped function between flow and cortisol release during chess play. *Journal of Happiness Studies*, *18*(1), 247–268. doi:10.100710902-016-9726-0

This research was previously published in the International Journal of Gaming and Computer-Mediated Simulations (IJGCMS), 12(1); pages 28-42, copyright year 2020 by IGI Publishing (an imprint of IGI Global).

Chapter 17
Persona–Scenarios in Game Development:
Communication Tensions Between Hearing Aid Users and Communication Partners

Harshada Patel

https://orcid.org/0000-0003-0175-1431

University of Nottingham, UK

Madeline J. Hallewell

https://orcid.org/0000-0002-2710-2176

University of Nottingham, UK

ABSTRACT

The 3D Tune-In project developed serious/leisure game applications to educate hearing aid (HA) users about how HA functionalities could improve hearing in different sound environments. The application development team had little prior experience catering for end-users with hearing loss. HA users and their communication partner were consulted regarding their communication difficulties and communication strategies in different environments. Participants reported many hearing problems, affective issues, problems with their HA, tensions in their relationship caused by hearing issues, and they noted a need for training in how best to use HAs. Persona-scenarios were created outlining user needs and goals and a user-requirements table detailed how end-users might interact with proposed applications, both of which were presented to developers during the initial application design period. Game developers identified that these resources positively influenced the development of their application. They were able to produce a useful and useable application for their new target user.

DOI: 10.4018/978-1-6684-7589-8.ch017

INTRODUCTION

Some of the most challenging outcomes of hearing loss (HL) are the extent to which it can affect people's ability to form and maintain interpersonal relationships and engage in meaningful/effective conversation, consequently straining existing relationships (Erber & Scherer, 1999; Heffernan, Coulson, Henshaw, Barry, & Ferguson, 2016; Heine & Browning, 2004; Preminger, Montano, & Tjørnhøj-Thomsen, 2015). The effectiveness and quality of communication between a person with HL and someone without is greatly affected by contextual factors such as type of environment, background noise and room echo as well as individual characteristics and behaviour (e.g. accents, facing each other when communicating etc.) and desired activities (Erber & Scherer, 1999; Hasan, Lai, Chipara, & Wu, 2013). Some environmental factors may constrain communication by influencing which strategies can be used to facilitate hearing; for example, people cannot face each other when travelling in a car.

The use of hearing aids (HAs) plays a significant role in the ability of those with HL to communicate (Guerra-Zúñiga, Cardemil-Morales, Albertz-Arévalo, & Rahal-Espejo, 2014). Achievement of a good fitting and post-fitting support are positively associated with HA use (Laplante-Lévesque, Dons Jensen, Dawes, & Nielsen, 2013; Solheim, Kværner, Sandvik, & Falkenberg, 2012). However, proper fitting and calibration of standard HAs is notoriously challenging to achieve, given the inherent differences in the nature of each acoustic context. Sound contexts may be subject to continuous change (e.g. the noise levels of a café may change depending on the number of people present and their activities), and the specific needs of HA users may vary (e.g. whether they want to converse or just listen) (Kuk, Bulow, Damsgaard, & Ludvigsen, 2004). Thus the HA fitting and calibration process is long-winded, requiring many audiologist appointments to allow HA users to 'test' the performance of their HA in different real-world sound contexts and discuss their experiences with the audiologist, who may then re-calibrate the HAs and conduct further assessment. Although some HAs allow users to change settings directly in different environments, Keidser et al. (2005) advise that only a subset of people with HL are viable candidates for these HAs, as their use requires a high level of understanding of both the limitations of their own hearing and also about what the settings do in each environment. Indeed, Laplante-Lévesque et al. (2013) identified that lack of knowledge about the functionalities of HAs resulted in sub-optimal HA use: many HA users leave their HA on the default setting, which is insufficient for hearing well in certain situations (de Graaff et al., 2018).

It is suggested that the HA user's satisfaction with their HA might be, to some extent, related to their level of social support (Singh, Lau, & Pichora-Fuller, 2015). Communication partners may, in some cases, be better placed to identify and objectively describe their partner's particular difficulties in different settings (Schulz et al., 2017). Research focusing on the frequent communication partners of people who wear HAs acknowledges the role of both parties in contributing to the psychosocial wellbeing (through effective communication) of each other (Barker, Leighton, & Ferguson, 2017; Brooks, Hallam, & Mellor, 2001; Erber & Scherer, 1999; Heine & Browning, 2004; Kamil & Lin, 2015; Lazzarotto et al., 2016; Manchaiah, Stephens, & Lunner, 2013; Preminger et al., 2015; Scarinci, Worrall, & Hickson, 2008; Vas, Akeroyd, & Hall, 2017). Communication partners may have learnt strategies to help facilitate conversations with someone with HL/HA users (Caissie & Gibson, 1997; Echalier, 2010; Manchaiah et al., 2013), but they may find it difficult to understand their partner's experience of HL or the effect of additional factors such as HA use, background noise and fatigue (Echalier, 2010). Communication partners may also experience fatigue in social interactions due to the additional effort required to converse with the person with HL (Vas et al., 2017). Both partners commonly experience frustration with the type and quality of communication and consequently both are at risk of feeling lonely and isolated (Echalier, 2010; Vas et al., 2017). Furthermore, the use of certain avoidance strategies, such as avoiding group situations or noisy restaurants or inviting friends to their home rather than going out, restricts not only the social experiences of the person with HL, but also of their communication partner (Echalier, 2010).

Our study was conducted within the context of an EU-funded project, 3D Tune-In (http://3d-tune-in.eu/). The goals of the project were to help people with hearing difficulties to correctly understand and use the available (yet often neglected) functionalities of their HA in everyday situations to improve their hearing, as well as increase empathy for HA users in those without HL (Eastgate, Picinali, Patel, & D'Cruz, 2016). As the majority of HAs on the market today (especially state funded) do not allow users to make changes to the calibrations of the HA, the project took a gamification approach, using a 3D binaural virtual environment and a Virtual Hearing Aid (VHA) to teach users how to improve their own experiences with HAs. In this way, users could make changes to the VHA in order to assess the difference made to their hearing without risk of making changes to their own HA which has been calibrated by their audiologist.

The innovative aspect of this project concerns the focus on enabling users to learn about their HA functionalities through exploring what effect these changes have in different realistic environments. The overall aim was for educating HA users such that if they were able to access customizable HA devices, they would be better informed about what changes they need to make in each setting, enabling them to make the adjustments more quickly. Dahl, Linander, and Hanssen (2014) proposed a similar solution involving a tabletop simulator used by the audiologist and their client in the clinician's office, which proved to be effective in helping HA users to better describe their problems in certain sound environments and improved the abilities of both parties to understand each other. However, the use-at-home service proposed in the 3D Tune-In project might suit the needs of HA users for learning to use their HA better than clinic based techniques such as that proposed by Dahl et al. (2014), or standard tutorials with clinicians in a clinical environment, which can easily be forgotten after leaving the clinic. Indeed, it is suggested that even where extensive HA "orientation" is offered, a significant number of HA users (40%) still report a lack of confidence in using their HAs (Kelly et al., 2013).

Three digital serious game applications (apps) (described below) were developed for adult HA users, which were built around a VHA which can be calibrated for the user's particular HL (Cuevas-Rodriguez et al., 2017). Across all of the apps, the VHA performs the same functions as a real HA, meaning that the user can remove their HA and use headphones. Within the apps, users are required to re-calibrate the VHA to improve their hearing in the different app contexts that simulate a real-life sound environment such as a busy restaurant or street. Users interact with the VHA similarly to how they might adjust settings on their mobile device or computer. In this way, users can experiment with different settings to learn more about how the different functionalities of HAs work in different environments, for example how changes to directivity might improve hearing in background noise. The apps are as follows:

- Play&Tune (Company 1): this app contains a number of game scenarios in which users are asked to identify either the location of a noise within the 3D space, for example a buzzing mosquito in a living room, or to identify the word(s) spoken in a noisy scenario, for example a waiter repeating an order in a busy restaurant. If the player doesn't hear well, they can adjust the built-in VHA until they can hear the stimulus sounds.

- Musiclarity (Company 2): this web application is a music rehabilitation service which allows users to change properties of music in order to improve their experience of music, for example increasing the vocals whilst reducing the bass sounds, or changing the directionality within the 3D space to hear the music from different directions. The app also guides users through the process of adjusting the functionalities of a HA to hear music better through utilising the built-in VHA.

- AudGam Pro (Company 3): this app is part of a software package designed to be used during hearing assessments and HA fitting by audiologists and their clients together. As users explore and carry out hearing tasks in virtual environments, audiologists are able to assess their hearing in a realistic environment, and users are able to assess the different calibrations made to the VHA by the audiologist in order to consider how these changes will affect their hearing in the real world.

A full description of each app is included in a public deliverable (see Hrafnkelsson & Levtov, 2017). The app developers did not have any prior experience of creating such apps for people with HL. As such, our research aim was to help them to understand the contexts in which people wear their HAs and how useful they find them, the hearing and communication challenges they experience in their daily activities in different acoustic and social situations, and the strategies they use with their communication partner to cope in these situations. Finally, we also wanted developers to understand the psychological impact of HL so that they could empathise with their new user-group.

MATERIALS AND METHODS

Data collection was carried out in two stages. Our approach was to first elicit user needs and goals through conducting paired interviews with HA users and one of their family members or friends with whom they communicate regularly. These interviews were carried out during the first seven months of the three-year project. HA users also completed a questionnaire. This approach provided an opportunity to gain an understanding of how HA users and communication partners experience their interactions in different everyday situations. This understanding was subsequently presented to the developers using persona-scenarios and user-requirements documents in order to assist the developers' vision for their apps and guide their development.

At the end of the project, once the apps had been released, we sought feedback from developers on the extent to which the persona-scenario and user-requirements information had aided the development of their app. Interviews were conducted with senior developers in order to capture their reflections on the way in which the information presented had helped or hindered the development of their app. The two aims for this paper are therefore as follows:

1) to identify problems and challenges faced by HA users and their communication partners in order to communicate this information to developers in such a way as to focus their efforts in developing apps;

2) to evaluate the effectiveness of the way that this information was presented to developers in giving them a clear idea of the target users of their apps.

Part 1: Persona-Scenario Development

Participants

Fifteen HA users (six females and nine males, aged 18+) from three countries (UK, Spain and Italy) participated in this study. In the age group 19-40, there were four pairs of HA user and communication partner, six pairs in the 41-60 age group and five pairs in the 61+ age group. Recruitment of participants in the UK was through personal communications and was assisted by a retirement village; recruitment and organisation of interviews in Spain was assisted by the Fundación Andaluza Accesibilidad y Personas Sordas; and recruitment, organisation and interviews in Italy were carried out by the University of Padova and the hearing association Ente Nazionale Sordi.

The recruitment criteria stipulated that participants must have mild to severe HL and be users of HAs (not cochlear implants or other devices which require surgery). All HA users had at least two years of experience with wearing HAs. There were many different causes of HL, including perforated eardrums, severe ear infections, ageing, nerve damage and surgery, varying in severity and the affected ear(s).

HA users were requested to recruit a communication partner (who did not have hearing difficulties) to participate with them in an interview. This partner was someone that the HA user communicated with on a regular basis, for example a spouse, friend, carer or their offspring. Demographic details were not collected from communication partners.

Method and Procedure

Participants were asked to attend the interview with their chosen communication partner. Prior to the interview, participants with HL completed a demographics questionnaire which also covered aspects related to their HL such as affected ear(s), length of time using HAs, and their self-rated quality of hearing whilst using their HA. During the interview, participants were asked questions according to a structured interview schedule and their responses were audio recorded. Participants were asked questions related to being in their home environment and were asked to choose one other context that was important to them from the following: shopping (n=2 pairs); restaurant/café/bar (n=7); cinema (n=0); walking along a busy road (n=2); or a travel/transport context (n=4).

The interviews were approximately 60-90 minutes in duration. For each context, the questions were focused on their experiences when the person with HL wears their HA(s). Areas of questioning for HA users concerned how often and how important the context was to them, specific details surrounding the performance of their HA in this context, their satisfaction with their communication and social practices, and whether they need more training in using their HA in this context. Questions directed at communication partners covered any adaptations they have made to be able to communicate in the context, what kind of difficulties they experience, and whether they had learned anything new about the HA user during the interview. Participants also were asked questions about their strategies to cope with hearing challenges in a particular context, a number of prompt cards were given as examples, and participants were encouraged to discuss these strategies along with any other strategies they use. Examples of prompts are as follows:

- I change the setting(s) of my HA(s);
- I ask the person to repeat what they said;
- I pretend to understand.

Writing the Persona-Scenarios and User-Requirements

The interviews and questionnaires generated a considerable amount of data, and presenting all of this data to the developers would have resulted in delays in the development process. On the other hand, presenting simply a table of user-requirements would have removed opportunities for developers to build an understanding of the target user group, which was one of the project aims. Persona-scenarios were selected as an effective means of condensing the information into an engaging and immediately understandable format, whilst providing an explanation for subsequent user-requirements.

There are many guidelines for writing personas and scenarios (e.g. Jacobs, Dreessen, & Pierson, 2008; Johansson & Messeter, 2005), although Madsen and Nielsen (2010) argue that a strong set of guidelines for using the methodology and creating persona-scenarios is still not established. The following basic requirements for persona-scenarios were followed in the present study: that the problems are described in a concrete and detailed manner; the problem should be presented in the beginning of the persona-scenario; design scenarios should have a happy ending; and the persona-scenario should include the use of the future system/product that is being designed (Madsen & Nielsen, 2010, p. 64). Crucially, the information contained must be based on user data.

The authors, who were researchers acting independently of the app development team, were jointly responsible for writing the persona-scenarios. For quantitative data (from the questionnaires), it was possible to use means and modes to represent the responses in order to build parts of the persona-scenarios, for example mean number of years with a hearing impairment and mean level of satisfaction with their HAs. For qualitative (interview) data an approach similar to a grounded theory analysis was taken, in which commonalities were sought between responses to questions within the structured categories of the interview schedule, i.e. the quality of their hearing with HAs, their problems in certain situations and strategies that the used to communicate well together etc. Exemplar cases were selected to appear in the persona-scenario in order to highlight common issues. Additionally, given the narrative, story-like nature of persona-scenarios, it was possible to select atypical cases of interest which would convey issues that may not have previously been considered by app designers. It was possible to present unique persona-scenarios that communicate both typical and atypical issues in order that game designers could consider how their applications and technologies can provide an inclusive experience for HA users and their communication partners/community. Further explanations and examples of the persona-scenarios developed for this project are described in (Patel et al., 2016).

The persona-scenarios were then synthesized into a user-requirements table (see table 1). In this table, the key details were set out as task requirements for the apps such as the nature of the background noise in each scenario (e.g. people talking, music, kitchen appliances and so on); the characteristics of the task and some examples of sound environments such as in a restaurant, living room, one-to-one conversations and so on. Each developer could then use this standard table as a basis for developing their ideas, which would be derived directly from user needs, but guided by their own priorities and interests. The process of creating this table involved identifying the problems that were included in the persona-scenarios and breaking these problems down into individual components. For example, in Figure 2, Jay finds it difficult to follow group conversations when he goes shopping because the announcements and other noises stop him hearing what he needs to hear. The suggested task would be to have a group conversation in a supermarket and the background noise would be the announcements, music and talking. The characteristics were elicited from considering the range of difficulties mentioned in the persona-scenarios. In this example, it would be understanding sequential speech and overlapping speech. Some further examples are provided in table 1.

Part 2: Developer Feedback on the Use of Persona-Scenarios as a Route to User-Requirements

A second aim of the study was to establish the value that the persona-scenarios and user-requirements added to the app development process. Senior developers from the three gaming/app companies involved in the project were interviewed by phone. The documents were re-sent to them prior to the interview to serve as a reminder of the information they had received. A structured interview schedule was used to gain feedback on the persona-scenarios and user-requirements. Developers were asked what they knew about HL and HAs before starting the project, and whether the development of their app had benefitted from using the user-requirements elicitation process. They were also asked whether the information was presented in a suitable format and whether they required any additional information in the initial stage of development.

Ethics approval for the both parts of the study was granted by the Faculty of Engineering at The University of Nottingham and by The University of Malaga. In line with local practices, no formal ethics approval was sought in Italy. However, researchers adhered to the procedures set out by the UK research team. The end-user interview protocol was originally developed in English and was translated into Spanish and Italian. Developer interviews were carried out in English and Italian, and were transcribed in English. Participants gave written informed consent prior to data collection.

Results

Persona-Scenarios

The persona-scenarios featured representative target users from the three age-groups of adult participants: 19-40, 41-60 and 61+. They detail typical HA use, limitations and challenges that people from each age group face in their daily activities and in their communication with others. They include personal information about the character, such as specific age, length of time wearing HAs, occupation, hobbies, experience with digital games and daily activities. They also contain information about the communication partner, such as age, occupation, interests, hearing status and relationship to the HA user (see Figure 1 for an excerpt[1]). Strategies mentioned by both the HA user and communication partners were also included for the home environment, and another context was chosen for each persona-scenario (see Figure 2 for an example).

The persona-scenarios also describe the initial ideas behind each of the three apps, including: gamification elements (e.g. reward mechanisms, gaming levels, estimated length of time taken to get through different levels); user interface requirements; interaction tools; game design (e.g. tasks to demonstrate functionalities, those to teach people how to calibrate their HA to meet the demands of a particular situation, or tasks to simulate hearing impairments to educate the general public about the challenges faced by those who are hard of hearing); and different acoustic environments (e.g. home, restaurant/café or walking along a busy road). They also detail the targeted age-group, the training goals of each app, a preliminary description of the tasks users will need to perform in the apps and how using the app will help them achieve transferable benefits (see Figure 3 for an excerpt). For this stage, it was important that game designers had already generated a concrete idea of their app in order to provide a supporting scaffold for further design work (Khaled & Vasalou, 2014). Once these details had been provided, their game was matched up to a persona-scenario of a HA user and their communication partner. This enabled the creation of scenarios in which the person appearing as the persona has used the game and has reached their goals or solved their problems related to communication.

Figure 1. Example of a persona-scenario of a 41-60 year old HA user

Domenico and Audrey

Domenico is 45 years old. He has had a hearing impairment for 10 years and has worn his current, state-provided hearing aids in both ears for 3 years. He has age-related moderate, high frequency hearing loss which was also a result of listening to loud music.

Domenico's hobbies are walking, watching TV, listening to music, running and he is in the Army Reserves. At work, he is responsible for providing customer services in a large workshop which has a lot of loud machinery.

Domenico uses his hearing aids for 9-16 hours per day and is motivated to wear them. His hearing is good with his hearing aids and he thinks they improve his hearing a lot. However he isn't satisfied with his hearing aids when taking part in his hobbies, sports and other interests, as in some environments they work well but in others he really struggles. Domenico doesn't have a problem with following a conversation with one person at home but does struggle to have a group conversation. He finds he has to look at Audrey and she will help him. Overall he is grateful for the hearing aids but he wishes they could be better and more flexible.

Domenico's wife, Audrey, is 43 years old; they have been married for 20 years. She works in Human Resources and her hobbies include walking, running and badminton and she is also in the Army Reserves. She doesn't have a hearing impairment. Domenico and Audrey have 2 children.

Audrey finds communication difficult if she is not in the same room as Domenico as he won't hear her, even with his hearing aids in. She has to find where he is in order to talk to him, which is frustrating as sometimes it would be easier to just shout to each other. Audrey also finds it difficult to act as the middle person when their children talk to him and he doesn't hear them. He'll look to her to explain but she doesn't always pass on all of the conversation.

User-Requirements Table

The persona-scenario information was condensed into a table of suggested tasks for developers to select and modify according to their preferences. Table 1 displays some examples of the suggested tasks.

Figure 2. Example of strategies used by the HA user and communication partner whilst out shopping

Jay and Steven: shopping

Jay goes to the shops 2 or 3 times a week. He doesn't particularly like shopping but it is a necessary task. He always wears his hearing aids when shopping as he cannot go anywhere without them. He is mostly satisfied with his hearing aids when out shopping but finds that background noise stops him from hearing conversations. The noises of speakers/announcements in shopping centres are particularly annoying.

He thinks that other people find it difficult to communicate with him when out shopping although they do try their best if they are aware of his problems. If people don't speak distinctly he tends to switch off from the conversation and if he is shopping with a group of people he can only concentrate on one conversation at a time. Indeed, Jay prefers people to speak one at a time because otherwise their speech jumbles together. As much as possible, Jay tends to avoid having conversations with others when he is shopping as it is so difficult to follow them. Jay relies on body language and asking people to repeat what they have said when out shopping.

Steven finds that he has to get closer to Jay when out shopping because otherwise Jay will not hear what he is saying to him over the background noise. Steven appreciates Jay's problems so although he would like to go shopping with Jay more often, he understands if Jay doesn't want to.

Jay has tried the loop in some shops but finds that it is not worth the bother. Jay finds it particularly difficult to communicate with the cashier; he understands most of what cashiers say to him except sometimes he can't hear them telling him the cost of what he is buying. He also finds it difficult to hear the cashier when he or she looks away from him so he would ask them to repeat what they have said. Cashiers and other people can help him by speaking more loudly and speaking face-to-face with him. Steven finds that he has to be close to Jay if he wants to talk to him and he tries to be face-to-face with Jay and raises his voice if he needs to speak to him when out shopping.

This table also included some coping strategies that were identified from the persona-scenarios that could be included in the app, such as asking characters to repeat themselves or repositioning themselves, and examples of the kinds of feedback users would require, such as asking the user if they can hear any distortions in the sounds they are hearing.

Developer Feedback on the Persona-Scenarios

Developers were interviewed at the end of the project to establish whether the persona-scenarios and user-requirements table had had an impact on the direction of their app development. Two of the developers reported that although they typically involve end-users in the development of the products, their involvement is informal and comes later in the process once a prototype is available. They typically elicit feedback from people close to them for example family and friends. One developer had worked

Figure 3. Example of a persona-scenario in which a HA user engages with the proposed app

Future scenario: Play&Tune

Jay is 68 years old and has a hearing impairment. During a recent appointment with his audiologist, Jay was told about a game called Play&Tune that could teach him how to calibrate a virtual hearing aid in different situations to improve his hearing.

Jay had never played computer games before and had no interest in them. His audiologist assured him that Play&Tune was not a typical video game, rather it was more of a training application with some simple elements of gaming, such as scoring points for progress. She told him that there was nothing complicated for him to install and that the game was easy to use even for older adults. He was given a flyer about the 3D Tune-In project which included details of a weblink to access the game.

When Jay got back home, he decided to try the game while he felt motivated. The 3D Tune-In flyer said that he could play the game on a touchscreen smart phone or on a tablet and that he could use typical touch gestures to control the game play and the game menu. He decided to play it on his iPad as it was easier for him to see things on a bigger screen. He typed in the weblink in the Safari browser and he arrived at the first page of the game.

He was told that he needed to wear headphones to experience a series of virtual scenes such as a restaurant with lots of people talking around him, or a noisy street, or a cinema and so on. He was told that he would experience 'wearing' a virtual hearing aid rather than his own hearing aid. He would have to change the settings of his virtual hearing aid in the different virtual contexts in order to hear more clearly.

with companies who had examined simple demographic information to build up profiles of the target audience, including information such as age, employment and wage bracket.

All developers therefore experienced this method of eliciting detailed user-requirements for the first time within this project. It was hoped that by providing more comprehensive information to them, they could gain a more extensive understanding of the challenges of the target population.

Prior Knowledge of HA Users

With the exception of one of the developers, most had not had any previous experience of developing apps for HA users and as such had limited knowledge of the specific issues faced by this population:

Interviewer: What did you know about HAs and HL before 3D Tune-In?

Table 1. Example tasks from the user-requirements table

Task	Background noise	Characteristics	Description or example scenarios
Individual speech	Talking and announcements	Normal speed and volume	Train station Airport
		Quickly	
		Quietly	
		Quickly and quietly	
Group conversation	Music	Sequential speech	Kitchen with radio on, living room with TV on
		Overlapping speech	
Localisation (source cannot be seen)	Estimating position, crowd noise	Single person shouting	This section is about hearing where sounds are coming from if the user cannot see them, as opposed to understanding speech.
		Non-speech source	
Music listening	Crowd noise	Understanding lyrics	Pop/rock song
		Differentiating instruments	Guitar from violin
		Hearing high frequency instruments	Violin
		Hearing mid frequency instruments	Cello
		Hearing low frequency instruments	Bass guitar
		Hearing quiet instruments	Harp

Company 1: Very little, no prior knowledge specifically about HAs at all really... I certainly can't remember going into it with any insight.

One developer had familiarity with HA users but had never developed an app for this population:

I have a lot of family with HL and I knew since I was a child how difficult it was to communicate with them. I knew about HAs – my family had used devices for a very long time – my uncle had used devices since he was very young. I've known about issues since I was very young and understood issues with stigma. I know new devices are smaller and can hide it in a better way. (Company 2)

Positive Impact of the Persona-Scenario Information

Mostly the feedback regarding the persona-scenarios was positive, and confirmed that the information was beneficial to the app development process by helping them to understand the target audience:

I wasn't aware that HA users just don't listen to much music. So there were those basic issues around it that made us think a bit more carefully... We probably had a more complicated idea in our heads to begin with than was necessary... the fact that HA users often just don't listen to any music because they just don't enjoy it any more, that was a revelation to us. (Company 1)

This developer described a scenario in which they discovered that some HA users do not listen to music. It was decided that their original idea would not address a very basic need of HA users to examine how they could start to enjoy music through changing HA settings. Another developer found the persona-scenarios useful to start off their design ideas:

We found that the [persona-scenarios] were an essential starting point for the design of the app…It has been challenging to understand the needs of people that live with such a disability. It was challenging indeed, but it [persona-scenarios] ended up being very useful as it allowed us to ultimately develop something useful and usable. (Company 3)

Learning

It was clear that the developers had learned about the target population from the user-requirements information and the project as a whole:

Somewhere along the process we realised there are far more fundamental things to be fixed about HA users experiences…It [the original app idea] was not even right for the demographic. That idea was not appropriate for them. (Company 1)

The most important thing is that people don't know how technology can improve their life. When 3D Tune-In started I thought HL is just a disability – I didn't know it's full of circumstances, variations, audiologists – it's a very big world. (Company 2)

Here, the developers particularly valued the contextual information provided by the persona-scenarios.

Challenges and Suggestions for Improvement

When asked about the format of the persona-scenarios in particular, it was evident that the volume of information presented was not ideal for two of the developers:

Sometimes there was so much information – to manage it wasn't easy. (Company 2)

In some cases, was a bit too verbose. (Company 3)

Whilst the others enjoyed the format, they would have benefitted from a wider target population/ user-groups:

More input from people who have done prior things to do with music and HL. (Company 1)

One developer suggested they might have benefitted from more direct contact with end-users:

If we had solved [some internal issues] earlier, we would have found useful to do more direct interviews with audiologists and end users in this stage (company 3).

Yet it is noted that overall, developers valued the humanness of the persona-scenarios that were presented to them, which is highlighted by the below quote:

I think it definitely adds the human element to it and you can directly imagine how your app will benefit them or how it will affect their lives. (Company 1)

Future use of User-Requirements Methods

Developers were asked whether they would use a similar method of eliciting user-requirements in the future. All reported that they would:

Yes, certainly, when it comes to the non-leisure games for sure, definitely going to try and get all kinds of end users into the mix as early as possible and just double check that we've got the right idea (Company 1).

Probably my way to work is different from 3 years ago thanks to the 3D Tune-In partners. My work is better – I'm going to use my experiences in other projects (Company 2).

Yes, definitely yes. I've learnt a lot in terms of involving end users in all stages of the development, from the early ones to the final summative ones. I've learnt about the importance of such involvement, which is essential for applications such as ours (Company 3).

It is worth noting here that user feedback is imperative in assessing the full extent of the impact of the persona-scenarios on the design of the apps. A full analysis of user feedback was conducted within the 3D Tune-In project, however the results of the iterative feedback process is not within the scope of this paper. Some initial findings relating to two of the apps have been reported in Hallewell et al. (2017) which suggests a positive response to early prototypes of the apps, specifically regarding the potential as an alternative to traditional audiological procedures and the potential impact on users' enjoyment of music.

Discussion

HAs can make a huge difference in the day-to-day life of people with HL and their communication partners. However HA technology can be complex, and as such, HA users are often reliant on their audiologist to ensure that the HA is optimally configured for each sound environment that they might enter. The 3D Tune-In project developed apps to help HA users to understand the functions of their HA to empower them to seek improvements in their hearing/communication experience, and to champion more autonomy over HA use. Communication partners were also consulted over the needs of those wishing to understand more about HL and HA use. In order to inform the development of these apps it was imperative to first develop an understanding of the needs of HA users and their communication partners, which was achieved through questionnaires and paired interviews, then producing persona-scenarios and user-requirements from the resulting data.

It was intended that an understanding of the activities and challenges of HA users and their communication partners could be harnessed to highlight gaps or needs which the 3D Tune-In apps could support. The data were presented to developers using a persona-scenario format and a user-requirements table, which presented suggested tasks based on the problems identified within these persona-scenarios. Our intention was to provide developers with information from which they could select salient problems and issues, which their proposed app might be best suited to address, and consider these during their own design process. For example, they could select the kinds of hearing tasks to include in their app depending on which tasks were more aligned to their initial ideas, for example varying the volume of speech in different levels of noise, or adjusting the frequencies of certain instruments when listening to music. The persona-scenario creation process allows app designers to more efficiently visualise how their apps might be useful to "real" people, and also to suggest how these people might go about using it to fulfill their goals. The interviews with developers suggested that the information presented to them in the persona-scenarios and user-requirements table assisted their vision for their apps and guided their development.

Case-studies of user-centered design are important for highlighting how the design process of products and services can be improved through focusing on the needs of the targeted user (Buckle, Clarkson, Coleman, Ward, & Anderson, 2006; Martin, Clark, Morgan, Crowe, & Murphy, 2012). We used one of the most common and well-regarded methods of detailing user information in gamification projects - the use of persona-scenarios- to indicate the needs of the target user(s) (Morschheuser, Hamari, Werder, & Abe, 2017). The persona-scenarios created during this study were intended to help the developers to understand their target user more clearly (Marshall et al., 2015), and envision how the target users would interact with the apps under development (Rosson & Carroll, 2009). The user-requirements table derived from these persona-scenarios then enabled developers to select concrete tasks that reflect real-life experiences of HA users.

It was acknowledged that the applications would evolve during the specification and development work. Indeed it was clear from the developer interviews that the persona-scenarios encouraged some major changes to the app concepts, one developer learned new facts about the user group which served to warn them that their initial designs would be ineffective or disengaging for the target users. The persona-scenarios and user-requirements were instrumental in ensuring that the evolution of the apps was directly focused on the target users, in order to produce a useable product.

One note of caution about the use of persona-scenarios was that some developers found the information too 'verbose'. We would argue that the story-like narrative or persona-scenarios can be more compelling than a simplified list of requirements (Grudin & Pruitt, 2002), and as such the length of the documents produced may be justified. Further, a thorough account of problems and issues is necessary when the user group is new to the developers, and in cases in which there is a need to build empathy with the user-group (Blanco, López-Forniés, & Zarazaga-Soria, 2017). A summary document of highlights from the persona-scenarios (user-requirements table) was presented to developers in this project, and would be recommended for future projects employing the persona-scenario format.

CONCLUSION

People who use HAs and their communication partners have complex problems relating to their communications in different sound environments. It is possible that some of the problems HA users commonly state result from not knowing how to correctly use their HAs' functionalities in specific contexts and for specific tasks. The use of apps such as those created during the 3D Tune-In project could be a practical and accessible approach to educating HA users to use techniques (such as changing the settings of their HA) to alleviate some of these problems. Yet designing such apps for HA users posed a challenge for the 3D Tune-In project, as these populations were not well understood by the designers.

We examined how HA users and their communication partners interact with each other in order to produce compelling persona-scenarios and user-requirements tasks to help developers to better understand the user group. This goal was achieved as evidenced by the comments of the developers, who admitted to not knowing enough about the target population prior to beginning the project, and highlighted that the development of their app had benefitted from gaining an understanding of users through reading these documents. In this project, persona-scenarios and the user-requirements table provided much needed information about HA users and their communication partners to assist in the development of the 3D Tune-In apps.

Funding Details

This research has received funding from the European Commission's Horizon 2020 Programme (GA 3D Tune-In No. 644051). This article reflects the authors' views. The European Commission is not liable for any use that may be made of the information contained therein.

ACKNOWLEDGMENT

We would like to thank Dr. Davide Salanitri of the University of Nottingham, Dr. Carlos Garre of the Universidad Rey Juan Carlos and Mattia Zaninoni of GN Resound, Italy for carrying out some of the end-user interviews; and Dr. Lorenzo Picinali of Imperial College London who conducted some of the developer interviews. Thanks also to the participants of the study.

Disclosure Statement

The authors receive no financial interest or benefit from the publication of this paper.

REFERENCES

Barker, A. B., Leighton, P., & Ferguson, M. A. (2017). Coping together with hearing loss: A qualitative meta-synthesis of the psychosocial experiences of people with hearing loss and their communication partners. *International Journal of Audiology*, 56(5), 297–305. doi:10.1080/14992027.2017.1286695 PMID:28599604

Blanco, T., López-Forniés, I., & Zarazaga-Soria, F. J. (2017). Deconstructing the Tower of Babel: A design method to improve empathy and teamwork competences of informatics students. *International Journal of Technology and Design Education*, 27(2), 307–328. doi:10.100710798-015-9348-6

Brooks, D. N., Hallam, R. S., & Mellor, P. A. (2001). The effects on significant others of providing a hearing aid to the hearing-impaired partner. *British Journal of Audiology*, 35(3), 165–171. doi:10.108 0/00305364.2001.11745234 PMID:11548043

Buckle, P., Clarkson, P., Coleman, R., Ward, J., & Anderson, J. (2006). Patient safety, systems design and ergonomics. *Applied Ergonomics*, 37(4), 491–500. doi:10.1016/j.apergo.2006.04.016 PMID:16753132

Caissie, R., & Gibson, C. L. (1997). The Effectiveness of Repair Strategies Used by People with Hearing Losses and Their Conversational Partners. *The Volta Review*, 99(4), 203–218.

Cuevas-Rodriguez, M., Gonzalez-Toledo, D., de La Rubia-Buestas, E., Garre, C., Molina-Tanco, L., Reyes-Lecuona, A., . . . Picinali, L. (2017). *An open-source audio renderer for 3D audio with hearing loss and hearing aid simulations.* Paper presented at the Audio Engineering Society Convention 142, Berlin, Germany.

Dahl, Y., Linander, H., & Hanssen, G. K. (2014). Co-designing interactive tabletop solutions for active patient involvement in audiological consultations. *Proceedings of the 8th Nordic Conference on Human-Computer Interaction: Fun, Fast, Foundational.* 10.1145/2639189.2639221

de Graaff, F., Huysmans, E., Ket, J. C. F., Merkus, P., Goverts, S. T., Leemans, C. R., & Smits, C. (2018). Is there evidence for the added value and correct use of manual and automatically switching multimemory hearing devices? A scoping review. *International Journal of Audiology, 57*(3), 176–183. doi:10.1080/14992027.2017.1385864 PMID:29017358

Eastgate, R., Picinali, L., Patel, H., & D'Cruz, M. (2016). 3D Games for Tuning and Learning About Hearing Aids. *The Hearing Journal, 69*(4), 30–32. doi:10.1097/01.HJ.0000481810.74569.d8

Echalier, M. (2010). *In it together: the impact of hearing loss on personal relationships.* Academic Press.

Erber, N. P., & Scherer, S. C. (1999). Sensory loss and communication difficulties in the elderly. *Australasian Journal on Ageing, 18*(1), 4–9.

Grudin, J., & Pruitt, J. (2002). Personas, participatory design and product development: An infrastructure for engagement. *Proc. PDC.*

Guerra-Zúñiga, M., Cardemil-Morales, F., Albertz-Arévalo, N., & Rahal-Espejo, M. (2014). Explanations for the non-use of hearing aids in a group of older adults. A qualitative study. *Acta Otorrinolaringologica, 65*(1), 8–14. doi:10.1016/j.otoeng.2014.02.013 PMID:24342699

Hallewell, M., Patel, H., Salanitri, D., D'Cruz, M., Levtov, Y., & Simeone, L. (2017). *3D Tune-In: Evaluating Applications Designed to Support Hearing Aid Users in the Customisation of their Hearing Experience.* Paper presented at the British Academy of Audiology's 14 th Annual Conference, Bournemouth, UK. http://3d-tune-in.eu/sites/default/files/3DTI_BAA-Poster_2_customize.pdf

Hasan, S. S., Lai, F., Chipara, O., & Wu, Y.-H. (2013). *AudioSense: Enabling real-time evaluation of hearing aid technology in-situ.* Paper presented at the 2013 IEEE 26th International Symposium on Computer-Based Medical Systems (CBMS). 10.1109/CBMS.2013.6627783

Heffernan, E., Coulson, N. S., Henshaw, H., Barry, J. G., & Ferguson, M. A. (2016). Understanding the psychosocial experiences of adults with mild-moderate hearing loss: An application of Leventhal's self-regulatory model. *International Journal of Audiology, 55*(sup3), S3-S12.

Heine, C., & Browning, C. J. (2004). The communication and psychosocial perceptions of older adults with sensory loss: A qualitative study. *Ageing and Society, 24*(1), 113–130. doi:10.1017/S0144686X03001491

Hrafnkelsson, R., & Levtov, Y. (2017). *D3.2 Application documentation (public report).* Retrieved from UK: http://3d-tune-in.eu/sites/default/files/articles/D3.2_ApplicationDocumentation.pdf

Jacobs, A., Dreessen, K., & Pierson, J. (2008). 'Thick' personas–Using ethnographic Methods for Persona Development as a Tool for Conveying the Social Science View in Technological Design. *Observatorio (OBS*), 2*(2).

Johansson, M., & Messeter, J. (2005). Present-ing the user: Constructing the persona. *Digital Creativity, 16*(04), 231–243. doi:10.1080/14626260500476606

Kamil, R. J., & Lin, F. R. (2015). The effects of hearing impairment in older adults on communication partners: A systematic review. *Journal of the American Academy of Audiology, 26*(2), 155–182. doi:10.3766/jaaa.26.2.6 PMID:25690776

Keidser, G., Limareff, H. S., Simmons, S., Gul, C., Hayes, Z., Sawers, C., Thomas, B., Holland, K., & Korchek, K. (2005). Clinical Evaluation of Australian Hearing's Guidelines for Fitting Multiple Memory Hearing Aids. *Australian and New Zealand Journal of Audiology, 27*(1), 51–68. doi:10.1375/audi.2005.27.1.51

Kelly, T. B., Tolson, D., Day, T., McColgan, G., Kroll, T., & Maclaren, W. (2013). Older people's views on what they need to successfully adjust to life with a hearing aid. *Health & Social Care in the Community, 21*(3), 293–302. doi:10.1111/hsc.12016 PMID:23373520

Khaled, R., & Vasalou, A. (2014). Bridging serious games and participatory design. *International Journal of Child-Computer Interaction, 2*(2), 93–100. doi:10.1016/j.ijcci.2014.03.001

Kuk, F., Bulow, M., Damsgaard, A., & Ludvigsen, C. (2004). Hearing aid fittings and the use of simulated sound environments. *Hearing Review, 11*, 42–49.

Laplante-Lévesque, A., Dons Jensen, L., Dawes, P., & Nielsen, C. (2013). Optimal Hearing Aid Use: Focus Groups With Hearing Aid Clients and Audiologists. *Ear and Hearing, 34*(2), 193–202. doi:10.1097/AUD.0b013e31826a8ecd PMID:23183046

Lazzarotto, S., Baumstarck, K., Loundou, A., Hamidou, Z., Aghababian, V., Leroy, T., & Auquier, P. (2016). Age-related hearing loss in individuals and their caregivers: Effects of coping on the quality of life among the dyads. *Patient Preference and Adherence, 10*, 2279–2287. doi:10.2147/PPA.S112750 PMID:27853359

Madsen, S., & Nielsen, L. (2010). *Exploring Persona-Scenarios-Using Storytelling to Create Design Ideas. In Human Work Interaction Design: Usability in Social, Cultural and Organizational Contexts.* Springer.

Manchaiah, V. K. C., Stephens, D., & Lunner, T. (2013). Communication partners' journey through their partner's hearing impairment. *International Journal of Otolaryngology, 2013*, 2013. doi:10.1155/2013/707910 PMID:23533422

Marshall, R., Cook, S., Mitchell, V., Summerskill, S., Haines, V., Maguire, M., Sims, R., Gyi, D., & Case, K. (2015). Design and evaluation: End users, user datasets and personas. *Applied Ergonomics, 46*, 311–317. doi:10.1016/j.apergo.2013.03.008 PMID:23578520

Martin, J. L., Clark, D. J., Morgan, S. P., Crowe, J. A., & Murphy, E. (2012). A user-centred approach to requirements elicitation in medical device development: A case study from an industry perspective. *Applied Ergonomics*, *43*(1), 184–190. doi:10.1016/j.apergo.2011.05.002 PMID:21636072

Morschheuser, B., Hamari, J., Werder, K., & Abe, J. (2017). *How to gamify? A method for designing gamification.* Paper presented at the 50th Hawaii International Conference on System Sciences Hawaii. 10.24251/HICSS.2017.155

Patel, H., Cobb, S., Hallewell, M., D'Cruz, M., Eastgate, R., Picinali, L., & Tamascelli, S. (2016). *User involvement in design and application of virtual reality gamification to facilitate the use of hearing aids.* Paper presented at the 2016 International Conference on Interactive Technologies and Games (iTAG), Nottingham, UK. 10.1109/iTAG.2016.19

Preminger, J. E., Montano, J. J., & Tjørnhøj-Thomsen, T. (2015). Adult-children's perspectives on a parent's hearing impairment and its impact on their relationship and communication. *International Journal of Audiology*, *54*(10), 720–726. doi:10.3109/14992027.2015.1046089 PMID:26083719

Rosson, M. B., & Carroll, J. M. (2009). Scenario based design. In A. Sears & J. Jacko, A (Eds.), Human-computer interaction: Development process (pp. 145-162). Boca Raton, FL: CRC Press.

Scarinci, N., Worrall, L., & Hickson, L. (2008). The effect of hearing impairment in older people on the spouse. *International Journal of Audiology*, *47*(3), 141–151. doi:10.1080/14992020701689696 PMID:18307094

Schulz, K. A., Modeste, N., Lee, J. W., Roberts, R., Saunders, G. H., & Witsell, D. L. (2017). Burden of Hearing Loss on Communication Partners and Its Influence on Pursuit of Hearing Evaluation. *Ear and Hearing*, *38*(5), e285–e291. doi:10.1097/AUD.0000000000000421 PMID:28338495

Singh, G., Lau, S.-T., & Pichora-Fuller, M. K. (2015). Social Support Predicts Hearing Aid Satisfaction. *Ear and Hearing*, *36*(6), 664–676. doi:10.1097/AUD.0000000000000182 PMID:26035144

Solheim, J., Kværner, K. J., Sandvik, L., & Falkenberg, E.-S. (2012). Factors affecting older adults' hearing-aid use. *Scandinavian Journal of Disability Research*, *14*(4), 300–312. doi:10.1080/15017419.2011.640411

Vas, V., Akeroyd, M. A., & Hall, D. A. (2017). A data-driven synthesis of research evidence for domains of hearing loss, as reported by adults with hearing loss and their communication partners. *Trends in Hearing*, *21*, 1–25. doi:10.1177/2331216517734088 PMID:28982021

ENDNOTE

[1]   Excerpts have been edited for the purposes of this paper.

This research was previously published in the International Journal of Game-Based Learning (IJGBL), 11(1); pages 1-16, copyright year 2021 by IGI Publishing (an imprint of IGI Global).

Chapter 18
Identifying Latent Semantics in Action Games for Player Modeling

Katia Lida Kermanidis

 https://orcid.org/0000-0002-3270-5078

Ionian University, Department of Informatics, Corfu, Greece

ABSTRACT

Machine learning approaches to player modeling traditionally employ a high-level game-knowledge-based feature for representing game sessions, and often player behavioral features as well. The present work makes use of generic low-level features and latent semantic analysis for unsupervised player modeling, but mostly for revealing underlying hidden information regarding game semantics that is not easily detectable beforehand.

INTRODUCTION

Player modeling has been attracting the interest of game design and development experts for several years, as a means to increase player satisfaction and immersion. According to the inclusive reviews in (Smith et al., 2011) and (Hooshyar et al., 2018), modeling techniques vary from empirical (data-driven) (Thue et al., 2007; Thurau & Bauckhage, 2010; Roberts et al., 2007; Geisler, 2002; Drachen et al., 2013), where the application of machine learning or statistical analysis to gaming data enables predictions of playing styles, to theoretical (i.e. analytical), mostly applicable to board-like games, where search and optimization techniques are used to determine the moves towards the best outcome (Bellman, 1965). The term 'play style' indicates the manner in which each player behaves while playing, i.e. the choices he makes, his reactions, his response time etc.

Regarding empirical approaches to player modeling, various learning techniques have been experimented with; supervised, like support vector machines for predicting difficulty adjustment (Missura & Gaertner, 2009), Bayesian networks for classification (He et al., 2008), statistical analysis of the distribution of player actions (Thawonmas & Ho, 2007), and unsupervised, like self-organizing maps

DOI: 10.4018/978-1-6684-7589-8.ch018

(Drachen et al., 2009), reinforcement learning (Kang & Tan, 2010), transfer learning (Shahine & Banerjee, 2007) and preference learning (Yannakakis et al., 2009). Supervised techniques (stand-alone or in combination with unsupervised approaches) have been gaining in popularity (Bisson et al., 2015; Luo et al., 2016; Min et al., 2016; Tamassia et al., 2016; Falakmasir et al., 2016; Gao et al., 2016) during the last three-four years, compared to purely unsupervised approaches (Drachen et al., 2009; Anagnostou & Maragoudakis, 2009; Cowley et al., 2014), mostly due to their improved performance. Dimensionality reduction techniques, other than self-organizing maps, have been experimented with for unsupervised modeling: Linear Discriminant Analysis has been applied to arcade-style as well as combat-style games (Gow et al., 2012), where match data are annotated with the players' identity to enable the supervised application of Linear Discriminant Analysis, and then k-means clustering groups together players of the same gaming style.

All previous approaches use a limited number of high-level game and player features to perform modeling, that are game-dependent (vary from game to game, and a game expert is required to define them) and whose impact on the player model is to some extent a-priori sensed. High level features indicate directly and almost explicitly the game status. High-level features in combat-style games may, for instance, include the number of weapons obtained, the number of shots performed, the number of spare lives accumulated. The high-level features pose significant demands on knowledge resources, while they minimize expectations to extract new knowledge and unforeseen relations and dependencies between game and player features. Low level features, on the other hand, are features that describe the morphology of the game terrain, at specific time intervals, and the game status needs to be indirectly deducted.

Latent Semantic Analysis (LSA) has been applied with significant success to several domains, other than IR, like essay assessment in language learning (Haley et al., 2005), intelligent tutoring (Graesser et al., 2007), text cohesion measurement (McCarthy et al., 2007), summary evaluation (Steinberger & Jezek, 2004), text categorization (Nakov et al., 2003). Although all previously mentioned LSA applications have been performed on text corpora, some approaches have proposed its use in different non-textual knowledge domains like board game player modeling (Zampa & Lemaire, 2002), complex problem solving (Quesada et al., 2001), gene function prediction (Done et al., 2010; Dong et al., 2006; Ganapathitaju et al., 2005), web navigation behavior prediction (van Oostendorp & Juvina, 2007), collaborative filtering (Hofmann, 2004), semantic description of images (Basili et al., 2007).

Latent Dirichlet Allocation (LDA) has been applied to several distinct modeling applications, like topic detection (Griffiths & Steyvers, 2004; Weinshall et al., 2013), tag recommendation (Krestel et al., 2009), entity resolution (Bhattacharya & Getoor, 2006), human action recognition in video streams (Deepak et al., 2013), spam recognition (Bro et al., 2009), satellite image clustering (Tang et al., 2013), flood event modeling (Aubert et al., 2013), source code analysis (Grant et al., 2013).

The present work proposes grouping similar playing styles together by modeling the semantics of the game domain. There are two possible ways for supplying domain knowledge (Lemaire, 1998): by hand, making use of domain experts' know-how, and automatically, by deriving the semantics from large corpora of "word" sequences, i.e. sequences of concepts that carry units of meaning related to the domain. The first approach is more accurate, but domain-dependent, while the second (adopted in the present work) is useful when no hand-crafted knowledge is available.

In an attempt to disassociate the player modeling process from the necessity of an already known high-level knowledge-based feature set, the present paper proposes:

- The use of numerous low-level generic screen-distributed features, relatively easily derived from any action game, that are raw (i.e. they are unprocessed and don't undergo any averaging/rate counts etc.); also, no sophisticated knowledge about the game is required (e.g. specific time lapses, specific player reactions, specific game frames and periods);
- The use of these features to model an action game domain knowledge, i.e. to semantically represent game states and game sessions;
- The application of LSA to the game term-document matrix in order to enable the revelation of hidden, previously unknown semantic relations among players, game states and sessions;
- The comparison of LSA to other semantic modeling approaches, like LDA, to note their differences in addressing the data sparseness problem.

It needs to be noted that all employed features are used to describe game states. Game states are screenshots of the game at specific time intervals. More details regarding the use of these terms are given in section 3.

The remainder of the paper is organized as follows: Sections 2 and 3 describe the theory behind LSA and its application to action games respectively. Section 4 presents LDA. Section 5 presents the use case game employed in the present work, all data collection modes, the respective experiments run, and the achieved results. The paper concludes in section 6.

LATENT SEMANTIC ANALYSIS

In Information Retrieval (IR) the most important data structure is the term-document matrix, where every matrix row corresponds to a vocabulary entry (the vocabulary or lexicon consists of the words/terms appearing in a document collection) and every matrix column corresponds to a document in the collection. Matrix cells may indicate term incidence (contain a Boolean value that denotes the presence or absence of a term in a document), term frequency (*tf* - denoting the number of times the term appears in a document) or more sophisticated weights that incorporate the discriminative power of every term, i.e. its ability to distinguish groups of documents based on their semantic similarity, like the widely used *tf.idf* metric, where *idf* is the logarithm of the inverse document frequency (*df* - the number of documents a term appears in). The larger the number of documents a word appears in, the weaker its discriminative power, i.e. its ability to semantically mark a document. The following formula defines *tf.idf*, *N* is the total number of documents in the collection:

$$tfidf = tf * \log\left(\frac{N}{df}\right) \tag{1}$$

In a realistic IR application scenario the number of rows and columns of the term-document matrix may reach tens or hundreds of thousands. LSA (Landauer et al., 1998) is a mathematical method, initially proposed for reducing the size of the term-document matrix in the IR setting, by applying Singular Value Decomposition (SVD). SVD decomposes the initial term-document matrix *A* into a product of three matrices, and "transfers" matrix *A* into a new semantic space:

A=TSD^T (2)

T is the matrix with rows the lexicon terms, and columns the dimensions of the new semantic space. The columns of D^T represent the initial documents and its rows the new dimensions, while S is a diagonal matrix (all non-diagonal elements have a zero value) containing the singular values of A. Multiplication of the three matrices will reconstruct the initial matrix. The product can be computed in such a way that the singular values are positioned in the diagonal of S in descending order. The smaller the singular value, the less it affects the product outcome. By keeping only the first k, i.e. the k largest, singular values, and setting the remaining ones to zero and calculating the resulting product, a low-rank approximation A_k of the initial matrix A may be calculated as a least-squares best fit. The rank of the new matrix A_k is equal to the number k of selected singular values.

As an interesting side effect, dimensionality reduction decreases or increases the cell values of matrix A_k, compared to those of A. It may even set the occurrence of words to higher than zero for documents that they initially did not appear in. Thereby semantic relations between words and documents are revealed that were not apparent at first (latent). It needs to be noted that LSA is fully automatic, i.e. the latent semantic relations are learned in an unsupervised manner.

LSA FOR ACTION GAMES

Unlike board-like and arcade games, action games have properties resembling those of complex/dynamic environments: causality (actions/decisions often affect subsequent actions/decisions), time dependence (environmental circumstances that affect actions/decisions vary over time), and latent, implicit relations between domain properties that are not straightforward.

The first challenge is the identification of the set of domain "words", corresponding to the collection vocabulary in the IR domain. In board and board-like games, like tic-tac-toe or chess, domain "words" are easy to identify. Boards may be viewed as grids of cells and each cell state (e.g. X/O/empty in tic-tac-toe) constitutes a "word" (Lemaire, 1998). In action games "words" are harder to identify. In the firefighting microworld of (Quesada et al., 2001) "words" are actions like appliance moves, or water drops. The definition of a game "word" depends on the intended use of the model. If the intended use is behavior prediction, a "word" needs to model a player's action, as the player's sequence of actions (in a given context) defines his behavior. Words need to be primitive carriers of domain knowledge and every word represents a distinct game state (a game screenshot at a given moment) in a unique manner. In the present work two ways for defining words are proposed. The first (henceforth the "holistic" approach) makes use of high-level game features (e.g. position of player ship, number of enemy ships etc) and measures their value for each particular game state. The concatenation of all feature values in a given game state is the word. The second (henceforth the "grid" approach) considers each game state to be a grid of cells, i.e. the game screen is divided into rows and columns so that the resulting cell size can roughly fit the game elements (spaceships, weapons, etc.). Each cell may or may not contain one or more game elements, i.e. game state semantics is acquired by combining the semantics of each cell in a given state. The number of possible state conditions equals (m is the number of cells, and n the number of game elements). A word is the concatenation of all cell conditions for the given state.

The second challenge involves the definition of documents. In IR, documents are meaningful utterances that carry information regarding their topic, author, genre etc. Similarly, game documents need to constitute complete and meaningful player "utterances", i.e. well-formed sequences of words that constitute complete descriptions of player actions or context conditions. Herein these descriptions address entire game sessions as these carry a complete meaning and the mark of each individual player. A game session is represented by taking a sample of the game state at constant pre-defined time intervals (i.e. every 500 msecs) and registering the sequence of words ("holistic" or "grid") that describe the sample. Each sample represents a game state at the specified time point.

After words and documents have been defined, the term-document matrix may be constructed. In this matrix each row is a word (i.e. game state) and each column is a document (i.e. game session). Two matrices are experimented with: one where each matrix element denotes the *tf* and one where it denotes the *tfidf* weight of a particular word in a particular document. The term-document matrices are very sparse, i.e. only very few words appear in more than one document and very few words appear in a document more than once. LSA is applied to the matrices in an attempt to address this sparseness and extract the knowledge lying underneath it.

LATENT DIRICHLET ALLOCATION

LDA (Blei et el., 2003) is a probabilistic process for modeling corpora. Documents in a collection are treated as distribution mixtures over 'topics'. 'Topics' are latent notions that are represented as word distributions $P(w|t)$. Given a document d, the probability that it involves a mixture of topics t is $P(t|d)$. The probability of a specific word w_i given a document d, can be calculated as:

$$P(w_i \mid d) = \sum_{j=1}^{t} P(w_i \mid t_i = j) P(t_i = j \mid d) \qquad (3)$$

where t_i is the latent topic and t is the number of topics, which is a-priori user-defined. LDA models the above distributions using Dirichlet priors from an unlabeled collection of documents. As a result, the process outputs a document-topic matrix and a term-topic matrix, i.e. a matrix containing membership probabilities of every document for every topic and a matrix with membership probabilities of every word for every topic respectively. Like IR, where topics are abstract concepts that are defined by sets of similar (synonym) words and (close in content domain) documents, in the game domain, topics are abstract concepts that are defined by sets of similar game states and sessions.

Unlike LSA, where the resulting feature-vectors are sometimes hard to explain, especially when they involve negative values, LDA probabilities on topics and documents are more straightforward to understand and make use of in other applications. Furthermore, LSA faces the effect of the 'bag of words' model, i.e. words are independent of each other and, no ordering (structure) information is retained, making it hardly straightforward for LSA to cope with causality and time-dependence.

LDA has been chosen for modeling the game semantics in this work, compared to similar methods, like word2vec/doc2vec modeling, due to its higher interpretability (LDA results in topic probabilities, while word2vec results in a vector of real numbers that are hard to interpret) and its globality[1]. In other words, LDA has the ability to model global dependencies (documents globally predict words), while, in word2vec, the modeled dependencies are local (one word predicts another word nearby). Given the complexity of the action game semantics, global dependencies need to be uncovered and are more useful.

EXPERIMENTAL SETUP: SPACEDEBRIS

The videogame used for the purposes of data collection is based on SpaceDebris (Anagnostou & Maragoudakis, 2009). The action takes place within the confines of a single screen, with alien ships scrolling downwards. There are two types of enemy spaceships, the carrier (enemy 1) which is slow and can withstand more laser blasts, and a fighter (enemy 2) which is fast and easier to destroy. The player wins when he has successfully withstood the enemy ship waves for a predetermined time. The game environment is littered with floating asteroids which in their default state do not interact (i.e. collide) with any of the game spaceships. In order to do so, an asteroid has to be "energized" (hit by player weapon). Also floating are shield and life power-ups which the user can use to replenish his ship's shield and remaining lives. The player's ship is equipped with a laser cannon which she can use to shoot alien ships. The laser canon is weak and about 4-5 successful shots are required to destroy an enemy ship (except for the boss which requires many more). The laser can also be used to "energize" an asteroid and guide it to destroy an enemy ship. A screenshot of the game is shown in Figure 1.

Figure 1. SpaceDebris

The participants included 10 players (74 game sessions, 10532 game states). Each participant had a 5-minute trial period for becoming acquainted with SpaceDebris. Then, he/she was given a short questionnaire consisting of three general gaming questions (about gaming experience, game type preferences and hours/day devoted to game play) and four specific questions about SpaceDebris (scale of gaming satisfaction, game style preference, preference in chosen weapons etc.). The questionnaire is used as an initial resource to categorize the gaming style of the player into one of four categories: novice (a player with little gaming experience and playing SpaceDebris without any particular style), tactical (a player keen on playing strategy or adventure games and when playing SpaceDebris makes wise use of the laser and power-ups), aggressive (a player keen on action games and when playing SpaceDebris fires constantly without frequent use of the power-ups), and defensive (a player keen on puzzle and internet games and when playing SpaceDebris does not fire or tries to avoid the enemies in order not to be killed). Afterwards, the participants played the game for 10 minutes, with the presence of a domain expert, who witnessed the player's gaming style and accepted or disputed the questionnaire's categorization. 29% of the game states belong to the novice class, 42% to the tactical, 19% to the aggressive and 10% to the defensive class. The class of a game state is given the value of the playing style a player exhibits on the particular game session.

"Traditional" Data Collection

For comparative analysis purposes, a first experiment was run using a dataset that is formed by a set of high-level features used traditionally in player modeling. Each feature-value vector represents an entire game session (i.e. 74 vectors in total), and the features (22 in number) denote:

- The outcome of the game session (win/lose);
- The session score value;
- The mean number of available life and shield upgrades during the session;
- The total number of life and shield upgrades performed;
- The minimum and maximum horizontal and vertical position of the player during the session;
- The total number of lasers fired by the player and by the enemies during the session;
- The total number of enemies killed by lasers and asteroids;
- The total number of enemies escaped;
- The total number of enemies very close to the player;
- The total number of enemies close to the player;
- The total number of enemies on screen;
- The total number of asteroids hit;
- The total number of visible asteroids.

```
shield <= 1969.482759
|   LifeUpgrades <= 26: Tactical (17.0)
|   LifeUpgrades > 26
|   |   MaxPosX <= 425: Tactical (9.0/1.0)
|   |   MaxPosX > 425
|   |   |   MaxPosY <= 116: Aggressive (7.0)
|   |   |   MaxPosY > 116: Tactical (2.0/1.0)
shield > 1969.482759
|   Result <= 0
|   |   LifeUpgrades <= 76
|   |   |   MaxPosY <= 49: Defensive (17.0)
```

```
|    |    |    MaxPosY > 49: Novice (3.0)
|    |    LifeUpgrades > 76: Novice (15.0)
|    Result > 0: Tactical (4.0/1.0)
```

Figure 2. Pruned decision tree from the traditional dataset. The tree expands left to right. Bracketed numbers at the leaves indicate (correctly/incorrectly) labeled examples at the given branch

```
shield <= 1969.482759
|   LifeUpgrades <= 26: Tactical (17.0)
|   LifeUpgrades > 26
|   |   MaxPosX <= 425: Tactical (9.0/1.0)
|   |   MaxPosX > 425
|   |   |   MaxPosY <= 116: Aggressive (7.0)
|   |   |   MaxPosY > 116: Tactical (2.0/1.0)
shield > 1969.482759
|   Result <= 0
|   |   LifeUpgrades <= 76
|   |   |   MaxPosY <= 49: Defensive (17.0)
|   |   |   MaxPosY > 49: Novice (3.0)
|   |   LifeUpgrades > 76: Novice (15.0)
|   Result > 0: Tactical (4.0/1.0)
```

Classification tests were run with several state-of-the-art classifiers (i.e. pruned decision trees, random forests and Support Vector Machines) on the Weka machine learning workbench (http://www.cs.waikato. ac.nz/ml/weka). Decision trees and random forests are used to demonstrate the features' impact on the gaming style, and the extent to which this knowledge is already known a-priori. As can be seen from the derived decision tree (Figure 2), the borderline of the player's position, the number of performed life and shield upgrades and the game result are closely related to the gaming style, information that is not so surprising, but can be sensed to some extent beforehand. The confusion matrix is shown in Figure 3. In this matrix rows show the actual gaming style derived from the questionnaire and the observation process described earlier (e.g. there are $25 + 2 + 2 + 0 = 29$ actual tactical game sessions), and the columns show the style predicted by the decision tree (i.e. of the 29 actual tactical games, 25 are correctly classified as tactical, 2 as aggressive, 2 as novice and 0 as defensive).

Figure 4 shows the confusion matrix when applying random forests and Support Vector Machines to the data (both learning schemata led to the same results). The meta-learning random forest schema and the SVM classifier, more sophisticated than the simple decision tree classifier, both reach 100% accuracy, showing thereby the relevance of the chosen features for modeling the particular game. Random forests were run choosing randomly 12 features and forming 100 decision trees in every run (Breiman, 2001). Support Vector Machines were run using a first degree polynomial kernel function and the Sequential Minimal Optimization algorithm for training (Platt, 1998).

Figure 3. Confusion matrix for the traditional dataset using a pruned decision tree classifier

a	b	c	d	← classified as
25	2	2	0	a = Tactical
3	3	2	0	b = Aggressive
4	1	15	0	c = Novice
0	0	0	17	d = Defensive

Figure 4. Confusion matrix for the traditional dataset using a random forest classifier and a Support Vector Machines classifier

a	b	c	d	← classified as
29	2	2	0	a = Tactical
3	8	2	0	b = Aggressive
4	1	20	0	c = Novice
0	0	0	17	d = Defensive

"Holistic" Data Collection

The game features for the holistic dataset and their value range are listed next:

- The number of enemies very close to the player (denoting imminent threat) (min: 0, max: 5);
- The number of enemies close to the player (denoting danger) (min: 0, max: 9);
- The total number of enemies on screen (min: 0, max: 13);
- The number of player lasers fired (min: 0, max: 5);

- The number of enemy 1 lasers fired (min: 0, max: 10);
- The number of enemy 2 lasers fired (min: 0, max: 10);
- The horizontal (X) and vertical (Y) position of the player (minX: -462, maxX: 462, minY: -334, maxY: 334);
- The number of life upgrades performed (min: 0, max: 1);
- The number of shield upgrades performed (min: 0, max: 1);
- The number of hit asteroids (min: 0, max: 6);
- The number of visible asteroids (min: 0, max: 8);
- The number of hit enemy 1 ships (min: 0, max: 8);
- The number of hit enemy 2 ships (min: 0, max: 8);
- The score value (min: 0, max: 8000);
- The number of the player's available life upgrades (min: 0, max: 3);
- The number of shields available to the player (min: 0, max: 100).

As explained earlier, a word is a string representing the concatenation of the values of all aforementioned features for a given game state, and the collected data resulted in 8458 distinct words. The feature values are discretized into at most ten value levels of equal distance. Even after discretization, the resulting term-document matrix consists of 98.4% zero elements, showing the sparseness problem.

"Grid" Data Collection

The game screen is viewed as an 8x11 grid. Table 1 shows the distinct states that a cell may be in. More than one of the distinct states may be combined to form the cell state. A word is the concatenation of the states of the 88 cells. The vocabulary consists of 10263 words, and, in this case, zero elements in the term-document matrix reach 98.8%.

To lessen the sparseness problem, another dataset was created, by merging the 25 distinct cell states into ten (see Table 2) and by reducing the granularity of the grid down to 4x5=20 cells. Vocabulary size drops down to 9694 words and the percentage of zero elements to 98.5%. The merging process inevitably leads to information loss, as different (though similar) game elements are treated as the same. All dataset files can be downloaded from http://di.ionio.gr/hilab.

LSA for Classification

All aforementioned term-document matrices are transposed so that rows indicate sessions and columns indicate game states. LSA is applied to all aforementioned term-document matrices. Experiments were run using 20, 40 and 60 latent semantic dimensions. The resulting *D* matrices depict the transformation of the game sessions (rows) into the new semantic space (columns). Performing classification experiments with the LSA datasets is not expected to lead to better results. As is claimed in the literature (Liu et al., 2004), running classification experiments using a dataset with latent attributes (dimensions) usually drops classification performance due to the unsupervised manner in which the latent dataset has been derived. Figure 5 shows the best results (confusion matrix) achieved with a latent dataset with the unpruned decision tree classifier.

Table 1. Grid distinct cell states

State ID	State Description
1	The cell contains an asteroid
2	The cell contains an "energized" asteroid
3	The cell contains the player's ship
4	The cell contains the player's ship being hit by enemy 1
5	The cell contains the player's ship being hit by enemy 2
6	The cell contains the player's ship being destroyed
7	The cell contains the player's ship firing a laser
8	The cell contains enemy 1
9	The cell contains enemy 1 being hit by a laser
10	The cell contains enemy 1 being hit by an asteroid
11	The cell contains enemy 1 firing a laser
12	The cell contains enemy 1 being destroyed
13	The cell contains enemy 2
14	The cell contains enemy 2 being hit by a laser
15	The cell contains enemy 2 being hit by an asteroid
16	The cell contains enemy 2 firing a laser
17	The cell contains enemy 2 being destroyed
18	The cell contains a player laser
19	The cell contains an enemy 1 laser
20	The cell contains an enemy 2 laser
21	The cell contains a life upgrade
22	The cell contains a life upgrade hit by laser
23	The cell contains a shield upgrade
24	The cell contains a shield upgrade hit by laser
25	Empty cell

Table 2. Grid distinct cell states – merged

State ID	Distinct Cell State Description - Merged
1	The cell contains an asteroid/energized asteroid
2	The cell contains the player's ship (firing a laser)
3	The cell contains the player's ship being hit by enemy 1 or 2
4	The cell contains enemy 1 or 2 (firing a laser)
5	The cell contains enemy 1 or 2 being hit by a laser/asteroid
6	The cell contains a player laser
7	The cell contains an enemy 1 or 2 laser
8	The cell contains a life/shield upgrade
9	The cell contains a life/shield upgrade hit by laser
10	Empty cell

Figure 5. Confusion matrix with decision trees for the holistic dataset with tf values, after applying LSA and keeping 40 semantic dimensions

a	b	c	d	← classified as
22	2	2	3	a = Tactical
3	2	3	0	b = Aggressive
7	1	5	7	c = Novice
4	0	0	13	d = Defensive

Figure 6 shows the confusion matrix when using random forests (parameters are the same like before), and Figure 7 is the SVMs confusion matrix with a fourth degree polynomial kernel function. The prediction weakness of the latent dataset is evident even with sophisticated learners.

Figure 6. Confusion matrix with random forests for the holistic dataset with tf values, after applying LSA and keeping 40 semantic dimensions

a	b	c	d	← classified as
24	1	3	1	a = Tactical
4	3	1	0	b = Aggressive
6	0	9	5	c = Novice
1	0	4	12	d = Defensive

Figure 7. Confusion matrix with SVMs for the holistic dataset with tf values, after applying LSA and keeping 40 semantic dimensions

a	b	c	d	← classified as
18	4	3	4	a = Tactical
3	4	0	1	b = Aggressive
8	2	7	3	c = Novice
2	1	1	13	d = Defensive

LSA for Clustering: Revealing Underlying Hidden Information

In order to identify the significance of the application of LSA, a similarity detection process between game sessions needs to be performed, other than classification. Metrics like the cosine similarity are widely employed for this purpose in the literature. Having constructed the term-document matrices, each game session may be viewed as a learning vector and k-means clustering is applied to the initial and the reduced dataset so as to group similar game sessions together in an unsupervised manner.

Choosing the number of clusters to equal the number of gaming styles, i.e. four, enables classes-to-clusters evaluation. Classes- to-clusters evaluation results in a confusion matrix that depicts to what percent sessions of the same style (class) are grouped into the same cluster. The confusion matrix for all initial datasets (before applying LSA) is the same regardless of the dataset type (holistic, grid or merged grid) and of using *tf* or *tfidf* weights, and is shown in Figure 8(b). Rows indicate actual gaming styles and columns indicate the clusters these were assigned to. For comparison purposes, Figure 8(a) shows the corresponding results for the traditional dataset. The difference in clustering performance is significant, clearly due to the large number of features in the term-document datasets. The boxed percentages of incorrectly classified instances are calculated as follows: In (b), for example, the majority of cluster 2 instances (28 in number) are tactical, so it is considered the 'tactical' cluster. No other cluster can be considered 'tactical', so all other tactical instance clusterings are errors. Also, all other non-tactical instances that have been clustered to cluster 2 are errors. So, the total number of errors is 44 out of 74 instances in total.

The remaining matrices ((c)-(t)) correspond to the LSA-transformed datasets. Though results are far from satisfactory when it comes to matching clusters to styles one-to-one (as already explained, this is not the primary concern of the proposed methodology anyway), several interesting findings are noteworthy. When the number of latent semantic dimensions reaches 60, clustering performance is the same as when no LSA is performed, i.e. no semantic information is hidden in the remaining singular values of the initial diagonal matrix that is not already captured in the first 60 singular values. Decreasing the number of singular values to 40 has a positive effect on clustering performance in most cases, while 20 dimensions seem to be insufficient to capture as well the semantic properties of the game. Regarding the holistic vs. the grid and the merged grid approach, it seems that the more "aggregate" (i.e. holistic) the nature of the dataset, the better the clustering performance, while the opposite holds for the "distributed" datasets. Intuitively, the latter require large amounts of data in order to overcome the bigger sparseness problem they face. Raw term frequencies seem to outperform *tfidf* scores in the "distributed" datasets, but not in the holistic dataset, where the *df* of the words varies significantly more and thereby makes their different discriminative power evident.

The subjective nature of the true play style assignment, the limited data, as well as the desire to investigate the semantic modeling process further, led to tests with a smaller number of clusters, i.e. 2. In this case, classes-to-clusters evaluation is not meaningful (a percentage of correctly clustered sessions is not provided). Figure 9 shows the formed clusters in relation to the game styles. What is interesting to observe is that for most datasets the majority of members of the first cluster are aggressive and tactical players, and of the second cluster defensive and novice players. The two formed clusters are interesting and can be explained, as novice players usually tend to play defensively, with no pattern or offensive strategy. On the other hand, aggressive and tactical players share the same confidence and are eager to win. The grid data captures this knowledge, while it is mostly lost in the merged grid, a sign of the information loss mentioned earlier. LSA helped reveal these unknown semantic similarities with low-level features even better than the high-level traditional dataset.

Another interesting finding is that the aggressive style seems to be the most difficult to model. While the other styles (especially the novice and defensive styles) show a more conforming behavior in the latent dimensions (almost no example has dimension values outside a specific limited range), some of the aggressive examples often show rebellious behavior and lie away from the majority of their co-clustered examples, given a latent dimension. This is partly attributed to the small number of examples of the particular class, and partly to the to-the-limit type of playing that aggressive players adopt, where borderline values of the latent features are often reached. This underlying semantics was not noticeable in the initial datasets, but came to light with the LSA analysis.

For experimental purposes the DBScan (Ester et al., 1996) clusterer has also been applied, as it is claimed in the literature to cope well with noisy data. DBScan is density-based and forms high-density regions into clusters. Pre-defining the value of cluster radius and the minimum number of objects required to form a cluster, the algorithm does not need to know the number of clusters beforehand, unlike k-means. Objects that end up not belonging to any cluster are considered as noise and remain unclustered. In our experiments the minimum number of objects was set to 8, as it was the number of objects belonging to the minority class (aggressive), and several radius values were experimented with.

The only interesting findings with DBScan were achieved with the traditional dataset (Figure 10). The higher the radius value, the fewer instances remain unclustered. A radius of 0.8 leads to the optimal confusion matrix and, interestingly, novice and defensive examples are mostly grouped together, something that k-means was able to reveal in the latent space only. Here this knowledge is derived from the traditional dataset; however, 17 instances (i.e. 23%) are left unclustered. The initial and the latent dataset lead to instances forming one cluster only, regardless of the radius size. These datasets are more complex, and multi-density, and DBScan neglects entire clusters and assigns them as noise (Ahmed, 2011).

Figure 8. Confusion matrices with 4-means clustering. The boxed score next to each matrix shows the percentage of incorrectly clustered instances.

0 1 2 3 <- assigned to cluster	0 1 2 3 <- assigned to cluster
21 1 7 0 I Tactical	1 0 28 0 I Tactical
4 0 4 0 I Aggressive	0 0 8 0 I Aggressive
0 15 0 5 I Novice	0 1 19 0 I Novice
0 2 0 15 I Defensive	0 0 16 1 I Defensive
(a) Traditional dataset 25.67%	(b) Initial datasets 59.46%

LSA - 20 dimensions	LSA - 40 dimensions	LSA –60 dimensions
0 1 2 3 64.86%	0 1 2 3 59.46%	0 1 2 3 59.46%
3 18 8 0 I Tactical	21 0 8 0 I Tactical	1 0 28 0 I Tactical
0 3 5 0 I Aggressive	3 0 5 0 I Aggressive	0 0 8 0 I Aggressive
0 18 1 1 I Novice	18 1 1 0 I Novice	0 1 19 0 I Novice
0 17 0 0 I Defensive	14 0 0 3 I Defensive	0 0 16 1 I Defensive
(c) Holistic-tf	(d) Holistic-tf	(e) Holistic-tf
0 1 2 3 64.86%	0 1 2 3 52.70%	0 1 2 3 59.46%
20 1 8 0 I Tactical	1 0 28 0 I Tactical	1 0 28 0 I Tactical
3 0 5 0 I Aggressive	1 0 7 0 I Aggressive	0 0 8 0 I Aggressive
17 1 1 1 I Novice	4 1 15 0 I Novice	0 1 19 0 I Novice
17 0 0 0 I Defensive	0 0 14 3 I Defensive	0 0 16 1 I Defensive
(f) Holistic-tfidf	(g) Holistic-tfidf	(h) Holistic-tfidf
0 1 2 3 59.46%	0 1 2 3 58.11%	0 1 2 3 59.46%
1 17 1 10 I Tactical	24 0 5 0 I Tactical	1 0 28 0 I Tactical
0 3 1 4 I Aggressive	4 0 4 0 I Aggressive	0 0 8 0 I Aggressive
0 19 0 1 I Novice	13 1 6 0 I Novice	0 1 19 0 I Novice
0 17 0 0 I Defensive	11 0 5 1 I Defensive	0 0 16 1 I Defensive
(i) Grid-tf	(j) Grid-tf	(k) Grid-tf
0 1 2 3 66.22%	0 1 2 3 64.86%	0 1 2 3 59.46%
5 18 0 6 I Tactical	8 0 21 0 I Tactical	1 0 28 0 I Tactical
1 4 1 2 I Aggressive	0 0 8 0 I Aggressive	0 0 8 0 I Aggressive
1 17 0 2 I Novice	4 1 15 0 I Novice	0 1 19 0 I Novice
0 17 0 0 I Defensive	4 0 12 1 I Defensive	0 0 16 1 I Defensive
(l) Grid-tfidf	(m) Grid-tfidf	(n) Grid-tfidf
0 1 2 3 62.16%	0 1 2 3 54.05%	0 1 2 3 59.46%
7 12 5 5 I Tactical	25 0 4 0 I Tactical	1 0 28 0 I Tactical
3 0 3 2 I Aggressive	4 0 4 0 I Aggressive	0 0 8 0 I Aggressive
1 9 10 0 I Novice	11 1 8 0 I Novice	0 1 19 0 I Novice
0 9 8 0 I Defensive	8 0 8 1 I Defensive	0 0 16 1 I Defensive
(o) Merged-tf	(p) Merged-tf	(q) Merged-tf
0 1 2 3 64.86%	0 1 2 3 60.81%	0 1 2 3 59.46%
5 17 6 1 I Tactical	5 0 24 0 I Tactical	1 0 28 0 I Tactical
0 3 4 1 I Aggressive	0 0 8 0 I Aggressive	0 0 8 0 I Aggressive
1 17 2 0 I Novice	4 1 15 0 I Novice	0 1 19 0 I Novice
0 17 0 0 I Defensive	1 0 15 1 I Defensive	0 0 16 1 I Defensive
(r) Merged-tfidf	(s) Merged-tfidf	(t) Merged-tfidf

Figure 9. Confusion matrices with 2-means clustering

0 1 <-- assigned to cluster	0 1 <-- assigned to cluster	
21 8 | Tactical	29 0 | Tactical	
4 4 | Aggressive	8 0 | Aggressive	
0 20 | Novice	19 1 | Novice	
0 17 | Defensive	17 0 | Defensive	
(a) Traditional dataset	(b) Initial datasets	
LSA - 20 dimensions	**LSA - 40 dimensions**	**LSA – 60 dimensions**
0 1	0 1	0 1
29 0 | Tactical	29 0 | Tactical	29 0 | Tactical
5 3 | Aggressive	7 1 | Aggressive	7 1 | Aggressive
0 20 | Novice	0 20 | Novice	0 20 | Novice
0 17 | Defensive	4 13 | Defensive	13 4 | Defensive
(c) Holistic-tf	(d) Holistic-tf	(e) Holistic-tf
0 1	0 1	0 1
29 0 | Tactical	29 0 | Tactical	29 0 | Tactical
5 3 | Aggressive	6 2| Aggressive	6 2| Aggressive
0 20 | Novice	0 20 | Novice	0 20 | Novice
0 17 | Defensive	4 13 | Defensive	12 5 | Defensive
(f) Holistic-tfidf	(g) Holistic-tfidf	(h) Holistic-tfidf
0 1	0 1	0 1
29 0 | Tactical	29 0 | Tactical	29 0 | Tactical
4 4 | Aggressive	4 4 | Aggressive	4 4 | Aggressive
0 20 | Novice	0 20 | Novice	0 20 | Novice
1 16 | Defensive	4 13 | Defensive	1 16 | Defensive
(i) Grid-tf	(j) Grid-tf	(k) Grid-tf
0 1	0 1	0 1
29 0 | Tactical	29 0 | Tactical	29 0 | Tactical
6 2 | Aggressive	8 0 | Aggressive	6 2 | Aggressive
0 20 | Novice	0 20 | Novice	0 20 | Novice
0 17 | Defensive	3 14 | Defensive	8 9 | Defensive
(l) Grid-tfidf	(m) Grid-tfidf	(n) Grid-tfidf
0 1	0 1	0 1
29 0 | Tactical	29 0 | Tactical	29 0 | Tactical
5 3 | Aggressive	5 3 | Aggressive	4 4 | Aggressive
0 20 | Novice	0 20 | Novice	0 20 | Novice
6 11 | Defensive	8 9 | Defensive	8 9 | Defensive
(o) Merged-tf	(p) Merged-tf	(q) Merged-tf
0 1	0 1	0 1
29 0 | Tactical	29 0 | Tactical	29 0 | Tactical
1 7 | Aggressive	8 0 | Aggressive	8 0 | Aggressive
0 20 | Novice	0 20 | Novice	0 20 | Novice
0 17 | Defensive	16 1 | Defensive	17 0 | Defensive
(r) Merged-tfidf	(s) Merged-tfidf	(t) Merged-tfidf

Figure 10. Confusion matrices with DBScan

0 1 <-- assigned to cluster	0 1 <-- assigned to cluster	0 1 2 <-- assigned to cluster
10 0 I Tactical	13 0 I Tactical	13 5 0 I Tactical
0 0 I Aggressive	0 0 I Aggressive	0 3 1 I Aggressive
0 12 I Novice	0 18 I Novice	0 1 18 I Novice
0 16 I Defensive	0 16 I Defensive	0 0 16 I Defensive
(a) Traditional dataset, r=0.5	(b) Traditional dataset, r=0.7	(c) Traditional dataset, r=0.8

0 1 2 <-- assigned to cluster	0 <-- assigned to cluster
15 6 7 I Tactical	29 I Tactical
1 3 3 I Aggressive	8 I Aggressive
19 1 0 I Novice	20 I Novice
16 0 0 I Defensive	17 I Defensive
(d) Traditional dataset, r=1	(e) Traditional dataset, r=2

Latent Dirichlet Allocation

Experiments with LDA were run on the Matlab Topic Modeling toolbox[2] that performs LDA with Gibbs sampling. The number of topics (T) was chosen to be 4 (the number of play styles) and 2 (for comparison purposes to LSA). According to the parameter default values suggested by the toolbox, the number of iterations was set to 500, the theta (topic distribution) and phi (topic-word distribution) hyperparameters on the Dirichlet priors were set to 50/T and 200/vocabulary-size, respectively.

Figure 11 shows the topic assignments of the game sessions for the initial grid and holistic datasets. For exploratory purposes, in matrices (a) and (d), the knowledge extracted from the LSA experiments is taken into account and results are depicted when only two styles are considered: aggressive-tactical and defensive-novice.

Figure 11. LDA topic assignments for the initial grid and holistic datasets

0 1 <-- assigned to topic	0 1 <-- assigned to topic	0 1 2 3 <-- assigned to topic
18 19 I Tactical	12 17 I Tactical	4 9 10 6 I Tactical
16 21 I Novice	6 2 I Aggressive	5 1 2 0 I Aggressive
(a) Initial dataset, Grid – tf	11 9 I Novice	6 2 5 7 I Novice
(Aggressive players are renamed	5 12 I Defensive	1 4 6 6 I Defensive
Tactical, Defensive players are		
renamed Novice), T=2	(b) Initial dataset, Grid – tf, T=2	(c) Initial dataset, Grid – tf, T=4
0 1 <-- assigned to topic	0 1 <-- assigned to topic	0 1 2 3 <-- assigned to topic
23 14 I Tactical	18 11 I Tactical	6 10 7 6 I Tactical
27 10 I Novice	5 3 I Aggressive	2 4 1 1 I Aggressive
(d) Initial dataset, Holistic – tf	13 7 I Novice	4 11 2 3 I Novice
(Aggressive players are renamed	14 3 I Defensive	3 13 0 1 I Defensive
Tactical, Defensive players are		
renamed Novice), T=2	(e) Initial dataset, Holistic – tf, T=2	(f) Initial dataset, Holistic – tf, T=4

Figures 12 and 13 show the percentage of words that belong to each of the four topics (T1-T4) for every game session (session ids 1-74 are depicted in the x-axis) for the holistic and for the grid data respectively. As can be seen, for most sessions, differences between their word-topic distributions are not immense, sometimes they are not even noticeable, leading to the 'unclear' confusion matrices of Figure 11.

Figure 12. Topic distribution of every game session for the holistic data

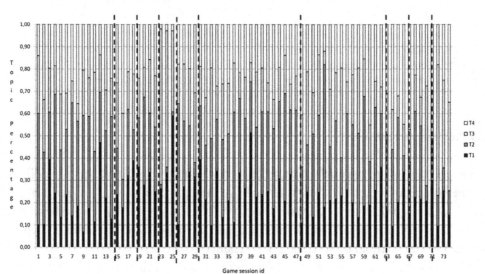

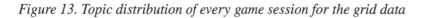

Figure 13. Topic distribution of every game session for the grid data

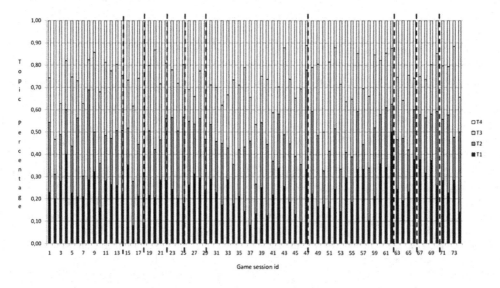

The dashed lines separate sessions between different players. At the player level, all players can be modeled using one or at most two topics, i.e. interestingly the vast majority of their sessions consist of words that belong to one or two topics at the most.

The increased sparseness in the data makes it hard for a probabilistic modeling algorithm like LDA to identify further sense-making concepts within the data in such a large feature space. Performance limitations of the Dirichlet-distribution based traditional LDA technique on sparse data has also been discussed elsewhere (Eisenstein et al., 2011). Furthermore, probabilistic modeling approaches usually rely on more data for more confident results.

CONCLUSION

Through a set of IR-inspired low-level features, LSA-based dimensionality reduction techniques and also a probabilistic modeling approach (Latent Dirichlet Allocation), the semantic domain of an action game is modeled, revealing dependencies and relations that are not easily detectable through traditional aggregate high-level feature vector representations. So, a set of approaches that are not-knowledge demanding and that can be easily applied to basically any action game without game expert knowledge, various plays styles can be identified, game domain knowledge may be discovered and players can be modeled, in a long-term goal to design games that are adjustable to the various gaming styles in an unsupervised, knowledge-poor manner. In fact, the knowledge-poor, generic nature of the proposed approach makes it applicable to games with a different purpose, apart from entertainment, namely serious games. In a learning environment, the proposed methodology can be applied to educational games to model students and learning styles, in an attempt to adjust the game to each student's profile and needs.

The four suggested classification categories (tactical, aggressive, novice, defensive) inherently pose limitations. Certainly, a player can belong to more than one style. A player may change his style over time, as he grows accustomed to the game. Also, a clear distinction among them is not always objective. These limitations, however, do not lessen the significance of the reported results.

The future research prospects regarding the detection of hidden semantic knowledge are significant. As already mentioned, LSA and LDA have inherent limitations (e.g. the effects of 'bag of words' modeling, and the data sparseness phenomena) (Anaya, 2011; Rizun et al., 2017). A larger dataset with more players, the inclusion of time- and causality-related features, and further exploration of the obtained model (e.g. word similarity apart from session similarity researched herein) can lead to the detection of unknown knowledge that may contribute significantly to intelligent player-centered game design. It can also ensure performance of higher quality for the probabilistic modeling approaches.

REFERENCES

Ahmed, R. (2011). *New Density-based Clustering Technique* [PhD Thesis]. Computer Engineering Department, The Islamic University of Gaza.

Anagnostou, K., & Maragoudakis, M. (2009). Data mining for player modeling in videogames. *Proceedings of the Panhellenic Conference on Informatics*, Corfu, Greece. Academic Press. 10.1109/PCI.2009.28

Anaya, L. H. (2011). *Comparing Latent Dirichlet Allocation and Latent Semantic Analysis as Classifiers* [Doctorate].

Aubert, A. H., Tavenard, R., Emonet, R., de Lavenne, A., Malinowski, S., Guyet, T., ... Gascuel-Odoux, C. (2013). Clustering flood events from water quality time series using Latent Dirichlet Allocation model. *Water Resources Research*, *49*(12), 8187–8199. doi:10.1002/2013WR014086

Basili, R., Petitti, R., & Saracino, D. (2007). LSA-based automatic acquisition of semantic image descriptions. *Proceedings of the Conference on Semantics and Digital Media Technologies* (pp. 41-55). Springer. 10.1007/978-3-540-77051-0_4

Bellman, R. E. (1965). On the application of dynamic programming to the determination of optimal play in chess and checkers. *Proceedings of the National Academy of Sciences of the United States of America*, *53*(2), 244–246. doi:10.1073/pnas.53.2.244 PMID:16591252

Bhattacharya, I., & Getoor, L. (2006). A Latent Dirichlet Model for Unsupervised Entity Resolution. *Proceedings of SIAM Conference on Data Mining* (pp. 47-58). Academic Press. 10.1137/1.9781611972764.5

Bisson, F., Larochelle, H., & Kabanza, F. (2015). Using a recursive neural network to learn an agent's decision model for plan recognition. *Proceedings of the 25th International Joint Conference on Artificial Intelligence* (pp. 918-924). Academic Press.

Blei, D. M., Ng, A. Y., & Jordan, M. I. (2003). Latent Dirichlet Allocation. *Journal of Machine Learning Research*, *3*, 993–1022.

Breiman, L. (2001). Random Forests. *Machine Learning*, *45*(1), 5–32. doi:10.1023/A:1010933404324

Bro, I., Siklosi, D., Szabo, J., & Benczur, A. (2009). Linked Latent Dirichlet Allocation in Web Spam Filtering. *Proceedings of the 5th ACM International Workshop on Adversarial Information Retrieval on the Web* (pp. 37-40).

Cowley, B., Kosunen, I., Lankoski, P., Kivikangas, J., Jarvela, S., Ekman, I., ... Ravaja, N. (2014). Experience assessment and design in the analysis of gameplay. *Simulation & Gaming*, *45*(1), 41–69. doi:10.1177/1046878113513936

Deepak, N. A., Hariharan, R., & Sinha, U. N. (2013). Cluster-based Human Action Recognition Using Latent Dirichlet Allocation. *Proceedings of the International Conference on Circuits, Controls and Communications* (pp. 1-4). Academic Press. 10.1109/CCUBE.2013.6718561

Done, B., Khatri, P., Done, A., & Draghici, S. (2010). Predicting novel human gene ontology annotations using semantic analysis. *IEEE/ACM Transactions on Computational Biology and Bioinformatics*, *7*(1), 91–99. doi:10.1109/TCBB.2008.29 PMID:20150671

Dong, Q., Wang, X., & Lin, L. (2006). Application of latent semantic analysis to protein remote homology detection. Bioinformatics. 22(3), 285-290. Oxford University Press. doi:10.1093/bioinformatics/bti801

Drachen, A., Canossa, A., & Yannakakis, G. (2009). Player modeling using Self-Organization in Tomb Raider: Underworld. *Proceedings of the 5th International Conference on Computational Intelligence and Games* (pp.1-8). Academic Press. 10.1109/CIG.2009.5286500

Drachen, A., Thurau, C., Sifa, R., & Bauckhage, C. (2013). A comparison of methods for player clustering via behavioral telemetry. *Proceedings of the Foundations of Digital Games*. Academic Press.

Eisenstein, J., Ahmed, A., & Xing, E. (2011). Sparse Additive Generative Models of Text. *Proceedings of the 28th International Conference on Machine Learning* (pp. 1041-1048). Academic Press.

Ester, M., Kriegel, H. P., Sander, J., & Xu, X. (1996). A Density-Based Algorithm for Discovering Clusters in Large Spatial Databases with Noise. *Proceedings of the Second International Conference on Knowledge Discovery and Data Mining* (pp. 226-231). Academic Press.

Falakmasir, M., González-Brenes, J. P., Gordon, G. J., & DiCerbo, K. (2016). A data-driven approach for inferring student proficiency from game activity logs. *Proceedings of the 3rd ACM Conference on Learning@ Scale* (pp. 341-349). ACM. 10.1145/2876034.2876038

Ganapathiraju, M., Balakrishnan, N., Reddy, R., & Klein-Seetharaman, J. (2005). Computational biology and language. In *Ambient Intelligence for Scientific Discovery* (pp. 25–47). Academic Press. doi:10.1007/978-3-540-32263-4_2

Gao, C., Shen, H., & Ali Babar, M. (2016). Concealing jitter in multi-player online games through predictive behaviour modeling. *Proceedings of the IEEE 20th International Conference on Computer Supported Cooperative Work in Design* (pp. 62-67). IEEE. 10.1109/CSCWD.2016.7565964

Geisler, B. (2002). *An empirical study of machine learning algorithms applied to modeling player behavior in a first person shooter video game* [MSc Thesis]. University of Wisconsin-Madison.

Gow, J., Baumgarten, R., Cairns, P., Colton, S., & Miller, P. (2012). Unsupervised modeling of player style with LDA. *IEEE Transactions on Computational Intelligence and AI in Games*, 4(3), 152–166. doi:10.1109/TCIAIG.2012.2213600

Graesser, A. C., Penumatsa, P., Ventura, M., Cai, Z., & Hu, X. (2007). Using LSA in AutoTutor: Learning through mixed-initiative dialogue in natural language. In T. Landauer, D. McNamara, S. Dennis, W. Kintsch (Eds.), Handbook of Latent Semantic Analysis. Academic Press.

Grant, S., Cordy, J. R., & Skillicorn, D. B. (2013). Using Heuristics to Estimate an Appropriate Number of Latent Topics in Source Code Analysis. *Science of Computer Programming*, 78(9), 1663–1678. doi:10.1016/j.scico.2013.03.015

Griffiths, T., & Steyvers, M. (2004). Finding scientific topics. *Proceedings of the National Academy of Sciences of the United States of America*, 101(Suppl. 1), 5228–5235. doi:10.1073/pnas.0307752101 PMID:14872004

Haley, D. T., Thomas, P., de Roeck, A., & Petre, M. (2005). A research taxonomy for latent semantic analysis-based educational applications. *Proceedings of the Conference on Recent Advances in Natural Language Processing,* Borovets, Bulgaria (pp. 575-579). Academic Press.

He, S., Du, J., Chen, H., Meng, J., & Zhu, Q. (2008). Strategy-based player modeling during interactive entertainment sessions by using Bayesian classification. *Proceedings of the 4th International Conference on Natural Computation,* Jinan, China (pp. 255-256). Academic Press. 10.1109/ICNC.2008.68

Hofmann, T. (2004). Latent semantic models for collaborative filtering. *ACM Transactions on Information Systems*, *22*(1), 89–115. doi:10.1145/963770.963774

Hooshyar, D., Yousefi, M., & Lim, H. (2018). Data-driven Approaches to Game Player Modeling: A Systematic Literature Review. *ACM Computing Surveys*, *50*(6), 90. doi:10.1145/3145814

Kang, Y., & Tan, A. (2010). Learning personal agents with adaptive player modeling in virtual worlds. *Proceedings of the IEEE/WIC/ACM International Conference on Web Intelligence and Intelligent Agent Technology,* Toronto, Canada (pp. 173-180). Academic Press. 10.1109/WI-IAT.2010.201

Krestel, R., Fankhauser, P., & Nejdl, W. (2009). Latent Dirichlet Allocation for Tag Recommendation. *Proceedings of the 3rd ACM Conference on Recommender Systems* (pp. 61-68). ACM.

Landauer, T., Foltz, P., & Laham, D. (1998). An introduction to latent semantic analysis. *Discourse Processes*, *25*(2-3), 259–284. doi:10.1080/01638539809545028

Lemaire, B. (1998). Models of high-dimensional semantic spaces. *Proceedings of the 4th International Workshop on Multistrategy Learning (MSL)*. Academic Press.

Liu, T., Chen, Z., Zhang, B., Ma, W. Y., & Wu, G. (2004). Improving text classification using local latent semantic indexing. *Proceedings of the International Conference on Data Mining* (pp. 162-169). Academic Press.

Luo, L., Yin, H., Cai, W., Zhong, J., & Lees, M. (2016). Design and evaluation of a data-driven scenario generation framework for game-based training. *IEEE Transactions on Computational Intelligence and AI in Games*, *99*, 1–1.

McCarthy, P. M., Briner, S., Rus, V., & McNamara, D. (2007). Textual signatures: identifying text-types using latent semantic analysis to measure the cohesion of text structures. In A. Kao & S. Poteet (Eds.), *Natural Language Processing and Text Mining* (pp. 107–122)., doi:10.1007/978-1-84628-754-1_7

Min, W., Baikadi, A., Mott, B., Rowe, J., Liu, B., Ha, E., & Lester, J. (2016). A generalized multidimensional evaluation framework for player goal recognition. *Proceedings of the 12th Annual AAAI Conference on Artificial Intelligence and Interactive Digital Entertainment*. Academic Press.

Missura, O., & Gaertner, T. (2009). Player modeling for intelligent difficulty adjustments. *Proceedings of the 12th International Conference on Discovery Science,* Porto, Portugal (pp. 197-211). Academic Press. 10.1007/978-3-642-04747-3_17

Nakov, P., Valchanova, E., & Angelova, G. (2003). Towards deeper understanding of the LSA performance. *Proceedings of the Conference on Recent Advances in Natural Language Processing* (pp. 311-318). Academic Press.

Platt, J. (1998). Fast Training of Support Vector Machines using Sequential Minimal Optimization. In B. Schoelkopf, C. Burges, & A. Smola (Eds.), *Advances in Kernel Methods - Support Vector Learning*.

Quesada, J. F., Kintsch, W., & Gomez, E. (2001). A computational theory of complex problem solving using the vector space model (part I): latent semantic analysis, through the path of thousands of ants. Cognitive research with Microworlds, 117-131.

Rizun, N., Taranenko, Y., & Waloszek, W. (2017). The Algorithm of Modeling and Analysis of Latent Semantic Relations: Linear Algebra vs. Probabilistic Topic Models. *Proceedings of the 8th International Conference on Knowledge Engineering and Semantic Web,* Szczecin, Poland (pp. 53-68). Academic Press. 10.1007/978-3-319-69548-8_5

Roberts, D., Riedl, M., & Isbell, C. (2007). Opportunities for machine learning to impact interactive narrative. *Proceedings of the NIPS Workshop on Machine Learning and Games*, Malaga. Academic Press.

Shahine, G., & Banerjee, B. (2007). Player modeling using knowledge transfer. *Proceedings of EUROSIS GAMEON-NA Conference,* Gainesville, FL (pp. 82-89). Academic Press.

Smith, A., Lewis, C., Hullett, K., Smith, G., & Sullivan, A. (2011). An inclusive view of player modeling. *Proceedings of the 6th International Conference on Foundations of Digital Games,* Bordeaux, France (pp. 301-303). Academic Press.

Steinberger, J., & Jezek, K. (2004). Using latent semantic analysis in text summarization and summary evaluation. *Proceedings of the Conference on Information Systems, Implementation and Modeling* (pp. 93-100). Academic Press.

Tamassia, M., Raffe, W., Sifa, R., Drachen, A., Zambetta, F., & Hitchens, M. (2016). Predicting player churn in destiny: A hidden Markov models approach to predicting player departure in a major online game. *Proceedings of the IEEE Conference on Computational Intelligence and Games* (pp. 1-8). IEEE. 10.1109/CIG.2016.7860431

Tang, H., Shen, L., Qi, Y., Chen, Y., Shu, Y., Li, J., & Clausi, D. A. (2013). A Multiscale Latent Dirichlet Allocation Model for Object-Oriented Clustering of VHR Panchromatic Satellite Images. *Geoscience and Remote Sensing, 51*(3), 1680–1692. doi:10.1109/TGRS.2012.2205579

Thawonmas, R. & Ho, J. (2007). Classification of online game players using action transition probability and Kullback Leibler entropy. *Journal of Advanced Computational Intelligence and Intelligent Informatics, Special issue on Advances in Intelligent Data Processing*, 11(3), 319-326.

Thue, D., Bulitko, V., Spetch, M., & Wasylishen, E. (2007). Interactive storytelling: A player modeling approach. *Proceedings of the 3rd Conference on AI and Interactive Digital Entertainment,* Stanford, CA (pp. 43-48). Academic Press.

Thurau, C., & Bauckhage, C. (2010). Analyzing the evolution of social groups in World of Warcraft. *Proceedings of IEEE Conference on Computational Intelligence and Games,* Copenhagen (pp. 170-177). Academic Press.

van Oostendorp, H. & Juvina, I. (2007). Using a cognitive model to generate web navigation support. *International Journal of Human-Computer Studies,* 65(10), 887-897. doi:. doi:10.1016/j.ijhcs.2007.06.004

Weinshall, D., Levi, G., & Hanukaev, D. (2013). LDA Topic Model with Soft Assignment of Descriptors to Words. *Proceedings of the 30th International Conference on Machine Learning* (pp. 711-719). Academic Press.

Yannakakis, G. N., Maragoudakis, M., & Hallam, J. (2009). Preference learning for cognitive modeling: A case study on entertainment preferences. *IEEE Transactions on Systems, Man, and Cybernetics. Part A, Systems and Humans*, *39*(6), 1165–1175. doi:10.1109/TSMCA.2009.2028152

Zampa, V., & Lemaire, B. (2002). Latent semantic analysis for user modeling. *Journal of Intelligent Information Systems*, *18*(1), 15–30. doi:10.1023/A:1012916523718

ENDNOTES

[1]   https://multithreaded.stitchfix.com/blog/2015/03/11/word-is-worth-a-thousand-vectors/
[2]   http://psiexp.ss.uci.edu/research/programs_data/toolbox.htm

This research was previously published in the International Journal of Gaming and Computer-Mediated Simulations (IJGCMS), 11(2); pages 1-21, copyright year 2019 by IGI Publishing (an imprint of IGI Global).

Chapter 19
Multi–Disciplinary Paths to Actor–Centric Non–Player Character Emotion Models

Sheldon Schiffer
Georgia State University, USA

ABSTRACT

Video game non-player characters (NPCs) are a type of agent that often inherits emotion models and functions from ancestor virtual agents. Few emotion models have been designed for NPCs explicitly, and therefore do not approach the expressive possibilities available to live-action performing actors nor hand-crafted animated characters. With distinct perspectives on emotion generation from multiple fields within narratology and computational cognitive psychology, the architecture of NPC emotion systems can reflect the theories and practices of performing artists. This chapter argues that the deployment of virtual agent emotion models applied to NPCs can constrain the performative aesthetic properties of NPCs. An actor-centric emotion model can accommodate creative processes for actors and may reveal what features emotion model architectures should have that are most useful for contemporary game production of photorealistic NPCs that achieve cinematic acting styles and robust narrative design.

INTRODUCTION

"Constructing characters" is a phrase that infers distinct meanings for two participants in the creative process of computer-based media. On one hand, for the narrative architect of video games or other kinds of narrative computational media, it is a semiotic process of fiction authoring where the character designer provides a written personal history. Three-dimensional or two-dimensional models of anthropomorphic shape combined with voice can also suggest agency in a game space. A weapon-wielding muscular humanoid with big bright eyes is well equipped for video game combat and all of the emotional expression players associate with fighting. Once audio-visual elements are programmed to react to user input, these elements can signify to the observant player an imagined persona. On the other hand, for the developer of video game computer code, "constructing characters" is a process of designing a system that uses

DOI: 10.4018/978-1-6684-7589-8.ch019

quantitative data derived from the game program, the computer operating system or from player input data to control or trigger character animation and voicing such that the player experiences the presence of a seemingly intelligent cohesive character identity. The result of the work of the designer and the developer is a composite signified that evolves in the player's mind over the time of game play.

The manner of construction for narrative architects of video games depends on mental processes of player participation. Over the course of game play time, the player may observe actions and behaviors of Non-Player Characters (NPCs) so that a pre-game play biography and an in-game "alterbiography" (Calleja 2009) combines the NPC's pre-game past with the evolving NPC actions the player witnesses or learns through game interaction since the start of the game. The manner of character construction for video game developers depends on computer languages whose frameworks contain data structures (primitives, classes, objects) and data behaviors (methods, functions) that can trigger and manipulate unique animations of the three-dimensional mesh model and its sound emanations (usually a voice) in ways that resemble the player's understanding of human and animal emotional expressions. These NPC animations and sounds must be recognizable by the player as specific to the NPC's type as a fictional narrative agent (human or non-human) and consistent with the character's role within the world of the game.

The study of character construction coincides with the related research in other disciplines. The late twentieth century coincidentally delivered strains of thought from disciplines that sought to provide taxonomies of two human endeavors – storytelling and emotion expression. Narratology addressed the former and evolved from literary theory and folklore studies to describe systematically the human perception and representation of stories in various media. The categorization of characters within stories based on a typology of roles and emotion sets afforded to those roles is one specialization within narratology. Cognitive psychology and its subdiscipline, Computational Cognitive Psychology, evolved as a reaction to Behaviorism and as an alternative explanation to the mental and emotional processes that drive human behavior. The categorization of human emotions as well as their neurological processes is one subdiscipline that Cognitive psychologist frequently consider. The two disciplines converge in computer game design because game character designers and game code developers both use models from which characters can be efficiently produced. These characters and their behaviors can be embodied as preconfigured audio-visual animation and sound synthesis systems for "static" characters or can be used in-game to spawn procedurally generated characters or behaviors.

This research focuses on NPC modeling rather than Player Character modeling for the benefit of taking a simpler problem before tackling the more complex Player Character with its additional set of variables that describe each player's unique persona and context. Daniel Vella initialized a discussion of the Player Character's implications on game narrative that can apply to related studies of NPCs (Vella 2014). A discussion of NPC modeling benefits from the character theories of Narratology and the emotion theories of Computational Cognitive Psychology because both examine the behavior of human or human-like agency. Narratology considers how foregrounding particular NPC behaviors in the context of an audio-visual story system forms the role of a character. These behaviors are a functional necessity for story development and an elaboration in the player's mind. Computational Cognitive Psychology considers how to represent in computational form, a simulation of the internal processing machinery of the emotive part of the human mind so that when one implements and embeds an emotion model in an agent such as an NPC, the sensory input will yield an expressive output as an appropriate behavior that simulates a coherent human-like character. To design an NPC model of emotion for video games, one must consider how emotions in characters are useful in the elaboration of narrative, and how they are generated by actors for use in animated characters.

BACKGROUND

Whether one considers video games as narratives or narrative systems, the fact a player *moves* through the time and space of a game world provides sufficient conditions to apply the frameworks of narratology. For games with NPCs, the player experiences over time the construction of character within her mind. Each interaction with an NPC is a momentary witnessing of in-game action with all of its semiotic unwrapping over the duration of gameplay. Cognitive Psychology recognizes that expression on the body, and in particular as seen on the face, belies the mental properties and emotional states of a person (Ekman 1997). It also communicates emotional meanings from the face of one person into the eyes of another. The latter function of emotion serves narrative expression in the visual arts through the agency of character. The degree to which facial expression effects game narrative depends on the complexity of expression, and therefore the degree of immersion and believability a player may experience. Thus, an effective NPC emotion model must strive for complex expressions.

Narrative Expansion Through Facial Expression Complexity

Seymour Chatman gives a comparative study of Maupassant's short story *Une Partie de campagne* (*A Country Excursion*) (Maupassant 2017) with Jean Renoir's rendition of the story in the film *A Day in the Country* (Braunberger & Renoir 1936). Chatman provides persuasive analyses of how emotions within characters as described by words in a literary narrative are interpreted through cinematography and editing to convey similar ideas in a film adaptation (Chatman 1980). Many of these emotional ideas that Chatman identifies depend on the framing of shots in the film where actors' faces communicate their emotional states. But cinema is not video game. In Renoir's film we are forced to see faces within a frame and in the order of a sequence of images. The dialectical process of montage allows the meanings of faces to be refined and elaborated by the image that precedes a facial closeup and by the image that follows. In video games, only cutscenes lock the player into seeing specifically framed and ordered images of faces. When the camera is released to the volition of the player, there are few if any cuts to other images. Once the camera is free to move in response to the player's will, there is no way for the game designer to be sure that the player sees anything in a particular order. An NPCs facial expression must convey its ideas independent of other objects in the viewing screen. The need for the player to maneuver and see an NPCs face must be embedded in the mechanic of the gameplay. While lighting, music and voice can reinforce the emotional state of an NPC as well as the mood of the game space, the facial expression itself must provide the emotional clarity the game designer intends. If the goals of characters steer their action, then the emotional expression on the face of NPCs reveal how the designer wants the player to understand the character's attitude toward their goals and the consequence of their action at a particular instance. (Later in this discussion, there will be a more robust elaboration of how Computational Cognitive Psychology informs the design of the internal workings of NPCs.)

But is there enough information from the face of an NPC to "move" the narrative and cause the player to decide something significant within a game? The answer depends on the resolution of the animation. A higher resolution facial animation provides the character designer more expressive possibilities. In the past, the concept of visual resolution has described the density of pixels for a given square of screen surface. But *animation resolution* describes the number of vertex groups of an NPCs facial mesh that move distinctly and simultaneously for a unique emotion expression. While this description does not yet provide a quantifiable ratio of dependent and independent variables (like pixels per inch, for example), it does communicate a problem in game animation that effects the player's experience. Game animation must render each frame in real time (usually 60 frames each second). A character with complicated expressions simultaneously moving many parts of a mesh, can demand a lot of parallel calculations of a graphics process, thus challenging the graphics processor to complete all necessary calculations within 1/60th of a second. Cinematic acting for NPCs depends on such computational power. But with complex animated facial expressions, players can observe more detailed expression; they can read more nuanced emotional information when observing NPCs up close. Chatman's close reading examines the polysemic phrasings of Maupassant's story with the polysemic cinematic expression of Renoir's filmed rendition. High resolution animation allows a similarly comparison between a character in a work of literature and its representation in a video game adaptation. Complex facial expression in game characters can allow the player to perceive NPC emotions in ways similar to human actors. NPC facial expression can then be used to effect narrative generation.

Augmenting the expressive capabilities of NPCs has the side effect of augmenting narrative expressivity of video games. Narratologist Uri Margolin defines *characterization* as a "human or human-like individual… capable of fulfilling the argument position in the propositional form DO(X) – that is, a Narrative Agent (=NA), to whom inner states, mental properties (traits, features) or complexes of such properties (personality models) can be ascribed on the basis of textual data" (Margolin 1986). The definition is applicable especially when examining the detailed form of a game character as seen in a single frame of video game play, in a model sheet typically produced in the preproduction stages of character design, or in a written biography of a video game character. In these video game text documents, signification occurs by inference. The character's behaviors are imagined by what its body looks like statically, and what has been reported about its past in the written form. Margolin continues by describing *character-building* in a narrative, which is an "accumulation of a number of traits" or trait clusters "from several successive acts of the NA [Narrative Agent]…" A built character is "a unified stable constellation" of traits experienced in narrative time. While Margolin had in mind primarily literary characters, the player likewise experiences NPCs during gameplay over time and observes their actions in much the same way, gradually building an idea of a character in mind.

When one thinks of actions in video game play, often the idea conjures dramatic movements that propel the body of the character or impact objects the character touches. These actions reveal internal and external states and features of NPCs through body gestures, postures and facial expressions. Facial expressions tell much about the internal mental states and actions of NPCs. Literary representations of emotion take the form either of direct predicate statements where the emotional state becomes the predicate or adverb (e.g. It is angry, charmed or It acts lovingly, scornfully) or are presented indirectly as actions or reactions in the form of a verb (e.g. It *flees* from fear, It *flirts* from arousal). Visual representations of character must use other means. Posture, gesture and facial expressions of emotion are the primary means of presenting emotion in NPCs. Early video games, much like early animation in the cinema were limited to a smaller vocabulary of emotional expressions because the processor speeds and workflow did not easily allow for much variation of expression. But more powerful graphics processors and modularized workflow allow for complex groups of simultaneous animations of different parts of an NPC face to form many more combinations and variations of emotional expression. By expanding the vocabulary of a character's emotive expression, the possible meanings derived by the player from an NPC's expressive system also expand. With more possible meanings entering the space of a narrative, the count of possible player experiences and interpretations grow as well. Thus as NPC emotional expressivity increases in combinatorial complexity with an expanding vocabulary of movements and gestures,

NPCs have the ability to evolve from expressing simpler cartoon-like acting styles where performative meanings are simple, discrete and the expressive variables show few dimensions, into a more robust cinematic acting style where expression is polysemic, often ambiguous and the expressive variables of the face have many more dimensions.

Agency and Acting

The "construction" or "building" of Non-Player Characters by the player within a video game borrows heavily from experiences with other non-ludic art forms, such as literary fiction and films, as well as perceived experiences of simulation systems, such as software. Theatrical and cinematic narrative depend on the appearance of willful actions of characters in a story world. *Agency* in drama is the apparent freedom of a character to act, react, not act, or sublimate desire to achieve a goal within a fictional world. Aristotle and many modern theorists of agency attribute voluntary goal acquisition as an underlying cause of human action (Charles 2017). For NPCs and Player Characters, Janet Murray translates the concept effectively. "Agency is the satisfying power to take meaningful action and see the results of our decisions and choices" (Murray, 1997). The definition of agency has extended itself into software engineering.

As NPCs in video games developed, likewise *agents* were run-time entities within software. The concept of *agency* in software engineering emerged commercially in the mid-1990s when software required run-time decisions to manage its states autonomously. Developers realized that software systems need agents to assess the state and behavior of a system's environment to autonomously manage the system in the background so that desired measurable states are maintained. Agents in software are distinct from other software components because they do not need to wait for a user to tell them what to do. Agents can have goals that they remember pervasively, and they can be provided readable and writable access to execute methods on other software objects to accomplish those goals (Maes, 1997).

Eventually, agents within software surfaced to interact with users directly using text, speech or character animation. They helped users accomplish software dependent tasks. These have been called *virtual* agents. The primary functional tradition of servitude for virtual agents limits their autonomy and their range of emotional expressivity. Virtual agents were not designed to entertain. But as computer games began to use facial animation for emotion elicitation of NPCs, an emotion model architecture was required. Animators provided basic iconic facial expressions of emotions and software developers integrated morph animations driven by emotion models adopted from virtual agents.

Virtual agents, however, were not originally embedded in artfully crafted interactive narratives, but were relegated to software assistance for users. As emotion models of Cognitive Computational Psychology were implemented into virtual agents, validation of virtual agent efficacy affirmed their use for pedagogical applications (Rickel and Johnson 1997, Lane et al. 2013). The implementation of the same virtual agent technology for video games was an obvious temptation. But the limitations of graphics processors, central processors and memory required a low bar of aesthetic expectations for players as demonstrated in the crude character designs of the first three decades of computer games. Player aesthetic expectations of autonomously animated NPC "acting" had to be simpler to adapt to technology limitations. Following comic book artists and non-photoreal animators before them, game character artists and developers more often mimicked the expressions in the cannon of Delsartean-based typology of facial and body models to create automated animations that could express basic recognizable emotions (Nixon 2010). Virtual agent emotion models could at best validate their ground-truth assumptions based on a player's recognition of an NPC emotion, an NPCs believability of the authenticity of expression, or the

NPCs social appropriateness. These three assumptions reflect the narrow range of expressivity a virtual agent could emote given the technological constraints on real-time 3D animation. These methods of emotion expression in agents do not consider the concept of complexity of animation expression, which can be defined as the number of simultaneous facial animations an NPC may elicit in response to stimuli as either an active or reactive expression. Simultaneous animations with higher resolution animation allow developers and animators to collaborate with actors and realize more complex emotion elicitation.

Behave Like a Human, Think Like a Machine

MIT Media Lab researcher Patti Maes in 1997 wanted agents of "intelligent software" to "sense the current state of its environment and act independently to make progress toward its goal" (Maes, 1997). While describing agents, Maes uses one of the underlying concepts of artificial intelligence laid out forty years before by Alan Turing in his notable 1950 essay "Computing Machinery and Intelligence" (Turing, 1950). Turing proposed that machines could think autonomously and learn from their environment and past actions. But four decades earlier, Turing went further than Maes. He proposed that machines could respond in human-like ways to elicit enough rapport to convince a user that the machine was human. Without stating so directly, his rebuttals redrafted the idea of what "thought" was, by allowing that the production of a thought can include distinctly "mechanical" methods. The notable proposal of a continuous state machine suggests that he at least intuited some types of "thought" were not finite states that depended on a combination of true (1) or false (0) relations but were gradients that allowed for a continuous range [0,1], much as basic emotional expression states are currently given normalized values, and much as emotion expression morphs are blended between each other (e.g. blendshapes). Turing anticipated that a machine may have to perform machine-like thinking to come to human-like results. "May not machines carry out something which ought to be described as thinking but which is very different from what a man does" (Turing, 1950)? Virtual agents, as Turing described in his essay, may process "thought" like a machine, but still elicit behavior like a human. Virtual agents are programmed to elicit emotional reactions like humans while processing input data mathematically, probabilistically and algorithmically.

Long before computers existed, French philosopher and mathematician, René Descartes reasoned how a machine could never think like a human (Descartes, 2006). Descartes decried in 1668 the "impossibility" of sentient AI. "...It is for all practical purposes impossible for a machine to have enough different organs to make it act in all the contingencies of life in the way in which our reason makes us act" (Descartes, 2006). The reasons he gave described the challenge of computing semantic correctness and social appropriateness with limited computing power and memory to process a wide range of meaningful expression combinations. The basic needs for semantic correctness and social appropriateness accomplish two things that humans do not always do well: *teaching* and *entertaining*. Both human activities require sensitive and dynamic awareness of the emotional state of the user. A detailed psychological model of the user or player is essential to direct the actions of an agent precisely and to measure the agent's effectiveness. A virtual agent with eyes must know where on the user's body of the elicitor it should look and gather input. It should also be able to interpret what that input means. Gestural and facial expression, with its potential for producing ambiguous meanings that trigger emotions, is what Descartes intuited as a combinatorial morass.

PEDAGOGIC AGENTS AND EMOTIONAL BEHAVIOR

Descartes was correct. Logical processes are not effective to make decisions if available information is not complete enough to find a rational conclusion, or if premises are contradictory. Cognitive psychologists and neuroscientists contend that "emotional intelligence" allows the mind to fall back on another process that is based on probabilistic reasoning (Damasio, 1998; Johnson-Laird & Oatley, 1992). The brain contains neural networks that use pattern recognition to provide probabilistic answers to situations that rational thought cannot adequately answer. By applying emotional reasoning methods in a virtual agent, it can "predict" or recognize patterns from machine-learned (ML) instances to make behavioral decisions.

"Socially Appropriate" Behavior

Rosalind Picard, a research pioneer in the field of Affective Computing, describes an emotionally intelligent agent as possessing "abilities to recognize, express, and have emotions, coupled with the ability to regulate these emotions, harness them for constructive purposes, and skillfully handles the emotions of others" (Picard, 2000). In the context of an animated video interaction, a three-dimensionally animated agent often moves and speaks in ways perceived as "socially appropriate" for the context of the user-agent relationship. It should demonstrate emotionally logical behavior, follow an expected cause-and-effect sequence, that would respond to the sentience of the user. The term socially appropriate (which is sometimes called "behaviorally appropriate") describes behaviors that fall within a normal range of variance of behaviors given a specific social situation with a known set of persons in specific types of relationships to a user (Price & Bouffard, 1974). The range of variance is affected by an expectation of satisfaction from a user and the culturally determined role the agent plays in the relationship with the user. For example, a virtual agent classmate in a learning application who assumes the role of a *peer* will likely behave with a broader range of appropriate behaviors than a virtual agent that is an *instructor* who assumes a role of pedagogic authority. Behavioral variance in virtual agents can constrain or expand user input as users adapt their decision-making variance to the variance expressed by agents (Yin & Sun, 2015). Additionally, some feature values of the human user are considered that can affect an agent's behavior – physical location, language, culture, gender, class, education level, age, sexual orientation, country of origin and ethnicity (Gratch, Okhmatovskaia & Duncan, 2006). A virtual agent can be designed to choose for vocalization variables: diction, prosody, volume, pitch and backchannel utterances or for facial expression variables: movement direction, velocity and acceleration so that it can reflect and respond in socially appropriate ways to the user. A designer's intention is for a virtual agent's elicitation parameters to effectively tune to the user's familiar behaviors so that it will maximize rapport during the interaction (Zhao, Papangelis & Cassell, 2014).

Virtual agents that teach or entertain, challenge the engineer to model its algorithms to accomplish a task that has no finite outcome of "correctness". A virtual agent with affective abilities should at least be able to fulfill each of Picard's criteria for emotional intelligence – emotion recognition, elicitation, and regulation – to accomplish its goal. For example, a virtual piano teacher must demonstrate a nomenclature in musical theory, but also must sense (by facial or vocal expression) if the student "feels" she is able to understand more complex or simple examples, or no examples at all (Picard & Rosalind, 2000). The virtual agent must decide if its own gestural and aural expression should be firmer and more resolute in posture and tone, or gentler and more accepting. A hospital-based virtual agent, called a

Hospital Buddy, provides companionship and reduces psychiatric side-effects of long-term patients. The Hospital Buddy must sense a level of trust to inquire from the patient perceptions of his hospital experience (Bickmore, Bukhari, Vardoulakis, Paasche-Orlow & Shanahan, 2012). Virtual immigration interviewers in the E.U. and the U.S. have been developed and tested for border crossings (Dormehl, 2018). They are designed to flag possible deception by visa applicants using affective biometric data, including facial micro-expressions, during inquiries for facts collected from an interview. The agent must choose questions that intend to trigger emotional responses in relation to known facts and to notice an absence of emotional response (Deahl, 2018). In all these examples of pedagogic virtual agents, they must sense the emotional state of the user and express itself in a socially appropriate way so that its tasks and manner prioritize the productive flow of information between computer to human, and back from human to computer.

Elicitation-by-Design

For this discussion here forward, the term *pedagogic* agent shall refer to didactic, interrogative, informative and simulative virtual agents (all characteristics of a teacher). Pedagogic agents are generally designed to elicit "controlled" emotional responses so that the messages they express produce a predictable experience from the user and for the developer. For pedagogic agents, emotional expression must carry an intended message and outcome so that the user's behavior leads to an interactive experience that enables the agent to gather the emotional information from the user as intended – surprises can defeat the software's purpose. Pedagogic agents are not free to express the full capacity of a human personality any more than a human could doing a similar pedagogic task. To accomplish this emotion-elicitation-by-design, the author of the agent must program to specification by biasing the emotion that the agent should demonstrate during an instance of human interaction. Pedagogic agents for the most part substitute a human service that the user is presumed to need. Once the user ceases to need the service, then a pedagogic agent can become an intolerable sycophantic nuisance. The "coached" emotion-elicitation-by-design approach often fails to convey authenticity because the emotional "results" performed in a scripted interaction are intended to synchronize with a developer-permitted pedagogic task to fulfill an anticipated user need rather than respond to the spontaneous emotion elicitation of the user.

Negative Personality Traits

Unpredictability, Immorality, Deceptiveness, Self-Loathing, Flippancy, Distractedness and Forgetfulness. The seven words are negative personality traits discouraged for any person assigned to a pedagogic role. Teachers, counselors, judges, doctors would not likely gain more clients if user reviews included descriptions with these negative characteristics. However, they are all attractive characteristics for fictional NPCs because they create inter-personal conflicts that test a player's beliefs and assumptions about the game world (and perhaps the player's world). While these characteristics may not be desired in a non-NPC emotion model (such as that of a virtual agent), each of them makes useful functional components in an NPC emotion model as it decides either what emotion its appraisal will select, or what elicitation it should animate.

Neuroticism

Sometimes the user appreciates hints of awareness of the negative characteristics in human behavior, or what is typically referred to in personality dimensions as "neurotic behavior" (Trull, 2013). Neurotic behavior from pedagogic agents (virtual or real) distract from the disingenuousness of a commercial-cum-social interaction. (Consider the cynical humor of flight attendants who joke about passenger attention during pre-flight announcements.) But neuroticism tolerance varies among users and contexts; it may contradict the social "believability" of the virtual agent (Malatesta, Caridakis, Raouzaiou, & Karpouzis, 2007). While humor for the user can be the result of an agent's neuroticism, it can be socially inappropriate for a user-agent relationship if the agent is pedagogic. Additionally, if the pedagogic agent has little or no awareness of human misdeeds or maladaptation, then a neurotic response would be implausible. Moreover, a pedagogic agent must have a narrow range of expressive variability to keep the user serviced and focused on the tasks of the software.

DISTINCT EMOTIONAL FEATURES OF NPCs

An entertaining agent gathers, processes, and elicits sentient information with greater freedom of emotional expression than a pedagogic one, much as an actor has more emotionally expressive liberty than a teacher. *Entertaining* virtual agents are found in games and interactive media where the agent is personified to express the features of its personality that serve the game world. For clarity, this author refers to entertaining virtual agents as NPCs. Their emotion-response algorithms receive relevant data from the player and game play space and elicit expressive data back into the game play environment for the player to observe and respond. A cycle of data exchange can create rapport or dissonance between player and NPC as the game evolves and as the NPCs role requires. The narrative "facts" revealed in this exchange can be distorted or omitted by the NPCs subjective filters, much as any fictional character does in other media. Furthermore, neuroticism may be welcome insofar as it fits the role required for the world of the game. NPCs are often designed to elicit from the player a wider range of emotional responses than pedagogical agents. Similarly, live action actors and comedians or animated cartoon characters provoke emotions that are not permitted from instructors or public spokespersons. An actor, through his character, can elicit rage, fear and disgust in "socially inappropriate" ways when playing a conflicted character. Pedagogic agents such as piano teachers or public health officials usually cannot; the roles of pedagogic agents rarely allow neurotic behavior. Spectacular neuroticism as a performative aesthetic of cinematic acting is a feature of cinematic acting insofar as game players also watch movies and expect a similar degree of performative complexity, emotional authenticity and celebrity attraction (Morgans, 2018; Stuart, 2016).

Cinematic Acting Style

The trend in the last half-decade has demonstrated strong interest in cinematic acting styles as games increase their ability to use higher resolution graphics, motion, and complex facial expression animation (Torres, 2014). Cinematic acting differs from theatrical acting in the production method. While performance preparation methods are very similar, cinematic acting requires the actor to deconstruct a performance into smaller units for each shot. Acting for animation of video game NPCs require actors to decompose further – down to the gesture, posture, or facial expression. To capture motion data for high resolution animation, increased computational power is needed to recognize the face, track its inflection, and predict its movement over time. Contemporary graphics processors allow for the capture of more complex and simultaneous emotion expressions. High-resolution animations support the aesthetic of cinematic acting styles in video games.

What are cinematic acting styles? Cinematic acting inherited many methods for training from theater. There are two dominant currents in cinematic acting styles. One works from a collective external vocabulary of postures, gestures and facial expressions that are loosely assigned to roles within a theatrical narrative. The task of the actor is to shape his own variation of a role as a set of expressions that convey the emotional expressions of a character for the specific narrative. This approach, often called the outside-in approach and is associated with performance theorist Vsevelod Meyorhold and Francois Delsarte, is highly adaptable between cultures and requires a studious actor to learn the emotive vocabulary of the target audience. The outside-in approach affiliates well with animation and its tradition of referencing a Delsartean taxonomy of physical expression, much like trained and practiced for silent film acting (Hart 2005). The other major approach requires a process of self-examination to identify existing emotional impulses from past lived experience so that when an actor in-character focuses on an action, the resulting emotion from obstructions or assistance are personally authentic. This inside-out approach has been affiliated with Konstantin Stanislavski and his Method approach as well as Sanford Meisner. In animated or live-action films, both currents of cinematic acting deploy complex simultaneous movements motivated by inferred psychological states that are used by actors to create character facial expression for motion capture or voice recording for video games.

For this research, both cinematic acting styles provide valuable methods for facial expression in video games as they connect the emotional source of actor expression to NPCs that move narratives forward. Games that aspire to cinematic high resolutions of image and movement, such as *Beyond Two Souls* (Quantic Dream 2013) and *The Last of Us* (Naughty Dog 2013), have shown substantial consideration of the aesthetics of cinematic acting through complex animations of the face. Therefore, the methods and techniques of cinematic acting, character development and performance deserve consideration as video games embrace NPCs with cinematic acting styles.

Responsiveness to Multiple Simultaneous Stimuli

The game player, attracted to cinematic acting, expects more complex animation to enrich the perceived emotional and intellectual life of the character. To develop cinematic acting for NPCs, its animation must move in complex ways that are consistent with the design of a complex screen performance; this means moving groups of vertices of an NPCs mesh in ways that represent a response from simultaneous stimuli from both external-physical and internal-mental sources. When we closely examine well-prepared actors that move in any fully developed performance style, such as naturalism or physical comedy, what makes a performance complex (and possibly "good") is when an actor responds to multiple stimuli almost simultaneously, from sources that are external-physical and also from sources that are internal-mental. Acting Theorist John Lutterbie draws from Cognitive Science as he describes the "acting instrument" as a Dynamic System Theory model that listens inside and outside the body, filters decisions through memory, then responds with complex movement, language and gesture (Lutterbie, 2011). Complexity increases when an actor listens, acknowledges and responds with "executive control" to multiple stimuli with an intensity that seems appropriate to the scene, role, its story, and its world.

Often attention to stimuli in the external-physical space appears to the player with a subjective internal-mental amplification or diminishment of intensity. As game designers deploy cinematic acting styles, the Player observes stimuli generated from the NPC that seems internal-mental and occurs simultaneously with stimuli from the external-physical space. That disparity of intensity creates a competition of focus for the NPC which results in polysemic expression. The player notices this distinction and imagines, often with pleasurable uncertainty and insatiable curiosity, what the actor is thinking or feeling. Often the most pleasure-inducing experience is an ambiguous facial expression, and the audience or player invents or projects her own meanings that caused the expression. This ambiguity of focus can be built into the NPC and is fundamental to how cinematic acting styles contribute to the expansion of the narrative space. No longer is the game limited to a visual physical space. Cinematic acting styles open the narrative to the mental space of the NPC. To achieve cinematic acting, NPCs require uniquely subjective filters and algorithms to idiosyncratically appraise and elicit reactions to the emotion-evoking entities it perceives.

Cinematic Mediation of Emotion Expression

Principal game characters are presented to the player base with spectacular trailers and posters, much modeled on theatrical film trailers. These advertising media reinforce character archetypes and stereotypes, and also create a set of behavioral expectations in the player before ever playing the game. Additionally, in-game NPCs are experienced by players as mediated persona through game video screens and speakers, much like film and television characters. Audio-visual moods and cues reinforce mediated emotional expressions in a game much as one observes in film and television (Smith, 2003; Wiley, 2003). The construction of mediated emotional expressions results from already familiar production methods of actor training, casting, rehearsal, recording and reperformance technologies that games use for their production. A facial expression on an NPC after a kiss or bullet to the back triggers an expected category of emotional response that can stand alone or come accompanied with sympathetic or dissonant music, sound effects or dialog. The combined facial expression and sound can affect the perceived meaning of the response and negate or affirm the expected response. These expectations do not precisely resemble real life but are a synthesis of memories of watching previous mediated experiences of similar events combined with real life memories. Actors are trained to express real emotions and to synthesize them with culturally preconceived expressions of real emotions.

Performative Mediation of Emotion Expression

Mediation is not only determined by industrial or societal norms through cinema. Mediation can also be the result of an actor's own imaginary construction of the character's mental processes as she believes the audience will perceive them. As each elicitation of an actor or NPC is presumably the result of the flow of emotion-evoking stimuli, it is an actor's detailed design of those mental processes for the character that provides actor-centric mediation of elicitation. Thus, what has here been defined as cinematic acting style for NPCs, with its complex mesh animations, is the result of an actor's invention of an internal emotion model that filters sensations, identifies them, prioritizes them, associates them with memories, maps sensations to affect definitions, and selects an elicitation in response that appears as an emotional facial expression.

EMOTION MODELING OF COGNITIVE COMPUTATIONAL PYSCHOLOGY

Performance theories that are foundational for cinematic acting share some concepts that describe the derivation of human emotion with those defined in the literature of Computational Cognitive Psychology. Psychologists Ortony, Clore and Collins were among the first to propose a human emotion model for simulation on the computer. While theirs was not intended for game development, it is easy to imagine that its deployment would sense emotion triggers in the game play space. The model would process the sensed data through its own character-specific filters, choose an emotion that describes the state of the NPC, and then elicit that emotion through an animatable face, body or synthetic voice. During the last thirty years, emotion models were designed to test the human affect processing system by observing them embedded in virtual agents more than NPCs. Computational Cognition Theories of emotion are collectively known as Appraisal Theories. To understand the rationale for an Actor-Centric emotion model for NPCs, a fundamental understanding of an Appraisal Theory framework for emotion models is helpful.

Appraisal Theory for NPCs

Computational Cognitive Psychologists for the most part agree that emotions are generated in response to an "appraisal" of the environment and its condition to affirm one's *beliefs*, provide access to fulfill *desires* and enable one's *intentions* (BDI). A person's environment is often laden with entities to appraise in ways that concern a person's physical and social survival and quality of existence. Appraisal occurs initially as a person assesses the immediate situation and its immediate impact (Ortony, Clore & Collins, 1990). And for some theorists, there is a *secondary* appraisal (reappraisal) where one considers how to cope long-term by accepting the situation as it is and adjust one's attitude about the situation. A person might then take action to change the situation in response (Lazarus, 1991).

Entities that have emotional effects on a person are either inanimate *objects*, animate *agents,* or consequential *events*. A person will judge an object's *likeability*, an event's desirability (of consequences), or an agent's (past, current or future) *praiseworthiness* (of actions) in terms that either favor positively or negatively one's own BDIs. Observing and evaluating an entity (object, event or agent) and its feature values registers an emotional appraisal along one or more dimensions of measurement. The values of these measurements are stored as *appraisal variables*. A fundamental scale of measurement is *pleasure* and *displeasure* within a range of [-1,1]. This dimension has also been interpreted as *aversion* and *attraction.* As a two-dimensional appraisal scale, *pleasure-displeasure* runs on the X-axis and rises with *arousal (intensity)* on the Y-axis within a range of [-1,1]. Originally known as the Circumplex Model of Emotion (Russell, 1980), it has been further refined as a 12-emotion unit circle with evenly divided expression positions called the Core Affect (Yik, Russel and Steiger, 2011), as shown in Figure 1. Core affect prioritizes the "basic" emotion positions in the unit circle. A three-dimensional scale variation includes *dominance* on the Z-axis within a range of [-1, 1] (Mehrabian, 1996) where dominance represents the degree to which a person can control the emotion from triggering impulsive elicitations that could be anti-social, unwelcomed or inappropriate, as shown in Figure 2. Most Computational Cognitive Models based on Appraisal Theories use either two- or three-dimensional emotion mapping, as found in Embodied Conversational Agent development (Malatesta, Raouzaiou, Karpouzis & Kollias, 2009). Using two- and three-dimensional emotion maps is known to provide a system modeled on closely observed human behavior. Emotion maps allow researchers to test a virtual agent accurately in relation to a human reference (Lisetti & Hudlicka, 2015; Gratch, Marsella, Wang, Stankovic, 2009).

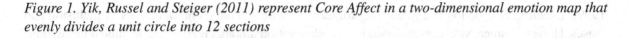

Figure 1. Yik, Russel and Steiger (2011) represent Core Affect in a two-dimensional emotion map that evenly divides a unit circle into 12 sections

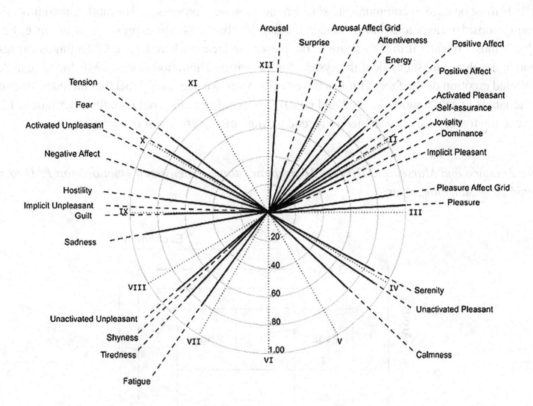

NPCs perceive entities with subjectively determined values of their feature variables based on their character-specific BDIs. For every entity that triggers an emotion, an algorithm must translate and map all the entity's feature values in a two-dimensional Circumplex, as shown in Figure 3, or a three-dimensional volume, as shown in Figure 4, to a coordinate point positioned by its appraisal variable values -- Pleasure, Arousal and (if in three-dimensions) Dominance (PAD). These two or three dimensional values are normalized within a [-1, 1] range of a unit circle or sphere.

Much of the distinction between appraisal theories is the structure of the emotion model, and therefore the path of stimuli signal through the model. Some theories emphasize memory and pattern recognition components in relation to goals and praiseworthiness, others emphasize reappraisal and changes of emotion response, while others emphasize the effect of stimuli on planning for goal acquisition. The resulting PA or PAD values may change as the appraisal process cycles through each appraisal or reappraisal over time. PA and PAD values infer a vector with a coordinate point at its tip. With each reappraisal cycle, the vector can move to a new position as the emotional state of the agent changes.

A coordinate point within a unit circle or sphere falls into a region or volume that is bounded by an emotion label. The idea of the emotion label is controversial. Some Computational Cognitive Psychologist prefer to abandon labels for emotions. The trepidation to work with emotion labels stems from the subjective quality of assigning a culturally determined word to an object (an emotion) only known by elicited effects in the body, and often repressed by the vagaries of culture (Russell & Feldman Barrett,

1999). Labeling an emotion is a linguistic problem rife with semantic contradictions of inclusion and biases. However, since NPC design depends on collaboration among creative and technical professionals, labels must be used to communicate software development processes. This author recommends the following considerations to avoid misunderstanding labeling emotion expression of the face. First, a developer must consider if in the culture of the player the face is where a specific feeling is expressed. Second, a developer must decide if the system for measuring elicitation (usually ML-based) can detect that labeled emotion on the face. Third, is the emotion word a categorical label that includes other more specific labels or is it a more detailed and descriptive word that does not contain other labels. Labels that are at the top of an inclusion hierarchy tend to draw more agreement of meaning.

Figure 2. Lance and Marsella (2010) use Mehrabian's three-dimensional emotion map PAD to show example emotional categories

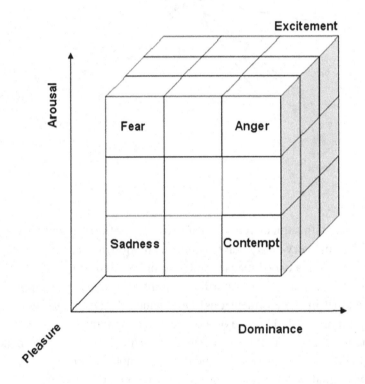

At the top of a hierarchy of emotion labels are "primary" or "basic" emotions. These are allegedly triggered by biological instinct and evolutionary necessity (Izard, 1992). If the label is not a primary emotion, then it is a secondary emotion. Some Cognitive Psychologist and Constructivist Neuroscientists believe that many emotions are contextually constructed, categorized and classified as expression concepts. Constructivists contend humans have a proclivity to express many emotions only if learned and permitted, and that some expressive characteristics may not be innate at birth (Quartz, 1999; Barrett & Satpute, 2013; Barrett, 2017). The labeling of patterns "nurtured" in context, explains the differences in emotion label meanings from one culture or social group to another.

Figure 3. Yik, Russell & Steiger (2010) use a 12-Point Affect Circumplex (12-PAC) model of Core Affect to plot the vectors of 30 mood words

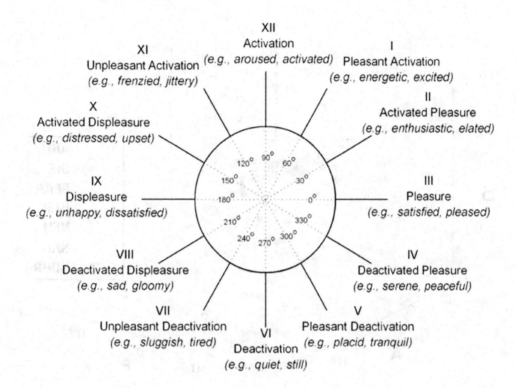

The components described in the various Appraisal Theory-based models are designed to best attain the principal objective or action of a person. Typically, object-action pairings are ascribed to an NPC. They could for example be assist player-character to attain goal, obstruct player-character to attain goal, obtain a game object or manage a game environment. If a virtual agent or NPC is intended to simulate the full psychological profile of a human, then a very complex model will be necessary to accommodate types of memory, learning, adaptation, natural and social reasoning, language acquisition and expression, motor-skill acquisition and adjustment, and other influences. Additionally, since reappraisal of an entity can be triggered by internal stimuli from memory, a scheduling algorithm must control the bussing of data through the components, thus allowing for more than one path through the system from sensation to elicitation, and allowing for interruption by cycles of signal between components.

SOLUTIONS AND RECOMMENDATIONS

For an NPC emotion model to accommodate the complexity of perceiving and processing multiple emotional entity categories of stimuli simultaneously, components that sense and process emotion-evoking entities must be built into the emotion model for sensing, evaluating, prioritizing and selecting affect. Ultimately, the path of either a sensation signal or a processed affect selection is controlled by algorithms that schedule the flow of data from sensation to appraisal to elicitation so that behavior is synchronized to receive new sensations and to reconsider past sensations (reappraisal) held in memory. Present sensa-

Figure 4. Zhang, S., Wu, Z., Meng, H. M., and Cai, L. (2010) use Mehrabian's three-dimensional emotion map to plot facial expressions of a talking avatar from an expression database

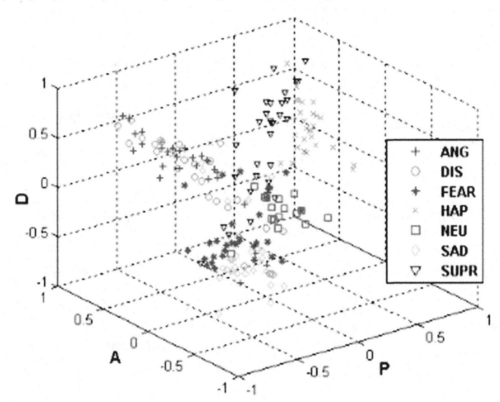

tions and memories compete for attention. Simultaneous appraisal and elicitation with reappraisal require parallel processing and scheduling to manage the complexity of computational processes. To achieve cinematic action and therefore high-resolution animated emotion expression, complexity in an emotion model must increase with the growth of more specific components and more non-linear scheduling of affect selection and elicitation.

An Actor-Centric Emotion Model

Extracting the principal points identified thus far, an actor-centric emotion model should have components that allow for the NPC performative characteristics. Arrays, structs or vectors serve to store immutable ordered data that describe the implicit biases of an agent. A Feed-Forward Neural Network (FFNN) provides the structure to algorithmically process input from multiple handlers-listeners or sensors into a gradient output that will result into an animated elicitation. These structures are used in Table 1 to describe how an emotional model may deploy the critical performative characteristics of an Actor-Centric emotion model.

A generic emotion model as shown below in Figure 5, presents the basic components of an NPC. This generic model was synthesized from the MAMID model developed by Hudlicka (2003), from the FeelMe model developed by Broekens and DeGroot (2004), and from the FAtiMA model developed by

Dias, Mascarenhas and Paiva (2014). The resulting model satisfies Picard's componential requirements. Table 2 elaborates on the function of each component.

Table 1. Data Structures and Algorithms for Performative Characteristics

Performative Characteristic	Data Structure(s)	Algorithmic Method(s)
Expression of Negative Traits	Arrays or vectors that store coefficients to alter values of post-appraisal dimensional vector	Receives post-appraisal signal as dimensional vector. Each dimensional value is multiplied by a coefficient C $\hat{I}$ ¡
Multiple Sensations Simultaneous Sensations	Multiple FFNNs or structs with object handlers-listeners and feature recognition array	FFNNs or structs receive signals from environment during same frame (appraisal instance).
Internal Stimuli	Array 1 stores feature values of significant objects from previous appraisals (memories). Array 2 stores relevant structures indexed by object type whose methods can trigger internal sensations.	If external stimuli are recognized as similar to significant objects in array 1, then method in structure of matching object type in array 2 triggers internal sensation.
External Stimuli	*Objects in game space:* Struct with vector representing feature values. Objects in player space: FFNN recognizes object and converts to vector representing feature values.	External stimuli are recognized as similar to objects in array 1, then method in structure of matching object type in array 2 triggers internal sensation.
Self-Oriented Goals	Data types that permit gradient values, such as 3D vectors. Or, any variable if the goal is not an emotional state or change in emotional state.	Method must check goal value and current state value. Difference may trigger new appraisal. Method might check player variables to decide to forgo action to serve self and instead engage player.
Modularity	Affect Derivation Component object or struct contains arrays or links to FFNNs. More modules increase ability to recognize more emotional entities.	Method switch can enable or disable modules as needed to minimize computational expense as agent changes state or space.
Scalability	Within Affect Derivation Component, increasing Affect Components allows for more granular sensitivity to variations of entity feature variables.	Method switch can enable or disable components as needed to minimize computational expense as agent requires greater sensitivity to entity feature variables.
Affective Loop	The entire emotion model runs as a process. It contains two cycles. *Cycle 1:* entirely internal and allows reappraisals. *Cycle 2:* partially external to the agent, allows the agent to send out elicitation and receive response from other agents or the player.	Scheduling of signal vector must allow for each component to complete its task. Must store in memory significant appraisals for subsequent recognition or reappraisal. Must regulate and prioritize competing signals to determine which should occupy appraisal bus: new signal or reappraisal.

Inside of the Affect Derivation component in Figure 5 is what is depicted in Figure 6. The generic emotion model uses FAtiMA's modularity feature. The Appraisal Components provide the Appraisal Frame the current values of each Appraisal Component's predictive result. This author proposes that each component consist of an FFNN that recognizes the entity and its emotion relevant feature variables and values to predict appraisal variable value for each affect from [0, 1]. For a facial emotion expression, that would be the gradient value of an emotion expression of which there is usually at least six expressions plus neutral.

Figure 5. A generic emotion model that combines features from MAMID (Hudlicka, 2003), FeelMe (Broekens and DeGroot, 2004) and FAtiMA (Dias, Mascarenhas and Paiva, 2014)

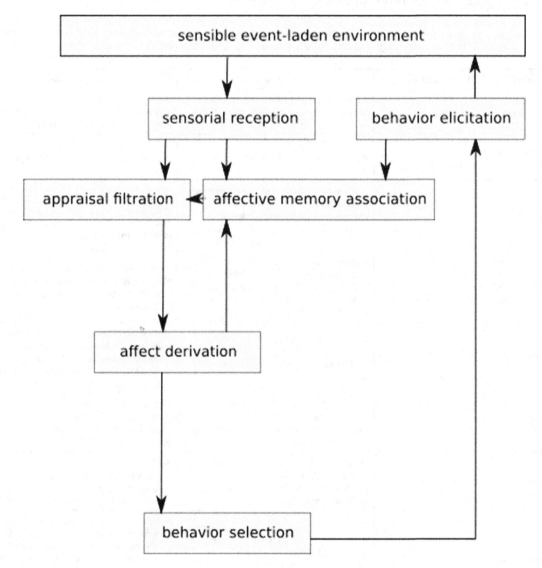

Each Affect Derivation Component consists of a data structure that receives input from an Appraisal Filter. The Appraisal Filter receives an appraisal signal that recognizes each emotion expression for each respective Appraisal Component. The filter will likely implement an object recognition neural network or an array of feature value ranges – both will process a vector whose elements and their values are within range to process and predict a meaning. For a facial emotion expression system, the Appraisal Filter will look for facial features in a video stream that fit the parameter values of an emotional expression on a human face. Then the signal must be sent to the appropriate Appraisal Component within the Affect Derivation unit. An Appraisal Component will evaluate a feature of the face that best indicates a value of a specific emotion expression type (happiness, anger, etc.). Then the Appraisal Component must use an emotion recognition FFNN to predict the expressive meaning of the signal. The resulting gradient value will reside in the Appraisal Frame. All Appraisal Frames will be evaluated to choose a final Affect Derivation for the appraisal instance. The resulting derivation will be the Affective State, which will make a Behavior Selection, and in turn trigger a Behavior Elicitation.

Table 2. Component descriptions of the generic emotion model in Figure 5

Component Name	Description
Sensible event-laden environment	Container of all events, objects and agents that can be sensed by emotional agent.
Sensorial reception	Events that are accepted by sensors.
Appraisal filtration	Filters perception of objects, agents, events in terms of beliefs, desires (goals) and intentions (BDI).
Affective memory association	Storage of perceptions, affects and elicitations.
Affect Derivation	Pleasure-Arousal-Dominance mapped emotion vector algorithm.
Behavior selection	Resulting animation of face indicating current emotional state.
Affective memory association	Storage of perceptions, affects and elicitations change the "rules" or "nets" (and don't maintain a memory of events.
Behavioral elicitation	The physical movement of the mesh as gesture or facial expression.

Figure 6. Detail of Affect Derivation Component from FAtiMA component (Dias, Mascarenhas, & Paiva, 2014)

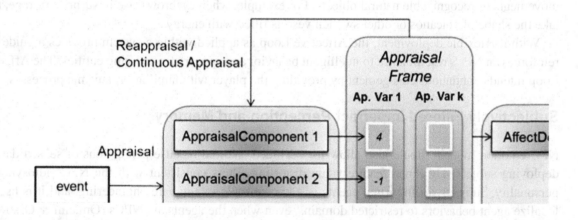

Applying the Affective Loop for Emotion Model Dynamics

A consistent theme in the discussion of emotion models is the idea that affectively relevant sense data runs a cycle between an agent and its environment. Sundström calls this cycle the Affective Loop (2005). The Affective Loop has three stages familiar to actors from improvisation and rehearsal exercises: 1) a human user elicits an emotional expression, 2) a system responds with an appropriate emotional expression, and 3) the human user internalizes and interprets the affective meaning of the eliciting system, and 4) the loop repeats. A similar concept is found in the Repetition Exercise of renowned theater director and acting teacher Sanford Meisner (Meisner, 1987). The three stages of the Affective Loop have parallel stages in the process of developing an actor's skill at finding authentic emotional responses to interactions with other characters, objects and events observed in a scene. The Affective Loop expands human-to-human interaction, as practiced in the dramatic arts, to a "design principle" of the Affective Computing domain that implements motion-capture-performer-to-computer and computer-to-player principles.

The Affective Loop design principles are interpreted for player to NPC interaction as follows from Sundström (2005). *Embodiment* is enhanced as the player's body expresses its affect through the game controller or other sensing interface. Some part of the player's elicitation data becomes input that the NPC's emotion system can sense. Likewise, the player can sense the NPC sensing the player, and sensing the NPC eliciting its organismic idiosyncrasies through its own body.

Flow is another attribute where, as the player interacts, there is a sense that there is always potentially a new sensation coming from which to repeat the Affective Loop. Or, an NPC can react to internal stimuli from memory. The emotion model not only repeats as loops, but it is always open for new stimuli from internal or external sources that allow each loop iteration to elicit distinct values.

Another Affective Loop attribute occurs when NPCs are designed with elicitation *ambiguity*. When there is more than one meaning and possibly more than one stimulus attributed to an NPC elicitation, the uncertainty can create interest in subsequent sense information with the belief that clarity of meaning will be revealed over time. Ambiguity is accomplished with facial expressions by always allowing multiple simultaneous stimuli sensations and appraisals causing distinct affect selections that can blend in the facial elicitation.

Lastly, *Natural-But-Designed Expressions* are characteristics that value elicitation forms found in nature, such as shapes of the face (eyes, mouth, ears) and their movements that resemble shapes and movements of recognizable natural objects. For example, when eyebrows rise in surprise or rage, they take the shape of volcanos or other swollen vessels filled with energy.

With its flexible deployment, the Affective Loop as applied within a system provides a guide that reinforces an NPCs resemblance to intelligent behavior and appearance of living entities. The Affective Loop intends continuous engagement by providing the player with familiar organismic processes.

Subjectively Filtered Imperfect Perception and Memory

NPC emotion models should also allow for occluded, skewed or false perceptions of sensed data by deploying subjectively tuned feature value distorting filters consistent with the NPCs idiosyncratic personality. Subjectivity in virtual agents is a known topic in software engineering, and it is used to localize agent behaviors to restricted domains, even when the agents are NPCs (Omicini & Ossowski, 2003). Designing subjectivity in an NPC then allows for building "imperfect", non-machine-like or organismic features that simulate human constraints on intelligence. Thus, rationality can be limited as the NPCs character design requires. Similarly, an NPCs memory can also be designed as "imperfect". Memories can be subject to disappearance, erosion and distortion over time. For an NPC to show signs of organismic entropy is for its memory to simulate decay and self-doubt as the game play proceeds. Furthering organismic limitations, an NPC may not always respond too quickly, nor should it always respond without the delaying force of anticipatory doubt, remorse or regret. Similarly, NPCs can reflect before choosing a course of action. They can likewise elicit a choice with temerity or tentativeness. People often mumble and stumble because they doubt their choices, forget their memories, become distracted by competing but pertinent stimuli, or fail to figure out a course of action in due time. Occasionally unclear elicitation is the result of an overloaded overwhelmed system. Such "imperfections" built into an emotion model make for NPCs that cause curiosity in players and reinforce the lifelikeness of the world that spawned them.

Modularity and Scaling of Emotion Resolution

Less an organismic and more a mechanical concern, the most adaptable emotion models are those that allow for modular components that increase the variety of sensible entities and the resolution of sensing input data. Modularized emotion models can allow an increase or decrease in the number of feature variables an NPC can sense, and an increase in the complexity of elicitation. Modularity gives a designer the ability to use the same model with fewer components for simple mass-produced NPCs, while for more complex supporting characters, and for very complex antagonists or "buddy" characters, more modules can expand the character's emotion complexity. Modularity also allows for real time scaling up or down, where if a complex character has a brief and simple appearance, its model can retain less data with fewer components, or vice-versa. Thus, when designing NPC emotion models, scale of entity detection and emotion elicitation may vary enormously, depending on the importance of a character in a game.

Like the limitations of scale, games provide circumscribed interactions with NPCs that reveal an incomplete view of a character. We get to know an NPC over time through a mediated context that serves the whole game. There is no need to model more than what the game design will allow the player to sense during anticipated game play time. A model needs to show only the emotions that the game mechanic allows. Like many forms of humanistic expression that comprise an art form, players must infer what they do not sense. And they cannot sense everything at once.

FUTURE RESEARCH DIRECTIONS

With an emotion model that is modular, it becomes conceivable to implement a procedurally generated emotion as part of a procedurally generated NPC and thus within a procedurally generated narrative system. Procedurally generated game components can become principal features of adaptive games that reshape themselves to the variables of the player. Adaptivity would require some mechanism that can categorically predict the features of the player so that generated game components would spawn in variations that best suit the designer's prediction of what the player needs to experience. A predictive system would require a robust machine learning algorithm that enables adaptivity in ways productive to the aesthetic of the game and player-designer relationship. From the perspective of the actor who must perform the character motion, it remains to be seen if the workflow proposed in this research is more or less consistent with the performance preparation process. This question needs further research and experimentation. Future work described is viable, reproduceable and could provide a new paradigm for production of photorealistic NPCs and cinematic acting in video games.

CONCLUSION

Enabled by processor innovations and the techniques of machine learning, photorealistic NPC design and development can adopt the performative aesthetics of motion picture acting with its complex facial animations. The challenge that lies ahead for developers is to design an emotion model and working process that adapts to existing entertainment methods and techniques. Past practices that relied on hand-crafted morph animations have provided remarkable accomplishments at creating life-like characters for computer games. However, animator-centric NPC emotion modeling based on morph animations is a cost prohibitive method for most game developers and designers. This research promotes a synthesis of the structures of emotion developed by Computational Cognitive Psychology with the most influential Performance Theories and acting training methods and practice toward the service of procedurally generated character and narrative. Future work will reveal if putting a human actor's creative process at the center of emotion modeling and the workflow of character design will make NPCs more enjoyable and closer to cinematic style acting for computer-based games.

REFERENCES

Bickmore, T., Bukhari, L., Vardoulakis, L., Paasche-Orlow, M. & Shanahan, C. (2012). *Hospital buddy: a persistent emotional support companion agent for hospital patients*. Academic Press.

Braunberger, P. (Producer), & Renoir, J. (Director). (1936). *A Day in the Country* [Motion picture]. France: Panthéon Productions.

Broekens, J., & DeGroot, D. (2004). Scalable and flexible appraisal models for virtual agents. In *Proceedings of the Fifth Game-on International Conference* (pp. 208-215). Academic Press.

Calleja, G. (2009). Experiential narrative in game environments in breaking new ground: innovation in games, play, practice and theory. *Proceedings of DiGRA 2009*.

Chatman, S. (1980). What novels can do that films can't (and vice versa). *Critical Inquiry*, *7*(1), 121–140. doi:10.1086/448091

Damasio, A. R. (1998). Emotion in the perspective of an integrated nervous system. *Brain Research. Brain Research Reviews*, *26*(2-3), 83–86. doi:10.1016/S0165-0173(97)00064-7 PMID:9651488

de Maupassant, G. (2007). *The Short Stories of Guy de Maupassant*. Black's Readers Service.

Deahl, D. (2018), The EU plans to test an AI lie detector at border points. *The Verge*. https://www.theverge.com/2018/10/31/18049906/eu-artificial-intelligence-ai-lie-detector-border-points-immigration

Descartes, R. (2006), A discourse on the method of correctly conducting one's reason and seeking truth in the sciences (I. MacLean, Trans.). Oxford University Press.

Dias, J., Mascarenhas, S., & Paiva, A. (2014). Fatima modular: Towards an agent architecture with a generic appraisal framework. In *Emotion Modeling* (pp. 44–56). Springer. doi:10.1007/978-3-319-12973-0_3

Dog, N. (2013). *The Last of Us* [Computer video game]. Sony Interactive Entertainment.

Dormehl, L. (2018), A.I. border agents could use machine smarts to tell if travelers are lying. *Digital Trends*. https://www.digitaltrends.com/cool-tech/ai-border-airport-virtual-agent/

Dream, Q. (2013). *Beyond Two Souls* [Computer video game]. Sony Interactive Entertainment.

Ekman, P. (1997). *What the face reveals: Basic and applied studies of spontaneous expression using the Facial Action Coding System (FACS)*. Oxford University Press.

Gratch, J., Marsella, S., Wang, N., & Stankovic, B. (2009). Assessing the validity of appraisal-based models of emotion. In *3rd International Conference on Affective Computing and Intelligent Interaction and Workshops* (pp. 1-8). IEEE. 10.1109/ACII.2009.5349443

Gratch, J., Okhmatovskaia, A., & Duncan, S. (2006, November). Virtual humans for the study of rapport in cross cultural settings. *25th Army Science Conference*, 27-30.

Hart, H. (2005). Do You See What I See? The Impact of Delsarte on Silent Film Acting. *Mime Journal*, *23*(1), 184–199. doi:10.5642/mimejournal.20052301.11

Hudlicka, E. (2003). Modeling effects of behavior moderators on performance: Evaluation of the MAMID methodology and architecture. *Proceedings of BRIMS*, 12.

Lane, H. C., Cahill, C., Foutz, S., Auerbach, D., Noren, D., Lussenhop, C., & Swartout, W. (2013). The Effects of a Pedagogical Agent for Informal Science Education on Learner Behaviors and Self-efficacy. In Artificial Intelligence in Education. AIED 2013. Lecture Notes in Computer Science, (vol. 7926). Springer.

Lazarus, R. S. (1991). Cognition and motivation in emotion. *The American Psychologist*, *46*(4), 352–367. doi:10.1037/0003-066X.46.4.352 PMID:2048794

Lisetti, C., & Hudlicka, E. (2015). Why and how to build emotion-based agent architectures. In R. A. Calvo, S. K. D'Mello, J. Gratch, & A. Kappas (Eds.), *Oxford Library of Psychology. The Oxford Handbook of Affective Computing* (pp. 94–109). Oxford University Press.

Lutterbie, J. (2011). *Towards a general theory of acting: Cognitive science and performance*. Palgrave Macmillan. doi:10.1057/9780230119468

Maes, P. (1997). Intelligent Software. *IUI '97 Proceedings of the 2nd International Conference on Intelligent User Interfaces*, 41-43.

Malatesta, L., Caridakis, G., Raouzaiou, A., & Karpouzis, K. (2007). Agent personality traits in virtual environments based on appraisal theory predictions. *Artificial and ambient intelligence, language, speech and gesture for expressive characters*, 7.

Malatesta, L., Raouzaiou, A., Karpouzis, K., & Kollias, S. (2009). Towards modeling embodied conversational agent character profiles using appraisal theory predictions in expression synthesis. *Applied Intelligence*, *30*(1), 58–64. doi:10.100710489-007-0076-9

Margolin, U. (1986). The doer and the deed: Action as a basis for characterization in narrative. *Poetics Today*, *7*(2), 205–225. doi:10.2307/1772759

Mehrabian, A. (1996). Pleasure-arousal-dominance: A general framework for describing and measuring individual differences in temperament. *Current Psychology (New Brunswick, N.J.)*, *14*(4), 261–292. doi:10.1007/BF02686918

Meisner, S. (1987). Sanford Meisner on acting. Vintage Random House.

Morgans, J. (2018). How video games cast actors just like movies do. *Vice*. https://www.vice.com/en_uk/article/gymde7/how-video-games-cast-actors-just-like-movies-do

Murray, J. H. (1997). *Hamlet on the Holodeck: The future of narrative in cyberspace*. MIT Press.

Nixon, M., Pasquier, P., & El-Nasr, M. S. (2010). DelsArtMap: Applying delsarte's aesthetic system to virtual agents. In *International Conference on Intelligent Virtual Agents* (pp. 139-145). Springer. 10.1007/978-3-642-15892-6_15

Omicini, A., & Ossowski, S. (2003). Objective versus subjective coordination in the engineering of agent systems. In *Intelligent Information Agents* (pp. 179–202). Springer. doi:10.1007/3-540-36561-3_9

Ortony, A., Clore, G. L., & Collins, A. (1990). *The cognitive structure of emotions*. Cambridge University Press.

Picard, R. W., & Rosalind, W. (2000). Toward agents that recognize emotion. *Vivek-Bombay*, *13*(1), 3–13.

Price, R. H., & Bouffard, D. L. (1974). Behavioral appropriateness and situational constraint as dimensions of social behavior. *Journal of Personality and Social Psychology*, *30*(4), 579–586. doi:10.1037/h0037037

Rickel, J., & Johnson, W. L. (1997). Integrating pedagogical capabilities in a virtual environment agent. In *Proceedings of the First International Conference on Autonomous Agents* (pp. 30-38). 10.1145/267658.267664

Russell, J. A. (1980). A circumplex model of affect. *Journal of Personality and Social Psychology*, *39*(6), 1161–1178. doi:10.1037/h0077714

Smith, G. M. (2003). *Film structure and the emotion system*. Cambridge University Press. doi:10.1017/CBO9780511497759

Stuart, K. (2016). Video games where people matter? The strange future of emotional AI. *The Guardian*. https://www.theguardian.com/technology/2016/oct/12/video-game-characters-emotional-ai-developers

Sundström, P. (2005). *Exploring the affective*. University of Sweden. http://www.diva-portal.org/smash/record.jsf?pid=diva2:1041047

Torres, S. (2014), Video game characters modeled after real people. *Venture Beat*. https://venturebeat.com/2014/06/28/video-game-characters-modeled-after-real-people/

Trull, T. J., & Widiger, T. A. (2013). Dimensional models of personality: The five-factor model and the DSM-5. *Dialogues in Clinical Neuroscience*, *15*(2), 135. PMID:24174888

Turing, A. (1950, October). Computing machinery and intelligence. *Mind*, *59*(236), 433–460. doi:10.1093/mind/LIX.236.433

Vella, D. (2014). Modeling the semiotic structure of game characters. *Proceedings of DiGRA 2014.*

Wiley, N. (2003). Emotion and film theory. *Studies in Symbolic Interaction, 26,* 169–187. doi:10.1016/S0163-2396(02)26012-3

Yik, M., Russell, J. A., & Steiger, J. H. (2011). A 12-point circumplex structure of core affect. *Emotion (Washington, D.C.), 11*(4), 705–731. doi:10.1037/a0023980 PMID:21707162

Yin, M., & Sun, Y. (2015). Human behavior models for virtual agents in repeated decision making under uncertainty. *Proceedings of the 14th International Conference on Autonomous Agents and Multiagent Systems.*

Zhao, R., Papangelis, A., & Cassell, J. (2014). Towards a dyadic computational model of rapport management for human-virtual agent interaction. In Intelligent Virtual Agents. IVA 2014. Lecture Notes in Computer Science, (vol. 8637). Springer. doi:10.1007/978-3-319-09767-1_62

ADDITIONAL READING

Feldman Barrett, L. (2017). *How emotions are made: The secret life of the brain.* Houghton Mifflin Harcourt.

Hudlicka, E. (2008, August). Affective computing for game design. In Proceedings of the 4th Intl. North American Conference on Intelligent Games and Simulation (pp. 5-12). McGill University Montreal, Canada.

Hudlicka, E., & Broekens, J. (2009, September). Foundations for modelling emotions in game characters: Modelling emotion effects on cognition. In 2009 3rd International Conference on Affective Computing and Intelligent Interaction and Workshops (pp. 1-6). IEEE.

Marsella, S. C., Carnicke, S. M., Gratch, J., Okhmatovskaia, A., & Rizzo, A. (2006, August). An exploration of delsarte's structural acting system. In *International Workshop on Intelligent Virtual Agents* (pp. 80-92). Springer, Berlin, Heidelberg. 10.1007/11821830_7

Popescu, A., Broekens, J., & Van Someren, M. (2013). Gamygdala: An emotion engine for games. *IEEE Transactions on Affective Computing, 5*(1), 32–44. doi:10.1109/T-AFFC.2013.24

Scherer, K. R., Bänziger, T., & Roesch, E. (Eds.). (2010). *A Blueprint for Affective Computing: A sourcebook and manual.* Oxford University Press.

Vick, E. (2009). *Emotion notions: Modeling personality in game character AI.* Cengage Learning.

Warpefelt, H., & Verhagen, H. (2015). Towards an updated typology of non-player character roles. In *Proceedings of the International Conference on Game and Entertainment Technologies.*

KEY TERMS AND DEFINITIONS

Affective Loop: A cycle of sensing and reacting between an agent and its environment. It models the process of human interaction with things external to the body.

Agency: The apparent freedom of a character to act, react, not act, or sublimate desire to achieve a goal within a fictional world.

Agent: (In software development) An artificially intelligent software object that can monitor a program's state and execute commands autonomously to achieve those goals. (In literary and performance theory) an object or being that appears to behave with an intention to achieve a goal. Actions taken toward goal attainment foreground the agency of the object or being.

Appraisal Variables: A set of values categorically assigned to objects that an agent senses that can affect the emotional state of the agent.

Computational Cognitive Psychology: A subdiscipline of Cognitive Psychology and Cognitive Science that draws from Neuroscience and Communication Theories to develop models of cognitive experience that can be programmed as computer-based application and tested with data collected from human subjects.

Emotion Model: An abstract representation of the components that comprise the process for an agent of sensing appraisal variables in objects, identifying objects, processing objects in relation to beliefs, desires and intentions, and eliciting emotions.

High Resolution Animation: An animation method, often assisted by motion capture technology, that uses very detailed movement to animate a photorealistic game character.

Non-Player Character (NPC): Characters in a video game, excluding the one performed by the player during gameplay.

Performative Mediation: The process of integrating information outside the domain of the game design for the construction of a character. An actor's personal experiences, an awareness of the distorting features of camera optics. These are external information that often is considered in an actor's performance preparation for a character and its role.

Player Character: The character in a game performed by the player.

Virtual Agents: An artificially intelligent software object programmed with an emotion model with the intent of teaching or assisting a user complete a task or learn a process.

This research was previously published in Bridging the Gap Between AI, Cognitive Science, and Narratology With Narrative Generation; pages 17-42, copyright year 2021 by Information Science Reference (an imprint of IGI Global).

Chapter 20
User Experience Design of History Game:
An Analysis Review and Evaluation Study for Malaysia Context

Seng Yue Wong

Centre for the Initiation of Talent and Industrial Training (CITra), University of Malaya, Kuala Lumpur, Malaysia

Simin Ghavifekr

Faculty of Education, University of Malaya, Kuala Lumpur, Malaysia

ABSTRACT

User experience (UX) and user interface design of an educational game are important in enhancing and sustaining the utilisation of Game Based Learning (GBL) in learning history. Thus, this article provides a detailed literature review on history learning problems, as well as previous studies on user experience in game design. Future studies on educational history games will benefit from this systematic review and analysis of current educational history games, as this article examines in detail which game features are the most effective in promoting engagement and supporting the process of learning Malaysian history. The results have revealed that mobile game applications with historical content can indeed be a meaningful way to create gaming experience, learning experience, adaptivity and usability, which can facilitate history learning through UX of playing history mobile games. The correlation results of these four dimensions have indicated four positive and significant relationships.

INTRODUCTION

South East Asia's video games market represents approximately 4% of global consumption. However, the region's global growth rate of video games is the fastest compared to any other regions in the world (MDEC, 2015). This tremendous enlargement of the game market in South East Asia truly offers immense opportunities for the industry to exploit, including the education field. Generation-Y is known

DOI: 10.4018/978-1-6684-7589-8.ch020

as the generation born between year 1980 and 2000. This generation is born into technology and often knows more about the digital world than their teachers and parents (Meier & Crocker, 2010). Today, they spend most of their time playing digital games which is enabled by the rapid growth in internet access and ownership of Information Communication and Technology (ICT) devices. Audio and video, film and television, games, Virtual Reality (VR) and Augmented Reality (AR) are the new ways of educating students nowadays. A clear understanding of the capabilities and shortcomings of video games in the education field helps in the design or development of potential games to meet the demands of its users.

For the past 40 years, many significant studies have proven that computer games have become a favourable past time activity and lately, serious gaming has been found to impact people's attitude, behaviour, skill acquisition and learning, thus attracting the interest of developers and researchers (Boyle et al., 2016; Khenissi et al., 2016; Raybourn, 2014; Vanisri & Roslina, 2015). Serious games can include role-playing experiences, social processes, immersive simulations for the exploration of interpersonal development, diplomacy, adaptive thinking, combat tactics, emergency response, governance, health, education, management, logistics, and leadership (Raybourn, 2014). Its ease-to-use, improved collaboration, innovation and production, the transformation from conventional educational methods to modern educational methods, contemporary software programmes, distance learning, the virtual learning environment and the increase of computer-based games for learning are the few factors that have led to the interest of utilising computer games, video games or serious games for learning (Khenissi et al., 2016).

Learning history has always been perceived as boring and static, and has traditionally emphasised on the memorisation of historical facts and chronological sequences of events (Angeli & Tsaggari, 2016). Furthermore, teaching history only focuses on information delivery without connections to our real life; thus, causing history to be unfairly promoted as a "death" subject. Nevertheless, history is vital as a learning subject for youngsters in order for them to understand national, political, social, religious and economic problems. Currently, the subject of history is listed as a compulsory pass subject in the Malaysian secondary level examinations. Since the immersive technologies such as the virtual world and augmented reality have been used in cultural heritage learning for the public, this is a great opportunity to motivate users to learn or gain knowledge in this way rather than receiving information passively. These technologies may enable students to visualise historical events and attract them to learn while playing the VR or AR games. The rewards system such as the unlocking of content and the gaining of experience points can increase their motivation to learn. This method has been practiced in museums, exhibitions, books and visual content (Mortara et al., 2014).

Thus, for this reason, game-based learning (GBL) or games with educational purposes, namely serious games are now very popular. The fun, amusing, compelling, and immersive experience, coupled with high engagement and flow are all crucial aspects that need to be studied and focused on either in current or future GBL studies. GBL or serious games have to be well-designed to increase learner engagement, an integral component of educational effectiveness (Kiili, de Freitas, Arnab & Lainema, 2012). According to them, the flow framework provides the principles for a good educational game design, which is based on associative, cognitive and situative learning theories and consists of engagement and pedagogic elements with the focus on feedback and flow principles. Therefore, the ultimate aim of game design is to create appealing experiences to users. User experience and user interface design of an educational game is important to enhance and sustain the utilisation of GBL in learning history. However, empirical studies on user experience in history games are scarce. History games are not widely available in the market. Most games may be related to history but are not for educational purposes. Furthermore, most of these games are developed for entertainment, fun and enjoyment purposes.

To address the knowledge gap, this study provides a detailed literature review on learning problems and solutions in the perspective of the history subject, as well as on previous studies related to user experience in game design. A mobile game application prototype was designed and developed for learning Malaysian history. To design the mobile game, the key architectural components, gameplay flow, mobile game use cases, and map of key architectural components to game requirements will be presented in this paper. Next, an evaluation study on user experience (UX) is conducted via this prototype to explore further about UX of historical mobile games. The study findings will be discussed, and a correlation model between four dimensions of user experience evaluation, which are gaming experience, learning experience, adaptivity and usability are proposed for the cultural and heritage learning of Malaysian history.

HISTORY LEARNING PROBLEMS AND SOLUTIONS

History learning, either at the primary school level or the secondary school level in Malaysia has long been perceived as a dull and boring subject. Students are unable to connect and sustain interest in learning history due to its nature– content-based or information-based learning with a lot of facts, dates, events, evidences that are irrelevant to students' daily lives (Angeli & Tsaggari, 2015; Lim, Chin, & Nabeel, 2011; Nor Azan, Azizah, & Wong, 2009; Sii & Soon, 2010; Voet & Wever, 2016). In Malaysia, the subject of history is made compulsory by the Ministry of Education and has to be taken in both primary and secondary schools. Students are not alerted by the importance of learning history and they study just because of examinations. However, the conventional teacher-centered learning method for the subject is the main contributing reason for this condition. Teachers use a single textbook and controls the question and answer strategy in the classroom (Angeli & Tsaggari, 2016; Sii & Soon, 2010; Voet & Wever, 2016). The heavy focus on chronological and factual information delivery which has no connection to the students' daily lives or experiences has caused the knowledge gap (Lim et al., 2011; Sii & Soon, 2010).

Since educational technology is important to be implemented in all subjects today, the use of multimedia in teaching and learning history has been studied (Angeli & Tsaggari, 2016; Lim et al., 2011; Sii & Soon, 2010). The utilisation of electronic materials via computer-based tools such as graphics, text, animation, movie and sounds are all combined in the presentation of historical facts. Besides that, teachers can also use videos and films to engage students in a more vivid and interesting learning environment. Within a computer-based multimedia system, students are capable to create their own digital portfolios and publish their podcasts and vodcasts in order to share their own historical facts and narratives (Angeli & Tsaggari, 2016). Lim et al. (2011) also studied the utilisation of social media such as Weblog in teaching and learning history.

Furthermore, there are many studies conducted on students' utilisation and attitude towards GBL in the education field, and most results have shown a very positive impact on teaching and learning (Watson, Mong, & Harris, 2011; Nor Azan & Wong, 2013). Out of 25,000 teachers in the United States, a researcher found that 65% of teachers are interested in the use of digital games or computer games in the classroom, and more than 50% of them would like to learn more regarding the integration of games in their teaching strategies (Project Tomorrow, 2008). GBL is an effective learning tool which uses action instead of narration to create personal motivation and satisfaction, accommodate multiple learning styles and skills, reinforce mastery of skills, and provides interactive context (Furio, Gonzalez-Gancedo, Juan, Segui, & Rando, 2013). The use of mobile devices as platforms for GBL also provide better learning experience as it allows users to access their games anytime and anywhere. In addition, educators can incorporate these powerful tools into their teaching, thus enriching and complementing students' skills via game play (Furio et al., 2013).

From these evidences, it is clear that immersive technology, virtual environments and AR via serious games have potential to support the process of learning history. AR consists of real-time interaction which combines real and virtual objects, and 3D registration (Furio et al., 2013). There are a variety of game types that can be adopted for learning history and cultural heritage such as puzzles and mini-games, simulation games, adventure and role-playing games, strategy games and action games (Mortara et al., 2014). Mortara et al. (2014) believed that the empathy of game character and plot may be very helpful for understanding historical events, different cultures, people's feeling, problems, behaviors, the beauty and value of nature, architecture, art and heritage. Thus, using GBL to teach history is not a new idea, but it needs a systematic review on it especially in the context of use, accuracy of historical facts, and the learning effectiveness which is highlighted in user experience and game design. The discipline of learning history is intended to develop higher-order thinking skills among students in order to enable them to synthesise historical events so that they will have knowledge of foresight and hindsight.

USER EXPERIENCE IN GAME DESIGN

GBL has to be well-designed in order to incorporate student engagement, a vital component of educational effectiveness. User interface (UI) is the medium of communication between players and a game. One of the problems in UI design is that not all users will perceive the UI as easy-to-use. If players perceive the UI as not easy-to-use, problems in terms of user experience will be raised. The culture may affect the path of people communicating with each other, thus the UI game design should be integrated with cultural values (Ratna, Noraidah, Nor Azan, Norlis, & Salyani, 2013). There are four elements of culture that have been studied, which are power distance index (PDI), masculinity (MAS), individualistic (IDV) and high context (HC) (Ratna et al., 2013). Some studies also claimed that GBL has to be designed properly to incorporate an engagement that integrates educational effectiveness, which has also become a challenge in balancing game play and learning objectives (Kiili et al., 2012).

User-centered Game Design (UCGD) is an advanced game design which consists of observational studies, conceptualisation, prototyping, and usability play-testing (Rankin, McNeal, Shute, & Gooch, 2008). The aims and advantages of game play are such as social interaction which supports learning processes and collaborative learning, as well as experience and learning outcomes. Despite of that, heuristics for game design is a set of usability principles used to explore a user's interface via an inspection technique and identify the usability problems. This technique can be used iteratively during game design process to uncover some game usability problems such as game play, engagement and storyline, but it is not comprehensive (Nor Azan & Wong, 2009).

User experience (UX) is often paralleled with usability (Kiili et al., 2012; Law & Sun, 2012; Saucken, Reinhardt, Michailidou, & Lindemann, 2013) which is focused on the interaction between people and products, the experience that results in a certain context of use, and the view on user product interaction from the emotional aspect. UX should be considered from the physical, sensual, cognitive, emotional and aesthetic perspectives (Kiili et al., 2012). According to Kiili et al. (2012), UX consists of three main elements which are users, artefacts, and tasks. UX emerges from the interplay between these three elements in certain context of use. A user's emotions, values and existing experience will determine how

Figure 1. Elements of user experience (UX)

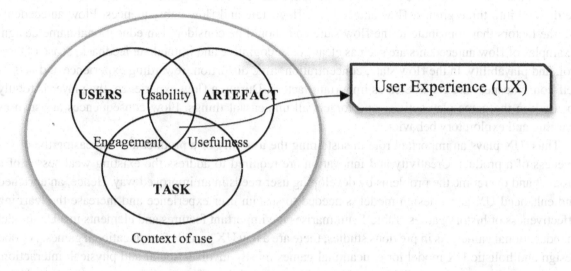

he/she perceives an artefact and the task at hand. Figure 1 shows the elements of UX from an individualistic point of view.

However, if we view the issue from another perspective, the UX interaction model has been enriched and used in a paper by Saucken et al. (2013) whose study was from the basic model, namely Customer Experience Interaction Model (CEIM). The CEIM emphasises four main elements which are user, usage, object and effect to provide a holistic view on the interaction between users and products. The UX Interaction Model (UXIM) consists of three UX-relevant parts; the interaction between user and product, the temporal perspective on experience and the surrounding environment, as well as the mental model as the user's inner representation of a product that strongly impacts UX. A user's expectation before the usage of a product, and the memory after usage are vital in UXIM. There are six principles embedded in UXIM: triggering perception via several senses, creating pleasant anticipation, meeting psychological needs, allowing for learning process, ensuring usability, and generating technical advances (Saucken et al., 2013).

Besides that, there is a study on UX for mobile game-based learning (mGBL) which consists of phases, components, steps and deliverables (Norshuhada & Syamsul, 2011). There are two layers in the model, where the first layer is called the general phase and consists of pre-production, production and post-production. In the second layer, there are components that should be included for each respected phase and are seen as fundamentals during product development. Activities in the model are specific steps or processes taken during product development. The mGBL engineering model is useful as it portrays the mGBL application in the Malaysian local context and it can be strengthened by applying some learning theories and approaches.

Furthermore, there is a review on the elements in UX of educational games based on ten existing UX models, including the mGBL above (Vanisri & Roslina, 2015). The paper identified seven obvious elements from the UX models and frameworks, which are social and physical, time, involvement, emotional and cognitive, game content, fun and flow factors, in sequence. They also expected that user's response to a product will change, and thus models should cover future expectations and recent trends to attract users' attention.

Kiili et al. (2012) studied on the flow experience for educational games. The elements of flow can be divided into three groups: flow antecedents, flow state and flow consequences. Flow antecedents are the factors that contribute to the flow state and should be considered in educational game design. Examples of flow antecedents are such as clear goals, cognitive and immediate feedback, sense of control, and playability. In the flow state, concentration, time distortion, rewarding experience and loss of self-consciousness are considered as important factors. During a flow-experience, the player is totally focused on the game-play activity and forgets all unpleasant things. Flow consequences are such as learning and exploratory behavior.

Thus, UX plays an important role in sustaining the usability of a product and increasing the effectiveness of a product. Creativity and innovation are required to address the existing weaknesses of a product and overcome the problems by developing user needs in an improved way. Hence, an enriched and enhanced UX game design model is needed to sustain user experience and increase the learning effectiveness of history games. Table 1 summarises the important features and elements in a UX model for educational games. As in previous studies, there are a few UX models for educational games. A good design and holistic UX model for educational games mostly involves social and physical, interaction, emotion, engagement, immersion components. Content and the effects or impacts of a product should be considered when designing the UX for educational games.

Table 1. Summary of existing UX models or frameworks for games

UX Model/ Framework	Researcher (Year)	Elements/ Features
UX model	Kiili et al. (2012)	User, artifact and task
Customer Experience Interaction Model (CEIM)	Saucken, Schroer, Kain, & Lindemann (2012)	User, usage, object, effect
User Experience Interaction Model (UXIM)	Saucken et al. (2013)	i. Interaction between user and product ii. The temporal perspective on experience and the surrounding environment iii. Mental model as the user's inner representation of a product that strongly impact on UX
User Centered Game Design (UCGD)	Rankin et al. (2008)	Observational studies, conceptualization, prototyping and usability play testing
Mobile Game Based Learning (mGBL) engineering model	Norshuhada & Syamsul (2011)	Phases: Pre-production, Production and Post-Production Each phase consists of components and activities
Elements of UX of educational games	Vanisri & Roslina (2015)	Social and physical, time, involvement, emotional and cognitive, game content, fun and flow factors
Flow Framework for educational game	Kiili et al. (2012)	Flow antecedents, flow state and flow consequences
UX for adaptive digital educational games	Law & Sun (2012)	Four UX dimensions: Gaming experiences, Learning Experience, Adaptivity and Usability

In this study, the authors adopted the four dimensions of the UX evaluation framework (Law & Sun, 2012) for adaptive educational games. Based on Table 1, previous studies on UX are numerous and involve different attributes for gameplay or gaming experience. The four dimensions that were used for this study's UX evaluations are gaming experience, learning experience, adaptivity and usability. Gaming experience are the observations of players' verbal and non-verbal behaviour that cover challenges, competence, flow, immersion, and positive and negative affect and tension (Law & Sun, 2012). Learning goals, content appropriateness, integration, feedback and extensibility, and media matching are attributes grouped under learning experience. Thus, learning experience is considered as players' perceptions on the educational value of a game; whether the game design can be used for learning or not (Law & Sun, 2012). Adaptivity means how players perceive hints, tips, rewards and encouragements offered. This dimension covers cognitive and motivational intervention, and game pacing (Law & Sun, 2012). Lastly, the usability dimension includes interface and interaction (Law & Sun, 2012).

DESIGN OF HISTORICAL MOBILE GAMES AND ITS KEY ARCHITECTURAL COMPONENTS

Eight key architectural components are used to design and develop historical mobile games. These eight key architectural components are mainly divided into three categories which are core mechanics, player objectives and player challenges. The eight key architectural components are exploration, story-based gameplay, complete chapter story, overcome challenges, quick time events, puzzles, retain syllabus information presented and arena scenes. Functional and non-functional game requirements were also reviewed. Table 2 shows the 9 functional game requirements (a to i) and 3 non-functional game requirements (j-l).

The following are the 8 key architectural components:

- **Exploration:** Exploration is one of the fundamental components in most video games. It allows for players to set their own pace while playing, therefore allowing players to have breathing room before the next challenge. It incentivises players to discover all the nooks and crannies that a game has to offer, therefore rewarding the player for self-propagated exploration. The project will incorporate exploration by creating an arena environment that will include characters, architectures and hidden pathways to encourage players to explore the arena.
- **Story-Based Gameplay:** A story-based gameplay will have its start and end points correlated to the game's own story, therefore all event triggers that further the story will be linked to the player's actions/inputs. All events between the start and end of the game serve to tell a story and lead a player towards the end of the game. The project will incorporate story-based gameplay in each chapter by having the player complete a series of actions from a given start point until the player progresses to the end of the game. The events that happen in between the start and end will serve to deliver the syllabus content to the player.
- **Complete Chapter Story:** When the player starts each chapter, the player is required to complete the chapter from start to end as there are no save points within a chapter.
- **Overcome Challenges:** While playing a chapter, the game will present various challenges to engage a player to be further immersed in the game. The player will have to overcome challenges in order to progress to reach the end point of a chapter. After a completion of a chapter, the player must also complete a set of ten multiple choice questions in order the gauge the information retained from playing that chapter. If a player replays the chapter, only the highest score achieved by the player will be stored. The score will then be stored locally in the application for future reference.

- **Quick Time Events:** A player is required to complete a set of input actions within a short time frame (tracing shapes and quick tapping), the failure of which will require the player to repeat the challenge until the challenge is complete.
- **Puzzles:** The player is required to complete a set of puzzles (card match and path finding), the failure of which will require the player to repeat the challenge until the challenge is complete.
- **Retain the Syllabus Information Presented:** While playing a chapter, the game will have certain instances where the player will be required to give an answer based on prior information given within the chapter itself, hence providing players an incentive to retain the information presented by the game.
- **Arena Scenes:** Arena scenes are the environment in which a player interacts with the game. It is where the actions of the player triggers events predetermined by the game. The environment of the game should include intractable characters and buildings to expand the exploration potential for the player.

Table 2. Functional and non-functional requirements for historical mobile games

Functional Requirements
a. Deliver history syllabus during gameplay via character dialog or in-game text. b. Allow player(s) to choose different chapters to play from the menu screen. c. Allow user(s) to view a player's progress of each chapter. d. All chapters are to be re-playable. e. Scenario Agent calls correct actions/challenges based on player input/pre- determined scripting. f. Track player(s) progress and understanding of each chapter and save data collected. g. Provide player(s) with a sense of exploration in the game. h. Provide player(s) with incentives and challenges to play the game. i. Reward player(s) for preferred action.
Non-Functional Requirements
j. Each chapter must not be over 20 minutes long in play length. k. Informational text (character dialogue, in-game text, etc.) within the game should be dispersed between player challenges and arena exploration. l. Include a variety of challenges (puzzles or quick time events) to diversify incentives for the player.

Table 3. Mapping of requirements to key architectural components

Key Architectural Component	Requirements
Exploration	a, b, d, g
Story-Based Gameplay	a, i
Complete Chapter Story	a, c, j
Overcome Challenges	h, i
Quick Time Events	e, h, l
[INSERT FIGURE 001]Puzzles	e, h, l
Retain Syllabus Information Presented	a, e, f, h, l
Environment	g, k

Table 3 shows how to map the requirements to the key architectural components. The game requirements are as listed in Table 2.

Use of Case Diagram and Gameplay Flow

The system analysis conducted had helped to determine which historical period was to be set for the game and is stretched into two chapters. The main game's mechanisms and storyline had been drafted and will be expanded upon in the section on system design. Lastly, the use of case diagrams and its specifications are designed and explored on to map out the requirements to the gameplay components. Figure 2 presents the use of case diagram for historical mobile game applications.

Figure 2. Use diagram for historical mobile game application

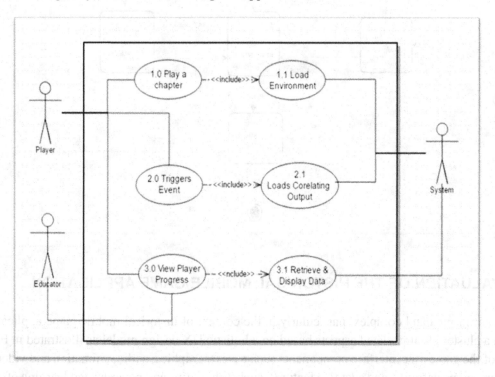

As the game was developed for mobile phones, the landscape view was selected (phone laying horizontally) as it allows for a larger range of screen space for larger dialogue area so that the text fits the screen comfortably. Typical phone screen sizes range from 2:3, 3:4, 3:5, 5:8, 5:9 and 9:16 ratios. Therefore, the developer needs to ensure that all the UI components in the game fit all screen sizes and do not intersect with the environmental (arena scene) components. Therefore, the game was developed based on the smallest phone ratio available and the UI and environmental components are fixed to ensure they don't intersect. The camera's orthodontic and the distance of game camera (consisting of UI component) from the environment will adjust according to screen size for optimal graphic display.

The colour theme for the game design is a palate of white backgrounds with bright colours (red, yellow, teal, etc.) to highlight borders, texts and buttons. The aesthetics of the game should be simple and accessible to as wide an audience as possible. Therefore, heavy stylisation (designing in such a way that is draws attention away from the object but instead to the design itself) for the graphic designs is discouraged. Figure 3 illustrates the proposed gameplay flow for the historical mobile game application.

Figure 3. Proposed gameplay flow for historical mobile game application

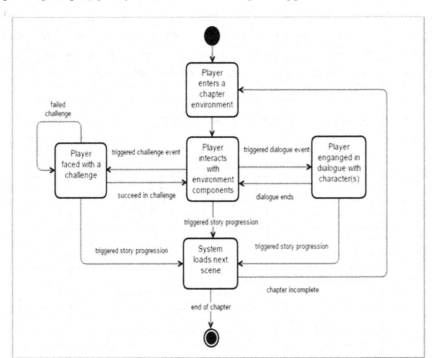

UX EVALUATION OF THE HISTORICAL MOBILE GAME APPLICATION

UX is multifaceted and complex, particularly in the context of historical mobile game applications. It is given a cluster of interrelated aspects based on a holistic UX design model as illustrated in Figure 4; quality of the game user interface components such as text, graphics, audio, animation and video; game characters, game narrative and adaptive features, such as hint, tips and rewards; and learning efficacy or learning experience that are affected by the quality of content delivered by the game. Moreover, some studies have stated that current UX evaluation methods have largely drawn from traditional usability approaches (Law & Sun, 2012).

USER STUDY SETTING

A prototype of a historical mobile game application was designed, developed and used to evaluate UX. Students from a secondary school had participated in this user study. They had to install the mobile game application prototype in their mobile phones or devices and play the history game for at least 2

Figure 4. Mapping diagram for the proposed history game features

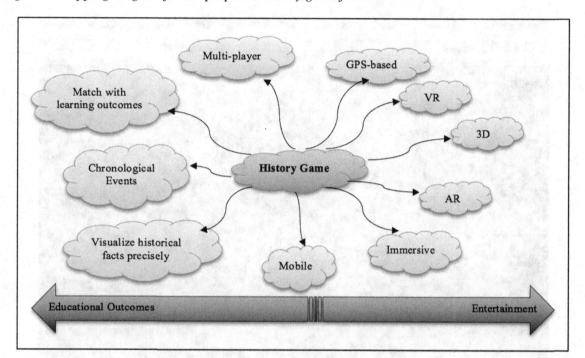

hours. After they had played the history game, they were guided to answer the evaluation test for UX of the game. This historical game prototype was developed to enable students to learn at their own pace while also establishing a more engaging learning process. The secondary school students can play each chapter and revisit those chapters to refresh their memory. Each session incorporates important historical facts into the game mechanics and story. The gameplay keeps the students engaged while delivering the learning content.

Figure 5 is one of the snapshots of the historical mobile game application prototype. This prototype game is structured as below:

- The prototype covers an important historical period in Malaysian history, which is the seventh chapter from the Form 4 textbook on the early culture of Malaya during the early Malay Kingdoms.
- There are two chapters for the period stated above which deliver the syllabus content through progressive story telling.
- Each chapter's average game session does not last longer than 20 minutes.
- Students' actions and behaviours during game play were evaluated and recorded into the player progress scene.

Figure 5. Snapshot of the historical mobile game application prototype

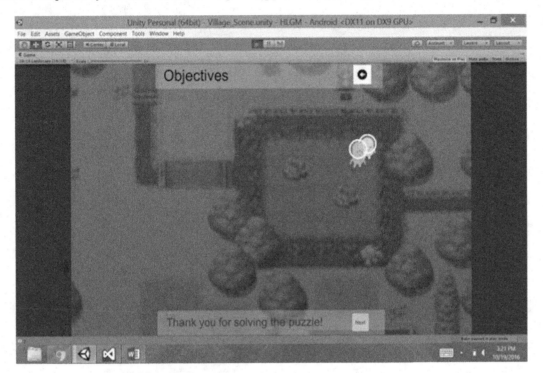

RESEARCH DESIGN AND PARTICIPANTS

The research is designed as an exploratory case study to explore the UX design model for a historical mobile game application. It involves 112 students (50 males and 62 females) who have played the prototype. They were chosen randomly from a selected secondary school. In this study, the participants were from the same school and their ages ranged from 16 to 17 years old as Form Four students (same age as 10th grade secondary level students). All participants had the experience of playing games, with 80.4% of them playing mobile games every day and the rest, two to three times per week.

INSTRUMENT AND MEASUREMENT

To understand the UX of the historical mobile game, data were collected via a questionnaire based on four dimensions: gaming or gameplay experience (G), learning experience (L), adaptivity (A), and usability (U). The instrument was modified from a previous study (Law & Sun, 2012). The questionnaire was employed to capture participants' background and demographic data as well as their opinion on the four dimensions mentioned above. A set of questions on age, gender, game experience which include the frequency of playing games, and game type preferences were presented. These background and demographic data were presumed to have influence on gameplay experience and performance.

Before the UX evaluation study, a pilot test was conducted to test the suitability of the terms used, arrangement of items, and arrangement of choices for each item. The pilot test was also used to determine the reliability and validity of the instrument. A total of 32 students with ages ranging from 16 to 17 years old (Form Four) from a selected secondary school had participated in the pilot test. The SPSS analysis results showed that the Cronbach's Alpha reliability coefficient value of this instrument is 0.812. This alpha value is satisfactory because it is within 0.65 to 0.95 (Chua, 2013), and means that all 12 items in the instrument is consistent, reliable and valid to be used to evaluate UX for the historical mobile game application. Table 4 shows the SPSS results of the pilot test for the 12 items in the instrument.

Table 4. The Cronbach's Alpha reliability test results for the UX evaluation instrument

Reliability Statistics		
Cronbach's Alpha	Cronbach's Alpha Based on Standardized Items	N of Items
.812	.823	12

Table 5 lists the questions asked in the questionnaire. The instrument consisted of twelve items based on four dimensions. A five-point Likert scale is used to test the level of satisfaction, effectiveness, likelihood and opinion (1-lowest to 5-highest) for the 12 tested items. The other 2 questions which require students to give suggestions, comments or recommendations to improve the history game are "What improvements would you suggest in terms of gameplay?" and "What additional features would you add that would improve the game?".

Table 5. Questions in the questionnaire based on gaming / gameplay experience, learning experience, adaptivity and usability

Item	Dimension(s)	Question
G1	Gaming / Gameplay experience	How enjoyable is the app as a game?
G2		How enjoyable is the gameplay in the app?
L1	Learning experience	How effective is the app for learning history?
L2		How well do you understand the historical contents after finishing a chapter?
L3		How interactive is this game compared to the way you learn history in your school?
L4		How well do you understand the chapter objectives?
A1	Adaptivity	How effective are the hints for you to play the game?
A2		How efficient is the engagement for you to play the game?
A3		How frequent do you replay the game?
U1	Usability	How well can you navigate the app menu & chapters?
U2		How easy is the usage of buttons in the app?
U3		How well do you learn to play the game?

UX EVALUATION RESULTS AND DISCUSSIONS

Demographic and Background Results

112 students which consisted of 44.64% males and 55.36% females have participated in the UX evaluation. Their ages are 16-17 years old, with a mean of 16.1. All of them are gamers, which mean that they have game experience and had explored digital games before. Of the 112 participants, 28 of them are at the expert level in terms of their gaming experience and 75% of them (84 students) are intermediate gamers. 53.6% of the participants have explored mobile games and 31.25% of them have played computer games. Besides that, 80.4% of the students have played console games, web games and Facebook games previously. To conclude the demographics or background study of this focus group's participants, with a mean of 16.1 years old, all of them have explored the game world and they play games quite frequently with the rate of at least 2-3 times per week and they are at least at the intermediate level of their gaming experience. Thus, their perceptions on their UX and satisfaction of historical mobile games are sufficient to contribute some deep insights on the historical game's UX design in the Malaysian context.

Gaming / Gameplay Experience

There are two questions included for gaming or gameplay experience dimension which are related to the participants' feelings or description about the historical mobile game. The mean for this dimension is 3.645 ± SD 0.933. This means that participants do not really enjoy the gameplay experience of the historical mobile game application. Due to lack of animation and disjoined graphics and themes, the participants felt not so enjoyed with the application as a game. Moreover, the gameplay complexity is simple as it only uses touch inputs. The participants felt that the challenges are easy to comprehend and overcome.

Learning Experience

For the learning experience dimension, a total of four questions were asked about the effectiveness of the game application in historical learning, how efficient the participants had learned the historical contents and understand the chapter objectives, and how interactive the historical mobile game is compared to the conventional method of learning history in school. The story in the historical game is consistent with the syllabus and follows a narrative flow. Each chapter has its own unique and specific narration. The mean score of this dimension from the participants' responses are 3.955 ± SD 0.838. They feel that the historical mobile game is more interactive than their current way of studying with a mean = 3.94 ± SD 0.809. Furthermore, the historical content in the mobile game is very high as the game is designed to deliver the same historical content as the history subject syllabus to the students.

Adaptivity

Adaptivity asks about the effectiveness of hints in the historical mobile game, engagement in the game, and how frequent the students replay the game as they adapt to the game. The participants can adapt to the history mobile game easily with a mean score = 4.07 ± SD 0.873, and they can engage in the historical mobile game easily with mean = 4.34 ± SD 0.778 for Question A2. The engagement level with the historical mobile game is high and it is supported by the natural flow of the story and challenges, although they did not enjoy the gameplay experience of the prototype.

Usability

The mean score for the usability dimension evaluation of the historical mobile game prototype = 3.857 ± SD 0.897, which is the highest score among the evaluated dimensions for UX of the historical game. This means that the usability of the historical mobile game is very high as it is easy to use and easy to learn. The participants can navigate well the game menus and chapters, easily use all the buttons in the game, and easily learn to play the game. These results also show that there are not many usability problems in this game. The participants did not have any usability problems such as cannot navigate to the selected chapter, cannot stop the game although the stop button was clicked on, cannot find the way to quit the game, and so on.

Other Suggestions to Improve UX of the Historical Game

To gather more data to improve the UX of the historical game, the participants also gave their suggestions to improve the gameplay experience. Most of the respondents suggest more engaging and interesting mini-games and stories for the historical mobile game to increase gaming experience and UX among the gamers. Some of the participants were quoted as following:

P1: "Mini-games need to be more challenging"
P2: "Implement strategy mini-games"
P4: "Write more relevant story for each chapter"
P7: "More interesting mini-games, like Candy Crush"
P8: "More interesting story"
P12: "Need to tie-in mini-game into the story"
P17: "Mini-games need to be more engaging"
P18: "Implement higher level of visual learning, such as adding in images of the historical figures, objects or location"
P20: "Mini-games should be more difficult and longer"
P22: "Story should be more interesting"
P35: "The game should be more challenging"
P57: "I prefer strategy games to learn history"
P78: "Multimedia effect should be extra"
P89: "I need more visual or virtual effects"
P102: "Engaged story plus visual effect"

However, there are some negative quotes from the participants' response, such as *P3: "Too many mini-games, not relevance/ similar between each mini-game"* and *P27: "...should have one main mini-game"*. Hence, the participants also suggested extra or additional features that are needed to improve the game. The following quotes are some responses from the participants:

P5: "Notes for each chapter…"

P6: "Bigger text size please…."

P10: "Summary of the chapter"

P13: "Additional link to other sources"

P18: "More variety of quiz questions"

P20: "Add more animations, audio……and visual learning"

P21: "A mind map of each chapter"

P25: "Short notes of each chapter"

P31: "Add animations and graphic effects"

P68: "Can add extra character in the game"

P92: "I need more visual and virtual effects"

P108: "Add some hints to play the games"

Relationship Between the Four Dimensions of UX in the Historical Mobile Game

Besides the evaluation study of UX via a history mobile game on the four dimensions above, these four dimensions were also analysed for the relationships between them. A correlation study on these four variables enabled the researchers to know whether there is a significant relationship between them or not. Due to the ordinal data collected in this study, Spearman's rho was used to calculate the relationship between these four variables. As mentioned above, UX was evaluated based on these four dimensions. To know further about these four variables' correlation coefficient, the Spearman correlation test was used to contribute further insights to improve history learning via mobile game applications. Table 6 tabulates the correlation results between learning experience, adaptivity, usability and gaming experience. From the results, there are three positive relationship with significant values = 0.000 between these four dimensions: (1) between usability and learning experience at 0.578 ($p<0.01$) with a significant value = 0.000; (2) between gaming experience and learning experience at 0.434 ($p<0.01$) with a significant value = 0.000; (3) between gaming experience and usability at 0.606 ($p<0.01$) with a significant value = 0.000. Furthermore, there is a significant relationship between adaptivity and gaming experience at correlation coefficient 0.213, with $p = 0.024$ ($p<0.05$).

Hence, there is a proposed model to show the relationship between these four dimensions which can be used to evaluate UX of the historical mobile game. Figure 6 has shown the proposed relationship model between adaptivity, gaming experience, usability and learning experience. From the correlation results, the authors suggest that the adaptivity of a game can affect students' gaming experience. The hints, tips, and reward system that are offered by the historical mobile game can increase students' enjoyment to play the game. They feel fun, happy, motivated, and challenged when they play the historical game. However, the usability problems had affected the students' gaming experience. Ease of use, navigation, the usage of screen buttons and a user-friendly interface are the main usability problems that may affect students' gaming experience. With a proper design and good navigation between game screens, students will feel that an application is easy to use, and hence play the historical game. Directly, students feel happy and enjoy playing the historical game. At the same time, these usability functions will increase students' learning experience too. For example, students can learn well when they feel that it is easy to play the game. If students gain gaming experience from the mobile game, they are gaining learning experience from the proposed relationship model in user experience model.

Table 6. Correlation results between the four dimensions in UX evaluation

Correlations			Learning Experience	Adaptivity	Usability	Gaming Experience
Spearman's rho	Learning Experience	Correlation Coefficient	1.000	.008	.578**	.434**
		Sig. (2-tailed)	.	.936	.000	.000
		N	112	112	112	112
	Adaptivity	Correlation Coefficient	.008	1.000	.003	.213*
		Sig. (2-tailed)	.936	.	.972	.024
		N	112	112	112	112
	Usability	Correlation Coefficient	.578**	.003	1.000	.606**
		Sig. (2-tailed)	.000	.972	.	.000
		N	112	112	112	112
	Gaming Experience	Correlation Coefficient	.434**	.213*	.606**	1.000
		Sig. (2-tailed)	.000	.024	.000	.
		N	112	112	112	112

* Correlation is significant at the 0.05 level (2-tailed)

** Correlation is significant at the 0.01 level (2-tailed)

Figure 6. The proposed model between adaptivity, gaming experience, usability and learning experience in user experience evaluation of the historical mobile game

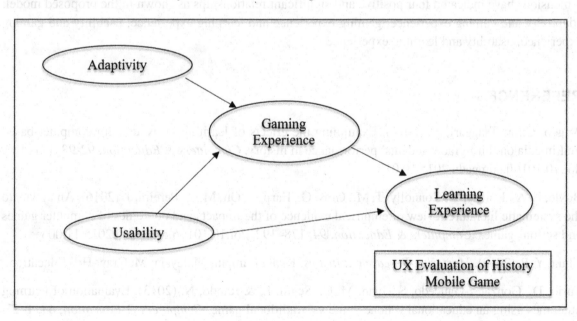

These four dimensions can be used for UX evaluations, but the relationship between these variables need to be countered to ensure that the UX of the game design is truly impactful or effective for history learning. This proposed model needs further investigation using the structural equation model method to analyze and test the complex relationships between these four dimensions. Future endeavors may be able to find the best fit model to support the proposed relationship, and it is useful to evaluate the UX for historical mobile games.

CONCLUSION

In conclusion, the use of case diagrams and its specifications are designed and explored in order to map out the requirements for gameplay components so to create an efficient mobile game application for Malaysian history learning. The proposed mapping of game requirements to the key architectural components is useful for mobile game application development in the future. This study has evaluated the UX of a mobile game application for Malaysian history learning from four dimensions: gaming experience, learning experience, adaptivity and usability. These four dimensions cover other crucial attributes of educational game from prior studies such as flow, challenge, immersion, competence (gaming experience), content appropriateness, learning goal, feedback, extensibility, media matching (learning experience), cognitive, rewards, motivations (adaptivity), interaction, and ease of use interface (usability). The results have revealed that the historical mobile game application can indeed be a meaningful mean to create gaming experience, learning experience, and adaptivity and usability, which can facilitate history learning through the UX of playing historical mobile games. The correlation results of these four dimensions have indicated four positive and significant relationships as shown in the proposed model: adaptivity and gaming experience; gaming experience and learning experience; usability and gaming experience; usability and learning experience.

REFERENCES

Angeli, C., & Tsaggari, A. (2016). Examining the effects of learning in dyads with computer-based multimedia on third-grade students' performance in history. *Computers & Education*, *92-93*, 171–180. doi:10.1016/j.compedu.2015.10.015

Boyle, E. A., Hainey, T., Connolly, T. M., Gray, G., Earp, J., Ott, M., ... Pereira, J. (2016). An update to the systematic literature review of empirical evidence of the impacts and outcomes of computer games and serious games. *Computers & Education*, *94*, 178–192. doi:10.1016/j.compedu.2015.11.003

Chua, Y. P. (2013). *Mastering Research Statistics*. Kuala Lumpur, Malaysia: McGraw-Hill Education.

Furio, D., Gonzalez-Gancedo, S., Juan, M. C., Segui, I., & Rando, N. (2013). Evaluation of learning outcomes using an educational iPhone game vs. traditional game. *Computers & Education*, *64*, 1–23. doi:10.1016/j.compedu.2012.12.001

Khenissi, M. A., Essalmi, F., & Jenni, M. Kinshuk, Graf, S., & Chen, N.S. (2016). Relationship between learning styles and genres of games. *Computers & Education, 101*.

Kiili, K., de Freitas, S., Arnab, S., & Lainema, T. (2012). The design principles for flow experience in educational games. *Procedia Computer Science, 15,* 78–91. doi:10.1016/j.procs.2012.10.060

Lim, H. L., Chin, H. L., & Nabeel, A. (2013). Using Weblog in cooperative learning to improve the achievement of history learning. *The Malaysian Online Journal of Educational Technology, 1*(3), 30–43.

Low, E. L.-C., & Sun, X. (2012). Evaluating user experience of adaptive digital educational games with activity theory. *International Journal of Human-Computer Studies, 70*(7), 478–497. doi:10.1016/j.ijhcs.2012.01.007

MDEC. (2015). South East Asia Game Industry Initiative. Retrieved from http://www.mscmalaysia.my/sites/default/files/pdf/booklets_brochures/GameIndustry_MDeC(FULL).pdf

Meier, J., & Crocker, M. (2010). Generation Y in the workforce: Managerial challenges. *The Journal of Human Resource and Adult Learning, 6*(1), 68–78.

Mortara, M., Catalano, C. E., Bellotti, F., Fiucci, G., Houry-Panchetti, M., & Petridis, P. (2014). Learning cultural heritage by serious game. *Journal of Cultural Heritage, 15*(3), 318–325. doi:10.1016/j.culher.2013.04.004

Nor Azan, M. Z., Azizah, J., & Wong, S. Y. (2009). Digital game-based learning (DGBL) model and development methodology for teaching history. *WSEAS Transactions on Computers, 8*(2), 322–333.

Nor Azan, M. Z., & Wong, S. Y. (2009). History educational game design. In *Proceedings of the International Conference on Electrical Engineering and Informatics* (pp. 269-275).

Nor Azan, M. Z., & Wong, S. Y. (2013). Design and evaluation of history digital game based learning (DGBL) software. *Journal of Next Generation Information Technology, 4*(4), 9–24. doi:10.4156/jnit.vol4.issue4.2

Norshuhada, S., & Syamsul, B. Z. (2011). Designing user experience for mobile game-based learning. In *Proceedings of the International Conference on User Science and Engineering (iUSEr)* (pp. 89-94).

Project Tomorrow. (2008). Speak Up 2007 for students, teachers, parents & school leaders selected national. Retrieved from http://www.tomorrow.org/docs/National%20Findings%20Speak%20Up%202007.pdf

Rankin, Y. A., McNeal, M., Shute, M. W., & Gooch, B. (2008). User centred game design: evaluating massive multiplayer online role playing games for secondary language acquisition. In *Sandbox Symposium,* August 9-10 (pp. 43-49).

Ratna, Z. R., Noraidah, S., Nor Azan, M. Z., Norlis, O., & Salyani, O. (2013). Development and validation of game interface with culture questionnaire: Graphic and animation. *Procedia Technology, 11,* 840-845.

Raybourn, E. M. (2014). A new paradigm for serious games: Transmedia learning for more effective training and education. *Journal of Computational Science, 5*(3), 471–481. doi:10.1016/j.jocs.2013.08.005

Saucken, C. v., Reinhardt, J., Michailidou, I., & Lindemann, U. (2013). Principles for user experience design: Adapting the tips approach for the synthesis of experience. In *Proceedings of the 5th International Congress of International Association of Societies of Design Research (IASDR)*, Tokyo, Japan, August 26-30.

Saucken, C. v., Schroer, C., Kain, B., & Lindemann, U. (2012). Customer Experience Interaction Model. In *Proceedings of Design Conference* (pp. 1387-1396).

Sii, C. H., & Soon, F. F. (2010). Effects of multimedia redundancy in history learning among 'deep and surface' students. *Asian Social Science*, 6(6), 119–127.

Vanisri, N., & Roslina, I. (2015). User experience of educational games: A review of the elements. *Procedia Computer Science*, 72, 423–433. doi:10.1016/j.procs.2015.12.123

Voet, M., & Wever, B. D. (2016). History teachers' conceptions of inquiry-based learning, beliefs about the nature of history, and their relation to the classroom context. *Teaching and Teacher Education*, 55, 57–67. doi:10.1016/j.tate.2015.12.008

Watson, W. R., Mong, C. J., & Harris, C. A. (2011). A case study of the in-class use of a video game for teaching high school history. *Computers & Education*, 56(2), 466–474. doi:10.1016/j.compedu.2010.09.007

This research was previously published in the International Journal of Distance Education Technologies (IJDET), 16(3); pages 46-63, copyright year 2018 by IGI Publishing (an imprint of IGI Global).

Chapter 21
Emotional Agents in Educational Game Design:
Heroes of Math Island

Mirela Gutica
British Columbia Institute of Technology, Canada

Stephen Petrina
University of British Columbia, Canada

ABSTRACT

Evaluating the subjective playing experience and engagement in learning is important in the design of advanced learning technologies (ALTs) that respond to the learners' cognitive and emotional states. This article addresses students' attitudes toward an educational game, Heroes of Math Island, and their responses to the emotional agent, an animated monkey. Fifteen students (seven boys and eight girls) from grades six and seven participated in this quasi-experimental study (pretest, intervention, post-test, followed by post-questionnaire and interview). This research presents a detailed analysis of students' subjective reactions with respect to Heroes of Math Island and to the underlying mathematics content, their learning gains and emotions triggered during gameplay, and design issues resulting from the evaluation of the game and of its emotional agent. The findings from this study inform how ALTs and educational games can be designed in order to be effective and provide emotional engagement, enjoyment, and learning.

1. OBJECTIVES

Educational games have a range of cognitive, emotional, motivational, and social benefits (Carvalho et al., 2015; Crookall, 2010; Ge & Ifenthaler, 2018). Video games designed to enhance or simulate educational experience are, in other words, advanced learning technologies (ATLs) (Conati, Jaques, & Muir, 2013; Rodrigo, et al., 2012). According to Aleven, Beal, and Graesser (2013), ALTs "provide a high degree of interactivity, reflecting a view of learning as a complex, constructive activity on the part of

DOI: 10.4018/978-1-6684-7589-8.ch021

learners that can be enhanced with detailed, adaptive guidance" and are capable of assessing or tracking learners' experiences, including learning strategies and affective states (pp. 929-930).

In "Why Games Don't Teach," Clark (2013) argued that "advocating games as a main or even frequent instructional strategy is misleading" and encouraged the development of a "taxonomy of games or game features that link to desired instructional outcomes" (p. 10). She noted the "insufficient well-designed experimental research on which to base many conclusions" (Clark, 2013, p. 1). Downsides are reported in literature, such as the appeal of video games as entertainment (Persico, et al., 2018) and the lack of correlation between playing video games as leisure activities and school cognitive tests, i.e., comprehension, math, school knowledge, and reasoning tests (Lieury, Lorant, Trosseille, Champault, & Vourc'h, 2016). Although Clark's argument for better alignment of game design with learning outcomes is valid and downsides should be considered, the educational literature presents evidence of the effectiveness of game-based learning (GBL) (de Freitas, 2013; Ge & Ifenthaler, 2018; Kiili, Ketamo, Koivisto, & Finn, 2014; Hosseini & Mostafapour, 2020; Partovi & Razavi, 2019; Spires, Rowe, Mott, & Lester, 2011). In a study that explored primary school children's technology acceptance, Camilleri and Camilleri (2019) reported that students recognized the usefulness and relevance of educational games played at school. However, important shortcomings result from design focused on content, as designers of educational games often "develop products that miss the most essential mechanism of engagement in games— the fun" (Granic, Lobel, & Engels, 2014, p. 74).

This article is derived from a larger study that involved the design and implementation of an educational game titled *Heroes of Math Island* (Gutica, 2014). Using design-based research (DBR), the larger study explored students' emotions during gameplay, learning gains, as well as their subjective attitudes towards the game and learning. We address in this article the following research questions:

- What are the students' subjective reactions to *Heroes of Math Island*?
- What are their emotional responses to the game and emotional agent?
- What are their levels of interest and achievement in the mathematics content after gameplay?

2. THEORETICAL FRAMEWORK

In this article, "affect," "affective state," and "emotion" are used interchangeably. Many contemporary scientists and theorists define emotion in a context of cognition and motivation (LeDoux, 1995; Ortony & Turner, 1990; Plutchik, 1984; Rolls, 1995). According to LeDoux (1996), "once emotions occur they become powerful motivators of future behaviors. They chart the course of moment-to-moment action as well as set the sails toward long-term achievements" (p. 20). The relationships between emotion and learning are varied and complex (Petrina, 2007, pp. 53-90). Astleitner (2000) empirically validated his theoretical instructional design approach employing five emotions— fear, envy, anger, sympathy, pleasure (FEASP)— and demonstrated the existence of a significant correlation between sympathy-related and pleasure-related instructional strategies and corresponding emotions in learners. Hascher (2010) stated that a positive environment is an "optimal precondition for holistic and creative thinking as it does not force the learner to cope with the situation but enables open-mindedness" (p. 15). However, this is a simplistic approach and the "valence of a mood or an emotion (being positive or negative) is only one aspect of its quality" (Hascher, 2010, p. 16). Educational research is well served by empirical and theoretical studies of emotion and learning (Astleitner, 2000; Ingleton, 2000; Hascher, 2010; Pekrun & Linnenbrink-Garcia, 2014).

Several researchers in the affective computing field argue that the only way to respond users' needs is to prompt them to sense and respond to cognition and emotion (Norman, 2005; Picard, 1997; Picard & Klein, 2002; Scherer, 2009). Past research on intelligent tutoring systems (ITSs) tended to privilege cognitive over affective needs by emphasizing cognition and "marginalizing affect" (Woolf, et al., 2009, p. 129). However, attention to emotion has been increasing (Baker, D'Mello, Rodrigo, & Graesser, 2010; Derbali, Ghali, & Frasson, 2013; Rodrigo, et al., 2012; Jaques, Conati, Harley, & Azevedo, 2014; Azevedo, Taub, Mudrick, Farnsworth, & Martin, 2016) (Schuller & Schuller, 2018; Tettegah & Gartmeier, 2016). Emotional agents (Scheutz, 2002) respond to learners' affective states, for example a child animation showing emotional facial expressions to provide motivational adaptive scaffolding in Ecolab (Rodrigo, et al., 2008) and "Scooter the Tutor" a dog animation designed to reduce "gaming the system" in Scatterplot Tutor (Rodrigo, et al., 2012, p. 226). Schuller and Schuller (2018) note that these agents are typically designed for "emotional recognition, augmentation, and generation" (p. 41). As several evaluations of pedagogical agents produced ambiguous results, attention should be shifted to "socio-emotional and relational variables" by complementing measures of learning outcomes with process measures, which are sensitive to the "situational demands" of interaction (Krämer & Bente, 2010, p. 71).

The design of affect-sensitive ALTs or emotional agents is complex as designers need to understand "cognition, emotions, motivation, aesthetics, communication, social interactions, sociology and technology" (Graesser, D'Mello, & Strain, 2014, p. 473). Although there is a large number of affect recognition and response studies, these studies tend to overlook learners' attitudes and subjective reactions during interaction with the learning environment. Designing for the appraisal and augmentation of emotions is quite challenging, as we explain.

3. DESIGN CONSIDERATIONS, METHODOLOGY AND PROCEDURE

This study consisted of three stages: (1) design of the game; (2) quasi-experimental study (pretest, intervention, post-test, followed by post-questionnaire and interview), and (3) affect analysis (emotion-labeling process and video annotations) performed by two trained judges (Gutica, 2014). The affect analysis and framework used to define the emotions analyzed in this study are described in details elsewhere (Conati & Gutica, 2016; Gutica & Conati, 2013). This article focuses on the quasi-experimental, post-questionnaire, and interview data. We also triangulate our results with affect analysis.

3.1. Game Design

Heroes of Math Island was designed on a gaming platform (Microsoft XNA) in consultation with two game designers. This allowed the implementation of rich game mechanics comparable to that of commercial video games. As we wanted to target an age group that enjoys playing games and is developmentally in a process of learning complex mathematics concepts, we designed the game for grades 5-7 students. Additionally, several other studies targeted the same age group (Conati & Maclaren, 2009; Conati & Manske, 2009; Rodrigo, et al., 2008; Rodrigo, et al., 2012). The math content (number factorization) was based on the curriculum taught in British Columbia (BC), Canada (BC, Ministry of Education [MoE], 2007). The game design uses a narrative (set on an island with a castle as the central site where students get challenges or "quests" from a king or queen). We drew on a range of design principles (Salen & Zimmerman, 2004), including avatars, non-player characters (queen and king), content design (a narrative accompanying each task), levels of difficulty, metaphors and semiotics (e.g., prime numbers are rocks that cannot be broken), and repeatability (a player will repeat a set of actions to gain mastery of a task). The idea of an island is popular in fantasy literature and educational adventure games or serious games (e.g., *Crystal Island*, McQuiggan, Robison, & Lester, 2008; Valenza, Gasparini, & Hounsell, 2019). *Heroes of Math Island*, like a range of mathematics educational games, provides a rich digital game-based environment (Broza & Kolikant, 2020; Chu & Fowler, 2020; Conati, 2002; Conati & Maclaren, 2009; Conati & Manske, 2009).

There are five possible challenges or quests in *Heroes of Math Island*: forest, mine, mountain, seashore, and swamp (Figure 1). Each quest is intended to include a set of activities. The mine quest is based on learning outcomes involving divisibility, prime numbers, and factorization in accordance with the provincial curriculum (BC MoE, 2007). Three activities — divisibility, prime numbers, and decomposition — each consisting of 25 exercises organized into five levels of difficulty containing five items, are included in the mine quest. The game progresses to the next level only if the student correctly solves all five exercises. The exercises are generated by the system based on the student's previous performance. In order to design this game, we conducted four usability studies involving a grade 6 student, a mathematics teacher for grade 6 (two studies), and two instructional designers. For the mine quest theme, the miners are sick and need help. Rocks represent numbers: prime numbers are represented by hard rocks that cannot be "decomposed." Composite numbers can be broken with picks. When decomposed correctly, the composite numbers transform into gold (Figure 2).

Figure 1. Heroes of Math Island

Figure 2. The Mine showing completed quest and happy monkey

On the island there is a library (the Wiseman's library) where students are sent when making mistakes. When students make mistakes, the game generates three levels of hints (a general hint acknowledging the error, a specific hint, and an example). The game design employs negative reinforcement for poor performance: on the fourth error, the player is sent to the library and the activity restarted. The Wiseman is not offering help in this version of the game (it will be expanded in the future). The game includes an emotional agent, represented by a monkey, presented in the next section.

3.2. Emotion Framework

The emotions considered in this study were selected based on emotion models found: (1) in the affective computing literature, i.e., the affect framework proposed by Graesser et al. (2006), which considers the following emotions: boredom, confusion, delight, engaged concentration (also known as flow), frustration, and surprise; (2) appraisal theories of emotions (i.e., OCC cognitive theory of emotion) (Ortony, Clore, & Collins, 1988) which consists of 22 emotion types emotions occurring during interactions as a consequence of events; and (3) emotion models found in the education literature: (a) Astleitner's (2000) model of emotions in the context of instruction (i.e., anger, envy, fear, pleasure, and sympathy) and (b) Ingleton's (2000) emotion model in learning (confidence, distance, fear, pride, shame and solidarity). Our final model included 12 emotions (plus neutral): boredom, confidence, confusion/hesitancy, curiosity, delight/pleasure, disappointment/displeasure, engaged concentration, excitement, frustration, pride, shame and surprise. The 12 emotions were used for emotion labeling by video annotations by two judges (the first author of this paper, and a student research assistant trained to perform the task). The study participants' emotions were labeled with a video annotation technique, using a 20-second granularity and reporting all emotions that occurred in each time interval. It is important to note that in open-ended questions and interviews, our participants did not describe their feelings with the set of emotions used by judges for affect analysis. We did not provide participants with descriptions of these emotions (Gutica, 2014; Gutica & Conati, 2013; Conati & Gutica, 2016).

The game includes an emotional agent, represented by a monkey (Figure 3). We designed the monkey to be continuously present on the bottom-right corner of the screen and play animations that express emotional states according to the student's score calculated as an average between an absolute score (number of mistakes minus number of correct responses) and the trend of the most recent actions performed by the student (i.e., 20 correct answers in a row will cause the level of difficulty to increase two times faster).

We wanted to explore if the monkey's presence and emotional reactions can encourage the student by mirroring what is happening in the game. The monkey displays a neutral state, two positive (happy and confident), and two negative (sad and frustrated) emotional states. All four emotions were carefully selected as being considered relevant to learning in the context of an educational game. The emotions happy and sad were selected from the OCC model of emotion as they are representative of emotions focused on consequence of events and are used in game interactions (Ortony, Clore, & Collins, 1988). The other two emotions were selected as being important for learning: confidence (Ingleton, 2000) the very positive emotion occurring as a consequence of concept achievement, and frustration (Graesser et al., 2006) the negative emotion that can often occur during problem solving. The monkey's expressions were designed by a graphic artist based on standard portrayals of emotions used in psychological tests and therapy (Creative Therapy Associates). These expressions are longstanding in the history of caricatures and comics, most definitively dating to Töpffer's (1845) illustrations in physiognomy. Emotional agents in the form of avatars also commonly adopt these facial expressions (e.g., Chen et al., 2012; Rodrigo et al., 2008).

Figure 3. Emotional States: Frustrated, Sad, Neutral, Happy, and Confident

3.3. Participants, Methods and Techniques

Fifteen students (seven boys and eight girls) from grades 6-7 participated in this quasi-experimental study. Participants for research were recruited with flyers posted in several locations (schools, daycares, and the post-secondary institutions where the authors are affiliated) and randomly selected. The mean age of participants (seven boys and eight girls) was 11.4 and the median age was 11. Quantitative and qualitative data were collected from the quasi-experimental study and videos of the participants.

The protocol used for experiments included a short tutorial. The tutorial was needed to bring participating students to the same level of mathematical knowledge regarding divisibility, prime numbers, and decomposition in prime factors. Total time for an experiment was 1 to 2-½ hours, and the time used for gameplay was 15 to 48 min (M = 32.3 min; SD = 10.3 min). The game interaction was videotaped (one video camera recorded the student's face and one recorded the computer screen). The pre- and post-tests were similar but not identical and contained 23 questions (12 divisibility, 5 prime numbers, and 6 number decompositions). The post-questionnaire was adapted to this study from one used in *Prime Climb* studies (Conati & Maclaren, 2009; Conati & Manske, 2009). The primary author conducted the experiments together with three student research assistants enrolled in an undergraduate computing program at the British Columbia Institute of Technology (BCIT), who were also involved in the design and implementation of the game.

The post-questionnaire blueprint is presented in Table 1. The rows correspond to the students' subjective attitude towards the game, mathematics and the monkey (emotional agent in this game): (a) affective domain, (b) cognitive domain, and (c) learning. Columns indicate the following domains: attitude towards (1) the game, (2) content (mathematics), and (3) the emotional agent. Intersection of rows and columns correspond to the themes of this study.

The post-questionnaire (see Appendix A) was composed of 48 Likert scale items: statements regarding the general game experience (14); statements regarding the enjoyment of the game experience (13); statements regarding learning mathematics in this game (7); statements regarding interest in video and math games and willingness to play the game again (10); reports of mastery of the three topics (divisibility, prime numbers and decomposition) before playing the game (3) and the attitude towards mathematics (1); and 5 open-ended questions.

Table 1. Questionnaire Blueprint (see Appendix)

	Affective	**Cognitive**	**Learning**
Attitude toward the game	1.1; 1.10; 2.1; 2.7; 2.11; 2.12; 2.16; 4.5; 4.6; 4.8; 4.10	1.5; 1.11; 4.12	1.6; 1.13; 3.1; 3.9; 4:11
Attitude toward math	1.7; 1.8; 2.8; 2.9; 2.13; 2.14;	1.8; 1.16	1.13; 3.1; 3.2; 3.3; 3.4; 3.6; 3.9; 3.10; 4.11
Attitude toward the monkey	1.3; 1.9; 1.12; 1.15; 1.17; 2.2; 2.3; 2.4; 2.5		

Some post-questionnaire statements were used to characterize more than one category. For example, the statement "I believe that I can learn math better by playing this game" is about learning and attitudes toward both the game and mathematics. However, for simplicity we analyzed each statement in only the most appropriate category, giving priority to the affective domain and learning.

Interviews were semi-structured for allowing for free discussion. The interview guide included a set of questions related to emotions, game design and learning. Issues noted during game interaction were clarified in interviews. Data collected from interviews were used to better describe, clarify and understand the findings resulting from questionnaires. After interviews, observers had a discussion and collaboratively wrote a report based on notes taken during experiments which provided a starting point for data analysis. We used descriptive statistics to analyze the data extracted from pre- and post-tests and questionnaires. We analyzed the open-ended and interview data using a deductive approach based on these themes of this study.

4. FINDINGS

4.1. Attitude Toward the Game

In order to evaluate the students' emotional reaction to the design of the game, we computed a summative histogram, with results from five questions related to game mechanics (e.g., aspects of the game related to the avatar, finishing the quest, the rocks' animations, and visiting the castle). The analysis concluded that only a small percentage of responses were not favorable: generally students found the game design enjoyable. Figure 4 presents the results.

Figure 4. Game design: Detailed histogram

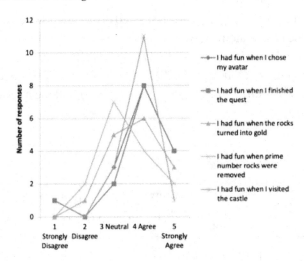

This finding is very important as many educational games lack the "fun" aspect of interaction (Granic, Lobel, & Engels, 2014). Students were asked during interviews to provide suggestions for improvement. They suggested adding more content to the game (quests), and including awards, leaderboards and game mechanics that are characteristics of video games targeting this age group (i.e., collecting items and "dressing their avatar").

4.2. Attitude Toward Learning

Students reported different levels of previous knowledge with respect to the three mathematics topics. More students reported a better grasp of divisibility than of prime numbers and decomposition. The null hypothesis of no difference between the pretest and post-test was rejected. One student did not write the post-test because he was too tired; therefore we computed the pre- and post-test scores for 14 students only. For these 14 students, there was a significant improvement from pretest (M = 77.7%; SD = 9.26%) to post-test (M = 83.6%; SD = 8.74%), t (13) = 3.17; two-tailed p = .007, d = 0.647). The Cohen's effect size value (d= 0.647) indicates a moderate to high practical significance.

Eight statements in the post-questionnaire addressed the students' perception of learning. One post-questionnaire item addressed the students' attitude towards learning prior to the gameplay ("I wanted to learn when I played the game") and six items addressed learning gains during and after gameplay, the overall impression ("I learned math when I played the game"), task accomplished ("I learned math when I finished the quest"), game design aspects related to learning ("I learned math when I got hints/ examples/harder question"), making mistakes ("I learned math when I made mistakes"), and social norms ("I learned math when I helped the miners"). One item addressed the students' belief that the game affords improved learning: "I believe that I can learn math better by playing this game." Figure 5 presents the computed histogram. We consider very promising that in the histogram, for all but one item ("I learned math when I got hints"), frequencies are concentrated towards "agree" and "strongly agree." Frequencies for the statement related to learning from hints are concentrated towards neutral, a finding that will be investigated in future research and will be taken into consideration in future revisions of the game.

From the group of 15 students, only one (Student 13) responded neutral to the overall statement related to learning "I learned math when I played the game," and 93.3% of students agree or strongly agreed: of the 14 students, 6 agreed and 8 strongly agreed. This was the same student who disagreed with the statement "I believe that I can learn math better by playing this game"; one other student was neutral, eight agreed, and five strongly disagreed. When Student 13 was asked how she would feel about the game if it would be improved, she responded that the game would not interest her unless the mathematical content were removed and replaced with "more fun learning material."

Figure 5. Learning: Detailed histogram

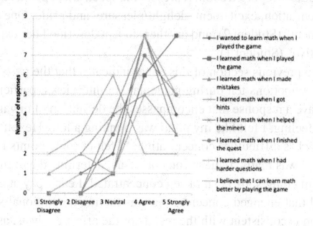

During the game, when experimenters observed that students were tired or struggled too much, they advised them to stop or replay the easier divisibility activity. It was interesting to notice that students were determined to finish the quest. None of the students in this group stopped before finishing the quest. Experimenters agreed that two students in particular were very tired during the gameplay, but did not want to stop, and managed to finish.

Interviews revealed the students' positive attitudes about the game: all but Student 13 agreed that they would like to study mathematics by playing the game. For example, Students 2 and 9 reported that the game is better than studying from textbooks. Student 6 believed that other students would also prefer this type of learning "because it is a game." Student 7 indicated that he would like to play the game to study for tests while Students 8 and 21 wanted to use the game to practice mathematics at school and home.

Student 18 reported that if each student would have a dedicated computer at school "then I would definitely say, we could use games like this one." Student 9 explained why she had fun: "Because I learned and I learned though a game and I like learning through games instead of just text book stuff." Even Student 13 (who disliked mathematics) agreed in interviews that she learned to some extent from the game: "Yes, I learned a little bit." It is important to note that Student 13 appeared to learn with the game as she improved her score by 4.3%, from 78.3% on the pretest to 82.6% on the post-test. She also was engaged during game play as engaged concentration was reported for her 48.5% by Judge 1 and 65.2% by Judge 2. She was observed only in few occasions expressing negative emotions: Judge 1 found her frustrated in few instances (6.1%) and Judge 2 found her confused but not frustrated (Gutica & Conati, 2013; Conati & Gutica, 2016).

Enjoyment and learning were generally reported together. Student 11 reflected on how gameplay enjoyment blended with learning: "I wanted to have [fun] and to learn more. And I like the game because it gave an opportunity to, like, do both." Student 15, who was neutral, clarified that she "didn't really care" if she had fun; however she learned "a lot."

4.3. Emotion and Learning

When asked what emotions they experienced during the game, participants generally responded happiness or having fun, and to a lesser extent confidence, confusion, frustration, and pride. We argue that the "happiness" state that students reported could represent the spectrum of positive emotions of confidence, curiosity, engaged concentration, excitement, delight/pleasure, and pride. One of the students reported "a sense of accomplishment" (Student 2), and another student described her experience with words like "interesting" and "effective" (Student 1).

Figure 4 included in a previous section of this paper indicates that the post-questionnaire responses are indicative of positive emotions felt during gameplay. In interviews, participants reported high engagement. Student 18 gave a response that encompasses the definition of engaged concentration "I felt like... it wasn't really a feeling, I felt like my mind was thinking a lot." He felt engaged with this game even though he generally has difficulties concentrating: "I felt at some points I felt a bit frustrated, and at some points I felt like I was really, I guess you could say, determined and my head was almost in it, when normally, when I'm doing stuff I can't keep concentrated, I can't pay attention to it."

Experimenters noted that engaged concentration was the main emotional state that students experienced. This observation is consistent with the results of the affect analysis, as engaged concentration was reported the majority of the time. It is important to note that these findings are in-line with the learning gains (the improvement from pre- to post-test), and the positive responses students gave to the post-questionnaire and during interviews.

The second most important affective state reported by judges was confidence, indicating that this emotion should be considered in future studies (Gutica & Conati, 2013; Conati & Gutica, 2016). The third most frequently reported state by judges (confusion/hesitancy, reported during emotion labeling 26% of the time) was also reported by some students. However, confusion is not considered an emotion that prevents learning (Craig, Graesser, Sullins, & Gholson, 2004; D'Mello, Taylor, & Graesser, 2007; Graesser, et al., 2006; Rodrigo, & Graesser, 2010).

Frustration is a negative emotion; however, during a learning process it may be "less persistent, less associated with poorer learning" (Baker, D'Mello, Rodrigo, & Graesser, 2010, p. 223). Frustration was observed to a lesser extent (only 5% of the time) during emotion labeling (Gutica & Conati, 2013; Conati

& Gutica, 2016). Some students reported frustration; however to a lesser extent: Student 7 responded that he felt "somewhat" frustrated; Student 9: "A few times I was a little frustrated, when I didn't get some of the rock things"; and Student 21: "It was fun, sometimes [I was] a bit frustrated, but it was a good game". Student 11 reported frustration with respect to the emotional agent's animations, which we will discuss in the next section. Frustration was reported in interviews in relationship to challenges encountered during learning (e.g., harder questions and making mistakes) and especially with regard to the negative reinforcement: when students made the fourth error and were sent to the Wiseman's library and the activity was restarted from the beginning. Our study demonstrates that negative reinforcement, a design element frequently used in video game design and ABA (Linehan, Kirman, Lawson, & Chan, 2011), is not an effective pedagogical technique as it can lead to frustration as we found from our participants. We did not ask the students how frequently they were frustrated. However, based on the overall positive responses given by students when asked if they learned during gameplay (Figure 5) and if they want to play the game again (Figure 6), and based on judges' observations, frustration seemed infrequent.

Another positive outcome of this study is that boredom, an emotion that is considered detrimental to learning (D'Mello, Taylor, & Graesser, 2007; Graesser, et al., 2006), was rarely observed; it was reported only 1.5% of the time in affect analysis. Only one student (Student 13) agreed with the post-questionnaire statement "This game was boring." In interviews, students did not report or complain of boredom, except for Student 13.

Figure 6. Boredom. Detailed histogram

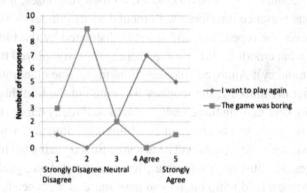

4.4. Emotional Agent

Mixed results were obtained with regard to the emotional agent: the monkey. We started from an assumption that the monkey (even displaying a simplistic and rudimental behavior in this version of the game) would be appealing and appreciated by students (Rodrigo et al., 2012). The usability studies conducted during the game design gave us confidence that the monkey would be liked by students. However, not all students liked the monkey: 53.3% of students disagreed or strongly disagreed to the post-questionnaire statement "The monkey was annoying," 26.6% of students were neutral, and 20% of students strongly agreed. Figure 7 presents the results.

Figure 7. The monkey was annoying. Detailed histogram.

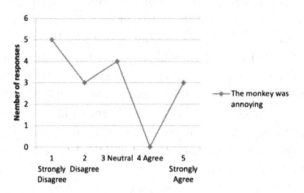

Interviews revealed two main issues related to the monkey: the agent's presence was either not observed or too distracting. For example, Students 2, 9, 10, 12, and 18 indicated that they did not notice the monkey during the gameplay. When asked if he noticed the monkey, Student 2 responded: "I noticed the monkey in the beginning, but when he was here, [I] less noticed [it] because I was thinking about the questions and I really didn't see it." Student 18 also did not notice the monkey: he reported in the open-ended item of the post-questionnaire: "I did not see the monkey react." In interviews he elaborated: "it did not bother me…I am not very observant." Similarly, Student 12 liked the monkey but did notice it less during the game: "Well I thought he was cute. Didn't see him very much though." Other students felt distracted (Students 4, 5, 6 and 13). Based on their responses, it appears that the money's animations and continuous presence interfered with mental focus. Student 4 observed and enjoyed the agent's animations; however she repeatedly said she was distracted by the blinking animation. To the statement "Please tell us what emotions did you experience when you played the game," she responded "Happy (because of the monkey); Annoyed (monkey blinking)." She elaborated during the interview: "I like the monkey just not the blinking, the monkey was cute but the blinking was annoying…. I was happy because the monkey kept making these really… he looked really happy, he was like confident. So I was happy and I was sort of annoyed at the monkey's blinking." Student 5 strongly disagreed with the statement "The monkey was annoying"; however he also mentioned during the interview being distracted by the monkey. He suggested: "Just do it one time [the animation], then, yeah, just smiling it'd work better. Like every five minutes, he'd jump up, so you have more of a chance to think." Student 13, also reported being distracted. She suggested: "Well, I think that, maybe, if the monkey got too annoying, there should be a stop button." She also agreed that having a monkey that participates in a different way in the game was more attractive to her; however, she was very clear that mathematics content would not motivate her to play the game.

Only three students agreed or strongly agreed to the statement "The monkey reacted correctly to my emotions": Student 8, Student 15 and Student 21. These students also strongly disagreed that the monkey was annoying. Student 8 elaborated in the interview:

Interviewer: Did [the monkey] respond well to what you were feeling?

Student 8: It did, it kinda was doing what I felt like. When I was failing I felt mad and the monkey felt sad, so it kinda made sense.

Student 6, who responded neutral, was supportive of the idea of an emotional agent responsive to student's performance bur criticized the animation design:" I kind of like the idea of him being sad or happy whether you get it wrong or right, but, it was a bit… normally his actions were really big, like, he could just make a little face." Student 11 liked the monkey without being able to give a reason. However, he did not consider that the monkey responded to his feelings and the way the agent was implemented created more frustration than good: "I felt frustrated when I was supposed to catch prime numbers from the last one but I got a little mixed up there and the monkey kept being sad and I was more frustrated." Student 21 in her interview reported the she did not notice the monkey "that much," except for confidence animation (she even made a face imitating the monkey's animation). The video confirms that Student 21, a strong mathematics student, avoided making mistakes and the monkey was in a happy or confident state all the time.

Students had mixed feelings regarding the inclusion of the monkey. Student 2 considered that having an emotional agent is beneficial and offered advice for future design: "I think the emotions are good and maybe even a voice too, like if you are doing good when he feels those emotions he could say like good job or keep trying, keep it up." Student 9 suggested that the monkey can participate in the game by offering hints: "If you are making too many mistakes then I would want to go to the Wiseman but if I got one wrong then instead of that thing popping up then maybe the monkey can give the hint." Student 7 suggested a fairly passive role for the monkey:

Interviewer: What would you like the monkey to do?

Student 7: Well, the monkey doesn't really do anything so just, maybe, just sit, and sitting there and watches I think.

Other students offered ideas of improvement of the monkey not necessarily related to emotions or the game mathematics content, but related to achievement and awards. Student 4 suggested collecting items for the monkey, Student 12 suggested that the monkey should wear different hats based on the student`s achievements in the game, and Student 21 indicated that the monkey should respond to the student's performance: "like at the end, once you see your score, and if you did really good then it would do a victory dance."

5. CONCLUSION

In response to the need for more empirical ALT and GBL research, this article addresses the design of an educational game (*Heroes of Math Island*) in the context of emotion and learning. By exploring students' attitudes toward the game and its emotional agent, and the affective states experienced by learners during gameplay, this article emphasizes the importance of taking emotions into account in designs for GBL. Exploration of gameplay with a focus on emotions may pave the road to a more long-term goal of responding to students' cognitive and emotional needs in promoting ALTs and GBL.

Data suggest that participants learned from their interaction with the *Heroes of Math Island* game, as there was a significant improvement from pre- to post-test and a moderate to high Cohen's effect size value. Another important finding is that students were highly engaged and determined to finish the "quest." These findings together with the improvement from pre-to post-test are important as evidence of learning gains in a context of increased attention and focus on the subject matter. Boredom, an emotion detrimental to learning was not observed and was reported by only one student, and frustration was infrequently observed or reported. These results are optimistic, indicating that the game mechanics and learning activities currently implemented in the game are adequate and attractive for this age group.

There are various limitations, including the number of participants. Although there was not a problem with the number of data points used for emotion analysis, data were collected and analyzed from 15 participants; the emotions identified or observed need to be tested on a larger sample. Second, the study took place in a laboratory and observers were present with participants. Methodologies used were appropriate for the age group but we acknowledge that participants may have felt compelled to report a positive sense of the game. A more extensive study should be conducted with participants and in a more naturalistic school setting. Third, the game used in this study incorporated a simplified agent; however findings can be used for design of ALTs and ITSs. Extrinsic motivators, such as emotional agents, prompts, and reward systems, are part and parcel of gameplay. Research is needed on participants' preferences and responses to these types of motivators in GBL.

Admittedly, we have to attend to the potential cognitive tutor to complement the emotional agent. As one of the students reasoned, "If you are making too many mistakes then I would want to go to the Wiseman." Culture and identity are increasingly important in the design of game agents, avatars, characters, and tutors (Demirdjian & Demirdjian, 2020; Harrell & Harrell, 2012; Petrina & Zhao, 2021). Research questions remain regarding the gender of agents in gameplay. For instance, is a wisewoman or wiseperson in gameplay merely symbolic or is there an effect for girls and women or gender non-binary players? Relations between players and avatars or agents appear to be gendered but much more research is needed (Lehdonvirta1, Nagashima, Lehdonvirta, & Baba, 2012).

Accounting for emotions in game design (e.g., the emotional agent) is critical for affect-sensitive ALTs. However, we found disagreement with respect to the emotional agent. The participants in this study offered feedback and suggestions for the future improvement of the emotional agent; the monkey's actions and contributions to gameplay need to be redesigned. Overall, we believe that this study offers a good starting point for future design of an agent that gives appropriate and timely emotional cues and responds to users' needs. More empirical research is needed for pedagogical agents and companions: what effect would a less intrusive, more useful agent have? The question is no longer whether educational game designers should include agents with or without emotions (Scheutz, 2002). The question is how well do agents augment, generate, and respond to players' emotional states during gameplay?

ACKNOWLEDGMENT

Components of the game's development were funded by the Social Sciences and Humanities Research Council of Canada and by the VP Research Seed Fund at British Columbia Institute of Technology (BCIT). There are no conflict of interest related to this study. Data collection was approved by the University of British Columbia's Research Ethics Board (certificate #H06-80670 and #H13-00245). We took all steps to protect the participants, ensuring that they were not disadvantaged and that the data have been anonymized. Raw data have not been placed in a repository.

REFERENCES

Aleven, V., Beal, C. R., & Graesser, A. C. (2013). Introduction to the special issue on advanced learning technologies. *Journal of Educational Psychology*, *105*(4), 929–931. doi:10.1037/a0034155

Astleitner, H. (2000). Designing emotionally sound instruction: The FEASP-approach. *Instructional Science*, *28*(3), 169–198. doi:10.1023/A:1003893915778

Azevedo, R., Taub, M., Mudrick, N., Farnsworth, J., & Martin, S. A. (2016). Interdisciplinary research methods used to investigate emotions with advanced learning technologies. In *Methodological advances in research on emotion and education* (pp. 231–243). Springer. doi:10.1007/978-3-319-29049-2_18

Baker, R. S., D'Mello, S. K., Rodrigo, M. M., & Graesser, A. (2010). Better to be frustrated than bored: The incidence, persistence, and impact of learners' cognitive- affective states during interactions with three different computer-based learning environments. *International Journal of Human-Computer Studies*, *68*(4), 223–241. doi:10.1016/j.ijhcs.2009.12.003

Barab, S., Scott, B., Siyahhan, S., Goldstone, R., Ingram-Goble, A., Zuiker, S., & Warren, S. (2009). Transformational play as a curricular scaffold: Using videogames to support science education. *Journal of Science Education and Technology*, *18*(4), 305–320. doi:10.100710956-009-9171-5

British Columbia Ministry of Education. (2007). *Mathematics, K-7*. https://www.bced.gov.bc.ca/irp/course.php?lang=en&subject=Mathematics&course=Mathematics_K_to_7&year=2007

Brown, J., Collins, A., & Duguid, S. (1989). Situated cognition and the culture of learning. *Educational Researcher*, *18*(1), 32–42. doi:10.3102/0013189X018001032

Broza, O., & Kolikant, Y. B.-D. (2020). The potential of rich digital game-based learning environments to promote low-achieving students' participation in mathematics. *International Journal of Game-Based Learning*, *10*(4), 40–54. doi:10.4018/IJGBL.2020100103

Camilleri, A. C., & Camilleri, M. A. (2019). The students' intrinsic and extrinsic motivations to engage with digital learning games. In *Proceedings of the 2019 5th International Conference on Education and Training Technologies* (pp. 44-48). New York, NY: Association for Computing Machinery. 10.1145/3337682.3337689

Carvalho, M., Bellotti, F., Berta, R., De Gloria, A., Sedano, C., Hauge, H., & Rauterberg, M. (2015). An activity theory-based model for serious games analysis and conceptual design. *Computers & Education*, *87*, 166–181. doi:10.1016/j.compedu.2015.03.023

Chen, G.-D., Lee, J.-H., Wang, C.-Y., Chao, P.-Y., Li, L.-Y., & Lee, T.-Y. (2012). An empathic avatar in a computer-aided learning program to encourage and persuade learners. *Journal of Educational Technology & Society*, *15*(2), 62–72.

Chu, M. W., & Fowler, T. A. (2020). Gamification of Formative feedback in language arts and mathematics classrooms: Application of the learning error and formative feedback (LEAFF) model. *International Journal of Game-Based Learning*, *10*(1), 1–18. doi:10.4018/IJGBL.2020010101

Clark, R. (2013). Why games don't teach. *Learning Solutions*. Retrieved June 10, 2019, from http://www.learningsolutionsmag.com/articles/1106/why-games-dont-teach

Conati, C. (2002). Probabilistic assessment of user's emotions in educational games. *Journal of Applied Artificial Intelligence*, *16*(7-8), 555–575. doi:10.1080/08839510290030390

Conati, C., & Gutica, M. (2016). Interaction with an edu-game: A detailed analysis of student emotions and judges' perceptions. *International Journal of Artificial Intelligence in Education*, *26*(4), 975–1010. doi:10.100740593-015-0081-9

Conati, C., Jaques, N., & Muir, M. (2013). Understanding attention to adaptive hints in educational games: An eye-tracking study. *International Journal of Artificial Intelligence in Education*, *23*(1-4), 136–161. doi:10.100740593-013-0002-8

Conati, C., & Maclaren, H. (2009). Modeling user affect from causes and effects. In *Proceedings of the 17th International Conference on User Modeling, Adaptation, and Personalization* (pp. 4-15). Berlin: Springer. 10.1007/978-3-642-02247-0_4

Conati, C., & Manske, M. (2009). Adaptive feedback in an educational game for number factorization. *Proceedings of the 14th International Conference on Artificial Intelligence in Education*, 518-583.

Craig, S. A., Graesser, A., Sullins, J., & Gholson, B. (2004). Affect and learning: An exploratory look into the role of affect in learning. *Journal of Educational Media*, *29*(3), 241–250. doi:10.1080/1358165042000283101

Creative Therapy Associates. (n.d.). Retrieved April 1, 2013, from http://www.ctherapy.com/Results_Pages/descriptions.asp?ProductID=PK100

Crookall, D. (2010). Serious games, debriefing, and simulation/gaming as a discipline. *Simulation & Gaming*, *41*(6), 898–920. doi:10.1177/1046878110390784

D'Mello, S. K., Taylor, R., & Graesser, A. C. (2007). Monitoring affective trajectories during complex learning. In *Proceedings of the 29th Annual Meeting of the Cognitive Science Society* (pp. 203–208). Mahwah, NJ: Erlbaum.

de Freitas, S. (2013). Towards a new learning: Play and game-based approaches to education. *International Journal of Game-Based Learning*, *3*(4), 1–6. doi:10.4018/ijgbl.2013100101

Demirdjian, C., & Demirdjian, H. (2020). The avatar as a self-representation model for expressive and intelligent driven visualizations in immersive virtual worlds. *International Journal of Applied Research in Bioinformatics*, *10*(2), 1–9. doi:10.4018/IJARB.2020070101

Derbali, L., Ghali, R., & Frasson, C. (2013). Assessing motivational strategies in Serious Games using Hidden Markov Models. In *FLAIRS 2013, Proceedings of the 26th International FLAIRS Conference*. St. Petersburg, FL: AAAI Press.

Design-Based Research Collective. (2003). Design-based research: An emerging paradigm for educational inquiry. *Educational Researcher*, *32*(1), 5–8. doi:10.3102/0013189X032001005

Ge, X., & Ifenthaler, D. (2018). *Designing engaging educational games and assessing engagement in game-based learning.* IGI Global. doi:10.4018/978-1-5225-5198-0.ch001

Graesser, A., McDaniel, B., Chipman, P., Witherspoon, A., D'Mello, S., & Gholson, B. (2006). Detection of emotions during learning with AutoTutor. I. R. In (Ed.), *Proceedings of the 28th Annual Meetings of the Cognitive Science Society* (pp. 285–290). Mahwah, NJ: Erlbaum.

Graesser, A. C., D'Mello, S. K., & Strain, A. C. (2014). Emotions in advanced learning technologies. In International handbook of emotions in education (pp. 473-493). New York, NY: Routledge.

Granic, I., Lobel, A., & Engels, R. C. (2014). The benefits of playing video games. *The American Psychologist, 69*(1), 66–78. doi:10.1037/a0034857 PMID:24295515

Gutica, M. (2014). *Designing educational games and advanced learning technologies: An identification of affective states for modeling pedagogical and adaptive emotional agents* (Unpublished PhD diss.). University of British Columbia, Vancouver, BC.

Gutica, M., & Conati, C. (2013). Student emotions with an edu-game: A detailed analysis. *Proceedings of the 5th International Conference on Affective Computing and Intelligent Interaction*, 534-539. 10.1109/ACII.2013.94

Harrell, D. F., & Harrell, S. V. (2012). Imagination, computation, and self-expression: Situated character and avatar mediated identity. *Leonardo Electronic Almanac, 17*(2), 74–91. doi:10.5900/SU_9781906897161_2012.17(2)_74

Hascher, T. (2010). Learning and emotion: Perspectives for theory and research. *European Educational Research Journal, 9*(1), 13–28. doi:10.2304/eerj.2010.9.1.13

Hays, R. T. (2005). *The effectiveness of instructional games: A literature review and discussion.* Retrieved 6 10, 2019, from http://oai.dtic.mil/oai/oai?verb=getRecord&metadataPrefix=html&identifier=ADA441935

Hosseini, H., & Mostafapour, M. (2020). Game on: Exploring the effectiveness of game-based learning. *Planning Practice and Research, 35*(5), 598–604.

Ingleton, C. (2000). Emotion in learning— a neglected dynamic. In R. James (Ed.), *Research and Development in Higher Education, 22, 86-99.*

Jaques, N., Conati, C., Harley, J. M., & Azevedo, R. (2014). Predicting affect from gaze data during interaction with an intelligent tutoring system. In *International Conference on Intelligent Tutoring Systems* (pp. 29-38). Springer. 10.1007/978-3-319-07221-0_4

Kardan, S. & Conati, C. (2013). Comparing and combining eye gaze and interface actions for determining user learning with an interactive simulation. *UMAP*, 215-227.

Kiili, K., Ketamo, H., Koivisto, A., & Finn, E. (2014). Studying the user experience of a tablet based math game. *International Journal of Game-Based Learning, 4*(1), 60–77. doi:10.4018/IJGBL.2014010104

Kiili, K., Moeller, K., & Ninaus, M. (2018). Evaluating the effectiveness of a game-based rational number training: In-game metrics as learning indicators. *Computers & Education*, *120*, 13–28. doi:10.1016/j.compedu.2018.01.012

Kolb, D. (1984). *Experiential learning. Experience as the source of learning and development*. Prentice Hall.

Krämer, N. C., & Bente, G. (2010). Personalizing e-learning: The social effects of pedagogical agents. *Educational Psychology Review*, *22*(1), 71–87. doi:10.100710648-010-9123-x

Lane, H. C. (2016). Pedagogical agents and affect. In S. Y. Tettegah & M. Gartmeier (Eds.), *Emotions, technology, design, and learning* (pp. 47–62). Elsevier. doi:10.1016/B978-0-12-801856-9.00003-7

LeDoux, J. E. (1995). Emotion: Clues from the brain. *Annual Review of Psychology*, *46*(1), 209–235. doi:10.1146/annurev.ps.46.020195.001233 PMID:7872730

LeDoux, J. E. (1996). *The emotional brain: The mysterious underpinnings of emotional life*. Simon & Schuster.

Lehdonvirta, M., Nagashima, Y., Lehdonvirta, V., & Baba, A. (2012). The stoic male: How avatar gender affects help-seeking behavior in an online game. *Games and Culture, 7*(1), 29-47.

Lieury, A., Lorant, S., Trosseille, B., Champault, F., & Vourc'h, R. (2016). Video games vs. reading and school/cognitive performances: A study on 27000 middle school teenagers. *Educational Psychology*, *36*(9), 1560–1595. doi:10.1080/01443410.2014.923556

Linehan, C., Kirman, B., Lawson, S., & Chan, G. (2011). Practical, appropriate, empirically-validated guidelines for designing educational games. *Proceedings of the 2011 annual conference on Human Factors in Computing Systems,* 1979-1988. 10.1145/1978942.1979229

Norman, D. A. (2005). *Emotional design: Why we love (or hate) everyday things*. Basic books.

Ortony, A., Clore, G., & Collins, A. (1988). *The cognitive structure of emotions*. Cambridge University Press. doi:10.1017/CBO9780511571299

Ortony, A., & Turner, T. (1990). What's basic about basic emotions? *Psychological Review*, *97*(3), 315–331. doi:10.1037/0033-295X.97.3.315 PMID:1669960

Papert, S. (1980). *Mindstorms*. Basic books.

Partovi, T., & Razavi, M. R. (2019). The effect of game-based learning on academic achievement motivation of elementary school students. *Learning and Motivation*, *68*, 1–9. doi:10.1016/j.lmot.2019.101592

Pekrun, R., & Linnenbrink-Garcia, L. (2014). *Introduction to emotions in education. International handbook of emotions in education*. Routledge.

Persico, D., Passarelli, M., Dagnino, F., Manganello, F., Earp, J., & F., P. (2018). Games and learning: Potential and limitations from the players' point of view. In *Games and learning alliance* (pp. 134-145). Springer.

Petrina, S. (2007). *Advanced teaching methods for the technology classroom*. Information Science Publishing. doi:10.4018/978-1-59904-337-1

Petrina, S., & Zhao, J. J. (2021). 3D Virtual learning environment for acquisition of cultural competence: Experiences of instructional designers. In G. Panconesi & M. Guida (Eds.), *Handbook of research on teaching with virtual environments and AI* (pp. 17–42). IGI. doi:10.4018/978-1-7998-7638-0.ch002

Piaget, J. (1952). *The origins of intelligence*. International University Press. doi:10.1037/11494-000

Picard, R. W. (1997). *Affective computing*. MIT Press.

Picard, R. W. (2000). Toward agents that recognize emotion. *Vivek*, *13*(1), 3–13.

Picard, R. W., & Klein, J. (2002). Computers that recognize and respond to user emotion: Theoretical and practical implications. *Interacting with Computers*, *14*(2), 141–169. doi:10.1016/S0953-5438(01)00055-8

Plutchik, R. (1984). Emotions: A general psychoevolutionary theory. In K. Scherer & P. Ekman (Eds.), *Approaches to emotion* (pp. 197–219). Erlbaum.

Prensky, M. (2001). *Digital game-based learning*. McGraw-Hill.

Prensky, M. (2003). Digital game-based learning. *ACM Computers in Entertainment*, *1*(1), 21–25. doi:10.1145/950566.950596

Rodrigo, M. M., de Baker, R. S., Agapito, J., Nabos, J., Repalam, M. C., Reyes, S. S., & Pedro, M. O. (2012). The effects of an interactive software agent on student affective dynamics while using an Intelligent Tutoring System. *Affective Computing*, *3*(2), 224–236. doi:10.1109/T-AFFC.2011.41

Rodrigo, M. M., Rebolledo-Mendez, G., Baker, R., Boulay, B., Sugay, J., Lim, S., & Luckin, R. (2008). The effects of motivational modeling on affect in an Intelligent Tutoring System. In *Proceedings of International Conference on Computers in Education* (pp. 49–56). Washington, DC: IEEE.

Rolls, E. T. (1995). A theory of emotion and consciousness and its application to understanding the neural basis of emotion. In M. Gazzaniga (Ed.), *The cognitive neurosciences* (pp. 1091–1106). MIT Press.

Salen, K., & Zimmerman, E. (2004). *Rules of play: Game design fundamentals*. MIT Press.

Scherer, K. R. (2009). Emotions are emergent processes: They require a dynamic computational architecture. *Philosophical Transactions of the Royal Society*, *364*(1535), 3459–3474. doi:10.1098/rstb.2009.0141 PMID:19884141

Schuller, D., & Schuller, B. W. (2018). The age of artificial emotional intelligence. *Computer*, *24*(4), 38–46. doi:10.1109/MC.2018.3620963

Shell, J. (2008). *The art of game design*. Elsevier. doi:10.1201/9780080919171

Spires, H., Rowe, J., Mott, B., & Lester, J. (2011). Problem solving and game-based learning: Effects of middle grade students' hypothesis testing strategies on learning outcomes. *Journal of Educational Computing Research*, *44*(4), 453–472. doi:10.2190/EC.44.4.e

Tettegah, S. Y., & Gartmeier, M. (Eds.). (2016). *Emotions, technology, design, and learning*. Elsevier.

Töpffer, R. (1845). *Essai de physiognomie*. Author.

Valenza, M. V., Gasparini, I., & Hounsell, M. da S. (2019). Serious game design for children. *Journal of Educational Technology & Society*, *22*(3), 19–31.

Woolf, B., Burleson, W., Arroyo, I., Dragon, T., Cooper, D., & Picard, R. (2009). Affect-aware tutors: Recognizing and responding to student affect. *International Journal of Learning Technology*, *4*(3-4), 129–163. doi:10.1504/IJLT.2009.028804

This research was previously published in the International Journal of Game-Based Learning (IJGBL), 11(4); pages 1-18, copyright year 2021 by IGI Publishing (an imprint of IGI Global).

APPENDIX

Table 2. Post-Questionnaire

	Disagree		Neutral		Agree
Scale 1. Do you agree with the following statements about your game experience?					
1. I wanted to have fun when I was playing the game.	1	2	3	4	5
2. The monkey was annoying.	1	2	3	4	5
3. The level of difficulty was right.	1	2	3	4	5
4. I wanted to learn when I played the game.	1	2	3	4	5
5. I felt upset when I did not answer correct.	1	2	3	4	5
6. I became curious about math (divisibility/prime numbers/factorization) by playing the game.	1	2	3	4	5
7. The monkey reacted correctly to my emotions.	1	2	3	4	5
8. I didn't care whether I had fun or not.	1	2	3	4	5
9. The game was too easy or too hard for me.	1	2	3	4	5
10. I was proud to see the monkey happy.	1	2	3	4	5
11. I wanted to learn math by playing the game.	1	2	3	4	5
12. I felt shame when I made mistakes and the monkey was sad.	1	2	3	4	5
13. I didn't want to think about math (divisibility / prime numbers / decomposition) when I was playing the game.	1	2	3	4	5
14. I didn't mind to see that the monkey was sad.	1	2	3	4	5
Scale 2. Please tell us what emotions you experienced when you played the game.					
1. I had fun when I chose my avatar.	1	2	3	4	5
2. I had fun when the monkey was happy.	1	2	3	4	5
3. I had fun when the monkey was sad.	1	2	3	4	5
4. I had fun when the monkey was confident.	1	2	3	4	5
5. I had fun when the monkey was frustrated.	1	2	3	4	5
6. I had fun when I finished the quest.	1	2	3	4	5
7. I had fun when I responded to math questions before play.	1	2	3	4	5
8. I had fun when I responded to math questions after play.	1	2	3	4	5
9. I had fun when the rocks turned into gold.	1	2	3	4	5
10. I had fun when prime number rocks were removed.	1	2	3	4	5
11. I had fun when I got hints.	1	2	3	4	5
12. I had fun when I got examples.	1	2	3	4	5
13. I had fun when I visited the castle.	1	2	3	4	5
Scale 3. Please tell us any other times you did not have fun: Do you agree with the following statements about your game experience?					
1. I learned math when I played the game.	1	2	3	4	5
2. I learned math when I made mistakes.	1	2	3	4	5

continues on following page

Table 2. Continued

	Disagree	Neutral			Agree
3. I learned math when I got hints.	1	2	3	4	5
4. I learned math when I got examples.	1	2	3	4	5
5. I learned math when I helped the miners.	1	2	3	4	5
6. I learned math when I finished the quest.	1	2	3	4	5
7. I learned math when I had harder questions.	1	2	3	4	5
Scale 4. I also learned math when: Do you agree with the following statements about your game experience?					
1. I was already good at divisibility before I played the game.	1	2	3	4	5
2. I was already good at prime numbers before I played the game.	1	2	3	4	5
3. I was already good at decomposition before I played the game.	1	2	3	4	5
4. I played video games before.	1	2	3	4	5
5. I like playing video games.	1	2	3	4	5
6. I played before math games.	1	2	3	4	5
7. I like playing math games.	1	2	3	4	5
8. This game was boring.	1	2	3	4	5
9. This game was more interesting than video games that I played.	1	2	3	4	5
10. This game was more interesting than math games that I played.	1	2	3	4	5
11. I would like to play the game again	1	2	3	4	5
12. I believe that I can learn math better by playing this game.	1	2	3	4	5
13. I would like to see more quests.	1	2	3	4	5
14. I like math.	1	2	3	4	5

Chapter 22
Designing a Minecraft Simulation Game for Learning a Language Through Knowledge Co-Construction

Joeun Baek
Boise State University, USA

Hyekyeong Park
Sancheong Middle School, South Korea

Ellen Min
Timberline High School, USA

ABSTRACT

The purpose of this chapter is to design a Minecraft simulation game where players can learn a language by communicating and negotiating meaning with other players. To achieve this, Gagné's events of instruction and Schmitt's strategic experience modules were adopted as a theoretical lens for simulation building. After the simulation game was designed, it was implemented to test its feasibility. The result shows that the simulation game has both the intended features of knowledge co-construction and the negotiation of meaning, as well as enjoyment of the game. The test result, however, also suggests that the simulation game needs more conditionals and loops in order for players to repeat their simulation game at any place and time.

INTRODUCTION

Minecraft is no longer a new tool in game-based learning. Teachers have been experimenting with different ways to use it in the classroom for some time. Some teachers use it to teach mathematic concepts like ratios and proportions, to experiment with science phenomena, and to experience cultural differences

DOI: 10.4018/978-1-6684-7589-8.ch022

in society, while others adopt it to support student creativity and collaboration. Minecraft also can be integrated indirectly to stimulate creativity, imagination, and collaboration in learning languages. For example, Marcon (2013) used Minecraft to get students to describe in writing the unique features of their characters. Uusi-Mäkelä (2014) included it for students write journal entries during game play, while Lorence (2015) had students write in-game books that could be loaned out to one another. As noted by Kuhn and Stevens (2017), Minecraft seems to be an ideal fit for language learning.

This chapter aims to show how one might design a Minecraft simulation where players can communicate and negotiate meaning during game play, as well as construct knowledge with other players. Additionally, the chapter will explore how to boost students' interests in learning a language through simulation game features, and essential expressions are introduced to help students become more fluent in everyday conversations. In Minecraft there are four real-life based themes that players experience through the simulation game play: Landmarks in the World, Having Fun in an Amusement Park, Attending a Party at a Friend's House, and Designing a Share House. While playing the simulation game and completing the various quests, players are encouraged to negotiate unfamiliar words or phrases and co-construct new knowledge by carrying out their individual or collaborative tasks. Since the four themes in the simulation game are related to real-life situations that players may have experience with, the players are led to learn essential expressions in natural and motivating ways. In order to meet the objectives of using Minecraft as described in this chapter, various learning theories related to role playing, and research on Minecraft use in the classroom, are explored. Gagné's (1992) instructional design model and Schmitt's (1999) Strategic Experience Modules are reviewed as the basis for building the simulation. After the simulation was designed, it was implemented to test its feasibility. Many non-English speakers have difficulty in learning English since they learn the language as an academic object rather than a communication tool. Moreover, they are often taught English expressions in fragmented and decontextualized ways. As a result, even though non-native English speakers may experience years and years of English education, they can be afraid of having conversations in English. The contribution of this simulation game in conjunction with language classes is to help language learners recognize English as a communication tool, acquire essential English expressions meaningfully and holistically in context, and apply what they have learned outside of the classroom by communicating fluently with other English speakers.

REVIEW OF RELATED LITERATURE

In this section, the basis for the main topic of this study, co-construction of knowledge, will be briefly introduced before looking at its theoretical background in the next section. First, a brief definition of co-construction of knowledge will be discussed and followed by how game play interactions are beneficial for learning in general or learning languages in particular. Then, how the features of knowledge co-construction are implemented within a designed Minecraft simulation game will be described.

Co-Construction of Knowledge in Language Learning

With a constant flood of information, it is impossible for people to store huge amounts of information in memory without some of it becoming meaningless. As a result, society does not look for polymaths, but rather for people who can create new information by sharing and understanding pre-existing knowledge through collaborative interaction. Co-construction of knowledge, which is the essential part of this information trend, can be defined in a variety of ways, as there are various common characteristics among the myriad of definition. Roschelle (1992) describes the co-construction of knowledge as the process people use to arrive at a shared meaning and description. This definition is theoretically supported by Ludvigsen (2009), who maintains that individuals make new meanings by employing or organizing their existing knowledge through actions and social interaction. This means that knowledge is newly formed when learners are interdependent and interact with each other during learning process (Säljö, 2010). To explain how co-construction of knowledge can be activated in learning activities, Vygotsky defined the Zone of Proximal Development as "the distance between the actual developmental level as determined by independent problem solving and the level of potential development as determined through problem solving under adult guidance or in collaboration with more capable peers" (Vygotsky, 1978, p. 86) to explain how co-construction of knowledge can be activated in learning activities. Tudge (1990) explains that this interaction with more competent peers can lead to highly effective cognitive development. The co-construction of knowledge can also encourage fostering added value, such as, the diverse perspectives that individuals can bring to a group process (Dillenbourge, 1999; Donato, 2004). Since learner interaction also occurs through revision and feedback, language learners can identify the strengths and weakness in their own language production, which results in language skill development (Dippold, 2009). Moreover, when collaborative activities are combined with games, they can improve learners' participation in learning activities and social skills (Fenstermacher, Olympia, & Sheridan, 2006).

The designed Minecraft simulation games basically motivate students to collaborate with each other through quests which are challenging or too difficult to complete alone. When players engage in the theme "The Landmarks in the World," they need to understand the information associated with each landmark in order to progressively take quizzes. The amount of information to memorize for each quiz might be overwhelming for one student, however, so students are asked to keep one piece of information in mind. Later, when students take quizzes collaboratively to complete the game quest, they share what they have memorized together in order to finish the game quiz. Additionally, learners in the game are encouraged to share their own understanding of the theme to complete the given quests successfully. For instance, in the beginning of the game "Designing a Share House," players enter a big empty room to figure out which materials they can use for decoration. Players will discuss the various items and determine which items they can utilize appropriately and share good items with other players so that they can build a better share house as a group.

Learning by Role-Playing in Minecraft

In this section, a sense of role playing will be briefly introduced, followed by features of the technique. Next, how role-playing produces positive effect on language learning and how the designed Minecraft simulation game has implemented features of role-playing (and its expected results in language learning) will be explained. Then the chapter will conclude with the use of Minecraft simulation games in classrooms and the role that teachers should have in mind.

Learning by Role-Playing

Although role playing as a learning strategy has been actively utilized in language learning classrooms, the application of massive multiplayer online role-playing games (MMORPGs) is controversial since many people are quick to think of the negative influence of games on learning rather than advantageous ones. Role playing in language learning basically has learners take the role of a particular person or character and act it out as if they were the real person or character. As Liu and Ding (2009) insist, role playing has many positive effects, especially on language learning, since the technique can animate the learning atmosphere and foster interest in learning the language and making its acquisition impressive. Dorathy and Mahalakshmi (2011) explain that role-playing does not only help learners deal with real-life situations and the use of daily expressions, but it also encourages learners to work together in order to understand each other. Furthermore, since role-playing can be organized around a particular student interest or need, the technique increases learner responsibility in learning and motivation. MMORPGs, which are the combination of role-playing and games, help learners participate in language learning in a meaningful way. As Peterson (2010) suggests, the features of MMORPGs have potential advantages in second language learning. For example, Role Playing Simulation games are able to provide network-based real-time text and voice chat. These functions help learners experience multiple communication channels with real-time feedback on the target language. Moreover, these functions facilitate learner-centered interactions, encourage active game participation, and enhance cross-cultural knowledge. Since simulation games give learners the chance to represent themselves with personal avatars, learners are likely to take more risks and have reduced inhibition regarding language use because they regard the avatar as a separate identity from their own in reality.

The designed simulation Minecraft game also contains not only the features of MMORPGs but has comparable effects on language learning as do other MMORPGs. Since Minecraft provides a real-time chatting function, players can communicate with each other to figure out the meaning of novel expressions. Furthermore, when players' breakdowns in communication occur while playing the simulation game, players can provide immediate feedback on language errors. Consequently, players not only learn new language items throughout the course of the game, but also have the chance to develop their English accuracy skills based on the linguistic feedback. Players can play the simulation game with minimal teacher instruction and are ultimately led to learner-centered interactions and active participation in the simulation game.

Minecraft in the Classrooms and Teachers' Role

Teachers have already been using Minecraft in a variety of subject areas. Students have created objects or built maps in Minecraft and kept journals about math and writing (Herold, 2015; Uusi-Mäkelä, 2014). Karsenti, Bugmann, and Gros (2017) observed social skill development, and Balnaves (2018) used Minecraft to build a world for students to play with that enabled global participation and increased intercultural competencies. Educators who have integrated Minecraft in their lessons have found successful results. Teachers have noticed that students were more motivated to do work and developed communicative and social skills (Petrov, 2014). Another key point to mention about Minecraft is that students were often engaged in unexpected ways. Aside from increased rates of assignment completion, for example, students who normally did not actively take a leading role in class were able to act as leaders within the game (Hulstrand, 2015). One main factor in ensuring the helpfulness of Minecraft is peer-to-peer collaboration, as more experienced gamers can use their skills to enable a smoother integration of the simulation game with all students (Hewett, 2016). However, varying levels of student experience—which, understandably, may be a point of concern—did not detract from learning. Players who were beginners at the simulation game, with some instruction, could follow along with the lesson relatively well (Callaghan, 2016).

Possible concerns, such as issues of time management or distractions, had little impact in a study of 168 middle school students. Students completed their objectives and tasks on time (Callaghan, 2016). Interestingly, one study noted that less content may be better in Minecraft; too much information can be overwhelming. It could be more effective to present a narrow range of topics but delve into the material more deeply (Steinbeiß, 2017). Although Minecraft facilitates more self-regulation and student-driven learning, the guiding role of the teacher should not be overlooked. That is, teachers' roles are ever more important in such an environment. Teachers are the main guiding figure in Minecraft learning, and players are eager to complete their tasks and show results to their teachers (Callaghan, 2016).

Not only are teachers paramount in enabling an effective use of the simulation game in learning, they are also crucial in getting such a program started in their classrooms. For maximum success, teachers should be fully supportive of the idea, and their teaching styles should be compatible with a student-centered approach (Petrov, 2014). Teachers should also be familiar with the simulation game and with knowledge of how social interactions and spaces within the simulation game function. However, many teachers are reluctant to use Minecraft in their curriculum, and part of this may stem from the gap between students' and teachers' video simulation game literacies (Kuhn, 2017). Many teachers have started projects to help bridge this gap. One group of teachers made an online space called TESOL (Teaching English to Speakers of Other Languages) EVO (Electronic Village Online), and another developed a 5-week MOOC (Massive Online Open Course) to help teachers become familiar with the simulation game (Kuhn, 2017).

Minecraft is viewed as an effective tool in multiple learning circumstances. It upholds principles crucial to effective learning by providing motivation, improving social and communication skills, and encouraging critical and creative thinking. Further research on how Minecraft benefits players, as well as on how to make it more suitable to teachers and learners, is promising.

Lessons from Minecraft Studies

The use of Minecraft in classroom environments has been explored in a variety of studies. Researchers have suggested various ways to integrate the game into curriculum, have offered insight into some of the benefits and drawbacks of doing so, and have proposed additional potential applications (Callaghan, 2016; Kuhn, 2017; Mail, 2015; Petrov, 2014; Steinbeiß, 2017). This research lends evidence to the theory that Minecraft is meaningfully contributive to language acquisition within real life situations.

Beneficial Qualities for Learning

Studies illustrate that teachers who play Minecraft generally view it as being a useful learning platform (Mail, 2015). Considering the unique advantages of Minecraft, it is not difficult to see why. Minecraft possesses the five principles that should be included in game-based learning: intrinsic motivation, learning through enjoyment and fun, authenticity, self-reliance and autonomy, and experiential learning (Petrov, 2014). Through these characteristics, Minecraft allows students to have a sense of control, provides motivation for success, and sets clear boundaries while simultaneously allowing exploration and creative thinking (Callaghan, 2016). Additionally, video games model real-life experiences instead of simply providing written or visual descriptions of them, which makes for a more hands-on approach than traditional classroom tools such as textbooks and worksheets (Bogost, 2011). Experiential learning meshes especially well with the "open and fluid nature of language learning"—in fact, Minecraft appears to be an "ideal fit for language learning" (Kuhn & Stevens 2017).

Minecraft, as a learning platform, is ultimately a blend of many conditions and/or characteristics that are necessary for proper learning, including entertainment, social skills, and creativity. Together, they make Minecraft an apt game to use in the classroom (Petrov, 2014).

Suggested Ways to Successfully Introduce Minecraft into Curricula

One way of introducing Minecraft to aid learning is to prompt where students play the game normally but with intermittent interruptions during which they must answer questions correctly to continue. Another way is to utilize in-game quests where tasks are given and accomplished within the Minecraft world (Mail, 2015). Prompting can be used in a fashion similar to flashcards which is most effective for asking trivia or relatively simple questions in order to practice knowledge recall, whereas in-game quests provide a more interactive, embedded approach to game-based learning (Mail, 2015).

Minecraft also has two modes of play to choose from: creative mode, which gives the player unlimited material and no danger of dying within the game, or survival mode, in which the player must gather material and defend themselves against possible threats in the game. Within the game, numerous "Modes" - or add-ons to the standard version of Minecraft - can be used to change the game as needed in terms of rules, content, design, or to fit to teachers' individual needs (Steinbeg, 2017). Furthermore, Minecraft allows educators to quickly and effectively design, modify, create, or delete experiments, and its capacity to have multiplayer modes and individual servers make it easy to collaborate and share content among teachers (Nebel et al, 2016). As we can see from the variety of ways that Minecraft can be implemented in educational programs, it is a flexible simulation game that can adapt to fit many different subjects and classes.

DESIGN METHODS

How the activities of gaming in Minecraft could be arranged for language learning is a question of identifying, selecting, arranging, and sequencing learning experiences for players. Gagné, Briggs, and Wager (1992) provide a robust framework for designing learning events and Bernd Schmitt's (1999) Strategic Experience Modules (SEMs) are good guidelines for players to have an optimal learning experience when playing Minecraft. Below are explanations of how the target simulation game follows their ideas and suggestions.

The Implementation of Gagné's Nine Events of Instruction

How Minecraft gaming activities can be arranged for language learning is a question of identifying, selecting, arranging, and sequencing the learning experience for players. Gagné, Briggs, and Wager (1992) provide a framework for designing learning. They developed a framework of nine general events that should take place during learning. This process is called Gagné's 9 Events of Instruction. The first event is gaining the attention of players with a stimulus that engages their minds. A good way to accomplish this is to present something that piques the players' curiosity such as a thought-provoking question. The second is informing players of the objectives. This gives players the motivation to learn by setting the level of expectations. The third is stimulating recall of prior learning. Players can then build upon their prior knowledge with the new material. The fourth is presenting the content. It is important to deliver the information in organized chunks through explanations and demonstrations using a variety of modes of media, such as combination of videos, texts, and images. The fifth is providing learning guidance through additional examples and other supportive materials. The sixth is eliciting performance or practicing. By practicing the new skill, learners solidify their understanding of the material and are more likely to retain the knowledge. The seventh is providing feedback. Players should receive immediate and specific feedback, but at this stage, the feedback should not be used to formally score the players. The eighth event is assessing performance. Players are given a final test or assessment, which should be completed without any help from the instructor. Mastery is generally considered to be achieved when the student gets 80% to 90% of the questions correct. The ninth, and final, event of the process is enhancing retention and transferring skills and learning for future application. Repetition and rephrasing of concepts are examples of content retention strategies.

To Gain Attention and Inform Objectives

In the amusement park, a Non-Playable Character (NPC) asks players a question, "Have you ever been to an amusement park?" Since most players are curious enough to visit the amusement park, this question not only helps players pay attention to the simulation game but also makes them more curious about the day's activities. The NPC introduces players to what they are going to do in the simulation game after getting their attention with the question "Have you ever been to an amusement park?" For example, the NPC says, "Today, you guys will have a great time in an amusement park going on fun rides, having food, and looking around the zoo." Through this interaction, players can understand what tasks they are required to do and how they are going to complete the objectives.

To Stimulate Recall of Prior Learning

In a friendly party, stimulating recall of prior learning naturally occurs when players are informed about the daily objectives. When players visit a friend's house, they can recall their personal experience of the same situation. This helps players understand the new information that they are gaining by relating the information to their own pre-existing knowledge.

To Present Contents and Provide Learning Guidance

In the Landmarks theme, players visit various famous places in the world. In each location, players will meet an NPC tour guide. The tour guide briefly explains where the landmark is and what additional information players should find out. After the briefing, players will figure out what to do to complete the quest based on some ideas from the NPC in terms of effective strategies for the simulation game. Guidance is offered to players such as following signs to get the required information easily. For instance, when players look around to gather information in Machu Picchu, they can find signs on the ground. Following the signs, players can easily get to other spots where they can find out more information about the landmark. Additionally, players can get some help if they do not understand some aspect of the landmark. All these devices provide instructional support for players' needs.

To Elicit Performance

In the Landmarks theme, activities are designed for players to look around and gather several pieces of information related to the landmark. By moving around the environment and reading information presented in signs, players can not only understand the landmark better, but they can also internalize new English expressions during the activities.

In the Share House theme, players' performance is elicited by letting them discuss how to decorate the house and delegate who decorates which parts. While discussing the design of the house and assigning a role to each player, players can internalize knowledge or English expressions related to the specific situation.

To Provide Feedback

In the Amusement Park theme, many chances are presented to players to communicate using the target language (English), and it also provides players with appropriate feedback regarding their activities and language use. For instance, players converse in English with the cashier when ordering some food to eat. While ordering food, players might experience a communication breakdown. In this case, through meaning negotiation or with the help of other players' linguistic feedback, players can successfully order the food they would love to have. This enables players to not only respond to the given request, but also improve their language skills through peer feedback.

To Assess Performance

Quiz stages are provided at landmarks in order to provide feedback and access players' performance. For example, after looking around Machu Picchu, players are led to a maze. There, they need to take quizzes related to Machu Picchu. With the quizzes, players can self-assess their understanding of Machu Picchu, and teachers can assess players' performance through their quiz scores.

Design for Players' Strategic Experience

Schmitt (1999) proposes five different types of strategic experience modules (SEMs) for learners. These modules can yield new insight into how to design learning experiences for game players.

The first type of experience is "Sense" the product (or game in this context) engages one or more of the customer's five senses: sight, sound, scent, taste, and touch. The second is "Feel": the product or service should elicit positive feelings from the customer in order to be successful. The third is "Think". Marketers should encourage customers to think creatively, which could potentially lead to a shift of their opinions on the company or product. The fourth is "Act". The marketing encourages customers to change their behaviors to incorporate the product in their daily lives. The fifth is "Relate," which allows customers to feel connected to a certain message presented in the company's marketing.

Experiential marketing is a methodology and concept that moves beyond the traditional "features-and-benefits" marketing. Experiential marketing connects consumers with brands in personally relevant and memorable ways. Schmitt (1999) proposed the strategic experiential modules (SEMs) as the assessment items of customer experience (Sheu, Su, & Chu, 2009).

Managers can use the different SEMs to create different types of customers. The term module has been borrowed from research in cognitive science and the philosophy of mind, referring to circumscribed functional domains of the mind. Modules have distinct structures and functions. The experiential modules in experiential marketing include sensory experiences, affective experiences, creative cognitive experiences, physical experiences, behaviors, and lifestyles, and social-identity experiences that result from relating to a reference group or culture. Each SEM has its own objectives, internal structure, and principles (Schmitt, 2015).

To create different experiences and achieve marketing goals, Schmitt proposed five Strategic Experiential Modules (SEMs): sensory experiences (Sense), feel experience (Feel), think experience (Think), act experience (Act), and relate experience (Relate). The definitions of strategic experiential modules are described as follows:

Module of Sense Experience (Sense)

This type of experience primarily derives from the five senses (sight, hearing, smell, taste, and touch). These senses can be exploited to affect the behavior of the customer. For example, pleasant music or delicious food elevates the value of an experience or product as perceived by the customer, increasing their interest in, and knowledge/usage of the product or service (Schmitt, 2012).

In the Minecraft theme "The Landmarks in the World," we constructed some iconic structures such as the Eiffel Tower and the Sphinx. We closely recreated the designs in order to provide student players with a sense experience. As a result, students can see a Minecraft version of the landmarks that resembles the original's distinctive features. These visual simulations make students feel more excited within the game, which can lead to higher motivation in learning during game play. In the map of "Attending a Party at a Friend's House," the game provides sensory inputs through various scenes in the game. Student players in the simulation game experience a variety of situations related to their daily lives. For instance, students visit a supermarket to buy some groceries for a party. Students will look for many items they need and can easily find in the supermarket, and these visual cues enhance students' motivation on the game. In "Designing a Share House," to enable a visually stimulating sense experience, the game begins in front of a share house that students need to decorate. The exterior of the building is decorative, and the elaborate exterior can make students feel excited since they will soon go inside the house. Moreover, since the exterior of the building is visually appealing, students will be motivated to decorate the interior in a commensurate fashion. In this way, the simulation game provides students with visual cues that enhance students' motivations to both play the game and learn. Lastly, in the theme "Having Fun in an Amusement Park," student players can experience many types of senses while playing the game. For instance, students can find rides similar to the actual rides in an amusement park such as roller coaster or merry-go-round. In addition to inspiring visual scenes, the game stimulates players with background music fitting to each activity. Through these visual and auditory cues, students will feel a great satisfaction in the game.

Module of Feel Experience (Feel)

This type of experience primarily stimulates the inner feelings and emotions of the customer. The presentation of experiential text, music, and images establishes a strong connection between customers and service/product providers, causing customers to resonate with the brand or product and have positive emotional responses (Kim & Perdue 2013).

In the map of the Minecraft game "The Landmarks in the World," the simulation game makes students feel satisfied by providing indirect experiences of visiting famous landmarks throughout the world.

Since the representations of the landmarks in the game are quite similar to the real structures, students will feel like they are traveling around the world. This exciting experience not only makes students motivated to learn, but also helps with a longer retention of language items used in the game. In "Attending a Party at a Friend's House," the game helps students feel satisfied by giving them several quests to complete. Before reaching the party host's house, students need to complete some tasks such as borrowing a DVD to watch and buying some food at a supermarket. When students reach the friend's house after the tasks are complete, the sense of achievement gives student players satisfaction in addition to confidence regarding their English skills. In the theme "Designing a Share House," the simulation game helps students experience happiness by letting them decorate the house based on their own preferences. After decorating the living room together, each student is given their own room to decorate individually. Since students can think about the interior of their own room and realize it by themselves, this will give them high satisfaction within the game and learning English through the game. In 'Having Fun in an Amusement Park', to provoke student players' inner feelings and emotions, the game offers students many opportunities to decide by themselves through discussion. For instance, in the beginning of the game students can negotiate which rides to go on, and after taking 3 rides, they will decide what to eat for lunch. Since students have many chances to employ their autonomy within the simulation game, their satisfaction and motivation on learning will be more advanced.

Module of Think Experience (Think)

Think experiences appeal to the intellect-oriented brand positioning and focus on action at awareness and knowledge level of consumer response by taking into account personal experiences, which help people connect with a brand and to make intelligent and informed purchasing decisions (Kailani & Ciobotar, 2015).

In the theme "The Landmarks in the World," to appeal to student players' intelligence, we have students take quizzes at the end of some landmarks such as the Sphinx and Machu Picchu. For example, after student players look around the Sphinx and collect information related to the place, students need to solve a riddle to move on to other landmarks. Since the riddle provides students with a slight intellectual challenge, students will feel intellectual satisfaction after solving it. In the theme "Attending a Party at a Friend's House," the game provides students with an intellectual challenge by letting them find the party host's house using spatial clues. For instance, student players get direction to the house from an NPC through dialogues. "Once you are out of the supermarket, you could find the bank. Keep walking straight ahead for 3 blocks. After you pass the library you have to turn left."

Using the clues students have to find the various locations, such as the library, and finally the party host's house. Therefore, this serves as an intellectual challenge for students furthering their satisfaction.

In "Designing a Share House," the map itself motivates players by letting them complete the tasks in their own creative ways. For instance, when students are to decorate the living room, they are given some conditions they need to carry on such as making a big screen to watch movies, a sofa to rest on, and a refrigerator to store food. Since the student roles and means of achieving these tasks are not directed, student players should think hard to complete the tasks, resulting in students' sense of achievement after finishing the work.

Module of Act Experience (Act)

This type of experience integrates numerous behavioral options, such as physical activities, living patterns, and interaction. Behavioral activities in the daily lives of a user leave a lasting impression or become a subconscious direct response (Chen & Lin, 2014).

We implemented "Module of Act Experience" in our Minecraft game as follows. In the map of "The Landmarks in the World," the game induces students' action by giving them quests to complete. Whenever students visit a landmark, they need to collect five pieces of information related to the place. That means, students are not passively given the information, but rather they must actively find it by moving around the virtual world. These activities help students learn better the information and related language expressions used in the simulation game, resulting in a more meaningful game and learning.

In "Designing a Share House," this map requires students to utilize the most autonomous actions compared to other themes in the game. Unlike the other themes where students perform activities within a ready-made-map, this theme provides students with an almost empty house. Therefore, students need to decorate the house based on their own decisions. Since students themselves are the ones who design and finish the map, students can feel a greater sense of achievement and satisfaction when they complete the quest.

Module of Relate Experience (Relate)

Relational experience marketing incorporates each of the other four experiences to integrate the product into social culture. It surpasses individual marketing, individual personalities, and emotions to connect the consumer to an ideal self, social culture, and to influence potential members of a social group (Sheu, Chu, & Wang, 2017).

Considering the Module of Relate Experience, our Minecraft game is designed as follows. In the map of "The Landmarks in the World," we implemented a famous landmark in Korea, Gyeongbokgung (a royal palace), for Korean players in addition to the landmarks elsewhere in the world. This custom landmark helps Korean students connect their local identity to the game. While looking at landmarks around the world, students feel like tourists. However, when they explore Gyeongbokgung, they will feel like local Koreans and feel proud of how beautiful the construction is, and how wonderful the traditional architecture is. This kind of localized experience makes playing the game more meaningful. In the theme "Attending a Party at a Friend's House," the simulation game helps students connect the game to their real lives, making them feel more excited and motivated to learn English and play the game. For instance, picking up a DVD to watch together and buying some food to share frequently occur in students' daily lives. Consequently, students feel learning English through the simulation game is more meaningful and valuable since it is possible for them to experience similar situations (i.e., hanging out with international friends and communicating in English) in the future. In "Designing a Share House," we devised for students to relate their personal experiences to the game by making them decorate their own room. Most students dream of their own places or houses. Students can realize their dream house through this theme, so this makes them feel happier within learning English through this simulation game.

A VILLAGE IN MINECRAFT FOR LANGUAGE LEARNING

Based on the reviews of theories related to language learning and the design of educational simulation games, a Minecraft simulation was designed and is presented below.

Getting Started with Landmarks

In the Landmarks, players are expected to learn about various landmarks in the world. While playing the simulation games, they will visit several famous landmarks. By looking around the landmarks, they will read and collect pieces of information related to each landmark. From the perspective of language learning, players should be able to negotiate the meanings of unfamiliar words they encounter and construct new knowledge in groups. Figure 1 shows the activity flow in Landmarks.

Figure 1. Activity flow in "Landmarks in the World"

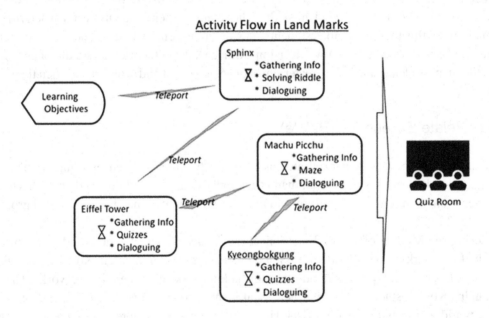

In the simulation game, the co-construction of knowledge including meaning negotiation occurs as follows. While looking around the Eiffel Tower and playing the simulation game, players are asked to keep in mind facts about the Eiffel Tower for quizzes later in the game. Then, players will delegate who memorizes which information. This encourages players to communicate and interact with each other more actively, and by having a specific role, players will be more responsible for completing the task and the simulation game overall.

Although each student has their own role to memorize a piece of specific information, players will help each other when they encounter challenging expressions such as "be named after" and "81-storey building" because they need to collaborate to complete the whole simulation game. To understand the meaning of difficult words, players will guess the meanings and share their ideas with the other players.

By doing so, players can develop an understanding of the meaning of the challenging words, and they will naturally co-construct knowledge about the Eiffel Tower (See Figure 2). Similar to the previous stages, players will assign a role to each group member and help each other to understand facts about the landmarks. While negotiating the meaning of incomprehensible words such as "emperor" and "plunder", players will use their own background knowledge or guess. If they cannot figure out the meaning, they can ask for help to a teacher or a teacher's avatar in the simulation game. In this case, the teacher decides whether the challenging words are key words students must understand. If so, the teacher gives hints so that players can figure out the meaning of the words by themselves. By doing so, players can learn the words' meaning, which is the result of negotiation of meaning and co-construction of knowledge.

Figure 2. The overview of "Landmarks in the World"

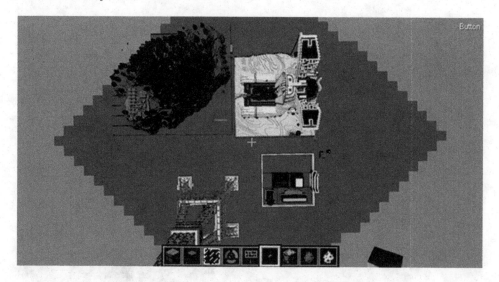

Having Fun in an Amusement Park

In the Amusement Park, players are expected to complete the given quests in an amusement park and zoo. While playing the simulation game, players will experience some typical situations they are likely to encounter when they visit a real amusement park or zoo. In the beginning of the simulation game, players will buy tickets for the ride. Also, they will order food in a cafeteria, and look around the zoo for certain animals. Since all of these situations based on experiences in their real lives, players will be more motivated to play the simulation game and learn new expressions in English. Figure 2 shows activity flow in the Amusement Park.

Players will be able to negotiate meaning and co-construct new knowledge in groups. In the simulation game, players will experience a variety of meaning negotiation and knowledge co-construction situations. For instance, players will discuss choosing a ride (See Figure 4). They also have chances to read the safety instruction before going on rides. If they do not understand some difficult words, they will negotiate the meaning by sharing each other's background knowledge. By completing quests, players will learn which expressions to use in each situation, resulting in co-construction of knowledge about the respective situations and the appropriate expressions in English.

Figure 3. Activity flow in "Having Fun in the Amusement Park"

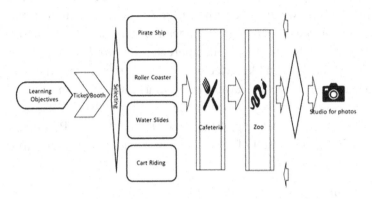

Figure 4. The overview of "Having Fun in the Amusement Park"

In the theme, numerous events for players require meaning negotiation and knowledge co-construction. Specifically, after being told about today's simulation goals, players move to a ticket box to buy tickets for rides. In the ticket booth, players will have a conversation with an NPC or a teacher's avatar about "buying tickets." The conversation will be about the cost, discounts, coupons, and so on. When players encounter some unfamiliar words or expressions, they have to negotiate the meaning of the words with other players or the teacher's avatar, and they will learn new expressions and understand the situation better. This interaction leads to co-construction of knowledge related to "buying tickets in the public places" such as amusement park and museums. When players go on three rides successfully, they will move to a cafeteria for lunch. There, players will discuss what to eat after reading the menu. While discussing the menu, players will learn some new words related to food through active communication. While ordering food, players are asked to talk about their food preferences, such as "What kinds of sauce do you like for your French fries?" When players need more explanation about the food, they can ask the clerk, and this naturally facilitates the negotiation of meaning. Through this series of activities, players will be aware of what to say in English when ordering food, which indicates construction of knowledge about "ordering food in a restaurant."

Attending a Party at a Friend's House

In the Amusement Park, players should be able to complete the tasks required to visit a friend's house. In the beginning of the simulation game, players are invited to a house party hosted by a friend. On the way to the friend's house, players stop by a DVD shop and supermarket. To complete the tasks, players need to use appropriate simulation game strategies and have conversations in English with other characters. Figure 5 shows activity flow to attend a party at a friend's house.

Figure 5. Activity flow in "Having a Party at a Friend's House"

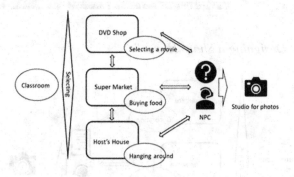

In this simulation game, players are exposed to various situations which have them negotiate meaning and co-construct knowledge. For instance, once players enter the supermarket, they walk around to find the items they need to buy. Some of the ingredients such as "beetroot" and "salmon" are unfamiliar to them. To figure out the meaning of the words, they negotiate the meaning with each other or they can get help from pictures.

In addition, players can choose one item they want to buy for the party as shown in Figure 6. To determine which item to purchase, players share ideas, which leads to active interaction and authentic communication. Throughout this whole process, players will negotiate the meaning of unfamiliar words and co-construct knowledge about "the name of some ingredient" or "expressions related to grocery shopping." Similar interactions may occur in the DVD shop where players can choose film titles to take to the friend's house.

Designing a Share House

As the activities in "Designing a Share House" mostly depend on players' personal preference and creativity, they provide a variety of opportunities to negotiate meaning and co-construct knowledge. In detail, players in the beginning enter a basement room to figure out what materials they can use to decorate the house. Figure 7 shows activity flow in a Share house.

Figure 6. A supermarket scene in "Having a Party at a Friend's House"

Figure 7. Activity flow in "Designing a Share House"

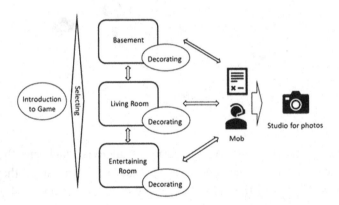

There, players will help each other understand what each item is and how it can be used to decorate the house (see Figure 8). During this process, players naturally have conversations regarding the items and when a student does not understand the exact usage of the item, other players can explain it in simpler terms by repeating the key words or using easier words. After figuring out the items to use, players move to the living room. Then they share ideas on how to decorate the house. For example, players assign which part each student will decorate and what type of items or materials they will use for the decoration. Players might have some misunderstanding due to some players' asymmetrical language competency.

In this case, players will help each other overcome any misunderstanding or miscommunication by giving feedback or using a simpler lexicon, all of which includes the negotiation of meaning. Since players will learn the name of items and how to use them for house decoration in addition to other new English expressions, they will co-construct the knowledge related to the given topic.

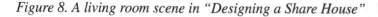

Figure 8. A living room scene in "Designing a Share House"

IMPLEMENTATION AS A PILOT TEST

After the simulation game was designed, two technology teachers and eleven students at elementary schools played the simulation game. They were told about the simulation game in advance and how it was developed. In addition, the objective of the simulation game was explained and the students were asked to play it and report any errors they found, and to make suggestions for the simulation game for learning a language.

Collection of Reviews

In order to collect review data, video was recorded during their gameplay and interviews with all participants were performed after their gameplay. Three research assistants who were trained in video recording participated in pilot game play to record gameplays of the participants. Researchers performed interviews with two teachers and eleven students. They played the simulation game for about sixty minutes. Interviews were also video recorded for analysis. Questions such as "how did you play the simulation game?" "were there any errors?" and "what recommendations do you have to revise it?" were asked. For teachers' interviews, a question about its effectiveness for language learning was added.

Analysis of the Data

The videos recorded during the participants' gameplay were analyzed and evaluated by researchers using the criteria in Table 1 below. Special attention was given to activities in navigating, communicating and gaming actions. The researchers observed the gameplay of participants and took notes when any notable actions of participants were found. The researchers discussed and summarized all observations.

Table 1. Criteria for evaluating gameplay video

Navigation	Communication	Gaming actions
Teleporting to	Talking to	Gathering information
Teleporting from	Asking	Decorating
Moving forward	Answering	Crafting
Moving backward	Negotiating	Buying
Turning left	Interacting with others	Selecting
Turning right		Dialoguing
Walking/Jumping		Quizzing
Running/Flying		Hanging around

The interview data was analyzed by researchers using questioning criteria in Table 2 below. Questions were created around how the simulation can help to learn a language, any errors found, and any recommendations for revising the simulation game. The answers were recorded, transcribed and summarized by researchers.

Table 2. Interview points in questioning

Contribution to Language learning	Errors	Revisions
Easy to learn languages?	Typing	Navigation
Active interaction in target language	Questioning	Interacting with colleagues
Real life situation	Answering	Gaming actions
Meaningful learning	Interacting with colleagues	Quizzes
Low affective filter	Interacting with objects	Maps
Long retention		Language learning
Reflecting English skills by interacting with others		Suggestions

Results from the Pilot Implementation

In the interviews, students reported that the intended features could be easily found in the designed Minecraft simulation game. Results from interviews and video observations are summarized as follows. Overall, players in the designed simulation game are encouraged to interact with each other through chat rooms for a variety of purposes. In the theme "Designing a Share House," players could have discussion time about how to decorate their shared house. In the discussion, players could assign a role to each other to decorate the whole house and talk about how to achieve the given quests, such as which material they are using and what furniture they have chosen. This interaction provided learners not only with a chance to communicate in the target language but also the opportunity for exchanging linguistic feedback or negotiating meanings when they did not understand each other. Moreover, every theme of the Minecraft simulation games had clear goals for players to complete. In the case of "The Landmarks in the World," players were asked to look around some landmarks in the world such as Machu Picchu and the Sphinx, and take quizzes after exploring the landmarks. Since the level of difficulty of the quizzes was slightly difficult for one player to handle alone, players were naturally required to collaborate with each other by assigning a role and helping others to understand unfamiliar words or phrases in the simulation games. Lastly, like typical RPGs, players in Minecraft also could have their own avatars. When playing with avatars, learners were less afraid of making mistakes since the avatar was not identified to their actual identity in reality (Chin, Oppezzo, & Schwartz, 2009). Consequently, this reduced inhibition allowed players to participate in the learning process more actively, leading to the enhancement of skills. Two technology teachers also reported that the simulation game should have more conditionals and loops so that players can repeat their simulation game at any place and time.

Implications and Revisions

Findings from the pilot implementation identified a few areas for improvement. There should be clear objectives for the simulation game presented *inside* of Minecraft. These could be hidden in the simulation or manifested overtly somewhere at the beginning of the simulation. If this simulation is used in conjunction with classroom teaching, teachers should consider allotting more time to each map inside the simulation. Lastly, interactions among players in terms of language learning should be more elaborately devised based on each map's purpose.

The designed simulation game has been revised as a result of the findings from the pilot implementation. In addition, some minor cosmetic revisions were made in regard to its appearance in color, arrangement of objects, and location of each map. Additionally, built-in dialogues were revised so that they were more visually appealing and could stimulate players' language learning.

CONCLUSION AND NEXT STEPS

A simulation is a goal-driven activity which occurs in a clearly described, realistic setting. As such, students in a simulation are given various tasks to complete, or problems to solve either alone or together. The information needed to complete the tasks and solve the problems is embedded strategically in the environment. To learn a language, a simulation can be a good tool where learners both play roles as characters, and themselves (Hyland, 1993). The authors wanted to stimulate language learning of learners by simulating the negotiation of meaning and knowledge co-construction in Minecraft. By adopting the 9 events of instruction from Gagné et al. (1992) and the strategic experience modules from Schmitt (1999), the authors designed a language learning simulation in Minecraft. These principles are expected to give learners an optimal experience and environment to play and communicate with others in a target language.

The designed simulation game was able to allow learners to practice a target language by constructing knowledge and negotiating meanings through game play. Based on the findings from the pilot, the simulation game was revised with more focus on language learning interactions. Researchers will start to collect more data when more students begin playing the simulation game. In addition, the simulation game will be tested to see if it is effective for language learning, and what can be done to iterate and revise the design in order to enhance players' language learning.

At the very least, the designed simulation game allows learners to develop experience in specific situations that also require them to apply the target language. However, the key to this simulation game is that it is a dynamic rather than fixed experience. The scenario can constantly be changed realistically as a result of player actions, and players must then also adapt to those changes. Thus, the simulation might work best with skilled speakers or trained instructors because the simulation game is a mechanism for learners to obtain real-time feedback on their actions. The inclusion of a qualified language speaker might be a future challenge in this simulation game.

REFERENCES

Balnaves, K. (2018). World building for children's global participation in Minecraft. In M. Ciussi (Ed.), *Proceedings of the 12th European Conference on Game Based Learning* (pp. 858-862). Reading, UK: Academic Conferences and Publishing International Limited.

Bogost, I. (2011). *How to do things with videogames*. Minneapolis, MN: University of Minnesota Press. doi:10.5749/minnesota/9780816676460.001.0001

Callaghan, N. (2016). Investigating the role of Minecraft in educational learning environments. *Educational Media International, 53*(4), 244–260. doi:10.1080/09523987.2016.1254877

Chen, S.-C., & Lin, C.-P. (2014). The impact of customer experience and perceived value on sustainable social relationship in blogs: An empirical study. *Technological Forecasting and Social Change, 96*, 40–50. doi:10.1016/j.techfore.2014.11.011

Chin, D. B., Oppezzo, M. A., & Schwartz, D. L. (2009). Teachable agents and the protégé effect: Increasing the effort towards learning. *Journal of Science Education and Technology, 18*(4), 334–352. doi:10.100710956-009-9180-4

Dillenbourg, P. (1999). What do you mean by collaborative learning? In P. Dillenbourg (Ed.), *Collaborative learning: Cognitive and computational approaches* (pp. 1–19). Oxford, UK: Elsevier.

Ding, Y. (2009). Perspectives on social tagging. *Journal of the Association for Information Science and Technology, 60*(12), 2388–2401. doi:10.1002/asi.21190

Dippold, D. (2009). Peer feedback through blogs: Student and teacher perceptions in an advanced German class. *ReCALL, 21*(1), 18–36. doi:10.1017/S095834400900010X

Donato, R. (2004). Aspects of collaboration in pedagogical discourse. *Annual Review of Applied Linguistics, 24*, 284–302. doi:10.1017/S026719050400011X

Dorathy, A. A., & Mahalakshmi, S. N. (2011). Second language acquisition through task based approach – role-play in English language teaching. *English for Specific Purposes World, 33*(11), 1–7.

Fenstermacher, K., Olympia, D., & Sheridan, S. M. (2006). Effectiveness of a computer-facilitated interactive social skills training program for boys with attention deficit hyperactivity disorder. *School Psychology Quarterly, 21*(2), 197–224. doi:10.1521cpq.2006.21.2.197

Gagné, R. M., Briggs, L. J., & Wager, W. W. (1992). *Principles of instructional design* (4th ed.). Fort Worth, TX: Harcourt Brace Jovanovich College Publishers.

Herold, B. (2015). Minecraft fueling creative ideas, analytical thinking. *Education Week, 35*(01), 12. Retrieved from https://www.edweek.org/ew/articles/2015/08/19/minecraft-fueling-creative-ideas-analytical-thinking-in.html

Hewett, K. J. E. (2016). *The Minecraft project: Predictors for academic success and 21st century skills gamers are learning through video game experiences* (Doctoral dissertation). Texas A&M University-Corpus Christi, College Station, TX.

Hyland, K. (1993). Language learning simulations: A practical guide. *English Teaching Forum, 31*(4), 16-22.

Jarvenoja, H., & Jarvela, S. (2009). Emotion control in collaborative learning situations: Do students regulate emotions evoked by social challenges? *The British Journal of Educational Psychology, 79*(3), 463–481. doi:10.1348/000709909X402811

Kailani, C., & Ciobotar, N. (2015). Experiential marketing: An efficient tool to leverage marketing communication impact on consumer behavior. *International Conference on Marketing and Business Development Journal, 1*(1), 281-287.

Karsenti, T., Bugmann, J., & Gros, P. P. (2017). *Transforming education with Minecraft? Results of an exploratory study conducted with 118 elementary-school students*. Montréal, Canada: CRIFPE.

Kim, D., & Perdue, R. R. (2013). The effects of cognitive, affective, and sensory attributes on hotel choice. *International Journal of Hospitality Management, 35*, 246–257. doi:10.1016/j.ijhm.2013.05.012

Kuhn, J., & Stevens, V. (2017). Participatory culture as professional development: Preparing teachers to use Minecraft in the classroom. *TESOL Journal, 8*(4), 753–767. doi:10.1002/tesj.359

Liu, F., & Ding, Y. (2009). Role-play in English language teaching. *Asian Social Science, 5*(10), 140–143. doi:10.5539/ass.v5n10p140

Lorence, M. (2015). School of Minecraft. *School Library Journal*. Retrieved from https://www.slj.com/?detailStory=minecraftedu-takes-hold-in-schools

Ludvigsen, S. R. (2009). Sociogenesis and cognition: The struggle between social and cognitive activities. In B. Schwarz, T. Dreyfus, & R. Herskowitz (Eds.), *Transformation of knowledge through classroom interaction* (pp. 302–317). New York, NY: Routledge.

Mail, T. M. (2015). In-game Minecraft quests for elementary education. *International Journal for Innovation Education and Research, 3*(8), 164–174.

Marcon, N. (2013). Minecraft as a powerful literacy prompt in the secondary English classroom. *Idiom, 49*(2), 35–37.

Nebel, S., Schneider, S., & Rey, G. D. (2016). Mining learning and crafting scientific experiments: A literature review on the use of Minecraft in education and research. *Journal of Educational Technology & Society, 19*(2), 355–366.

Peterson, M. (2010). Massively multiplayer online role-playing games as arenas for second language learning. *Computer Assisted Language Learning, 23*(5), 429–439. doi:10.1080/09588221.2010.520673

Petrov, A. (2014). *Using Minecraft in education: A qualitative study on benefits and challenges of game-based education* (Unpublished master's thesis). University of Toronto, Ontario, Canada.

Pusey, M., & Pusey, G. (2015). Using Minecraft in the science classroom. *International Journal of Innovation in Science and Mathematics Education, 23*(3), 22–34.

Roschelle, J. (1992). Learning by collaborating: Convergent conceptual change. *Journal of the Learning Sciences, 2*(3), 235–276. doi:10.120715327809jls0203_1

Säljö, R. (2010). Learning and technologies, people and tools in coordinated activities. *International Journal of Educational Research, 41*(6), 489–494. doi:10.1016/j.ijer.2005.08.013

Scarcella, R. C., & Oxford, R. L. (1992). *The tapestry of language learning: The individual in the communicative classroom.* Boston, MA: Heinle & Heinle.

Schmitt, B. (1999). Experiential marketing. *Journal of Marketing Management, 15*(1-3), 53–67. doi:10.1362/026725799784870496

Schmitt, B. (2012). The consumer psychology of brands. *Journal of Consumer Psychology, 22*(1), 7–17. doi:10.1016/j.jcps.2011.09.005

Schmitt, B. (2015). Experiential Marketing: A new framework for design and communications. *DMI 40th Anniversary Issue 2015, 25*(4), 19-26. doi:10.1111/drev.10298

Sheu, J.-J., Chu, K.-T., & Wang, S.-M. (2017). The associate impact of individual internal experiences and reference groups on buying behavior: A case study of animations, comics, and games consumers. *Telematics and Informatics, 34*(4), 314–325. doi:10.1016/j.tele.2016.08.013

Sheu, J.-J., Su, Y.-H., & Chu, K.-T. (2009). Segmenting online game customers – The perspective of experiential marketing. *Expert Systems with Applications, 36*(4), 8487–8495. doi:10.1016/j.eswa.2008.10.039

Steinbeiß, G. (2017). *Minecraft as a learning and teaching tool - Designing integrated game experiences for formal and informal learning activities* (Unpublished master's thesis). University of Oulu, Oulu, Finland.

Tudge, J. (1990). Vygotsky, the zone of proximal development, and peer collaboration: Implications for classroom practice. In L. Moll (Ed.), *Vygotsky and education: Instructional implications and applications of sociohistorical psychology* (pp. 155–172). Cambridge, UK: Cambridge University Press. doi:10.1017/CBO9781139173674.008

Uusi-Mäkelä, M. (2014). Immersive language learning with games: Finding flow in MinecraftEdu. In *Proceedings of ED-MEDIA 2014: World Conference on Educational Multimedia, Hypermedia & Telecommunications.* Chesapeake, VA: AACE.

Vygotsky, L. (1978). *Mind in society.* Cambridge, MA: Harvard University Press.

Woolfe, R. (1992). Experiential learning in workshops. In T. Hobbs (Ed.), *Experiential training: Practical guidelines* (pp. 1–13). London, UK: Tavistock/Roudledge.

KEY TERMS AND DEFINITIONS

Gagne's Events of Instruction: In 1992, Robert Gagné and his colleagues developed a nine-step instructional process that includes (1) gaining attention, (2) informing learners of objectives, (3) stimulating recall of prior learning, (4) presenting the stimulus, (5) providing learning guidance, (6) eliciting performance, (7) providing feedback, (8) assessing performance, and (9) enhancing retention and transfer.

Knowledge Co-Construction: A premise that learners can learn and grow from social interaction.

MMORPG (Massively Multiplayer Online Role-Playing Game): An online game-playing environment where a large number of people can participate simultaneously.

Negotiation of Meaning: A process that people go through to reach a clear understanding of each other. In second language acquisition, it is defined as an attempt to overcome comprehension problems.

Role Play: The act of imitating the character and behavior of someone who is different from oneself.

Schmitt's Strategic Experiential Modules: A framework for enhancing participants' experiences, including sensory experiences (SENSE), affective experiences (FEEL), creative cognitive experiences (THINK), physical experiences, behaviors and lifestyles (ACT), and social-identity experiences that result from relating to a reference group or culture (RELATE).

Simulation Game: Computer games in which players are provided with a simulated environment. Such games contain a mixture of skills, chances, and strategies to simulate an aspect of reality.

This research was previously published in Teaching, Learning, and Leading With Computer Simulations; pages 181-208, copyright year 2020 by Information Science Reference (an imprint of IGI Global).

Chapter 23
Design of a Web3D Serious Game for Human Anatomy Education:
A Web3D Game for Human Anatomy Education

Robson R. Lemos
Universidade Federal de Santa Catarina, Brazil

Poliana F. Pereira
Universidade Federal de Santa Catarina, Brazil

Cristiane Meneghelli Rudolph
Universidade Federal de Santa Catarina, Brazil

Bruna S. Bueno
Universidade Federal de Santa Catarina, Brazil

Arthur V. Batista
Universidade Federal de Santa Catarina, Brazil

Patricia J. Fiuza
Universidade Federal de Santa Catarina, Brazil

Karolini R. Conceição
Universidade Federal de Santa Catarina, Brazil

Samira S. Mansur
Universidade Federal de Santa Catarina, Brazil

ABSTRACT

The use of 3D web-based models allows researchers to explore interesting characteristics searching for the increase of quality in the anatomy education. This chapter aims to present the design of a serious game for human anatomy education that can assist the students in the understanding of the anatomical structures as well as the relationship between them in a virtual environment. The digital game design and development was carried out in partnership with specialists in human anatomy for the study of the lower limb bones (skeletal system), vessels and arteries (cardiovascular system), and lower limb skeletal muscles (muscular system). A case study was performed with students of physiotherapy undergraduate program in the course of anatomy through usability assessment techniques. Based on the results obtained it was possible to identify fundamental and innovative features that have to be present in the design of serious games for the teaching of health sciences.

DOI: 10.4018/978-1-6684-7589-8.ch023

INTRODUCTION

Human anatomy is an indispensable course and the foundation of all clinical studies. The goals of anatomy teaching are, at the very least, to know the anatomical structures and the relationships between them; recognize anatomical structures through imaging techniques; and, understand the anatomical bases of Pathology (Corredera & Santana, 2003). The knowledge of the anatomy is fundamental for the formation of health professionals and comprises the macroscopic study of the organs and systems that make up the human body, using its own terminology and descriptions from innumerable anatomical studies (Bastos & Proença, 2000). Due to its interdisciplinary relationship, the knowledge associated to human anatomy becomes imperative as a foundation in the professional courses of health programs (Neves, 2010). Improving the teaching resources applied to the teaching of anatomy tends satisfactorily for the direction of actions, stimulates the student's participation as an active subject in the search for new information, promoting indispensable support to the teaching-learning process (Guiraldes *et al.*, 1995).

The traditional teaching of human anatomy involves two distinct moments: the exposition of theoretical concepts and definitions of the systems and organs of the human body; and, the practical approach, which, through anatomical pieces and cadavers in the laboratory, allows to study the general characteristics and their interrelationships. Among the different methods used in teaching anatomy, can be cited studies on previously dissected anatomical pieces, anatomical models, interactive virtual environments, general purpose software and even social media (Lopes &Teixeira, 2018; Nuland & Rogers, 2016; Hennessy *et al.*, 2016).

However, the immense anatomical nomenclature can make complex the learning of the course for the students, therefore, leading to a weak learning experience, being responsible for the origin of negative connotations in relation to the subject and resulting in a superficial approach to the learning process and even being able to lead students to dropout the course (Smith *et al.*, 2016). In that scenario, virtual environments for anatomy teaching play a large role in learning by providing a new study environment other than the anatomy laboratory (Richardson *et al.*, 2011).

A great applicability of virtual environments is based on the fact that the virtual tool replaces the use of anatomical models and, within certain organic systems, replaces the cadaveric anatomical parts itself. The preservation of small and fragile anatomical structures such as blood vessels and nerves, which require a perfect dissection for a satisfactory visualization by the students, is one of the great challenges of the anatomy laboratories. In addition, another difficulty that anatomy laboratories face is the mechanical wear of corpses and cadaveric preparations during anatomy classes. The cost of maintaining an anatomy laboratory is high since the preparation of an anatomical piece for study involves the use of large quantities of reagents as well as dissecting materials and technical work. Moreover, it is a major obstacle for laboratories to obtain bodies for the teaching of anatomy.

Based on that, virtual tools and digital games have been gaining space in theoretical and practical classes of anatomy, which are being increasingly used by teachers as a tool that, through its playful aspect, arouses a great interest of the students and excludes most of the issues during the learning process. In addition, virtual tools not only enhance teaching-learning but also enhance the potential of the course content.

The use of games in the educational context can be called serious games, and usually aims at learning (Birkenbusch & Christ, 2013). With the development of new technologies, games have become an ally of the classroom, allowing the educational environment to move away from traditional teaching and starting to function within the information. Therefore, the use of games to train, learn and perform real activities in virtual environments can improve students' performance, as it allows the experience of individually produced learning experiences according to the style of the student (von Wangenheim, 2008).

Focusing on health there is a great opportunity to incorporate the use of games in the anatomy course, serving as a facilitator resource for student learning. Thus, by combining geometric models of the human anatomy with customized software, students can have access to new ways of interacting with anatomy that could not be achieved through static images or traditional anatomical models (Ma *et al.*, 2012). The study of anatomy including the three-dimensional (3D) interpretation of the relationships between structure and function represents a fundamental component in the teaching of several areas of health and sport science (Allen *et al.*, 2016; Brown *et al.*, 2012).

Web3D is a generic term used to refer to any type of three-dimensional (3D) graphics technology supported by the World Wide Web (WWW). Currently, there are a range of applications that are characterized as virtual environments for the Web.

In this study, it is presented a virtual environment aimed at teaching human anatomy of specific parts of the skeletal system, cardiovascular system, and muscular system. For that, the Web3D serious game entitled EducaAnatomia3D (EducaAnatomia3D, 2018) was developed, which aims to assist the teaching of students in the health area. The digital game design was carried out in partnership with specialists in Human Anatomy who assisted in the identification and addition of important concepts within the context of the anatomy study to assist with the understanding of the structure and function of the lower limb bones (skeletal system), vessels and arteries (cardiovascular system), and lower limb skeletal muscles (muscular system).

In the program of Physiotherapy, the study of the human anatomy is introduced in the Anatomy I course. For that, case studies were organized with students of the Physiotherapy program in the Anatomy I course for the use of the serious game, through usability assessment techniques found in the Human Computer Interaction (HCI) research area.

The main goal of this chapter is to present the design of a serious game for human anatomy education and to investigate the relevance of serious games for the anatomy teaching. For that, a first version of the Web3D serious game EducaAnatomia3D was developed, so that the following research question could be answered through the use of evaluation techniques: Web3D serious games for interactive virtual teaching of anatomy are relevant in the process of learning concepts associated with structure and function?

BACKGROUND

Recent relevant studies and surveys related to virtual environments for anatomy education were identified in the literature. The studies were classified in the following related areas: serious games for health sciences education, virtual environments for anatomy education, and virtual and augmented reality for health sciences education.

Serious Games for Health Sciences Education

Girard, Ecalle, and Magnan (2013) main objective in the study was to review through a meta-analysis the results of experimental studies designed to examine the effectiveness of serious games. The authors point out that one of the main limitation of the evaluated studies was the inconsistent use of the concept of "control group". According to the authors opinion, the best way to prove effectiveness to any type of training is to compare it with at least one group that receives no training and a group that receives training using a different type of training material. Based on the evaluation of the studies, the authors basically explained that the effectiveness of serious games has not yet been proven and that future studies need to address the question of the transfer of acquired knowledge and skills. According to the studies evaluated and the arguments found in those studies regarding the positive effect of engagement on the students the authors concluded that serious games might be powerful tools for learning. However, based on the observations of the authors there is a clear lack of empirical studies investigating the effectiveness of serious games in learning.

Wattanasoontorn, Boada, García, and Sbert, (2013) performed a systematic review of the literature on serious games for health and proposed a classification of serious games based on the following topics: The main purpose of the game (entertainment and teaching or health), stages of the disease being treated (health monitoring, detection, treatment, rehabilitation and education), and the type of end users in the game (general population, patients and health professionals). According to the authors, the development of a serious game involves different processes, technologies and specialists. It is also mentioned that, in the case of serious games special attention must be paid to the content provider. Meaning that the content providers needs to provide the information related to the game and also share their expertise to define game parameters such as the level of difficulty or the proper rewards and obstructions. Finally, the authors mention that an important part of the game development process is the target player specification. In this way the game design strategies and levels of the challenges need to be carefully considered in order to provide suitable rewards and obstacles.

Ricciardi and Paolis (2014) performed a comprehensive review of serious games in health professions. The authors compared serious games with traditional simulators taking into account four fundamental factors: entertainment factor, development costs, development time, and deployment costs. According to the authors, in the serious games the users are entertained by the need to improve their performance which is normally measured by some type of scoring mechanism and by the challenge to reach some type of goal. For game development, the supporting technology is widely diffused and it is available in desktops and mobile devices. Based on that, the authors observed also that development costs, development time and deployment costs were reduced if compared to costs of traditional simulators. Serious games were classified by application area such as: surgery, odontology, nursing, cardiology, first aid, dietitian and diabetes, and eMedOffice (e.g., serious games to teach medical students). The authors found that the application area of first aid had the highest number of developed serious games. According to the authors, one possible explanation for that is because continuous training is very important for health professionals and that serious games have a lower cost to achieve that goal.

Virtual Environments for Anatomy Education

Focusing on the field of human anatomy education and presenting general information of the systems of the human body, two virtual environments can be emphasized: Biodigital Human© (2018), and Complete Anatomy© (2018). Normally, virtual environments for anatomy general study purposes such as Biodigital Human© (2018) and Complete Anatomy© (2018) usually do not include information associated with the structure and function of the three-dimensional representation of the position of bony landmarks.

Attardi and Rogers (2015) presented a pioneer study in the realization of the first description of a fully online third-year year undergraduate anatomy course including live broadcast and interactive laboratory components with 3D anatomical models. The study was performed at Western University,

London, Ontario, Canada. The online course was designed to run in parallel with a traditional face to face course. The lectures of the face to face course were broadcasted to online students using a web collaborative software (web conferencing software) along with an interactive whiteboard. The same collaborative software was used to present laboratory demonstrations in which 3D virtual anatomical models were manipulated by the Netter´s 3D © Interactive Anatomy software. On top of that, online materials for the central nervous system were available through a website containing 360° images of plastinated prosected brain specimens. In that way, different types of interaction were explored during the online course, such as student-instructor and student-student interactions. According to the authors, based on the course design the software adopted to manipulate 3D virtual anatomical models was used by the students along with the laboratory instructor to facilitate student-content interactions. Based on the student's grades obtained by both group of students, the authors concluded that previous student academic performance, and not course delivery format, predicts performance in anatomy.

Berney, Bétrancourt, Molinari, and Hoyek, (2015) investigated the interplay between learning material presentation formats, spatial abilities, and anatomical tasks. The authors conducted two experimental studies. The first study was conducted to explore how presentation formats (dynamic vs. static visualizations) support learning of functional anatomy. And, the second study was conducted to investigate the interplay between spatial abilities (spatial visualization and spatial relation) and the presentation formats regarding the functional anatomy of the upper human limb. The dynamic visualization for functional anatomy is important because it allows to specify the spatial organization of elements and how it occurs the change with time. According to the authors, dynamic visualization models can help resolve spatial difficulties found when learning anatomy through static visualizations however they might be difficult to process by the novices. The authors found interesting interaction characteristics between presentation formats and spatial relation ability for some specific anatomical tasks.

Azer and Azer (2016) investigated studies exploring 3D anatomy models and their impact on learning for health sciences students as well as the current quality of the research that has been done in that area. A systematic review of the literature was performed and the main inclusion criteria was studies that were able to assess the impact of using 3D anatomy model on the student learning process. Several factors affecting learning by 3D anatomy models were investigated. Some important factors were taken into account: Factors related to the 3D model such as design of the 3D software and availability of visual and auditory information; factors related to learner characteristics such as innate visual space ability and prior orientation to 3D technology; and, factors related to the curriculum and learning environment integration of the 3D tool with other components in the curriculum and anatomical region studied. The authors concluded that students favored the use of 3D anatomical models and that in general the students found the 3D models more satisfactory when compared to traditional anatomy teaching. However, the authors found no solid evidence that the use of 3D anatomy models is superior to traditional teaching. The authors concluded that more studies exploring 3D anatomy models are needed to investigate the impact of those techniques on learning using appropriate evaluation tools.

Virtual and Augmented Reality for Health Sciences Education

Huang, Rauch, and Liaw (2010) presented the use of Web-based 3D technologies along with virtual reality features for learning applications. Two case studies were presented to investigate virtual reality for learning purposes of anatomy. The authors used constructivist learning as the pedagogical methodology for the development of the virtual reality application. The authors proposed four designed principles to be considered when building educational applications, such as: learning from interacting with an artificial real environment, learning from problem solving to promote creativity, motivating learners to learn, and virtual reality as a scaffolding tool for learners to learn. The authors mentioned that when educators apply virtual technology to educational design settings they need to consider how a learning theory influence the learning process. Based on that, the authors concluded the study presenting a guideline for effective use of virtual reality for learning purposes.

Ferrer-Torregrosa, Torralba, Jimenez, García, and Barcia (2015) presented a study in the development and evaluation of a tool for anatomy education based on augmented reality technology. Students of seven private and public Spanish universities were divided in a control group and an experimental group. The anatomical region adopted in the study was the human lower limb. The control group received traditional teaching lessons supported by books and videos. And, the experimental group received the same traditional teaching lessons but additionally used the ARBOOK augmented reality tool. A specific questionnaire was applied in both groups of students as part of the case study. After the data analysis of the results the authors concluded that the ARBOOK group obtained better scorings in the questions regarding attention-motivation, autonomous work and three-dimensional comprehension tasks.

Küçük, Kapakin, and Göktaş (2016) developed an application to study neuroanatomy topics by using mobile augmented reality technology. The main goal of the study was to evaluate the effects of learning anatomy using the mobile augmented reality application through academic achievement and cognitive load. In the case study two main groups of medical students participated of the study. An experimental group that used the mobile augmented reality application and a control group that used printed books to study neuroanatomy topics. According to the authors, the mobile learning application helped students learn better by exerting less cognitive effort. They also mentioned that the possibility to have a real-time interaction with the environment enable students to structure their knowledge and to complete the learning tasks. As future work the authors suggest to integrate the augmented reality applications with different learning approaches, such as: problem-based learning, game-based learning and collaborative learning. Also, one of the main obstacles mentioned by the authors was the development of 3D multimedia content because the instructors usually do not have the required level of skill needed to develop 3D modeling.

MAIN FOCUS OF THE CHAPTER

The main objective of this chapter is to present the design of a serious game for human anatomy education that can assist the students in the best possible way in their studies and in the understanding of the anatomical structures as well as the relationship between them in a virtual environment. Some issues, controversies, or problems must be observed during the design and evaluation process of a virtual learning environment for students in the health area.

Issues, Controversies and Problems

In the specific case of the design of serious games or virtual environments for Anatomy education the following issues, controversies, or problems must be observed:

- For the students to deal with the immense anatomical nomenclature that can make complex the learning of the Anatomy course, it is important to provide additional virtual learning tools that can be easily available and that present an interactive interface to stimulate the student's participation;
- For the students to learn the anatomical structures and the relationship between them it is important as part of the learning process the understanding of the concepts associated with structure and function;
- For specialists in Human Anatomy and students that have to deal with small and fragile anatomical structures, which require a perfect dissection for a satisfactory visualization, it is important to make available alternative ways of learning such as tools to explore anatomical structures in an interactive virtual 3D environment.

In general, the design of a serious game or an interactive virtual environment for anatomy education that is suitable to students in the health area is a possible first step in the direction of dealing with those issues. Another important step is the use of evaluation techniques to investigate the relevance of virtual environments for Anatomy Education since there are still controversies about the use of this type of approach in the literature (Azer & Azer, 2016).

SOLUTIONS AND RECOMMENDATIONS

The proposed solutions and recommendations to deal with the possible issues, controversies, or problems presented in the previous section is to design, develop, and evaluate a Web3D serious game for human anatomy education.

The use of Web3D technologies makes easy access to the virtual environment through a web browser in which nowadays all students have access. The design, development, and evaluation of a serious game for human anatomy education have to have the participation during the usability engineering life cycle of software developers, specialists in human anatomy, and target users (students in the health area).

The collaboration in a multidisciplinary team in the development of a serious game is important to make sure that the learning process such as the understanding of the concepts associated with structure and function are taken into account during the design for the techniques adopted for the presentation of the content and the assimilation of the content.

Moreover, a tool that is able to handle small and fragile anatomical structures in an interactive virtual 3D environment can be really appreciated by the students in the health area in order to obtain the necessary motivation during their studies and comprehensive understanding of the anatomical structures and the relationships between them.

Designing a Web3D Serious Game for Human Anatomy Education

The adopted methodology for the EducaAnatomia3D consists of an applied and technological research. It was also adopted the Digital Game-based Learning (DBGL) methodology, which, according to the literature, helps to overcome learning problems. The DGBL model (Zin *et al.*, 2009) subdivides the game design into two main parts. The first part corresponds to the presentation of the content of the study. And, the second part corresponds to the presentation of learning techniques to assimilate the content. In the context of the EducaAnatomia3D, the first phase of the game is the presentation of the content of a particular anatomical system and the second phase of the game is the assimilation of the content making use of game learning techniques.

The EducaAnatomia3D contains the functionality for managing user information, creating virtual classrooms and ranking process. It has also the functionality for studying specific parts of the skeletal, cardiovascular, and muscular systems. In the skeletal system it is possible to study the structure of the lower limb bones where the first phase (presentation of the content) and the second phase of the game (assimilation of the content) are currently available to the students. In the cardiovascular system, it is possible to study the structure of vessels and arteries. And, in the muscular system, it is possible to study the structure of the lower limb skeletal muscles. In both, cardiovascular and muscular systems, the first phase of the game (presentation of the content) is functional and the second phase of the game (assimilation of the content) is currently under development.

For the Web3D serious game project, it was carried out the data modeling and the interface design. The data modeling is mainly to manage the user registration information, the creation and elimination of virtual classrooms, and the ranking of the users as well as the ranking for each classroom and the overall ranking of the game. And, the interface design is mainly to provide the best user experience possible during a serious game session. The main functionalities added to the game design interface corresponds to the management of the user data, creation of virtual classrooms, ranking process, and the interactive virtual environments for the skeletal, cardiovascular and muscular systems.

For data modeling, the conceptual model was first elaborated based on entity-relationship diagrams. In order to do that, tables were needed to represent the information associated with each user and the virtual classrooms. In addition, the logical model for the identification of the primary key, as well as the types and size of each attribute was elaborated. And, finally, for the description of the physical model, the tables containing its attributes were created. Regarding the database, it was chosen MySQL© and for the Web application to be able to query the database, the PHP© language was adopted.

For the interface design, the conceptual design model, the prototype of the conceptual model and the detailed design of the user interface were developed. In this way, for the serious game design, technologies have been adopted for Web application development such as HTML5, CSS, and Javascript for the development of the interaction interface. In order to allow the interaction with 3D objects Web3D technology was used through the framework BabylonJS (framework for building 3D games using WebGL, WebVR, and Web Audio). The 3D objects responsible for the representation of the anatomical structures were obtained from the BodyParts3D© database (Mitsuhashi *et al.*, 2009) (with permission "BodyParts3D, © The Database Center for Life Science licensed under CC Attribution-Share Alike 2.1 Japan").

For the skeletal system, the evaluation of the serious game in the teaching environment was carried out through a case study with students of the Anatomy I course from the Physiotherapy program at Universidade Federal de Santa Catarina (UFSC), Brazil. In order to verify if the interaction with the interfaces, such as the interfaces for presentation and assimilation of the anatomy content, are attractive and easy to use by the users, it was adopted usability evaluation techniques found in the HCI area through usability tests using satisfaction questionnaires. The protocol for the case study, the consent form free and informed, and the satisfaction questionnaire were approved by the ethics committee and research at UFSC and by the Plataforma Brasil (Plataforma Brasil, 2018). Moreover, for the data analysis, a descriptive analysis was used based on the results obtained with the satisfaction questionnaires.

Managing Users, Virtual Classrooms and Ranking

The serious game EducaAnatomia3D allows to manage the user registration information, the creation and elimination of virtual classrooms, and the ranking of the users in the game.

Figure 1. Sign in and sign up page (a) and the user information page (b) (in portuguese)
Source: Prepared by the authors, 2018

(a)   (b)

As part of the management of the user information, the user first needs to register in the EducaAnatomia3D. The user can sign in or sign up in the serious game through a pre-existing Facebook or Google account (Figure 1(a)). In addition, the user can register a new account by providing an e-mail and password. From the creation of the account, additional information is required, such as: Institution of Origin, Study Program, Age Group (ages ranging from 0-14, 15-24, 25-34, 35-44, 45-54, and 55-years), City, and Country (Figure 1(b)). After completing the registration, the users will have access to the account data, virtual classroom information and the overall game ranking in the main page of the EducaAnatomia3D (Figure 2).

In the virtual classrooms management, the user can access "All Classrooms" or "My Classrooms" ("Todas Salas" or "Minhas Salas" in Portuguese) (Figure 3). In the option "All Classrooms" the user will have access to a list of virtual classrooms that are still available. Those virtual classrooms may have public or private (where a padlock icon is shown) access. The classrooms where the users can have access will show an option to "Enter" ("Entrar" in Portuguese). As soon as the users sign in a virtual classroom they can start the game as a member of that group and them in-game score will be counted in that particular virtual classroom. In the option "My Classrooms" it will show a list of virtual classrooms that the user is currently participating.

Assuming that the user signed in the virtual classroom entitled "sala andrew huxley" the user will have access to a list of users who currently participate in the classroom and from that point the user can start the game as a participant of the classroom (Figure 4).

Now, assuming that the user wants to create a virtual classroom to play with some colleagues, that can be accomplished through the selection of the plus sign icon (+) (Figure 3). From that point, the user will have to enter the name of the new virtual classroom (e.g., "amigos do pilates") and its form of access (i.e., public or private).

Figure 2. Main page (in Portuguese)
Source: Prepared by the authors, 2018

Figure 3. All classrooms (in Portuguese)
Source: Prepared by the authors, 2018

Assuming that the new virtual classroom entitled "amigos do pilates" was created the user can then add players to the classroom. By selecting the "add players" option ("Adicionar Jogadores" in Portuguese) (Figure 5(a)), the list of all players registered in EducaAnatomia3D will appear and the owner of the classroom will be able to include the players in the list. That type of functionality is interesting at the time of creating a private classroom by a student or professor. In this way the owner of the virtual classroom can define a group of users for a specific virtual classroom (Figure 5(b)).

Figure 4. Participating of a classroom (in Portuguese)
Source: Prepared by the authors, 2018

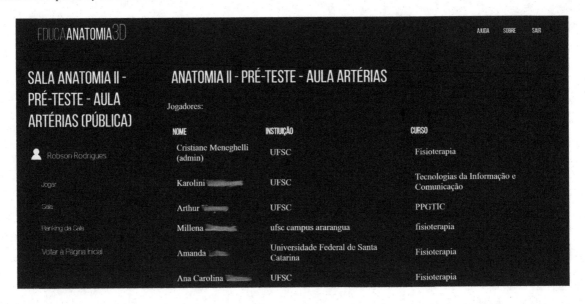

Figure 5. Managing your own classroom. Adding players (a) and List of available players (b) (in Portuguese).
Source: Prepared by the authors, 2018

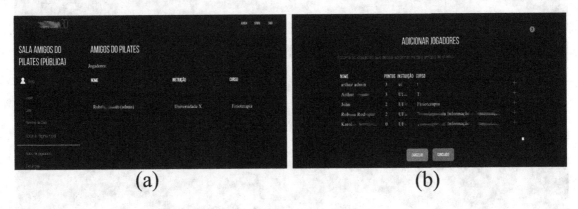

At the moment that the user is participating in a virtual classroom, the user can check the classroom ranking in the option "Classroom Ranking" ("Ranking da Sala" in Portuguese) (Figure 6(a)). And, in the main page (Figure 2) the user can always check the overall ranking of EducaAnatomia3D (Figure 6(b)). After the process of choosing to participate in a classroom the user can choose which anatomical system (e.g., skeletal, cardiovascular or muscular system) wants to study for a session of the game.

Figure 6. Classroom Ranking (a) and Overall Ranking (b) (in Portuguese)
Source: Prepared by the authors, 2018

(a)   (b)

Designing the Skeletal System

The digital game design was carried out in partnership with specialists in Human Anatomy who assisted in the identification and addition of important concepts within the context of the anatomy study to assist with the understanding of the structure and function of the skeletal system. Based on that, in the content presentation of the skeletal system, the human skeleton is first presented as a whole (Figure 7). Then based in the sequence of events normally adopted in the classroom, the content is subdivided in the following sections: skull, chest, spine, upper limb, and lower limb.

Figure 7. Content presentation phase for the skeletal system (in Portuguese)
Source: Prepared by the authors, 2018

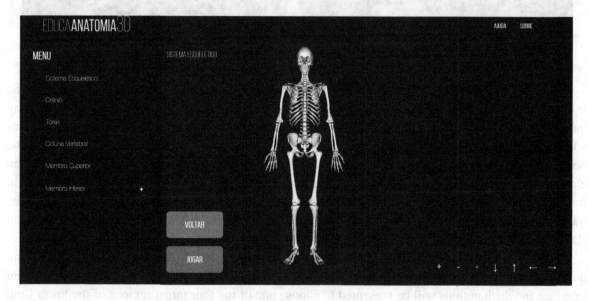

In the case of the lower limb bones, they are subdivided in four regions as follows: Hip, Thigh, Leg, and Foot. The specialist in Human Anatomy assisted with the addition of the concept associated with three-dimensional representation of the position of bony landmarks. The interface to the content presentation phase of the serious game allows visualization and interaction of the geometric representation of the anatomy, representing the lower limb of the human skeleton (Figure 8). When the mouse triggers an element on a specific part of the lower limb, the selected 3D object will be set with a highlighted color and the other 3D objects will be set with a transparency color. From the selection of the object, is presented in the interface the content of the course of anatomy referring to the selected bone.

Figure 8. Content presentation phase for the lower limb bones (in Portuguese)
Source: Prepared by the authors, 2018

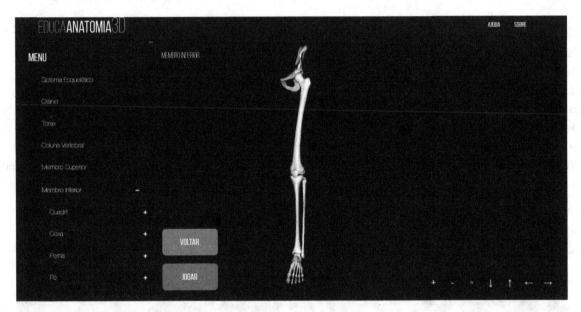

A unique feature of the serious game is its ability to capture essential concepts in the study of the lower limb of the human skeleton at undergraduate level in health sciences such as the location of bony landmarks (Authors, 2018). To this end, the location of each bony landmark of the lower limb was added to the geometric representation of the anatomy with the aid of anatomists. The locations of the bony landmarks are represented by 3D spheres and, when the mouse triggers a particular sphere of an element, the name of the bony landmark is displayed. The location of the bony landmark is important for the students' understanding of the function and structure of bones and the position of origin of the muscles and insertion of the tendons which are responsible for the movement of the human skeleton (Dangelo & Fattini, 2017) (Figure 9).

After the content presentation phase of the study, the user can test their knowledge by answering questionnaires in the content assimilation phase. To accomplish that, the game will take the user to an interface in which options will be presented to choose one of the four target regions of the lower limb (e.g., hip, thigh, leg, and foot). Following the choice of the lower limb region, a digital roulette wheel is presented for sorting the number of questions to be answered (e.g., 5, 10, 15, and 20) (Figure 10).

Figure 9. Content presentation phase for the lower limb bones (in Portuguese). Location of the bony landmarks.
Source: Prepared by the authors, 2018

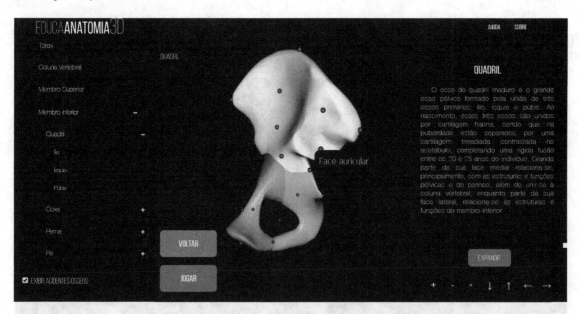

Figure 10. Content assimilation phase. Digital roulette wheel (in Portuguese).
Source: Prepared by the authors, 2018

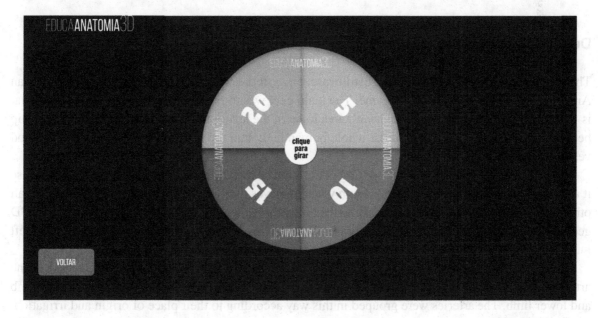

From the draw with the digital roulette wheel, the user will start the questionnaire corresponding to the selected region (Figure 11). Questions are key items for proposing in-game challenges. There are currently 131 questions in total, related to the four regions of the lower limb. For each question answered the game will display a message regarding the user´s response. After completing the questionnaire, the results of the correct and incorrect answers are presented.

Figure 11. Content assimilation phase. Questionnaire for the Foot region (in Portuguese).
Source: Prepared by the authors, 2018

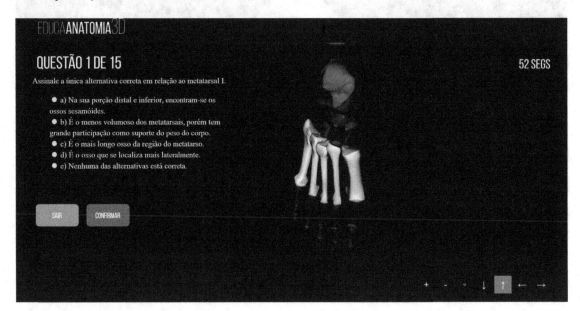

Designing the Cardiovascular System

The presentation of the content for the cardiovascular system was design in collaboration with Human Anatomy specialists for the serious game. The main goal was to present the content in such a way that is meaningful for the students of the health area to learn the anatomical structures and the relationship between them. First, it is presented the whole human body and the main organs along with the blood vessels (Figure 12).

For the cardiovascular system the starting point is the heart. The heart is an important organ because it acts as a contractile-propellant pump, from where it leaves the aorta artery, which will give rise to all other arteries, being responsible for boosting the blood for the whole body (Figure 13). Based in the 3D geometric representation of the heart it contains the following arteries: pulmonary trunk, right lung, left lung, arch of the aorta and ascending part of the aorta.

Based on that, the blood vessels are subdivided in arteries and veins (Figure 14). In the case of the arteries, they are subdivided in five regions as follows: head and neck, thorax, abdomen, upper limb and lower limb. The arteries were grouped in this way according to their place of origin and irrigation.

Currently, the interface to the content presentation phase of the serious game allows visualization and interaction of the geometric representation of the arteries in the cardiovascular system. Arteries are in the group of anatomical elements that are small and fragile anatomical structures, which require a perfect dissection for a satisfactory visualization in the Anatomy laboratories. When the mouse triggers an element on a specific part of the artery in the human body, the selected 3D object will be set with a highlighted color and the other 3D objects will be set with a transparency color. From the selection of the object, it is presented in the interface the content of the course of anatomy referring to the selected artery (Figures 15 and 16).

Figure 12. The cardiovascular system (in Portuguese)
Source: Prepared by the authors, 2018

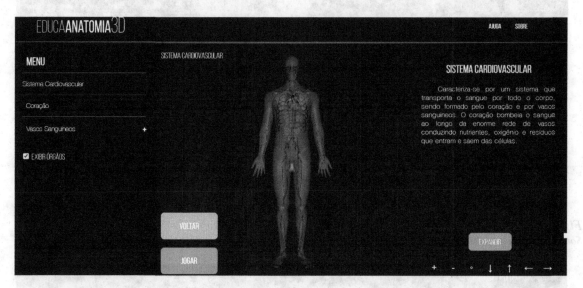

Figure 13. Anatomical structure of the heart (in Portuguese)
Source: Prepared by the authors, 2018

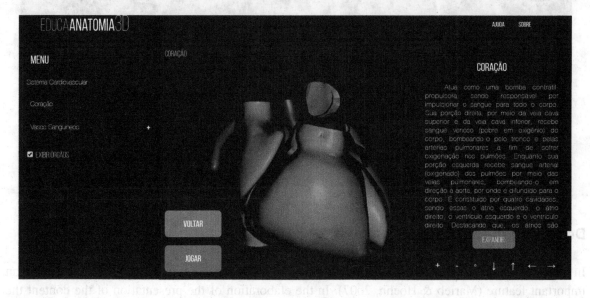

Figure 14. Subdivision of the blood vessels in arteries and veins (in Portuguese)
Source: Prepared by the authors, 2018

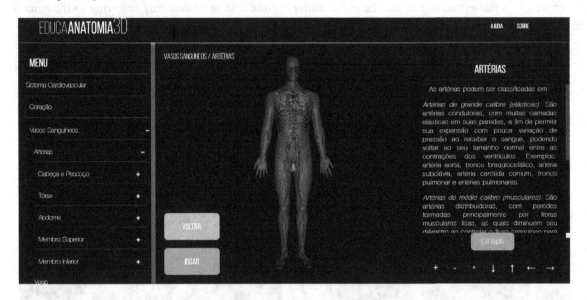

Figure 15. Femoral artery from the lower limb region (in Portuguese)
Source: Prepared by the authors, 2018

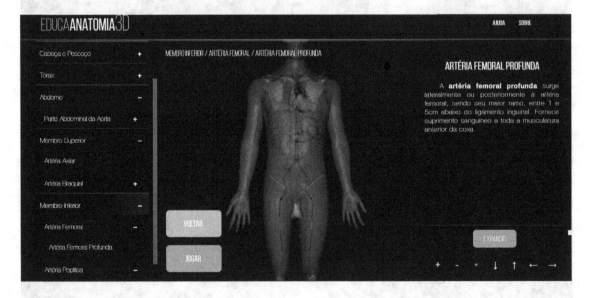

Designing the Muscular System

In most mammals, muscles represent more than 40% of the whole body mass which corresponds to an important feature (Marieb & Hoehn, 2007). In the elaboration of the presentation of the content the help of the specialists in Human Anatomy is important for the correct determination of the origin and insertion of the muscles and the concepts associated with the structure and muscular function in the study of anatomy.

Figure 16. Intercostalpost artery from the thorax region (in Portuguese)
Source: Prepared by the authors, 2018

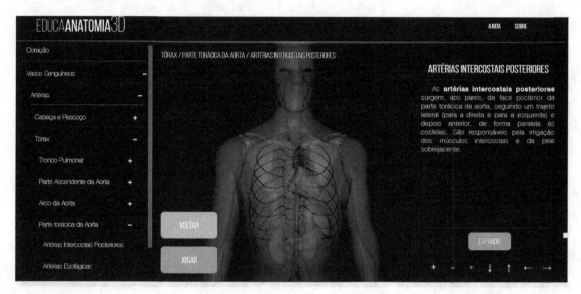

In the content presentation of the muscular system, the human body is first presented as a whole. Then based in the sequence of events normally adopted in the classroom, the content is subdivided in the following sections: head and neck, thorax, abdomen, back, pelvic joint, perineum, upper limb, and lower limb (Figure 17).

In the case of the muscles in the lower limb, they are subdivided in four regions as follows: gluteal, thigh, leg, and foot (Figure 18).

Figure 17. Skeletal muscles of the lower limb (in Portuguese)
Source: Prepared by the authors, 2018

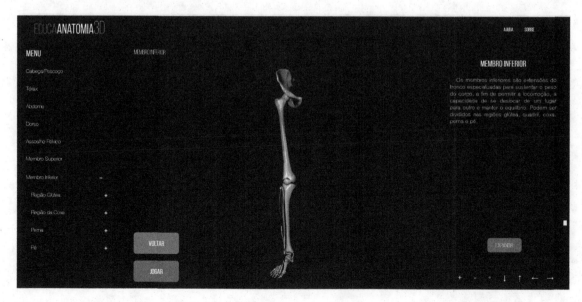

Figure 18. Skeletal muscles of the thigh region (in Portuguese)
Source: Prepared by the authors, 2018

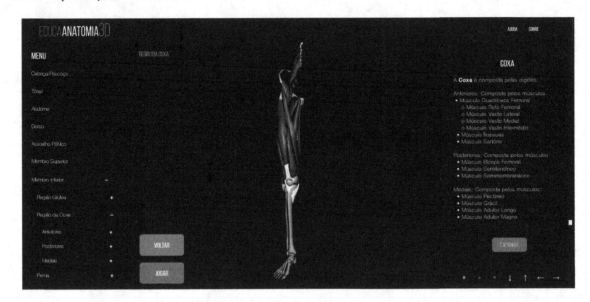

When the mouse triggers a muscle on a specific part of the lower limb, the selected 3D anatomical structure will be set with a highlighted color and the other 3D anatomical structures will be set with a transparency color. From the selection of the object, it is presented in the interface the content of the course of anatomy referring to the selected muscle. In the case of the skeletal muscle it is important to show the corresponding skeletal system as well as the origin and insertion of the muscle (Figure 19).

Figure 19. Rectus femoris muscle of the thigh region (in Portuguese)
Source: Prepared by the authors, 2018

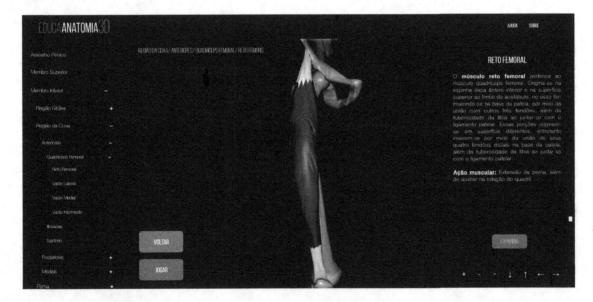

Performing Usability Evaluation for the Educational Game Development Cycle

As part of the educational game development cycle, usability evaluation tests are performed. Students of the Physiotherapy program in the Anatomy I course participated in a case study for usability evaluation of the EducaAnatomia3D for the lower limb of the skeletal system. The attendance was of 31 students being 22 women and 9 men and from the age range of 16 to 52 years old. In the particular course, most students have a level of experience with serious games or virtual educational environments considered to be intermediate. The professor of the course, who has extensive experience in teaching Anatomy, also participated in the case study.

For the presentation of the serious game EducaAnatomia3D in a computer lab, the students were asked to sign the Term of Free and Informed Consent, so the game could be applied. After one hour and forty minutes playing the game, the students and the professor answered the satisfaction questionnaire for the usability evaluation.

In order to measure the quality of the user interaction with the interface, usability tests were performed through satisfaction questionnaires. Bosse et al. (2016) presents a systematic mapping of instruments for evaluating serious games. In this study, a satisfaction questionnaire was elaborated which adopts the five usability factors suggested by the Usability Measurement Inventory questionnaire (Sumi, 2018). The five usability factors for this study seek information from the user, regarding: affect, control, learnability, efficiency, and helpfulness. In this context, the student satisfaction questionnaire was elaborated making a total of 12 affirmations in which the users should position themselves, noting one of the five alternatives presented at the end of each question according to the Likert scale of 5 points: 1 - Disagree Totally, 2 - Disagree, 3 - No Opinion / Not Sure, 4 - I agree, and 5 - I fully agree (Table 1). Also, the questionnaire contains three open questions, where the students and professor provide their opinion regarding the interaction with the interface.

Table 1. Satisfaction questionnaire

1. The use of the serious game in general was a satisfactory experience.
2. During the use of the serious game it was possible to explore the concepts associated with the human lower limb and to conduct the questionnaires for the content assimilation through a minimum set of operations.
3. The serious game was important for performing activities related to the assimilation of the content in the Anatomy course.
4. The serious game interaction interface was easily understood.
5. There was no need to stop the proposed activity in the face of obstacles in the interaction with the interface.
6. I have not encountered errors related to the serious game from the start to the end of the activities.
7. As a serious game user it was possible to visualize and interact with the human lower limb elements in an intuitive way.
8. The serious game presented an interface with the teaching terminology for Human Anatomy in a consistent manner.
9. The information provided by serious game was satisfactory for understanding the structure and function of the main elements of the lower human limb.
10. Regardless of the regularity of use of the serious game the functionalities of the interaction interface were easy to memorize.
11. The information presented in the interface of the serious game was sufficient for its use.
12. During the use of the serious game the messages and warnings were sufficient for the understanding during the study of the presentation and assimilation of the topics of the lower limb through questionnaires.

In the descriptive analysis, it is investigated the results obtained with the evaluation by the students and for the professor of the Anatomy I course. For the satisfaction questionnaire carried out by the students and the professor, 5 usability factors were adopted. The usability factors adopted, corresponding to the questions presented in Table 1, are as follows: (i) Affect: questions 1, 6, and 7; (ii) Control: questions 2 and 10; (iii) Learnability: questions 3 and 9; (iv) Efficiency: questions 4, 5, and 8; And, (v) Helpfulness: questions 11 and 12.

The results of the satisfaction questionnaire for students of Anatomy I are presented in Figure 20. Regarding the average of the usability factors obtained, the highlight of the results with the highest average was for the category Learnability, related to the ease of interaction and understanding of the content, with 4.66. Next, the Efficiency category with an average of 4.54, Control category that the environment provides and Helpfulness, both with 4.48, and, finally, the Affect category with 4.43.

Figure 20. Average usability factors for the serious game
Source: Prepared by the authors, 2018

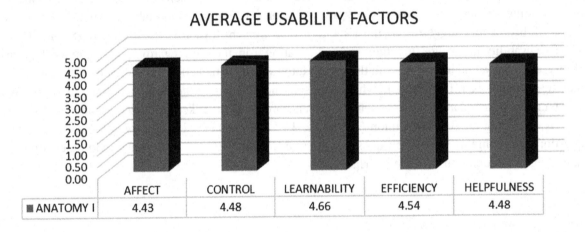

In addition, three open questions were included and the main observations pointed out by the students and professor are presented below:

- **Question 1: What are the Benefits or Advantages While Using the Game?** (i) Students: The main benefits cited were that the game allows the learning, from representations of the lower limb in 3D, in an interactive, dynamic and playful way, facilitating the study. (ii) Professor: The main observations were that the student has the opportunity to study anatomy through a web browser without necessarily needing to attend the laboratory in the teacher assistant hours and unlike a traditional classroom, students become more active during the learning period through the serious game, which keeps the attention (focus on learning and ability to concentrate) for a longer time than that of the classroom. Students who find it difficult to memorize the anatomical terms can use the game as an auxiliary tool for the assimilation of the content.

- **Question 2: What are the Difficulties or Disadvantages While Using the Game?** (i) Students: The main difficulties cited were regarding the understanding required to answer some questions of higher complexity level in the maximum time of 60 seconds. (ii) Professor: The professor described that the only disadvantage at first, is that students in particular with reduced knowledge of virtual learning applications including 3D interaction features may need an initial adaptation period to interact with the game in an efficient way.

- **Question 3: What are your Suggestions for the Improvement of the Game?** (i) Students: As for suggestions for improvement, the students cited that it would be interesting to add questions by adopting different presentation formats, to add more anatomical system in the serious game, as well as to include options to choose a maximum time to answer a certain number of questions. (ii) Professor: Finally, the professor mentioned that it would be interesting to add more playful characteristics in the content presentation phase in order to stimulate the student even more for a complete learning and to better enable them to answer the questions in the content assimilation phase. And, in the content presentation phase another suggestion was to allow the visualization of the names of the foot bones during the interaction with the 3D scene.

FUTURE RESEARCH DIRECTIONS

Future work intends to explore more intuitive and playful forms for the content presentation phase such as the introduction of gaming techniques as part of the interaction with the 3D objects representing the anatomical models. At the same time, in the content assimilation phase additional gaming techniques will be explored.

For the existing anatomical systems in the EducaAnatomia3D (i.e., skeletal, cardiovascular and muscular system) more anatomical structures will be added. Also, additional anatomical systems have been investigated for future releases of the game as part of the collaboration with Human Anatomy specialists including information and mechanisms to explore the understanding of its function and structure.

In some anatomical systems, it seems to be more suitable to apply techniques for interaction and visualization such as virtual and augmented reality. Currently, it has been investigated the use of virtual and augmented reality in the Web3D serious game for the nervous system.

Another research area that can be explored in the EducaAnatomia3D is Learning Analytics. For that, the data modeling for the game is been adapted to take into account data obtained during a game session by the users. When the EducaAnatomia3D is able to collect data for that purpose during a game session, data mining algorithms will be implemented and Learning Analytics techniques will be applied. Therefore, the EducaAnatomia3D team will be able to identify for example, which areas the users need to improve their performance or which parts of the serious game need to be redesign to get users more motivated in their studies.

As part of the educational game development cycle, usability evaluation test will continue to be performed for the anatomical systems as well as learning evaluation tests in order to investigate the impact of the serious game EducaAnatomia3D in the learning process of the students in the health area.

CONCLUSION

The serious game EducaAnatomia3D aims to facilitate the teaching of Anatomy, allowing a new form of aid for studies and tests of the knowledge in that area. There are serious games and virtual environments available in the literature for teaching and learning the course of Anatomy (Biodigital, 2018; Complete

Anatomy, 2018). However, the approach in the design of serious games and virtual environments for the teaching of Human Anatomy found in the literature usually presents several systems of the human body from the point of view of a 3D atlas.

The serious game was design for the study in the health sciences area with the assistance of Human Anatomy specialists. The design team was composed of software developers, specialists and end users (students in the health area). This multidisciplinary team was responsible for the design of the skeletal, cardiovascular and muscular system.

In the case of the skeletal system, the information associated with bony landmarks allowed to explore important features in understanding the function and structure of bones. In this way, the serious game EducaAnatomia3D presents an innovative component in the design of games enabling students of health sciences to make use of a virtual environment for teaching and learning where the presentation and assimilation of the content take into account concepts associated with function and structure of bones.

In general, the application received a satisfactory score in the usability tests and interesting suggestions for possible improvements to make the experience for students more complete and interesting. Thus, the serious game EducaAnatomia3D has proved to be relevant as part of the learning process of concepts associated with bone function and structure.

It was observed, from the analysis of the results of the use and evaluation of the serious game by the group of students of Anatomy I, that the game helped to introduce the concepts regarding the anatomy of the lower limb and helped the novice students to understand the three-dimensional (3D) relationship of bony landmarks with regions of the lower limb.

Finally, the usability evaluation tests, as part of the educational game development cycle, applied in the Physiotherapy students have proven to be very helpful in the understanding of the health students profile. Basically, through the answers and suggestions in the satisfaction questionnaire it was observed in the case study that the students really appreciated a well prepared Human Anatomy content and a great number of questions on the subject. It was also observed that the students appreciated the ability to interact, navigate, and visualize 3D objects representing anatomical models with meaningful information in a serious game environment. All those observations helped the EducaAnatomia3D team in the design decision making process based on a better understanding of the target users.

REFERENCES

Allen, L. K., Eagleson, R., & de Ribaupierre, S. (2016). Evaluation of an online three-dimensional interactive resource for undergraduate neuroanatomy education. *Anatomical Sciences Education*, 9(5), 431–439. doi:10.1002/ase.1604 PMID:26990135

Attardi, S. M., & Rogers, K. A. (2015). Design and implementation of an online systemic human anatomy course with laboratory. *Anatomical Sciences Education*, 8(1), 53–62. doi:10.1002/ase.1465 PMID:24920278

Azer, S. A., & Azer, S. (2016). 3D anatomy models and impact on learning: A review of the quality of the literature. *Health Profession Education*, 2(2), 80–98. doi:10.1016/j.hpe.2016.05.002

Azuma, R. T. (1997). A survey of augmented reality. *Presence (Cambridge, Mass.)*, 6(4), 355–385. doi:10.1162/pres.1997.6.4.355

Bastos, L. A. M., & Proença, M. A. (2000). A prática anatômica e a formação médica. *Revista Panamericana de Salud Pública*, 7(6), 395–401. doi:10.1590/S1020-49892000000600007 PMID:10949901

Berney, S., Bétrancourt, M., Molinari, G., & Hoyek, N. (2015). How spatial abilities and dynamic visualizations interplay when learning functional anatomy with 3D anatomical models. *Anatomical Sciences Education*, 8(5), 452–462. doi:10.1002/ase.1524 PMID:25689057

Biodigital. (2018). *Biodigital Human©*. Retrieved January 22, 2018, from https://www.biodigital.com/about

Birkenbusch, J., & Christ, O. (2013). Concepts behind serious games and computer-based trainings in health care: immersion, presence, flow. In *Serious games and virtual worlds in education, professional development, and healthcare* (pp. 1–14). IGI Global. doi:10.4018/978-1-4666-3673-6.ch001

Bosse, R., Soares, A. V., & da Silva Hounsell, M. (2016, March). Serious Games for Balance Improvement: A Systematic Literature Mapping. WorldCIST, (2), 73-82. doi:10.1007/978-3-319-31307-8_8

Brown, P. M., Hamilton, N. M., & Denison, A. R. (2012). A novel 3D stereoscopic anatomy tutorial. *The Clinical Teacher*, 9(1), 50–53. doi:10.1111/j.1743-498X.2011.00488.x PMID:22225894

Complete Anatomy. (2018). *Complete Anatomy©*. Retrieved January 22, 2018, from https://3d4medical.com/apps/complete-anatomy

Corredera, B. M. & Santana, P. L. (2003) Relevancia de la anatomia humana en El ejercicio de la medicina de assistencia primaria y em el estudio de las asignaturas de segundo ciclo de la licenciatura em medicina. *Educación médica*, 6(1), 41-51.

Dangelo, J. G., & Fattini, C. A. (2017). *Anatomia humana sistêmica e segmentar*. São Paulo: Atheneu.

EducaAnatomia3D. (2018). EducaAnatomia3D - Jogo Sério para o Ensino da Anatomia Humana. Retrieved March 23, 2018, from http://labanatomiainterativa.ufsc.br/ea3d

Ferrer-Torregrosa, J., Torralba, J., Jimenez, M. A., García, S., & Barcia, J. M. (2015). ARBOOK: Development and assessment of a tool based on augmented reality for anatomy. *Journal of Science Education and Technology*, 24(1), 119–124. doi:10.100710956-014-9526-4

Girard, C., Ecalle, J., & Magnan, A. (2013). Serious games as new educational tools: How effective are they? A meta-analysis of recent studies. *Journal of Computer Assisted Learning*, 29(3), 207–219. doi:10.1111/j.1365-2729.2012.00489.x

Guiraldes, D. C., Oddó Atria, H., & Ortega, F. (1995). Métodos computacionales y gráficos de aopyo al aprendizaje de la anatomía humana: visión de los estudiantes/Computer and graphic methods of support to the human anatomy learning: the students point of view. *Revista Chilena de Anatomía*, 13(1), 76–71.

Hennessy, C. M., Kirkpatrick, E., Smith, C. F., & Border, S. (2016). Social media and anatomy education: Using twitter to enhance the student learning experience in anatomy. *Anatomical Sciences Education*, 9(6), 505–515. doi:10.1002/ase.1610 PMID:27059811

Huang, H. M., Rauch, U., & Liaw, S. S. (2010). Investigating learners' attitudes toward virtual reality learning environments: Based on a constructivist approach. *Computers & Education, 55*(3), 1171–1182. doi:10.1016/j.compedu.2010.05.014

Küçük, S., Kapakin, S., & Göktaş, Y. (2016). Learning anatomy via mobile augmented reality: Effects on achievement and cognitive load. *Anatomical Sciences Education, 9*(5), 411–421. doi:10.1002/ase.1603 PMID:26950521

Lopes, P. T. C., & Teixeira, C. N. (2018). *Ensino de anatomia humana: comparação entre três métodos de estudo.* Retrieved January 22, 2018, from http://www.efdeportes.com/efd175/ensino-de-anatomia-humana-tres-metodos-de-estudo.htm

Ma, M., Bale, K., & Rea, P. (2012, September). Constructionist learning in anatomy education. In *International Conference on Serious Games Development and Applications* (pp. 43-58). Springer. 10.1007/978-3-642-33687-4_4

Marieb, E. N., & Hoehn, K. (2007). *Human anatomy & physiology.* Pearson Education.

Mitsuhashi, N., Fujieda, K., Tamura, T., Kawamoto, S., Takagi, T., & Okubo, K. (2008). BodyParts3D: 3D structure database for anatomical concepts. *Nucleic Acids Research, 37*(suppl_1), D782-D785.

Neves, M. V. S. (2010). *Uma nova proposta no ensino de Anatomia Humana: desafios e novas perspectivas* (Master dissertation). Fundação Oswaldo Aranha.

Plataforma Brasil. (2018). *Plataforma Brasil.* Retrieved January 22, 2018, from http://plataformabrasil.saude.gov.br/

Ricciardi, F., & Paolis, L. T. D. (2014). A comprehensive review of serious games in health professions. *International Journal of Computer Games Technology, 9.*

Richardson, A., Hazzard, M., Challman, S. D., Morgenstein, A. M., & Brueckner, J. K. (2011). A "Second Life" for gross anatomy: Applications for multiuser virtual environments in teaching the anatomical sciences. *Anatomical Sciences Education, 4*(1), 39–43. doi:10.1002/ase.195 PMID:21265036

Smith, C. F., Finn, G. M., Stewart, J., & McHanwell, S. (2016). Anatomical Society core regional anatomy syllabus for undergraduate medicine: The Delphi process. *Journal of Anatomy, 228*(1), 2–14. doi:10.1111/joa.12402 PMID:26612335

Sumi. (2018). *Software Usability Measurement Inventory©.* Retrieved January 22, 2018, from http://sumi.uxp.ie/

Van Nuland, S. E., & Rogers, K. A. (2016). The anatomy of E-Learning tools: Does software usability influence learning outcomes? *Anatomical Sciences Education, 9*(4), 378–390. doi:10.1002/ase.1589 PMID:26671838

von Wangenheim, R. P. C. G. (2014). O Uso de Jogos Educacionais para o Ensino de Gerência de Projetos de Software. *Fórum de Educação em Engenharia de Software, 37.*

Wattanasoontorn, V., Boada, I., García, R., & Sbert, M. (2013). Serious games for health. *Entertainment Computing, 4*(4), 231–247. doi:10.1016/j.entcom.2013.09.002

Zin, N. A. M., Jaafar, A., & Yue, W. S. (2009). Digital game-based learning (DGBL) model and development methodology for teaching history. *WSEAS Transactions on Computers*, 8(2), 322–333.

KEY TERMS AND DEFINITIONS

3D Models: Mathematical representation of a three-dimensional object.

Augmented Reality: Technology that has the ability to merge real world and virtual world by combining human senses with virtual objects.

Human-Computer Interaction: It is the study of how people interact with computers.

Serious Games: Games used for purposes other than mere entertainment.

Usability: The effectiveness, efficiency, and satisfaction with which specified users achieve specified goals in particular environments.

Virtual Reality: Technology that has the ability to visualize 3D objects and to provide an interactive environment that reinforces the sensation of an immersion into a virtual world.

Web3D: Generic term used to refer to any type of three-dimensional (3D) graphics technology supported by the World Wide Web (WWW).

This research was previously published in the Handbook of Research on Immersive Digital Games in Educational Environments; pages 586-611, copyright year 2019 by Information Science Reference (an imprint of IGI Global).

Index

N

S

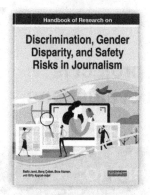
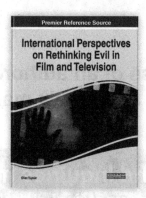

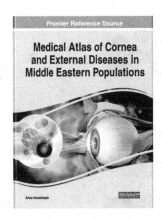

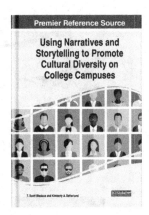

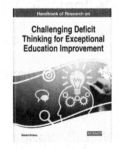

Printed in the United States
by Baker & Taylor Publisher Services